WILLIAM HEINEMANN

A Century of Publishing 1890–1990

WILLIAM HEINEMANN

A Century of Publishing 1890 - 1990

JOHN ST JOHN

HEINEMANN : LONDON

William Heinemann Ltd
Michelin House, 81 Fulham Road, London SW3 6RB

LONDON   MELBOURNE   AUCKLAND

First published 1990
© Diana St John 1990
Postscript © Octopus Publishing Group Ltd 1990
ISBN 0 434 66654 8

Photoset by Rowland Phototypesetting Ltd
Bury St Edmunds, Suffolk
Printed in Great Britain
by St Edmundsbury Press Ltd, Bury St Edmunds, Suffolk
and bound by Hunter and Foulis Ltd, Edinburgh

CONTENTS

[v]

Contents

Contents

BOOK III: 1945–1961

Contents

Contents

ILLUSTRATIONS

EDITOR'S NOTE
AND ACKNOWLEDGEMENTS

The author of this book had been closely involved with Heinemann as an editor and director for more than thirty years. His most lasting achievement as a publisher was the creation and sustained development through the 1960s and 1970s of a distinct list and division within Heinemann for specialized non-fiction books. These were for a long time officially classified as 'technical books': an imprecise term, as his field was much wider, including, besides many textbooks on specific technical subjects, business management, company and industrial history, food and wine, religion and philosophy, and others; his constant goal being to acquire and successfully publish good books combining aspects of science or technology with an expansive human dimension. John St John had the discrimination and perseverance to enable him to build up a first-class and profitable list by signing up and working with authors who, though experts in their own subjects, were largely unknown to the public and, in some cases, novices in the art of writing books. Many of the books which he and his colleagues commissioned years ago remain today (often in editions regularly updated and revised) at the core of the thriving list of Heinemann Professional Publishing (the name of the Octopus division that has inherited the old 'technical books' list).

Shortly after John St John retired in the early 1980s, the Heinemann board invited him to write this centenary history; a task which he accepted on the condition (freely granted) that he would have unrestricted access to all records and liberty to express whatever opinions he chose. He worked almost without interruption for more than three years, interviewing former and present staff and authors and tirelessly researching not only the Heinemann archives and library but also scores of collections of books and documents in private and public hands in the U.K. and the U.S.A. He delivered a substantially complete typescript of more than two hundred thousand words in the autumn of 1988, only weeks before his unexpected death on 2 December.

It is for his readers to judge how well he discharged this huge task of distilling such diverse material embracing literary, business, and personal histories into a coherent, entertaining and instructive narrative. As his editor who has helped to prepare the typescript and seen it through the press, I would like only to draw attention to three facts regarding its contents. One is that this book is designed to be the history of William Heinemann Ltd, the fiction and general publishing company founded in 1890, and only incidentally of the Heinemann Group of Publishers which came into being after the Second World War; it may be noted in particular that the history of Heinemann Educational Books Ltd has been extensively covered in *In Pursuit of Publishing* by Alan Hill (John Murray/HEB 1988). The second point is that (understandably to those who knew him) John St John scarcely mentions his own crucial editorial role during the last quarter of the Heinemann century; a defect which this brief notice, together with a few editorial footnotes or interjections, must serve, however poorly, to redress. The third point is to record another omission from John St John's text: that of any coverage of the six years following the takeover of Thomas Tilling by BTR in June 1983. As I know from many conversations with the author, he had determined to cover this recent period, which he viewed as current events rather than history, not in detailed narrative but in a more summary and (as he put it) 'philosophical' manner. That intention he was sadly prevented from fulfilling but a short postscript has been added, beginning on page 619.

Scores of people generously gave of their time and knowledge during the preparation of this book and John St John would certainly have recorded here his sense of gratitude to them all.

First must come his wife, Diana, who read and commented on the whole typescript during all its stages, helped to check the quotations, and consistently acted as a staunch ally of the entire project from its inception, patiently sharing her home for about four years with bulging boxes and cabinets of research material.

I would like also to record our gratitude to the following people whose specially valuable contributions, in some cases spread over a considerable period of time, are known to me: the late Phyllis Alexander, Alewyn Birch, Grace Cranston, A. Dwye Evans, the late A. S. Frere, Roland Gant, Dr Humphry Gyde, Tara Heinemann, Alan Hill, Maire Lynd, Charles Pick, and D. L. Range.

Editor's Note and Acknowledgements

In addition we are grateful to the following for agreeing to be interviewed by John St John: Chinua Achebe, the late Barley Alison, Elizabeth Anderson (Mrs Roantree), Peter Barnard, the late John Beer, Vincent Brome, David Burnett, the late Victor Canning, Catherine Cookson, OBE, David Elliot, Sir John Elliott, Judith Elliott, Graham Greene, OM, Sir Rupert Hart-Davis, the late Bill Holden, the late Nigel Hollis, Reginald Keel, David Machin, Dr Edwin Maddison, Simon Master, James Michie, Malcolm Muggeridge, Barbara Noble, Anthony Powell, CH, Derek Priestley, Eric Rabbets, Janice Robertson, Max Reinhardt, Tom Rosenthal, Peter Ryder, MBE, Carol Smith, Nigel Viney, Graham Watson, the late Mary Whitehead, and Hugh Williamson.

We gratefully acknowledge the help given by the librarians and staff of the Library of Newcastle-upon-Tyne, Reading University Library, Stanford University Library, California, the Houghton Library at Harvard University, the Library of the University of Iowa, the New York Public Library (Berg Collection), and the National Library of Canada, Ottawa.

We are grateful to the following for permission granted to reproduce copyright material: Mrs Eva Reichmann for a quotation from "Whistler's Writing" in *Yet Again*, for an extract from a previously unpublished letter by Max Beerbohm to Sydney Pawling, and for a cartoon by Max Beerbohm; A. P. Watt Ltd on behalf of the National Trust for extracts from two previously unpublished letters by Rudyard Kipling to William Heinemann; and to Laurence Pollinger Ltd (representing the Estate of Frieda Lawrence Ravagli) for extracts from three letters and a quotation from *Phoenix* by D. H. Lawrence.

Roger Smith

BOOK I
1890–1920

1

Starting with a Bang

The opening entry in the cash book of William Heinemann, book publisher, records that, on 2 January 1890, £500, his initial capital investment, was paid into a newly opened bank account. Facing it on the opposite page, the first payment out of the new account was £300 to the author Hall Caine, being the advance of royalties for his novel, *The Bondman*. This had previously been turned down by Chatto & Windus, who had published his earlier novel, *The Deemster*, and also by Cassell's who felt it was 'too gloomy' and that Hall Caine's request for £400 'outright' was excessive. It took Heinemann only a month to publish it with a print of 3,000. As was customary at the time, it was first issued in three volumes, mainly for the libraries, at a price of £1 11s.6d., but by October a cheap one-volume edition was announced at 3s.6d.

The fledgling firm's first book was an immediate, triumphant success. The romantic saga about two half-brothers, Michael Sunlocks and Red Jason, set in the Isle of Man and Iceland invaded by the Danes, appealed to the late Victorian taste for melodramatic tales of adventure and violence, lush sentimentality and passion. Some of the Press went so far as to hail it as a companion volume for the Bible, and compare it to the *Odyssey* and to the best of Victor Hugo; *The Times* declared that it was 'impossible to deny originality and rude power to this saga, impossible not to admire its forceful directness and the colossal grandeur of its leading characters'. In the opinion of none other than Mr Gladstone *The Bondman* was 'a work of which I recognize the freshness, vigour and sustained interest, no less than its integrity of aim'. It reprinted continually and was to go on selling for years, eventually reaching a total of over 450,000 copies. Hall Caine's later novels were to perform even better and provide the firm with the kind of financial underpinning that only comes from a regular bestselling author. With inspired insight young Heinemann decided that his telegraphic address should be named after the *The Bondman*'s hero, and 'Sunlocks, London' appeared on the firm's notepaper until in the 1980s telex and facsimile replaced the telegram.

There is said to be no such thing as good luck in publishing and it is undoubtedly truer to say that selecting Hall Caine as his first published author was a demonstration of William's uncanny nose for books that the reading public, or a substantial section of it, needed. Popular novelists did not, however, fuel his foremost motivation to set up as an independent publisher. He was primarily concerned with weightier, scholarly works, for the most part non-fiction, as the structure of his early spring and autumn lists makes clear; but before describing their contents it is necessary to introduce William Heinemann himself because the types of books he published grew very directly out of his personality and background.

Born on 18 May 1863, he was twenty-seven when he opened his business in two rooms on the second floor of 21 Bedford Street on the fringe of Covent Garden vegetable and fruit market, connecting it with the Strand. The building still stands, though it is now part of Moss Bros, the outfitters. It was a very ordinary Victorian office building, though it boasted a grand marble staircase. The ground floor was occupied by a bespoke tailor and the first floor by the Camera Club. The new firm's capital (£2,000 by the end of 1890) was supplied by William's father, Louis Heinemann, a director of Parr's Bank who had a substantial competency as one of the earlier users of the electric telegraph on the London produce markets. Heinemann senior was a native of Hanover but had been naturalized as a British subject some years before the birth of William, whose mother, Jane (née Lavino), came from Lancashire. William was the eldest of three brothers and two sisters. Both parents were Jewish by descent, but the family had been Anglicans for two generations. Although they now lived in Lancaster Gate, north of Hyde Park, William had been born on a farm owned by his father in Surbiton, which was then in the country.

Though raised in England, William, unlike his brothers, was essentially a cosmopolitan, largely as a result of his unorthodox education. After a spell with a tutor in London he was sent away to study at Dresden *Gymnasium* and elsewhere in Germany. Abroad he became fluent in French as well as German and to a lesser extent in Italian; and in fact there was always a noticeable trace of a foreign accent in his English, which was nevertheless perfectly idiomatic. He was well read in Continental literature, loved its art and music, and considered most of the British to be relatively Philistine. P. Chalmers Mitchell, who knew William from the age of twenty-one and who later became one of his authors, was a guest at Lancaster Gate during the Christmas vacation of 1884. He recalls that 'Willie differed in appearance very little then from his outward personality even in later life. He was rather short, with small hands and feet (of which he was proud), a rather large, round head, sleek dark hair, getting thin on top, and a small moustache. His eyes were dark, a little protruding and with a merry twinkle. His mouth was small, with delicate, firmly-held lips. He had a tendency to embonpoint, and, especially when he was excited, the slightest of stutters gave a characteristic to his speech. Like good conversationalists, when in friendly argument he usually overstated his case, and was fond of making preposterous assertions "on his honour". . . .'

In that Christmas holiday 'Willie took me to a prize-fight in a Shoreditch public house (the butler was our guide), to music-halls and theatres, to night-clubs and restaurants. And when we were doing nothing else we played *écarté* and talked. Willie, by the way, enjoyed a moderate game of poker and was a good player, with some luck, excellent power of observation, but not much dash. But he liked still better the tables at Ostend and Monte Carlo, where he played *trente-et-quarante* for fairly high stakes. . . . We talked of everything under the sun, of sex and philosophy, of persons and plays, of countries and languages, in the way young men talk. . . . He had the gift of affectionate friendship, coming to me to discuss his troubles, and always ready to help or to listen to me. Sometimes it happened, I might not see him for long intervals, but whether after hours or months, we always met in unbroken intimacy. There was no better companion for a weekend at Brighton, in Paris, at Boulogne, Ostend, or Monte Carlo, or for a longer trip in the Cévennes or the Loire Valley. He was always gay and good-tempered, fertile in getting the best local food or wine out of a country inn and ready to enjoy luxury or make the best of temporary inconvenience.'[1]

William's earliest ambition was to be a professional musician, a pianist or possibly a composer but, deciding that he lacked the necessary talent to be a really great artiste, he turned to his second love, literature, and became in 1879 apprenticed to the erudite publisher, Nicholas Trübner. With experience of scholarly bookselling in Göttingen, Hamburg, and Frankfurt, Trübner had come to London to work for Longman, and later, in 1852, started business on his own account in Paternoster Row. To begin with, he had published some fiction, including four of Charles Reade's best novels; but, to quote from Heinemann's own obituary of his employer, he soon 'turned to graver subjects – to linguistic and philosophical literature. The success he had in these branches was more than adequate, and his *Oriental Series* and the *English and Foreign Philosophical Library* include works of the greatest scholars and the profoundest thinkers of the age. . . .' In particular, Trübner's firm became 'the literary intermediary between Europe and the East'.[2]

William began at the bottom, behind the counter in Trübner's front office, receiving visitors and taking orders from the booksellers' runners. He gained practical experience of every phase of publishing from routine selling and publicity to buying paper and dealing with printers' estimates. His interest in and grasp of technical details were to contribute to many of his future successes. He always took meticulous pains over the appearance of his books, over the quality of the paper, typeface and binding, and his brain seemed to be equipped with a built-in computer when calculating production costs. He also of course became involved on the editorial side of Trübner's and compiled his own learned bibliographies such as *A Bibliographical List of the English Translations and Annotated Editions of Goethe's Faust* and *An Essay towards a Bibliography of Marlowe's Tragical History of Doctor Faustus* – both published in *The Bibliographer (1881–4)*. After Trübner's death in 1884, Heinemann was largely responsible for managing the business, but left when it amalgamated with Kegan Paul, Trench & Co.

His experience at Trübner's and of the kind of books they published must certainly have influenced the shape of the more scholarly sections of his own list, but he was not yet ready to start it and he equipped himself further with several more years of travel on the Continent which built the connections with publishers in France, Germany, Scandinavia, Russia, and Italy, which were to lend such a distinctive character to his own publishing.

The Early Lists –
Whistler, *The Heavenly Twins*,
and a Victorian *Spycatcher*

Publishing in the 1890s was on a very much smaller scale than it is today: in 1889, the year prior to Heinemann's opening, new titles totalled 4,694 (compared with 43,188 in 1988), together with 1,414 new editions and reprints (compared with 14,594). The reading public was likewise far smaller and there were few public libraries, though the privately owned subscription libraries such as Mudie's and W. H. Smith's flourished and, as will be seen, dominated the fiction market. There were also of course fewer publishers, but it was a period of expansion and increasing competition, and the decade saw the arrival of several other important new imprints besides Heinemann, among them T. Fisher Unwin, Hutchinson, John Lane, Edward Arnold, and Gerald Duckworth. The main centre for publishers was Paternoster Row, near St Paul's, but Arnold's and Macmillan's were also in Bedford Street, though the latter's offices were soon taken over by Dent's, and Duckworth's were round the corner in Henrietta Street.

There was just enough room on the second floor at Number 21 for Heinemann's staff consisting of W. Ham-Smith, who had followed him from Trübner's and was made business manager (at £18 15s.0d. a month), and an office boy, though after a year they were joined by a secretary, Miss Pugh (at only £4 6s.8d. a month, but perhaps she was part-time). He must have worked them hard. The scope and rapid growth of the early Heinemann list are shown by the advertisement to the trade on 10 October 1890, reproduced on p. 11. Such an assembly of titles was only made possible because from the outset he must have had a clear concept of what he wanted to achieve and because he knew his way round literary London. As well as being a polymath, Heinemann enjoyed society. He was a familiar figure at first nights and the opera, at private views, and on the upholstered benches at the Café Royal. With his clipped moustache and careful dressing hinting at the dandy, he was the complete man-about-town. At lunchtime at Romano's they always reserved his special table and in later years the Metropole, Brighton, was renowned for its *Sole Heinemann*. The preponderance of his list was too serious to be influenced markedly by the Gay Nineties, but they were reflected in his personal life in which his social and publishing lives were intermeshed. Some of his friends became authors or advisers and, conversely, quite a few of the authors and advisers became his intimate friends.

This was particularly true of James McNeill Whistler, whom Heinemann had met at various dinner-parties. Despite the considerable difference in their ages, an unusual sympathetic resonance linked Heinemann with the tetchy, celebrated American painter whose glittering and caustic conversation was said to equal his mastery of canvas. It was this that inspired one of the firm's earliest, most original books: Whistler's *The Gentle Art of Making Enemies* (1890). Before being commissioned it had already been the subject of much publicity because of a dispute with an American newspaperman, Sheridan Ford, who had made a collection of Whistler's writings, letters to the Press, etc, and was only prevented from publishing them after being sued by Whistler in a law court in Antwerp. The final assembly of provocative, combative letters, articles, and other sallies against the vested interests of the Art world effervesced with wit, subdued irony, and pointed implications; they were accompanied by comments and reflections set in small type in the margins. The blurb spoke of *The Gentle Art . . .* as being 'pleasingly exemplified in many instances, wherein the serious ones of this earth, carefully exasperated, have been prettily spurred on to indiscretions and unseemliness, while overcome by an undue sense of right'. The reader was treated, for example, to the details of Whistler's famous battle with Ruskin who had written that he had seen and heard much of Cockney impudence before now but never expected to hear a coxcomb ask two hundred guineas for flinging a pot of paint in the public's face'. Whistler had sued for £1,000 damages but, after a great many arguments and counter-arguments by counsel, obtained no more than the satisfaction of the verdict and damages of one farthing.

The Gentle Art . . .'s typeface, paper, and binding in buff and gold were selected in close consultation with the author, who also helped with the layout and decorated its 350 pages with numerous drawings of butterflies, each of which somehow expressed the meaning of a paragraph as they fluttered, danced, mocked, triumphed – or drooped their wings over the farthing's damages. This unprecedented collation was issued in two editions, one 'printed on handmade paper, signed by the author, and limited to 150 for England'. This sold for 31*s.6d.*, the standard edition for 10*s.6d.*

Its publication caused a sensation and amused admiration, and it did much to establish Heinemann in his first year. Some years later Max Beerbohm, still at Charterhouse when *The Gentle Art . . .* was published, wrote that 'Whistler was that rare phenomenon, the good talker who could write as well as he could talk. Read any page . . . and you will hear a voice in it and see a face in it and see gestures in it. And none of these is quite like any other known to you. It matters not that you never knew Whistler, never even set eyes on him. You see him and know him here. The voice drawls slowly, quickening to a kind of snap at the end of every sentence, and sometimes rising to a sudden screech of laughter; and, all the while, the fine fierce eyes of the talker are flashing at you, and his long, nervous fingers are tracing extravagant arabesques in the air. No! you need never have seen Whistler to know what he was like. He projected through printed words the clear-cut image and clear-ringing echo of himself. He was a born writer, achieving perfection through pains which must have been infinite for that we see at first sight no trace of them at all.

'Like himself, necessarily, his style was cosmopolitan and eccentric. It comprised Americanism and Cockneyism and Parisian *argot*, with constant reminiscences of the authorised version of the Old Testament, and with chips of Molière, and with shreds and tags of what-not snatched from a hundred-and-one queer corners. It was in fact an Autolycene style. It was a style of the maddest motley, but of motley so deftly cut and fitted to the figure, and worn with such an air, as to become a gracious harmony for all beholders.'[3]

At first glance the 1890–93 Heinemann lists may seem to have been wildly eclectic, but steadily a clearer structure emerges, based on fiction, aimed principally at the subscription libraries, balanced by heavyweight series for the most part thought up and commissioned in the office. These included *The Complete Works of Heinrich Heine* (1892–1905), translated by Charles Leland in eight volumes and later supplemented with four further volumes translated by T. Brookshank and Margaret Armour. There were also *The Great Educators*, an ambitious series, eventually in ten volumes, by recognized experts on Aristotle, Loyola, Alcuin, Froebel, Pestalozzi, and others; *The Posthumous Works of Thomas De Quincey*, together with two volumes of his correspondence and other records; *Heinemann's International Library* (see page 16); *Heinemann's Scientific Handbooks*, which included manuals of *Bacteriology* and of *Assaying Gold, Silver, Copper*; and the start of a sumptuous series of art books. All this within the first four years! Among this framework were the large number of titles, many of them one-off, opportunist ventures, to be found in any general publisher's list, which defy classification. It is difficult to understand how or why some of these were thought to be viable – for example, *The Word of the Lord upon the Waters* (1892), sermons composed by a German army chaplain, Dr Richter, and 'read by His Imperial Majesty the German Emperor while at sea on his voyage to the Land of the Midnight Sun'.

There were three other titles from those early lists, all written under pseudonyms or anonymously, that demand to be mentioned because of their particular contribution to the rapid establishment of the new publisher. It needed courage to accept *The Heavenly Twins* (1893) by an unknown authoress, Madame Sarah Grand – the pseudonym of Mrs Frances McFall – because it had already been rejected by Cassell, where Meredith read it, and several other firms. Heinemann's regular reader, Daniel Conner, liked it and thought it 'admirably written', though he also found it 'daring and original . . . and so unconventional, so altogether outside the ordinary track of fiction that, in the absence of anything with which it can be compared, any criticism of it becomes extremely difficult'. He recommended, however, that 'the passages of medical detail ought to be cut out or, at any rate, softened. The whole subject matter of these chapters is extremely unpleasant. . . .' These pages dealt honestly with the dangers of syphilis and the immorality of the Contagious Diseases Act, and it is not known to what extent they were 'softened', but the book was published and was a sensational success with record-breaking sales. Apart from its wit and psychological insights, one reason for its appeal was that Sarah Grand's views reflected those of the 'New Woman' and her plot illustrated the evils of the double standard of morality for men and women. It made an impact on the more progressive thinking of the age.

Desperate to get it published, Sarah Grand originally sold the copyright to Heinemann for £100, but when its surprisingly large sales were apparent he gave her a new contract by which she was to be paid 'the most favoured royalties' and handed her a cheque for £1,200, the amount already earned on the new basis. She went on to write six other books for him, including the semi-autobiographical *The Beth Book* (1898). Much of the rest of her life was, however, devoted to women's rights and municipal politics, including several years as the mayor of Bath.

Another valuable discovery was Robert Hichens, whose *The Green Carnation* (1894) appeared in Heinemann's Pioneer Series. One weekly

declared it was 'the most impudent piece of fiction we have ever met with'. It was a scintillating satire on the literary and artistic world of the day with thinly disguised versions of George Moore, Augustus Sala, Sarah Grand, and others; but the main victims were Oscar Wilde and the Aesthetic Movement. It was before his trial, but rumours about Wilde's private life were then persistent and *The Green Carnation*, while making no distinct charge, reinforced them and hinted at sinful practices. The character of Esmé Amarinth is immediately recognizable: 'Nothing is so unattractive as goodness, except, perhaps, a sane mind in a sane body'; or when Amarinth tells Reggie: 'I will be brilliant for you as I have never been brilliant for my publishers. I will talk to you as no character in my plays has ever talked. . . . Let me be brilliant, dear boy, or I feel that I shall weep for sheer wittiness, and die, as so many have died, with all my epigrams inside me.' His character, Mrs Windsor, could have stepped straight out of a Wilde play: 'The train has been punctual for once in its life. How shocked the directors would be if they knew it, but, of course, it will be kept from them'; or when she reports that someone's mother 'lives in Canterbury, where she does a lot of good among the rich.'[4]

Hichens at his first interview with Heinemann was very impressed: 'What a clever man! He was a true cosmopolitan, a live wire if ever there was one, a searcher after new paths, a man with a will of his own, a man of more than good taste, an extraordinarily well-read man, as sharp as any man in the huge city of London.'

Heinemann explained that he'd felt it necessary for the manuscript to be checked for libel by his solicitor, George (later Sir George) Lewis, but it was felt not to be actionable. Heinemann advised, none the less, that it would be wiser to publish it anonymously, adding:

'"Then it will be attributed to half the well-known authors in England. And the sale will soar."'

'I followed his advice and the book came out anonymously. On the day of publication there was an article about it in the *Daily Telegraph* . . . and the sales began at once. The journalists tried to find out who was the author and many names were put forward; among them the names of Oscar Wilde himself; of Marie Corelli – because she had written anonymously *The Silver Domino*; of Mr Alfred Austin, afterwards the poet laureate; and of various others. Then an amusing thing happened. I received one morning, handed in together, two telegrams. One was signed "Oscar", the other was from Lord Alfred Douglas. I can't now remember the exact wording of them. But Oscar Wilde's told me that "all is discovered" and suggested instant flight on my part to escape his vengeance. And Lord Alfred's told me that I was unmasked and had better go into hiding. Both telegrams were burlesque and merely good jokes. And Lord Alfred's was followed almost immediately by a visit and an invitation to go out to dinner. . . ."[5]

It was Lord Alfred at that dinner who revealed to a group of journalists at the next table that Hichens was the author. His cover blown, his name appeared on the next edition. Hichens went on to write seven more novels for Heinemann, including *Flames* (1897) and *Bella Donna* (1909); but intermittently he was also published by other firms.

The third bestselling *coup* was the publication of *Twenty-five Years in the Secret Service* (1892) by 'Major Henri Le Caron', the pseudonym of Thomas Beach, who had been an accomplished government spy and uncovered the intrigues of the Irish-American Fenians. Scotland Yard particularly wanted to know about the relationship with the Irish Home Rule Party. What were held to be his sensational discoveries made him an important witness for *The Times* when their articles on 'Parnellism and Crime' were investigated by the Parnell Commission of 1889. Parnell was exonerated and his letters were found to be forgeries. All this enabled Le Caron to write a Victorian equivalent of *Spycatcher* (commissioned by Heinemann Australia nearly a century later). Not that the Victorian government attempted to ban it; the Unionist Press was delighted with the book as evidence in their campaign against Home Rule and it led to several actions for alleged libel, mainly brought by Irish MPs, one of which led to booksellers and libraries refusing to handle the book until steps had been taken to remove the offending words; but by then it had reached its sixth edition.

Rudyard Kipling wrote to Heinemann from America: 'Caesar! *what* a splash Le Caron is making! I'm delighted to hear that you have a libel suit on hand. It's good – better than any other kind of advertisement.'[6] He was concerned, however, about Heinemann wanting to quote his own opinion of Le Caron's book: 'Your book-list is mighty strong and should sail ahead without any help of mine. Le Caron alone ought to be a good revenue. O Lord, Lord! To think of the amount that man has chucked away thro' not knowing how to write it up. I'd ha' given three months' pay to have been at his elbow while he was getting the book ready.'[7]

Mentor and Partner:
Gosse and Pawling

Although the impress of William's personality stands out clearly on every facet of his list, he was a wise delegator and from the outset enrolled excellent advisers. Regular readers, either on the staff or freelance, included Daniel Conner and F. M. Atkinson, as well as men of the calibre of Edward Garnett and Walter de la Mare. Ideas and advice came also from Arthur Symons, W. E. Henley, and several others. Most of them came from the intellectual circle he normally inhabited, his business and social lives overlapping. Whether lunching at the Savoy, sipping champagne during theatre intervals, as a guest at dinner-parties, at musical evenings, or weekend house-parties in the country, he was always the publisher, seeking new talent, learning from literary and theatrical gossip. His own dinner-parties were noted not only for the food and wine but also for the conversation and accomplishments of the company.

Two men in particular played substantial roles throughout his thirty-one years as an eponymous publisher: Edmund (later Sir Edmund) Gosse as chief adviser, as reader and author; Sydney Pawling who in April 1893 joined the firm as a full-time partner. Gosse of course was the Man of Letters *par excellence* – or, as H. G. Wells put it, the 'official British Man of Letters'. He became a leading critic with an influential column in *The Sunday Times*. He knew 'everyone' in many walks of life. Every Sunday afternoon Edmund and Nellie Gosse were At Home, first at 29 Delamere Terrace, near Little Venice, and later at 17 Hanover Terrace facing Regent's Park. Among the regular attenders were Henry James, George Moore, Thomas Hardy, Max Beerbohm, Edward Marsh, Austin Dobson, Theodore Watts-Dunton, to mention but a few. Lanky with gold-rimmed spectacles and a drooping moustache, Gosse worked as a translator at the Board of Trade and from 1904 onwards as Librarian to the House of Lords, a position which gave him ample time to pursue his literary concerns and to conduct his correspondence on embossed, official cream-coloured notepaper.

Gosse was a talented raconteur and an accomplished lecturer,

[14]

duchesses being said to fill the front row of his audiences. He enjoyed being a patron to young poets and novelists and being able to acclaim a new talent. He was kindly and devoted to his friends, but he could be quick to take offence. He tended to pomposity and self-importance. Inevitably, a man of his influence was not without enemies and there were those who, with some justice, found his writings guilty of numerous inaccuracies. Introducing her monumental life of *Edmund Gosse*, Ann Thwaite writes that it has become customary to deride him: 'There have been regular suggestions that Gosse, far from being the pillar of Establishment Bloomsbury abhorred, had in fact been involved in the T. J. Wise forgeries and had been a secret homosexual, as well as being malicious, snobbish and a hopelessly unreliable scholar. He certainly had "a genius for inaccuracy", in Henry James's phrase. But he possessed far rarer qualities than accuracy. Raymond Mortimer attempted to set the record straight in *The Sunday Times* in 1949, a hundred years after Gosse's birth. "How trivial are the inaccuracies for which he was attacked compared with the felicity of his style, the width of his allusions, above all the gusto of his bookishness." Thirty-five years later this tribute sounds dated. We do not use words like "felicity", "gusto", or even "bookishness", without reservations and inverted commas. But I have shared Mortimer's pleasure in reading Gosse's criticism.' She also quotes T. S. Eliot's comment: '"The place that Sir Edmund Gosse filled in the literary and social life of London is one that no one can ever fill again, because it is, so to speak, an office that has been abolished." But it seemed, the more I looked into it, that Gosse had held that office well, and performed functions that still need to be performed by those who care about literature.'[8]

No one could have been more suited to advise a new young publisher in the 1890s. The senior by fourteen years, Gosse was the ideal mentor, in a position to provide elder-brotherly wisdom as well as to assess and bring in new talent. In a letter to Heinemann immediately after a close colleague's death, he wrote: 'After a shock of this kind it always seems at first as though everything would go at once to pieces; after a few days one perceives that the status quo is very tenacious.'[9] After Heinemann had suffered a difficult interview with a visitor, Gosse admonished him: 'Of course I do not know your side of the matter. But do you not think that it is very injudicious to be so violent? It seems to me that nothing is gained and much lost by your want of self-command. You will end by doing some irresponsible injury not to yourself only, but to us all. I hope you will not think that I speak in any spirit but that of real affection and sympathy with you. If you could only learn to moderate your transports!'[10]

Gosse was a frequent visitor at 21 Bedford Street and in the very early days when Heinemann was abroad he almost seemed to be holding the 'editorial fort'. As well as industrious, he was methodical and meticulous. Reports and proofs always arrived punctually and he was correspondingly intolerant of delays and carelessness by others, especially printers. These attributes, added to his linguistic skills, made him the ideal editor of the first of William's large-scale, office-originated projects: Heinemann's International Library, a series of translations of foreign novels which already by 1894 contained seventeen titles by authors ranging from the Norwegian of Björnstjerne Björnson (*In God's Way*) and the French of Guy de Maupassant (*Pierre and Jean*) to the Russian of Goncharov (*A Common Story*) and the Spanish of Juan Valera (*Doña Luz*). Gosse wrote an introduction to each volume and called the Library 'a guide to the inner geography of Europe . . . a series of spiritual Baedekers or Murrays'. Aware of British chauvinist and puritanical sensibilities, especially among buyers for the subscription libraries, the trade Press advertisements emphasized that the translations would consist only of books that 'combine literary value with amusing qualities of manner and matter, all that can justly give offence being excluded'. The International Library was the forerunner of the other translations of Continental fiction which were to be one of the cornerstones of Heinemann's prosperity (see pages 77–82).

Sydney Pawling was first met by William at Mudie's circulating library, where he was an important buyer, having worked there since he was fifteen, his uncle and guardian being Charles Mudie, the library's founder. Potentially Mudie's were any fiction publisher's most important customer and on that first occasion William was excited to pick up a large initial order, said to be for 3,000 copies, of his first book, *The Bondman*, and further orders for it followed. He soon sensed, however, that Mudie's were not giving him the orders merited by other titles and he heard rumours that Sydney Pawling had taken a personal dislike to him. Typically, William, far from being downcast, went out of his way to interest Pawling in his new venture and started to invite him to comment on new manuscripts. A few of his handwritten reports survive. They are models of their kind, combining literary judgment with a very experienced assessment of the size and type of the book's market. Among them is a report on *The Irrational Knot*, a novel submitted by George Bernard Shaw which received an unambiguous thumbs-down: 'Being without doubt a clever man he is likely to write a clever book and being young will probably improve on his already published work, but this Ms. I consider to be the low water-mark of his powers: some of it is clever, some of it is dull. The main thesis was fresh seven years ago when this was written and the book might then have read fairly well on that account, in spite of its faults of crudeness and absence of sustained power on the main subject. Today however the thesis is old – it has been better treated and it is too much to expect that you should pay for and publish this bald early work of a man whose reputation would suffer.' Pawling went on to say that the story was dull and colourless; the hero was a 'machine-like working man . . . who bears quite smilingly and with the serenity of a dummy his sister's loss of virtue and his wife's elopement with another man'; the author may have read about the ways of Society but 'too evidently had never lived in them, though most of the action lies in Belgravia'. *The Irrational Knot* was nevertheless published by Constable in 1905.

It was Pawling, however, who strongly recommended the publication of two of Heinemann's bestsellers: Le Caron's *Twenty-five years in the Secret Service* and Sarah Grand's *The Heavenly Twins*. With his experience of assessing books Pawling was just the kind of man Heinemann needed for his fast expanding business, and so early in 1893 he invited Pawling to become a partner. The offer was at once accepted because after fifteen years he was becoming bored with the staid, restricted atmosphere of the library. A good mixer – the cliché fits exactly – he liked the idea of dealing with authors and of pitting his judgment against the more challenging risks of publishing.

Financially the business was already doing quite well. After a profit of £70 1s.5d. in its first year, this increased to £1,049 6s.2d. in 1891 and to £3,656 18s.11d. in 1892 – this amounted to 27½ per cent on sales of £13,278 which was so good that one wonders at the accuracy of the valuation of unsold stock! By the end of 1982, capital and undrawn profits had increased to £6,923. The new partner brought £1,399 15s.9d. into the business and after various adjustments and writing down of stock the opening capital of the partnership came to £5,883 – £3,975 owned by Heinemann and £1,908 by Pawling. Profits were to be split ⁷⁄₁₂ths for Heinemann and ⁵⁄₁₂ths for Pawling.

The partnership was cemented at a celebratory dinner at the Conservative Club, an occasion which caused some raised eyebrows because of this austere establishment's 'desecration' by anything so commercial. The alliance with Pawling was in every sense a shrewd move: as well as his literary judgment and his connection with Mudie's he was a figure of impeccable respectability and social substance, qualities that counted for much in late Victorian England. The two partners complemented each other well. Over the years many who knew the firm have commented upon the contrast between their characters. Pawling, thirty-one, had, unlike Heinemann, been brought up conventionally. Handsome with an impressive moustache, curled no doubt with Hungarian pomade, and with a large physique, he was a great sportsman. Heinemann took no interest in games apart from some very amateur croquet, whereas Pawling was a stalwart of the Hampstead cricket club and had even on three occasions played for Middlesex. He was reported to be the fastest bowler in England, and it was told how he once matched himself against his friend, the 'demon' Spofforth, to bowl across the entire length of the Essex County Ground; Spofforth's ball reached the rails but Pawling's did one better by rebounding three yards as well. He also played in Sir James Barrie's team and captained the Publishers in their first match against the Authors at Lord's. Later he became the MCC's honorary treasurer.

Gosse used to call him the 'handsome Saxon' and Arthur Waugh wrote that 'it would be impossible to imagine a more complete contrast than this great, blonde athlete presented by the side of the little black-haired, bright-eyed, effervescing Heinemann; and it was only one more proof of his hawk-like sense of his own and his business needs, that Heinemann should have seen by instinct that Pawling who, to begin with, did not like him at all, was just the man he wanted to counterbalance and direct his own mercurial and impatient brilliancy.'[11] Similarly, Alfred Stevens, who joined the staff after working at Mudie's, recorded that 'Pawling's temperament was diametrically opposite to Heinemann's at almost every point. Certainly his manner was sometimes a little gruff, but you always had the impression that this was a mask which he used as a protection for his generous nature and big, soft heart.'[12]

Pawling's sobriety and cool judgment must often indeed have provided a corrective to the volatile Heinemann's panache, flair, and intuition. It was Heinemann inevitably who received all the acclaim and publicity, but it would be a mistake to think of Pawling, because he kept in the background, merely as the wise, patient administrator. Heinemann was often away, in Paris where he kept an apartment, or in America, and it was

Pawling who kept the organization going, but he also discovered many of the firm's best authors. He was very discerning and it used to be said that it was easier to sell a manuscript to Heinemann than to his partner; but in fact they worked closely together and most decisions to commission or reject an author were taken jointly.

Kipling and Balestier, a Challenge to Tauchnitz, Ouida

Another of William's important early business associates was the American Wolcott Balestier, but their work together was short-lived, being tragically and suddenly ended by typhoid. Balestier was also joint author of the only original novel Heinemann published by Rudyard Kipling, *The Naulahka* (1892). Balestier, dispatched to London in 1888 at the age of twenty-seven by the American publisher John W. Lovell, in order to cement and develop relationships with English writers, had set up an office at 2 Dean's Yard, Westminster. In particular, he was able to offer decent contracts to authors who had suffered from their work being extensively pirated in the States. Pale, tall, with delicate health, he soon made friends with many well-known authors and won over their support. Henry James wrote of his 'extraordinary subtlety of putting himself in the place of the men – and quite as easily, when need was, of the women of letters'.[13]

Balestier probably first met Kipling at the home of Mrs Humphry Ward, the novelist, but it was Edmund Gosse who advised him of the importance of Kipling, then still something of a young prodigy. At first Balestier dismissed the possibility, but before long made contact with Kipling in his rooms in Villiers Street and they at once took a strong liking to each other. Balestier rapidly arranged for John W. Lovell Inc. to publish an American authorized version of all Kipling's works including some new collections, among them the *Barrack-Room Ballads*, as well as work that had hitherto been pirated. It was at Balestier's office that Kipling is reported to have first met his sister Carolyn (Carrie) and was very taken with her.

Balestier was in addition a writer with three novels published in the States. They possessed no great distinction, but it was a bond. The experience and inspiration of the two young men (Balestier was four years older) sprang from very different sources: the great expanses of the American heartland with its 'moving frontier', pushing ever farther westwards; the expanses of India with its teeming people, temples, animals, rajahs, mystery, and white colonial life. Leon Edel has helped explain how it was that Kipling felt the need for a partner. 'That Kipling, so powerful in his craft, should accept as a collaborator an amateur, even though in some ways a skilful journalist, may seem curious if we judge the collaborator with professional eyes. But such a collaboration – unless it relates to hackwork – is usually an act of friendship, a partnership of the spirit, an act of love. There was also its practical side. Balestier had convinced Kipling that what the author of *The Ballad of East and West* needed was to write – with him – a novel of East and West. . . . If Balestier had neither the verbal endowment nor the required imagination, he had his own concretions of experience and he made the collaboration work. Reading the American's clumsily written newspaperish tales, we sense a Kiplingesque temperament which does not possess Kipling's literary power.'[14]

Balestier wrote the first section laid in Colorado, and Kipling the Indian section based on his visits to the Princely States of Rajputana, full of tension, corruption and sloth, and, for the ruling families, incredible riches. The story centred on a priceless jewel. The depiction of Kunwar, the ruler's young son, threatened with secret poisoning, was masterly. The result was not one of Kipling's finest books, though recently it has been rated more highly and Kipling included it in his collected works.

Although almost certainly William knew Kipling quite well, it is probable that he secured the contract for *The Naulahka* because Wolcott Balestier had joined with him to launch the English Library, an ambitious project to challenge Baron Tauchnitz's virtual monopoly of limp-bound books by British and American writers sold on the Continent. A small limited company was set up: Heinemann & Balestier, the other two directors being Heinemann's close friend at the Lyceum Theatre, Bram Stoker, and W. L. Courtney, an influential journalist on the *Daily Telegraph*. Arthur Waugh – later to be the father of Alec and Evelyn and head of Chapman & Hall – who had been engaged by Balestier, was made company secretary. He gives a good picture of the young Heinemann in action: '. . . whose mercurial energy seemed indomitable. Nothing turned the edge of his keenness; he would gyrate through his office during the day, reducing his small staff into terror, and the next moment bending, all smiles and compliments, over a woman novelist; or lending an entirely patient ear to the preposterous scheme of some literary charlatan. No doubt he could not have bottled up his impatience if he had not let it loose upon his underlings; and, when the explosion was over, it left no ill-feeling behind. He continued to explode and cool again until six o'clock had struck. . . . The next morning he was early at his desk, as fresh as the spring breeze. His nervous force must have been tremendous; but it made the going hard for his companions, more especially as he was a very tyrant in defence of his own judgment, and could not bear to listen to a contrary argument.'[15]

The English Library was launched with Kipling's *The Light that Failed* as its first title. Others followed with extraordinary rapidity, among them reprints by George Meredith, Henry James, S. Baring Gould, Hall Caine, R. L. Stevenson, J. M. Barrie, Jerome K. Jerome, Oscar Wilde, and many others. Kipling contributed several more, including *Soldiers Three* (No. 57) and *The Jungle Book* (No. 167). It was an impressive undertaking, typical of Balestier's verve and energy, and yet Heinemann was getting annoyed with him for spending too much time away from the office, a weekend at his rented house on the Isle of Wight with Henry James extending to many days: 'Your idea', Heinemann stormed, 'of running a London office from the Isle of Wight is about as sensible as steering a ship in a storm from the top of a lighthouse.'

For three months Balestier did not work at Dean's Yard, leaving everything to the able young Waugh, and then in November 1891 he set off for Leipzig to consult Albert Brockhaus, the English Library's German agent. He was exhausted and when he reached Dresden was taken ill with a virulent form of typhoid. Carrie, his elder sister, went out to him at once and Waugh tells us that 'she knew that he was very ill, and the way she knew struck me as poignantly pathetic. He needed the attendant to bring him something, and his sister rang the bell. Nobody came, and she turned to ring again. "She'll come as soon as she can", he said faintly; "don't hurry her!" In health he had never brooked a moment's delay. "I knew then", said his sister to me afterwards, "that he must be very ill indeed." The crisis came on the twenty-first day of the illness – on the 6th December 1891; and he was not strong enough to fight it. The news that he was dead, within a few days of his thirtieth birthday, seemed for the moment to hold time motionless, "like Joshua's moon on Ajalon". We could only look blankly into one another's faces, wondering what was to happen next.'[16]

Heinemann and Henry James went to Dresden for the funeral. Kipling was in Ceylon, though before Christmas he sailed for home. He had received a wire from Carrie Balestier: 'Wolcott dead. Come back to me.' Kipling came and they were married at All Souls Church, Langham Place, scarcely five weeks after the funeral. Henry James acted as father and gave the bride away and Edmund Gosse was best man. Heinemann was among the very few others who attended the ceremony.

Meanwhile the English Library continued to be run by Waugh, but the first year's accounts were very disturbing. With the exception of two of Kipling's, none of the books had paid their way, as Waugh records: 'The entire venture was on an unstable basis. Baron Tauchnitz knew very well what the Continental rights in an English novelist were worth, and he had been dealing fairly with his clients. We had taken them away from him by paying twice or three times as much; but the market could not justify the speculation. Again, the Baron printed the books himself on the spot in his own printing works, and he printed cheaply. Most of our books had been given to the best and most expensive printers in Edinburgh and London; and, finally, the whole organization was handicapped by the commission of a German agent. The rivalry had been attempted too hastily, and launched without counting the cost. For the moment the shareholders were reassured by promises of retrenchment; but any competent auditor, overhauling the figures, would have seen at once that the eventual bankruptcy was only a question of time.'[17] On top of this, Lovell Inc. in New York was declared bankrupt and only a cheque from Heinemann delayed the loss of the Dean's Yard office. By mid-1893 Heinemann had decided there was no point in throwing good money after bad, in reinforcing failure, and the English Library was wound up. Heinemann, after all, had his hands full enough with other ventures.

Wolcott Balestier, however, was remembered by Heinemann in the publication of *The Average Woman* (1892) which contained three of his novellas, and by a novel, *Benefits Forgot* (1892). The former also carried a lengthy biographical sketch, as only Henry James could write it, which helps to convey something of Balestier's unique, magnetic capabilities. 'He was a man of business of altogether peculiar genius, and it was in this light that he figured, with singular intensity, to a large number of charmed, befriended people during the part of his brief life in which I judge that he had lived more than in all its preceding time, the three crowded London years that began in December 1888. . . . I speak of his having "figured" in London, because he was from the first, in his bright young ingenuity, his suggestion of immediate capacity, an apparition essentially salient. This is what he remained to the end, unmistakably an influence exotic and curious, dropped down from without, not thrown up from within. He made London, on the ground on which he dealt with it, so extraordinarily his own that the contrast between the spirit and the matter, the agent and the medium, could only grow more striking and, if I may frankly say so, more amusing . . . and it was given to him, moreover, to encounter the human, not to say the supposedly literary spirit, bared of its appetites. He saw many realities and had already learned not to blink many uglinesses. Young as he was, he had perceived what was of the essence. . . .'[18]

Edmund Gosse penned a somewhat less convoluted memoir for the *Century Magazine* in 1892, later reprinted privately, in which he wrote of Balestier's business resource and literary promise and the speed with which he was able to 'conquer a place of influence in the centre of English literary society. . . . What was so novel and so delightful in his relations with authors was the exquisite adroitness with which he made his approaches. He never lost a shy conquest through awkwardness or roughness. If an anthology of appreciations of Wolcott Balestier could be formed, it would show that to each literary man and woman whom he visited he displayed a tincture of his or her own native colour.'[19]

Balestier was also responsible for bringing to Heinemann *The Tower of Taddeo* (1892) by one of the most established best-selling authors of the day, Ouida (the pen-name of Marie Louise de la Ramée), with forty-five novels under her belt, perhaps the best known being *Under Two Flags*. There were occasions when she had been ridiculed for over-writing and for the extravagance of her characterization, but for the young firm to be able to add her to the list was a *coup* indeed. Unfortunately Ouida herself took a different view and in an angry letter to *The Times* (22 November 1892) she claimed that the book had been obtained by 'unfair, secretive, and perfidious means'. Balestier, she asserted, had merely purchased the European and American rights for Lovell Inc. of New York and she would never have dreamed of allowing it to appear under the imprint set up in opposition to her old friend Baron Tauchnitz. She'd also had no idea that her agreement with Lovell could allow it to be published in London by Heinemann. She was incensed that it was to be published in three volumes instead of one. 'Mr Heinemann states with impudent indifference that he is not acting illegally. This is very probable. Few treacherous, mean, and unjust actions are punishable by law. I can only repeat that I have never had, and never shall have, any voluntary connexion with his firm; that to see this little story in his London and Leipzig lists is distressing, injurious, and offensive to me; and that, if the general rule of *de mortuis & c.*, prevents the full expression of my views concerning the deceased person who Mr Heinemann has seen fit to mourn as a Marcellus, I must, in justice to myself and to the little Florentine tale of an old tower, say herein that in the arrangement for its production I was completely overreached by a singularly sharp Yankee.'[20]

The next day *The Times* printed a lengthy reply to this outburst from Heinemann which began: 'The battle with Mme Ouida were fairer could one employ the weapon she employs. Fortunately, the courtesy due to a lady prevents one from throwing mud. . . . Her very animosity defeats her object, and the recipient of her blows smiles when she would fain make him smart.' In the course of a recital of technicalities he demonstrated that the contract, written in her own hand, gave him the right to publish. He also pointed out that Ouida had unreasonably demanded no fewer than seven consecutive revises of the proofs of the whole book, and concluded sourly: 'For my part, the natural regret that Mme Ouida should not in future have any "voluntary connexion" with my firm is somewhat tempered by the experience of the last few months, while this book has been going through the press.'[21]

Once again an encouraging, if somewhat sexist Kiplingesque note came from America: 'Your letter says everything that a man could say to carry conviction. . . . 'Tis a stale old whore any way and I suppose her book sales are running down and she wants to lift 'em. . . . It's a sweet sight to see a woman doing business as a man and *then* claiming all the advantages of the sex.'[22]

Young Heinemann uses Hall Caine
to Kill off the Three-Decker

Chronology provides the backbone for any history, but the complex of happenings and influences with which it is fleshed out are not always readily disciplined by a timescale; and yet unless there is some method of grouping and classification their presentation becomes indigestible. Deciding what to include and exclude is also of course necessary. During the course of a century there have been literally thousands of Heinemann authors and tens of thousands of titles to choose between, and selection of the severest kind has been unavoidable if this history were not to degenerate into little more than a dry-as-dust catalogue – though selection always brings the risk of distortion.

History is usually as much an essay as a record of events, and this one is no exception. This is not, however, intended to be a work of literary criticism and yet mere description can be unpalatable and tedious without comment or interpretation, which in turn tend to govern what events and, in particular, which authors are to be included. Some, in fact far too many, authors and individual titles choose themselves, but others need to be included for a number of very different reasons. Can, for example, an author who is now no longer read and is virtually forgotten, and whose work would, by today's criteria, be found dull and unacceptable, be omitted even though he or she contributed a stream of very successful novels? Conversely, should not room be found for an author with no more than a single title but which with hindsight is seen to have been significant, though at the time in terms of numbers sold or finance it was a flop? Then what about an author without either great literary or commercial value, but whose publication was noteworthy for some quite other reason? – such as a libel action.

Many of the authors not included in the body of the text will, however, be found in Appendix A at the end of the volume. Their consignment thither has meant taxing, frequently painful, decisions. Among them will be found some whose names are unquestionably established but whose contribution to the Heinemann list has been minimal. The authors selected for the text are grouped under the generic headings found in any publisher's catalogue (Fiction, Drama, Biography, etc.) and, for the most part, they appear within one or other of the chronological divisions during which the bulk of their work was published. So far as possible, the full range of an author's books are treated together, though some (e.g., Edmund Gosse, John Masefield, Max Beerbohm, Somerset Maugham) spill over irresistibly into more than one division or, more likely, subject category.

All the above considerations have influenced the choice of the authors included in this chapter – a mere handful of the novelists published by Heinemann up to the 1914 World War which marks a natural watershed. Hall Caine was obviously the first to choose himself and more needs to be said about him; but, first, it is necessary to give some attention to the role of the Victorian circulating libraries because of their domination of the fiction market. Chief among them, as already mentioned, was Mudie's. Founded in the 1840s, its clientele were largely 'carriage trade'. The Ionic pillared entrance hall in New Oxford Street was on most days crowded with frock-coated gentlemen and floral-hatted ladies, clasping majestic volumes and chattering about their latest choices, bolstering or de-molishing literary reputations. Mudie's main but slightly down-market rivals were the libraries at the branches of W. H. Smith's. Early in the twentieth century further competition grew, especially from Boots's branch libraries and the Times Bookclub. Public libraries, run by local authorities, were still on a very much smaller scale, though by 1913–14 they held 11.4 million volumes in stock compared with only 1.96 million volumes in 1884–85; similarly by 1913–14 the populations of areas served by libraries amounted to 60 per cent of the total compared with only 23 per cent in 1881.

Heinemann's business was scarcely four years old when he played a decisive part in revolutionizing the library trade. Until then the trade custom was to issue novels first in three-volume editions (or 'three-deckers' as they were often called) at a normal price of £1 11s.6d. (with discount actually 15s.) which was too expensive for most people and so they were attracted to the circulating library with its annual subscription of one guinea. If Mudie's and Smith's approved of a novel, they bought out virtually the whole of the first edition, even though at an artificially inflated price. This had very obvious financial attractions for the publisher, but on the other hand the system gave the libraries a monopolistic power which enabled them to influence, if not dictate, the kind of fiction which was published. In defence of the three-decker it was said that the high price and relatively small initial print-run enabled publishers to issue works by 'serious' authors who would otherwise never be in print. Against this it could be argued that three-deckers fostered too much windy, moralizing, prolix prose, padded out in order to go the distance.

Another weighty criticism was that people who were not library members had to wait anything up to twelve months before the issue to bookshops of the standard 6s. one-volume edition and even longer for the usual 3s.6d., 2s., or even 7d. or 6d. editions. The time gap between the three-volume and one-volume editions was, however, being speedily reduced, giving the libraries less time for their exclusive service or in which to dispose of stocks they had finished with. Eventually, Mudie's and Smith's acted together and dispatched letters to publishers asking that the price of novels in sets should not be more than 4s. per volume, and that the cheaper reprints should not appear until twelve months after the date of first publication. The recently formed Society of Authors took a very different view and, finding 'themselves almost unanimously opposed to the continuance of the three-volume system', considered that 'the disadvantages of that system to authors and to the public far outweighed its advantages; that for the convenience of the public, as well as for the widest possible circulation of a novel, it is desirable that the artificial form of edition produced for a small body of readers only be now abandoned; and the whole of the reading public should be placed at the outset in possession of the work at a moderate price. . . . During the first six or twelve months after the publication of a novel the author is shut off from the whole of the reading public (except the subscribing part of it). When the time comes for the issue of a single-volume edition he has to face the fact that 60,000 subscribers, meaning perhaps 240,000 readers, have already made themselves acquainted with his book, and that the old three-volume copies are offered to the public at half-a-crown or three shillings apiece.'[1]

Many publishers seemed uncertain what to do, but the *Publishers' Circular*, then the leading trade journal, was opposed to the libraries' proposed 'revolution in literature, so far as fiction is concerned. The occupation of two-thirds of our novelists would be destroyed at a blow, and the remaining third would be compelled to accept considerably lower terms than they now receive. For publishers could not possibly continue to pay present prices or present percentages to authors while making a reduction of something like twopence halfpenny in the shilling to libraries.' The journal went on to ask if the three-volume was doomed and to warn that 'as soon as it becomes the practice to issue novels at once in cheap editions, the public will forsake the libraries and flock to the booksellers'.[2] Instead the journal supported the idea that the circulating libraries should solve their problems by putting up their own prices. The same issue reported that 'Mr William Heinemann strongly protests against the action of the libraries. Writing to the *Daily Chronicle*, he says: "If at the present moment the libraries, by the larger output of literature, offer their subscribers so much wider a range from which to select books, is it not reasonable that subscribers for this class of literature, at least, should pay a trifle extra? A shilling or two per annum from each subscriber would solve the whole difficulty, and would not – as would the carrying out of the present suggestion – reduce to destitution a considerable number of quite worthy and not unuseful writers. They may be in no way contributors to literature, but they cater for a public with little or no appreciation for literature, requiring simply to be pleasantly and innocently amused."'.[3] Heinemann also proposed that libraries should make some difference in price between good books and bad ones.

The impracticality and other objections to making such invidious choices were only too obvious, but he also suggested that long novels might be published in four volumes apiece. It was therefore surprising that very soon afterwards it was left to him to give the publishing trade the lead it needed by announcing that 'Mr Heinemann has much pleasure in announcing that Mr Hall Caine's New Novel, *The Manxman*, will be issued on 15 July 1894 in One Volume, crown 8vo, price 6s.' Beneath was a special announcement emphasized by three asterisks: 'There will be no edition in three vols.' This was not actually the first novel he had issued in this manner – there had been a few earlier ones issued initially at 5s. in his Crown Copyright Series – but it was the first time that an explicit disclaimer of a library edition had appeared, and publishing history normally credits him with having killed off the three-decker novel. Six months later in an interview with the *Publishers' Circular* he confirmed that he 'believed greatly in the single-volume form of publication for popular fiction, and since the circular addressed to the publishers from the libraries I have not published any novels in three volumes. This, however, does not mean that I shall not do so. . . . Six-shilling novel volumes of fiction are, however, selling remarkably well, but, of course, it may only be a boom for a time. At this price such works seem to sell better than at a lower, provided, of course, they are well got up and worth the money.'[4]

His pioneering gamble paid off; because *The Manxman* sold around 400,000 copies. Hall Caine wrote ecstatically from his machicolated Greba Castle in the Isle of Man: 'The superb cheque with the accounts came all right. They are splendid! One is almost afraid to hope for such returns again. The receipts of the book thus far have more than realized your own and Pawling's great predictions of two years ago; in fact, with America and the serial they reach nearly five figures. I confess that the amount almost terrifies me. You have worked splendidly for the book and your judgment was entirely right when you made the other books 6*s*.'[5]

The Manxman's complex story of the love of two friends for the same girl was another powerful blend throbbing with passion, tragedy, ambition – and yet it was also edifying and intensely moral. It catered perfectly for the mass reading market which appeared with the growth in literacy since the 1870 Education Act. Altogether Hall Caine wrote thirteen books for Heinemann. Several of them were 'blockbusters' with, for the period (up to 1917), prodigious sales, viz. *The Manxman* (1894) 397,966; *The Christian* (1897) 643,228; *The Eternal City* (1901) 702,212; *The Prodigal Son* (1904) 368,225. Many were serialized before publication, published in America, and translated into many European languages. Stage and silent film versions also brought in large sums. He claimed that his earnings by his pen were larger than those of Dickens, and perhaps only less than those of Scott. At his death he left £240,000, which was then a fortune. He played a very active part in promoting his own books, sending the office a stream of letters in tiny crabbèd handwriting, insisting on more advertising and advising on circularization and other methods of publicity. Ernest Whyberd, who worked behind the counter at 21 Bedford Street, recalls that 'he had a genius for advertising and could sell his own books better than anyone else. He looked upon himself as the second Shakespeare, I should think, for he tried to look as like him as possible. He had a neat Elizabethan beard, hair swept back from his forehead, and he dressed in a long black cloak, a flowing tie and a black wideawake hat.'[6] He was known as one of the firm's most difficult and time-consuming authors; but of course his personal quirks had to be put up with, though Heinemann himself did not always set a good example. Once, following a heated argument, he brought the interview to an abrupt end by holding open his office door for Hall Caine to depart: 'Your name', he barked, 'should be *Hell* Caine!'

An indication of the difference then in popular taste and interest is given by the strongly religious, evangelical character of his bestsellers, often with Biblical themes. He described the fundamental idea behind some of them as being 'the possibility of the absolute regeneration of the human soul. As against the theory of the domination of heredity, I have attempted to illustrate the miraculous power of atonement. I take this to be of the essence of the Christian faith, expressing itself for men like John Bunyan in the word "conversion".' With other books it was 'the unity of religion and the spiritual brotherhood of mankind'.[7] Publication of *The Christian* caused a religious furore. The newspapers carried angry letters from clerics, but other letters were full of praise. Of course all of this acted like adrenalin on its sales, though Hall Caine genuinely seems to have found the attacks very upsetting, as he makes clear in several letters: 'The truth is that the literary class was against me. Success of their own kind hurts them. . . . The wise journalists would write a better book than *The Christian* if they knew how. They don't know how, and that's why they are journalists.'[8] A few days later: 'I am getting many letters calling on me to stick to my guns. Of course the parsons are the most unscrupulous. This I expected. . . . But I cannot speak about all the base fighting without letting the book down. As Pawling truly says, my best is in the novel. Let the blackguards tear at that.'[9] In a letter to Bram Stoker he complains that 'the penalties of success are terrible. Every base and low down dodge which it is possible to practise on a man seems to have been practised on me. Private letters and telegrams printed, lies of the most outrageous kind told, and all the other tactics of the devil brought into play. . . . An experience like this makes one realize how large a part malignity plays in life, and it takes all one's time not to become bitter and hard. It is the cruellest passage of life I have ever gone through. I feel as if I want a spiritual bath, that I may plunge in and come out again clean of all the foulness that has been flung at me.'[10]

With *The Woman Thou Gavest Me* (1913), which sold over 100,000 on subscription and was translated into twelve languages, Hall Caine fell foul of the libraries, who often acted as self-appointed guardians of public morality. The Circulating Libraries Association, whose purpose was to hamper books which 'transgressed the dictates of good taste', placed it on the list of books not to be supplied to customers unless it was specially asked for. The trouble with this novel appears to have been that it made a married woman describe how she seduced her lover who, up to the time of her nightly visit to him, had at least respected her married state. Again there were angry protests and interviews in the Press and invaluable publicity which helped turn the book into another bestseller, but Hall Caine indignantly denied that he wanted this kind of publicity and pointed out that if as many or more books were sold through, or in spite of, being censored, the act of censoring was even more indefensible. In particular, it prevented his book from reaching young women readers largely for whose benefit he wrote it. He appears to have been affected by the beliefs of the Suffragist Movement then reaching one of its peaks, because he defined the underlying concept of *The Woman Thou Gavest Me* as 'the equality of the sexes according to natural law, as opposed to the inequality which human law, and too often the churches, have imposed upon woman, to her age-long and most terrible martyrdom'.[11]

Although knighted by a presumably admiring sovereign, Hall Caine's literary reputation soon faded after his death in 1931. *The Concise Cambridge History of English Literature*, published in 1941, dismisses him tersely: 'The numerous novelistic melodramas of T. H. Hall Caine must rest unnamed'.[12]

Zangwill, Wells, Conrad, and other Novelists

Assessed by today's literary criteria, it is not difficult to dismiss Hall Caine and many other Victorian and Edwardian writers, though at times posterity makes an unnecessarily harsh judge. There is certainly no justification for underestimating a writer like Israel Zangwill who with *Children of the Ghetto* (1892) was one of Heinemann's earliest recruits and who went on to contribute twenty-six more books. They included six plays, essays, and a book of poems, as well as novels. In his studio portrait photograph he looks, chin on hand, unblinkingly at the lens through small pince-nez from a long, almost equine face with hair parted in the middle –

the questioning, mournful, rabbinical stare as Jewish as his name. Many of his other novels and collections of short stories were also about the Jewish community of London's East End: *The King of the Schnorrers* (1894) which had pictures by Phil May; *Dreamers of the Ghetto* (1898); and *Ghetto Comedies* (1907). There was plenty of Yiddish humour and whimsical jesting; but there was also sadness, and his fiction was in part a vehicle for his ideas. These were also embedded in his plays: H. R. Nevinson in *The Nation* described *The Melting Pot* (1909) as 'a new and vast idea presented with all the power of art, irony, tragedy and domestic situation. . . . One of the greatest dramatic productions of our age . . . a grand theme, treated with almost pathetic seriousness, and illustrated by all the crash of movement and human passion such as the noblest drama has always demanded.' William Archer in *The Star* wrote that *The Next Religion* (1912) was 'a splendidly vivid epitome, one may almost say, of the spiritual struggles of the age'.

Zangwill was personally involved in the struggle for women's suffrage and other liberal causes, being the founder of a Jewish social movement and theory known as 'territorialism' which at one time competed closely with Herzl's Zionism. Zangwill's life-style was very different from Heinemann's – he lived modestly, mostly in the country, and felt more at home in London's Bohemia than in the Savoy Grill – but their shared Jewish background must have made a bond, though one wonders how far Heinemann shared some of his ideas – not that as a publisher he ever felt it essential to profess the beliefs of all his authors. Zangwill was by no means a particularly profitable author, but a serious list needed an author whom G. K. Chesterton, for example, called 'a great artist', whose characters were likened by Holbrook Jackson to Falstaff and Micawber, and who in Paris was hailed as 'one of the vast European intelligences of this epoch'. His personal predilections apart, from the beginning Heinemann knew that it was quality far more than bestsellers which made a firm's true reputation and was its ultimate justification.

With *The Time Machine* (1895) the firm entered into a long but quarrelsome and spasmodic relationship with H. G. Wells which ended in 1945 with his last book (see page 404). *The Time Machine* was his first novel and was introduced by W. E. Henley, who planned to serialize it in the *New Review*, then just launched and financed by Heinemann (see pages 147–9). Under Henley's guidance the text was considerably improved and Heinemann agreed to publish it with the relatively generous advance of

£50, a starting royalty of 15 per cent, and a guaranteed first printing of 10,000 copies. This early essay in science-fiction not only contained some fine imaginative writing but it also pointed to the kind of writer Wells was to become. The conflict between the Eloi and the Morlocks, and especially the second voyage to a more distant future when the sun was dying and life had become all but impossible, struck the note of pessimism found in some of his work and undermined the complacent Victorian belief in the inevitability of progress; though in the short term it is true to say that Wells was an optimist.

Wells meanwhile signed contracts for further books with Dent and Methuen, but the next year Heinemann published his third novel, *The Island of Doctor Moreau* (1896) with its terrible prophecy of what science without ethics, science for science's sake and when in evil hands, is capable of. Emboldened by the healthy sales and the reception given to *The Time Machine*, Heinemann increased the advance to £60 and let the royalty grow from 15 to 20 per cent after the sale of 5,000 copies. The Press reaction to *Doctor Moreau* was not, however, uniformly favourable and when he received his royalty statement Wells doubted its accuracy: 'I do shrink from the bother of litigation and on the other hand I don't care to let the matter pass simply because you are defiant and troublesome. It's rather a case for the Authors' Society than for me as it affects the general body of authors. I'm busy now but I will consider the whole question at my leisure and let you know then what line I take.'[13] Some weeks later he wrote: 'You not only bother an author to ask for what is due to him, but you are uncivil over the payment. You say you overpaid me for the Moreau. . . . Do you really think you lose by me? If so, I am prepared to do this in order that you may not complain to that effect further. *I will pay back every penny I have ever had from [you] for the book rights of* Time Machine *and* Moreau, *buy all stereo plates, copies and so forth at the valuation of any independent and competent person* on condition that all existing agreements between us are cancelled. I think that is a fairly generous offer of release to you. If you don't accept it, I hope you will at least have the grace to apologize for that "overpaid".'[14] But the quarrel was made up and his titles remained in the list.

In *The War of the Worlds* (1898), with its invasion by Martians only halted by their lack of immunity to earthly bacteria, Wells reached a new peak of success and international fame. James Pinker, now his agent, was able to drive a hard bargain, but it was the last of Wells's novels the firm was to publish. He had already started to earn his reputation as the author with the largest number of publishers under his belt, though in 1910 with *The New Machiavelli* he nearly came back. Macmillan's were due to publish it but at the last moment held back because it was so 'improper', though it came out later that a much bigger worry was the possibility of libel actions because of the recognizable verbal portraits of Sidney and Beatrice Webb, Arthur Balfour, and others. Sir Frederick Macmillan took the very unusual course of himself offering it to Heinemann, but the latter felt bound to tell Wells that 'it was certainly one of the most brilliant books I have read for years and one which has given me the greatest possible pleasure in reading . . . but it was so charged with a dangerous (and perhaps libellous) atmosphere' that he dared not risk taking it on.[15] Wells wrote back to say that he was very sorry, but added: 'there's a note of personal resentment and distrust in yours that troubles me. I parted with you on Tuesday on such good terms and in such good spirits that I can't help asking you anyhow to keep friends. Your distrust really does me an injustice. If you will look up our correspondence you'll see I've made you very definite offers to bind myself to you and leave you free and that I've made all sorts of variations with the idea of meeting you. No doubt the fun of bargaining got the better of me on Tuesday; it's my loss anyhow, so there's no reason for making a personal estrangement of it.'[16] *The New Machiavelli* was in the end published by John Lane at the Bodley Head. It did well but Wells did not remain with him. It is doubtful if at the time Heinemann could have understood just what he was losing; those first three novels by Wells are still in the Heinemann catalogues of the 1980s.

Although Joseph Conrad was a Pole, he belongs in this chapter and not in the section devoted to European authors, because he always wrote in English rather than in Polish or French, his first and second languages. His third novel, *The Nigger of the 'Narcissus'* (1897) was published by Heinemann but like Wells he then soon went elsewhere – Dent mainly, but also T. Fisher Unwin and Methuen. Publishing history shows that it is one thing to recognize genius, but it is quite another to hold on to it. *The Nigger* was introduced to the firm by Edward Garnett and it was Pawling who accepted it and arranged for it to be serialized in the *New Review*. Conrad had been thirty-seven when he abandoned a life at sea for literature, as he explains in the preface to *The Nigger* which appeared in the American edition – written of course long before the arrival of Black consciousness: 'From that evening when James Wait joined the ship – late for the muster of the crew – to the moment when he left us in the open sea, shrouded in sailcloth, through the open port, I had much to do with him. He was in my watch. A negro in a British forecastle is a lonely being. He has no chums. Yet James Wait, afraid of death and making her his accomplice, was an impostor of some character – mastering our compassion, scornful of our sentimentalism, triumphing over our suspicions. But in this book he is nothing; he is merely the centre of the book's collective psychology and the pivot of the action. Yet he, who in the family circle and amongst my friends is familiarly referred to as the Nigger, remains very precious to me. For the book written round him is not the sort of thing that can be attempted more than once in a lifetime. It is the book by which, not as a novelist perhaps, but as an artist striving for the utmost sincerity of expression, I am willing to stand or fall. Its pages are the tribute of my unalterable and profound affection for the ships, the seamen, the winds and the great sea – the moulders of my youth, the companions of the best years of my life. After writing the last words of that book, in the revulsion of feeling before the accomplished task, I understood that I had done with the sea, and that henceforth I had to be a writer.'[17]

The Nigger was declared by the critics to be a masterpiece, but it did not appeal to a wide public and made little money either for publisher or author, who for years found it a struggle to live by his pen. The firm also published *Typhoon and other Stories* (1903) after which Conrad also committed himself to Heinemann to write *The Rescue*, though he found this impossible to finish until much later in life. This meant that he was in debt to Heinemann for the advance, Pawling having to write to J. B. Pinker as late as March 1914 to draw attention to an outstanding balance of unearned advance amounting to £311 1s.9d. Conrad always felt guilty about this: '. . . poor Heineman[n]', he wrote to William Blackwood in 1900, '(who had been awfully decent to me) has nothing to show for his decency but a few receipts for moneys paid out to and half a novel which is hung up to ripen – I trust. He seemed very anxious to see it. I am not enthusiastic about it myself but it seems to have hit Heinemann's readers in a soft spot. . . .'[18]

The only other book by Conrad published initially by Heinemann was a novel written jointly with Ford Madox Hueffer (Ford Madox Ford) called *The Inheritors* (1901), a *roman à clef* with a political theme. Hueffer wrote the basic text and Conrad's contribution was to polish and 'to give each scene a final tap'. The collaboration, as might be expected, led to considerable stress for them both, but they badly needed the money: Hueffer describes how 'William Heinemann – the most generous and wise of publishers, a Jew at that – would hand out an unexpected cheque on the top floor of 21 Bedford Street whilst the writer kept Pawling – a blonde Christian but much more like a publisher than his Semitic partner – interested as well as he might with a description of the plot of *The Inheritors*. . . . Then Conrad would come in, buttoning his overcoat over the cheque; Mr Pawling would throw up his hands in horror and exclaim to the writer: "You've let him get at that ass William again. By God, that is not cricket!" '[19] When the joint effort was accepted Conrad wrote to Edward Garnett: 'Jove! What a lark! I set myself to look upon this thing as a sort of skit upon the sort of political (?!) novel fools of the N.S. sort do write. This is in my heart of hearts. And poor *H*. [Hueffer] was in dead earnest! Oh Lord. How he worked! There is not a chapter I haven't made him write twice – most of them three times over. This is collaboration if you like! Joking apart, the expense of nervous fluid was immense. There were moments I cursed the day I was born and dared not look up into the light of day I had lived through with this thing on my mind. H. has been as patient as no angel has ever been. I've been fiendish. I've been rude to him; if I've not called him names I've *implied* in my remarks and the course of our discussions the most opprobrious epithets. He wouldn't recognize them. 'Pon my word it was touching. And there's no doubt that in the course of that agony I have been ready to weep more than once. Yet not for him. Not for him.'[20]

At first *The Inheritors* received favourable reviews, but later ones were negative and sales were poor. Hueffer records that 'it caused no excitement; even to ourselves it caused so little that the writer cannot so much as remember opening the parcel that contained the first copies. . . . It was received by the English critics with a paean of abuse for the number of dots it contained. . . . One ingenious gentleman even suggested that we had cheated Mr Heinemann and the public who paid for a full six-shilling novel with words all solid on the page.'[21]

Hueffer, as Ford Madox Ford, was later published by various other publishers, but years afterwards the firm issued his autobiography, *It was the Nightingale* (1934). It handled no more original works by Conrad, though his collected works in twenty volumes appeared between 1921–27, published jointly with Doubleday, accompanied by *Notes on my Books* (1927), consisting of prefaces, extracts from correspondence and other unpublished material, and also the *Life and Letters of Joseph Conrad* (1927) by M. Jean-Aubry. At first William had resisted the idea of a collected edition and talked scathingly of 'merely the supplying of "book furniture"', but the project went ahead and Conrad wrote to F. N. Doubleday that 'nothing would give me greater pleasure than to see the English issue in Mr Heinemann's hands. I have preserved a very vivid sense of that firm's friendly attitude towards my earlier work. They did everything that was possible to give a chance to *The Nigger of the "Narcissus"* – a pretty hopeless book at that time; and later, when I failed in my engagement to them, they treated me with a delicate consideration which I am not likely ever to forget.'[22]

Two more authors only will have to suffice to represent the novelists taken on by the firm up to the end of the century. E. L. Voynich wrote only four books for Heinemann and one of them was after a gap of forty years – *Put off thy Shoes* (1946) – but the first, *The Gadfly* (1897), turned out to be one of those unexpected successes that appeal to and justify the gambling instinct in any good publisher. It sold prodigiously for years and went into many editions, was published in America, and there were several translations. The firm revived it in 1973. Though first taken for a man, Ethel Lilian Voynich was young and Anglo-Irish, a former governess and music teacher, married to a Polish scholar who had become a revolutionary in the struggle for freedom from Russian rule, and had been exiled to Siberia. From him and his circle of friends she learned about the methods and spirit of underground tactics described with such dramatic detail in *The Gadfly*, though its setting was not divided Poland but the Italy of the Risorgimento and the early years of Mazzini's movement. A romantic tale of adventure with a strong, magnetic central character, it also depicted clearly the various and sometimes conflicting elements in the Italian revolutionary movement and the causes of unrest that gave rise to it. The Press at once recognized that they were reviewing something remarkable: 'It is more deeply interesting and rich in promises than ninety-nine out of every hundred novels' – *The Academy*. 'Altogether real and admirable is the personality of the bitter, biting, mocking, suffering Gadfly, untameable, unrelenting, and always "game" – a living man that will force the most unwilling reader's sympathy' – *The Bookman*. 'Exciting, sinister, even terrifying, as it is at times, we must avow it to be a work of real genius, which will hold its head high among the ruck of recent fiction' – *St James's Gazette*. There were many more equally good and Heinemann must have been glad that he had postponed publication until after Queen Victoria's Jubilee: writing to *The Gadfly*'s American publisher, Henry Holt, on 15 May 1897, he explained that because of it 'there is an absolute stagnation of business, such a stagnation as I have never known before. People are thinking of nothing but the pageant that is to come, and there is positively not the ghost of a chance for any book that is published now . . . the whole week will be one of riot and fun-making here; in fact, I believe most businesses will be closed. . . .'[23]

The last writer in this section is Flora Annie Steel, who supplied Heinemann with twenty-one titles, the best-known being about India, where she went as a young married woman in the 1860s, her husband being in the Indian Civil Service. Untypically she learned the local languages and gave medical help to Indian women, later becoming an inspector of schools. Her books are based very much on what she saw and learned for herself. The most famous, *On the Face of the Waters* (1897), was, however, about the Indian Mutiny of 1857. It had been turned down by Macmillan but Heinemann at once recognized its importance. There are plenty of the expected ingredients of a novel – jealousy, a mistress, and violent action – but it is 'faction' rather than fiction, and the historical events are seen from both sides: what Heinemann's reader in a very positive report calls 'the natives' as well as the British. It had sold 46,000 copies during its first three years and she was soon celebrated enough to be lionized whenever she came to London.

For the last thirty years of her life she lived at home, mostly in Scotland and Wales, and five of her novels have British backgrounds; there were also volumes of short stories; *Marmaduke* (1917), partly about the Crimean War; a children's book – *The Adventures of Akbar* (1913); *The Complete Indian Housekeeper and Cook* (1898) written with Grace Gardiner, again based very much on her own experience as a supportive European wife in the East. She was devoted to animals and, against Heinemann's better judgment, wrote *A Book of Mortals* (1905), which she described as a 'record of the good deeds and good qualities of what humanity is pleased to call the "lower animals". Collected by a Fellow Mortal'. It was dedicated to Angelo, her dachshund puppy, was well illustrated; but at 10s. too expensive, and it was a flop.

Violet Powell (see also pages 444–5) has written for Heinemann an enjoyable life of *Flora Annie Steel, Novelist of India* (1981), which provides a few vignettes of Heinemann as a person: when *On the Face of the Waters* 'hit the jackpot, excited telegrams came flashing to Flora from her publisher, but besides this business success their personal sympathy increased. This included Heinemann's love of good living. Flora considered him to be a true *gourmet*. She devoted careful attention to providing him with *sole au vin blanc* for which he had the highest standard. Even a visit to the Steels' Highland home was made delightful to a man indifferent to sport by the dish of *perdrix aux choux* which greeted him on arrival.'[24] Violet Powell also describes a dinner-party given by Heinemann, recorded by another of his authors, Mrs C. A. Dawson Scott (see page 53). Flora and her daughter, Mabel, were guests, among whom were also Whistler and Gosse. Heinemann was then living in Whitehall Court: 'This massive group of buildings has seen many literary encounters, besides possessing fine views over the Thames Embankment. From here Mrs Steel had watched a procession of motor cars, driven past in triumph to celebrate the abrogation of the law decreeing that a man with a red flag must walk in front of these dangerous monsters. Flora obviously appreciated this actively demonstrated liberation. With her interest in house decoration and her knowledge of Eastern art, she must also have been pleased when Heinemann abandoned the current fashion for crowding rooms with heavy imitations of Oriental furniture. Thrown out with the furniture was a gallery of photographs of actresses, mostly in parts from the plays of Ibsen. . . .' Violet Powell goes on to report that 'it has even been suggested in Flora's family that she would have welcomed Heinemann as a son-in-law. His age was appropriate, his vitality was enjoyed by many friends, but he has a Punchinello quality which made his frequent pursuit of ladies slightly grotesque. As it happened the dinner-party to which Mabel, then in her twenties, accompanied her mother would hardly have furthered any courtship. After dinner, Whistler, seated on a stool in the centre of the company, poured forth the champagne of his conversation. Attempts by Gosse to maintain his own conversational reputation by catching the party's ear with a rival story were deftly parried. There was no need for Whistler to employ a verbal *addio del marito*. Both in strategy and tactics Gosse was completely outclassed.'[25]

In her memoirs, *The Garden of Fidelity*, Flora Annie Steel recalls how Heinemann gave colourful backing to her support for Women's Suffrage: '. . . all my life I have been keen, not so much on the rights, as the wrongs of women. I spoke a good deal, and twice, though I never was a militant, I solidly refused to pay rates and taxes – for I owned a weekend cottage at

Aberdovey – on the ground that I was not a citizen. But my refusals were really great fun, and we had quite a festival when they came to sell me up. The village was tremendously interested, sympathetic, and excited, and there was loud cheering the first time when my publisher, Mr Heinemann, bought in the first lot which was put up, for £10 – more than the whole of my rates! And it was only the first chapter, in manuscript, of *On the Face of the Waters*! But I had put it in a big envelope emblazoned with some of the fine compliments with which the book was greeted. One of them, I remember, was: "Many an officer would give his sword to write military history as Mrs Steel has done".'[26]

D. H. Lawrence Discovered
but soon Lost

'I wonder whether any publisher can, in the case of the majority of the books he publishes, give a logical reason for his faith – books, of course, on which he "puts his money and his name". . . . Personally I could do so but rarely, and with the choice of the untried author's work it is mostly only a matter of instinct.' Writing in the journal *Literature* in June 1900, Heinemann was reaffirming his distrust of the processes of non-rational assessment when selecting fiction. 'On looking critically at the flowers that attract one's literary tendrils one is humiliated as a purveyor and business man with the catholicity of one's tastes, with the swaying inclinations of one's foolish instincts, and the lamentable absence of good, hard reason.'

Heinemann was also chary of being influenced by literary fashion. 'I think it has comparatively little to do with it, and that the only sure guide to success is the consideration of freshness and novelty, either in subject or in treatment, or in *genre*. The only justification I have ever found for the assumption that fashion favours one class of novel today and a different class tomorrow is that every striking work of literature or art engenders in the lazy worker the vision of a welcome *pons asinorum*, and with the unthinking reader a comfortable wish for "more of the same".' Heinemann was never much concerned with the needs of the 'unthinking' reader. 'Too often the very elementary axiom seems to be forgotten that the reader is in search of a novel experience or sensation with each new book, and that it is useless to try and interest him in the same sort of story, or character, or surroundings, over and over again. . . . I remember the appearance of a novel dealing with an unhackneyed and interesting problem of some particular relations between men and women, and it had hardly reached its *n*th edition when a great many novelists burst upon the world with books dissecting that very same problem. Then there appeared a religious novel dealing with special phases of religious faith and religious doubt, and these same phases at once served as quarries for all the little quarrymen who happened to be standing by, and happened to see gold in the quartz as it broke under the strokes of the original quarryman's pick.'

As his list demonstrated, he was open to all kinds of fiction, whether it had a contemporary or an historical setting, whether it offered merely a good read or had pretensions to serious literature, but provided only that its standards were high and it was true to human realities. 'My experience would seem to lead me to believe that the success of tomorrow may grow on any branch of the tree of fiction, and that a medlar may be as palatable as a cherry. . . . In the novel of tomorrow I would hope for excellence of character drawing, absorbing interest of plot, breadth in covering the canvas, and style in painting details, the conflict of fate and temperament, humour and pathos, despair and hope – in short, the whole gamut of human experience. Are these *desiderata* new? Will they ever be old? Assuredly not! No, I will never believe that there are fashions in fiction, or in any other form of imaginative creation. There is only one thing that changes, and that is the standard of excellence. . . . Let any author offer me a novel that excels in *any* particular – let his work be of *any* school – he will not find me difficult to convince that his and his only for the nonce is the novel towards which the tendencies and the taste of the day are gravitating.'[27]

No fashion was being followed when Pawling decided to take D. H. Lawrence's first novel, *The White Peacock* (1911). He was recommended to Heinemann by Ford Madox Hueffer, who wrote a fulsome letter which Lawrence passed on when offering the manuscript, then titled *Nethermere*. The letter warned that 'with its enormous prolixity, the book sins against almost every canon of art as I conceive it . . . but I am not so limited as to fail to appreciate other schools than my own, and I can very fully admire your very remarkable and poetic gifts. I certainly think you have in you the makings of a very considerable novelist, and I should not have the least hesitation in prophesying for you a great future, did I not know how much a matter of sheer luck one's future always is.'[28] The manuscript was delivered to the office by Violet Hunt, Hueffer's mistress and herself a Heinemann author (see page 53). Lawrence, she recalled, 'seemed to regard me as a sort of literary godmother ever since, as reader, I brought his poems to Joseph Leopold's notice in the *English Review*.... He considered me, in this game he did not understand, a good business woman, "a better prospector of Tom Tiddler's Ground than I ever hope to be".... "Billy", Mr Heinemann, was away, talking to Book Congresses in Berne, where his coadjutors always sent the kind publisher with a soul, when he had been accepting too many worthless – as far as saleableness went – novels out of the goodness of his heart and consideration for the poor author by whom, after all, publishers must live.

'Mr Pawling read *The White Peacock* – he read it in two days. So I think there was nothing much wrong with the book in the way of being a selling concern. Two days later I had occasion to see him about a book of my own and he said to me negligently, as he was bowing me out: "I'll take your friend's book." He was really jumping at it. He had a *flair* – better than Billy's even. Of course he did not let on how pleased he was to get it and I was thankful on my client's behalf to obtain the exceedingly – as things are now – humble advance he offered.... "Take it or leave it!" Tom Tiddler's Ground indeed!'[29]

The royalty was 15 per cent and there was an option on his next novel, but a condition was that Lawrence had to make some alterations based on the report of F. M. Atkinson, then resident reader and general editor who had been introduced to the firm by George Moore. Four months later Lawrence sent in the revised manuscript, explaining: 'I think I have removed all the offensive morsels, all the damns, the devils and the sweat. I hope nothing of the kind remains. My own skin is not super-sensitive so I can hardly judge what will make delicate people dither. But to my fancy, it is now all quite suitable even for the proverbial jeune fille – a kind of exquisite scented soap, in fact.'[30] *Nethermere* was disliked as a title and Lawrence was in despair over finding an alternative, sending numerous suggestions to Atkinson, among them those 'designed to give a truly rural odour and at the same time a touching picture of the futility of agitated humanity: "Lapwings" (sad, lamentable birds – recall my effusions) – "Pee Wits" (the same) – "The Cry of the Peacock" (a discordant row of selfishness triumphant – please refer to the keeper-graveyard-Lady

An[nabel] scene?) "The White Peacock" to wit . . .'.[31] Unfortunately at this point the letter is torn, though ten days later he wrote to Atkinson saying that ' "The White Peacock" must be shot: it is a bird from the pen of Wilkie Collins or of Ibsen – "Now droops the milk-white peacock like a ghost" – Nay, I would not for worlds capture *that* poor creature and haul it round in a "one-object show".'[32] Instead he preferred 'Tendrils' but it seems that in the end the publisher must have made the decision.

Publication was expected in September or October and Lawrence was keen to get his hands on the proofs. In mid-July he begged Atkinson to intercede with Pawling to hurry them up: 'He is a large and weighty man of affairs: in his presence I feel like an extinguished glow-worm under a lamp-post: when I think of writing to him, the stopper dives into the neck of my bottle of words, and there sticks firm. I am an ass.'[33] Delays were caused by the text being reset by the American publishers, Duffield, and, as Lawrence recalls, 'at the last minute, when the book was all printed and ready to bind: some even bound: they sent me in great haste a certain page with a marked paragraph. Would I remove this paragraph, as it might be "objectionable", and substitute an exactly identical number of obviously harmless words. Hastily I did so. And later, I noticed that the two pages, on one of which was the altered paragraph, were rather loose, not properly bound into the book.'[34]

Publication was eventually in January 1911, though Lawrence was able to place an advance copy into the hands of his mother, who was very close to death. 'She looked at the outside, and then at the title-page, and then at me, with darkening eyes. And though she loved me so much, I think she doubted whether it could be much of a book, since no one more important than I had written it. Somewhere, in the helpless privacies of her being, she had wistful respect for me. But for me in the face of the world, not much. This David would never get a stone across at Goliath. And why try? Let Goliath alone! Anyway, she was beyond reading my first immortal work. It was put aside, and I never wanted to see it again. . . .'[35]

For a first novel the critics' reception of *The White Peacock* was very favourable. The scenes reflecting his own youth in the Midlands; the working-class characters; George, the farmer's son, the tragedy of his broken affair with Lettie, his marriage with Meg, his collapse into drunkenness . . . offered entirely new insights, though criticisms were made of his rambling construction, its length, its morbidity. A bad review appeared in *The Times* which made Lawrence feel 'cut down like a poppy that gives only one red squint out of the pod before the mowing machine trips him up'.[36] The *Observer* review was more representative: beyond the shortcomings it recognized 'a confusing, strange, disturbing book; but that it has the elements of greatness few will deny'.[37]

The first printing of 1,500 copies was followed by a reprint of 1,000, but that was all. It was far from being a bestseller, and yet it was undoubtedly a *succès d'estime* and Heinemann wanted some short stories and verses; but he was very cool about the next novel, *The Trespasser*. Lawrence told Edward Garnett, with whom he had become very friendly and who by then was reading for Duckworth, that Atkinson after three months had written: ' "I have read part of the book. I don't care for it, but we will publish it". I wrote back to him "No, I won't have that book published. Return it to me".'[38] A year later it had still not been returned. 'Atkinson promised to do so, and said "I have never finished it. It's your handwriting, you know." – a sweet smile. "Perfectly legible, but *so tedious* – a sweet smile. That's all the criticism he ever ventured.'[39] Once when Lawrence was having lunch with Garnett, Atkinson was in the same restaurant. 'Garnett doesn't like Heinemann's people', he wrote to Louie Burrows to whom he was then engaged, 'so he was beastly sarky with him. I hate Atkinson – I don't go to Heinemann's because I don't like the sneering, affected little fellow. . . . I am afraid I have offended Heinemann's people mortally. . . . They are mad, and they are sneery. I don't like them.'[40]

Atkinson left soon afterwards and was succeeded in January 1912 as resident reader by Walter de la Mare, but Lawrence continued to be disenchanted with the firm. *The Trespasser* went to Duckworth. Heinemann also dithered over the poems and after six months sent them back 'without a word except "Your manuscript is herewith returned". . . . De la Mare says he strongly recommended them to Wm H – and that Atkinson had done so. But I suppose the verses also shocked the modesty of his Jew-ship.'[41] The final break came with Heinemann's rejection of *Sons and Lovers* (then called *Paul Morel*). Walter de la Mare also had doubts about it: 'I don't feel that the book as a whole comes up to Lawrence's real mark. It seems to me to need pulling together: it is not of a piece. But the real theme of the story is not arrived at till half way through. . . . The best in it is of course extraordinarily good.'[42] Heinemann himself was also worried that it would be banned by the libraries. He may have been right, though Lawrence had been very willing to revise it, as indeed he did for Duckworth. Such a classically mistaken rejection merits being quoted in full: 'I have read *Paul Morel* with a good deal of interest and, frankly, with a good deal of disappointment, especially after what you wrote to me with regard to your feeling about the book and the view you took that it was your best work. I feel that the book is unsatisfactory from several points of view; not only because it lacks unity, without which the reader's interest cannot be held, but more so because its want of reticence makes it unfit, I fear, altogether for publication in England as things are. The tyranny of the libraries is such that a book far less outspoken would certainly be damned (and there is practically no market for fiction outside of them).

'In declining this manuscript, with many regrets, I would like to say that I am a great admirer of your writing, that certain parts in *Paul Morel* strike me as good as anything I have ever read of yours; but as a whole it seems to me painfully mistaken, if for no other reason than that one has no sympathy for any character in the book. A writer must create interest in his characters. Even, after a while, one's interest in Paul flags – while in its early part the degradation of his mother, supposed to be of gentler birth, is almost inconceivable.

'I need hardly say that I shall at all times be glad to read anything of yours, and it is a real disappointment to me to have to decline this book. The manuscript goes back to you in a separate parcel, registered.'[43]

The letter came at a particularly bad time, Lawrence being desperately concerned over being able to hold on to Frieda Weekley, her husband imploring her to return to him and her children. Lawrence unburdened himself to Garnett, wishing that Heinemann's 'name be used as a curse and an eternal infamy', though it is not clear how much of the rest of the letter was directed at Heinemann or at Weekley: 'Curse the blasted, jelly-boned swines, the slimy, the belly-wriggling invertebrates, the miserable sodding rotters, the flaming sods, the snivelling, dribbling, dithering palsied pulse-less lot that make up England today. They've got white of egg in their veins, and their spunk is that watery it's a marvel they can breed! God curse them, funkers. God blast them, wish-wash. Exterminate them, slime. . . . They deserve it that every great man should drown himself. But not I (I am a bit great).' There was plenty more, but also an almost contrite PS: 'And Heinemann, I can see, is quite right, as a business man.'[44] A decade later he wrote that he realized what an immense favour Heinemann had done him in publishing his first novel. 'As a matter of fact he treated me quite well.'[45]

[45]

Heinemann himself thus let *Sons and Lovers* also go to Duckworth, though years later the whole Lawrence canon was to return to the list (see pages 259–60). The justification for describing the early connection with him at such length is not only because it was Lawrence, but because its ups-and-downs, the delays in reaching a decision, the trouble in finding a title, the last-minute corrections, the neglect of the author, show vividly that the publishing process then was very similar to, and prone to, the same mishaps and shortcomings as it is today. It would be poor and unconvincing history to make out that everything in the house of Heinemann was always rosy. Heinemann himself was brilliant at recognizing potential greatness, but he was too apt to let it slip through his fingers, and there were occasions when, like all publishers, he was blind to it. It is easy enough to say this with hindsight, but it has to be recorded that among other authors whose early work he rejected were James Joyce, Edgar Wallace, Gertrude Stein, P. C. Wren, and Compton Mackenzie, who recalled that when he met Heinemann four years later he seemed very surprised: ' "I always regretted you did not give me the opportunity of publishing your first book."

' "But I did, Mr Heinemann", I told him.

' "Did you?", he asked in a tone which suggested he thought I must be making a mistake.

' "Yes, I sent it to you after Mr Henry James wrote to ask you in 1909 if you would give it your attention. The typescript came back to me in three days."

'One may read of a brow darkening, but I had never observed the phenomenon until that morning in William Heinemann's room on Bedford Street. . . .

' "I must have been away in France", he muttered.

'And as I . . . left him I felt somebody at Heinemanns was in for it presently.'[46]

As we have seen, Heinemann legitimately earned a reputation as a publisher who was prepared to take risks, even with a book that others felt was morally improper. On the other hand he in turn rejected some titles on moral grounds that were later taken on by houses that were no less respectable. Strindberg, for example, was consistently rejected by Heinemann on moral grounds. But like his competitors he could never afford to forget the censorship exercised not only by the libraries but also by the authorities. There was the threatening example of *Passion Fruit*

(1912) by Charles E. Vivian. After the court had pronounced it obscene the police came round to Bedford Street and burned the remaining stock on the office stove.

Moore, Maugham, Galsworthy, and the Incredible *Dop Doctor*

By the time he moved over to Heinemann, George Moore was already well established, particularly after the publication of *Esther Waters*, which was highly praised and the subject of another battle with the librarians, who saw fit to limit its circulation. His first book on the Heinemann list was *The Lake* (1905), the short novel about Father Gogarty who drove a young unmarried schoolmistress out of the parish because she was pregnant. Troubled by his conscience, he starts a correspondence with her and gradually discovers that he loves her. Much of the book is filled with their letters and the priest's anguished imaginative reveries by the lakeside. Moore obviously identified with him closely. The critics praised his lyrical descriptions of the Irish landscape, and its smooth narrative style earned him the sobriquet of an Irish Turgenev. His most important contributions to the list were, however, autobiographical. *Memoirs of My Dead Life* (1906) were followed by *Hail and Farewell*, a trilogy: *Ave, Salve, Vale* (1911–14), described by many as his finest work. From the romantic, rambling reminiscences of his childhood in County Mayo at Moore Hall, the family's country seat; of his ten years learning to paint and much else in Paris; the establishment of the Irish Literary Theatre; from the yarns, satire, intimate conversations with women, and much, much else emerges his own extraordinary personality which is exactly mirrored in his very distinctive style. The 1914 autumn catalogue called it 'a masterpiece of malice touched with beauty'.

The firm also published a dramatic version of *Esther Waters* (1913) and another play, *The Passing of the Essenes* (1930), on the Paul–Jesus theme, but because of what was described as a 'misunderstanding' Heinemann did not publish the very successful biblical story, *The Brook Kerith*, which went to Werner Laurie. Moore enjoyed revising his books and seeing

[47]

them reissued as 're-orchestrations'. Thus *Lewis Seymour and Some Women* (1917) was a rewritten version of *A Modern Lover*, published in 1883; the new one led to an unsuccessful libel action and a dispute with Moore over who should pay the costs. A very original and charming volume of literary criticism appeared with *Conversations in Ebury Street* (1924) and there were other reorchestrations, but these culminated in the twenty volumes of his uniform edition (1924–33).

Flashy, entertaining, querulous, infuriating, a bit of a card, George Moore was often a time-wasting burden to the occupants of 21 Bedford Street. There was the occasion when he got his knife into Conrad, describing him to the office manager as 'a piece of Stevensonian wreckage floating in Henry James's slops'. With his proofs he was notorious for being demanding, exacting, obstinate and finicky. He insisted that all his books were set by hand instead of by a monotype machine, and his corrections were so voluminous that he had to be furnished with galleys with extra wide margins. All this inflated the cost of manufacture and the price to the public, though this was made more acceptable by tricking out his books with hand-made paper, deckled edges and marbled board bindings.

A writer like George Moore is particularly difficult to sum up but his very idiosyncratic talent has been very perceptively placed by Desmond Shawe-Taylor: 'The contemplation of his work as a whole induces a feeling of completeness which is due not merely to the care with which each individual book is shaped and polished, but to the impression that here for once is an artist who has fully explored and expressed his genius, who has realized the whole extent of his spiritual demesne, cultivating every acre of his own soil without once venturing across the walls into alien land. . . . Moore's comprehension of life was instinctive rather than intellectual. . . . It was a mind that reached profundity neither in the metaphysical apprehension that makes saints or philosophers or great poets, nor in the vast understanding of humanity that endows the supreme dramatists and novelists with the creative gift of a god. He resembled rather an observant old gentleman who takes a bus ride into the remotest suburbs and slums of humanity, seeing all and rejecting nothing, but clutching tightly in a benevolent palm his return ticket. That ticket, whose possession shut him out from the company of Balzac or Tolstoy, guaranteed his return not only to Ebury Street, but to the centre of all things – to the core of George Moore.'[47]

William's scorn for literary fashion and his reliance on his publisher's instinct are demonstrated in his acceptance of William de Morgan's *Joseph Vance* (1906). Though he was sixty-six, it was his first novel. He had spent all his life as a not very successful artist, a member of the Pre-Raphaelite Brotherhood who earned a living making stained-glass windows and pottery in Chelsea. The manuscript ran to 500,000 words, written in a heavy mid-Victorian fist partly on torn scraps of paper and backs of envelopes. It had been rejected by Hodder & Stoughton as being 'too long and too much in the roundabout style fashionable in Thackeray's time'. But Henry Lawrence, of Lawrence & Bullen, publishers with small resources, recognized its quality and, while he felt unable to publish it himself, he took it round in a cab to 21 Bedford Street, with a strong recommendation. Subject to an extensive reduction in the book's length, William was not long in making up his mind to take a chance, thereby gaining himself a bestseller; and almost overnight the elderly author to his bewilderment found himself to be famous. This fictional 'autobiography' was in many ways old-fashioned and it reminded people of Dickens, *viz.*, *The Spectator*: 'No book has appeared for long in which lovers of the classic tradition in classic fiction are likely to find such generous entertainment.'

It was followed by *Alice for Short* (1907), *Somehow Good* (1908), *It Never Can Happen Again* (1909), and five others. Part of de Morgan's skill lay in his ability to blend a multitude of trivial details to create a character. He pictured them surrounded by the penumbra of their pasts and futures. As *The Bookman* put it in 1910, 'He cannot even see a shivering, withered old crone serving out a ha'p'orth of baked chestnuts over her charcoal fire without reflecting that those skinny, claw-like hands were once the beautiful hands of a young girl; he is never content to sketch the least significant of his characters in outline only, he must needs give you the whole man and the whole woman by deliberately linking up their todays with their yesterdays, so that you know their dispositions, the environments that shaped them, the motives that actuate them, and can guess how they will behave in a given crisis before the crisis is upon them.'[48] His stories were often romantic but he was a great realist. In *It Never Can Happen Again* he tells the reader to 'be good enough to note that none of the characters in this story are picturesque or heroic – only chance samples of folk such as you may see pass your window now, this moment, if you will only lay your book down and look out. They are passing – passing all day long – each with a story. And some little thing you see, a meeting, a parting, a quickened step, a hesitation and a return, may make the next hour the turning-point of an existence. For it is of such little things the great ones are made. . . .'[49]

The inspiration of much of his work came from his own life and the people and streets of London, though in his fourth book, *An Affair of Dishonour* (1910) he broke new ground by leaving Victorian England for his plot and carried the reader back to the days of Charles II, of duels, the Plague, dissolute country gentlemen, mistresses and witchcraft; but it was almost certainly his complex and skilfully entangled re-creations of Victorian England that made him so popular. Financially as well as creatively he must have been among the most rewarding authors on the list. Although he received large and tempting offers from other publishers, he always remained faithful to the man who had given him his first chance.

Luck as well as publisher's instinct probably accounts for the prodigious success of *The Dop Doctor* (1910) by the unknown Richard Dehan. There were eighteen reprints of the first 6s. edition; eight reprints of a 2s. edition first issued in 1913; five of the 3s.6d. edition first issued in 1918; at least eight colonial (export) editions; and various others up to 1940, making a total of thirty-seven impressions and 229,877 copies sold. In addition, it was also successfully published in America with a different title: *One Braver Thing. Dop* is Afrikaans for 'drunk' and the central character, Owen Saxham, was a dissolute physician involved with the lovely heroine, Lynette Mildare, in the hectic events in the Boer War leading to the siege of Gueldersdorp. It ran to over 500 pages and it was at once acclaimed by a wide Press; *Spectator*: 'A vividly interesting novel. . . . Readers who do not mind having the horrors of war laid naked before their eyes will be intensely interested by Mr Dehan's book, and will be unable to read without a thrill his accounts of the adventures and escapes of the heroic defenders of the historic little town.' *Observer*: 'A great novel. The author has written a fine and moving tale, wide in its range, deep in its sympathies, full of the pain and the suffering, the courage, and truth of life.' *Daily Express*: 'Pulsatingly real – gloomy, tragic, humorous, dignified, real. The cruelty of battle, the depth of disgusting villainy, the struggles of great souls, the irony of coincidence, are all in its pages. . . . Who touches this touches a man.'

The identity of Richard Dehan remained a mystery. No one connected with South Africa knew him, though he was obviously personally familiar

HEINEMANN'S LIBRARY OF MODERN FICTION

FALSE BALANCE IS AN ABOMINATION

JUST WEIGHT A DELIGHT

Autumn, 1909

THE WHITE PROPHET
    By Hall Caine. In 2 Vols. 4s. net.

THE STREET OF ADVENTURE
    By Philip Gibbs. In 1 Vol. 3s. net.

THE SCANDALOUS MR. WALDO
    By Ralph Straus. In 1 Vol. 3s. net.

HEDWIG IN ENGLAND
    By the Author of " Marcia in Germany." In 1 Vol. 3s. net.

IT NEVER CAN HAPPEN AGAIN
    By William De Morgan. In 2 Vols. 6s. net.

LORD KENTWELL'S LOVE AFFAIR
    By F. C. Price. In 1 Vol. 3s. net.

BELLA DONNA
    By Robert Hichens. In 2 Vols. 4s. net.

BEYOND MAN'S STRENGTH
    By M. Hartley. In 1 Vol. 3s. net.

A SENSE OF SCARLET
    By Mrs. H. E. Dudeney. In 1 vol. 3s. net

FURTHER VOLUMES TO BE ANNOUNCED LATER

21 Bedford Street, London, w.c.

with the veld and the war. Was he perhaps a journalist hiding behind a pseudonym? It was two years before it was revealed that the author was Miss Clotilde Graves, approaching fifty and with a heart condition. She was stout and always wore black. Eventually she was confined to a wheelchair and retired to a convent. Although it was a first novel, she was previously well known as a playwright with sixteen plays produced in London and New York, and also as a contributor to magazines and newspapers. At a meeting with Heinemann and Pawling they put great pressure on her to trade on her reputation, but she was adamant that she wanted a '*nom de guerre* to serve as my mask when the thoughts, reflections, experiences and griefs of a lifetime, contained between the battered leaves of eighty-seven notebooks and wrought into the chapters of a novel, should be sent out into the world'.[50] John Dettmer remembered that the original edition had 'the usual khaki-coloured dust jacket with the window punched in the back to show the title and author on the book's spine, but that the wrapper of the cheaper 2s. edition struck a new note. It was one of the first, if not the very first, to have an all-round pictorial jacket instead of just on the front. It illustrated a rather sad episode, a man kneeling at the rudely constructed grave of his wife somewhere out on the veld. A sombre scene but effective and most appropriate to the times.' Richard Dehan went on to write fourteen other books of short stories and novels, many of which did well, and one, *That which hath Wings* (1918), was a sequel to *The Dop Doctor*, but not surprisingly that kind of incredible success cannot easily be repeated.

Throughout the firm's history there has been a group of authors who regularly turned in novels of good or better quality and which might be described as the 'bread-and-butter' of the list. Occasionally they also contributed a volume of poems or stories for children. Their correspondence, where it still exists in the firm's archive, is for the most part not illuminating, being largely concerned with proofs, book titles, complaints about theirs receiving insufficient attention in the firm's Press advertisements, and money – a starting royalty of 20 per cent, increasing to 25 per cent after the sale of 5,000, was by no means uncommon. Several of them went on being published after William's time, but they are now largely forgotten, though occasionally their work gets revived. It would be tedious to describe each with much detail, though the following will have to represent many others. In each case their first novel for Heinemann and one other is given: E. F. Benson, 20 titles: *Mammon and Co.* (1899), *The*

Luck of the Vails (1901); Mrs Henry Dudeney, 15 titles: *The Maternity of Harriott Wicken* (1899), *A Large Room* (1910); Mrs Belloc Lowndes, 18 titles: *The Heart of Penelope* (1904), *Letty Lynton* (1931); J. D. Beresford, 6 novels: *Goslings* (1913), *The Camberwell Miracle* (1933); Eden Phillpotts, 13 titles: *Brunel's Tower* (1915), *A Human Boy's Diary* (1924); C. Amy Dawson-Scott, 10 titles: *Idylls of Womanhood* (1892), *Wastralls* (1918); Violet Hunt, 5 titles: *White Rose of Weary Leaf* (1908), *Tales of the Uneasy* (1911).

This chapter ends with two novelists taken on in William's day who were for many years to be cornerstones of the list: John Galsworthy and W. Somerset Maugham. The first four books by Galsworthy were published by T. Fisher Unwin, Duckworth, and Blackwood, under the pseudonym of 'John Sinjohn'. He was then still feeling his way and the first novel with the true Galsworthian flavour was the first to be published by Heinemann: *The Island Pharisees* (1904). Though weak in structure, it made full use of satire to indict the complacency of English society, its wealth and respectability. Galsworthy had asked Edward Garnett and Conrad for their opinions of the manuscript, and it was the latter who wrote that he had presented it to Pawling: 'I was delighted to find him extremely well-disposed towards the book. Heinemann himself, I understand, was doubtful, not of the value but of the expediency. However that's his normal attitude towards every new work and in your case is no obstacle to publication by them. . . . P. himself seems to think that a hit is by no means impossible.'[51]

A contract was signed and it appeared to mixed reviews, but with his next book, *The Man of Property* (1906) it soon became clear that a new major novelist had arrived. This opening volume of what sixteen years later would become *The Forsyte Saga* (see pages 245–6) portrayed how the prosperity of the upper middle class in England towards the end of the 1890s was based on its sense of property. Irene, Soames Forsyte's wife, is trapped and yet he cannot possess her heart as he does his shares and dividends. Nearly all the reviews were favourable and in the same year he repeated his success with his first play, *The Silver Box*, though this and the succession of plays which followed were published by others, mostly by Duckworth. A major novel appeared thenceforth every other year: *The Country House* (1907), *Fraternity* (1909), *The Patrician* (1911).

The reception was again on the whole very favourable, but it was not matched by sales, as he complained in a letter to Pawling in August 1911: 'I daresay you are disappointed with the sales of *The Patrician*, and I am also. I cannot believe that something could not be done to put renewed life into them. There does not seem to be any advance to speak of on *Fraternity*, although the book was admittedly more likely to be popular. I don't understand it.' He went on to ask if the travellers were taking enough trouble as he never saw his books on railway bookstalls and hardly ever in a shop window. Did they perhaps mistakenly think he had insufficient popular appeal? 'I feel that I am the sort of author about whom a publisher soon says: "Oh! yes – Galsworthy – superior sort of stuff – will only reach a certain circulation", and then gives it up. But I don't accept that view of my own writing; it has this distinction (among many others) from the work, say, of James, Meredith, or Conrad – that it is absolutely clear in style, and not in the least exotic, and can be read by the average person without straining the intellect. I feel that from *The Man of Property* 5,000 to *The Patrician* 8,000 is a very discouraging rise. . . . I seem to feel that both you and Heinemann have become perhaps discouraged, perhaps a little indifferent. If that is the case, I had better know.'[52] In an earlier letter he had emphasized the same point: '. . . my plays have had a considerable sale, and have widened my circle of readers. Still in the future I do hope that every effort will be made . . . not to sit down with the idea that I'm an intellectual, advanced, or whatever you may call it author and can only be read by the few. In this connection I hope due attention is paid to the papers that cater for Socialists – though I am not one myself.'[53] For the same reason he was frequently pressing Heinemann to arrange for very cheap editions of his books, even if it meant selling the rights to another publisher such as Nelson.

Although possessed of such a strong social conscience and so critical of class hypocrisy, he was chary of using his books as vehicles for his ideas. Writing to Heinemann about the manuscript of *The Freelands* (1915), he explained: 'I'm quite with you as to being far more concerned with the work of art than the lesson conveyed. . . . You are very likely right but I have to keep my head and watch out that you don't stampede me into betrayal of the book's significance – a significance that belongs all the way through. . . . There isn't really, I think, "theory" in the book, so much as the working bias of a temperament that revolts always against the direct imposition of one will over another. And, since it is cardinal to my view of art, that a work of art must bear the distinct impress of the maker's temperaments – must carry a definite flavour, this book – *selon moi* – would not be a work of art if the working bias were left out.'[54]

There were five other Galsworthy books published in Heinemann's lifetime, together with his less significant publications, but further discussion of his work belongs properly to Book II (pages 245–9).

Before he joined up with Heinemann, W. Somerset Maugham had already published four novels with T. Fisher Unwin, one of which, *Liza of Lambeth* caused quite a stir. It stemmed from his experience of maternity cases in the London slums after he had qualified as a doctor at St Thomas's. His next novel, *Mrs Craddock*, was however turned down by publisher after publisher, including Heinemann, because they thought it was improper, but Robertson Nicoll, a partner in Hodder & Stoughton, was sufficiently impressed with it to urge Heinemann to reconsider it – presumably because he had already gained a reputation for taking on more risky ventures. Heinemann read it himself and agreed to publish it provided, as so often, the more shocking passages were deleted. To modern taste these were surprisingly innocuous and had to do with an amorous meeting between Mrs Craddock and a young man, such as 'Flesh called to flesh, and there was no force on earth more powerful.'

Mrs Craddock was published in 1902 and was considered to be his most mature work to date, though in a preface to a later edition he dismissed it as a period piece: 'Some absurdities in this book have really been too much for me and I have cut them out, but I have left others, though they made me smile and blush, because I thought they belonged to the period; and if the book has any merit (which the reader must judge for himself) it is that of a faithful picture of life in a corner of England at the end of the nineteenth century. Women then wore long dresses and long hair; and men top hats and frockcoats. The Boer War had not yet been fought and every Englishman knew that he was a match for ten Frenchmen. It was the end of an era, but the landed gentry, who were so soon to lose the power they had so long enjoyed, were the last to have a suspicion of the fact. They were very conscious of their gentility and they had only disdain for the moneyed class that was already beginning to take their place. They were for the most part narrow, stupid and intolerant; they were prudish, formal and punctilious; they had outworn their use and few can regret that the course of events has swept them out of the way.'[55]

Next came the *The Merry-go-round* (1904) with a print of 3,000 and good reviews. There was an advance of £60 in respect of royalty of 15 per cent up to 2,000 copies sold and 20 per cent thereafter; for the colonial edition the author got 3*d.* per copy. Royalties in those days were a good deal higher than they are today, but this was probably not an unreasonable deal. Maugham liked Heinemann personally and said that he 'made a hard bargain with the young authors, but if they stood up to him and wrung better terms out of him, he would laugh and say "Well, you're not a bad businessman." '[56]

After the publication of a travel book about Andalusia, *The Land of the Blessed Virgin* (1905), Maugham became disenchanted with the firm because they had sold only 2,000 copies of *The Merry-go-round*. He also decided to get rid of his agent, William Colles, and was introduced to James Pinker by Arnold Bennett: 'Would you like to place my new novel for me? It is very different in style from my previous work; it is very light and is supposed to be humorous. It is quite moral. Heinemann has published my last three books but I am tired of him. . . . I am sick of playing third fiddle to Hall Caine.'[57] Pinker signed him up with Chapman & Hall for *The Bishop's Apron*, but with *The Explorer* (1908), after some haggling to obtain better terms including an advance of £150 and a starting royalty of 20 per cent, he returned to Heinemann's and stayed with them for the rest of his life, despite many tempting offers from rival firms. Like virtually all authors Maugham continued to grumble about insufficient advertising, but he came to an arrangement whereby he himself paid one third of the advertising costs, provided their total was correspondingly increased. Another curiosity was his insistence on the impression of his special sign 'against the evil eye' on the front of the binding, something which Heinemann appears to have resisted because in one letter in November 1911 Maugham asks him to agree to it 'with a cheerful spirit and not in the resigned and melancholy humour your letter indicates.'[58]

Meanwhile he had started on his career as a playwright. Hawking six full-length plays round London theatres, at first he found it difficult to find anyone to take him on until *Lady Frederick* was staged at the Court in the autumn of 1907. It was a sensational success and managers competed for the rights in his other plays. The next year he broke all records by having four plays running simultaneously in London; and others followed, nine of them also being published by Heinemann including *Lady Frederick* (1911), *Jack Straw* (1911), *Penelope* (1912), and *Landed Gentry* (1913). They were just what the Edwardian stalls wanted – witty, smart, sardonic, well constructed, and cynical without being uncomfortably committed.

Overnight, Maugham found himself wealthy as well as fashionable. He moved into an elegant house in Mayfair, joined the Savile Club, and started to collect theatrical paintings. His prosperity also enabled him to resist making cuts to placate the puritanical. In August 1914 he told Heinemann: 'I am aware that in the past I have compromised too much with what others have thought the public taste. . . . Many writers are forced by poverty to consider whether this or that will hurt the sale of their books; their position is very difficult and one can only sympathize with them if they find compromise necessary; but I think it would be disgraceful if I allowed any such thoughts to influence me. There are very few of us who can afford to break the bonds which the circulating libraries have placed on the contemporary English novel (bonds which have made it an object of contempt on the Continent) and it behoves such as can to do so. You have done your part . . . and you should not mind if I now try to do mine.'[59]

This letter appears to have referred to *Of Human Bondage* (1915), one of his greatest novels. Desmond MacCarthy has written that 'it is an unflinching description of the drizzling growing-period of life, when much is hoped for and little attained, written with admirable directness and insight into the pinchings of poverty, the ache of desolation, the bitterness of humiliation, and the bewilderments of passion to which the mind does not consent. . . . One might, too, have expected the hero of *Of Human Bondage* to become a novelist to whom the glamour cast by passion was beautiful and pathetic, but by whom passion itself would be likely to be depicted as brief, ruthless and empty, and Nature, both within and without a man, as a force indifferent to man's welfare, yet ultimately his master – in short, such a novelist as Somerset Maugham.'[60]

The decade ended with *The Moon and Sixpence* (1919), inspired by Gauguin's self-exile in Tahiti, one of his most enduring popular successes. More will be said about Maugham in Books II and III. A few of William's other discoveries, such as Henry Handel Richardson, Joseph Hergesheimer, and R. B. Cunninghame Graham who straddle both periods will also be covered in Book II.

On the Bedford Street Pay-Roll
the Windmill Colophon

The expansion of the business continued steadily during its first decade, so that by 1903 the catalogue listed 766 titles in print (and 459 authors), compared with 251 titles in 1894 (and 170 authors). Although for the first two years annual turnover was not recorded in the general ledger – gross profit or loss on each title was recorded instead – from 1892 onwards turnover increased steadily to reach an annual average of about £40,000. The following table also shows how profits fluctuated considerably, though some of the variations may have resulted from inconsistent bases of stock valuation. The profit figures include the accumulated interest on the partners' capital:

	Turnover	Profit
1890		£ 70
1891		1,049
1892	£13,278	3,657
1893	20,409	4,224
1894	34,345	6,890
1895	21,290	2,902
1896	23,878	1,859
1897	45,739	10,415
1898	39,653	8,416
1899	37,562	6,251
1900	40,069	4,848

The two rooms on the second floor of 21 Bedford Street were soon much too small, and by stages the floors occupied by the Camera Club and the bespoke tailor were taken over. Eventually when room had also to be found for *The World's Work* and *Bon Ton* magazines (see Chapter Six), the entire building was acquired, and rooms were occupied in the neighbouring buildings. The stock was housed in the cellar, which extended a long way back, and also in the cellar next door. In charge of the stock and a staff of four was Alfred Maddison with the rank of publisher's foreman. He also acted as security officer, living in a flat on the top floor, and kept rabbits in a little yard at the back. His son, Dr Edwin Maddison, told me of his childhood there. As they used the office staircase, he knew most of the staff and in which room they worked:

'Mr Heinemann originally had his own office at the front of the first floor, reached by a magnificent marble staircase, but he later moved to a room at the back, the front room being allotted to the readers. Pawling, who gave me a cricket bat which I still have, and Chalmers Roberts of *World's Work* were on the second floor. Unusually for those days, lady secretaries were employed. Carbon paper was used but all the foreign correspondence was copied in a press onto tissue sheets of large copy-books. As well as Ham-Smith, the general manager, there was C. A. Bang, a Dane in charge of the foreign department, and a chief accountant called Muir, aided by three clerks. He was succeeded by Gatfield who married the telephonist who operated an internal switchboard with the wires coming down through the roof.'

The main entrance led straight into the trade counter for the book-sellers' 'collectors'. It also acted as a reception point for visitors. In charge was Ernest Whyberd assisted by John Dettmer, who began as office boy at the age of fourteen for six shillings a week and, apart from the trenches in 1914–18, stayed with the firm for seventy-three years! Whyberd also spent most of his working life with the firm and, as receptionist, was on friendly terms with many of the authors.

'Mr Heinemann's first instructions to me were that no one was to be allowed to go up to see him without first being announced. If he did not want to see them for any reason, it was my job to think up some tale to put them off. I then had to report back to him just what I had told the caller; and I found him very matey in this connection. The first time I saw John Galsworthy he arrived in the office with a lovely Old English sheepdog. Fortunately Mr Heinemann was also a dog lover and they all settled down happily together. William Nicholson, on the other hand, always arrived on a bicycle and would take his clips off before going up to see Mr Pawling. . . . Then Edmund Gosse caused me a bit of trouble because he complained that my "s" looked so like an "o" that his name on a parcel of books looked like "Goose". After that all his labels had to be typed. . . . Ellen Terry lived just opposite the office. She would often come to the counter to buy books and as she got older she became very forgetful. My instructions from Mr Heinemann were that she could have any books she wanted, and "don't ask her for the money".'

Whyberd also remembers how, while Pawling would travel to the office in a hansom cab, Heinemann arrived every morning in his own carriage and pair, with coachman and footman. 'Often he kept them waiting all morning and then would decide to walk to lunch. At that time he lived in a street off Park Lane and during the summer he had a house at Merton Court where he entertained many of his authors.' Whyberd described him as brilliant, lively and intelligent but, like others, remembered his fiery temper. 'When anything went wrong, he could be so furious that he could hardly speak. But once the row was over he never mentioned the subject again. He particularly disliked people who made excuses and he enjoyed letting them get tangled up in their own explanations, for it was impossible to fool him. But he had a wonderful capacity for relaxation: he would slump down in his chair for a short time and would then stand up completely refreshed. As far as I was concerned he was generous to a degree. When my kid had scarlet fever in the early days of the war he paid all the expenses, including travelling to see him in hospital and a fortnight's convalescence at Southend.'[1]

John Dettmer remembered the green carpet in William's office and how he wrote many of his letters by hand at a roll-top desk by the window. But he also spoke of the short outbursts of temper. 'Some of the staff were so frightened that they would try and hide. He would stamp his little feet and his bulbous eyes would start out of his head, but then suddenly he would be completely docile. Bertie Woods, in the manufacturing department, was particularly apt to annoy him, and about once a month would be sacked. Bertie would return to his family's printing business in Islington, but then Mr Heinemann would have to beg him to return.' On these occasions Pawling would act as a true partner and soothe everyone down. He was readily approachable and known for his kindliness.

Staff wages appear not to have been over-generous. As reader, the talented Edward Garnett, for example, received only £3 to £3 10s. a week for an exacting amount of reading, editing, and correcting. But his position was never very secure, Garnett explaining to his father that '"as Pawling's protégé I have, from the first, been looked upon by Heinemann with some jealousy, and he has now taken an opportunity of putting his own man in my place.'"[2] This was an intentional, and with hindsight a mistaken, dismissal, William's letter to Garnett (2 July 1901) seeming more than a little tainted with hypocrisy: 'I am more than fully alive to the fact that the salary we are paying you now is hardly adequate to your qualifications and your work, and I am also aware that I require soon – and shall require even more in the future – a certain editorial assistance which is somewhat outside your lines. Under these circumstances I cannot afford further to burden any "reading budget" by offering you a salary such as I should like to offer you. This consideration has led us to revise the whole question of reading, paragraphing, editing, etc. and we have come to the conclusion that it will suit our purposes best to remould our arrangements entirely. Under our new arrangement we could, I fear, even less than in the past offer you what is so unquestionably your due, and we think therefore that it will be best if you at your own convenience and in your time dispose of your work elsewhere. In depriving ourselves of your services we are more than conscious of their great value, and we beg to thank you very cordially for the efficient, original, and devoted manner in which you have conducted our affairs. Your relations with our authors have certainly been entirely satisfactory to ourselves.'[3]

In charge of production were a Mr Lowe and Herbert Clarke, though William himself took a close interest in the appearance of his books and often achieved high standards, many of the best being printed by Ballantyne, Hanson, & Co, with headquarters in Edinburgh. Heinemann books usually looked 'modern' for their own period. He was not scared to experiment, such as using the reverse side of the cloth for the binding in order to achieve a distinctive effect. He was a perfectionist. On one occasion he insisted on having 2,000 copies of a book destroyed because of a relatively minor blemish. With reservations he had great faith in the qualities of British craftsmanship. 'There is unquestionably a certain foundation for the charge of monotony in the get-up of modern English books', he wrote to the *Publishers' Circular*, 'and yet more novel ideas, in format, type, scheme of illustration, &c. originate in England than in any other country. . . . This is the case notwithstanding the fact that English publishers have great difficulty in fighting the conservative stolidity of English manufacturers, for in book-making as in every other branch of manufacture we are inclined to consider as acceptable today that which has seemed good in the past. The fact remains that English paper and English type are the best in the world, and that while half the *éditions de*

Crown 8vo,
In Five Vols.

Price
6s. each

THE NOVELS OF DOSTOEVSKY

Translated by CONSTANCE GARNETT

THE BROTHERS KARAMAZOV · THE IDIOT
THE POSSESSED   CRIME AND PUNISHMENT
THE HOUSE OF THE DEAD, ETC.

FIODOR MICHAILOWITCH DOSTOEVSKY was born in Moscow in 1821, and died at the age of sixty, after a varied career during which he contributed some of its greatest features to Russian literature.

His books have been translated into many different European languages, notably of course into French and German, and through them they have reached English readers. But a translation through another language is but a distant relation to the original, and is always unsatisfactory for any one wishing to make the acquaintance of the works of a true literary artist. It is, therefore, with special satisfaction that Mr. Heinemann announces a translation of the works of another of the great Russian Classics by Constance Garnett, whose translation of the works of Turgenev and Tolstoy are among the finest translations ever made in English, and have as such been specially honoured by the British Government.

Large
Crown 8vo

Price
6s. net

ON THE ART OF THE THEATRE

By GORDON CRAIG.   Fully Illustrated

MR. GORDON CRAIG has worked hard and enthusiastically to attain a measure of improvement in "stage craft." He aims at perfection in scenery —lighting and artistic presentation. This book is not merely an exposition of his ideals, but is of great practical value as a record of actual experiences. The leading theatres on the Continent, more especially in Germany and Russia, have been happily influenced by him. He has recently returned to England, and it is hoped that this book will assist the author in his intention of developing his views in London, so that our theatres may benefit by his splendid work, as many theatres on the Continent have done.

Uniform
with " The
Plays of
A. W.
Pinero "

Prices
Cloth
2s. 6d. ;
Paper
1s. 6d.

THE PLAYS OF W. S. MAUGHAM

AS a dramatist Mr. Maugham possesses in a rich degree two most important qualifications, he can draw human character and write vivid, witty, and pointed dialogue ; also he has undoubtedly mastered the whole art of construction.

The work of few dramatists has produced so much spontaneous applause and held the interest of the audience so strongly as the plays of Mr. Maugham.

Mr. Maugham makes no efforts in rhetorics or high-flown phrase with the usual poverty stricken thought underneath ; simplicity is throughout the keynote of his dramatic vein, and a keen instinct for the essentials of life.

I. A Man of Honour   II. Lady Frederick   III. Jack Straw

20

PUBLISHED BY WILLIAM HEINEMANN LONDON

luxe that are sold in America are manufactured in England, very few books of luxury come to England from America. . . . The best illustrations I have ever used in my art publications are made in England – the best in photogravure and lithography, and in process. Unfortunately one meets constantly with the inability of English art printers to cope with big contracts, and is driven abroad; but rather than go abroad for the manufacture of my books I have had to employ five firms to print the plates of one single book. English establishments capable of turning out first-class lithographic work are similarly limited in number and capacity, so that one is frequently forced to turn to Germany for that class of work. But in this branch also the very best work is unquestionably done in England. We suffer from a want of skilled labourers in these trades, not of skilled labour and achievement.'

His intense interest and delight in fine book production were expressed in a typically ironic and yet touching conclusion to this letter when he took pride in an unnamed book merely described as 'the work of a writer of first-class importance, illustrated by one of the first living artists. It was manufactured entirely in England and I should like to compete with it before any competent jury. . . . It is, and will remain, I fear, a joy and happiness to me, because up to the present day I have only sold four copies of it, but such as it is I consider it the best produced book I have ever issued, a book which I – in the unprofitable possession of almost the whole edition – venture to declare the equal as far as production is concerned of any modern printed book.'[4]

Was it his personal taste which was responsible for much of the good typography and layout of the firm's catalogues, particularly those between 1906 and 1914? Because of the length of the blurbs and the inclusion of four-colour plates by Rackham and others they must have been a heavy expense. Surviving leaflets testify to the value William put on direct-mail promotion. Exceptional importance was also attached to Press advertising, which was usually the largest single item in the overheads. In 1910 he told an interviewer that 'though the bad organization of our book-trade forces us to rely too much upon it, advertising is extraordinarily effective in selling a book. Of course no one who knows his business advertises at random. There is an art in that, as in everything else. We may not aim at the individual reader, but we can aim pretty accurately at a class. Like gunners we can calculate our range and drop our shells with tolerable precision, even over an unseen target. Of course there is a great deal, too,

[63]

in the choice of the weapon – the particular paper we select in order to get at a particular section of the public.

'Emphatically, advertisements have more influence than reviews. The glory of reviewing is departed – it is not what it used to be. I don't mean to say that it is less able. I think, on the contrary, that the average ability of reviewers is steadily rising. But for some reason or other the review has ceased to bite on the public mind as it used to. The days are past when a single article in *The Times* or the *Spectator* could make the fortune of a book. These romantic incidents don't occur nowadays. Our reviewers are excellent critics, but for some reason or other they don't excite such interest in the books they deal with as the reviewers of the past seem to have excited.'

Reviews, even good ones, could sometimes hamper sales. 'How often you feel you have got out of a review all that you want to know about a book, and need not trouble about it any further? The function of the literary weekly, or the literary page of the daily paper, is largely to give people a superficial acquaintance with current literature, while saving them the expense of book-buying and the time involved in book-reading. I really do not know why we publishers support – as we do, almost entirely – the literary weeklies. They are of no proportionate service to us, either as organs of criticism or as mediums of advertising – except, perhaps, those that are practically trade organs. . . . If they are effective organs of publicity at all, it is only in the case of a very special class of books. For getting at the great reading public, the popular newspaper is alone effective. It is so effective that well directed advertising will often counteract the harm done by the most damaging review, even in the most influential paper.'[5]

In building up the firm's image an important part was played by the colophon which appeared on title pages, the spines of the binding, and in advertisements. The original colophon consisted of a simple monogram of William's two initials, but this was soon followed by a more elaborate monogram designed by Whistler in an oval-pointed frame carrying the words: *Scripta Manent* (see figure). It was not very satisfactory and would not have looked out of place on the breast pocket of a sportsman's blazer. It was replaced in 1897 by the famous windmill, a woodcut made by William Nicholson who gave it to Heinemann as a present. Tradition has it that it was copied from the windmill at Rottingdean which overlooked North End House where Nicholson was then living. Because of this connection the firm has donated money for the upkeep of the mill and in 1968 A. Dwye Evans, then the company's chairman, unveiled a plaque attached to the mill stating that 'The windmill is the original from which William Nicholson made his drawing for William Heinemann, the publisher, in 1897 and which became the Heinemann colophon'.

Unfortunately experts have raised doubts over the design's provenance, claiming that, though stylized, the Heinemann colophon is clearly based on a post-mill whereas the Rottingdean mill is a smock-mill. Furthermore, Edward Craig, in an introduction to a recent (1980) reissue by the Whittington Press of Nicholson's *An Almanac of Twelve Sports and London Types*, has written recently how his father (Gordon Craig) one day 'was showing me some old prints that he had stacked away in a portfolio and among them was a superb seventeenth century bird's eye view of a battle taking place somewhere in Holland: armies were investing a city from every quarter, and in the foreground was a cluster of windmills. "Look", said father, selecting one particular mill, "that's Nicholson's mill – I remember him tracing it off that very one." And there is was, delicately etched and quite inconspicuous until Nicholson had turned it into what is

now almost an heraldic badge. It started as a bookplate, a gift to the publisher, then it went through a number of states as Heinemann's trademark.'[6] Colin Campbell, an expert on Nicholson, believes that it must have been Callot's 'Siege of Breda', a bird's-eye view which is full of windmills. Gleeson White, writing in a special number of the *Studio* for the winter of 1898–9 also speaks of Nicholson's woodcut of the windmill as a bookplate and it was reproduced in colour.

Whatever its provenance, the Heinemann windmill has for long existed in its own right and still stands for the distinctive character of the firm's publishing. On the cover of his 1919 catalogue William printed the windmill in the centre of this very apt truism: *Non minima pars eruditionis est bonos nosse libros*.

Some Americans:
Crane, James, Sinclair,
London, Robins

From the outset American writers featured in Heinemann's lists and he worked closely with American publishers, most of them, as today, in New York. The addition of copies for the US to the print run, whichever side of the Atlantic the book was typeset and/or printed and bound, meant a sizeable reduction in basic costs and in the case of specialized titles could make a book just viable. The efforts of British publishers were, however, seriously impeded by American pirating of their editions, US copyright law being of little help because it insisted that copyright could be recognized only when the book had been typeset in the States. Later this was made more onerous because a new copyright bill decreed that the book had to be printed and bound in the States as well. Books in foreign languages were treated more favourably in that they were given provisional copyright protection for the first twelve months.

Heinemann, on one of his visits to America in order to buy and sell rights, managed single-handed to moderate this naked piece of protectionism. Acting independently but in contact with the British Publishers Association, he argued with their opposite numbers in the US and also with the American Typographical Association, getting them to agree in principle to provisional copyright protection for a period of sixty days for any book printed abroad in the English language – not as generous as for foreign books, but it would afford British publishers a breathing-space in which to negotiate rights deals without the threat of pirating. This concession was eventually inscribed in a new 1909 American Copyright Bill and Heinemann was publicly thanked and praised by his fellow UK publishers and presented with the trade's blue riband.

In June 1893 he had also appointed his own personal New York representative, Paul Reynolds, to help negotiate rights deals as well as scout for new talent. He started off as a publisher's agent only, but eventually became literally a double agent, handling authors as well, though there is no reason to think that he used his dual role dishonestly. One of the American authors he represented was Stephen Crane, who joined the Heinemann list in 1895 with *The Red Badge of Courage*. He was only a month short of twenty-four when this celebrated novel about the American Civil War was published; written from the point of view of a private soldier, it has been described as perhaps the best fictional study in English of fear. It brought him overnight fame and it was followed by *The Little Regiment and Other Episodes of the American Civil War* (1896); *The Black Riders* (1896), a volume of poems; and *Maggie: a Girl of the Streets* (1896), a naturalistic novelette culled from his experience as a journalist of American city life – he described New York's Bowery as his 'artistic educator' and once, after testifying on behalf of a woman he had seen being charged unfairly with soliciting, the police ran him out of town. Setting off from Jacksonville to report the Cuban insurrection against the Spanish, he joined a tug carrying arms to the Cubans, but this foundered and he only got to shore in a lifeboat. This experience was the basis of the title piece of a collection of brilliant short stories, *The Open Boat* (1898).

In 1897 he came to England and told Heinemann that he thought it was high time that he saw a little fighting for himself. He wanted to test what he had written in the *Red Badge* against reality. He was going to Greece to report the Greek/Turkish War for the *New York Journal* – Pawling was to arrange for him also to cover the war for the *Westminster Gazette*. But the war fizzled out and he came back and settled for a while in England with Cora Jackson, whom he'd met in Jacksonville where she was the madame of a brothel and the undivorced wife of the son of a former British Governor-General of India. Heinemann also published two novels, *The Third Violet* (1897) and *Active Service* (1899), but tragically Crane contracted tuberculosis, then a major killer, and died at twenty-nine. In the UK Crane's books never sold well, with the exception of *Maggie* and *The Red Badge of Courage*, a classic certain to preserve his name for posterity.

Crane was very far from being a Man of Letters. He had little formal education. He was never happier than in the saddle of a horse. While he must have absorbed influences from contemporary literature, he was a completely natural, unselfconscious writer. He was a fervid admirer of Conrad's *The Nigger of the 'Narcissus'* and also of the man himself, to whom he had been introduced by Pawling over lunch. After it the two tramped the streets all afternoon, ending up for supper at Monico's. Conrad likewise admired Crane's talent, even to the point of envy. Though he once wrote to Edward Garnett about the limitations of Crane's impressionist style, close on twenty years after Crane's early death Conrad paid tribute to his 'wonderful power of vision, which he applied to the things of this earth and of our mortal humanity with a penetrating force that seemed to reach within life's appearance and forms the very spirit of their truth. His ignorance of the world at large – he had seen very little of it – did not stand in the way of his imaginative grasp of facts, events, and picturesque men. . . . He knew little of literature, either of his own country or of any other, but he was himself a wonderful artist in words whenever he took a pen into his hand. Then his gift came out – and it was seen to be much more than mere felicity of language. His impressionism of phrase went really deeper than the surface. In his writing he was very sure of his effects. I don't think he was ever in doubt about what he could do.'[7]

Conrad also wrote an introduction to *Stephen Crane: a Study in American Letters* (1923) and much later the firm published, in conjunction with Knopf, a *Stephen Crane Omnibus* (1954) which contained 'all that anyone but an expert student will care to read'.

Although Henry James spent most of his adult life in England and became a British subject in 1915 shortly before his death, he properly counts as an American writer. He had been friendly with Heinemann for some years and in 1895 decided to join him, leaving Macmillan's because for his last book they had reduced his already modest advance. His hopes of better rewards do not seem, however, to have been realized, though his books with Heinemann included important titles such as *The Other House* (1896), *The Spoils of Poynton* (1897), *What Maisie Knew* (1898), and *The Two Magics* (1898) which contained *The Turn of the Screw* – James himself dismissed this as a 'down-on-all-fours pot-boiler'. After the publication of *The Awkward Age* (1899) he appointed Pinker as his agent – an action which thoroughly annoyed Heinemann, who declared that he considered James as a personal friend and balked at the idea of dealing with what he considered to be a parasitic intermediary (see pages 92–5). It is also feasible that Heinemann was not all that distressed to see James go, as his books probably made little, if any, money and it is in part only hindsight that makes his loss seem so serious.

Pinker then signed him up with Methuen's, who, with one exception, published all his future novels. They treated him rather more generously, though; after seven novels his unearned advances came to £672 out of a total of £1,600. Although he lived in some style in his superb house in Rye, money continued usually to be a problem. Despite the break, he wrote three travel books for Heinemann with illustrations by the American artist Joseph Pennell: *A Little Tour of France* (1900), *English Hours* (1905), *Italian Hours* (1909). In the catalogue James's idiosyncratic style seems to have affected the blurb writer: 'It is impossible to describe the brilliance of Mr James's words, darting to the point, full of humour, pathos, colour, and distinction; supple as the fingers of a conjurer, turning, twisting, beautiful as the places they describe. With touches, irresistible and incomprehensible [*sic*] he raises before us the Stones of Venice, more entrancing than Ruskin ever made them. . . .' James had once described Heinemann as 'the most swindling of all publishers', and he seems to have had a very legitimate grouse because, while preparing the third of the travel books, he found it necessary to write to Heinemann that 'I have been waiting in vain for you to give some sign of remembrance that all this while I have had from you in respect to its two predecessors . . . not only not a single shilling but no account, report, statement or explanation of any sort. Have your losses on my volumes of fiction swallowed all profits, for me, of these books too, and is that to be the case with these *Italian Hours* as well? . . . I have had these several years considerable sums from Houghton Mifflin & Co., semi annually, on the American sales of each.'[8] His letter written a week later suggests inefficiency rather than duplicity on the part of the firm: 'I can find no record nor précis of any contract or agreements between us about these two books, and I seem to remember none – nothing but more or less informal letters which I seem not to have kept. . . . I can only hope Pennell hasn't consumed all my profits.'[9]

Over the years he continued to correspond with and meet Heinemann, though on one occasion he was recorded as grumbling that he had to entertain him to luncheon 'as if he hadn't done me enough bad turns',[10] but on another he wrote warmly from Rye: 'I shall be delighted to see you any time you can, on any strange monster of transport familiar to men of fashion, get yourself conveyed hither. Except for three or four days from August 1st next, I cherish the fond hope of not being obliged to leave this place for weeks, for months to come. But it would be always well to make me a signal of your approach.'[11] The firm's archive contains several of his letters which, though in parts indecipherable, would delight any devotee of Jamesian prose style. One more example will have to suffice to show his ability to hone and refine a mundane business letter and turn it into a literary *objet de virtu*. In October 1914 he was merely thanking Heinemann for allowing another publisher to reprint five of his short stories: 'I greatly appreciate the amenity and philosophy of your reply. It really may render me a service much greater than the size of any sacrifice it involves for yourself. My plan, as excogitated some time back, is really quite a different thing, and a more workable one on the basis of *all* the things consistent with it, from, and than, your own simpler idea. And it isn't after all, I may add, as if it could have been at all in the bosom of the gods that yours should perceptibly enrich you, any more than mine is likely to do that for yours gratefully. . . .'[12]

Of the ninety books written by Upton Sinclair William published only seven and they were all early ones, though they included one of the few that is now generally recognized as an American classic, *The Jungle* (1906). Because he used his novels in order to expose social outrage and as vehicles for his beliefs as a very committed socialist, he was apt to be dismissed as a propagandist. *The Jungle* was of course propaganda of a very necessary sort, but it also bears the hallmark of great literature alive with unforgettable human beings, as we read about the Lithuanian immigrant family of Jurgis Rudkus, hooked on the American Dream, going to work in the appalling Chicago stockyards. The horror of their sufferings and tragedies are only too believable, but what also emerges is the heartlessness of the social system that exploits and debases them. In his autobiography Sinclair recalls how when collecting material for *The Jungle* 'for seven weeks I lived among the wage slaves of the Beef Trust, as we called it in those days. . . . I went about, white-faced and thin, partly from undernourishment, partly from horror. It seemed to me I was confronting a veritable fortress of oppression. How to breach those walls, or to scale them, was a military problem. I sat at night in the homes of the workers, foreign-born and native, and they told me their stories, one after one, and I made notes of everything. In the daytime I would wander about the yards, and my friends would risk their jobs to show me what I wanted to see. I was not much better dressed than the workers, and found that by the simple device of carrying a dinner pail I could go anywhere. So long as I kept moving, no one would heed me. . . . For three months I worked incessantly. I wrote with tears and anguish, pouring into the pages all the pain that life had meant to me.'[13]

In America *The Jungle* at once made the headlines. Sinclair was invited to the White House and became world-famous. The book was translated into seventeen languages, becoming a bestseller in London as well as New York. Heinemann gave it a full page in his list as 'The Unforgettable Book of 1906'. The reviewers likened Sinclair to Zola and thirty-one-year-old Winston Churchill wrote a two-part article about the book in T. P. O'Connor's magazine, in which he said that *The Jungle* had 'agitated the machinery of a State Department; and having passed out of the sedate columns of the reviewer into leading articles and "latest intelligence", has disturbed in the Old World and the New the digestions, and perhaps the consciences, of mankind. . . .'[14]

Among the firm's other Sinclair titles were *King Midas* (1906) and *The Journal of Arthur Stirling* (1906), which Sinclair claimed helped to launch the Nietzsche cult in America. There was also *The Fasting Cure* (1911), based on his own self-treatment which he had found mentally as well as physically beneficial and which the blurb claimed had 'the recommendation of many of the more advanced members of the Faculty'. The next year saw the publication of *Love's Pilgrimage* (1912), a case record of a marriage, largely his own, and of what happens when it is 'entered into in utter ignorance of all its practical problems. . . . Both parties had been taught very little, and most of that was wrong.'[15] The remark in the catalogue that 'Mr Sinclair wields no timid pen, none of the important realities are omitted or glossed over' almost certainly reflects fears about charges of obscenity. Heinemann had sent him a number of suggested cuts, all of which Sinclair accepted, though he resisted two of them. It appears that Heinemann was concerned about putting in asterisks to indicate where the cuts had been, because he wrote that he 'would much rather give up the whole thing than appear as a mutilator of a work of art'.[16] Sinclair replied: 'I am disposed to feel that I do not want the book published in an expurgated edition without some brief statement to the effect that it is expurgated in the form of a preface.'[17]

Everything seems to have been agreed, and yet five months later Sinclair, hearing from a friend that Heinemann had still got cold feet, sent a protest at the long delay in publication and decided that if necessary he would be prepared to sue. Although *Love's Pilgrimage* came out in London the next year, it was the last of Sinclair's books that Heinemann published, apart from a very much later book, *Boston, August 22nd*, which came out sixty-six years later in 1978. It is not known what part, if any, the fuss about the expurgation or, more likely, the delay in publication played in the loss of another major author.

The connection between a writer's work and his upbringing, background, life experience, and beliefs is more than usually clear in the case of Jack London. His deprived childhood, his early jobs as an oyster pirate and an able seaman on a whale-hunting schooner, his prospecting for gold in Alaska, his experience of poverty, all help to explain his sympathies with the exploited masses, his attraction to the ideas of Darwin, Nietzsche, and Marx, and his hopes of some kind of socialism; on the other hand, his struggle to succeed as a writer, his accumulation of wealth and his eventual involvement with the problems of owning and running a large ranch in California are at the root of his passionate belief in individualism and, later, his support for American oil interests and the ideology of the exploiters.

By the time of his death at forty he had written forty-four volumes – novels, plays, short stories, essays – and six more were published posthumously – though inevitably with such an output their quality was uneven. Heinemann published only nine titles, but among them were some of the most important, including *The Call of the Wild* (1903) in which Buck, the dog, exchanges a comfortable background for the harshness of the Klondike gold diggings; but because he is a super(man)dog he survives brutality and hardship and joins a pack of wolves, ending up as their leader. Similarly Wolf Larsen in *The Sea Wolf* (1904) is a powerful individualist with great strength and skills, though he could not survive in modern society. *The War of the Classes* (1905), *Tales of the Fish Patrol* (1906), and *Martin Eden* (1910) each in their different ways stem from his experience and beliefs. Somewhat self-consciously, the blurb stated that 'these studies may be called socialistic. One of his own sentences best illustrates the appeal he makes: "Socialism now presents a new spectacle to the world, that of an organized, international revolutionary movement. It is surely time that the capitalists knew something about this Socialism which menaces them."'

His books sold well. *The Call of the Wild*, for example, was still in the list in 1955 and had sold over 130,000 copies. London must have been pleased with Heinemann's performance because in December 1908 he wrote suggesting that he should take over the UK rights of all his future books, including the sale of serials, in the same way as the American Macmillan Company had always done, and pay him an agreed monthly sum on account of royalties. The negotiations were complex, particularly over the transfer of British Empire rights, but in March 1910 full agreement was reached and contracts were exchanged, the monthly payment having been operating already for some time.

The arrangement was, however, doomed. It seemed as if his personal background and life experience affected his relationship with his British publisher just as much as it did his writing. Pawling seems to have become the focus of his aggression. After only ten months London issued an ultimatum because 'I cannot deal with Mr Pawling any more, nor can I deal with any other representative of your house who is dictated to by Mr Pawling, or who in any way apes Mr Pawling's ways. If you say so, and if you feel that my experience with Mr Pawling is not unique, if you feel that I am the erring one, kindly proceed in the shortest possible way to bring our contract to a close. Rather than continue to have any further contact with Mr Pawling, I should prefer never to print another book of mine in England.'[18]

It is possible to understand how the individualist, arrogant, hard-drinking London found it difficult to accept the letters and attitudes of conventional, self-assured, upper-class, cricket-playing Pawling. The firm may or may not have been inefficient, but the letter received by Pawling himself is so vituperative and extraordinary that it merits quotation at some length, if not in full: 'In reply to yours of January 5, I sometimes wonder if you think that in your dealings with me you feel that you are compelled to play a sharp and baffling game of business enterprise. As a business man and a horse trader, these things might go with me; but being neither a business man nor a horse trader, but just an ordinary common-sense sort of a man, they don't go. I have no patience with bafflement nor with cleverness . . . you tell me that you consider you are serving my best interests by not rushing out books at too short intervals. At the same time you have a contract with me under which you are to publish all my books. At the present moment, of books unpublished by me in the United States but finished, and of books published in the United States which are not published in England, you are precariously close to ten (10) behind the schedule. If, despite the contract, which covers all my books, you cannot keep up with this schedule, the best thing for both sides to this matter is to quit the arrangement. A better thing would be to let me deal with Mr Heinemann directly. You, Mr Pawling, may be a very excellent Englishman; but you're not the right kind of Englishman to meet an American like me. I am quite confident that I can deal with Mr Heinemann, but I cannot deal with you. There is a smack of the shop and of petty cleverness about you, and of small caddish ways, that turns my gorge. From the beginning of my correspondence with you, after I finished my correspondence with Mr Heinemann, you dealt with me in the spirit of a Jew Pawnbroker trying to buy several moth-eaten under-shirts from an impecunious sailor. Now, we can't go on this way. Personally, my feeling is that if ever I should meet you, I should pull your nose. . . .

'Let me deal with Mr Heinemann. Let me deal with a man. Let me deal with somebody who has enough decency to tell me what is being done with my stuff, what books are being published, what books are proposed to be published, etc., etc. Please take this letter as the expression of one who is temperamentally not akin to you. You and I live in different worlds and talk different languages. I care never again to howl on your doorstep, and I wish never again to have you slink under my window when I'm trying to sleep. Kindly show this letter to Mr Heinemann, and deliver to him the rest of our correspondence from A to Z. If you don't, I'll see that I get to Mr Heinemann by other means. As it is, I refuse further to be treated in the absurd and preposterous way in which you treat me.'[19]

It was left to Heinemann to reply to this paranoid effusion which he did unerringly and with immaculate coolness. After a formal opening sentence he said he would 'refrain from commenting upon the unaccustomed want of restraint in that communication, for I must assume that it was written in a moment of quite unnatural excitement. It is not our habit to receive such communications or to permit them to be addressed to any member of our firm. . . . I have taken the pains of reading the correspondence that has taken place between you and Mr Pawling and I feel that if his letters have sometimes seemed to you vague, he has laboured under

considerable difficulty from the fact that you have frequently left enquiries of his unanswered and at other times have assumed knowledge on
his part he could not possess.' There followed four typed pages of
explanation and justification which are very convincing. He ended by
emphasizing that to achieve what London wanted 'requires time,
patience, and in your case a great clarifying of the situation, which has
been badly if not irretrievably hurt by the fact that your stories have been
handled by so many different agents and that your name has drifted about
in various catalogues. We will, if you wish it, continue to do our best for
you, and I believe that in time you would reap the benefit of our
endeavours; but it is quite impossible to work if friction exists, and under
no circumstances can I tolerate such letters as you have addressed to Mr
Pawling. I must leave you now to judge for yourself, and I have no doubt
that when you have done so, whether we continue or not, you will wish to
withdraw expressions which are entirely indefensible.'[20]

London had no such wish. His riposte to this placatory but firm letter
made it impossible for the relationship to continue. In his reply Pawling
was likened not only to a cad and Petticoat Lane huckster, but suffered
insult in the form of 'a little story that occurred down South. A Northerner
who had never seen a skunk was inquiring as to what a skunk looked like.
The white master said that a skunk looked like a pussy-cat – in fact, he
thought, if anything, the skunk was handsomer than a pussy-cat. And he
referred the matter to his negro servant who replied: "Well, Massa, you
may think a skunk is hansomah than a pussy-cat, but I say that handsome
is as handsome does." Pray pardon me, but if your Mr Pawling stinks, who
that are overtaken by the smell may not announce that they have smelled
him?'[21]

To lose an author who writes letters like that is understandable; but it
has to be recognized that, whereas Heinemann was brilliant at discovering
and contracting the up-and-coming authors of his day, too often he failed
to hold on to them. Too many moved elsewhere: Kipling, Conrad, Wells,
Lawrence, James, Sinclair . . . though of course others of great import
stayed or moved from other publishers. Undoubtedly in the case of each
departure there were special reasons – maybe it was inefficiency, carelessness, overconfidence, or meanness – but it happened too frequently for
easy justification.

The last author in this section, Elizabeth Robins, was a competent but
not a major novelist and she merits inclusion on other counts. She might

fit equally well into the section on drama but, more important, she happened to be the woman whom Heinemann loved more than any other. It is not my intention to depict the personal amatory lives of any other of the top executives in the firm's history, but on occasions with its founder an exception does seem to be justified. His personal and publishing affairs were intermingled so frequently, and this was particularly true in the case of Elizabeth Robins. Born in Louisville, Kentucky, in 1862, the year before William, at eighteen she had begun as an actress in New York and with the Boston Museum Company. She married another actor in the company, George Richmond Parks, but two years after the wedding he committed suicide by jumping into the Charles River at the stroke of midnight, wearing a suit of armour to weigh himself down. Soon after this she came to England and established herself as a serious actress, becoming best known for her appearances in Ibsen's plays, with which Heinemann was very much involved (see pages 117–21). At the same time she started to write under the pseudonym of C. E. Raimond with Heinemann as her publisher. Her first novel had the curious title of *George Mandeville's Husband* (1894). Because she did not want her real name known in the office Heinemann explained that he couldn't draw up an official agreement and asked her to send him a letter, which he could lock up in his private safe, authorizing him to arrange for its publication with a royalty of 15 per cent and an advance of £50. The full proceeds of any American rights would be hers. Other novels and a collection of short stories followed, including *The Open Question* (1898), described as a 'tale of two temperaments' which dealt with eugenics, suicide, and Suffragists, with whom Elizabeth Robins had become actively involved. Friendly with Emmeline and Sylvia Pankhurst, she became a committee member of the Women's Social and Political Union and other bodies. She also wrote a play, *Votes for Women*, which in 1907 she turned into a novel, *The Convert*, published by Methuen.

The identity of C. E. Raimond became widely known and her later books were issued under her own name. Meanwhile her brother, Raymond, had joined the gold rush on the Klondike and, worried about him, she decided to go there herself, arranging for a magazine to finance her journey in return for some articles. Although her stay in Alaska was brief, as well as persuading her brother to leave, she collected material for some short stories and two very successful books: *The Magnetic North* (1904) and *Come and Find Me* (1908). Some memoirs – *Both Sides of the*

Curtain (1940) – were published by the firm many years later, but the last of her books to be issued by William himself was *Where are you Going to?* (1913), which was centred on the tragic lives of two young sisters, the author's 'idyllic exordium being in admirable contrast to the catastrophe round which the story is woven'.

Among the surviving correspondence covering many years between author and publisher, as well as the usual information about proofs, cheap editions, *et al.* and at least one tiff about an increased advance, are paragraphs and indeed whole letters in which William reveals his feelings for her. An undated letter from Paris talks of his eagerness to see her again, to spend 'one and many evenings together ... and of this camaraderie of ours. You have never, my dear friend, realized how much everything I do and think takes an odd relationship to yourself – how I seem to look to you and lean on you through the years.'[22] A letter from Algiers in March 1897 describes a trip into the desert and how he is writing 'basking in the shade of the palm trees – because the sun is too hot. The roses are in full bloom, strawberries to perfection, and asparagus. Also the sea seems bluer than it ever was before – but perhaps that is my fancy and I am really thinking of your eyes which are bluer and more beautiful by far than the sea or sky above.'[23] Early the next year, Robins confided to a woman friend that he had proposed to her for the last time. She quoted from his letter: 'I am going to ask you once more, and I am never going to ask again. .... I have made up mind not to be a homeless Bohemian any longer. If you say "No" this time, I must find the next best who will say "Yes".'[24]

Sadly, as we shall see later, William had to settle for 'the next best'.

Björnson, the Russians, Magda Heinemann, and other Europeans

William's European background and connections, coupled with the advice and editorial expertise of Edmund Gosse, were reflected in the regular commissioning of translations of works by European authors. Gosse also devised and edited an ambitious series of short histories of the literatures of fifteen nations and/or languages (1897): Europe was represented by eight volumes covering French, Spanish, Italian, German, Hungarian, Bohemian and Russian; there were separate volumes on Chinese, Japanese and Arabic literatures; on Ancient Greek, Latin and Sanskrit; the series was completed by volumes on American and Modern English literatures. The last was written by Edmund Gosse himself and among other well-known contributors were Gilbert Murray (Greek) and Richard Garnett (Italian).

Another major Gosse project was the launch in 1901 of the Century of French Romance, later renamed Masterpieces of French Romance. Twelve of the most famous French authors were each represented by a single volume containing one of their best known stories: e.g., Stendhal (*The Chartreuse of Parma*); Victor Hugo (*Notre-Dame of Paris*); Flaubert (*Madame Bovary*); Daudet (*The Nabob*); Jules and Edmond de Goncourt (*Renée Mauperin*). The Goncourts also appeared elsewhere in the list with a two-volume selection from their *Journals*. Among other French authors were two books by Emile Zola: *The Attack on the Mill and Other Sketches of War* (1892 and *Stories for Ninon* (1895); and Romain Rolland's four-volume novel, *John Christopher* (1910–13), translated by Gilbert Cannan (the author himself of three novels for Heinemann).

Cannan also translated the two volumes of *Heinrich Heine's Memoirs* (1910), culled from his works, letters and conversations, about whom the catalogue wrote as having possessed more than simple genius, but also 'the heart of a disappointed man and the bitterness of one who, though he has attained success, has been wounded in the battle of life. The bitterness is there, but he sang the tender passions in a more melodious key than any other poet of the Romantic movement. Yet he savoured his writing with Gallic salt, caustic and biting.' Goethe was represented by *Wilhelm Meister's Theatrical Mission* (1913), a first draft of his great work and in which there were considerable differences from the final version. *The Poems of Schiller* (1901) were also in the list.

Fluent in Norwegian and Danish, and as an expert on the area, Gosse introduced several Scandinavian writers, among them Björnstjerne Björnson. At first Björnson distrusted Gosse because he suspected, almost certainly wrongly, his views on Norwegian politics and because Gosse was friendly with his arch political/literary rival, Ibsen; Gosse had been critical of Björnson's writing and even called his poetry that of a 'vulgar stump orator', but later he admitted that he had failed to comprehend the meaning of Björnson's more recent work. Following his two novels in the International Library (see page 16), Gosse edited his collected novels in thirteen volumes (1895–1909).

Undoubtedly the most important and enduring contribution Heinemann made to British understanding of European literature was the commissioning of translations by Constance Garnett, the wife of Edward, of the great Russian novelists. She had started to learn Russian from Felix Volkhovsky, one of a group of exiles with whom she and her husband had become friendly. In their circle was also Prince Kropotkin, a leader of the second phase of European Anarchism (see also pages 107, 114) and Sergei Stepniak, a romantic Tartar who had fled Russia after confessing to knifing a general. Stepniak did much to encourage Constance with her Russian and helped her to revise her first translations – in fact they fell in love though two years later Stepniak was killed on a level crossing. She sent her first translation, Goncharov's *A Common Story* (1894) to Heinemann who accepted it, gave her a fee of £40, and asked her next to translate Tolstoy's *The Kingdom of God is Within You* (1894). It was about this time that she paid the first of two visits to Russia, and for the next thirty-five years she was never without a Russian book to translate. Next came Turgenev. Starting with *Rudin*, she went on to translate the *Complete Works of Ivan Turgenev* (1894–99) in fifteen volumes – two more volumes being added in 1919–23. While there had been occasional translations of his books before, this was the first time they were made available together. Not only did they sell well but Turgenev's approach and style had an influence on much English writing.

Constance Garnett's translations of three of Tolstoy's works followed: *Anna Karenina* (1901); *The Death of Ivan Ilyitch and Other Stories* (1902); *War and Peace* (1904). That year she made her second visit to Russia and in 1907 when the convention of the exiled Russian Social Democratic Party was held in London, met Lenin, Trotsky, and Stalin. Lenin impressed her but on the whole she was scornful of the Bolsheviks, though the next year Heinemann published her translation of Constantine Feldmann's *The Revolt of the Potemkin* (1908).

They were brilliant, but her Tolstoy translations lost the firm money, though even for *War and Peace* she received only £300. When negotiating the contract for her next assignment, *The Novels of Dostoevsky* (1912–21) in twelve volumes, she asked for a small royalty after the sale of a certain number of copies, but William felt bound to resist, or at least postpone the proposal: 'I have on principle nothing against it, but you will realize that I must also take into consideration the frightful failure of the Tolstoy translations, and the horrible loss they have entailed, eating up so far most of the profit on Turgenev. I should rather say that after three years I would see how we stand and pay you a further fee if I find my Russian translations have been sufficiently successful to warrant it. At the present moment the Tolstoys balance the Turgenevs, and I am hoping that Dostoevsky will recoup and pay me; but that of course is a gamble. . . .'[25]

The Dostoevskys had a remarkable impact. For some he became a cult figure. Middleton Murry claimed that *The Brothers Karamazov* was 'one of the most epoch-making translations of the past, one to be compared with North's Plutarch'. Virginia Woolf wrote: 'Constance Garnett's translations were a crucial influence on the novel for after reading *Crime and Punishment* and *The Idiot*, how could any young novelist believe in characters as the Victorians painted them?'[26] Despite Constance Garnett's immense reputation, during most of her professional life she earned relatively little – though eventually she was awarded a Civil List pension. Her years of painstaking work affected her already weak eyesight and at times she had to rest her eyes, wear blue spectacles, and employ a secretary to read aloud and write for her. In April 1915 she raised once again with William the possibility of a modest royalty as well as the fee for the Dostoevsky translations, reminding him of his promise that when 1915 was reached he would 'go into the matter in a liberal spirit'.

'When I began translating Turgenev, you agreed to pay royalties of 10 per cent on all vols sold after the first 2,000, in addition to 9 shillings per 1,000 words on publication. Since then I have been translating for you for 20 years and my work has been uniformly praised by all the critics, both English and Russian, and has in fact gained me a reputation rather unusual for a translator. Yet I am actually being paid less for what I am doing for you now than for the work I did in 1895 when I had no name and no experience.'[27] William did increase her rate of payment from 9s. to 12s. per 1,000 words, but in a letter to Edward Garnett in December 1915 he was still resisting a royalty: 'I have not the slightest doubt that you want to be quite fair to both parties, but to me it seems extraordinary how little able you seem to realize that there are two sides to the question of my arrangement for the publication of Dostoevsky. . . . I have always said I would reconsider the matter when the series was complete and I was able to see how the books sold as a set. . . .' Dostoevsky so far showed a loss of

£166 14*s.6d.* The war was going to increase production costs. No, he couldn't pay a royalty as well as increase the rate per 1,000. Not that this bald statement of fact in the least 'took away from the consideration of Mrs Garnett's work as worth the highest praise. . . . I am happy and have always been proud to publish Mrs Garnett's work and I shall always hope to publish it'.[28] But this didn't happen. It is likely that dissatisfaction with the financial return dampened William's enthusiasm for her proposed translations of Chekhov's stories and plays. These went instead to Chatto & Windus, who followed on with her translations of *The Works of Gogol* and *The Memoirs of Herzen.*

William must have regretted losing her. Although there were other translators from Russian – or from Russian via French or some other language – she was easily the best for more than a generation. Perhaps Conrad put his finger on one reason for her extraordinary talent after Constance had dedicated Turgenev's *A Desperate Character* to him: 'She is in that work what a great musician is to a great composer – with something more, something greater.'[29] Her own estimation of the comparative values of her translations is also illuminating: 'I should like to be judged by my translation of *War and Peace.* But Tolstoy's simple style goes straight into English without any trouble. There's no difficulty. Dostoevsky is so obscure and careless a writer that one can scarcely help clarifying him – sometimes it needs some penetration to see what he is trying to say. Turgenev is much the most difficult of the Russians to translate because his style is the most beautiful.'[30]

A few other Russian works were commissioned from different translators, including Chekhov's *The Steppe and Other Stories* (1915); *The Plays of Turgenev* (1924); various minor works by Tolstoy such as *The End of the Age – on the approaching revolution* (1906); Gorki's *The Orloff Couple and Malva* (1901) – and much later *Reminiscences of my Youth (my Universities)* (1924); and *Reminiscences of Leonid Andreyev* (1931) – the last was translated by Katherine Mansfield and S. S. Koteliansky.

Another writer with whose works Heinemann battered at the walls of British insularity was Gabriele d'Annunzio. This Italian poet, novelist, dramatist, journalist, patriot-politician was famous throughout Europe and it was high time we knew about him. In the firm's promotional booklet Arthur Symons, one of his translators, introduced him as 'the idealist of material things, while seeming to materialize spiritual things. He accepts, as no one else of our time does, the whole physical basis of life, the spirit which can be known only through the body, the body which is but clay in the shaping or destroying hands of the spirit . . . he takes nature very simply, getting sheer away from civilization in his bodily consciousness of things, which he apprehends as directly, with however much added subtlety, as a peasant of his own Abruzzi.' Twenty years later d'Annunzio, the gilded young writer who told no stories but wrote only about states of mind, revelling in a sensual riot of language, was to become also a man of action, the 'poet-airman' who urged war against Austria and, against the wishes of the Allies, seized Fiume and headed a short-lived city-state with its own army. But the novels and plays which Heinemann published were more concerned with the study of love, 'the analysis of that very mortal passion which beats at so many of the closed doors of the universe. He has shown us the working of the one universal, overwhelming, and transfiguring passion, with a vehement patience, and with a complete disregard of consequences, of the moral prejudice.'

For once Gosse disapproved. Thanking William for this booklet, he remarked that his play, *The Dead City* (1900), which had just been published 'has the same odious thesis that d'Annunzio always affects – namely, that merely physical infatuation, sheer lust in short, is a sufficient excuse for every species of ingratitude, disloyalty, cruelty. This runs through every book he writes, and makes him, to my mind, the most odiously immoral and disgraceful of modern authors. Not one of the Frenchmen has gone so far as he in the deification of mere cowardly sexuality.'[31]

Altogether Heinemann published eight d'Annunzio titles: three other plays: *Gioconda* (1901), *Francesca da Rimini* (1902), *The Honeysuckle* (1915); and four of his novels: *The Triumph of Death* (1898), *The Child of Pleasure* (1898), *The Virgins of the Rocks* (1899), *The Flame of Life* (1900). The translator of the last of these was a young Italian woman, Magda Sindici, who two years earlier, while still in her 'teens, had written a novel, *Via Lucis* (1898), under the pseudonym of Kassandra Vivaria. A publicity paragraph in the trade press announced that it had 'a somewhat romantic interest, for it is the only work of the author that will ever reach the public; and it seems certain that the nature of its reception will never come to the author's knowledge although she is still living – to judge from her portrait, – in the very prime of health and youth. The book was written under great stress, and as indicated by its title, *Via Lucis*, represents the struggles and efforts of a young girl in her attempt to find the true way of happiness. In this instance, "Vivaria", the *nom de plume* under which the book appears, has apparently found this happiness in the bosom of the Roman Catholic Church. When the book is published she will, in all probability, have taken the final vows for life in a convent so strict in its precepts that no rumour from the outside world ever penetrates its wall.'[32] This may well have been a crude publicity stunt because a year later, on 22 February 1899, this retiring author became Mrs William Heinemann.

Magda Sindici was the daughter of the Cavaliere Sindici of Porto d'Anzio; her mother's origin was Scottish. Most of William's friends thought he was incredibly lucky to marry someone so much younger than himself who was also beautiful, lively, and with a good mind of her own. He seems to have been besotted with her, and yet a week before the Roman Catholic wedding in Anzio, he wrote a painful letter to Elizabeth Robins: 'The fatal 22nd. draws nearer and nearer and somehow I am constantly haunted with thoughts of you, dear soul, in your little flat in London, knowing full well how frequently your thoughts also are directed towards Rome. You have been to me (I pray to God you always will remain) so sweet and loyal and good a friend that it seems almost impossible that another should be on the point of becoming even nearer to me than you have ever consented to be. . . .' He hopes that she will as far as possible allow his wife to get to know her, and the letter ends: 'I know that it will always be a satisfaction for you to know that there is at least one man in the world who is a better man than he would ever have been – through your friendship and help.'[33]

After the honeymoon in Sicily they went to Paris and stayed in the little flat Heinemann kept in the Palais Royal where Magda immediately went down with measles. It was symbolic of the unhappy months ahead. Back in London she was at first a delightful hostess and seemed to enjoy getting to know William's friends, but this didn't last. According to his old friend Chalmers Mitchell, 'Magda tried to be good, but wasn't. She was bored, which Willie thought intolerant, and rude, which offended him as he was the soul of good manners and had been accustomed to grace such tables with a princely affability. But, worst of all, she made him laugh at them afterwards and infected him with her own distastes, a difficult position, as with some of them he continued to have professional relations. And so, socially, the couple almost ceased dining out and entertained largely and informally at home. Their luncheons and dinners, dances and suppers were the gayest and best-served in London, and no one was invited except

[83]

to the taste of Willie or of Magda or of both. There was an unexpected result. Willie had always been the leader at his own parties. But Magda was even more of an international, a better linguist, with a wider knowledge of European art and letters, of music and food; she had a quicker wit and, where the company pleased her, an even more charming manner. She was young, alluring, and now beautifully dressed. She beat Willie at his own game, sometimes made him seem one of the duller guests in his own house, in short, not to put a fine point on it, offended his vanity.'[34] Magda seems to have realized some of this, for she confided in Elizabeth Robins that she was a 'terrible influence for Willie – he *says* he is happy and I know his deep love. But my presence and mental and emotional attitude towards the things of life and art have decomposed his sense of joy which was the best thing in him, and taken all the keenness away from the edge of his enjoyment of those things. I have turned an optimist into a pessimist, and surely that is a wrong thing to do.'[35]

Magda seems to have been an exemplification of the self-conscious bitch. There is an account of how at one of William's dinner-parties she failed to put in an appearance until halfway through the meal when she entered still in furs, hat and veil. When William asked what had happened to her, where had she been, she at first ignored him until, exasperated, she retorted: 'Willy, darling, if you ask me again, I shall tell you!'

Gwen Gabriel who later joined the staff at Bedford Street, but who was earlier employed by Magda who had started some sort of dress business, remembers her as having many faults: 'She was always in debt; she was incurably improvident; she would spend the housekeeping money on other things and then try to borrow from the servants to buy things for a party. Worse, she was unfaithful; worse still, she had more than one lover and was light-hearted about it. William eventually discovered the state of affairs by chance, and the more he probed the worse he found it. . . .'[36] The debts grew month by month. In any case William's establishment had inevitably expanded. As a bachelor, though he spent most of his income, he had lived in a service flat with one man-servant, the faithful Payne who stayed with him for the rest of William's life, but now he kept up a house, a carriage and a coachman, a chef and kitchenmaids, a secretary as well as a maid for Magda, and then more servants to wait on the others. There must have been the traditional marital rows over money, but Magda then began to borrow secretly from most of his friends. She also gambled on the Stock Exchange and this helped for a while to pay off debts, but there were those who said that William accepted these explanations too easily and there were hints of her making half-promises to some of her lenders which she never intended to keep.

There is evidence that William became very depressed. In 1901 he was ordered by his doctor to go to the Mediterranean 'to rest and think of nothing'. He still wrote to Elizabeth Robins; in 1904, for instance, from Paris, telling her that he had tried to have a good time there but had failed. 'Now I often despair and wonder if the fight is worth it all and what the end will be.'[37] In 1903, four years after the wedding, William was so desperate that he filed a petition for divorce but subsequently withdrew it and settled for a deed of separation instead, after which Magda went to live in Paris. Two years later, however, he decided a divorce was essential, presumably because of the continuing debts. Reading between the lines of *The Times* report, it is clear that a fake co-respondent had been fixed up: 'In consequence of rumours which reached him the petitioner had "Mrs Thompson" watched, and it was ascertained that she was frequently visited at her hotel by an elderly gentleman, M. Dimitri Monnier. It was subsequently ascertained that she daily accompanied him to the Café de Paris, at the angle of the Avenue de l'Opéra and the Rue Louis Legrand, where they spent hours together *en cabinet particulier*. There they were followed by detectives and, after some trouble with the *maître d'hôtel* and his waiters, who had endeavoured, first, to wall up the detectives with tables, screens and chairs, and secondly to shut them up in another *cabinet particulier*, they established the fact that the respondent and co-respondent had for several hours been locked in together drinking champagne and coffee.'[38] At the end of a farce which sounds to have been worthy of Feydeau a decree nisi was pronounced.

When, ten years later, Hall Caine ran into Magda in Rome, she admitted that she had 'voluntarily provided the co-respondent in return for a payment of £2,000 as a reward for not defending the divorce suit'. She also 'painted the portrait of a most deeply injured and entirely blameless person – well, not a Virgin Mary, but at least an entirely pure woman who had never at any time been guilty of unfaithfulness and who respected her soul too deeply to be guilty of falsehood under any circumstances. All the same she made admissions – she had lost her head, been a trying person for any husband, did not know the value of money, etc. . . . to tell the truth I found the little lady just as interesting, just as clever, just as charming to meet as before.'[39] This £2,000, or possibly yet another £2,000, cropped up two years after the divorce when she was summoned in the London bankruptcy court with liabilities of £16,691 against assets estimated at £695: 'The greater part of the £2,000 from her husband seemed to have been paid over to a solicitor in whose business she was to have an interest. This transaction had not been satisfactorily explained. The solicitor had lately been adjudged bankrupt and had absconded . . . the Official Receiver reported that she had brought on her own bankruptcy by rash and hazardous speculation, and unjustifiable extravagance. . . .'[40] In perhaps the bitterest of his letters to Elizabeth Robins, William spoke of Magda's treachery and infamy 'being screamed from the housetops . . . in all my suffering I have often wondered if I ought ever to have married at all, when I knew that you could not join me.'[41]

Royalties –
Heinemann's Lifelong Antagonism
to Literary Agents

In the Edwardian England of the new century the list continued to burgeon and the business to expand, the number of titles in the catalogue increasing from 766 in 1903 (and 459 authors) to 1,635 in 1914 (and 985 authors). Turnover likewise grew but, as the table below indicates, profits declined and reached a low point in 1902 with a profit of only £381 which, after £1,095 had been written off the valuation of publishing rights, became a loss of £714. For the first time a loan from the bank was sought and the following year additional capital of £12,000 was introduced by a new partner, H. L. Weinberg, though it is not clear to what extent he participated actively in the running of the business. He received ⁴⁄₁₆ths of the profits, Heinemann getting ⁷⁄₁₆ths and Pawling ⁵⁄₁₆ths. It will be seen that business soon picked up with a turnover that expanded steadily to reach £58,214 in 1909, though the profits continued to fluctuate:

	Turnover	*Profit*
1901	£46,225	£2,695
1902	36,471	381
1903	37,980	2,805
1904	50,147	2,855
1905	51,079	4,082
1906	55,046	5,806
1907	56,358	4,991
1908	52,085	7,713
1909	58,214	2,639
1910	56,113	4,867
1911	58,904	3,889
1912	59,938	3,557
1913	74,237	5,406

At the end of 1909 Weinberg withdrew from the partnership, so that at the close of 1910 the balance sheet showed total capital and withdrawn

[87]

profits invested by the two remaining partners amounting to £41,300 –
£24,400 owned by Heinemann and £16,900 by Pawling.

In some respects Weinberg was succeeded by Nigel de Grey, who,
though he introduced £3,000 capital, does not appear to have had the
status of a full partner – he was entitled to 5 per cent interest as well as 7½
per cent of net profits, though exempted from sharing in losses. De Grey
had joined the firm in 1907 to succeed Alice Pugh as William's secretary,
but subsequently became manager. Few had a better opportunity of
observing William at work from such close quarters and an extract from
the contribution he made to Frederic Whyte's memoir of Heinemann
deserves to be quoted: 'W.H. was a born publisher – by far the most
brilliant man that I have known in the profession. We often hear of the
"flair" of a publisher – I have known two men who possessed it. Other
men I have known of excellent judgment, fine literary sense, astonishing
breadth of knowledge, excellent trade experience, shrewd business capability. I should say that Heinemann had none of these things in the highest
degree, and most certainly not the commercial force that builds a great
industry. But among publishers he stands to me *facile princeps* – in that he
had an almost unerring instinct for the right book. Failures we often had,
like every other publishing business in the world, some of them ignom-
inious, many more glorious – but short and long his "flair", there is no
other word, was extraordinary. His books were for ever setting the literary
world a-talking, in part because he added to his other quality (if it is not
the same one) the knack of starting the talk, but much more because he
found the new things that people wanted to discuss. He was as a rule a
little ahead of the general trend, and so led the van in the newest direction.
All very intangible, this, for the layman, but easily appreciated by fellow-
publishers. . . .'

De Grey goes on to present a picture of 'a man of unbounded vitality,
bursting with energy, irritable to a degree, impatient, dominating, violent
in his temper, keen, quick, mentally so active that he would often seem
inconsequent, exacting of service to others, intensely difficult to serve,
with moods that varied almost from hour to hour, a man who at times
seemed unbearable, yet whose faults one forgot for the sake of his
wonderful qualities. He could turn the whole of his business into a
bear-garden – the place would seethe and ferment with his driving-
power, and, half an hour later, at luncheon, maybe, he would be the
delightful host, amusing, charming, full of knowledge of the world,

[88]

exercising on his guests a peculiar fascination of which I for one have not the power to convey the sense. As can be imagined, such a man was no organiser of a commercial concern. He was no builder of a machine. His business prospered because it had the goods to deliver. He drove it along by the force of his personality. . . .'

Like so many of Heinemann's contemporaries, including his closest friends and admirers, de Grey seemed to have been continually conscious of William's Jewishness – before the Nazi holocaust a measure of what today would be considered veiled or open anti-Semitism was looked upon as perfectly respectable. He was surprised when Heinemann told him that 'he hated the commercial side of the business. I had always felt that he enjoyed a bargain, and there is no doubt that, when occasion demanded, he bargained well. Like nearly all Jews, his sense of honesty was strong. If he bargained hard, he held to his bargain absolutely. He was quick as lightning with figures, with a wonderful "nose" for a mistake, even though his arithmetic was often faulty. With authors he was as a rule generous, with the young especially so. He was a hard fighter. I have seldom known him to admit defeat if he was really in earnest. If he thought his opponent was trying to get the better of him by unfair means he was merciless. I do not think he was ever sentimental.'[1]

William's Jewishness also intrigued Lytton Strachey, who was a fellow guest at a house party at the Northumberland castle owned by Edward Hudson, the proprietor of *Country Life*: 'I found him a fascinating figure . . . one that one could contemplate for ever – so very very complete. A more absolute jew face couldn't be imagined – bald-headed, goggle-eyed, thick-lipped; a fat short figure, with small legs, and feet moving with the flat assured tread of the seasoned P. and O. traveller. A cigar, of course. And a voice hardly English – German r's; and all the time somehow, an element of the grotesque.'[2]

There is plenty of evidence that William was liked and respected by most of his authors, not only the successful ones, but his mercurial temperament not infrequently led to acerbic brushes. The American publisher, George H. Doran, tells in his memoirs how his editor and reader, Coningsby Dawson, had one of his books, *The Garden Without Walls* (1913), published by Heinemann. A success in the States, it fell flat in the UK: 'Dawson visited London and roundly reproached the discerning Heinemann who so affronted Dawson that their association was abruptly terminated; for Heinemann's advice to Dawson was to accompany

[89]

him to Boulogne, where he would have awaiting Dawson a motor-car and a *cocotte* from Paris. Dawson was to make a month's tour of France accompanied by this personable creature, and then Heinemann assured him he would be competent to write of life'.[3] William himself told a dinner of the London Booksellers' Society how 'one gentleman whose drama in blank verse he had declined had asked him to meet him outside England according to the Continental fashion. Which he supposed meant pistols or swords. He might tell them that he left his office for weeks in fear and trembling.'[4]

As we have seen, Heinemann tended to be more generous with royalties and advances than was Pawling. It would be very difficult to gauge the extent of the firm's generosity or meanness in relation to other publishers, but it is probably safe to assume that on the whole the rates offered and accepted were those determined by the normal processes of competitive trading, though some authors were undoubtedly lost because they were offered more elsewhere. This was not unconnected with William's lifelong antagonism to most literary agents, but before coming to this it is necessary to give some indication of the rates prevailing at the time. As late as the 1880s the royalty system was far from widespread. Most books were sold either outright for a fixed sum; or they were published on a 'half profits' basis; or they were published on 'commission' with the author paying all the costs of production and promotion. It was only with the establishment of the Net Book Agreement (see pages 145–6) in 1900 that a firm basis was provided for paying royalties, but from the outset Heinemann had rewarded most if not all of his authors by this system.

On the whole, rates of royalties were then higher than they are today. Some new authors might receive 10 per cent, but the commonest rate was probably 15 per cent; 20 per cent and even 25 per cent were by no means unknown. The rates on 'colonial' editions, bound in paper for export only, were lower (e.g., 3*d.* to 6*d.* per copy sold of a 6*s.* novel). These terms can be illustrated by a random selection of titles, the royalty rates shown being those at which the bulk of copies were sold: Sarah Grand, *The Heavenly Twins*, 20 per cent; Israel Zangwill, *King of the Schnorrers*, 17½ per cent; Hall Caine, *The Christian*, 25 per cent; Robert Hichens, *The Green Carnation*, 15 per cent; Le Caron, *Twenty-five Years in the Secret Service*, 10 per cent; Henry James, *The Spoils of Poynton*, 15 per cent; A. W. Pinero, *each play*, 10 per cent; H. G. Wells, *The Time Machine*, 15 per cent. Earlier or later titles by these authors may well have been at lower or higher rates.

A more detailed analysis of the contract for a single title gives a clearer picture. In the case of Galsworthy's *The Man of Property* (1906), for example, when he was relatively unknown, the key points were:

> royalty of 15 per cent on the retail (published) price on all copies sold, 13 copies counting as 12;
>
> advance of royalties of £50, payable on publication;
>
> on colonial sales: 3*d*. per copy sold;
>
> on a 6*d*. edition: ½*d*. per copy sold;
>
> on a *Times* Book Club edition (1,200 copies): 7½ per cent royalty;
>
> on an American edition (Putnams): 10 per cent royalty on the American retail price on the first 1,000 copies, 12½ per cent to 3,000 copies, 15 per cent thereafter. (These terms were not standard, the split on American royalties frequently being 85/15 or 75/25 in favour of the author);
>
> income arising from minor rights such as translations, Continental editions, etc. to be shared equally.

The eleven clauses of this contract were very similar to those in a contemporary one, but there was far less elaboration, so that it was scarcely half the length. The earliest Heinemann contracts were even shorter.

Heinemann's start in business coincided with a growing militancy among authors and followed soon after the foundation of the Society of Authors in 1884. Its membership had grown from the initial 68 members to more than 900 in 1900, and it rose to 2,500 by 1914. It was a phenomenon that could not be ignored and from the outset it was respectable as well as authoritative, with Tennyson as president and Matthew Arnold, T. H. Huxley, Charles Reade and Wilkie Collins as vice-presidents. Sir Walter Besant, a mainstay of the Society, edited its journal, the *Author*. Gosse was a member of its council and for a while of its committee of management, but in 1895 he fell out with them because he accused some popular authors of being too greedy and of 'killing the goose that lays the golden egg. . . . Often, when a very successful novel is published, you would find, if you looked beneath the surface, that the author had got the publisher's heart in a little hand-mill, and every now and then was giving it another turn, and then peeping in to see whether he was still alive, and then giving another little turn, squeezing out, drop by drop, royalty blood. . . .'[5]

The young Heinemann made no bones about his opposition to the new body, but he also recognized its good, if mistaken, intentions. In the course of a letter published by the *Athenaeum* in December 1892 he claimed that the Society was 'a trades union more complete, more dangerous to the employer, more definite in its object, and more determined in its demands than any of the other unions – conducted, besides, with intelligence, with foresight, with purity of purpose, but unquestionably and avowedly against the publisher. No one has had better opportunity than myself to test the courteous spirit and fair dealing of the Author's Society, and I will be second to none in acknowledging the services rendered by Mr Besant and his colleagues in certain directions. But with all deference, I will say that they have done harm, too – not voluntarily, but accidentally. I will not dwell on a number of very inaccurate and very unreliable handbooks which they have published, because I do not fancy that these have penetrated very far, so that the errors they contain can hardly become very widespread. But I will at least mention the surprise felt by our American confrères at the lethargic attitude of the London publishers when the Authors' Society takes upon itself to judge as to the proper way a book should appear, the proper remuneration the author should receive ("if he respects himself, and if the publisher is honest"!), and best of all when it calculates the cost of publication, &c., with a disregard to that heavy item – our working expenses – which is delicious in its airiness. In the latter function the position of the Authors' Society is as naïve as if we publishers were to sit down and write fiction or poetry instead of publishing what others have written.'

He went on to give examples of what he considered to be unreasonable demands by authors and concluded by arguing that, of late, authors' prices had 'gone up by leaps and bounds; that royalties are actually being paid which, with the increase in the cost of production, leave to the publisher barely his working expenses; and that they, as well as printers and binders, have a trades union which has formed a decided front, determined on concerted action, not perhaps *against* us, but *for* themselves'.[6]

Brushes with the Society of Authors continued throughout most of his professional life, but his antipathy to the Society was nothing when compared with the acute antagonism he felt for another new arrival, the literary agent, and in particular for A. P. Watt, by repute the founder of their occupation, who dominated it during its formative years. Watt rapidly enlisted a galaxy of successful authors among his clients, including Wilkie Collins, Arthur Conan Doyle, Rider Haggard, Thomas Hardy, and Rudyard Kipling, to mention but a few. Heinemann threw down the gauntlet with an attack in the *Athenaeum* in 1893 in which A. P. Watt was the thinly disguised target: 'This is the age of the middleman', he thundered. 'He is generally a parasite. He always flourishes. I have been forced to give him some little attention lately in my particular business. In it he calls himself the literary agent. May I explain his evolution?

'*The Origin*. You become a literary agent by hiring an office; capital and special qualifications are unnecessary; but *suaviter in modo* must be your policy, combined with a fair amount of self-assertion. You begin by touting among the most popular authors of the moment, and, by being always at hand and glad of a job, you will soon be able to extract from them testimonials which, carefully edited, make up a seductive prospectus to send out broadcast. You must collect these testimonials with zest, just as the pill-doctor or the maker of belts electropathic. It does not much matter how much you pester quiet people for them, as long as you get your circular together. You have made one author wealthy (*you*, not his work; oh no, not his work!) who was poor before; another has found you invariably reliable; and a third has tried you two years ago, and has never been anywhere since.

'*The Business*. You commence by taking in a weekly paper, in which you follow carefully every author who has hitherto been unsuccessful, who is just beginning to succeed, and who has found a friend in some publisher, whose endeavours and efforts and work have at last helped to bring him into recognition. You must lose no time in despatching your circular to this author, telling him that he has been shamefully neglected in the past, that you can double, treble, increase his income tenfold, if he will only allow you 10 per cent of this income for doing so. . . .'[7]

While continuing to avoid dealing with Watt, William's attitude softened a little with the establishment of other agents. He always resented their intrusion between his authors and himself, but he had to recognize that, to keep and acquire the authors he wanted, the agent could not be ignored. In fact he developed relatively cordial and extensive relations with several, including James B. Pinker, who started up in 1896 and was noted for mothering his authors and on occasion lending them money to see them over a difficult patch; C. F. Cazenove; Curtis Brown;

and in particular W. M. Colles, whose Authors' Syndicate was closely associated with the Society of Authors which otherwise for years seemed to have been as antagonistic towards literary agents as were most publishers, presumably because they saw them as rivals. It is significant too that Heinemann saw fit to appoint a literary agent, Paul Reynolds, as his permanent representative in New York.

Despite some softening in his attitude Heinemann continued throughout his life to attack agents and, though some leading publishers were more accommodating, almost certainly he usually spoke for the majority of the other firms. Probably the most deeply considered analysis of his reasons why he felt literary agents served neither publisher nor author nor literature appeared in *The Author* in 1901. Despite its length, a reasonably full extract needs to be recorded:

'1. *The Publisher*. – (a) Because the literary agents prevent that free and intimate intercourse between author and publisher which is from my experience of unquestioned mutual advantage.

'(b) Because I have not found literaray agents scrupulously honest in their dealings.

'(c) Because I resent the implied imputation that the publisher might take advantage of the author. . . .

'(d) Because I do not consider it in the interests of *my* individual business or in the interests of publishers in general that one of us should be played off against the other, as is the habit and practically the *raison d'être* of the literary agent.

'(e) Because no author would be so quixotic as to employ a literary agent if he did not hope to get as much more out of the publisher as the agent's commission represents.

'2. *The Author*. – (a) Because I believe it to be in many instances of advantage to authors to be in personal communication with their publishers.

'(b) Because I consider it *infra dignitatem auctoris* to assume that he cannot take care of himself should he really come into contact with an overreaching publisher. . . .

'(c) Because the author's agent is successful only after an author's reputation has been established by the publisher, but never with a young and unknown writer, so that he merely comes in for an enormous share of profits. . . .

'(d) Because the author's agent fosters in authors the greed for an immediate money return . . . at the cost of all dignity and artistic repose. . . .

3. *Literature.* – (a) Because I do not consider it to be in the interests of literature that books be put up to auction. . . .

'(b) Because it is certainly very much against the interests of literature that authors should be pledged and sold body and soul to syndicates and publishers. . . .

'(c) Because of the fact that it discourages the publisher from taking up new authors, if they are, as soon as he has borne the first risk and launched them, to be put up to public auction. . . .'[8]

Today, when agents play such a dominant role in publishing, much of this will sound impossibly high-minded, self-satisfied, and at times hypocritical. A letter to another publisher in March 1917 makes William sound quite paranoiac: 'My theory is that when once an author gets into the claws of a typical agent, he is lost to decency. He generally adopts the moral outlook of the trickster, which the agent inoculates with all rapidity, and that virus is so poisonous that the publisher had better disinfect himself and avoid contagion.'[9] There were other, more rational examples, such as when in 1918 William drew attention in the *Publishers' Circular* to an attempt by W. P. Watt to suborn several of his young authors on behalf of another, unnamed publisher. John Murray, Stanley Unwin, and others applauded William's exposure, but enough has been said in this chapter to convey his basic unshakeable antagonism to agents. As succeeding chapters will show, he seems to have set a pattern for the firm, particularly as manifested in the 1960–70s, though there have of course been considerable variations in attitude and for the most part the literary agent has had to be accepted as a necessary, if irritating, reality. James Hepburn opens his excellent study of the rise of the literary agent, *The Author's Empty Purse*, with Heinemann's classic attack in the *Athenaeum* and towards the end asks: 'Are we then to infer that Heinemann's attacks on agents and A. P. Watt in particular in 1893 tell us more about Heinemann himself than about the problems of literary agency?' A few lines further down he suggests that 'perhaps Heinemann's animus was fair, and was doubly fair when W. P. Watt tried to take away some of his young authors'.[10]

The Fine Arts – Pennell, Nicholson, Rackham

From the outset William published books about the fine arts and artists and he also soon became noted for books containing the work of contemporary artists, in particular William Nicholson and Arthur Rackham. As expected of someone with his Continental background, among the earliest was a translation by Eugénie Sellers of Adolf Furtwängler's *Masterpieces of Greek Art* (1895). The German text was shortened, tightened up, and illustrated on a lavish scale. It was a work said to have had a considerable influence on the course of classical archaeology and was a considerable success. It was followed by several other books on ancient classical art, especially Franz Wickhoff's *Roman Art* (1900) which at the time likewise exerted much influence on classical studies and dealt in particular with the application of Roman principles to early Christian painting. Two other pioneering art books were Emile Michel's *Rembrandt* (1894) and Corrado Ricci's *Correggio* (1896). They were again profusely illustrated; the latter, for example, had 37 full-page plates and 190 text illustrations. 'By issuing this book', *The Times* commented, 'Mr Heinemann has done much to take away the reproach of English publishers, who have been justly charged with falling behind their foreign rivals in the matter of illustrated books upon art.' At £2 2s. it was inevitable that these books were too expensive for many pockets, and in 1895 it was decided, as with *Rembrandt*, to issue *Correggio* in monthly parts at 2s.6d. each.

This method of marketing appears to have worked satisfactorily, for it was continued with other expensive titles, for example, *Great Masters, 1400–1800* (1903) by Martin Conway: originally £5 5s., it was not only available in fortnightly 5s. parts but alternatively could be paid for on an instalment plan. Publication usually depended on co-editions in other countries, particularly France, Holland, and Germany as well as America, and the quality of reproduction at these prices was also made possible by improved methods of printing by photogravure. Six publishing houses, for example, combined to issue the Ars Una series (1909), each volume of which dealt with the art and architecture of a single country: Great Britain and Northern Ireland; Northern Italy; Spain and Portugal; France;

Egypt; Flanders. Each volume had about 600 illustrations and originally sold for as little as 6*s*. each. Other titles were aimed at a more limited, recherché clientele, as with *The King's Pictures* (1905), published 'by command of His Majesty King Edward VII', with a descriptive text by Lionel Cust, Surveyor of the King's Pictures and Works of Art. The two volumes were available to subscribers at 20 guineas net or 26 guineas if bound in full morocco. The classified catalogues listed a separate collection of books on Applied Art which included the long-running series of *Little Books about Old Furniture* (1911–22) by J. P. Blake and A. E. Reveirs-Hopkins, and books on old clocks, lace, old glass and lustre ware, and French fashions.

The American artist Joseph Pennell and his wife Elizabeth form a bridge between books about artists and books by artists. Together they wrote *The Life of James McNeill Whistler* (1908). It was during the period when Whistler, shattered after the death of his wife, used often to stay at William's flat in Whitehall Court that the Pennells became intimate with him. When William persuaded Whistler to have his life written he chose the Pennells as authors with whom he felt he could work, though he died before they had done little more than collect material. After his death there was a trying lawsuit in which Whistler's executrix tried to prevent the book going ahead, but this was won and the book, lovingly written, was a success. Mrs Pennell recalls how Heinemann 'read all the proofs, not for, but with me day after day. He debated every debatable point. He corrected, suggested, argued. He went over the revise, the page proofs, the arrangements of the illustrations. . . . We had endless and violent arguments with him when he endeavoured to edit us. We were not as convinced as he that his style was superior to ours, not as eager to sacrifice anything in our book to his literary flourishes. But we quickly learned one of Heinemann's good points as an over-sympathetic publisher. "The best thing about Heinemann", Joseph Pennell would often say to me, "is that he has no memory." And it was true. Eventually, we seldom protested when he elaborated on the margin of MSS. or proofs. But as soon as he was gone we rubbed out the elaborations and he never knew the difference, convinced probably that the chief merit of the book was due to him.'[11]

As well as making the illustrations for the European travel books by Henry James and W. D. Howells (see page 69), Joseph Pennell had written a study of *The Jew at Home* (1892), based on drawings made during a summer and autumn spent travelling around Austria and Russia which,

The Times remarked, 'gave a vivid impression of the Hebrew in all his native squalor and ugliness'. William's family were upset about the publication of this book, but their protests arrived too late. Later the firm published three of Joseph Pennell's books of drawings with accompanying texts he made of the *Panama Canal* (1912) and *The Land of Temples* (1925). There was also his *Pictures of the Wonder of Work* (1916). Elizabeth Pennell by herself also wrote a travel book and *The Lovers* (1917) about the tragedy of a young couple when the husband falls in Flanders.

The Pennells always remained close friends with William, but Joseph's relationship with him was often stormy, particularly over production details. To quote at random from some of William's letters to Joseph in 1913–14: 'I am in a little despair. We talk things over and come to a perfectly clear understanding as to what we are to do, and then you seem to repent of any understanding we have come to and raise difficulties.'[12] 'It seems almost a joy to you to make things difficult. I have made every experiment you asked me to make, and the time wasted has been wasted simply in order to satisfy you.'[13] 'I think we had better chuck the "Temple" book, if you will not be satisfied with anything we do. The proofs on the yellow paper are an enormous improvement . . . try and help in times of stress instead of indulging in outbursts of impatience.'[14] 'If I had many authors as unreasonable as you are, I should give up my business as a publisher.'[15] Joseph was never one for understatement: when sending six prints, he insisted that 'no damn experiments are to be played with them – no one is to spit on them – drop acid on them – smash them as is the custom and habit of the photo-engraver . . .'.[16] Back home in America he wrote to William about the miseries of prohibition in some of the States: 'Hunting for drink is the only chasse, spur, suit or occupation at present indulged in by the few native Americans left in this God-forsaken women-governed, dry, sentimental, hypocritical hen hole – the worst curse I could curse you with: wish you may go dry.'[17]

It was Whistler who recommended William Nicholson to Heinemann, having seen his woodcut of Persimmon, the Prince of Wales's horse. At their first meeting Nicholson suggested making twenty-six woodcuts for *An Alphabet* (1898), each letter showing a single figure, e.g., 'A was an Artist; B for Beggar; C for Countess . . . ending with Z for Zoologist.' There were three editions: a *de luxe* portfolio, limited to twenty-five copies, printed from the woodcuts direct, and delicately coloured by hand by the artist, priced £21; a library edition of colour lithographs of the original woodcuts on Dutch hand-made paper, mounted on brown paper and bound in cloth, price 12s.6d.; a popular edition of colour lithographs on cream heavy wove paper, price 5s. *An Alphabet* was aimed at adults as well as children but, so as not to offend the sensibilities of the latter, 'E for Executioner' and 'T for Topers' were replaced by the less disturbing 'E for Earl' and 'T for Trumpeter'. Nicholson was paid £5 for each woodcut and sixpence for colouring each sheet; he was also given a 10 per cent royalty on all copies sold after the first edition. This amounted to 5,000 copies, but the popular edition was so popular that it had to be reprinted twice within two months.

Although Nicholson had little experience of woodcuts and was self-taught, he possessed an extraordinary and original feeling for the medium. Another commission followed immediately, *An Almanac of Twelve Sports* (1898), each month illustrated with figures taking part in 'January, Fox Hunting; February, Coursing; June, Cricket; October, Golf'; and so on, all very hearty, traditional English sports. When Nicholson showed the first woodcuts for the *Almanac* to Kipling, he liked them so much that he suggested that he should write short verses to go with them – which of course delighted Heinemann, though he advised Kipling to tone down some of the lines: thus under 'Coaching', the picture for August, the lines:

Youth on the box and Liquor in the boot,

My Lord drives out with My Lord's prostitute.

had to be suitably amended. In a flowery, joky letter of thanks, Heinemann wrote: 'Never assuredly before was a young artist more generously thanked by a "brother in arms". But what am I – *l'homme d'affaires* – to say to your demands? Has the impeccable "What's his name?" taught you so inadequately what every little precious word you write is worth? Seriously I cannot accept the thing at such a figure. It is worth much more to *me* at least and therefore I've thought (unable to trace the Byron–Murray figures) of a 'Pound a Line' & here's my cheque. You must be very considerate & generous please with me in my delirium and just say it's alright. I am now and always your debtor & now for once at least (how I wish it were for ever) Your publisher, Wm. Heinemann.'[18] The *Almanac* was as before sold in three versions with the popular edition at 2s.6d.

Next came the publication of Nicholson's famous Diamond Jubilee woodcut of Queen Victoria. Marguerite Steen, Nicholson's biographer, explains why this portrait was so significant: 'The Queen Empress had invariably been presented with every device of pomp and panoply that could conceal from the notoriously truth-disliking public eye the fact that Victoria of Great Britain and India was a dumpy old woman whose dignity (which none who saw could deny) derived from her own perfect conviction of her own omnipotence.

'It was William [Nicholson] who first had the temerity to present this unheroic old figure just as it was: an animated tea-cosy, walking an Aberdeen in the gardens of Kensington Palace. He did it lightly, unmaliciously, and in terms that would startle, yet, on second thoughts, appeal to the British public. Plastered with jewels, the Garter ribbon bulging over her improbable bust, Victoria was all very well; but here was a nice old lady who would offer them tea and inquire after their rheumatism if they happened to drop in when passing the palace! In place of their old illusion William gave them a new illusion; it was bound to be a success . . . but Heinemann did not see it in that light at all. The sensitive Teutonic nose smelt *lèse-majesté*; he did not want to publish it.'[19]

Luckily Pawling thought differently and saw its merits. So did W. E. Henley who wanted to have it 'doubled in half' as a double-page insert in the *New Review* (see pages 147–9). Heinemann relented and later regretted his misjudgment and there followed the two sets of *Twelve Portraits* (1899 and 1902) of, as well as Victoria, people such as Sarah Bernhardt, Cecil Rhodes, Sir Henry Irving, the Kaiser, Henrik Ibsen. . . . Each set was sold for 21s. in a portfolio or separately at 2s.6d. each. They were also inset in issues of the *New Review*.

Nicholson was now much better paid, but some time later he wrote to Heinemann to say that 'I have often wept in the dawn to think I only got £10 10s. for my little queen with which you have papered the world. I remember so well how you hated the idea of her and predicted failure and often I have wondered that you haven't sent me £1,000 hush money by a black-masked messenger boy – even now I would pay the boy at this end.'[20]

Nicholson's brilliant spell as a wood-engraver was very brief, because once established and earning enough he turned to his main love, oil painting. There were, however, three more projects for Heinemann during this prolific period: the twelve woodcuts of *London Types* (1898) with accompanying quatorzains by W. E. Henley – Heinemann suggested including more women; *The Square Book of Animals* (1900), with rhymes by Arthur Waugh, which is a genuine children's book – Kipling had tried his hand, but gave up, telling Heinemann that 'all N's animals are practically extinct in Great Britain, their places being supplied by New Zealand lamb; Argentine beef; Ostend rabbits; Rouen ducks; and Continental poultry generally. The only way I tried it, my verses became so deeply political (not to say protectionist) that I stopped';[21] lastly there was a portfolio of sixteen colour lithographs entitled *Characters of Romance* (1900), including Don Quixote, John Silver, Jorrocks, and Miss Havisham. Though they were very skilful, they seemed to lack the incisiveness of the woodcuts and lost Heinemann money. Nicholson designed a few bookjackets including that for Magda Heinemann's translation of d'Annunzio's *The Flame of Life*. In the sale after Heinemann's divorce Nicholson bought the sumptuous bed which he had lavished on Magda. It had belonged previously to an eighteenth-century French courtesan.

As already described, Nicholson made Heinemann a present of the drawing of the windmill which was adopted as the firm's colophon. Later he did a children's book, *Clever Bill* (1926) and seven colour plates, endpapers and the jacket for the bestselling *The Velveteen Rabbit* by Margery Williams (1922).

As many of them were illustrated, this is a logical point at which to say something about the firm's children's books, though they were relatively few in number. The best-known is almost certainly *The Secret Garden* (1911) by Frances Hodgson Burnett, with illustrations by Charles Robinson. The mysterious attractions of the garden kept locked for ten years, until the little orphan girl with the help of a friendly robin finds the long lost key and explores the tangled plants and the carpet of sweet flowers run wild, help to explain why this tale has endured down the generations. But there is also a powerful story with a happy moral ending when the garden itself turns the sullen girl into a wholesome bright little person and also cures her invalid boy cousin. Burnett's biographer, Ann Thwaite, also makes the point that it is a 'book of the new century. Far from encouraging the attitudes instilled in Frances as a child ("Speak when you're spoken to, come when you're called . . ."), it suggested children should be self-reliant and have faith in themselves, that they should listen not to their elders and betters, but to their own hearts and consciences. Someone once said that you could learn the elements of pruning roses from *The Secret Garden*, and another large part of the attraction of the book is its exactly accurate descriptions of real gardening. Frances was always good

15

at detail. She knew children liked it. It is not enough to mention they have tea, she once said, 'you must specify the muffins'.[22] It is significant that her best known children's books, including the earlier *Little Lord Fauntleroy*, published before Heinemann set up in business, were enjoyed by adults as much as were her novels and plays. Heinemann came in towards the end of her life, but published five more of her books including *The Shuttle* (1907) and *The Little Hunchback Zia* (1916).

Some of the books written for children are included, where relevant, on other pages, but among others which might be mentioned were *The Story of Chanticleer* (1913) adapted from the French of Rostand and illustrated by J. A. Shepherd; *The Playmate* (1907) and other stories for boys by Charles Turley; Jean de Bosschère's *The City Curious* (1920) and *Beasts and Men: Christmas Tales of Flanders* (1918). In 1917 there was an attempt to found Every Child's Library of 'Charming Gift Books for Boys and Girls, Brimful of Exciting Incident and Adventure', but after a few titles it seems to have petered out, and one year there was an inexpensive *Happy Annual* (1907) by Cecil Aldin and John Hassall. Aldin was also responsible for those sentimental/humorous drawings of dogs as seen in several money-making publications such as his *A Gay Dog* (1905) about a bulldog who follows the pursuits of the smart set and has adventures at Ascot, Henley, etc.

By far the most illustrious books for children came, however, from Arthur Rackham. Although he worked for other houses, his main publisher was Heinemann, issuing seventeen of his large-scale illustrated volumes. His first book for the firm was Washington Irving's *Rip van Winkle* (1905) which established him as a leading decorative illustrator with his fertile imagination for the odd, the grotesque, and queer folk, imps and fairies, and for eerie landscape and especially gnarled tree roots and branches exuding menace. His illustrations seem to overwhelm the texts, even though most of these were classics. They can be divided roughly into two categories: those for children, though grown-ups also loved and collected them, such as *Alice's Adventures in Wonderland* (1907), though some thought it was almost blasphemy to try and match Tenniel; *Aesop's Fables* (1912); *Mother Goose: Old Nursery Rhymes* (1913), for which his approach was different and had the 'delicacy of cherry blossoms'; *Cinderella* (1919) and *The Sleeping Beauty* (1920), in which most of the illustrations were black-and-white silhouettes and the tales were retold by the firm's joint manager, Charles Evans.

ARTHUR RACKHAM'S
BOOK OF PICTURES

15s.
net.

Cr. 4to. 44 plates in colour with descriptive tissues and an Introduction by Sir A. T. Quiller-Couch. Also a large paper edition, limited to 1,000 copies, for Great Britain and Ireland, numbered and signed by the Artist. £2 2s. net.

NOTE.—This Collection will never again be issued in its entirety.

MR HEINEMANN will publish in the autumn Mr Arthur Rackham's *Book of Pictures,* consisting of forty-four coloured reproductions of water-colours, oils and pastels, representing the artist's work from the early days to the present. It will be the most representative book of Arthur Rackham's work, with a value quite of its own for collectors and all interested in English Art. The quaint picturesqueness of some of Mr Rackham's works, the exquisite draughtsmanship and daintiness of line of others, his charming colour schemes make of this work a veritable picture gallery—representative of the most popular draughtsman of our day.

Also illustrated by Arthur Rackham, *uniform in size and price:*

WAGNER'S RING OF THE NIBELUNGS. *In two volumes, each 15s. net:*
    I. Rhinegold and The Valkyrie. II. Siegfried and The Twilight of the Gods.

A MIDSUMMER NIGHT'S DREAM. William Shakespeare.

RIP VAN WINKLE. Washington Irving.

INGOLDSBY LEGENDS. R. H. Barham.

LONDON · MCMXIII   WILLIAM HEINEMANN

Symbolism, conscious and unconscious, is clearly at work in much of his work for children, as indeed it is also in that for grown-ups, such as the two volumes illustrating *The Ring of the Niblung: Rhinegold and the Valkyrie* (1910) and *Siegfried and the Twilight of the Gods* (1911). Rackham is said to have been influenced by various people from the Pre-Raphaelites to Aubrey Beardsley, but his interpretation of this Teutonic folklore suggests powerfully, as does much of his other work, the influence of Dürer, Menzel, Hans Thoma and other artists of the German school. Adults were presumably uppermost in mind in the illustrations for Milton's *Comus* (1921), and Swinburne's *Springtide of Life* (1918) and in other titles.

It was normal practice with Rackham's books to increase the printing numbers by making a sheet or plate deal with an American publisher and for the illustrations alone with European firms. Special limited editions were issued on handmade paper, numbered and signed by the artist and sold at a much higher price. Most of the books carried line drawings on the text paper as well as four-colour half-tones on art paper inserts, Rackham being particularly good at adapting his technique to the new methods of printing. But he dominated the text as well as his medium, as he made clear in a lecture he gave at the Author's Club: 'An illustration may legitimately give the artist's view of the author's ideas; or it may give his view, his independent view, of the author's subject. But it must be the artist's view; any attempt to coerce him into being a mere tool in the author's hands can only result in the most dismal failure. Illustration is as capable of varied appeal as is literature itself; and the only real essential is an association that shall not be at variance or unsympathetic. The illustrator is sometimes expected to say what the author ought to have said or failed to say clearly, to fill up a shortcoming, and not infrequently he has done so. Sometimes he is wanted to add some fresh aspect of interest to a subject which the author has already treated interestingly from his point of view, a partnership that has often been productive of good. But the most fascinating form of illustration consists of the expression by the artist of an individual sense of delight or emotion aroused by the accompanying passage of literature.'[23]

No one could be more different from Rackham than Max Beerbohm, whose caricatures and cartoons were, like his writing (see pages 138–44), unique and 'incomparable'. Altogether the firm published six volumes of them, chosen from a very large output – 2,093 are listed in Sir Rupert

Hart-Davis's published catalogue of his caricatures[24]. There is of course an intimate connection between his writing and drawing, one being very much an extension of the other, which is underlined by his extraordinarily apt and often exquisitely funny captions. Both drawings and captions often display his love of parody. By means of the subtlest and telling distortion and exaggeration he conveys instantly the idiosyncrasies of his subjects. Not trained by any art school, he perfected a style entirely his own and the delicate use of soft colours. The prettiness itself is relevant and enhances the humour. In his famous drawing of Tennyson reading aloud to Queen Victoria, the colours in the carpet and wallpaper are both pleasing and mock mid-Victorian taste in furnishings.

A distinction has to be made between his cartoons and caricatures. The former are political and sociological and convey his distrust of democracy, of Labour's attitude to poets, of the future; and they gently mocked every kind of pretension and humbug. The caricatures make up a gallery of many of the public people of the day – statesmen, artists, philosophers, royalty, writers and men of letters. Most of them were still alive, though he also drew real or imaginary figures from the past, particularly the mid-Victorian age of Carlyle, Swinburne and the Pre-Raphaelites, and *Rossetti and his Circle* (1922). Although the drawings could be lethal, their criticism was usually implied rather than overt and his victims seldom became enemies and were usually proud to be drawn by him. Many were Heinemann authors: George Moore is shown being presented by W. B. Yeats to the Queen of the Fairies; Henry James's essay on d'Annunzio inspired the drawing of the artist kneeling by two pairs of shoes, a man's and a woman's, outside a shut bedroom door in the corridor of a 'promiscuous' hotel; a grotesque fur-coated Pinero with an enormous eyebrow jutting from a bald, egg-shaped head and reflected in a series of mirrors to symbolize that his plays were becoming repetitious. Gosse was a favourite subject, as in the riverside scene, being taken by a miniature Algernon Swinburne to see 'his great new friend Gabriel Rosetti' and in a scene at the Board of Trade during office hours being caught by Joseph Chamberlain composing a ballade with Austin Dobson. Among other Heinemann authors caricatured were Hall Caine, Cunninghame Graham, Maurice Hewlett, Robert Hichens, and John Masefield.

The first collection of Beerbohm's drawings published by the firm was *The Poets' Corner* (1904) which was followed by *Fifty Caricatures* (1913), and other volumes in the 1920s, but let us leave the last word with Max, from his essay on 'The Spirit of Caricature': 'Such laughter as may be caused by a caricature is merely aesthetic. It corresponds with such tears as are shed at sight of a very beautiful statue. . . . Tragedy, said Aristotle, purges us of superfluous awe, by evocation, and comedy likewise purges us of superfluous contempt. Even so might idealism of a subject purge us of superfluous awe for it, and caricature purge us of superfluous contempt. . . . Caricature never has had moral influence of any kind. . . .' He ends by saying that 'the perfect caricature is that which, on a small surface, with the simplest means, most accurately exaggerates, to the highest point, the peculiarities of a human being, at his most characteristic moment, in the most beautiful manner'[25].

<hr>

Historical Works and the Backhouse 'Forgery'

<hr>

The authors of books on historical subjects were predominantly European as were their subjects. The history of France, the country which Heinemann looked upon as a second home, was particularly well catered for with three major series. G. Lenotre, the pseudonym of Louis Gosselin, the specialist on the French Revolution, contributed four volumes such as *The Last Days of Marie Antoinette* (1907) and *A Gascon Royalist in Revolutionary Paris, 1792–95* (1910). This period was also covered by a translation of the Anarchist Prince Kropotkin's *The Great French Revolution, 1789–93* (1909) which the *Daily News* described as being full of 'militant ideas, a book which will compel its readers to think. It is a history with a purpose and is at once a plea and an interpretation.' The six volumes of *The National History of France* (1916–36), edited by F. Funck-Brentano, surveyed close on a thousand years of French history 'in which the concision of a textbook and the variety of a French memoir are deftly combined'. Funck-Brentano wrote *The Middle Ages* himself; other volumes included *The Century of the Renaissance* by L. Batifol and *The Consulate and the Empire* by Louis Madelin. Most ambitious was the Versailles Historical Series (1899) in no less than eighteen volumes, at a guinea apiece, which contained memoirs, the correspondence of noted persons belonging to the different European courts, 'giving graphic descriptions of court life, state secrets, and the private sayings and doings of royalty and court attachés'. The whole project was translated and arranged with numerous photogravures by Katherine Prescott Wormeley. Among the unusually lengthy titles, most of which were introduced by C. A. Sainte-Beuve, were *Memoirs of Madame de Motteville on Anne of Austria and her Court*; another was *The Correspondence of Madame, Princess Palatine, Mother of the Regent; of Marie Adelaide de Savoie, Duchesse de Bourgogne, and of Madame de Maintenon, in Relation to Saint-Cyr*; and to give the series a little spice, *The Book of Illustrious Ladies* by the Abbé de Brantôme.

One wonders how this kind of project was marketed and how well it really did. There is no doubt that the weighty *The World's History – a Survey of Man's Record* (1901–7), edited by the German Scholar H. F. Helmolt, only just avoided being a financial disaster, despite a tie-up with an American publisher. Its eight Super Royal 8vo volumes, starting with *America and the Pacific Ocean* and concluding with *Western Europe since 1800 – The Atlantic Ocean* were enriched with coloured plates and maps, some of them pull-outs, and numerous black-and-white illustrations. All this must have involved a sizeable capital investment, but each volume sold for only 15*s*. or in half-morocco for 21*s*. The project was certainly prestigious. The *Saturday Review* declared that 'it is difficult to give too much praise to the enterprise and public spirit of Mr Heinemann in placing these volumes within the reach of the English-speaking public in so attractive a form. . . . We do not know which to admire most, the erudition upon which it is based, the broad philosophical standpoint from which it is composed, or the boldness with which its novel conclusions are reached. It is a monument. . . .'

The British public were not very impressed, at least to the extent of forking out their 15*s*. a volume, but rescue came in the form of a deal with Harold Harmsworth, a personal friend of William's and brother of Lord Northcliffe, proprietor of the *Daily Mail*. The idea, originally conceived by Arthur Mee, a Harmsworth editor, was to expand Helmolt's history with contributions from top British scholars, and to increase the illustrations to a total of 10,000, so as to make forty-eight fortnightly parts, to be sold at sevenpence each through the *Daily Mail* and other outlets controlled by Carmelite House. In return for the translated text and the maps and illustrations in his six volumes Heinemann was to receive a royalty of a halfpenny on each part.

This with luck might pay off Heinemann's loss on the project. When Arthur Mee chaffed William that he would end up with an extra £20,000 for his old Helmolt stuff, the latter ridiculed the prospect, saying he would be very unlikely to get as much as £10,000.

'If you should get £10,000', Arthur Mee retorted, 'will you give me a motor-car?'

'You bet I will! I'd be only too happy.'

The sale of the part-works had only reached the halfway mark, when a magnificent, new Martini car arrived at the entrance to Carmelite House with Mr Heinemann's compliments. By the time all the part-works were sold, Heinemann's royalty had reached over £20,000.

The comprehensive category of History, Biography, and Memoirs in the 1914 classified catalogue lists 216 titles. The following, picked more or less at random, may indicate its scope. The five volumes of Guglielmo Ferrero's *The Greatness and Decline of Rome* (1907–09) covered 450 BC to 41 AD, but concentrated on the later years and the age of Julius Caesar. Ernest Renan contributed *Studies of Religious History* (1893). In a Great People's Series, Martin S. Hume wrote on *The Spanish* (1901) and Arthur Hassall on *The French* (1902). Eastern Europe was catered for by Georg Brandes's *Poland: a Study of the Land, People, and Literature* (1903) and six books by K. Waliszewski such as *The Story of a Throne: Catherine II of Russia* (1895), *Ivan the Terrible* (1904), and *Paul I of Russia* (1913). Then there was Count Arthur Gobineau who as well as writing on the Italian *Renaissance* (1913) – which dealt with Savonarola, Caesar Borgia, Julius II, Leo X, and Michael Angelo – wrote what with hindsight we can see as the very sinister *The Inequality of Human Races* (1915) because it became one of the formative influences in Hitler's *Weltanschauung* and his concept of the Master Race.

The last title to be discussed in this section is the remarkable *China under the Empress Dowager* (1910), hailed everywhere as being of the greatest importance, though its success was tarnished with accusations that much of its contents was fraudulent. Its two authors were J. O. P. Bland, for many years correspondent of *The Times* in China, and Sir Edmund Backhouse, an eminent sinologist who had lived many years in Peking. Something of a legend in his own time, he lived as a recluse and – with a wispy beard and silk robe – looked like a mandarin. Backhouse had worked for the British Secret Service and had been involved in negotiations with the Chinese Government, becoming the confidant of the

Empress Dowager Tzu Hsi. Almost the last of the Manchus, she had ruled for fifty years and was largely blamed for the anti-foreign agitation which culminated in the Boxer Rising. The book showed an intimate knowledge of life and politics at the Chinese court. Use was made of a number of state papers and hitherto secret documents. The catalogue announced that the core of the work was the diary of His Excellency Ching Shan, a Manchu scholar who had held office as Assistant Secretary of the Imperial Household. 'This most vivid and thrilling human document gives a daily and detailed account of the thoughts, words and deeds of the Empress and her immediate advisers from the beginning of the Boxer Rising to the day when, the relief forces having entered Peking, the diarist was brutally murdered by his own son.' It was in Ching Shan's deserted house that Backhouse claimed to have discovered and rescued the diaries 'in the nick of time'. Backhouse supplied the raw documents and the translations which Bland skilfully turned into a very readable text.

Trouble began when G. E. Morrison, then chief *Times* correspondent in Peking, spread rumours around literary London that Backhouse had faked these key diaries. Heinemann was understandably alarmed, particularly as Morrison had made this accusation to the editor of the *World's Work* periodical published by Heinemann (see pages 149–50), telling him that 'it was the work of Backhouse's "boy"'. Heinemann wrote to Bland and Backhouse saying that the matter must be cleared up, as the allegation could do the book irreparable damage. Bland naturally challenged Morrison, who was then evasive and denied it, but soon afterwards began to repeat it verbally.

It was difficult for even an expert to know who was telling the truth, but Hugh Trevor-Roper in his life of Backhouse, *Hermit of Peking*, has investigated the case in detail and recorded the different opinions of sinologists over the years as to the diaries' authenticity. After various pundits had expressed their belief in them it was not until 1936 that their authenticity was again seriously questioned by William Lewishon, a British journalist who was a good Chinese scholar. Others supported his convincing arguments and most experts came to agree that the diaries must be a forgery. Trevor-Roper after many pages of discussion writes: 'Once we agree that the diary, as produced by Backhouse, is a forgery, we have no alternative but to regard his story of its discovery as fantasy; and if a man gives, and persists in, an entirely fictitious account of his acquisition of a forged document, there is no moral reason for supposing him incapable of forging it himself. Conversely, whoever forges a document must also provide it with a history which presupposes that it is genuine; and that history must of necessity be a forgery too.'[26] Trevor-Roper supports the evidence of forgery with many strange examples of Backhouse's double-dealing in other spheres: 'We who have seen him palming off forged scrolls on libraries, forged contracts on manufacturers, forged "curios" on individuals, forged letters of recommendation, forged reports of high-powered interviews, imaginary arms, imaginary battleships, imaginary libraries, imaginary pearls, all explained by elaborate, detailed, self-glorifying fantasies . . . certainly we need not boggle at a forged diary explained by a fanciful scenario in the desolate house of its alleged author. Such a forgery may have demanded unique, even incredible skill. But Backhouse evidently had that skill.'[27]

After the initial fuss had died down Heinemann had no doubts about following up a very successful book with Bland and Backhouse's *Annals and Memoirs of the Court of Peking* (1913), covering three hundred years of secret history of China's rulers, from the last days of the Mings to the decline and fall of the Manchus. Again the text was based on state papers, private diaries of court officials, and 'from Chinese books printed for private circulation'. Bland alone also wrote several other books for the firm on China, Japan, and South America.

Shackleton, Nordau, Montessori, Suffragettes, and even Freud

There are of course many books which do not fit into any of the rough categories so far covered, but there is space to mention no more than a few representative titles in order to indicate the parameters of the rest of the list. There were, for example, some outstanding books on exploration and travel, the most celebrated being Ernest Shackleton's *The Heart of the Antarctic* (1909). Heinemann was behind the expedition from the start, offering an advance of £1,000 which would become £5,000 if they reached the South Pole, in return for all the book and serial rights with the exception of four articles in the *Daily Chronicle*. When they just failed to reach the Pole and planted the Queen Alexandra Union Jack 'almost within sight of it', Heinemann cabled Shackleton that he would nevertheless pay the larger amount. He then demonstrated his talent for promoting and exploiting a key book. Immediately he took the train to meet Shackleton in Brindisi in the south of Italy, stopping off at Paris to sell the book to Hachette and some articles to *l'Illustration*, and arranging for a formal welcome to the explorer. On the way back he managed to prevent anyone from entering Shackleton's carriage while he examined the photographic and other material. Back in London he engineered a continuous stream of publicity for the returning national hero and launched the book at a banquet during Ascot week. The first edition of 10,000 copies at 36s. was rapidly exhausted. There were also 350 numbered copies of a *de luxe* edition on hand-made paper with a special watermark, bound in vellum, and signed by every member of the shore expedition – priced at ten guineas net. There was a school edition, the first of Heinemann's Hero Readers 'to kindle in youthful minds the desires to excel and to lead, manliness and fortitude'; and a school prize edition handsomely bound in blue cloth and gold. For the expert there were four fat volumes of *Scientific Reports of the British Antarctic Expedition*. Simultaneous publication of the main edition was organized in nine European countries as well as America.

When Shackleton set off on his last Polar expedition in 1914–17 it was recorded in *South* (1919), accompanied by many photographs and maps. His aim had been to cross Antarctica from the unknown side, south of South America, to the comparatively well-known side south of New Zealand. This was not accomplished, but it led to even more suspenseful adventures and hardships – their ship frozen up and imprisoned for nine months in drifting ice until it was crushed and sank; twenty-eight explorers and seventy dogs marooned on a piece of ice floating 346 miles from land; the dogs killed for food while their piece of ice got smaller and smaller; putting to sea in three small boats until they reached Elephant Island; and much, much more – as the catalogue stated, 'an epic of the ice which will be read and remembered for an example as long as our Empire exists'.

Although Constable had published the major book by Fridtjof Nansen, the Norwegian Arctic explorer, Heinemann followed it with his *In Northern Mists* (1911), a two-volume history of the gradual discovery of the Northern wastes from the earliest times of the Norsemen, leading to the legendary lands of the West and voyages to 'Wineland the Good' which established the prior claim of the Icelanders to have reached America before Cabot and Columbus. It was followed by his account of his journey *Through Siberia: the Land of the Future* (1914). That considerations other than profit motivated William to back the explorers was testified by Sir Douglas Mawson, author of *The Home of the Blizzard* (1915), the story of the Australian Antarctic expedition of 1911–14. 'Financial gain was never foremost in his mind', Mawson wrote to C. A. Bang. 'National and literary merit in propositions put before him was always sufficient to enlist his sympathy. In such cases he would be eager to assist and . . . indeed do all that was financially in his power towards its realization. . . . In my own case I can only say that his personal co-operation was one of the factors that carried the Australian expedition on to success.'[28]

There were books for the ordinary traveller to various parts of the United Kingdom and Europe, but more inspiring were two by the intrepid Gertrude Bell: *The Desert and the Sown* (1907) about Syria and *Amurath to Amurath* (1910) about her journey to Asia Minor. According to the *Daily Telegraph*, 'very few travellers possess the literary equipment of Miss Bell, and not one travel book in a decade can boast the vigour, the fine characterisation and the nervous distinction which mark its pages . . . her book is no less valuable as a work of reference than it is attractive and picturesque as a study in national character.' Particular interest in South Africa, stemming from the Boer War, Heinemann catered for with titles like *The Transvaal from Within* (1899) by J. P. Fitzpatrick, 'a private record of public affairs', which was reprinted at least seven times. Then there was John A. Buttery's *Why Kruger Made War or Behind the Boer Scenes* (1900).

Among books on sociology/philosophy was the Hungarian Max Nordau's *Degeneration* (1896), with which it is unlikely that William personally had much sympathy. Brilliantly written, it caused a sensation for its assault on the Decadents and the ideas associated with the *Yellow Book*, Wilde, and Beardsley. Nordau's theory was that most of what was conspicuous in contemporary art, literature, and life was but proof of physical and psychical degeneration. The *Daily Telegraph* typically praised it as 'a powerful antidote to many prevailing modes of thought'. In every age there is always someone who appeals to society's innate conservatism by declaring that it is going to the dogs. When William took Nordau to lunch with Gosse, he didn't make a good impression. 'He talks very fluent

English', Gosse wrote to a friend, 'and very intelligently, but I should think he might become a frightful bore. He has got hold of a new formula for crime, for ill-doing of every sort – it is "parasitism". A burglar robs you and knocks you down, because he is a parasite. Well, that you can follow. But a man that has a prostitute is a parasite also, because he does to her, for money, what she does not want to have done. That is more difficult. In short, he seems a learned empiric, a kind (really) of brilliant humbug, and I should think had possibilities of boredom quite stupendous. The Y.V. [the Young Voluptuary, Heinemann's nickname] who has only had 24 hours of him yet, looks pale with exhaustion (he won't go to bed, and then rises at 5!) already, and he is to stay a week.'[29] Poor William found himself in an embarrassing situation when he invited Bernard Shaw to meet Nordau over another meal, because a few days earlier Shaw had published a coruscating attack on *Degeneration* and felt he ought to warn Heinemann: 'I summed him up as a "pretentious ignoramus" after demonstrating his inadequacy at great length. . . . He doesn't interest me as a critic, because he knows nothing about art and literature, and I do. . . .'[30] Nevertheless there were at least ten impressions of *Degeneration* and Heinemann published two more of Nordau's books: *Conventional Lies of our Civilization* (1895) and *Paradoxes* (1896), followed by three of his novels.

Other titles in this sub-category were, for its time, an enlightened Modern Criminal Science Series (1911), each written by a European expert, including the famous Cesare Lombroso. William's ear must have been very close to the European intellectual ground because he also took on Sigmund Freud – *On Dreams* (1914), though one wonders why nothing else; Benedetto Croce – *The Essence of Aesthetic* (1921); and Prince Kropotkin – *Mutual Aid* (1902) which was reprinted in a new edition 'to meet the wishes of the author who has had many applications for the book in a cheaper form from working men's clubs and institutes'. Like any good general publisher, William by no means agreed with or even sympathized with the ideas of all his authors. It was only very rarely that he felt it necessary to disavow them publicly, as happened in the case of Lady Constance Lytton's *Prisons and Prisoners* (1914). A militant suffragette, she was arrested in Newcastle for throwing stones at a demonstration, but she was convinced that she had been released because of her title. She therefore cut off most of her hair, disguised herself as an ordinary working woman with the assumed name of Jane Warton, and was arrested again, in

William Heinemann

Sydney Southgate Pawling, July 1907

Liverpool. She was sentenced for breaking the governor of Walton gaol's windows. This time she served her sentence, was forcibly fed and because of her treatment suffered a heart attack. 'Jane Warton' was billed as joint author of this account of her experiences which also amounted to important criticism of the state of women's prisons. William must have admired her extraordinary courage, but felt bound to print the following note at the start of the book: 'The Publisher hopes that fault will not be found if he disclaims agreement with some of Lady Constance Lytton's views expressed in this volume, notwithstanding the fact that he is glad to offer it to the public. He feels that personal disagreement over details should not hinder him from publishing this splendid story of heroism and unselfishness.' The 'New Woman', as we have seen, kept cropping up in Heinemann novels and there was at least one other straight book about the movement: Rosa Mayreder's *A Survey of Woman's Problem* (1912), translated from the German.

Relatively few other books were published on contemporary politics and affairs, but mention must be made of Norman Angell's *The Great Illusion* (1910) which earned the right to be called a classic. Written primarily in terms of the Anglo-German situation, it was not so much a plea for disarmament but was designed to show that an understanding between the two powers was not only possible, but also of practical benefit. The military seizure or destruction of the wealth and trade of either side would inevitably involve the conqueror. Military power was therefore an economic futility. He also wrote *The Foundations of International Polity* (1913) and *Prussianism and its Destruction* (1914). Two fast-selling political parodies were *Clara in Blunderland* (1902) and *Lost in Blunderland* (1903), both written under the terribly obvious pseudonym 'Caroline Lewis' – in reality M. H. Temple, J. Stafford Ransome, and Harold Begbie. On the death of Lord Salisbury all references to him had to be removed.

It would be tedious to describe the various books on cooking, gardening, sport and games to be found on any general publisher's list and of which there were in any case only a few; but an exception may be made in two instances: *A Guide to Modern Cookery* (1907) by Georges Auguste Escoffier, in charge of the kitchens at the Carlton Hotel, which rapidly became recognized as the basic text on *haute cuisine* for professional chefs. This first edition was followed by revised versions in 1911, 1926, 1957, and 1981 when an entirely new translation from the French was made (see page 557). Secondly, the breadth of William's publishing grasp was demonstrated once again by his decision, as someone for whom physical sports held no attractions, to initiate a monumental *Encyclopaedia of Sport and Games* (1911). Its four volumes, originally issued in fortnightly parts over eighteen months, were embellished with colour plates and 2,000 photographs and drawings. They ran alphabetically from Vol. I, A to Cricket; II, Crocodile to Houndbreeding; III, Hunting to Racing; IV, Rackets to Zebra.

Science was one of the weakest categories, though there was a popular Conquest of Science series, mostly written by F. A. Talbot on the Air, Lighthouses, Moving Pictures, etc.; and William's old friend P. Chalmers Mitchell, who became an FRS and secretary of the Zoological Society, wrote engagingly on *The Childhood of Animals* (1912). He also edited two books by the director of the Pasteur Institute, Elie Metchnikoff: *The Nature of Man* (1904) and *The Prolongation of Human Life* (1907), 'optimistic essays' which expounded the thesis that human life is not only unnaturally short but unnaturally burdened with physical and mental disabilities. Analysing the causes, he gave his reasons for hoping they could be counteracted by a 'rational hygiene'.

Although in a sense many Heinemann books could be said to be popular education, only a very few were textbooks designed specifically for schools, though there were some important titles on educational method. The typically ambitious series on Great Educators in ten volumes dealt with Froebel, Aristotle, Rousseau, Arnold, Loyola, Pestalozzi, and others. Then there was Marian Gibb's *Guide to Marie Chassevant's Method of Musical Education* (1914) in four volumes accompanied by boxes of movable signs, a keyboard diagram, and other apparatus; H. Caldwell Cook's educational method known as *The Play Way* (1917); and, most important of all, the series expounding the pioneering system of education of very young children developed by Maria Montessori, a large project in which C. A. Bang was much involved. The basic text, *The Montessori Method* (1912), included an account of the practical application of her principles in the 'children's houses' she established in Rome; this was followed by *Dr Montessori's Own Handbook* (1914) and *The Advanced Montessori Method* (1917–18), issued in two parts and which extended it to children between seven and eleven years old. The series was crowned with a more theoretical work with the forbidding title *Pedagogical Anthropology* (1913).

Ibsen, Pinero – but Shaw Rejected

William's creative energy and mastery of diverse interests were demonstrated no more remarkably than in connection with the theatre. During the first few years of the firm he somehow found time to participate not only as publisher but also as impresario and playwright. At the start of the 1890s there were some twenty playhouses of standing in London. It was very much the age of the actor-manager, above all of Henry Irving at the Lyceum. With honourable exceptions, the fare they offered was conventional: scenically elaborate productions of Shakespeare, domestic dramas and farces adapted from the French, spectacular melodramas, and at Christmas even more spectacular pantomimes. There were of course also music-halls and Gilbert and Sullivan. But things were starting to change: Oscar Wilde's *Lady Windermere's Fan* and Bernard Shaw's *Widowers' Houses* were both produced in 1892 and other plays by them followed rapidly. Ibsen was slowly becoming better known: *A Doll's House* was produced in 1889, followed two years later by a sensational production of *Ghosts*; though, because of the strict censorship by the Lord Chamberlain's office, this had to be staged privately by J. T. Grein's newly formed Independent Theatre.

This genuinely moral play about hereditary syphilis was met with almost universal abuse from the Press – the *Daily Chronicle* called it 'revolting, suggestive and blasphemous'; the *Observer*: 'a putrid drama, the details of which cannot appear with any propriety in any column save those of a medical journal'; in a two-column attack the *Daily Telegraph* likened the play to an open drain, a loathsome sore unbandaged, a dirty act done publicly, or a lazar-house with all its doors and windows open. But it was also praised and welcomed excitedly by a small but influential group, including many in Heinemann's immediate circle. When Shaw wrote his famous polemical *The Quintessence of Ibsenism*, the lengthy battle between the Ibsenites and the traditional theatre had been joined – between on the one hand those who felt the need for a theatre of honesty and realism, that would tackle the ills and hypocrisies of society, and on the other the complacent advocates of the 'well-made play', the commercial guardians of humbug.

Few plays were published because once one was available in printed form it was an open invitation for it to be pirated on the American stage, but the passing of the American Copyright Act of 1891 gave the necessary protection and Heinemann was among the first publishers to take the fullest advantage of the change. His respect for Ibsen determined him to become his main publisher in the English language and here he was supported by Gosse, who in 1873 had first introduced Ibsen to English readers. Ibsen's new play was *Hedda Gabler*. In 1890 Heinemann offered £150 for the full rights, provided the proofs of the original Norwegian could be sent to Gosse, who was to translate it, as soon as they came off the press. Ibsen was happy to accept, telling Gosse that he felt 'much bounden to Mr Heinemann for so liberal an honorarium' and spoke of his 'deep joy and satisfaction at seeing how my writings increasingly win an entry into the immense territory of the English-speaking peoples, in which a foreign author generally has such difficulty in establishing a foothold'[1]. To safeguard the stage as well as the book rights, on 11 December 1890 Heinemann published an edition in Norwegian, limited to twelve copies, as well as Gosse's translation six weeks later.

Unfortunately there were other Ibsen admirers already in the field, and this smart move provoked an attack from William Archer, the noted critic, who was the editor of a collected English edition of *Ibsen's Prose Dramas* published by Walter Scott. The first four volumes had already been issued. Under the heading 'A Translator-Traitor. Mr Edmund Gosse and Henrik Ibsen', Archer, normally a very mild person, launched in the *Pall Mall Gazette* a terrible attack, declaring that not only was it 'one of the worst translations on record' – it seems that it did have its shortcomings – but that 'some months ago I waived in Mr Gosse's favour a position of advantage which I held in regard to *Hedda Gabler* . . . on the explicit understanding that the privilege I thus transferred to him could not and would not be used to impede Mr Walter Scott in completing his edition of *Ibsen's Prose Dramas* under my editorship'. Archer's ending was withering. 'To find a parallel for Mr Gosse's conduct in this matter, I need to go no farther than the play itself. Yet the parallel is not exact. It was by chance, not through an act of courtesy, that Hedda became possessed of Lovborg's manuscript; and having become possessed of it, she did not deface, stultify and publish it – and then claim copyright. She did a much less cruel thing – she burned it.'[2]

It wasn't poor Gosse's fault. There must have been a misunderstanding between Heinemann, who thought he had bought all rights, and Ibsen, who thought he had sold him the first rights only. The conflict appears to have been settled amicably because Archer's translation appeared as volume 5 in the Walter Scott series. The dispute paradoxically also had the effect of drawing Archer into Heinemann's orbit so that Archer and Gosse worked together on the translation of the next play, *The Master Builder* (1893).

It was probably about this time that William first met and became so deeply attracted to Elizabeth Robins, the American actress who was to become one of his authors (see pages 75–7). She had appeared in the London production of *A Doll's House* and, as owner of the English stage rights, William backed her in the first London production of *Hedda Gabler* in April 1891 at the Vaudeville Theatre, in which she took the lead part. Once again the critics tried to demolish it – the *Daily Telegraph*: 'It was like a visit to the Morgue. . . . There they all lay on their copper couches, fronting us, and waiting to be owned. . . . There they all were, false men, wicked women, deceitful friends, sensualists, egotists, piled up in a heap behind this screen of glass, which we were thankful for. . . . What a horrible story! What a hideous play!' *Pictorial World*: 'Hideous nightmare of pessimism . . . the play is simply a bad escape of moral sewage-gas. . . . Hedda's soul is a-crawl with the foulest passions of humanity.'[3] Despite the Press, the play did very well. Originally put on for only five matinées, the theatre manager transferred it to the evenings; when it ran for five weeks and was taken off at the peak of its success. The direction was perceptive, but the most plaudits went to Elizabeth Robins. William Archer, who never allowed his admiration for Ibsen to cloud his objectivity, wrote: 'In rapidity and subtlety of intellect, I find it hard to think of a woman in the whole range of the drama who can rival Hedda Gabler; and Miss Robins makes us feel throughout that her own mind could work as rapidly as Hedda's. She played upon her victims with the crisp certainty of touch of the consummate virtuoso. Behind every speech we felt the swift intellectual process that gave it birth. . . . Miss Robins never forgot that Hedda is neither a hypocrite nor a fiend. I do not hesitate to call her performance in the last act the finest piece of modern tragedy within my recollection. Sarah Bernhardt could not have done it better. . . .'[4] Shaw was also enthusiastic and after seeing her performance from the back of the pit 'in company with a large and intelligent contingent of Fabians' told her that 'I never had a more tremendous sensation in a theatre than that which began when everybody saw that the pistol shot was coming at the end. . . . You were sympathetically unsympathetic, which was the exact solution of the central difficulty of playing Hedda.'[5]

William committed himself to *The Master Builder* without even knowing what the play was about, but nevertheless was worried that a rival might capture it and so, prevailed upon by Elizabeth, he travelled to Norway and came back with the rights virtually in his pocket. The proofs of the Norwegian edition were again dispatched in batches and there was another token Norwegian edition, but to make doubly sure of the stage rights, William booked the Theatre Royal, Haymarket, for the morning of 7 December 1892; stuck up a theatre bill at the entrance; and a strange cast which included himself, Gosse, and Elizabeth Robins, read the play in Norwegian, which some of them could not understand, in front of an audience of four people.

When after difficulties a theatre was found for the real performance, *The Master Builder* was greeted by the usual hostile Press, though Elizabeth's performance as Hilda Wangel was probably her most famous part. Again with William's support she had been instrumental in getting the play produced and later he backed her with a loan of £500 to put Ibsen on in New York. He was by no means her only admirer. John Masefield wrote her numerous love letters. She enjoyed a close but presumably platonic relationship with Henry James, with whom she exchanged numerous letters which she herself published.[6] In 1897 she joined William Archer in forming the New Century Theatre to sponsor non-profit productions which led James's biographer, Leon Edel, to write that 'her secret love affair with the critic William Archer – a story yet to be told – was a kind of collaboration in the theatre as much as a passion, a case of mutual professional respect transmuted into affection'[7]. Shaw too admitted having been in love with her and how after making overtures to her was 'flung out of the vehicle into the mud, with wheels flying over me this way and that and horses dancing and stumbling on my countenance'[8]. It can be argued that she manipulated men, including Heinemann, to her advantage; but this may well be unfair and is indeed contradicted by an undated letter in which she told him: 'I am blaming myself all day for not being *en garde* of late – am most of all remorseful that in the face of your pointblank question about the future last night I laughed and evaded instead of giving you a truly honest answer as I have always done before. I would be very much to blame if I allowed you to go away with the idea that I was likely to think any differently of my future today than I did months ago so far as "marrying" is concerned. I would not speak of this except that I feel you might one day reproach me with a lack of candour.'[9]

With Ibsen's other plays the same procedure took place, with Archer apparently as the main translator. The culmination was *The Collected Works of Henrik Ibsen* (1906–12) in twelve volumes, entirely revised and edited by Archer, who also wrote introductions to the plays. Three other titles complete the firm's Ibsen bibliography: *The Life of Henrik Ibsen* (1890) by H. Jaeger; *A Commentary on the Works of Henrik Ibsen* (1894) by H. H. Boyesen; and a burlesque of the playwright titled *The Pocket Ibsen* (1893) in which F. Anstey of *Punch* presented a collection of his 'best known dramas, revised, and slightly rearranged'.

In addition to plays by Zangwill, Maugham and Galsworthy already referred to and a cheap forty-volume edition of Shakespeare included in Heinemann's Favourite Classics, other dramatists of note to be found in the list were the Belgian, Maurice Maeterlinck – *The Princess Maleine and the Intruder* (1892); The German Gerhart Hauptmann – *The Weavers* (1899), *The Sunken Bell* (1900); and, of particular importance to the firm, Arthur Pinero. The year, 1891, when he allied himself with Heinemann to publish his plays coincided with a key moment in his career. By then he had earned himself an outstanding reputation as a master of well-constructed farces, though less mechanical than their French models, of sentimental comedies, and 'unpleasant' plays with an element of tragedy. He produced many of his own plays and directed them with the skill of a master technician. Out of the numerous plays of this earlier period the best-known today are probably *The Magistrate*, *Dandy Dick*, *Sweet Lavender*, and *The Weaker Sex*.

With the Ibsen debate starting to rage, Pinero turned to the 'problem' play and in 1893 staged his most famous play, *The Second Mrs Tanqueray*. Opinions among critics and theatrical historians have disagreed as to what extent he was really influenced by the Master. Holbrook Jackson contrasts the views of Shaw and Archer: 'Bernard Shaw was not deceived by this quasi-modernism. In 1895 he wrote . . . "No doubt the success of *The Second Mrs Tanqueray* . . . seemed to support the view that the new style had better be tried cautiously by an old hand. But then *Mrs Tanqueray* had not the faintest touch of the new spirit in it; and recent events suggest that its success was due to a happy cast of the dice by which the play found an actress [Mrs Patrick Campbell] who doubled its value and had hers doubled by it." William Archer took a more lenient view of the situation. He referred to it in 1893 as "the only play of what may be called European merit which the modern English stage can yet boast", and he went on to advise Pinero's fellow-craftsmen to follow the lead set by *The Second Mrs Tanqueray*, because Pinero had "inserted the thin end of the wedge", and "I firmly believe", he said, "that not only the ambition but the material interests of our other dramatists will prompt them to follow this lead, and that, therefore, we are indeed on the threshold of a new epoch."

'That proved to be true. *The Second Mrs Tanqueray*, although it was not of the "advanced movement", was really part of the movement. It was the first effect on the English stage of the influence of Ibsen and the propagandists of the modern drama . . . above all it possesses a masterly stage technique which alone makes it worthy to be considered with the works of great modern masters.'[10]

Adding Pinero as well as Ibsen to his list showed that William was a modern master among drama publishers. Pinero insisted on a special arrangement whereby the printed text of each new play was available for sale in the theatre on the first night. This was made possible because of the clear-headed self-assurance with which he worked: as Pinero explained to a correspondent, 'it is my practice to have my plays "set up" by the printer, act by act – that is, when I have finished my first act it is put into type before I begin my second. I follow the same course with the second, and so on. Very rarely do I make any alteration in these acts once they are in print.'[11] Among his later plays to be published were *Mid-Channel* and *Trelawny of the 'Wells'*, still regularly revived and which uniquely expresses our own as well as Pinero's love and enchantment with the theatre.

Despite his fame, Pinero's plays were not bestsellers, as William explained to Shaw when rejecting his hitherto unacted plays. Years later Shaw told Frederick Whyte, who was then preparing his memoir of William, that 'I wanted to have them in print because I was making my living as a theatre critic, and therefore could not offer them in the usual way to the managers. Only by publishing them could I put them on the market without putting myself in an awkward position. Indeed, I must have proposed their publication, and not he to me, for I distinctly recollect calling on him one day to discuss the matter. He disposed of it very effectually by first telling me that nobody bought plays except the people who gave amateur performances of them, and then proving this by showing me the ledger account of Pinero, whose plays he published at eighteenpence apiece. And, sure enough, all the items were for little batches of copies consisting of one for each character in the play and one for the prompter. . . . This was conclusive, as the amateurs of that day never touched plays unless they had seen them performed by fashionable actors and actresses whom they longed to ape.'[12] For this reason Heinemann did not become Shaw's publisher, a decision he might later have regretted, though Whyte records that William's memory played him a trick when he indignantly denied having taken it. But Shaw bore William no grudge, continued to have the greatest respect for him and remembered him as 'a sensitive little man, with character enough to back his own judgment, and judgment enough to succeed as a publisher. Publishing is such a mixture of routine and gamble that it is possible for a man whose ability is literary rather than commercial to succeed in it if he has courage (or folly) and judgment. He came at a time when his big competitors (Bentley, Macmillan, Longmans, Smith Elder, Blackwood) had buried the able old rascals who built them up, and fallen into the hands of men who were mostly only the sons of their fathers. Among them W.H. shot to the top by simple gravitation just as Jonathan Cape would have done.'[13]

Bedford Street was in the thick of theatreland, as it turned out of the Strand, then the main centre for playhouses. The actors' Green Room Club and Ben Greet's Academy of Acting were a few doors down the street. Round the corner was the Garrick Club with its strong theatrical connection and not far away was Henry Irving's Lyceum. For many years Irving's literary and business manager was Bram Stoker, author of *Dracula*. A close friend of William's, he often dropped in at the office. He wrote five less celebrated novels for the firm and his *Personal Reminiscences of Henry Irving* (1906). Earlier Heinemann had published the great man's addresses on *The Drama* (1893). Likewise Herbert Beerbohm Tree contributed a small book on *Some Interesting Fallacies of the Modern Stage* (1892). Later came that classic by the revolutionary master of stagecraft, Gordon Craig: *On the Art of the Theatre* (1911). Among theatrical memoirs were Sarah Bernhardt's *Recollections* (1905) and *My Double Life* (1907).

It was a theatrical list that any publisher might envy, and one can see how it grew out of William's personal involvement behind the West End curtains. This chapter would not be complete, however, without referring to the plays he wrote himself. Originally William had decided to make his début in his own list, and an announcement appeared among his forth-coming titles for autumn 1894; but they were actually published by his friend, John Lane, at The Bodley Head. J. W. Lambert, its historian, tells how 'one day, after Lane had set up shop on his own, William Heinemann dropped in for a chat. Lane had just seen Heinemann's autumn list, congratulated him, but added: "There is one book on your list which ought to have come to me, and I feel rather resentful at seeing it among *your* books." With his habitual slight stutter, Heinemann replied "M-m-m-my dear Lane, I'm so sorry. Which one?" "*The First Step* by William Heinemann, of course." "Oh", said Heinemann modestly, "*You* wouldn't have taken it." "Of course I would", said Lane. And so, according to this pleasing story, Heinemann transferred his book to Lane's list, along in due course with two more plays, *Summer Moths* and *War*.'[14]

The First Step was due to be staged by the Independent Theatre, but then the Lord Chamberlain's office refused to give it a licence. The dialogue was deemed to be too utterly 'frank', though reading it today it is difficult even to guess at what was being objected to. Although it was next planned to stage it before what was technically a private audience, over which the Lord Chamberlain had no jurisdiction, none of the owners of available theatres would consider letting their premises for such a play without a licence. William therefore had to be content with having *The First Step* presented only in book form, and this also appears to have happened to the other two plays. In the prelims, he added a note of protest which made the point that the censor in 'requiring, with ladylike niceness, a good character for the frail heroine, not only deprived the play of its pur-pose, but rendered it, if not positively *im*moral, *un*moral, to say the least.'[15]

His efforts as a playwright did not, however, pass unnoticed. Reviewing *Summer Moths* in the *Daily Chronicle*, William Archer both praised and disparaged it. Shaw's lengthy review in the *Saturday Review* was riddled with complex paradoxes and had even more of the texture of the curate's egg. In the opening sentence he wondered 'whether Mr William Heinemann is the coming dramatist', but then immediately went on to state that 'it is a play which confesses to a quite exceptional lack of specific talent. It is not adroitly constructed; it is not witty; it shows no mastery of language – not even normal fluency; and it deals with common sorts of common men and women without venturing on a single stroke of rare individual personality. . . . So much, and no less, any artist-critic must say for the relief of his starving soul after a meal of *Summer Moths*. But he does not thereby dispose of the play in the least; on the contrary, he only lays bare the secret of its importance. If Mr Heinemann were an artist of brilliant and facile specific theatrical talent, he would do what our popular dramatists do: that is, pour another kettle-full of water on the exhausted tea-leaves of romance and idealism, and make the pale decoction palatable by all sorts of innutritious sweets and spices and effervescents and stimulants. Luckily, he is as incapable of doing this as Millet was of painting like Bouguereau or Fortuny.' After contrasting him with Pinero, Wilde, Maupassant, and others, Shaw declares that it is his deficiency in all the fashionable talents that makes him give Heinemann 'my most respectful attention, and I am particularly careful to indulge in none of those prophecies of extinction which were so confidently launched at Wagner, Ibsen and Meredith . . . he has done the right thing in giving up literature and the specific talents, and beginning to drive as hard as he can at real life. Out of that anything may come.'[16]

The following week Max Beerbohm, who had taken over the column from Shaw, attacked him as well as Heinemann for saying anything good about an imitation of Ibsen and a bad one at that. He ended: 'Bad imitations of Ibsen will do no good, however seriously one may take them. Such a play as *Summer Moths* will do no good at all. One should not encourage feeble work at the expense of fine work. To do so is a mistake in policy as well as in criticism. And one should not go about making other people's publishers ridiculous.'[17]

As a publisher William had certainly stuck his neck out, but of course it grew out of exceptionally broad shoulders. Six years later he welcomed Max's first book to his list.

Poets: Naidu, Hope,
'Fiona Macleod',
Masefield, Swinburne

During the early years of the firm, novelists and other authors were likely, as we have seen, also to write verse and were, compared with today, much more likely to get it published. There were also a few others on the list who were primarily poets, among them two women who lived in, and whose inspiration came from, India. The first was Sarojini Naidu, who lived in Hyderabad and was married, with four children, to the only doctor in the Nizam's state. During most of her life she suffered from bad health, including malaria, but this did not prevent her from being very active in politics and social work as a friend of Nehru and Gandhi.

As a sixteen-year-old student at King's College, London, and later at Girton, she met Gosse who described her as being 'unlike the usual English maiden of that age as a lotus or a cactus is unlike a lily of the valley. She was already marvellous in mental maturity, amazingly well-read, and far beyond a Western child in all her acquaintance with the world.'[18] When she showed him some of her poems, he was impressed with their technical skill, but very wisely he told her that what was needed was not a '*réchauffé* of Anglo-Saxon sentiment in an Anglo-Saxon setting, but some revelation of the heart of India, some sincere penetrating analysis of native passion, of the principles of antique religion and of such mysterious intimations as stirred the soul of the East long before the West had begun to dream it had a soul . . . to be a genuine Indian poet of the Deccan, not a clever machine-made imitator of the English classics'[19].

She evidently took Gosse's advice, though it was Arthur Symons who suggested that her poems be collected and published and who wrote the introduction to her first volume, *The Golden Threshold* (1905), which appeared when she was twenty-six. A Hindu, her verses make clear how much she also loved the Muslim culture of her native Hyderabad:

> See how the speckled sky burns like a pigeon's throat
> Jewelled with embers of opal and peridote.
>
> See the white river that flashes and scintillates,
> Curved like a tusk from the mouth of the city gates.
>
> Hark, from the minaret, how the *muezzin*'s call
> Floats like a battle-flag over the city wall. . . .[20]

The Golden Threshold was an immediate success in Britain as well as India, the praise from *The Times Literary Supplement* being not untypical: 'Wisdom, passion and humour, we find them all in her poems . . . her poetry seems to sing itself, as if her swift thoughts and strong emotions sprung into lyrics of themselves.'

Some Poets

She possessed the self-confidence of a well-heeled high-caste Brahmin, and told Heinemann that she was the only upper-class woman around the Muslim court of the Nizam who dared visit the mosque unveiled. It appears that William on a trip to India stayed at her home, and her letters suggest that they were close friends, though none of his replies are to be found. Amid news of the progress of her writing, queries about publication dates and reviews are long, descriptive, often flowery accounts of her family and feelings: 'Our daily life, if we but follow the simple rules of our forefathers, is so full of poetry; from the invocation of the sun god at dawn by the men and the worship by the women of a household of the goddess Lakshime to the very food, the first few morsels of which are consecrated to the Eternal Giver and the ancestors, and the last morsels of which are left in the brass platter or plantain leaf for the ants and humble sharers of the eternal life. These beautiful and symbolic and uplifting things are dying out of our daily life, and alas: but in my own home and in my husband's home they are observed and faithfully fulfilled.'[21] She tells William about 'helping to arrange tableaux for the British Resident's wife' and how her house is the centre of so many activities, because she knows everyone from 'bejewelled and rose-veiled Begums with gold anklets to quite humble schoolmasters and poor students'[22].

In another letter she writes about her little girl being taken ill and how 'cholera, smallpox, typhus and malaria are raging and at last, at last plague has begun. . . . I have volunteered to go and nurse the patients at the plague camps, and my husband has been good enough to promise I shall do so if really necessary.'[23] Her husband is the 'severest of her critics, he and my father, and their ideals of me are so high that they scarcely ever give me praise, even when you and Mr Gosse are enthusiastic'. It is clear she loves and reveres her husband, but thinks 'he is not a popular man because he is so uncompromisingly straight and honest and a little rugged. The poor adore him. . . . There was once, not long ago, a terribly bad man here, an incalculably dangerous man and a blackmailer, who when he was dying sent for my husband to heal him. "Dr Naidu, I sent for you because you are the only one I can trust. You have always treated me with contempt when all others feared me, and so I know that my life is safe in your hands".'[24]

There were two other volumes of Naidu's poetry: *The Bird of Time* (1912) and *The Broken Wing* (1917), in which some of her verses spoke of her ill health and exhaustion:

Oh fate, between the grinding stones of pain,
Tho' you have crushed my life like broken grain,

Lo! I will leaven it with my tears and knead
The bread of hope to comfort and to feed

The myriad hearts for whom no harvests blow
Save little herbs of woe.[25]

She was then thirty-eight and, indeed, from then on she gradually gave up poetry and offered herself to India's non-violent struggle against the British, including a spell in prison. On a visit to America in 1929 she still referred to herself as a 'singer of songs', but she wrote nothing more of much account. Was it because she was too occupied with other things, or was the poetic taste of the post-war world inimical to her simple, but lushly emotional lyrics?

The love affair of the literate British with the romantic features of their Indian empire was a continuing source of profitable books. Laurence Hope became well-known overnight with *The Garden of Kama and Other Love Lyrics* (1901). It was not clear to what extent they depended on the Indian originals, but they were said to possess 'an oriental luxuriance of passion'. They also showed the technical influence of Swinburne and other contemporary Western poets. *Literature* declared that they were 'impregnated with the fascinating atmosphere of the land of the Moghra and Oleander flowers, and at the close of every lyric we feel that the artist has achieved its purpose'. The *Athenaeum* said that they 'caught admirably the dominant notes of Indian love-poetry, its delirious absorption on the instant, its out-of-doors air, its melancholy':

The Fireflies shall light you,
And naught shall affright you,
Nothing shall trouble the Flight of the Hours.
Come, for I wait for you,
Night is too late for you,
Come, while the twilight is closing the flowers.

Every breeze still is,
And, scented with lilies,
Cooled by the twilight, refreshed with the dew,

The garden lies breathless,
Where Kama, the Deathless,
In the hushed starlight, is waiting for you.[26]

At first it was not known that 'Laurence Hope' was the pseudonym of a young English woman, Adela Nicholson, who had settled in Madras after marrying a Colonel Malcolm Nicholson of the Bengal army. A further selection, *Stars of the Desert* (1903), was also successful, but then her husband died and two months later, it was learned from Madras that, prostrate with grief, she had 'died by her own hand of poisoning by perchloride of mercury'. A third volume, *Indian Love* (1905) was published posthumously.

As might be expected, William played his part in the great Celtic revival. It wasn't restricted to Yeats and the Irish, for there were parallel awakenings in Scotland and Wales. The most important work came from Fiona Macleod and, though she was first published by Moray of Derby and Patrick Geddes of Edinburgh, Constable, and others, two years after her death Heinemann published her *From the Hills of Dream: Threnodies, Songs and Later Poems* (1907) and three years later he proudly announced the publication of *The Collected Works of Fiona Macleod* (1909–10) in seven volumes, among them being her first work, *Pharais* (vol. I); *Under the Dark Star: The Dominion of Dreams* (III); *The Winged Destiny* (V). The poems, prose, and drama were one of the finest expressions of the Celtic movement's neo-romantic, mystical quest for the transcendental ideal of beauty and truth. As the poet says in *Green Fire*: 'The world without wonder, the world without mystery. That indeed is the rainbow without colours, the sunrise without living gold.'

It wasn't until after her death that it became widely known that 'Fiona' herself was a myth and was really William Sharp, himself a well established poet, novelist, and critic. The secret had on the whole been well kept, even to the extent of answers to letters in disguised handwriting, phantom visits to London, and a false entry in *Who's Who* which gave her favourite recreations as boating, hill climbing, and listening. The legend was that Fiona was a young woman endowed with the dreamy Celtic genius whose work reflected the inspiration of ancient Celtic paganism and a rapturous worship of Nature.

Together with the *Collected Works* Heinemann published a very sympathetic *Memoir of William Sharp* (1910) by his wife, Elizabeth Sharp, which among much else endeavoured to explain the nature of his *alter ego* and various theories as to why it was necessary. There is no doubt that it was, because the literary transvestism certainly released a powerful creative vein that was different from and superior to that expressed by Sharp himself. Elizabeth Sharp explains that the 'E.W.R.' to whom the first Fiona Macleod romance is dedicated was a beautiful woman he met while they were staying in Rome and who became his muse. 'There, at last', she wrote, 'he had found the desired incentive towards a true expression of himself, in the stimulus and sympathetic understanding of this friend. . . . This friendship began in Rome and lasted throughout the remainder of his life. And though the newer phase of his work was at no time the result of collaboration, as certain of his critics have suggested, he was deeply conscious of his indebtedness to this friend, for – as he stated to me in a letter of instructions, written before he went to America in 1896, concerning his wishes in the event of his death – he realized that it was "to her I owe my development as 'Fiona Macleod' though, in a sense of course, that began long before I knew her, and indeed while I was still a child", and that, as he believed, "without her there would have been no 'Fiona Macleod'" '.

'Because of her beauty, her strong sense of life and of the joy of life; because of her keen intuitions and mental alertness, her personality stood for him as a symbol of the heroic women of Greek and Celtic days, a symbol that, as he expressed it, unlocked new doors in his mind and put him "in touch with ancestral memories" of his race. So, for a time, he stilled the critical, intellectual mood of William Sharp to give play to the development of this new found expression of subtler emotions, towards which he had been moving with all the ardour of his nature.'[27]

Immediately after his death one or two friends he cared for greatly received this note: 'This will reach you after my death. You will think I have wholly deceived you about Fiona Macleod. But, in an intimate sense this is not so: though (and inevitably) in certain details I have misled you. Only, it is a mystery. I cannot explain. Perhaps you will intuitively understand or may come to understand. "The rest is silence". Farewell.'[28] A companion series of five volumes of *The Selected Writings of William Sharp* was published in 1912.

October and Other Poems (1920) was the only title published by the firm for Robert Bridges, the Poet Laureate, but the prolific works of his successor to this illustrious post, John Masefield, were nearly all issued by the firm, and they included drama and prose (see page 220) as well as poetry. His early work had been published by Elkin Matthews, Sidgwick & Jackson, Grant Richards, and others, though most of this was later reissued in various forms by Heinemann. *Dauber* (1913), one of his great narrative poems, was the first on the Heinemann list. Drawing on his own experience in the training ship *Conway* and as an apprentice aboard the *Gilcruix* battling with storms when rounding the Horn, he created the character of the sensitive painter with a love for the sea who at first is alienated from the rest of the crew but as a seaman wins their acceptance through his courage, though it is all wasted when he is blown by a gust from the topsails to be killed on the deck. It was followed by *The Daffodil Fields* (1913) which came close to sentimental melodrama and was not so well received, though it sweetly evoked the English countryside.

His greatest popular success was *Reynard the Fox or The Ghost Heath Run* (1919). As well as conveying the excitement and cruel drama of the chase, it creates Chaucerian pictures of country life at all social levels – the grooms, stable hands, huntsmen, trainers, a publican and barmaid, the parson, the doctor, the squire, young ladies and children. Written soon after the devastation of the trenches, it is a study in survival, because the first fox escapes. It was very well received by the critics and the first edition of 3,000 copies was soon reprinted, to be followed by an illustrated version. Its companion narrative poem, *Right Royal* (1920), told the story of a point-to-point steeplechase. It was full of gusto and suspense but, perhaps, because the verse itself was not of the same standard, it did not have the same success.

Volumes of Masefield's shorter poems were also published, such as *Lollingdon Downs and Other Poems with Sonnets* (1917) and there were four volumes containing plays, in verse as well as prose, though he was most involved with the non-commercial theatre. They included the verse play, *Good Friday* (1915), and the Japanese tragedy, *The Faithful* (1915). Masefield's later works will be discussed further on in this book (page 224), as for many years he was to remain one of the most significant as well as valuable items in William's literary legacy.

Apart from Shakespeare the largest element in Heinemann's poetry list was Swinburne, the firm having acquired in 1917 the copyright in his published and unpublished works. Hitherto many had been published by Chatto & Windus, and between 1917–19 Heinemann took over their remaining stock, though the full scheme of publication and republication was delayed by the war. Gosse, who wrote a life of Swinburne for Macmillan, was at the heart of what can only be called the 'Swinburne industry', together with the notorious T. J. Wise who was a skilled literary forger and who duped Gosse together with several others – though Gosse was never to know this, as Wise's exposure came six years after Gosse's death. Together they edited *The Posthumous Poems of Algernon Charles Swinburne* (1917), followed by two volumes of *The Letters of A. C. Swinburne* (1918), and *Selections from A. C. Swinburne* (1919). All this culminated in the Golden Pine edition of *The Works of A. C. Swinburne* (1917–25) in seven volumes and separate editions of his plays, prose and other works. Steps were also put in hand for the final definitive edition edited by Gosse and Wise known as the Bonchurch, but not published until 1925–27 (see page 289).*

Belles-Lettres and *Fin de Siècle* – Max Beerbohm

In the 1890s and the early years of this century there was a category of books which today is virtually extinct, though similar contents may turn up in other forms. In catalogues they appeared beneath the heading 'Essays and Belles-Lettres' and they were allied with volumes of poems – or, more often, verse – and anything that could be fitted loosely or precisely into the category of Literature. Heinemann's had its share of Belles Lettres *et al.*, its exemplar, its prototype, being Edmund Gosse who contributed books of poetry, criticism, literary history and what may be best called 'literary portraiture', essays of all kinds, as well as autobiography and a small amount of fiction. His criticism and thus his reading was prolific. For years he wrote regular articles for *The Sunday Times*, some of which were collected in book form as in *Silhouettes* (1925) and *Books on the Table* (1921; 1923). The firm also at intervals published seven volumes of his essays, though these were mostly on literary topics and the dividing line from criticism was blurred. They included *Gossip in a Library* (1891),

*The Heinemann archive contains some still-unpublished works by Swinburne – or Wise.

Questions at Issue (1893), *Collected Essays* (1912), and *Some Diversions of a Man of Letters* (1919). The *Spectator* summed up his reputation well when it wrote that his 'literary criticism has ever and again been illuminated by portraits of writers drawn by his pen from life, which have proved candles, by whose light it has been delightfully amusing, and often subtly profitable, to read their works. They are vividly alive and their traits are noted by an eye which seizes readily upon what is imposing and every observation is recorded by a hand skilful in composition.'

Gosse also wrote full-scale biographies and histories including *The Life and Letters of John Donne* (1899) in two volumes and *Modern English Literature* (1897). The latter carried illustrations as did the much more ambitious project, *English Literature: an Illustrated Record* (1903). This was written jointly with Richard Garnett, who worked at the British Museum library and was the father of Edward. It could be justly described as an Edwardian coffee-table book, its four large volumes being richly illustrated with pictures of authors and facsimile reproductions of manuscript pages. Garnett wrote the first two volumes: *From the Beginnings to the Age of Milton* and Gosse in the other two covered *From Milton to the Age of Tennyson*. Garnett also wrote *Essays of an Ex-Librarian* (1901).

Gosse composed much poetry, particularly when younger, and though, as Quiller-Couch commented on his collection *In Russet and Silver* (1894), he 'does all things becomingly', he was depressed that he never managed to be recognized as being among the first rank. An article in the *London Mercury* in 1923 somewhat damningly praised his verse by saying 'it is good enough to remind us of something yet better, for his choice of subject, in his natural tendency to an equable, unstartling felicity, as well as his love of English landscape, his poetry has been akin to the purest and happiest of Tennyson's. Poetry has been a refuge rather than a passion; it has had his reverent ceremonial homage, but not his whole heart.'[29] Heinemann published two other volumes of his poems: *The Autumn Garden* (1908) and *The Collected Poems* (1911) as well as reprints of his pre-1890 volumes. Although Gosse himself called it a 'fantastic sort of poem', *Hypolympia* (1901) was more prose than poetry, a masque in which gods of Ancient Greece held conversations. The critics treated it badly, though a few thought it was a masterpiece. Another disappointment was his novel *The Secret of Narcisse* (1892), a romance set in medieval France. The superficial theme was the creative artist pitted against a philistine society, but there were other, sexual undertones.

Gosse also wrote books for other houses, but Heinemann provided his main outlet and, moreover, published what is likely to remain his enduring masterpiece, *Father and Son* (1907). Initially it was issued anonymously, though the catalogue announcement added 'but the writer will doubtless be recognized as an author who has been prominently before the public for the last quarter of a century'. This may have been an attempt to stimulate curiosity and therefore comment, but in any case the author's identity soon leaked out and his name was added to the title page for the fourth impression in March 1908. In a far less outspoken age the need for anonymity is clear from the original announcement which stated bluntly that 'this is a record of the religious struggle which took place fifty years and more ago between a well-known scientific investigator, who was also an Evangelist of the old extreme type, and the soul of his only child. It was the design of the Father, from the Son's earliest hour, that he should be brought up in "the knowledge and love of the Lord" and should be dedicated exclusively to God's service. The book describes the failure of that plan, the causes of failure, and the ultimate disruption of hearts. . . . Although his Mother was taken from him early in his childhood, her figure animates the earlier pages of the record with a vivid and strange illumination of piety. In this book, with outspoken candour and directness, an attempt is made to constitute the modes of life in an old-fashioned Puritan family of a type which no longer exists, and to show the resistance which it offered to all forms of modern liberty, in thought and action. There was a mixture of comedy and tragedy in the situation, and the heartrending pathos of a crisis where the comedy is superficial and the tragedy internal has been faced unflinchingly. It is offered as a "document" in the history of the religious evolution of our age.'

When he first read the manuscript Heinemann thought it ended too soon and pressed Gosse to add some more. He agreed and in sending in the final chapter he wrote: 'I cannot thank you enough for so very kindly urging me to write it. Had I not done so, the book would not merely have ended too abruptly, but in quite the wrong key.'[30] He clearly must have benefited from William's editorial guidance, for three weeks later he wrote: 'I greatly appreciate your great good-nature in putting up with all my bother. I hope you don't look upon me as a sort of minor Hall Caine! With your fatherly help, I believe this little book will have a great success.'[31] And it did! Most of the reviews were excellent, though Gosse, like many authors, groused about inadequate advertising and in letter after letter kept pressing for more sales effort: 'You are very stingy about presentation copies. I thought you promised to be liberal in distribution. The book will be an utter failure if you don't take a personal interest in it.'[32] Only ten days after publication he told William that 'I am getting fearfully depressed, but my sheet-anchor is in your energy'[33]; and after another ten days he ended a letter to Pawling: 'Well, in the bargain and partnership between us, I have done my part. Now it is your part, as the distributing agency for a knowledge of it. If you will take a real interest in spreading curiosity about it, it ought to sell in thousands. If you grow languid about it, because it does not sell at once, automatically, you will do me a great injustice.'[34]

It is of course never easy to understand exactly why a tiny fraction of books endure to become classics. Ann Thwaite, Gosse's biographer, helps make it clearer in the case of *Father and Son* as in this short extract from a long chapter: 'One of the virtues of the book is that the father is not less valued than the son; his strengths are given full due; his humanity confronts us as much as his fanaticism. Indeed, the book takes much of its power from what Edmund rejected. Henry Tonks . . . saw "that monstrous father" as "one of the most terrible people the world has produced". More readers saw that this was not so, that his "ruinous errors" were due to his creed and not to his character. Haldane wrote that he was filled with reverence for the father, "so single-minded and distinguished in character". Lady Londonderry could sympathize with a parent's feelings and the pain of finding out that the child would always think differently. It was in no ironic spirit that Edmund was able to talk of the book as a monument to his father, "a good and even great man, whose character was too powerful not to have its disconcerting sides". . . .

'In 1907 it seems that the "modern" period is beginning. *Father and Son* feels modern in tone, in a way that one of its few antecedents – Mark Rutherford's *Autobiography* – does not. 1907 was the year of the publication of *The Longest Journey* by Forster, of Synge's *Playboy of the Western World*, Belloc's *Cautionary Tales* and James Joyce's first book, albeit a conventional one, *Chamber Music*. It was the year Auden and MacNeice were born. Accustomed as we are to the great variety of autobiographical confessional writing of the twentieth century, it is quite difficult to realize just how original *Father and Son* is. There had to be a strong feeling in the nineteenth century that private life should be private. It was not only Tennyson who thanked Almighty God that the world knew nothing of

Shakespeare but his writing, and that he knew nothing of Jane Austen. Gosse himself says that "the peculiar curiosity which legitimate biography satisfies, is essentially a modern thing and presupposes our observation of life not unduly clouded by moral passion or prejudice". Harold Nicolson, quoting this . . ., found it strange that Gosse, who laid no particular stress on form, believing the form of a biography less important than its content, went on to produce the most "literary" biography in the English language. Nicolson called *Father and Son* "a masterpiece in which, by consummate power of selection, the author has been able to combine the maximum of scientific interest with the maximum of literary form".[35]

In many ways a European equivalent to Gosse was the industrious and celebrated Danish critic Georg Brandes, who joined the list in 1898 with two substantial volumes of *William Shakespeare: a Critical Study*. His object was to trace Shakespeare's mental and spiritual history through his works. In the opinion of the *Athenaeum* 'no other single work on Shakespeare includes so much, and so much that is valuable. There is no side of his subject which he neglects. He is both an antiquary and a critic. . . . He has brought to bear a judgment well-balanced and vigorous and a mind liberal and independent.' A weighty tool in Heinemann's campaign to educate the insular British to appreciate the virtues of European culture was provided by the translation of Brandes's six volumes devoted to the *Main Currents in Nineteenth Century Literature* (1901–05). He also wrote *Critical Studies of Henrik Ibsen and Björnstjerne Björnson* (1899); on the pioneer of economic Socialism, *Ferdinand Lassalle* (1911); on *Friedrich Nietzsche* (1914); and an autobiographical *Recollections of my Childhood and Youth* (1906). Not surprisingly he was also one of five contributors to an inexpensive Contemporary Men of Letters series, writing the volume on *Anatole France* (1908).

A representative *fin de siècle*, literary all-rounder was Arthur Symons, poet, playwright, translator, anthologizer, critic, contributor to literary journals, and editor of the short-lived but important *Savoy*, with a similar mission to that of *The Yellow Book* and noted for its publication of the drawings of Aubrey Beardsley. Holbrook Jackson described Symons as the 'poet of the music hall, the café and the *demi-monde*, literary impressionist of towns, and penetrating critic of the writers of the decadence of France and England'[36]. His first book for Heinemann was his study of *The Symbolist Movement in Literature* (1899) which showed his acute understanding of French literature, a book which had a decided influence on Joyce and Pound. Symbolism stood for Art possessing a transcendental power and he became spokesman for 'art for art's sake' and for the quest for 'the universal science of Beauty'. Art and morals had nothing to do with each other. Among his other works published by Heinemann were two volumes of *Poems* (1901–02); a strange little 'morality' issued as *The Fool of the World and Other Poems* (1906); three verse dramas titled *Tragedies: The Harvesters, The Death of Agrippina, Cleopatra in Judea* (1916). Some of the best of his dramatic writings were collected in *Studies in Elizabethan Drama* (1920).

Heinemann had close connections with John Lane and The Bodley Head's *The Yellow Book*. Henry Harland, its editor, was a Heinemann novelist – *Mea Culpa* (1891) and *Mademoiselle Miss* (1893) – and Symons together with many of Heinemann's authors and personal friends were contributors to the early numbers and so was the romantic young Hubert Crackanthorpe. He was noted for belonging to the 'realist' school and owed much to Maupassant and Ibsen. Heinemann first published his *Wreckage* (1893) with seven short stories which, according to his contemporary, Richard Le Gallienne, 'was one of the sensations of the period. Crackanthorpe's concern was not with his prose, but with the faithful presentation of human character and story, as close to the bare fact as possible, with no intrusion whatever of the writer's temperament. A scrupulous, almost fanatical, "objectivity" was his artistic aim. . . . One felt that his characters and situations were presented too much in a vacuum. Some suffusion of his austerely suppressed self might have endued it with more magnetism.'[37] There followed more stories in *Sentimental Studies and a Set of Village Tales* (1895), but not many months later Crackanthorpe, in trouble with a wife and a mistress, disappeared in Paris until the corpse of this attractive, boyish, brilliant man of thirty-one, so full of promise, was retrieved from the Seine. It looked like suicide but it could have been an accident. Posthumously Heinemann published his *Last Studies* (1897).

There has to be a limit to the number of Bellelettrists who can be included, but a few lines must be found for Maurice Hewlett. He was best known for his historical novels such as *The Fool Errant* (1905), described as being the 'memoirs of Francis-Antony Strelley Esq, citizen of Lucca'; and *The Little Iliad* (1915) which was illustrated by Philip Burne-Jones. But he also wrote things like *Pan and the Young Shepherd* (1906), 'a pastoral' in two acts; and the long poem, *The Song of the Plow* (1916), which

[137]

recounted the history of the 'governed race' in England and expressed his passionate belief in the peasantry as the country's only hope.

Another obvious candidate for this chapter is Max Beerbohm. Not only was he justly called 'incomparable', but the form of his output was very varied: parodies, short stories, satires, verses, essays of every size and shape, cartoons (dealt with on pages 105–7), and his only but outstanding novel, *Zuleika Dobson* (1911). This was his first title with Heinemann, though he was already well known for his frivolous trifle 'A Defence of Cosmetics' contributed to *The Yellow Book*, published by John Lane, and for his second book *The Works of Max Beerbohm*, the preposterous title for a writer twenty-four years old. He was already a familiar among the writers connected to 21 Bedford Street, a close friend of Maugham, and a guest at Gosse's literary parties. *Zuleika* marked the start of a long relationship with the 'Eternal Volatile' (a private nickname for Heinemann) who 'is a very amiable publisher, and our communications are of an exquisite amenity'[38]. For *Zuleika* Heinemann gave him an advance of £400 in respect of a 20 per cent royalty. The extravaganza, based on his time at Oxford, about the most attractive woman in the world, a conjurer to boot, who descends on the university in Eights Week so that every undergraduate falls for her and drowns himself because his love is not requited is, like most of Max's work, too subtle to be conveyed in any words but its own. Wherever she went, in whatever country, men fell for her madly: 'Prince Vierfunfsechs-Siebenachtneun offered her his hand, and was condemned by the Kaiser to six months' confinement in his little castle. In Yildiz Kiosk, the tyrant who still throve there conferred on her the Order of Chastity, and offered her the central couch in his seraglio. She gave a performance in the Quirinal and, for the Vatican, the Pope launched against her a Bull which fell utterly flat.'[39]

David Cecil, one of his biographers, suggests how *Zuleika* 'exhibits in the most extreme form his characteristic blend of the pretty and the comic. A delicate rococo, frolicsome prettiness, flaunts itself through every paragraph, informing image and description, making itself heard in every dancing and lingering cadence of Max's prose. But so also is every page saturated with his comic sense; sometimes rollicking and farcical, sometimes sharply satiric, sometimes taking wing in a flight of whimsical nonsense. But it is always present; never for an instant is he serious. His tone is sustainedly ironical: his prettiness never softens into sentiment. . . . Neither is his satire ever serious. He is not out to castigate or

correct human folly. . . . Most of his jokes are directed against dandyism
and university institutions, two of the things that pleased him most in
life. . . . *Zuleika Dobson* is an outstanding example of his characteristic
propensity to laugh at what he loved and to love what he laughed at.'[40]

With all his books Beerbohm took an insistent, not to say pernickety,
interest in their appearance. From his home in Rapallo poured letters full
of instructions as to typefaces, width of margins, binding cloth, the
positioning of a heading. In July 1911 he wrote: 'it is generous of you to
leave with me the final decision as to the format of Miss Dobson. . . . I
have been looking at all such novels as I have here, one with another, with
a deepening gloom: oh those dreary, utilitarian, *mesquin* pages! All very
well, no doubt, for simple go-ahead stories; but how hard on, how fatal to a
story interspersed through and through with passages of sheer decoration
and disquisition. And gradually, it has been borne in on me that at all
hazards I must ask you to let Zuleika go forth into the world with that
width of margin which suits her leisurely and belles-lettresque (what a
word!) nature.'[41] There were inevitably a few misprints in the finished
copies which caused him to send Ballantyne's, the printers, a letter
'couched in cold and calculated fury'. He also wrote to Pawling: 'As to that
world "inexpell*a*ble", Messrs Ballantyne's impressive invocation of half-
a-dozen dictionaries and "the custom of 120 years": I know very well that
dictionaries spell the word with an *a*, and I further assume that Messrs
Ballantyne's proof-readers have for 120 years been instructed to correct
in proof any dubious spelling. Of *Zuleika Dobson* I had two proofs. In
neither of them was "indispell*i*ble" queried or corrected. Had it been so, I
should have written *stet* for the "i", and (as my nature is keen and
communicative in such matters) have explained that for good reasons of
Latinity "indispell*a*ble" is as vile and harrowing a word as "inelegable"
would be, or "inaud*a*ble", or "inevit*i*ble", or "ar*i*ble". The proof-reader,
having had no right to suppose at the last moment that *I* had been lax too.

'As to general typography I am very ready and glad to believe that all
those swaying lines, those letters bobbing up, those letters slipping down,
and other defects over which I had to expend so much time in correcting
the proofs, and which have not been wholly purged away from the
published book, were due simply to "a slight inequality in the alignment
of this particular fount". In all friendliness, then, I implore Messrs
Ballantyne to abandon this particular fount (evidently our old friend the
fons et origo malorum) for ever and ever, or to use it only on very special

occasions – as when they are called on to print *The Confessions of a Dancing Dervish*, for example, or *The Random Memories of a Palsied Hottentot*. If they yield to my entreaty I will make a design of their Managing Director as noble as anything on the Parthenon Frieze.'[42]

Zuleika was received with rapturous acclamation and so was his 'weaving' of *A Christmas Garland* (1912), his collection of parodies of famous authors, including Belloc, Wells, Shaw, Hardy, Bennett, Galsworthy, Conrad, Gosse, Moore. . . . The author of *Max in Perspective* (1921), Bohun Lynch, surmised that 'even easy and obvious parody of peculiar style may be clever and amusing, but there is much more than mere cleverness in these. Anybody with a knack for mimicry can exaggerate the salient eccentricities of an exceptional manner of writing, but in *A Christmas Garland* the parody is twofold: the style and the method of construction is imitated, but not too grossly caricatured; and, better still, the treatment, apart from the actual subject of each parody – which is Christmas – is recognisable as the potential treatment of each separate victim. Mr Beerbohm might be described as a devil who has temporarily possessed these writers. In "Some Damnable Errors about Christmas" Mr G. K. Chesterton is made to say . . . "We do not say of Love that he is short-sighted. We do not say of Love that he is myopic. We do not say of Love that he is astigmatic. We say quite simply Love is blind. We might go further and say, Love is deaf. That would be a profound and obvious truth. We might go further and say, Love is dumb. But that would be a profound and obvious lie."' Lynch goes on to quote from the parody of Kipling, titled 'P.C.X 36', which makes fun of his trick of displaying technical knowledge in an acutely nonchalant fashion: '"Now when Judlip sighs the sound is like unto that which issues from the vent of a Crosby boiler when the cog-guages are at 260 degrees F. Judlip, moreover, flashes "his 45-c.p. down the slot of a two-grade Yale." In fact, is it nonsense? And, after all, the following verse does more than merely recall *Barrack-Room Ballads*:

> "Then it's collar 'im tight,
>   "In the name of the Lawd!
> "'Ustle 'im, shake 'im till 'e's sick!
>   "Wot, 'e *would*, would 'e? Well,
> "Then yer've got ter give 'im 'Ell,
>   "An' it's trunch, trunch, truncheon does the trick".'[43]

The trouble with Beerbohm is that he is so irresistibly quotable and there is no more space in which to deal properly with his other titles such as the stories in *Seven Men* (1919) which included his satire of the Decadent Movement in 'Enoch Soames' and of fashionable Edwardian society in 'Maltby and Braxton'. Then there were the essays as in *And Even Now* (1920) and much later in *Mainly on the Air* (1946) and *A Variety of Things* (1953); and several other titles including *Max in Verse* (1964). A second premature collected works, this time in ten volumes, was issued between 1921 and 1928.

Heinemann and the Book Trade –
President of the PA

As seen in other chapters, Heinemann was a great believer in the virtues of marketing books in groups – collected works of individual authors, 'libraries', special series. One of the longest running was Heinemann's Favourite Classics, originally issued at 6*d*. in cloth and 1*s*. in leather, both with a photogravure frontispiece; this 'dainty series of reprints of some of the gems of English literature' ranged from the works of Addison to Macaulay, from Milton to Tennyson. In other series the same title would often be presented to the public – or rather different publics – in different guises and/or at different prices. American authors would thus sometimes be billed as part of the Dollar Library of American Fiction; other novels were grouped together in the Pioneer Series or the Kit-Cat Library or the Acme Library of Popular Fiction – several if not all these titles had originally appeared as standard 6*s*. novels. The Works of Shakespeare appeared, with introductions by Georg Brandes, in 40 volumes among Heinemann's Favourite Classics, in 12 volumes as the Garrick Shakespeare, and in 12 volumes bound in blue buckram with gilt lettering as number three in the Pickering Club Classics. The Club was limited to 375 'bibliophile' members and aimed to specialize in classical works which, 'by reason either of their bulk or their lack of delicacy, are ordinarily issued in emasculated editions'. Each set was numbered and the type distributed after the completion of printing. Twenty-five sets were printed on the 'finest Dutch hand-made paper, with duplicate sets of plates, forming an *édition de luxe* of very exceptional magnificence'. The earlier two sets comprised 16 volumes of the Works of Henry Fielding with a critical appreciation by W. E. Henley and 19 volumes of the Works of Samuel Richardson with an introduction by Austin Dobson. The Pickering Club does not appear to have been much of a success because it soon disappeared from the catalogue.

With very many novels it was standard practice, once the demand for the original 6*s*. edition had begun to decline, to re-issue it at 3*s*.6*d*. or 2*s*. or

1s. or even 7d. Occasionally another publisher, such as Nelson and Warne, would be licensed to include it in his low-priced series, but normally the right to issue cheaper or cheap editions was jealously guarded. Interviewed in 1904, Heinemann stated that 'the sixpenny edition is simply the publisher's measure of self-defence against the cheap magazine. It ranks with periodicals rather than books. The work published in sixpenny editions is probably, on the average, better than the matter supplied in the cheap magazines; and anything that tends to beget and foster the habit of reading – be it sixpenny editions, circulating libraries, public libraries, or what not – is in the long run good. The reading habit is like the opium habit; once acquired, it cannot be shaken off.'[1]

Heinemann was very aware of the different layers of the novel-reading public, and how it was changing and expanding. In the same interview he argued that there was an unintelligent as well as an intelligent reading public. 'The intelligence of the middle and lower-middle classes, in the matter of book-buying, is on the whole improving. I don't know that I can say as much for the wealthier classes. Many a man, where his father would have spent a pound on books, will now spend a guinea on an opera stall, and sixpence – or fourpence-halfpenny – on a magazine. On the other hand, people of moderate means have now much more encouragement than they had a generation ago to form their own little libraries. Look how execrable was the manufacture of books during all the middle years of last century. A reasonably attractive edition of a classical author was scarcely to be had for love or money. Now – within the last fifteen years or so – the improvement has been enormous. . . . It is not only good in itself. It helps current literature as well by enabling people, at a reasonable expenditure, to form the nucleus of a handsome and attractive private library. Though I'm afraid I must admit that a good many people buy the Shakespeares and Scotts and Macaulays, with which the press teems, rather as furniture than as literature. . . . But I think we may take it that most book-buyers buy to read; and I believe that the number who buy intelligently to read intelligently is increasing year by year. . . . There is always a steadily growing public to appeal to – not only owing to actual increase of population, but to the spread of education. Remember, it is only a little over thirty years since the first Education Act was passed.'[2]

Heinemann never forgot the difficulties and needs of the booksellers. In the case of nearly all books except novels he was happy, for example, to supply copies on 'sale or return', provided he knew the bookseller to be trustworthy. On the other hand he was scathing about the shortcomings and backwardness of most booksellers compared with those on the Continent, especially Germany. 'You may think it is a paradox, but it's not far from the literal truth, that many booksellers in England never see a book of any value or importance, but live entirely by peddling novels, old and new. The book-trade will never be in a thoroughly healthy condition until we have a body of selected and trained booksellers all over the country, to whom we give depots of books on sale or return, and say to them "Now, sell these – don't merely wait till people come to buy them, but *sell* them – that is your business!" English booksellers, with rare exceptions, have never realized, or have forgotten, that bookselling is no mere mechanical function like handing out tickets for the Twopenny Tube, but is a calling that demands a great deal of intelligence, enterprise, and skill.'[3]

The main part of a good bookseller's business, he believed, should be not selling to chance customers but to regulars who can be reached by means of prospectuses and in many cases by putting the actual books in the hands of people he knows are likely to want them. 'Look at our scores of large towns inhabited mainly by people of means and leisure – who ought to be the backbone of the reading public – and you will find that there the bookselling trade is conducted with incredible negligence and stupidity. Ask a bookseller in any well-to-do seaside resort, for instance, whether he has even a list of possible customers for special professional books, and he will tell you that he has never thought of keeping one. But every German bookseller has not only a list, but a carefully classified list of his *clientele* and can tell at a glance how many he can rely upon to buy this book, how many to buy that. To take an obvious example, he knows that such and such a doctor is a throat specialist: he sends to his house, without waiting for an order, a new book on diseases of the larynx; and if the doctor doesn't want it, he fetches it away again in a day or two. Another doctor is a chest specialist: to him he sends a book on the Nordrach open-air cure – and so forth.'[4]

It was a truism that a healthy, profitable bookselling trade was essential if publishers were also to flourish. Nothing did more to prevent this ideal from being realized than underselling both by booksellers and publishers. Fierce, unregulated competition was causing both to cut their own throats. As Heinemann put it in December 1892, 'The general rule remains that bookselling is about as profitable as the backing of horses, with less chances and similar risks. To reduce these risks to the narrowest limit is, of course, the steady aim of all in the trade, and the result is that, with the exception of a small number of firms of high standing and with a large turnover, they become daily less inclined to stock books. Our travellers visit them regularly, and, in order to get a "line", they have to offer books at reductions which amount in some cases to 50 per cent off the published price. Those publishers who issue series at 6s., or 3s.6d., or 2s.6d., or 2s. find, with the increased number of these issues, a corresponding disinclination on the part of the trade to take up new volumes. Better terms are, therefore, offered as an inducement, with the result that we are at the present moment cutting prices to an extent that will land us all in the workhouse, if we do not make some timely and united stand against this increasing danger.'[5]

What this had led to was that publishers had to price their books at least 25 per cent higher than was otherwise necessary in order that booksellers could pass on an attractive discount to their customers. The obvious answer was to stabilize prices, so that booksellers were able to adhere to the published retail prices established by the publishers. This could be achieved only if publishers and booksellers – and both parties among themselves – agreed to operate this in principle. This necessity was a prime reason for the formation of the Publishers Association in 1896 in which William, though much younger and less experienced than colleagues like John Murray and C. J. Longman, played a leading part.

After two years of negotiation with the Associated Booksellers of Great Britain and Ireland the new body was able on 1 January 1900 to report the signing of the Net Book Agreement which laid down that books were to be sold, at least for the first six months, at the full price. At first it applied only to books priced at above 6s. and to non-fiction, and it was not until April 1916 that novels were also included, so that the 6s. novel was normally sold to the public less 25 per cent discount: i.e., for 4s.6d. There also remained certain other categories of non-net or 'subject' books, as is the case today with school textbooks. The severest test to the Agreement was the insistence of *The Times* Bookclub library to sell books to the public at a discount after being loaned only as few as a couple of times. The Publishers' Association declared the Club 'black' and the great 'Book War', as it became known, had started. Many publishers refused to supply the Club, and *The Times* used its columns as artillery. The conflict lasted two years (1906–08) before peace was negotiated with the new proprietor of *The Times*, Lord Northcliffe. William had vigorously attacked the Bookclub for breaking the Net Book Agreement but it was he, together with Frederick Macmillan, who succeeded eventually in reaching a settlement with the Bookclub, on behalf of the Publishers' Association, at a meeting in his own office at 21 Bedford Street. The Net Book Agreement was saved.

William's nonpareil qualities of vitality, coupled with the clarity with which he seemed to see and explain his objectives, enabled him to devote a great deal of his time to the politics of publishing in parallel with building up a new firm. It is beyond the scope of this history to include this aspect of his life beyond recording that, after serving on the Publishers Association's Council from the outset, he was elected Hon. Treasurer in 1906 and became President in 1909. For seventeen years he was Britain's regular representative at meetings of the International Congress of Publishers which took him to meetings at Brussels, Budapest, Milan, Leipzig, and elsewhere. His capacity for languages and grasp of such recondite subjects as international copyright made him invaluable.

It was in his capacity of President that during a speech at a large trade gathering he floated a novel idea that was to have practical consequences for the firm. He opened an attack on 'the production of worthless books and books that have been artificially spun out to bulk within covers at 6s. which contain in reality little more reading matter than the old-fashioned 1s. book contained. Gentlemen, we have all seen 6s. novels of less than 40,000 words, and we have seen others exceeding 300,000 words. It may be objected that quantity is not a criterion of literature, but a man who pays 4s.6d. for a book and expects five or six evenings' entertainment from it, feels cheated if he gets through it in a couple of hours. There is in the whole range of commerce no commodity for which the public is asked to pay indiscriminately one price, whether it be a pound or an ounce that is offered.

'To those who would still object that quantity has nothing to do, or should have nothing to do, with literature, I should like to reply that quality is often ignored in the fixing of the price of a novel. The ripe work of experience brings, in the shape of a novel, no more money than the slipshod writing of young ladies and gentlemen who can afford to spend £50 or £100 on the production of a few hundred copies of their foolish vapourings. Out of this indifference to quantity and quality in the

The office at 21 Bedford Street, Covent Garden

William Heinemann in his office about 1913

William Heinemann in 1920 – the last year of his life

publication of novels has grown a habit in the retail trade of distinguishing too little between what is worth selling and pushing and what had better be left unrecommended. . . . We must not forget that the sale of every bad and unworthy novel is a nail in the coffin of 6*s*. novels as a class.'[6]

That autumn Heinemann took the risk – and it was a considerable one – of putting into practice his own preaching with the launch of the Heinemann Library of Modern Fiction, each title with one or two volumes at different prices per volume, according to length. The format was slightly smaller than that of the ordinary 6*s*. novel and bound in thin instead of thick boards, but with good cloth and gilt lettering. The first title was Hall Caine's *The White Prophet* in two volumes at 4*s*. each, and there were nine other new titles, all by established authors, most of them in one volume at 3*s*. net, though William de Morgan's *It Never Can Happen Again* ran to two volumes at 6*s*. each.

Unfortunately this much praised attempt to fit the price to a book's merit and length was a failure and was not repeated – the libraries, for example, would not touch the de Morgan because it broke their 6*s*. barrier. It was, however, a typical and courageous example of William's restless enterprise.

New Review, World's Work, Gazette du Bon Ton

In the years before the First World War literary journals played a more important part in the development of new talent, and one associated with a book publisher could be an asset. Heinemann undoubtedly felt the need for one. Only four months after starting up in business he announced that he had taken over *East and West*, 'a magazine for all', from Ward & Downey Ltd. The May 1890 number was declared to be the start of a new series but it does not seem to have survived many issues. For some years he also helped distribute, and rented an office to, the *North American Review*. A much more important venture was the *New Review* which he took over with the January issue of 1894. Until then it had been distributed by Longmans, Green & Co, though it was owned and edited by Archibald Grove, Liberal MP for West Ham. Its contents were then worthy but remarkably dull. After a short while Grove relinquished control and W. E. Henley became editor from January 1895, being backed by a group of literary/political friends who may also have put up some money and acted as a board of directors, to relieve Henley of the daily editorial grind. They included George Wyndham, Herbert Stephen, Lord Windsor, and Charles Whibley. Beerbohm called these supporters 'Henley's regatta'.

Henley had been a brilliant editor of the *Scots* (later *National*) *Observer* and was of course well known as a poet and critic. Though hampered by ill-health and lameness resulting from tuberculosis and with a reputation for caustic, even violent opinions, he was much loved and respected. He was all for realism and had no time for the ivory tower or for decadent aesthetes. For young Heinemann he was certainly a catch, and soon proved his worth by assembling an impressive list of contributors, including Verlaine, Arthur Symons, W. E. Gladstone, Stephen Crane, Maurice Hewlett, W. B. Yeats, Wilfrid Scawen Blunt, and many others. As we have seen, his serials provided a launching pad for the novels of Wells and Conrad; he also ran Arthur Morrison's *A Child of the Jago*. There was, however, soon friction with his board who begged him to be more discreet and in his keenness to shock Victorian proprieties not to go too far ahead of the paying public. The inclusion of one story in which the seduction of a housemaid was described in fuller detail than was customary at the time was said to have caused the circulation, which had been slowly and laboriously creeping up, to drop like a stone. Henley evidently thought differently, on one occasion grumbling that 'my directors have landed me for about 100 pages of Henrietta James. So I fear the *N.R.* will scarce survive the year'[7] – this referred to the serialization of *What Maisie Knew*. Almost from the start there had also been recriminations with Heinemann. 'The truth is, I fear – and so do we all – that Billy H. doesn't know his business. He is all right with books: but as for magazines! – It is a rude awakening from that pleasant dream of his competence in which we've lived since the beginning of the year. . . . The truth is, he is too bloody cultured: he wants to edit the magazine – not to sell it.'[8]

The *New Review* was losing Heinemann more money than the prestige it brought justified – at least £1,000 had to be written off – and in December 1897 at the end of Henley's fourth year he ceased to be editor and Heinemann ceased to be publisher, though it continued under

George Wyndham and in a very different form and with a different title –
the *Outlook and New Review* which later became simply the *Outlook*.

Until his death in 1903 Henley seems to have remained on good terms
with William, who published his *Hawthorn and Lavender* (1901), a lyric
parable of the seasons. He also contributed 'A Song of Speed' to the
World's Work magazine (see below), inspired by his delight in his first
experience of motoring. A melodramatic farce, *Macaire* (1895), written
jointly with his old friend R. L. Stevenson, had appeared, but the plan to
edit the *Letters of Lord Byron* never went beyond the first volume (1897)
because of copyright difficulties.

A magazine with a very different character and which was to endure for
close on thirty years was the *World's Work*. It was founded by its editor,
Walter H. Page, and published by Doubleday, the New York book
publishers (eventually Doubleday, Page). In 1913 Page became American
ambassador in London and stayed during most of the First World War. At
the suggestion of Henry Chalmers Roberts, an American journalist,
Heinemann decided to launch an equivalent magazine in London;
though, while there was an exchange of articles, its contents were on the
whole different and it remained an entirely distinct enterprise. The
London editor was Henry Norman, MP, who in the first number,
December 1902, elaborated on the significance of its lofty sub-title, 'The
New Illustrated Magazine of National Efficiency and Social Progress'.
Quoting a remark of the Prince of Wales that 'the Old Country must buck
up', he explained that each month the *World's Work* would 'present a
picture of the activities of the world – particularly of the British world – in
public life, in foreign affairs, in commerce, industry, science, invention,
literature, art and social life. . . .' It would be inspired by the conviction
that 'the education and well-being of the people form the surest foundation of national prosperity. It will regard the Empire as the personal
concern of every citizen, and its security and development as indissolubly
dependent on his own character and aims.' But 'the world's work cannot
be successfully carried out without the world's play' and so there would be
articles on sport (but not professionalism which degrades), on books, and
subjects, including work, to interest women. It was launched with much
réclame with an 'Important Subscription Scheme', with a 'Prize of £100
Cash', 'of Special Interest to Newsagents'.

It is difficult to convey its character and flavour because no modern
magazine is remotely like it. It had a large format, 112 pages of good art

paper, and plenty of half-tone illustrations. It cost a shilling a month, quite a lot for those days and therefore it would have appealed to a high-minded middle-class and lower-middle-class readership, but less sophisticated and quite different from that of the literary journals. A small selection from the first twelve issues may help indicate the contents: 'The Coming of the Motor Car'; 'Alien Immigration'; 'Fish-Farming in Scotland'; 'The Marvellous Story of Helen Keller'; 'The Negro Problem in the United States'; 'Remodelled Noses'; 'The King's Visit to Portugal'; 'Behind the Scenes at Golders Green Crematorium'; 'Higher Education'. The last was written by Sidney Webb. Among the contributors to later issues were Clemence Dane, J. B. S. Haldane, Lady Astor, Philip Snowden, Arnold Lunn, St. John Ervine, Rudyard Kipling, and T. P. O'Connor.

The monthly treadmill of editing and administering a big magazine from the cramped premises at Bedford Street must have caused many problems, but it was a project in which William believed profoundly, even to the extent, as happened in some years, of losing money. At the end of 1903, Chalmers Roberts took over the editorship, a post he relinquished only in 1930. Then in 1913 the magazine was hived off as a separate company called The World's Work (1913) Ltd, the directors being Heinemann, Pawling, and Chalmers Roberts, who had forty-nine per cent of the shares. William's cousin, John Heinemann, who had joined the main firm the year before, was made company secretary. Dead magazines are more easily forgotten than the books of dead established authors, but this history would be incomplete without stressing the important part it played in the firm's affairs throughout over a quarter of a century.

Completely different again and displaying the catholicity of William's taste was his other monthly, the *Gazette du Bon Ton*, launched by the firm in 1914. It was advertised as 'The most expensive magazine ever published', at 10s. a month or £4 4s. for a yearly subscription. This luxury product was issued simultaneously in Paris, Berlin, New York, and London, and it is likely that Heinemann, who became involved only with the thirteenth issue, were essentially distributors, although the *Gazette* had its own office at Bedford Street. After an opening tribute to the artistic geniuses of the Italian Renaissance the launching announcement asked: 'Are we on the threshold of a twentieth century renaissance, in the sense that we are putting into our daily service and using for the adornment of everyday life the brains and inventions of the geniuses of our day? Artists are proud to contribute to the beautifying of all objects of luxury; and from the first impetus given to art handicraft by William Morris in England a feverish competition has sprung up in all countries to adorn the things around us – what we see, what we touch, what we wear.' The *Gazette du Bon Ton* was 'the joint product of the artist and the refined dressmaker, jeweller, furrier, carriage and car builder'. The illustrations were a very special feature. 'Here is no confusion of tints inevitable in photographic reproduction; but each picture is hand-coloured exactly in imitation of the artist's original – a real picture, in fact, not a mere reflection of lifeless mannequins.' To launch such a luxury project on the eve of a European war was bad luck, but it is not clear for how many issues it survived.

The Loeb Classical Library –
Entry into Medical Publishing

One of the most important and enduring of William's achievements was the creation in 1912 of the Loeb Classical Library which close on eighty years later is still flourishing and adding new titles to the total of 470 (1988). Dr James Loeb was a wealthy American banker of German extraction who had settled down near Munich, where he lived for the rest of his life, apart from a short period in Switzerland when America entered the First World War. The original idea came from Salomon Reinach, of the Institute of France, but Loeb, apart from providing the finance, kept in close touch from a distance except during long patches of mental illness. In practice Heinemann and his staff formulated and managed the whole project in return for a 15 per cent commission on net receipts, though for William personally the motivation must by no means have been entirely financial. It was the kind of scholarly challenge that excited him.

Loeb had always envisaged it as an expression of the best of Anglo-American scholarship and the books, supplied from London, were published simultaneously in America, first by the Macmillan Co. of New York and later by Putnam – Heinemann's commission being altered to 10 per cent on the manufacture of copies for America and 5 per cent on American receipts. The editors were T. E. Page, formerly of Charter-house, and W. H. D. Rouse, of the Perse School, Cambridge. They were soon joined by Professor Edward Capps, of Princeton. The books, usually issued in two annual batches of seven or eight pocket-sized volumes, were bound in green for Greek titles and red for Latin. The original text was printed on the left-hand pages with the English translation facing it. Most of the translations were new and the aim was to ensure that they were literate as well as accurate. To use Dr Loeb's own words: 'To make the beauty and learning, the philosophy and wit of the great writers of ancient Greece and Rome once more accessible by means of translations that are in themselves real pieces of literature, a thing to be read for the pure joy of it, and not dull transcripts of ideas that suggest in every line the existence of a finer original from which the average reader is shut out, and to place side by side with these translations the best critical texts of the original works, is the task I have set myself.'

The original plan, on an almost heroic scale, was to include everything of any importance from the time of Homer to the fall of Constantinople. As well as the standard authors such as Thucydides and Xenophon, Aristotle and Plutarch, Cicero and Pliny, Seneca and Tacitus, were lesser known figures like Boethius on *The Consolation of Philosophy* and Theophrastus on plants. For the theologian there were handy versions of the Apostolic Fathers, Augustine's *Confessions*, and works of the Venerable Bede. There were also ancient novels and tales of adventure, such as Apuleius' *The Golden Ass* (*Metamorphoses*) and the story of Daphnis and Chloe with its picture of country life on Lesbos. It was never, from the outset, a dry-as-dust collection, and this may help to explain the Loeb Library's quite extraordinary success.

Another significant departure was the acquisition in 1913 for £3,300 of an existing publisher of medical books, Rebman Ltd. It was a short list of some hundred titles, but it covered most of the standard medical disciplines with quite strong sections on diet, dentistry, ophthalmics, and dermatology; there were several titles dealing with sexual problems, including a translation of the latest edition of Krafft-Ebing's monumental *Psychopathia Sexualis*. There were also eight titles on Electricity and Röntgen Rays and a couple of learned journals. Somehow this going concern, together with its manager, Hugh Elliot, was squeezed into space next door at 20 Bedford Street.

In 1917 a new company was formed, William Heinemann (Medical Books) Ltd, which formally purchased the business from the partnership of Messrs Heinemann (£1,257) and Hugh Elliot (£1,047), though this

GAZETTE DV BON TON

The most expensive magazine ever published.
Issued monthly. Price 10s. net per month, or £4 4s. for yearly subscription.

ART, FASHION AND LUXURY.

IN the great era of Italian Renaissance the princes and the wealthy had in their pay artists to make beautiful their surroundings; the houses they lived in, the utensils they used, the armour with which they protected themselves, the clothes they wore, were the fabric of the great geniuses of the period—Benvenuto Cellini, Bramante, Leonardo da Vinci, Michael Angelo and others.

Are we on the threshold of a twentieth century renaissance, in the sense that we are putting into our daily service and using for the adornment of everyday life the brains and inventions of the geniuses of our day? Artists are proud to contribute to the beautifying of all objects of luxury; and from the first impetus given to art handicraft by William Morris in England a feverish competition has sprung up in all countries to adorn the things around us—what we see, what we touch, what we wear.

Lallique has provided the fair sex with jewellery such as has not been seen since the great days of Florence: men like Bakst, Barbier, Marty, Iribe, Drian and Delvaille have been proud to design the clothes worn by fashionable women. The "Gazette du Bon Ton," the joint product of the artist and the refined dressmaker, jeweller, furrier, carriage and car builder, etc., will be made a mirror in which all arts are reflected. Here is no confusion of tints inevitable in photographic reproduction; but each picture, is hand-coloured exactly in imitation of the artist's original—a real picture, in fact, not a mere reflection of lifeless mannequins.

Besides gowns, every accessory to a woman's toilet is dealt with—lingerie, boots, parasols, veils and hats, fans, and also the carriages and motor cars in which the élégante drives, while children's and men's clothes are not neglected.

"The Gazette du Bon Ton" is an expensive publication, expensive to produce and expensive in its aim to be the true mirror of all that is smartest and most elegant in the social life of our day.

Two volumes have now been published, the third begins with the January number, and this is the first to be issued simultaneously in Paris, Berlin, New York and London.

Illustrated prospectus with specimen hand-coloured plate on application.

and the new company were financed with a debenture of £3,300. Elliot, who had 45 per cent of the shares, became managing director with a salary of £300 a year and the secretary was Heinemann's export specialist, C. A. Bang, who became increasingly involved with the medical list. It was already profitable in a small way, a net profit of £551 being returned by 1920.

Publishing in the Great War

The eve of the outbreak of the First World War found William in Leipzig on a visit to an international exhibition of books and graphic arts – he was responsible to the Board of Trade for the British section. It meant a hurried, difficult return home which is conveyed in these extracts from an account he wrote for the *World's Work*: 'I left German territory on the second day of mobilization. My experiences were interesting because, in command of their language, I was able to speak to many Germans in different stations of life and to witness conversations in hotels, cafés, &c. . . . Strolling through the crowded streets of Leipzig at night, I noticed a total absence of the military which is usually so prominent a feature in all German towns. There were few students to be seen in their gay caps – partly because not many remain at the University during the vacations, but principally, I was told, because the older among them are already *militärpflichtich* and had had to report just as the regular soldiers immediately on publication of the proclamation.

'In the Grimmaische Strasse there were thousands of people flowing up and down even at midnight, and there were endless little knots and groups – mostly girls and women – eagerly discussing the topic of the hour – all of them grave and concerned. There was a complete absence of laughter and all faces seemed set, either with grim determination or with a curious look of vacant apprehension. I heard no loud words and no music until about one in the morning when close to my hotel I passed a café from which came the sound of a patriotic song played by an orchestra and sung by many voices.'

He found the book exhibition to be empty, a 'city of deserted palaces', among them the 'beautiful little Tudor pavilion which had been set up in the heart of Germany, through its dignity and refinement a monument of British art and culture, standing apart from the garish exhibition houses round it'. He decided that he would be wise to return home. 'In the dining-car I sat at a table with two very young Germans of good family.

They were apparently aspiring artists living in Berlin . . . but they had both been called up and were on their way to take farewell of relatives. . . . They talked of Secessionist and Cubist painters, of art criticism and poetry. They quoted Oscar Wilde's remarks on the privileges of youth and they knew Bernard Shaw's works far better than I did. They drank one another's health in soda water, wished one another speedy promotion, and protested that they would go to the Front with no sense of danger and fear. . . . They had little doubt that war was coming and were certain of victory – if only one knew what England would do. It was inconceivable, they assured themselves, that the country of Wilde and Shaw would fight with the half-civilized hordes of Russia. Even if they did not join their German cousins as they should do, surely they would at least remain neutral. "Blood", they quoted, "is thicker than water".

'We got to Frankfurt three hours late. The platforms were littered with mountains of luggage, the station packed with the densest mass of people I have ever seen. . . . In the morning the station was in the hands of the military, but we left punctually and my only companions in the first-class carriage were an aged couple who insisted on having all windows closed though the heat was oppressive. . . . At the Belgian frontier we were marched out of the country through rows of soldiers to gain the Belgian train after walking two kilometres in pelting rain carrying our luggage.'

William's concluding impression was that the German nation had gone into the war with little enthusiasm, with no real hatred of her enemies, and with little knowledge of the possible consequences. 'I was told that the war was the work of the Kaiser and the military party. That a people so highly civilized, so honourable, should approve of the insult its Executive offered Great Britain in supposing that we should break our treaties and betray our allies for the sake of gaining their favour is inconceivable. If things don't go smoothly with the German armies and navy there is a horrible day of reckoning in store for the epileptic megalomaniac who has challenged the world.'[1]

For William with his German origins and friendships with so many civilized Germans, with his great love for France and Paris (which he considered to be his second home), the war and the complacent jingoism in London must have caused a particular bitterness and grief. There were days when the windows and door of 21 Bedford Street were plastered with horse manure and cabbage leaves and he became very conscious of his German name. During the first months, when exceptionally depressed, he even thought of changing it, but in other moods he declared that it was a name to be proud of, as much respected in the world of letters as that of Rothschild in the world of finance. F. Tennyson Jesse, a close friend who had already written her first novel for Heinemann – *The Milky Way* (1913) – and had been taken on as a reader, recalled that 'the war was the worst thing that ever happened to Heinemann. He was one of the people whom it made perfectly miserable and ill, and yet he conducted himself throughout it in a way that made his friends unhappy. He was a man with an arrogant mentality and, knowing he had a German name and German blood, he was determined not to appear over-anxious on the matter to his disadvantage. The result was that, in his anxiety to avoid the ultra-Britishness that so many men of German extraction flaunted during the war, he went, by a curious inversion of pride, to the other extreme. Though he was, I knew, perfectly loyal, he indulged in a good deal of rather foolish talk with the idea of showing that he was not afraid to be what he was and who he was, and so devoted were his friends – perhaps even misguidedly so – that instead of talking to him straightly we all combined to try and protect him from the difficulties in which he might have found himself. He took an almost impish delight in arguing that the Germans were the finest soldiers, and so on and so on, although I know no one who took the English reverses in the war more to heart than he did.'[2]

Essentially, though, William was strongly in favour of the war effort and even talked about 'Huns'. At a lunch party he gave early in 1914 he accused Walter Hines Page, the American ambassador, of being 'so damned neutral that you don't mind who beats the Germans'. His wartime lists also showed clearly where he stood. From the front line came five books by Philip Gibbs (later Sir Philip) who was among the best of the war correspondents. Gibbs describes in his memoirs how the first, *The Soul of War* (1915), was written when 'my own mind had been scorched by its flame. I was obsessed by the depths of the tragedy I had seen and haunted by the drama in the fields of France and Belgium, not knowing when I wrote it that there were still nearly four more years to go with increasing fury and increasing slaughter of which I was to be a witness and recorder. William Heinemann took a chance in publishing that book. It would not have been passed by military censorship, and to this day I don't know how it escaped that inquisition, for it was realistic and unsparing in its revelation of human agony in time of war by civilians as well as soldiers, and expressed views about war which to say the least of it were not in tune with official propaganda. "It's a dangerous book", said Heinemann over a dinner table to which he had invited me when I made a dash back to England from France and Belgium. He had an idea that we should both get in trouble about it, but he was willing to take the risk because he had read it, he said, with extreme interest and emotion.'[3] But nothing happened and the book was widely praised and after its publication Gibbs was appointed one of the five war correspondents on the Western Front. His next three war books were *The Battles of the Somme* (1917), *From Bapaume to Passchendaele* (1918), and *Open Warfare; the Way to Victory* (1919). Inevitably their approach was somewhat more subdued because of the military censor, but *Realities of War* (1920), written without hindrance, was a profound summing-up of an experience that had 'utterly changed him'. It was presented 'not only as a warning of what will happen again – surely – if a heritage of evil and of folly is not cut out of the hearts of peoples'.

John Masefield worked with the Red Cross in France and served in a hospital ship during the fearsome 1915 campaign in the Dardanelles. This led to *Gallipoli* (1916), in which he used to the full his narrative powers, though some felt he made too much of the horrors. It was also very successful in America and aroused much support for the Allied cause. He also wrote an account of the early fighting on the Somme, *The Old Front Line* (1917). Other war books included titles such as *Fighting in Flanders* (1914) by E. Alexander Powell; *Outwitting the Hun* (1918), by Lieut. Pat O'Brien; *On Active Service* (1914) by Major G. P. A. Phillips, furnished with a 'waterproof pocket-book and pencil, containing essential information for subordinate leaders'; *War Nursing* (1918), 'what every woman should know', by Charles Richet. There were also quite a few titles which discussed the politics and background to the war, such as *The Schemes of the Kaiser* (1917) by Madame Adam (Juliette Lamber); *Men around the Kaiser* (1913) by Frederick William Wile; and *Belgium under German Occupation* (1919) by Brand Whitlock, US Minister to Belgium. Notable also was the much read anonymous (W. B. C. W. Forester) *From Dartmouth to the Dardanelles* (1916).

Women, too, contributed to the war list. F. Tennyson Jesse left Bedford Street for France to write about the Women's Army in France, the WAACs, the FANYs, the VADs, without glamour or false heroics, but with considerable insight – later she became a regular contributor to the list, being perhaps best remembered for *A Pin to See the Peepshow* (1934).

There was also E. M. Delafield's study of women, *The War-Workers* (1918), which, though fiction, was tellingly realistic; and the first book by Enid Bagnold, *A Diary Without Dates* (1918), culled from her experience as a VAD in a wartime hospital. Much later she recalled in her *Autobiography* (1969), that 'the Royal Herbert Hospital when I was first there was staffed by old-time Sisters in scarlet capes who inherited from peace the idea that men in bed were malingerers. At the opening of the war men lived on meat and died on the gravy: there was no light diet. When a man died his bed was emptied, his mattress taken away to be disinfected. No attempt was made to see that the visiting parents didn't arrive to behold the empty wire of the bed. This attitude shocked me more than the plight of the men themselves. I kept a diary of such shocks. . . . When *A Diary Without Dates* was published, I was sacked from the hospital by the Matron in the first half-hour of my day.'[4] Her book caused a great stir and the *Daily Mail* backed up what she claimed with a leader. The firm had added a writer who would add lustre to its list throughout her long life. Next she went to France as a voluntary driver with the French army which led to a novel, *The Happy Foreigner* (1920), a love story set against the grim Armistice landscape of prostrate France. William's talent for recognizing quality was also shown by his signing up two of the most original war poets: Robert Graves with *Fairies and Fusiliers* (1917); and Siegfried Sassoon. William sent the latter, on leave from France, an enthusiastic handwritten letter accepting his first selection of poems, *The Old Huntsman and Other Poems* (1917). On publication day Sassoon was recuperating from a 'relatively unserious hurt' in a London hospital and a copy was sent by hand and William paid him a visit. There rapidly followed his *Counter-attack and Other Poems* (1918) and *The War Poems of Siegfried Sassoon* (1919).

Quite apart from specific wartime titles, books continued to be published and new authors taken on (see other chapters), but inevitably turnover declined during 1914–18. In 1915 it fell by a third to £42,507 and there was a loss of £269. No sales figures can be traced for the other war years, but by 1917 the firm was again able to report satisfactory annual profits (including partners' interest on their capital):

Profit

1915	£1,483
1916	1,574

Profit

1917	5,569
1918	8,168
1919	6,247

It will be seen that by 1917 things had really started to improve and for the rest of the decade results were well up to pre-war levels.

In the early war years publishers' economics were not seriously affected, but in the later stages the government restrictions on imports and sinkings by German submarines reduced the import of paper and esparto grass and prices started to soar. As the trenches demanded more men there were serious shortages of skilled labour in printing works and elsewhere. The Government set up a Royal Commission on Paper, charged with controlling its distribution, prices, and the import of raw materials, but it was ineffective so far as publishers were concerned. Its very existence frightened paper manufacturers into precautionary increases. In April 1916 Heinemann was appointed by the PA to prepare a report which he wrote with typical frankness. As well as establishing that paper prices had already doubled, he declared that 'in view of the fact that the Paper Commission has shown no sign of trying to alleviate, by careful husbanding of the national resources, the hardships inflicted through a national necessity, the conclusion is forced on me that the Commission is mischievous as far as the publishing business is concerned. Certainly it has failed in distributing evenly the burden of the War on all those concerned in the making and use of paper.'[5] Shortage of labour in the mills coupled with speculators made things even worse, so that by the Armistice prices had more than doubled again, though some years later they eventually fell, to settle somewhere near double pre-war prices. Shortage of other raw materials such as strawboard as well as of binding and printing staff also contributed to the rise in costs.

Eventually all this led to an increase in the price of the 6s. novel (for which the public paid 4s.6d.) to 7s. and 7s.6d. (on which the public received no discount). Despite this, in order to cover expenses, the publisher had to sell at least double the number of copies compared with before the war, whereas if he sold as few as 500/600 copies out of a first print of 1,000 he would still not suffer a loss, thus making it much easier to take a chance on an unknown author. After the war he needed to sell about

1,800 copies out of 2,000 printed to break even. For his business to be profitable, it was essential to have a proportion of bestsellers and plenty of reprints and cheap editions.

The shortages and the resulting economic factors of course affected Heinemann and he too lost male staff. De Grey, Dettmer, Reeves (in sales), Whyberd, and others left one by one for the Forces. Maddison was put on to munitions. At one point there were only two men left, apart from the two partners. They were the joint managers, C. A. Bang, who was Danish, and C. S. Evans, who in 1914, at the age of thirty-one, had joined the firm from Edward Arnold, the educational publishers; earlier he had spent five years as an elementary schoolmaster. He was also something of an author, writing *Nash and Some Others* (1920), various textbooks, and compiling for the firm *An Anthology of Patriotic Verse* (1914). But it was as an editor and publisher that he was destined to play a major part in the firm and that his greatness lay, as will be seen in succeeding chapters.

With the absence of men the firm depended more than ever on women. Mrs Whyberd, for example, took over from her husband at the trade counter and others took on unaccustomed roles. A formidable newcomer in 1918 was Louisa Callender. Very large, with chestnut hair, and a memory like a filing cabinet, even when young she had 'presence'. She soon became William's secretary and personal aide, and later worked for Pawling and C. S. Evans. It was to take many years, however, before she was elected to the board, or before women, so many of whom did so much to keep the firm afloat during 1914–18, began to take their rightful places in the firm.

As part of his personal war effort, William circulated documents such as the petition by his author Romain Rolland, to be signed by men of letters and artists against the wanton destruction of historic monuments by the Germans. Then the 1918 autumn list opened with a powerful *Plea for Books*, written by Edmund Gosse. William put the copyright at the disposal of other publishers. Its final paragraph read: 'If you do not intend to allow the tension of the war to harass your spirits beyond all endurance, temper that distress by the sedative of reading. At this moment, whatever is stinted and discouraged, the production and dissemination of literature ought to be directly protected by the State. What will be the profit to us if we gain the whole world and lose our own souls? So far from placing vain and tiresome obstacles in the way of the publication of literature, our rulers would be wise to take it under their special guardianship. There is no weakening of the national effort, there is no vain expenditure of material and of energy in keeping alive the generation of books. It is a national benefit to pour oil into the lamp by which the hunted spirit of Man may trace its path over the dark moorland to victory.'[6]

Heinemann's Encroaching Blindness and Sudden Death

For William the worst tragedy of the war was the death in action at Ypres of his cousin, Captain John Heinemann. He was twenty-six. Having no children of his own, William had taken him into the business in 1912 with the idea that he should one day take it over. He wrote a painful obituary for the *Publishers' Circular*. It reads like thousands of others written in those years, but it was none the less true and it conveys something of William's grief: 'His taste and critical faculty were remarkable for one so young, and his capacity for hard work and the taking of pains was quite out of the ordinary. His vitality was remarkable, and so was the energy with which he threw himself into anything he undertook to do. He thereby struck others sometimes as 'slapdash' and impetuous, but he had *flair* and therefore seldom went wrong, either in judgement or in "the pace of doing things".'

William explained how when John first enlisted in September 1914, he was three times rejected because of bad eyesight, but 'ultimately he found an unobservant oculist'. He won his commission within a month. 'He loved his men and was loved by them. His letters from the Front were full of concern about them, and of characteristic little touches of their intercourse. Like many others, he dreaded the hardships of trench life more than the enemy's bullets: "In the first line of all", he wrote, "the dug-outs had fallen in, and all the ground was a mere swamp. The officer's dug-out in which I reigned supreme was leaning at an angle of 65 degrees, and threatened me with imminent burial, while inside the only things showing above the flood was the top of the table, though underneath were a sandbag bed and, I believe, a couple of forms and several odd boxes. . . . But sticking on there was nothing to the agony of the communication trench leading back to the support line, which it took something over two hours to cross with half a company the night we were relieved. The mud sucked at your waders, and you were tired before you got your first foot out and were ready for the next step. The distance was something under 400 yards. . . .'[7] John Heinemann was shot through the brain while superintending a wiring party, and died as he was carried out of the trench.

Those who knew him well said that William never got over John's death. In the last years of the war, he worked as hard as ever, there were signs that his health was beginning to fail. He wrote bravely to Paul Warburg, who was looking after Dr Loeb's affairs, that 'my eyes are giving me a great deal of trouble (which is a serious matter for a publisher), but I have no difficulty in adapting myself to being read to when manuscripts come in which require particularly good sight. I have read manuscripts every night for thirty years and that has at last told on me, but I am now taking things very much easier and spending a lot of time in the open air. . . .'[8] Somerset Maugham recalled having noticed a book of braille in William's office. 'Oh yes, I am studying it while I still have the chance.' A friend, Theodore Byard, was engaged to read to him and help with his foreign correspondence. In July 1920 he went to Harrogate to take the waters and have medical baths, but the weather was so foul that he came home. Writing to Gerard Harry, a Belgian friend, to thank him for the part he had played behind the scenes arranging for William to be awarded the *palmes d'or* of the Belgian Crown for the 'conspicuous services' he had rendered to the Belgian cause during the war, he asked to be forgiven 'for practising the typewriter on you. I am learning to write on it, and levy from my friends the tribute of having to read my blunders – enemies won't. . . . I find my spelling goes to the dogs when I face the keys.'[9]

In the last months the decline in his general health became obvious to everyone, but he continued to work and to entertain. Fran Tennyson Jesse remembers how when she dined with him a week before he died and was trying to cheer him up, 'he had suddenly got really frightened about himself and his failing eyesight; and he seemed to be feeling better than he had for some time; but he said to me wistfully, "Do you think I shall ever be able to enjoy life again? That's what I want to know." And in that sentence you have the keynote to his life. . . . For he had the greatest enjoyment for the actual business of living of any man I ever met, and this enjoyment of his was so dependent upon other people, the other people in his vicinity, enjoying life also that as far as lay in his power he saw to it that they did. . . . No one who knew him well could ever forget him, and no one could ever fill exactly the place that he filled in the hearts of all of us.'[10]

His actual death was sudden and unexpected. On the 5th October when his valet, George Payne, went to call him at eight-thirty, he found him lying on the floor by the bed, which had been slept in. He was fifty-seven. At the inquest his doctor said that, although he had been suffering from a chronic nervous disease which would eventually have made him completely blind, the cause of death was a heart attack. An independent post-mortem showed that there was no question of suicide.

Tributes poured in and there were long laudatory obituaries. There was no doubt that British publishing had lost one of its greatest pioneers. His estate was valued at £33,780 with net personalty of £32,578; rather less than might have been expected but he had been generous all his life, travelled widely and lived very well. He left £500 to the Publishers Association as a reserve fund to meet any emergency where the interests of British publishers were threatened; £500 went to the National Book Trade Benevolent Fund, of which he had been President; Pawling inherited his personal papers and various pieces of silver donated by authors, including a Georgian cream jug and toast rack given by Whistler and bearing his butterfly; and there were other small legacies. Subject to the life of his mother and his two sisters, half of his residuary estate went to the Royal Society of Literature to establish The Heinemann Foundation of Literature which would give an annual prize up to £200 for a work of real worth. Fiction would not be 'excluded but the judges were requested to bear in mind that the testator's intention was primarily to reward classes of literature which are less remunerative, namely poetry, criticism, biography, history, &c.' One quarter of the income was intended for the payment of members of the jury. This prize is still regularly awarded and provides a most suitable memorial. But he will always be best remembered by the firm which still bears his name.

BOOK II:
1921–1945

8

Effendi to the Rescue

The sudden death of Heinemann created a void with threatening possibilities, not excluding that of the firm being absorbed by a rival nor even its total liquidation. As the surviving partner with forty-five per cent of the equity, Sydney Pawling had an option to purchase Heinemann's controlling share from his estate. But where was the money to come from? As it happened, a solution was found even before the funeral. Shortly before Heinemann's death the New York publisher F. N. Doubleday, together with his wife and son Nelson, had arrived in London and were looking forward to having dinner with William. They had also agreed to have a business meeting with him at 21 Bedford Street. On arrival there Doubleday was horrified to find a notice posted on the office front door, saying that Mr Heinemann had died during the night.

He found Pawling in a state of shock and when Doubleday enquired if there was anything he could do to help, both the uncertain future faced by the firm and Pawling's own financial problem gradually became clear. Above all Pawling needed to find someone he trusted to make use of his own option and purchase William's share. Would it by any chance be of any interest to Doubleday, Page & Co? It would give them control of the firm, but he would of course be prepared in practice to continue running it.

A deal was agreed, at least in principle, in a very short time. Later, Doubleday described it as the riskiest decision of his career. Without any previous experience of running an English publishing house and with little acquaintance with its executives apart from Pawling himself, to decide to take over the control of a business from the other side of the Atlantic was indeed an 'impulsive action which was far from sensible'[1]. On the other hand Doubleday possessed the shrewdness as well as the vision to recognize the value and great potential of what he was being offered. He had known William for nearly thirty years and, though they had frequently disagreed, they maintained a curious kind of friendship.

They had sold each other books and there was the continuing link provided by the *World's Work* magazine. In particular, he had a considerable respect for William's literary judgment – 'he had a faculty for picking the best and worst books in the literary market. A glance at the Heinemann catalogue shows how clever he was.'[2] It was a good bargain. William's share cost Doubleday £25,000, purchased in gold valued at $3.40 to £1.

An announcement of the new Anglo-American partnership was placed in the December issue of the *Bookseller*, emphasizing that 'Pawling retains control of the London business, and will continue the character and traditions of the firm obtaining during the past thirty years. . . . It is confidently hoped that this co-operation will prove an added benefit to the literature of both countries, and ensure an increasing output and opportunity for the works of British, American, and foreign authors.'[3]

The smooth words of the PR handout did not exaggerate. In character the two firms were not dissimilar, their main strength being soundly written books aimed at a large public, though this kind of generalization can be misleading because Doubleday had authors of the calibre of Kipling and Conrad to match the more intellectual parts of William's list. It was Kipling who had given Doubleday the nickname 'Effendi' by which he was always known. This play on his initials is a Turkish title meaning Chief. Doubleday, Page and Co. were a little younger than the Heinemann firm, being formed in 1897 first as Doubleday and McLure, the latter handling a magazine division. When McLure left to run Harper Bros, his place was taken by Walter Page. Several members of Effendi's family helped to run the firm, including his brother Russell, who was editor-in-chief, and his son Nelson, who was followed in turn by Nelson Doubleday junior.

The mutual advantages and the rationale that underpinned the transatlantic partnership were undeniably sound, and yet there was an immediate danger that several of the best Heinemann authors might leave because of the fear that the firm would lose its old identity and be ruined by Yankee efficiency methods and grasping commercial standards. Charles Evans warned Effendi that Galsworthy in particular was antagonistic to the takeover and had even advised Evans himself to look for another job. Americans, Galsworthy declared, were only interested in profits, though with Heinemann they were unlikely to achieve them. Evans had managed to persuade Galsworthy to suspend judgment and suggested that Effendi should meet him over lunch, in order to dispel his fears and to convince him that the imprint would remain unchanged, that no Americans would be joining the staff, nor would any English executives be asked to resign.

That meeting proved to be a turning-point. Doubleday recalled: 'I shall never forget that lunch as long as I live. It took place at the Automobile Club. I had just come off the deep and for almost the first time in my life had been deadly seasick; but the engagement was made and I was bound to keep it. Galsworthy was delightful. I did not tell him what I lived through from course to course; every moment I feared would be my last, and that my stomach would do me in. Fortunately, I became so much interested in talking with Mr Galsworthy about our plans, and he seemed so much interested in hearing of them, that I forgot about my stomach and dismissed it completely for the time being. Much to my gratification – and I have never ceased to be thankful for it – Galsworthy seemed to think that our plans were not foolish, and one of the most important literary people in England has been a faithful and helpful friend from that day to this. His influence was of overwhelming importance. . . .'[4]

Another lunch invitation from Jonathan Cape, who had recently established his own imprint, was less reassuring. Cape told him bluntly: 'You can hardly expect to make a success of your management of the Heinemann business; it will certainly fail, the conditions being entirely unfavourable, and I only want to tell you that, when you do fail, I stand ready to take it over.'[5]

A public inauguration of the new partnership took the form of a dinner at the Bath Club in honour of Arthur Page, editor of the *World's Work* in the USA and son of Doubleday's original partner, the late Walter Page, who had also served as a popular US ambassador in London during the World War. With turtle soup, Sole Princesse Olga, Tournedos Rachel, Poulet Souvaroff, Soufflé Marquise, and Paillettes Parmesanes, washed down with Lafite 1906 and Taylor 1904, no expense was spared. Literary London was well represented, as the guests were not limited to Heinemann authors and included Arnold Bennett, T. P. O'Connor, J. C. Squire, St John Adcock, Sir Hall Caine, Sir Arthur Pinero, Arthur Rackham, and relative youngsters such as Robert Graves and Siegfried Sassoon. There were even three agents present, including the formidable Pinker.

The main toast was proposed by Hall Caine with characteristic rodomontade: 'This is a gathering of the Heinemann clan, its chieftains, its captains, and its soldiers. I have belonged to it for thirty-one years. Indeed, I am the oldest surviving member. . . .' After a fulsome welcome to Arthur Page as a representative of a new kind of Anglo-American alliance, Caine went off at a tangent to expatiate on the currently gloomy state of authorship. Never had the commercial side of authorship been at so low an ebb. 'The enormous increase in the cost of manufacture, added to the limited range in the price which the public is able or willing to pay for books, has almost crushed authorship, as a profession, out of exist-ence. A little more and it would be quite extinguished, and literature would neither be a walking-stick, nor a crutch but something like a coffin.' Some great change in book publishing was needed, and he hoped that the new combination would bring this about.

Replying at even greater length and proposing Pawling's health, Arthur Page was expansive on the bonds that linked the two countries and spoke of a London club with four categories of members: Englishmen, Col-onials, Americans, and Foreigners. 'The principal export of this island is ideas, chiefly in printed form. Everyone in America reads British books. The British point of view is not foreign in the slightest to us. It is not only that the language is the same, but so far as books are concerned, the yearly ration of brain food is the same on both sides of the water. I was much struck the other day to see in Mr Pawling's records that ninety-five per cent of the books he published last year were also published in the United States. I do not believe that England takes the same high percentage of American books. But I recognize that custom, like large bodies, moves slowly. The continuous change of ideas – that is the tie that binds.'[6]

Pawling concluded with similarly warm sentiments and paid traditional tribute to the loyalty and support of his colleagues; but this proved to be false optimism, for in its early months the newly constituted firm was to be faced with some unnerving problems. Perhaps the worst was that Charles Evans, finding it difficult to get along with Pawling, was thinking of accepting the offer of an attractive job with Cassell's. He had confided in Edmund Gosse, who advised him to leave but to stand out for 'good and far-reaching terms for yourself. Don't slip out of the frying-pan into the fire. . . . Don't make yourself cheap. It is highly altruistic of me, I think, to encourage this move, for my affairs at 21 B.S. will go to rack and ruin when once you are gone! But I shall be heartily delighted if I can see you properly appreciated at last.'[7]

Gosse realized that Evans was by far the most important member of staff when it came to literary assessment and maintaining good relations with authors. Luckily Effendi had also discerned his value, but he had a hard time convincing him that he ought not to leave.

'Evans, if you stay, I will guarantee that you will be happy and your wife will wear diamonds.'[8]

Evans in the end relented on the basis of more generous terms and other conditions, and some years later Effendi was indeed to present his wife with a souvenir mounted with diamonds.

Gosse himself had also quarrelled with Pawling because of the sale in New York of some of his private correspondence with William. 'I thought it shocking,' he wrote to Evans confidentially, 'and so does everyone to whom I mention it. I waited for him to say something. He was silent, and so at last – without any heat or emphasis – I asked him to explain. After some delay, I received a letter from him in which he curtly declined (after "reflection", he said!) to give me any apology or explanation. I wish you to know this, because the matter may very possibly be misrepresented to you. This is all that has passed between Pawling and me, and I am sure you will understand how painful it is to me, after my long and confidential friendship with Heinemann, to have been treated in this way. At the same time, I do not want to prejudice you in any way, or to induce you to "take a side". I only want you to realize that I feel myself deeply injured, and that I cannot continue an acquaintance on these terms.'[9]

That one of the architects of the Heinemann list should feel like this was serious indeed, though in the end Gosse agreed not to desert it. The letters he referred to must have been part of the 'private papers and collection of autographs' left to Pawling in Heinemann's will 'absolutely for his sole and separate use but knowing that he will deal with the same with discretion and not publish any of the same prematurely'. Gosse's complaint suggested that other items in the firm's archive might also have been sold in New York. While researching this book, I eventually tracked down at the Grolier Society the catalogue of some five thousand letters addressed to William Heinemann auctioned at the American Art Association (later taken over by Sotheby's) in New York on Friday, 13 January 1922. In addition to eighty-one letters written by Gosse, which fetched $17.50, there were letters from James Barrie, Aubrey Beardsley, Max Beerbohm, Joseph Conrad, John Galsworthy, Thomas Hardy, W. E. Henley, Henrik Ibsen, Henry James, George Moore, Ouida, Bernard

Shaw, Leo Tolstoy, Oscar Wilde, James McNeill Whistler, and many others. Gosse had every reason to be affronted, particularly as the copyright in a letter belongs to the sender and not the recipient. A surprising number of the letters have been discovered at various American academic libraries, but what amounts to the heart of the firm's archive during its early years disappeared in that sale. One can also but wonder about the fate of the 'portfolios, diaries, biographical sketches and the manuscript and copyright of an unpublished Reminiscences' also willed to Pawling. Extensive enquiries have produced nothing, though there were rumours that they had been burnt.

Not long after this sale it became increasingly clear to his London colleagues that Pawling was not well. He was behaving strangely and everyone was on edge. Out of loyalty they hesitated whether to inform Effendi; but according to Doubleday's own account this was unnecessary: 'One day in the Spring of 1922 I was dressing, when a tremendous impression came over my mind which I have never been able to account for. My vision indicated that Pawling was sick and the whole Heinemann business in danger. I turned to Florence and said: "There is something the matter with Heinemann's; I think we had better take the next steamer and go over and find out what is wrong." This we did, and I telegraphed in advance to Pawling, hoping that he would play golf with me. When we arrived we found Byard, Charley Evans and Henry Roberts waiting for us at the train in a state of excitement. They said that Pawling, who was at the moment in a nursing home, had acted very queerly and put everyone on the qui vive, and they felt that they could not undertake to go on in the situation in which they found themselves; namely, that Pawling had the authority to order anything he chose, and they could not induce him to change his point of view, which they thought indicated nothing short of madness.'[10]

Pawling was under the medical care of Sir Thomas Horder, but he insisted on holding on to his position as head of the firm, even though it was obvious that it was now beyond his capacity. Diplomatically, with Horder's help, an arrangement was made by which he was prevented from doing the firm serious harm, and this was to operate until he had fully recovered. He never did. His condition deteriorated and he died at the age of sixty-one on 23 December 1922. He was buried in Hampstead, not far from the cricket ground where he was once said to have developed into the fastest bowler in England. Obituaries in *The Times*, *The Sunday Times*, and the trade Press paid tributes to his popularity as well as his capability as a publisher. Doubleday maintained that secretly Pawling hated Heinemann, but the *Publishers' Circular* probably summed up the essence of their relationship more accurately: 'There could hardly have been a more ideal partnership. Pawling had a steadiness of aim and a fine business instinct which was a good balance to his partner's brilliance. . . .'[11]

A Limited Company – Byard Succeeds Pawling

Before Pawling's death the partnership had been transformed into William Heinemann Ltd with an authorized capital of £80,000, divided into 35,000 participating preference shares and 45,000 ordinary shares. Doubleday, Page & Co. had owned £22,500 ordinary and Pawling £18,000 preference. Pawling's shares (less £2,000 which he had borrowed) were purchased by Doubleday to give his widow a gross sum of £16,000 plus £1,600 by way of interest for 1923. This meant that after two years the firm had become an American subsidiary, apart from £5,000 invested by its English directors.

Meanwhile, despite the two deaths, a stagnant book market, and a damaging strike throughout the trade over a five shillings a week wage reduction, the firm prospered during the early 1920s. Several of the authors enlisted by William were still at the top of their form, including John Masefield, Somerset Maugham, and John Galsworthy. The only author of note to leave (for Cassell) was Hall Caine, whose *The Master of Man*, his last Heinemann title, had an initial print of 100,000. The loss of William's very first author, whose swashbuckling popular yarns sold literally in millions and one of whose titles, *The Deemster*, had by then achieved fifty-two editions, was a commercial disaster, but it did not worry Doubleday: '. . . of all the bores and thick-headed idiots that I ever knew, he took the palm. His books were entirely out of key with the whole Heinemann business, but they had been very successful and the profits, I think, induced Heinemann with his thrifty mind to keep on with Hall Caine, especially as poor Pawling had to do all the dirty work. I had several interviews with Caine, and Nelson did some talking, and we were both convinced that his material would be less valuable as time went on, and in any event would not add to the dignity or the quality of our list.'[12]

With Effendi as chairman, the board of the newly formed William Heinemann Ltd now consisted of Charles Evans, with the curious title of Secretary – though he later became Managing Director; Arthur Page; and a relative newcomer, Theodore Byard, who was put in overall charge and eventually had the title of 'Resident Chairman'. Byard had next to no experience of publishing, having previously been a successful professional singer as well as serving as a subaltern in India and during the Great War. Through his music and love of painting and literature he had become a very close friend of William who, knowing him to be a good linguist, had in 1920 invited him to join the firm and help out with the foreign department which, because of his failing eyesight, he could no longer deal with personally. A tall, imposing figure with swept-back greying hair, private means – which included a weekend cottage in Milford, Surrey and a house in Venice complete with gondola – it is understandable why Effendi singled him out for the top London job. Very much a man of the world, Byard must have exuded reliability and could be expected to act responsibly on his own and, when necessary, decisively. He made a good partner for the creative, mercurial, highly strung Evans. Indeed they seem to have worked well together, sharing decisions about the day-to-day running of the business and, at least in the early years, about commissioning titles. By means of monthly reports and budgets they maintained regular contact with New York which was strengthened by personal visits in both directions; these also helped to familiarize them with Doubleday procedures and managerial methods which were far more meticulous than anything the English firm had been used to.

Faced with accounting realities, Effendi was quick to realize that the firm's finances were decidedly 'shaky and by no means conservatively managed'.[13] More money had to be ploughed in – a total of $140,000 by mid-1923 on which no interest was paid. The firm's own bankers refused to help, but it was borrowed without any difficulty from another bank with which Doubleday ran an account, though Effendi was astonished by the old-fashioned and amateur banking methods compared with New York, including the use of cumbersome two-foot-square, thousand-page ledgers instead of cards. When giving a promissory note for £10,000, Effendi was asked to sign a lengthy printed form, part of which he found to be unintelligible. The bank manager, not having read it for twenty years, also failed to understand it. The bank's legal expert was summoned but he was out at lunch and another employee was brought in who was equally baffled. In the end the manager suggested it would be simpler to cross the passage out.

A Doubleday expert came over to help B. F. Oliver, the cashier, to reorganize his accounting methods and to tighten up the office organization. The book stock was depreciated by £8,000. Salaries were increased, particularly of the humbler staff, and this brought its own reward in greater output. For the senior staff Effendi wanted to introduce a 'Net Results Club' as was operated in New York, which would share five per cent of the profits between five or six heads of departments; regular dinners would be held at which they could talk about the business and divide the money up equally. To his surprise the proposal met with little enthusiasm and it took Effendi nearly a year to unearth the reason:

'It seems that among these people there were various classes; one man regarded his social position as more important than that of another; and I finally discovered, after many conversations, that they objected to the whole scheme because everybody was put on the same basis. I was frankly appalled to discover this situation, but accepted it and said nothing; and the matter was dropped and no Net Results Club was started'[14]. A year later, however, Effendi learned that the senior staff now regretted their negative reaction and the club was started after all.

It must have been difficult for an American to grasp the strength and complexity of the class differences among the Heinemann staff, and how often these impeded the smooth running of the business. Once Oliver confided to Effendi that in his opinion Britain was a nation of snobs: '"For instance, a man in a high position with a title would snub Mr Pawling; Mr Pawling, being the head of our business, would snub me; and I, being the head of a department, would snub my inferiors. I think it is important", he said, "that you should realize this, because it accounts for so much that otherwise you would not understand."'[15]

Effendi also recalls how at Bedford Street 'a certain head of department came into my office one morning in his usual respectful manner. According to custom, he would not take a chair unless I invited him to do so, so he stood before me and said that he had something private about which he wished to talk with me. When I asked what it was, he said that a certain head of another department had sent a messenger asking him to come and call upon him in his office in another part of the building. "I regard this as an impertinence", he said, "as my social position is infinitely superior to his".

'"Sit right down", I said, "and I will go and see our friend and find out what he wants".

'His embarrassment was naturally intense, but I forced him into a seat, went to see the man who had the suggestions to make, talked them over with him, and brought back the message to the department head who had been so touchy.'[16]

At Christmas every member of staff received an extra week's salary and a dinner was held attended by everyone from Theodore Byard down to the most junior packer, sitting and eating together on at least outwardly equal terms. Arnold Gyde, then head of the editorial department, recalls his first Heinemann Christmas dinner in 1923 at the Florence Restaurant, Wardour Street. As the office closed at six and the dinner did not begin until eight, most of the men spent the interregnum in the pub and were well away when they sat down with a bottle of red wine and white wine in front of each place. Mr Byard 'pronounced a discourse which was warmly cheered, but no one could make head or tail of it when the shorthand notes of it were deciphered the following morning. Then Charley [Evans] sat down before a funny little piano and gazed at the copy of the song which Sophie [Gyde's wife, Sophie Wyss, who became a celebrated singer] was going to sing, blinked twice, and closed the music with a smile. It was far too late to read complicated notes. In the end I think they contented themselves with *Home Sweet Home*. . . .' As with many office parties attended by normally respectable staff unused to high living and the sudden release from customary restraints, the evening ended in messy debauchery. 'A lot of the fellows had no memory at all of what happened. Many passed out. Ernest Whyberd, then manager of the packing and dispatch department, improvised a sort of stretcher squad, had the chaps carried out feet foremost and laid out in an adjoining room. . . . One was so ill that they dared not send him home, but took him back to the office and laid him out on Charley's sofa.'[17]

Skeletons in William's Cupboard

Among a number of skeletons in William's private cupboard was a personal agreement between him and James Loeb over the subsidizing of the prestigious Loeb Classical Library. This showed clearly that Loeb had been wrongly charged with expenses which were not his liability to the extent of some £3,000. Sam Everitt, a senior Doubleday executive, wrote asking if Loeb could be assuaged by the reimbursement of half this sum, but Byard felt strongly that it would be wiser to come clean and pay the whole debt. 'I can assure you that this job has been one of the most unpleasant and difficult I have ever undertaken; in fact, the prospect of tackling Loeb about it made me positively ill and I had to put off going for a week. . . .' Byard had decided that it would be easier to see Loeb in person and travelled to St Moritz where he was then living. 'After the first shock had passed over, I did tentatively suggest that possibly lawyers might consider that we were not technically responsible for the strange performance of W. H. Loeb immediately took this up and said this might be so, but no honourable firm like Doubleday, Page & Co would consider falling back upon such technicalities in a big question of morals such as this. I therefore shut up.'[18] Loeb was therefore paid back the full £3,000 in six annual instalments and the Classical Library continued to flourish under the editorship of T. E. Page and W. H. D. Rouse, who were joined by Professor E. Capps of Princeton. Putnam continued to distribute the Library in the States. By the end of the decade it had expanded to 200 volumes.

Another continuing problem was the pressure from literary agents for unrealistic advances linked with threats to withdraw authors. William's long-standing quarrel with Watt was supposed to have been made up, but he continued to make authors restless. Denis Mackail had been advised straight out to leave, being tempted by offers of larger advances. Difficulties over Maurice Baring's new contract were such that Byard feared that he too would be lost. The younger members of the Watt family were brazen, one of them telling Evans that if he thought they could persuade Galsworthy to move, he would try to do so at once.

Effendi was, however, firmly against big advances. Pleased with sales for 1922 of £133,000 (compared with £71,000 for 1913 and a wartime £43,000 in 1915) he wrote – aboard S.S. *Olympic* during a gale – that he was convinced that this change for the better 'came not through going out and buying authors by large advances in a scramble for the very latest, but mostly by organization of the selling side of the business – which brings me to the point of my publishing philosophy; namely, that the fashion of letting Brown (who thinks us back numbers) and other literary agents and often authors push us into speculative advances doesn't fill the bill and bring lasting success. In all my talks I did not hear once of any publisher who had the reputation of getting twice as many sales out of a given book as any other publisher, but always of a publisher who paid twice as much percentage of royalty, or twice as much advance, or both. These are the literary agents' heroes.

'If this is true, and I believe it is, we have a chance of developing our market for a comparatively small list to the limit of sale, to make a reputation along rather different lines and more substantial ones. I have no figures by me, but I believe that the money and effort we have put into the expansion of the selling and pushing has cost us not more than half what the big advances would have come to and yielded twice as much. Then, too, if we had followed the Curtis Brown line, our statement would have looked very different. Our stock would have been less clean and our position not nearly so healthy and encouraging.'[19]

Effendi certainly had little time for agents and once remarked that the relationship between agent and publisher was the same as that between knife and throat. Evans, while trying to keep relationships with agents sweet, would probably have agreed. He was particularly adamant on the need to preserve unhampered contacts between publisher and author. 'I have never yet admitted,' he wrote to Eric Pinker, 'and I never will admit, even though a book is accepted from an author through an agent, that a publisher must hold all communication with that author through the agent, except in matters connected with terms and the payment of royalties. On this latter point I never transgress . . . even though the author himself raises such matters with me. . . . The amount of money to be spent on advertising and the details of that advertising are matters for the publisher himself to decide, and if the author has any observations to make or suggestions to put forward, they should rightly be put forward to the publisher direct, and not through the agent, whose function begins and ends, it seems to me, with the transaction of the author's financial affairs. I feel this so very strongly that if there were any general tendency among the agents to step into the intimate details of the publisher's business I should think it a matter for serious consideration by the Publishers Association.'[20]

After eighteen months' trading Effendi was convinced that the Heinemann annual list tended to be too large and was carrying too many titles over which capital and publishing effort were spread too thinly. While he had ambitions, even visionary long-term plans for Heinemann, he was against any immediate expansion. This seemed to relieve Byard, who replied: 'I should never have volunteered to suggest going slowly, unless it had originally come from you as I should have feared your putting it down to our humdrum, sticky old English ways; but now that you have made the suggestion and ask my opinion about it, I want to say that it comes to me as a relief. This endeavour to increase the size of Heinemann's rapidly has always seemed to me dangerous. Our reputation is that of a quiet, distinguished firm which has not gone in for huge undertakings such as are associated with Cassell's and Hodder's.'[21]

A brake on expansion was the increasing cost of production. The firm's cost of sale in 1922 was 42.4 per cent, which was then considered much too high; but all publishers were suffering from a considerable rise in basic costs compared with the halcyon days before the war. Writing to *The Times* in July 1921, Geoffrey Williams, President of the Publishers Association, pointed out that 'the cost of printing is approximately two and three-quarter times what it was in 1914, paper (of an inferior quality) costs over double what it did in 1914, binding (also of an inferior quality) costs rather more than three times what it did in 1914, while the total cost of a large edition of a small book works out at about 180 per cent above the 1914 figure, and publishers' establishment charges and the cost of advertising have kept pace with other items in their upward course'. He ended by complaining that 'wages are the dominant factor, and unless they fall, not by a mere 10 or 20 per cent, but by a substantial amount, it is impossible to hope for any material reduction in the price of books'[22].

The public of course complained that book prices were too high. The standard pre-war price of 4s.6d. for a novel had now become an almost standard 7s.6d. Opening a discussion on 'Are Book Prices Too Cheap?' at the recently formed Society of Bookmen, Charles Evans seemed to disagree with the President of the Publishers Association. He suggested that 'the question might fairly be asked, "Can a book ever be too cheap?" He would reply that if the price made it necessary that producers of all grades employed in its production were insufficiently paid, it certainly might be. This was no doubt in some cases the fact before the war. At the same time, if the public had enough money to buy books, the price within certain limitations was not the most vital element in their circulation. If books were cheaper, more might be sold, but if the prices were higher the standard might be higher. Publishers were certainly not to blame for high prices, for publishing was perhaps the most unremunerative of businesses which required similar knowledge and ability. . . . After all, books had not been increased in price as much as other things. He thought that today the market for books was greater than ever. It was not likely that books would ever again be as cheap as they were before the war, for increased costs were lessening very slowly and it was unlikely and undesirable that wages would ever fall to the pre-war level.'[23]

For the first time in sole charge, in conjunction with Byard, of what was to be published, Evans did not find it difficult to agree with Effendi that the firm was publishing too many unprofitable titles. He provided a telling analysis of each category of title published during the eighteen months between January 1922 and June 1923:

Novels: In the course of a year out of 57 new titles, 9 made a net profit, after charging 30 per cent of sales revenue to overheads; 29 made a gross profit, which in some cases approximated to the 30 per cent overhead and in other cases fell a good deal away from it; 19 books made a dead loss. Some of the losses would probably eventually be made good, but there were quite a few which should never have been taken.

Plays: Out of 13 plays published, 3 made a profit; 2 came home; and 8 were a dead loss. The profit makers were Flecker's *Hassan*, Macleod's *Immortal Hour*, and a play by Masefield. The lesson to be learned was that, apart from very exceptional circumstances, plays should never be published.

Poetry: Out of 20 books of poetry, 2 made a profit (both by Masefield); 9 came home; and 9 were a dead loss.

Limited editions: Thirteen out of 14 titles made a profit.

Translations: All 8 non-fiction titles made a loss. Translated fiction was equally unprofitable. The lesson to be learned was that, if there were ever any money in translations, that time had gone by.

Travel: Out of 9 titles, 4 made a profit; 4 came home; and 1 made a loss.

Biography and Memoirs: Out of 13 titles, 6 made a profit; 4 made good; and 3 made a loss.

During 1922 altogether 129 titles were published, of which 32 made good money – £2,882 out of total profits of £5,335, including backlist. In other words 25 per cent of the books published made 52 per cent of the profits. Evans summed it all up: 'It is clear that we must not go out to get a greater turnover merely by publishing more books. I realize fully that in the case of the books that have made a loss, not only is the loss to be paid, but also the amount of time which has been expended in the manufacturing, sales, publicity, and other departments . . . in future we must raise our standard, publish fewer books and better ones, and especially devote more attention to the selling of those books we do publish.'[24]

Many of the books in this analysis must have been commissioned in Heinemann's day, but this kind of hard-nosed thinking was to have an influence on the publishing programme of the next few years. William's brilliance, his bravado and enthusiasm for what he felt was worthwhile was to give way gradually to safer publishing, centred on a broad core of readable middle-class, middle-brow fiction, though the annual total of new titles (and new editions) showed only a temporary decrease (viz: 1921 – 92; 1922 – 117; 1923 – 136; 1924 – 112; 1925 – 98; 1926 – 96; 1927 – 100; 1928 – 159; 1929 – 226; 1930 – 212). However clearly defined – and in practice this is almost impossible – a publisher's list can often turn out to be very different from his intentions. With good luck his hopes for its quality may be exceeded or with bad luck frustrated. There is always the chance of the unexpected masterpiece and the book that becomes a bestseller for no very discernible reason. In the years which followed among Heinemann's large and varied lists these truisms were substantiated.

The World's Work and Frere-Reeves

London's relationship with New York was on the whole very amicable and the major decision-making was smooth, though often Byard's correspondence sounded sycophantic and was overlarded with flowery expressions of adulation which may have cloaked his own insecurity in running what was still an unfamiliar business. But there were occasions which caused strong differences of opinion and on which Byard did not hesitate to write frankly and to stand his ground. One of these arose over the British edition of *The World's Work* magazine which, though still influential, was ailing financially, with a circulation of 7–10,000. It needed greater attention. Since 1913 it had been an independent company – with Henry Chalmers Roberts, who owned forty-nine per cent of the shares, as chairman and managing director as well as editor; but in 1920, despite having moved next door to 20 Bedford Street, its affairs were inevitably entwined with those of the main firm, Byard and Evans being also World's Work directors. With a good deal of logic Effendi suggested in mid-1923 that the magazine should come completely under Heinemann's control; he was particularly worried lest it should grow into an expensive separate organization. The alternative to incorporation, he suggested, could be to sell the magazine or close it down. Byard strongly resisted all three possibilities, especially incorporation. He knew that Chalmers Roberts could be very tiresome and was noted for shouting at the staff, and Byard admitted frankly that 'his personal relationships with Roberts are, to say the least of it, unpleasant and difficult'[25]. The burden of the magazine's losses falling on Heinemann was completely unacceptable and he was particularly concerned over the additional strain it would mean for Evans, as he explained to Arthur Page: 'I do not know whether you and the rest of the Garden City people realize how very much the running of this business depends upon Evans – that is to say our department of it – mine and his. There is as yet no one below him capable of taking his place should he be ill, and since you have been away we have had several instances of the great gap existing between him and the next person. Evans has had a great deal of illness at home and has been unable to depute work here which he should have been able to give to someone else. He has worn himself out until he is in a very nervous condition.' He went on to deplore any further involvement by Evans or himself because it 'would be a continual worry and nervous strain so long as Roberts is part of the combination'[26].

Byard won the argument and The World's Work continued as a separate unit, though steps were taken to improve the magazine's quality. Its title was changed to *The World Today*; Alan Bott became managing editor under Roberts; and later Arnold Bennett was enlisted as editorial consultant. The separate company's turnover was increased by taking on the UK distribution of a handful of pulp publications, mostly from the Doubleday stable. With titles such as *Frontier Stories*, *West*, *Health Builder*, *Great War Adventures*, *Tales of Wonder*, *The Master Thriller* series, and a fortnightly collection of short stories, they were decidedly downmarket but they made money. They would never have been tolerated under the Heinemann imprint, but they set a pattern and were the forerunners of many book titles which the main firm itself would have been ashamed to publish but could not afford not to. The chief credit for the success of this new enterprise went to the newly appointed business manager at The World's Work, Alexander Frere-Reeves.

As a future Heinemann chairman, under the name he later adopted of A. S. Frere *tout court*, the somewhat bizarre manner of his appointment is not without relevance. It was at a luncheon party given by Countess Russell, the author of bestselling *Elizabeth and her German Garden*, that Frere-Reeves first met Effendi, who was her American publisher, though Macmillan published her in the UK. Frere-Reeves, after a tough war in the Suvla Bay landing in Turkey and as a pilot in the Royal Flying Corps, had taken a degree at Cambridge where he had edited *Granta* and was then working in a junior capacity in the features department of the *Evening News*. As Frere-Reeves described it, 'the company at the luncheon was very grand and as well as Doubleday it included Bernard Shaw and John Middleton Murry. Shaw inevitably monopolized the conversation, though their hostess was adept at puncturing his comments whenever she felt like it. At the end of the meal Effendi asked me if I knew anything about book publishing. I shook my head.

'"Well, that makes two of us – at least I know nothing about English publishing, though I have just committed the indiscretion of buying a London publishing firm. Elizabeth has spoken warmly about you and as neither of us know anything about it, how would you like to join me and see if we can make a go of it?"

'Taken aback, I wasn't sure if he was joking, but it sounded an attractive idea. I asked if I could think it over.

'"You won't have much time for that, because I sail for New York tomorrow morning. Let me know this evening. At Brown's Hotel."

Back in Fleet Street, his editor tried to dissuade him, but Frere-Reeves had already decided to chance his luck. He was shown up to Effendi's suite at the hotel where he was alone with his wife Florence and J. M. Barrie.

'"This young man, Barrie, is going to join me in running Heinemann. What d'you think of that?"

'Barrie put on a remote, fawn-like act of being startled. "Know nothing about him." Barrie gazed at me, "But he is exceedingly fortunate."

'I asked politely how Effendi could be so sure I had decided to accept, but he brushed this impatiently aside. "Of course you have! Otherwise you wouldn't have turned up." There were so many questions I wanted to ask, particularly about salary, but Effendi obviously felt the interview was over. "Just go round to 21 Bedford Street. Ask for Mr Evans. He'll fix you up. I've told him about you and he'll be expecting you."

Evans wasn't, and John Dettmer behind the counter announced that he never saw anyone without an appointment, but eventually Frere-Reeves was admitted. 'Charley was sitting at an incredibly untidy desk. His cold blue eyes gave me an unfriendly stare. He was Welsh to the backbone. What then did I want? I asked if he had heard from Mr Doubleday.

'"What have you been saying to Mr Doubleday?" Disconcerted, I replied that I didn't remember saying anything to him except that I would take the job going at Heinemann's. "Oh, he offered you a job, did he? Well, you need to know that the only person in a position to hand out jobs is myself. What's more, I have nothing for you."

'"But Mr Doubleday seemed to think that I could start fairly soon – even right away."

'Evans then asked what I knew about publishing and I had to admit that it was very little. "In that case there's no more to be said. Doubleday is now on the Atlantic and, besides, he has no say on what goes on in this office – at least not yet. Good day to you."'[27]

This was the appalling start to what was to be an unhappy and difficult relationship lasting over twenty years. Apparently jobless, Frere-Reeves stumbled out into Bedford Street, running almost literally into the arms of H. Chalmers Roberts, whom he already knew. When told of Frere-Reeves's plight, he took him for a comforting lunch at the St James's club. He confirmed that he would never get a job out of Evans, who was worried about his own future and knew little of what was going on. Roberts, however, promised to try and fit Frere-Reeves into the World's Work company, not on the magazine itself, but perhaps helping to increase the sale of the various pulp publications which were in effect dumped surplus copies left from Doubleday's print runs. If the UK sale of any of them could be pushed over 10,000, it would be enough to justify importing plates and print over here with a more satisfactory profit.

Despite Frere-Reeves's newspaper experience and his editorship of *Granta*, it was clear that Roberts was not going to admit an ambitious potential rival near the editorial chair. It was therefore, for the moment at any rate, starting on the road as a rep. or nothing. Provided with a motorbike with a coffin-shaped sidecar capable of holding several hundred sample copies, Frere-Reeves set out to visit wholesalers and newsagents on tours covering the whole of England and Wales, and Scotland as far as Edinburgh. His efforts were very successful and helped to establish pulp literature as a permanent part of the firm's list.

When Effendi was next in London, Frere-Reeves complained that he had been misled, but he was assured that there would still be a place for him in the main firm. After a week of accompanying Mrs Doubleday on a round of literary parties he was told to follow them back to New York on the *Berengaria*, so that he could learn the basic techniques of publishing and the methods used at the Country Life Press at the Garden City. There he found himself sharing a desk with Ogden Nash, then a Doubleday reader, and over several months gained first-hand experience of printing, binding, packing and dispatching, promotion and accounting. Weekends were often spent at Effendi's home at Oyster Bay and he made good friends with the key Doubleday executives.

When he returned to London it was therefore as Effendi's protégé and, despite a frosty welcome from Evans and Byard, he became World's Work's business manager; by early 1924 he was playing a big role in Heinemann as well, including the sales department, then in the charge of an old hand, C. E. Reeves. Frere-Reeves's progress was facilitated by the departure of C. A. Bang. Despite Bang's twenty-two years' service, latterly as Joint General Manager, and his recent award of the OBE, Byard, and possibly Evans as well, decided that they now had no use for him. Getting rid of Bang was unpleasant and nearly led to litigation, but his lawyers eventually agreed to a basic severance payment of £1,200.

A strengthened sales and promotion department was organized with four representatives on the road. Leslie Munro, the London traveller and a future sales director, was understudy to C. E. Reeves, whose health was not good. Munro was also involved in setting up the Book Publishers' Representative Association (BPRA). Effendi believed that more turnover could be squeezed out of the list and advocated that the advertising budget be increased. In 1923 it was 3.6 per cent of turnover, compared with Doubleday's own ratio of 6.1 per cent. He was particularly keen on opening up new markets as well as expanding existing ones.

Resisting Effendi's continuous pressure for more sales, Byard would sometimes seek refuge in the different approaches to life in the two countries. 'It does seem to me that with your American policy – undoubtedly a very fine one – of developing the organization first at considerable expense, you must expect a considerable time to elapse before the sales go up in ratio to the increased expenditure. The English system – doubtless old-fashioned and contrary to all American ethics – is to increase sales gradually and let the organization develop as the sales come in. I am only pointing this out as it has been at your suggestion, both here and in World's Work, that these increased expenditures to which you refer have been incurred. We should never have had the courage to do it on our own account. Increased sales cannot come so quickly in this old country as in America, and you must therefore expect the results of your fine organizing schemes to be longer in realization than on the other side of the Atlantic.'[28]

Effendi continued to promote Frere-Reeves's interests, suggesting in 1925 that he should finally leave The World's Work and become an understudy to Byard and Evans. They continued to prevaricate, arguing that The World's Work still needed him, but after Frere-Reeves had paid another long visit to the Garden City Effendi tactfully but firmly made clear who was boss. 'While he was over here we have devoted a great deal of time and study to putting before Frere-Reeves all the essential problems of the publishing business, and you know that our ideas are somewhat different from those held by most publishers. He has been a willing scholar, and from my point of view has learned a great deal. I should like to feel that I have your co-operation, which is absolutely necessary, in taking him in the camp when he gets home. . . . He has a very great love for good books which should stand him in good stead; and under your helpful suggestion I am sure he will develop in a way which will give you all satisfaction. Of course, as you know, I feel that there are no bounds to the success that Heinemann can achieve, provided always that we have an organization which represents the spirit and enthusiasm to carry it to greater glory. Pardon these Fourth of July expressions, but they really mean a lot to me.'[29] It took until 1928, but by then Frere-Reeves was so well dug in that he was elected a member of the Heinemann board.

The Medical Company Retained

Another difference of opinion with Effendi arose over the future of the medical company, also run from 20 Bedford Street. A majority interest having been purchased from Rebman in 1913, it was managed by Hugh Elliott, who owned the other forty-five per cent of the shares. Its list was small but, despite the war years, Elliott had by 1923 converted a pre-war loss into a reasonably satisfactory annual turnover of £12,000, though part of this came from the sale of lymph for vaccination against smallpox! Elliott would have liked, in conjunction with Bang, with whom he was very close, to buy out Heinemann's shares and Effendi was in favour of getting rid of a small company whose future he considered hazardous. He also disliked not owning all of it, because this meant that Heinemann received only fifty-five per cent of profits but would in practice have to stand the whole of any losses. Byard was bitterly opposed to the sale, arguing cogently that the medical company admirably fulfilled William's plan to widen the firm's list and give them a footing in a scientific discipline, an activity, what's more, that 'did something solid for the benefit of mankind . . . to lop off this part of our business at the present time is bound to give rise to talk – and you can take it from me that Bang would not go out of his way to combat any gossip against our interests.' The medical company was doing very nicely, making a profit, and becoming increasingly well regarded by scientific opinion. Why sell it? 'If the medical company were to go, it would, in my opinion, be advisable to start another.'[30]

This time it was Effendi who gave in and the medical company in its relatively small way continued, with ups and downs, to flourish. What would turn out to be a significant step was the appointment of Dr Johnston ('Barney') Abraham, a well-known surgeon and author of the bestselling *The Surgeon's Log*, as an adviser. As so often happens, it was the result of a casual remark when Evans was lunching with Abraham at the Savage. As

Barney remembers it: 'Charley had just come back from the Isle of Man, completely exhausted by Hall Caine, who for years used to insist on his going over there for a month at a time, tidying up his latest novel. It was a custom started in Willie Heinemann's time, and Willie had always grudgingly agreed to it because Hall Caine was a bestseller. The one person who wasn't considered by either at the time was Charley. And now it seemed, though Heinemann was dead, Charley himself was still carrying on of his own accord. I remember saying to him:

'"You know, Charley, you should watch that chap Hall Caine. In one of his novels, *The Christian*, I think, there was a chapter where the nurses held a dance in the operating theatre! Shades of Lister – an operating theatre! What a blah! What you want is a medical adviser to protect you from bloomers like that, now that Willie's gone and you're in the saddle."'[31]

This led to Abraham being invited to visit Bedford Street twice a month to give advice on medical manuscripts and offers of medical books. His visits became more and more frequent until in 1931 he became a director of the medical company and eventually, in 1942, its chairman and managing director.

9

The Building of the
Windmill Press

By 1925 Effendi's health was beginning to fail; it was to fluctuate severely
for the rest of his life, but his imaginative energy never weakened. He
combined a talent for 'thinking big' with knowing what was practicable.
Above all he was determined to create a British equivalent to the Country
Life Press at Garden City, Long Island. Conditions at Bedford Street
were unpleasantly cramped. A move to larger central London premises
would inevitably mean an increase in overheads. What about moving to
the edge of London instead? Effendi's answer was to have two new
premises – town and country – though, first, he had to wear down not
unexpected caution from Byard and Evans. The advantages of moving to
the country, within an hour's journey from central London, were summarized as: office space would be much cheaper and working conditions
would be superior; despite extra costs for deliveries, so would warehouse
space and there need be no limit to expansion; against this, contact with
authors would be more difficult and Evans at least would need to be in
London on two or three days a week.

The decision to start the firm's own printing works and bindery was on
an altogether different scale. This had obvious attractions and in theory
books could be produced more cheaply, but to erect a plant with sufficient
capacity would mean a sizeable investment. Experience at Country Life
suggested, however, that a well-managed press could be very profitable in
its own right. The whole venture – press, warehouse, and offices – would
entail raising an additional £100,000, and it was decided to increase
capital partly in the form of preference shares. Anything more could be
borrowed from Doubleday, Page and Co.

An earlier plan was to start a small 'private' press, producing a few
high-quality books, employing only four or five men, similar to the
Kelmscott and Fanfrolico presses, and to this end in 1925 a period house
called Well Farm, near Banstead, Surrey, was actually purchased, but
the scheme proved unworkable because it was impossible to obtain

permission for even such a small industrial development from the local rural district council. Typically, it was the failure of this scheme which fired Effendi with the idea of the infinitely bigger press, the private one being forgotten and Well Farm sold. A thirty-acre site was found a few miles away where there were no planning objections. Heavily wooded with beech, oak, and elm, astride a small down, slap in the middle of what was to become the Green Belt, several miles from the nearest village or town of any size . . . it was an odd place to build a factory and warehouse. The absence of other buildings was, however, exactly what Effendi wanted and the site cost only £300 an acre.

According to what may be partly legend, the site was finally decided on when Effendi took Rudyard Kipling and T. E. Lawrence to inspect it. They were accompanied by the two architects, Lord Gerald Wellesley (later the Duke of Wellington) and Trenwith Wills. Sitting in a wood carpeted with bluebells, picnicking on smoked salmon and champagne, they examined the first plans of what was to be the Windmill Press. Occupying three sides of a square, with reddish brown brickwork and white painted windows, some with fanlight tops, it was designed as a fine exercise in Neo-Georgian. Surrounded by shrubs and formal flower beds against a backdrop of woods, it would look more like a country club than a printing works and warehouse – and again this was exactly what Effendi wanted. As with the press on Long Island, it was to be an adornment and not a defacement of the rural landscape, with as many of the trees preserved as possible. Effendi's two guests were greatly taken with the scheme. T. E. Lawrence urged that the ground-floor windows of the print shop should reach down to the ground so that the staff could see the gardens and enjoy the maximum sunshine. Kipling suggested a small ornamental pond with a fountain and later supplied water lilies and goldfish from his own pond at Bateman's. The fountain was built with an elaborate stone base against the building's central wall and incorporated the foundation stone laid on 10 June 1926 by Effendi; it bears the inscription *'Quid sapientia locupletius?'* ('What is richer than wisdom?') Above it in the centre of the wall was an escutcheon carved in stone with rococo scrolls surrounding the windmill colophon, flanked by 'W' and 'H'. The pediment of the impressive doorway on the left of the entrance court was carved with the word 'Office'; it opened on to an elegant double staircase with curving ironwork banisters painted blue. On the opposite side of the court an identical doorway, surmounted by the inscription

[190]

'Press', took you straight into the rhythmic clamour of machines and the smell of printer's ink.

Building started in November 1926 and was completed a year later. The London staff moved down in January 1928 and the stock, in charge of Whyberd, head of the dispatch department, followed over a period of five weeks. It was a severe winter and the new building was surrounded with snowdrifts. Understandably the office staff were very worried about the move and the long daily journey, either by steam train, followed by a walk across fields from Kingswood station, or by the newly opened Underground to Morden where a private bus conveyed them the ten miles to the press. Their lives would be dislocated, but jobs were scarce and the bulk of the staff agreed to give it a try. Salaries were raised and they soon became delighted with the ideal working conditions and most gradually moved into houses or lodgings within easy reach, the firm helping with removal expenses. A canteen supplied a solid lunch for one shilling (coffee one penny extra), though the directors and important visitors used a private dining-room. In charge of the canteen – and also of the staff's 'physical and moral welfare' – was Gwen Gabriel, an old friend of William's who had earlier worked at Bedford Street. Handsome and in chic overalls, she was very popular and was to be the press's mother figure until the 1950s. Effendi's best memorial as a model employer was the large sports ground and its pavilion which was also used for social events and amateur theatricals.

Grace Cranston, then in the circularizing department, recalls the pioneering *esprit de corps* of those first months: 'Snow was lying everywhere. The building hadn't dried out and was very cold. We worked in our coats the whole of that first winter. Nevertheless there was a palpable feeling of excitement and exhilaration. It was new and it was a long time before dull routine clamped down on us again. . . . Football started the very first Saturday we were there. The girls followed soon after with netball. And in the evenings, when work was finished for the day, we set up the ping-pong table (as it was called in those days) in the middle of the general office. We had all sorts of activities – chess, Indian clubs and darts and, when the weather improved, rambles in the lovely countryside. . . . There were still a good many rats about. One of the builders told me that they had to keep their sandwiches in tin boxes when they were working on the press or the rats would climb up and remove them from their bicycle baskets. In those early days the men would organize rat hunts on Saturday afternoons with as many terriers as they could muster.'[1]

The Windmill Press was formally opened by John Galsworthy on 23 May 1928 before a distinguished literary gathering. Effendi was not well enough to sit on the platform but heard the speeches from an adjoining room with the door left ajar. It was raining hard and everyone was crammed into the boardroom to hear Galsworthy, looking very nervous and partly inaudible, utter his flowery congratulations. 'When a ship is launched our hearts go out not only to the designer and constructors of the great new creature, but to the captain, the officers, and the crew; to all those who will live and move and have their being thereon, whose fortune and very lives are bound up with its life and fortune. And so it is, at the launch of this building, which, though it never move from its moorings, will share fortune with all who work here; to it and to them, with a certain emotion, we wish good luck; may they all have the health, the prosperity, and the happiness which he who conceived this great removal designed to give them. . . . Those of us present, and absent, whose books in future will from cover to cover take shape between these walls, will feel, I am sure, an intimate satisfaction in knowing their work goes forth from such a place. . . . Much fine work has been done in the shadow of the windmill, and many caps have been flung over it. Unlike some windmills that I know, it is in good repair; stronger in build, and more sensitive to every wind than it ever was. Out of the fellowship born today with the Windmill Press still finer work will be done, and more caps will be flung over the windmill; for in the making of good books it is good that the world should be well lost now and again.'[2] He was seconded by J. C. Squire, the picturesque doyen of the twenties' literary establishment, who in a facetious speech upset everyone by making no reference to Effendi and remarking that it was the authors who make the money and it was the publishers who spent it on bricks.

The visitors were shown round the high book stacks in the warehouse, and on the ground floor were able to watch each stage in the production of books from composing room to machine room and bindery. In charge of production was B. F. Oliver, a large and fair-haired Yorkshireman with a genial smile for everyone. Until then he had been the company's cashier and secretary and knew nothing about printing. His appointment resulted from one of Effendi's quixotic, intuitive assessments. With advice from two experts from Garden City, John Hessian and Donald Macdonald, and part-time typographical aid from Gerald Meynell of the Westminster Press who had succeeded Stanley Morison, Oliver learned rapidly – not that no mistakes were made, one being the removal of all the cedillas from a French translation because they were thought to look untidy!

To begin with, a large second-hand Scott rotary caused a lot of trouble, but before the official opening all the other equipment was in action: other essential items consisted of one Monotype and two Linotype composing machines; three Miehle flat-bed presses; some perfectors, which printed on both sides of the paper; a foundry capable of making flat-bed casts for reprints and curved plates for the rotary; a bindery employing mainly female labour; and two marine oil engines for making the plant's electricity. The first book to be printed was a novel, *Bread and Honey* by M. Linford.

The plant employed some 70 people, which with the 80 office and other staff, made a full complement of 150. Grace Cranston reports 'some jostling for precedence in the relationship between the staff upstairs and downstairs. The office staff had no doubt believed at the beginning that they were better educated, better dressed and superior in all ways. But it soon transpired that the printers had as high – or higher – an opinion of themselves. They were at that time the aristocrats of the trade unions, and they had a staunch and well-deserved pride in their work as craftsmen. Even prouder were the compositors.'[3] The production staff had been recruited with surprising ease, considering the distance from London; although the press was one-and-a-half miles outside the officially recognized area, full London rates were offered. The good working conditions and amenities encouraged them to stay. The typographical union was very co-operative, but at the outset the binders' union made trouble because of the firm's refusal to recognize a closed shop. After the union had prevented potential employees from starting work, a meeting took place between their leaders and Byard, Oliver, and Frere-Reeves. Byard's report to Effendi reflects employers' attitudes and prejudices during the years following the General Strike: 'Three revolting creatures appeared to represent the men – most unworthy specimens of the working classes. One was a fat, podgy creature, with an enormous swelling half the size of his head on one side of his neck; another was a horrid little adenoidal Hebrew; the third was a more respectable but rather uninteresting Englishman. I tried hard to feel like you, and I flatter myself that between us I think we got a pretty solid victory. It took two hours, and it looked at first as though there could be no compromise, but after long arguments and pointing out to them that we were doing as much, and a great deal more, than they could possibly have expected from any other employers for their men, they finally – aided by a cup of tea and the fact that Oliver drove them in his car to the station – went away pretty well agreed to leave us alone. . . . The unfortunate thing is that 70 or 80 per cent of the best workers in this country are union men, and pretty loyal ones too, and they are apt to make the lives of non-unionists who work with them excessively uncomfortable. As you will know, it is hard to prove victimisation, but undoubtedly in a quiet way this takes place everywhere. However, by sticking to this open house arrangement, we have retained absolute control of Kingswood and shall not be bothered with Fathers of the Chapel and all sorts of internal and interfering regulations from the union.'[4]

By the third month of operation the new press was showing a profit and turning out some 2,000 completed books a day, together with 12,500 copies of each issue of the *World's Work* magazine. From its birth the Kingswood venture was a success. What's more, it showed the world that the House of Heinemann was in the van of industrial enlightenment along with Cadbury's Bournville and Lever's Port Sunlight. This was recognized by reports in the Press. 'Here is an important business which is transplanting its workpeople from the fogs of London to the free air of the countryside', wrote F. Yeats-Brown in a rapturous account for the *Spectator*. 'Here are employers with vision and vigour, here are fine buildings, fine machinery, above all, here are happy men and women – delightful material for a journalist after the difficulties and depressions of South Wales. . . . Here, encircled by bluebell woods, they may rest their eyes occasionally on something prettier than corrected galley-proofs, and if they open the window, between spells of work, they may exchange chatter of the Linotype for the song of blackbirds.'[5]

Ninety-nine Great Russell Street

A new era had indeed begun, but it took all of Effendi's persuasive sinews finally to convince Byard and Evans that Bedford Street was not good enough for the vision he had of the new Heinemann of the future. In April 1927 he put the matter bluntly: 'Bedford Street is to me anathema – a down at the heels, narrow-chested affair whose only tradition goes back to the German and the Jew. It may have had many literary associations, but it is certainly inefficient for its purposes, and to most people extremely unattractive. You have asked me many times why I didn't bring Mr Kipling to the office. Perhaps you may remember that I did once, and he wasn't particularly impressed. If you will compare Bedford Street with St Martin's Lane and Macmillan's, the reason will be obvious. I think you and Charley have got so used to this old rookery and running up and down stairs that it has some charm for you which no one else feels. You have got to move sometime, and why not while you are making other changes? I am not greatly impressed with what the other publishers think of staying on in Bedford Street. They all prophesied failure when we went into Heinemann's, and I sometimes think that they regard any change as a calamity. . . . My purpose in talking about a large house was that I have the greatest faith in the development of the Heinemann business, not only the branches that are in existence now, but others that will come; and if it costs a few hundred pounds to get a larger place than we really need, I for one do not object to the expenditure. . . . Your position will be more dignified, and you should, I think, have a habitation suitable to your achievements.'[6]

It was undoubtedly Effendi's ability to think big and to take a long, ambitious view of the future that led to the leasing of elegant new offices at 99 Great Russell Street, close by the British Museum in literary Blooms-bury. The rent was £1,500 a year plus rates and taxes. Built towards the end of the seventeenth century, it was a fine William and Mary mansion, with richly moulded cornices and the original panelling in the major rooms and on the staircase, above which the ceiling carried a painting by an unknown Italian artist depicting Bacchus, Venus, and Cupid. It was believed that it was once occupied by the Hon. Topham Beauclerk, a grandson of Charles II and Nell Gwyn, and his artist wife Diana. Eccentric, somewhat dissipated, with exquisite taste and the possessor of an immense library, a friend of Johnson and the *haut ton*, Beauclerk might be thought to provide a very suitable ghost for a publisher's premises, and indeed this was made much of by the publicity department. Unfortunately, however, it was later discovered, in 1935, by Ethel Sutton, a member of the editorial staff, that the Beauclerks had almost certainly inhabited numbers 100–102 next door, then known as Thanet House. A plaque on the wall of Number 100 now confirms this.

Number 99's spacious panelled room at the rear of the ground floor was ideal for a publisher's parties and Charles Evans's similar grand room on the first floor could be calculated to overwhelm even important authors. Suitably impressive furniture was chosen by Mrs Byard. Some of the smaller rooms were poky, but the Loeb Classical Library had a room of its own. The World's Work had two, but the medical company had to share a room with the secretaries. Editorial and Publicity were mainly at Kingswood, which for many years was in fact the firm's power centre and the venue for board meetings. Inevitably there had to be a great deal of tiring commuting between the two establishments, though communication was eased by a private telephone line and a daily van which was used primarily to service the trade counter in Number 99's basement. In moving its warehouse and administrative centre outside London, Heinemann was decades ahead of other London publishers who were later to make similar moves. Kingswood certainly had many advantages, but the physical division of the company also brought its own special problems, particularly when after the Second World War the power base steadily shifted back to London.

10

The Nose for a Good Book

Kingswood was also the venue for the weekly meetings, attended by key members of staff, around which the firm's activities revolved. Decisions were made on book prices, printing numbers, jackets and publicity, reprints, and much else. Arnold Haskell, who, starting soon after Kingswood opened, worked for five years as a reader before making his name as a prolific writer on ballet, recalls that 'whatever happened, these weekly meetings were good for a laugh as when one of our travellers informed the dignified Byard that the sales of a certain book could be said to *flunctuate*, or when one of our bright young men suggested that the one-volume six-novel edition of Jane Austen be advertised as "The Austen Six"'[1]. Rupert Hart-Davis, who also began his publishing career in the Kingswood editorial department at £2 a week, told me that the weekly meetings were very tedious, though he agreed that they were not without giggles, such as when Byard kept referring to *Into the Abyss* by John Knittel as '*Into the Abbess*'. On another occasion he wanted to know where on earth was this place scheduled as 'B'ham' on the Midlands representative's report.

Hart-Davis used to travel down each morning in Haskell's Austin Seven. The latter's father was very rich and gave him £5,000 a year so long as he did some work. Haskell was an exceedingly rapid reader and he reckoned that in his five years with the firm he reported on over five thousand manuscripts. 'The main trouble is caused by the very many border-line cases competently written, publishable but rather dull. C. S. Evans was marvellous with these doubtfuls, able to gauge whether the author's next book would be really worth while or if he had put everything into this first attempt. . . . Once when I reported enthusiastically on a novel he took it home for the weekend and returned my report with the comments: "I agree with you; an excellent book but if you examine it carefully I think you will find it has been translated from the French and someone is trying to pull a fast one." He proceeded to set out the data and afterwards I was able to confirm it. The whole episode gave him enormous pleasure since he adored detective stories.'[2] When Haskell asked Evans on what principle a report should be made, he replied: '"No one can tell if a book will please the public or not. I want a straightforward personal opinion on the book's merits, that is the only type of reading that is any good for this firm." His reply was in sharp contrast to the American publisher, George Doran, to whom I was loaned for a London visit. When I asked him the same question the reply was "Will it ring the bell?" and when I looked puzzled, "Will it pay the rent?"'[3]

Haskell worked hard but he seems to have enjoyed Kingswood. 'Isolated as we were in the country with directors only visiting us once a week, discipline was by no means rigid. As long as the safe did not remain too full and the reports were satisfactory when a harrowing post-mortem took place on a novel that we had rejected and that was selling well elsewhere, we were left entirely free. We forgathered for long under-graduate discussions on every subject under the sun, rehearsed for amateur theatricals or ragged, sometimes noisily. A great feature of the editorial was a steeplechase track under chairs and over tables.'[4] Security was lax and not a few books were pinched by the staff, among them one young man who, volume by volume, smuggled out a complete set of the Loeb Classical Library. With Frere-Reeves by then a director, Evans had to acknowledge the value of his energy and other merits, but their love-hate relationship was obvious to the young Haskell. 'Frere-Reeves and Evans not infrequently took different points of view over a manu-script, and this occasionally placed members of the reading staff in a position which called for some diplomacy, though at the same time it was undoubtedly stimulating. I remember reading *The Specialist* with Frere-Reeves and both of us roaring with laughter at that superb piece of "folklore". The sequel was that I had to read it aloud to Evans over the traditional glass of sherry and try to explain to him why it was funny. I did not succeed and the firm lost a money-spinner. Reeves and Evans were equally charming and their widely different qualities were com-plementary, a fact to which the sustained and often brilliant success of the firm owed a great deal. Evans looked on publishing as a one-man business in which the books published reflected his own particular taste. Reeves looked ahead as a businessman and was also more in touch with the younger generation.'[5]

Editors were given scope to discover and foster their own authors, subject to a final decision by Evans, if not the whole board. Haskell, for example, introduced *Theatre Street* (1930) by Tamara Karsavina and *The Sculptor Speaks* (1931) which he wrote himself in the form of a dialogue with Jacob Epstein. Hart-Davis, on the other hand, described to me how he tried unsuccessfully to introduce his uncle Duff Cooper's life of Talleyrand: 'Evans said he was too busy to read it and told me to give it to Frere-Reeves who in turn said it was no good at all. This was lucky for me because when later I moved to Cape I was able to offer it to them and it was a tremendous success.' Most books had their own sponsors who nursed them through all the stages of copy preparation, blurb and jacket, and catalogue description. Not that the editors worked in watertight compartments; they relied on the enthusiasm of the whole staff to make a book go.

Head of the editorial department was Arnold Gyde who joined the firm in 1925 after being invalided as a regular army officer. Badly wounded in France, he had written under the pseudonym of 'Casualty' a book about his experiences called *Contemptible* which was published by the firm in 1916. A convivial, often flushed man who loved racing, cricket, booze and anecdotes as much as he did Schumann or a novel with a strong story-line, he was known for his rumbustious enthusiasm for the book of the moment, though he found it difficult to remember its title or its author's name. Grace Cranston, who acted as his secretary, remembers how he employed an elaborate system of nicknames – thus, 'Fitz-Blood Buff-Orpington was Fitz-Adam Ormiston. He had a habit of suddenly dictating letters in the corridor from a distance of twenty yards: "Dear Bill, What did I tell you? This book is a wow! If you will only start it I can guarantee you a sleepless night" . . . and you might send a line to that charming man – you know his name – the one who's always tight after three o'clock. Tell him that if he will only read this wonderful book he will find enough stories in it to keep him and his paper going for the rest of his life.'[6] He was well known in Fleet Street's Press Club and also handled much of the publicity, which later became his chief assignment. His punchy, innovative missives to the Press and trade became known as 'Heinemann's Gyde to Literature.'

Among the other editorial staff in the twenties and early thirties were Warren Shaw-Zambra, who handled foreign manuscripts and translated the Kaiser's memoirs. Then there was Arthur Barker, who later set up his own imprint. An unusual but entertaining young member was Edmond Segrave, who had just left a Roman Catholic seminary on discovering a lack of vocation. He was noted not only for his knowledge of the classics, useful when checking Loeb Classical Library proofs, but also for his ability to dance and sing while balancing a tumblerful of water on his head. Haskell remembers an elaborate practical joke which 'came about through Edmond's gift as a calligrapher. He could copy any handwriting without difficulty. Arnold Gyde had been boring us all about the marvels of Henry Handel Richardson. So we sent him a letter signed by her name saying that her niece, Lottie Ostrahan – I take an author's pride in the name – would be coming down to visit the works on a certain day, and would he kindly entertain her? As the whole office was in the secret we were able to intercept his reply without much difficulty. Gyde set off to the station in a staff car, and Lottie, an excellent actress, arrived. The joke proper began at tea when I set out to be deliberately rude to her, upsetting a cup over her dress, laughing in the wrong place, contradicting her flatly, and so on. Wherever Gyde piloted his honoured guest some mishap or other occurred. He tried to tell her that I was quite a decent chap as a rule but had recently taken to drink; but it was of no avail, and finally she left in a great huff saying she would tell Auntie about our lack of hospitality. We deserved a violent scene for the dreadful afternoon we had given him, but his invincible good humour and his relief at hearing the truth made him enjoy the joke as much as we did.'[7] In later years Segrave became a highly effective editor of *The Bookseller*.

William's custom of employing outside literary advisers and readers continued, though from 1923 his old personal office in Bedford Street had been occupied by a resident reader, James Whitall, an American who was having a prolonged love affair with England and who had previously worked on *The London Mercury* with J. C. Squire; he had also translated for the firm François Mauriac's *The Kiss of the Leper* and Gérard de Nerval's *Daughters of Fire*. In his memoirs he makes clear how he realized while with Heinemann the importance and enormous responsibility of a publisher's reader. 'I developed a certain amount of speed in reading likely efforts, and it was not long before I learned to dispose of the useless ones after several hasty dips into their frequently illiterate and almost always pathetic pages. Sometimes the ineptitude of a work that could obviously never be printed was very beguiling and I would read on and on in fascinated absorption, with a possible bestseller on the top of the pile beside me. My job as resident reader was in one respect an important one. I found that any recommendation of mine as to the acceptance of a book was always carefully considered, but publication was never undertaken without further readings in and out of the office. This was shared responsibility, but the other recommendations, fifty times as numerous and sometimes only one word long, represented my primary function, and in its performance I was supported by no one. In other words, if a masterpiece or a bestseller were rejected by Heinemann's, the blame would fall squarely upon my shoulders and I watched other publishers' lists with an eagle eye for the appearance therein of books I had declared to be unpublishable or unsaleable. My first experience of this sort gave me a nasty turn, and I shall not soon forget the misery I lived in until the reviewers corroborated my opinion. Later, when I learned that the publisher of the book had paid for his mistake by selling less than a hundred copies, the incident took on a very different significance and I could almost look forward with equanimity to repetitions of it. These occurred, of course, but my strengthened self-confidence did not diminish the misery of that first period of suspense. My employers assured me that no reader was infallible, citing instances where men far more experienced than I had made expensive errors of judgment, but the sight of an announcement of the publication of one of my rejected manuscripts never failed to give me a sense of impending tragedy.'[8]

Whitall captures the to-and-froing of a busy publisher's office: 'Conferences with Evans or Byard and occasional meetings with authors of varying degrees of eminence provided the necessary breaks in the monotony of my day. Rare glimpses of Conrad showed him to have aged noticeably . . . his face was pale now, and I was oddly shocked to find that the tracery of delicate lines upon it had disappeared. The two flights of stairs to Evans's room seemed to exhaust him. John Galsworthy, Edmund Gosse, Maurice Baring, Clemence Dane, Tennyson Jesse and many others were frequently in the office. . . . The seclusion of my office was, through the inadvertence of the people on the ground floor, sometimes violated by authors who imagined that a word to the reader before or during his perusal of their works would be advisable. If they had only known! [George] Moore, though not in this category, was frequently more annoying than the most unpublishable aspirant. Closed doors were as nothing to him, and his favourite objective was the book-keeping department, whence he would climb the stairs to infuriate Evans with some demand based on information wrested from an awe-stricken clerk. On the rare occasions when he departed without favouring me with a visit, I had only to emerge from my room to be made fully aware of his recent presence; the harassed appearance of those who had had to deal with him and the ruffled atmosphere of the office in general were unmistakable. Moore was important to his publishers and they did their best to be patient with him even when his behaviour was past all forgiving. Once when carefully enthroned at a table in the room adjoining my office for the purpose of autographing pages for one of his limited editions, he decided to be annoyed because he was not importantly alone. To the other occupant of the room he addressed these peculiarly ill-chosen words in a voice that clearly betrayed his feelings: "I am very busy signing these pages for my book. Would you mind going away? I cannot be disturbed." No immediate notice being taken of his unusual request, he persisted, thinking to settle the matter forthwith: "I am George Moore. Will you please go away?" And he enforced this disclosure of his perfectly apparent identity with the swish of a fat arm. Whereupon the man across the room raised his handsome head, smiled, and said: "My name is John Galsworthy and I am signing pages for a book too." I do not need to add that it was the author (also perfectly recognizable) of *The Forsyte Saga* and not Mr George Moore who took himself off in search of a quieter place."[9]

Part-time advisers included Walter de la Mare; Harry Graham, author of many humorous books and for long an adviser to Arnold's when Evans was there; and Desmond MacCarthy, enlisted by Byard in 1924. Mac-Carthy's reputation was already formidable and it was hoped that he would attract good authors to the Windmill. It was arranged that he should attend the offices each Thursday afternoon and Friday morning and read no more than two or three manuscripts a week. He shared the room with Whitall, who found his advice of immense value. 'Desmond was an expert in the solution of manuscript difficulties and he could perform miracles of clarification with novels which showed promise but could not be published as they were. I remember a session with the young writer of a story which Desmond had said was like a ball of wool after a kitten had been playing with it. The session lasted four hours, the young man put in another month's work on his manuscript and a successful book resulted.'[10]

In 1928 another well-known littérateur, the novelist Frank Swinnerton, was enrolled on a similar basis. He brought with him years of experience, mainly acquired at Chatto's. 'The publisher's reader', he wrote, 'must have no vagaries. His prejudices must all be sunk when he takes up a manuscript. A dislike of the author must not influence him. Neither may he allow himself the satisfaction of refusing a book which attacks his idols. He must not have idols, in fact. He must combine enthusiasm with calm; caution with boldness. He must be patient, wary, shrewd; he must know something upon every subject; he must be acquainted with all literatures, and, preferably, with several languages. He must understand the book trade, must have a very easy familiarity with the work of all living authors, so that he knows how they are "ranked" by critics and how they are "rated" by the libraries. He must himself be a critic able to appreciate both the unfamiliar and the conventional. And he must never make a mistake.

'He is expected to mark down a bestseller at sight, and to distinguish between work that is immature through excess of genius and work that is crude through congenital incapacity. He is to be a hack and an explorer, the brains of a publishing business and the anonymous and frequently ill-paid servant of his employers. At all times, in all circumstances, he should have his stethoscope pressed close to the heart of the public, so as to know when that heart jumps a beat. If it jumps a beat, or if the beat quickens or slackens, a change in literary fashion is imminent, and the professional reader must be ready to anticipate any change of fashion, and ready to discount mere fluctuations of pulse.'[11]

Creative Flair of Charles Evans – Priestley, Brett Young, Somerset Maugham

Each post added to the heaps of unsolicited manuscripts from unknown and usually hitherto unpublished authors. The Kingswood staff and their part-time advisers knew that at the most five per cent were worth a second opinion and that less than one per cent were likely to be accepted, but they all had to be read – or at least skimmed – and, if of any particular value, a synopsis was prepared. Throughout its history Heinemann's readers, often unknown and poorly paid, have been the first to meet and recognize the talent that has made the imprint successful. Sated though they were with words, with eyes weary from untidy and often well-thumbed typed or sometimes handwritten pages, the chance of spotting literary merits as well as what may or may not sell has always depended in the first instance on their discernment and taste. Inevitably, in the unceasing flow of material potential bestsellers were sometimes missed by the readers or, even when they were spotted, were rejected by the directors, who of course held the ultimate responsibility – a burden largely shouldered by Charles Evans.

If anyone possessed that indefinable quality known as 'publisher's flair' it was Evans. His literary and commercial judgments meshed well together. Unlike some celebrated publishers he actually read manuscripts carefully himself. He didn't merely – to use the give-away phrase – 'read into them'. He understood and liked authors and in turn they liked him. He was strengthened by an untiring curiosity. John Masefield described him as 'a man of varied interests. He worked very hard at Egyptian studies, at jazz music. . . . But was there anything at which he did not work hard? He gave me always the impression that he was over-working. He was interested in people, in the theatre, in the cinema, and in every branch of literature. I used to wonder if he ever went to bed. He would do a full day at the office or at the works or both; then to dinner with somebody, then to the theatre, perhaps; then back to some manuscript, or problem. If he ever took any rest, he never seemed rested.'[12] David Higham, as a literary agent, respected his judgment and shrewdness, but described him as a man 'who lacked much physical charm but had a way with him that drew affection from most of those who came to know him well, men as well as women. The women wanted chiefly, I think, to mother him, though he had a wife and half a dozen children. He had, himself, the air of a child almost, a certain simplicity, a naïvety of which he was never ashamed; and beneath all that a warm and genuine heart, a generous one, too.'[13]

His staff respected him, but knew he could be very difficult and temperamental. Small, fast-talking and shrewd, he was still very much the schoolmaster. It is probable that only Frere-Reeves actively disliked him, and yet Arnold Gyde, who must have known him as well as anyone in the office, recorded in his private journal: 'Charley was in better spirits at Kingswood in the morning, but he was down on me for overriding the reader's advice and getting John Clayton's novel *Silver Swan* published. "It's not good enough for our lists", he says to me with bitterness and venom. Then he begins to attack me on a more vulnerable point . . . it gives him the chance to repeat twice more what he has said thrice. The idea, of course, is to prove to me that I don't know anything about a book, and to prove it to others too. It has made me very miserable.'[14] Other entries about Evans in Gyde's journal are far from charitable: 'How the world would laugh at him if it saw him at these meetings. The successful publisher Charley Evans! A bald and bespectacled little fright, with twitching hands and eyes – suspicious, bankrupt of any kindly thought, and supremely anxious that nobody shall get any credit for anything'[15]; and again 'Nobody dropped a failure quicker than little Charley.'[16] Hart-Davis, who recognized Evans's great ability, spoke of him as 'a petty little man. When I worked for him, if I ever did anything he felt he should have done himself, he complained that I was stealing his thunder.'

Evans's nerves, his insomnia and general ill-health including high blood-pressure, culminated in a major breakdown towards the end of 1927. He was sent on a long convalescent holiday, sightseeing in Egypt, followed by some weeks in Rapallo and a visit to Somerset Maugham, then at Beaulieu-sur-mer on the French Riviera. Byard wrote to Effendi: 'His breakdown was, as you know, a very serious one, not owing to any particular shock, but was the result of many years of overstrain going back to the time when he was at Arnolds, and was also due to the fact that he is unable to depute and is consequently and inevitably always overworked. All his friends have seen this breakdown coming for a long time. Now it seems to me that a breakdown which comes from a long strain is a far more serious matter than one which is owing to a shock, and I am beginning to be very doubtful whether Charley will come back in a fit condition really to be the live wire of Heinemanns, especially in view of all the new developments. I gather from his letters that he is better, but he felt the heat very much in Egypt and apparently had one quite nasty attack whilst he was out there. It appears that the veins of his forehead swelled up to the centre of his head like cords, and he had to have ice packs on for several hours. Of course, this may have been due to the heat, but I rather doubt it as he says himself that he had on a large solar topee; and the heat in January is not intense. I am therefore rather afraid that this may be the forerunner of other attacks of this kind. . . . Should he have another breakdown in a few months' time (which God forbid!) we should be faced with an extremely difficult situation. If this should happen, I imagine it would take him at least six months or a year to get right.'[17] Effendi was of course very sympathetic and invited him to prolong his holiday and stay with him at Nassau, and there was even talk of seeking a potential substitute. But after a couple of months Evans came back effectively recovered, though he seemed ready enough for Frere-Reeves to continue handling many of the responsibilities he had assumed in Evans's absence.

Evans's outstanding talent was being able to recognize potentially successful 'broadbrow' fiction, stories which promised a good long read and which probably reflected his personal taste as well as that of a large middle-class public. It was through him that in the later 1920s and throughout the 1930s Heinemann dominated the bookshops and libraries. It is doubtful if its list could be said to reflect strongly the 'Jazz Age' or the 'Roaring Twenties' or the 'Bright Young Things' – they published Michael Arlen's *The London Venture* (1920) and five more of his charmingly mannered books about London *à la mode*, but they missed out on *The Green Hat* – though it cannot be gainsaid that several of the firm's blockbuster novels succeeded in presenting drab inter-war realities. Galsworthy's *A Modern Comedy* (1929), according even to Beatrice Webb, gave 'a remarkable description of England after the war'[18] and few books provided a more telling picture of the depressed regions of industrial England than J. B. Priestley's *The Good Companions* (also 1929), with Jess Oakroyd's dried-up kipper in the opening chapter in Bruddersford and its sordid theatrical boarding-houses, or his description in *Angel Pavement* (1930) of Smeeth, the elderly decent little man working as chief clerk in the City veneer business wrecked by the eruption of a hard-faced capitalist trickster.

Although the firm had by then published three previous books by Priestley – *The Open House* (1927), a book of essays, and two novels, *Adam in Moonshine* (1927) and *Benighted* (1927) – none of which had been strikingly successful, Evans, as soon as he read the first part of *The Good Companions* immediately recognized that it was a winner. His letter merits reproduction in full: 'During the weekend I read the first part of *Good Companions*, and the only thing I can say is, bless you! In a desert of aridity which I have been traversing for the last six months, your book stands out as a green and pleasant oasis. There is not a line of it that I could have wished away, and I am certain that if you go on as you have begun, we are going to produce a book that the world has got to reckon with. Appreciation so enthusiastic as this may seem strange to you after my lukewarm reception of your two other books; but this is ever so much bigger than either. It has the true creative spirit in it. It has humour, humanity and exuberance – three of the very rarest qualities in the fiction of our time.

'May I add one little word of warning? Do not let facility take the place of creation. You are a very facile writer, my dear Priestley, and you can do standing on your head what other writers can only achieve with blood and tears. Do not let that facility run away with you. I have in mind one particular passage – the description of the concert in the singing room. It is all easy and pleasant reading, but I do not think it is quite on an equality with the really creative quality of the rest of the book. This kind of thing has been done many times before. I hope you will forgive this one isolated criticism. For the rest, you can go forward with confidence. I do not think I ever doubted that you were going to be a really great novelist, but I am sure of it now. I am eager to read some more. Do let me have the next section as soon as it is ready. When do you think we can publish?'[19]

In his happy reply the very next day Priestley commented: 'I am of course deliberately breaking with everything that is characteristic of highbrow fiction of the moment, the vague crowds of clever idlers, the dreary futility, and all the rest of it. Let's have some Real People, says I.'[20]

Evans's prognosis proved to be completely correct, though the book's performance must have exceeded his most extravagant hopes. It started slowly and even looked like being a flop, but after a few months it suddenly took off and was selling 3,000 copies a day so that extra vans and staff had to be hired. The first relatively high printing of 10,000, with a published price of 10s.6d. – a lot of money in those days for a novel – proved so inadequate that it had to be reprinted 8 times in 1929; 9 times in 1930; 5 times in 1931; 4 times in 1932; 5 times in 1933; twice in 1934; and at least once every year until the wartime paper shortage caused a temporary break. Almost overnight Priestley had become a 'popular' writer in every sense. His mammoth, picaresque, often sentimental tale provided maybe the kind of enjoyable escape that the public yearned for during the gloomy years of the Depression – and this is exactly how he saw it. Asked at the time why he wrote it, he replied: 'Well, of course, I wrote it for applause, for money, for fame, for all the usual things and the usual reasons. But really I wrote it for fun. I made up my mind to write a novel that I myself could enjoy, even if nobody else ever did. I never sat down to write without telling myself that if other people did not like it, they could lump it. I meant to enjoy myself and I did. . . . I came to the end of my huge tale, not with a sigh of relief but with a sigh of regret. We had all such fun together.'[21] His personal experience of violence and tragedy, with most of his friends killed in the war in which he was wounded himself and with a young wife dying of cancer leaving him with two young children, gave him the need for 'a holiday from anxiety and strain and tragic circumstances'.

According to Evans, Priestley was still a gauche young man and would turn up at Heinemann parties in ill-fitting clothes. He was uneasy with the kind of literary lady who asked his opinion of, say, Virginia Woolf. 'He had two methods of dealing with them: either to remain easy or to get drunk and "talk 'em down". They didn't stand a chance once Jack got going!' He was now not only an established writer with for the first time a good income, but he was becoming 'Jolly Jack', the pipe-smoking Englishman, the grumbling radical and moralist who deplored the loss of the values and habits of the society in which he had grown up. He seemed to enjoy the part but it was an oversimplification – as was shown by *Angel Pavement*, which followed in 1930. This did not enjoy quite the same runaway success. It was a very different novel from *The Good Companions*. Not only was it set in a sharply observed London, but it was realism rather than escapism, concerned with the colourless existence of underpaid, exploited typists, cashiers, and young clerks, but who none the less themselves escaped into private fantasies.

Critics have considered *Angel Pavement* to be his finest novel, but throughout his long career they tended to underrate him. 'The novel was hardly his true medium', *The Times* was to write in his obituary, 'and he was an occasional novelist, as some excellent writers of verse have been occasional poets. Even at its best, as in *Angel Pavement*, his fiction is marred by an essayist's diffuseness.'[22] He was very aware of how the critics assessed him: 'There is a tendency in highbrow critical circles here', he once wrote to Frere-Reeves, 'to regard me as a good dramatist but negligible as a novelist. Often in critical articles on the English novel I am never even mentioned. I have never advanced great claims for myself as a novelist; nevertheless I believe this attitude towards my fiction to be wrong and to be based chiefly on ignorance. . . . I'm getting a little tired of being regarded as having no literary significance, when – in spite of being a popular figure – I could write most of these people out of their homes and down the street.'[23] In *Margin Released*, one of his collections of reminiscent essays, he wrote: 'I am too conventional for the avant-garde, too experimental for Aunt Edna; too extroverted for the introverts, too introverted for the out-and-out extroverts; a low-brow to high-brows, a high-brow to low-brows.'[24]

Whether or not it was his true medium, Priestley continued to write successful novels, as well as a profusion of essays, plays, and broadcasts. In the 1930s Heinemann published a further 24 of his titles, comprising 7 novels: *Faraway* (1932), *Wonder Hero* (1933), *Albert Goes Through* (1933), *They Walk in the City* (1936), *The Doomsday Men* (1938), *Let the People Sing* (1940), and *I'll Tell you Everything* (1933) – the last jointly with Gerald Bullett – all but the third sold very well, though nothing like as well as *The Good Companions*; there were no less than 13 published plays, including *Dangerous Corner* (1932), *Laburnum Grove* (1934), *Eden End* (1934), *Time and the Conways* (1937), *Johnson over Jordan* (1939); there were also 2 volumes of autobiography; 1 book of essays; and *English Journey* (published jointly with Gollancz in 1934), a travel book with harsh reportage of the effects of mass unemployment and the sapping of the vitality of the land of hope and glory. There was also a continuing flood of more ephemeral articles, film work, lectures, etc.

In *Midnight on the Desert* (1937) Priestley describes himself well: 'I take no thought whatever about a career, make no plans far ahead, but do whatever I want to do, with no reference to its possible dignity or lack of it. I have a restless nature, easily bored, and so I flit from one kind of work to another, partly sustained by a very genuine interest in the technical problems of all forms of writing. I have always wanted vaguely to be an all-round man of letters on the 18th Century plan, which allowed or commanded a man to write essay or poem, novel or play, just as he pleased. This is good fun, but it may not be good business. If you want to play for safety, keeping the career on a steady course, you will do the same thing over and over again – painting two cows in a field, two cows in a field – until at last they write, for the school books, "Nor can we omit a consideration of the leader of the two-cows-in-a-field group. . . ." And there you are in your pigeon-hole, and not unlike a stuffed pigeon.'[25] With so many outlets for his talents, it is no wonder that this fluent, tetchy writer with the independent stance of an old-fashioned radical could never be fitted into a neat critical pigeon-hole, but for his publishers he was for fifty years to provide a cornerstone for their spring and autumn lists.

Another of Charles Evans's broadbrow bestsellers was Francis Brett Young. His best-known novels were set in the Midlands, a region which took in the coalfields of the Black Country and the countryside bordering the Severn Valley. His early life as a doctor perhaps accounts for his exceptionally acute observation of individuals, but he was also adept at weaving them into a sound, leisurely narrative against romantic land-scapes, enriched with what was called 'lyrical nostalgia'. Although earlier published by Collins and Martin Secker, it was his first book for Heinemann, in 1927, *Portrait of Clare*, that was a major success and won the James Tait Black prize. It was succeeded the next year by *My Brother Jonathan* (1928) which, like several of his novels, was partly autobio-graphical. During the 1930s one bestseller followed after another, includ-ing *Mr and Mrs Pennington* (1931), *The House Under the Water* (1932), *White Ladies* (1935), *Deep Sea* (1936), *Portrait of a Village* (1937), and *Dr Bradley Remembers* (1938). They were all in a similar vein: copious, pleasant, and very British. They made ideal stock for the big subscription libraries such as those run by Boots, Harrods, and W. H. Smith. Critical judgment asserted that most of his novels could be improved by drastic cutting – several ran between 600 and 800 pages – but subscription libraries liked big books, because they took longer to read and there-fore had a low 'volume-per-monthage' (compared with the twopence or threepence per volume downmarket libraries which needed short novels with a high 'volume-per-monthage'). Another fertile theme stemmed from his war service in the RAMC with a Rhodesian regi-ment during Smuts's East African campaign; this resulted in *They Seek a Country* (1937) and *The City of Gold* (1939), which dealt with the Great Trek, the founding of Kimberley, and other events down to the Jameson Raid, books which were also very long and yet as always accomplished.

Brett Young's relationship with Evans was close and even dependent. His letters are full of pleas such as 'I hate not talking over plans with you before I begin, and wish you could dash down for a night to make up my mind for me.'[26] After completing *They Seek a Country* he believed, as it turned out quite mistakenly, that Evans had not read it properly. He was so upset that his wife, Jessica – who acted as his assistant-cum-manager – wrote secretly to Evans: 'It happens to be the first time you have not given him what he has always counted on, your valued opinion. . . . It is as though something were missing for him, as he has always absolutely hung upon the words you have said about each different book.'[27] He was not an easy author. More than once, when he felt his books had not been given enough publicity or some minor thing went wrong, he threatened to find another publisher, but his large and regular sales ensured that he was treated as a VIP, being allowed the use of the private flat at the top of Great

Russell Street and being sent proofs in stages before a book was finished – and he insisted they were in page and not galley. Jessica was undoubtedly also a woman to be reckoned with. There are conflicting accounts of one visit to the office when Charley could not take his eyes off Francis's multi-coloured knitted stockings, which he wore with plus-fours. When Jessica noticed his interest, he pretended to admire them and a few weeks later was taken aback to receive a parcel containing some multi-coloured stockings for himself with a note from Jessica, saying that she had been unable to find a similar pattern and so, instead, she was sending a pair of Francis's. She was afraid they were rather heavily darned . . . but he wore them while he was writing *Mr and Mrs Pennington*!

Shortly after the death of Galsworthy in 1933 the *Daily Mail* offered a fifty-pound prize for an essay on 'Who are our Future Literary Giants?' to be assessed by a distinguished panel of judges. The winning entry argued that Galsworthy's mantle had fallen upon Francis Brett Young: 'John Galsworthy's place in the hearts of the English reading public can only be taken by someone who is as English as Galsworthy was. He must be very different, for no literary giant may tread in his forerunner's footsteps. First, his work must stand as a memorial to the beauty of the British countryside and to the genius of its people. . . . He must have travelled; he must know the world. Also, he must know more of life, death, of struggle, failure and success than the average man can know. No sooner are these conditions put on paper than the answer suggests itself. Francis Brett Young can fill all of them. . . . In face of all his natural gifts, developed by hard work and circumstance, most of his contemporaries will soon be forced to hail him as a literary giant.'[28]

It was a marvellous piece of free publicity, but the excitement in the office was short-lived when it was discovered that the prize-winning author was Captain Arnold Gyde, Heinemann's publicity expert who had submitted the essay privately. Soon it was said on Fleet Street and in the trade that he had engineered the whole thing, that it was no more than a stunt. Worse, a furious letter arrived from Somerset Maugham, complaining that he had been overlooked, that he was never given the star treatment he merited, and therefore the time had come for him to find another publisher. He was even instructing his agent, Watt, to arrange also for the transfer of all his earlier titles. Horrified, Evans telegraphed that he was coming to see him and took the next train to the French Riviera. He arrived to learn that Maugham had departed on a motor tour.

Eventually Evans ran him to earth in Aix. Luckily he was easily pacified and Evans joined him on his tour to Avignon and Arles before taking the train back to London.

Discussing the claim to have succeeded Galsworthy, *The Times* at the end of Brett Young's life uttered the mandarin observation that 'although the designation was not altogether apt, it implied quite justly that Brett Young achieved a certain breadth as a novelist rather than depth. The temptations of popularity, it may be said, stood in the way of his achieving more. . . .'[29] The fact remains that each of his books sold well, and he produced a mammoth volume at least once a year. By the standards of the 1970s onwards this figure was still large, while not exceptionally so, but in the 1930s it was considerable when the reading public was very much smaller, and it was before the days of vast paperback sales (the first Penguins were launched only in 1935). There were also fewer translation and other subsidiary rights, but on the other hand most copies were sold at the full hardback price of seven-and-sixpence or eight-and-sixpence – or five shillings when they were eventually issued in the firm's Severn collected edition of Brett Young's works – and, relative to the value of money and the lower rate of taxation, commercially successful writers were undoubtedly wealthy.

Before Brett Young became a bestseller he lived very cheaply in the sunshine of Anacapri. C. P. Snow, in his preface to Jessica's biography of her husband, published by Heinemann in 1962, discussed comparative wealth between the wars: 'The writers went abroad partly, of course, because it was cheap to live: but also it was part of the romantic conception of the artist which, in the twenties, was still very much part of the air. On the whole they did themselves better, lived more lavishly, than their successors. This was partly a matter of fashion; it was then more a matter of literary economics. Successful writers were more prosperous in the twenties than they had ever been before or are ever likely to become again.'[30] This was also largely true of the thirties. After the success of *My Brother Jonathan* Brett Young was rich enough to return to England and, after a spell in the Lake District, to purchase Craycombe House, a country seat overlooking the Avon Valley above Evesham. This compared with Priestley's thirty acres surrounding the marble-floored Kissing Tree House at Alveston in Warwickshire, with Kipling's Batemans in Sussex, or Walpole's place in Cumberland, or Somerset Maugham's elegant Villa Mauresque at Cap Ferrat. Brett Young also owned a seaside home at

Talland, near Looe in Cornwall. A Heinemann bestselling author could certainly afford to live it up.

To lose Somerset Maugham would of course have been a disaster, because he was then at the height of his powers, Heinemann between the wars publishing no fewer than 32 of his titles, including 15 plays, among them *The Circle* (1921), *Caesar's Wife* (1922), *Our Betters* (1923), *The Breadwinner* (1930), *For Services Rendered* (1932); as well as 17 novels, collections of short stories, and essays, including *The Painted Veil* (1925), *The Casuarina Tree* (1926), *Ashenden* (1928), *Cakes and Ale* (1930), *The Narrow Corner* (1932). To hold on to a successful author can quite often be as difficult as discovering a new one. Over the years Heinemann has probably lost no more than it has gained authors from rival firms. The reason for the moves frequently were complex and hard to understand, among the commonest being unreasonable demands by agents for bigger advances and dissatisfaction, whether or not justified, with the amounts and effort expended on promotion.

These and other problems have on many occasions been solved or, better, avoided by the trust and closeness of the link between the author and an individual in the firm. With top authors this has usually been the chairman or managing director, though it may sometimes be the editor who normally handles his or her work. Writing is a lonely trade, and authors, including the most inspired and proficient, usually look to the publisher to provide not merely objective criticism but also reassurance. Understandably the bestselling authors have always received VIP treatment, involving a multitude of small personal favours. Sales representatives ensure that their latest book is given impressive displays in the bookshops prior to one of their visits to London or any major centre. But the relationship often goes very much deeper and leads to genuine friendship. In the case of 'Willie' Maugham this was certainly true of Evans and, particularly in later years, of Frere-Reeves, who also paid visits to the Villa Mauresque, though he told me that 'Charley didn't know too much about them!' Eventually Frere-Reeves was to buy a nearby holiday villa for himself.

In *A Writer's Notebook* (1949) Maugham remarked that he did not think success had gone to his head because he had always expected to be successful. He certainly wanted generous royalties and advances and could reasonably expect them. He also demanded maximum advertising and promotion. He once wrote to his agent in New York that 'there is only one way I know by which a publisher can guarantee success, and that is by giving so large an advance that it is necessary for him to do everything he can for the book in order to get his money back. . . . I have been with Heinemann in London for twenty years and have resisted very substantial offers to leave them. . . . I am not so anxious to make a large sum of money out of a book as to have it as widely read as possible. I seek distinction rather than lucre.'[31]

The more consciously intellectual contemporary critics tended to think of Maugham as second-rate with a penchant for clichés; as a writer who merely possessed a knack for telling a good story and turning out well-made plays. They were apt to label him as being flippant, cynical, superficial, and, with that most dismissive epithet, 'competent'. His reaction was typically waspish: 'It has seemed strange to me that so many people concerned, though only at second hand, with the arts should regard competence with so little favour.'[32] As the astonishing extent of his achievement became apparent and maybe as literary fashions changed, he grew in stature, so as to present his publisher with the ideal and rare combination of a first-class craftsman, one who is not aiming merely to entertain, and a large, ever increasing readership. By 1933 Desmond MacCarthy was able to write in a pamphlet put out by the firm, 'It may not seem at first sight so surprising that such a writer should have won back the admiration of intellectuals as that he should have kept that of the common reader. Yet this is only unexpected to those who have not taken the trouble to observe what it is the public wants. It is a mistake to suppose that they only want happy day-dream fiction. They lap up any quantity of that soothing drug, and it is easy to provide, but they also love stories of actual life, even though these may be coloured by a pessimism they repudiate. Who, after all, has enjoyed a wider or more lasting popularity as a story-teller than Maupassant? And who was more pessimistic? Only such a writer must be one who *can* tell a story, who himself prefers stories with a point and can convey in immediately intelligible words whatever he describes. He must not be allusive but direct in statement. And if he sets out to write about reality, it must be a reality he has felt and seen himself. Above all, he must be intensely interested in men and women, though they disappoint him; and he must never be bored – no, not even with his own boredom. Just as it is the *genuine* fatuity of wish-fulfilment fiction which secures its success (everybody knows it is hopeless to try to write a sentimental bestseller with tongue in cheek), so it is the sincerity of the realist which holds the larger public, as it also does the few. Somerset Maugham possesses all the gifts essential in a popular realist.'[33] Being very professional, Maugham was also an ideal author in that his type-scripts were always meticulous. Frere-Reeves told me: 'After delivering them he would not expect any communication about them or want to discuss them until he received the proofs. Not that one ever did need to raise any points because everything was always perfect.' The proofs were returned promptly with very neat corrections. His attitude was: 'I've written the book. Now it's your job to publish it. I don't want to hear about it from now on." That was our relationship.' For eighteen years his proofs were also checked by his old friend Eddie Marsh (later Sir Edward and private secretary to three Prime Ministers: Asquith, Chamberlain, and Churchill). A Heinemann author himself and a translator of La Fontaine's *Fables* (1924), he supplied pages of copious notes on Maugham's proofs. 'Maugham was astonished to see that Marsh, so lenient in society, was a despot when it came to grammar. In fact, Marsh called what he did "diabolization", the art of finding fault and being as carping as possible for the eventual benefit of the work. "His comments are by turn scornful, pained, acid and vituperative", Maugham complained. "No obscurity escapes his stricture, no redundance his satire, and no clumsiness his obloquy. I think few authors could suffer this ordeal and remain per-suaded that they wrote tolerably well.'[34] Marsh refused any payment for his many hours of work and insisted that he did it only for pleasure.

The proofs of *Cakes and Ale* (1930) led to a literary *cause célèbre*. A set was sent to Hugh Walpole, chairman of the recently formed Book Society. In the middle of the next night Frere-Reeves was woken by an angry and agitated Walpole demanding that the publication be stopped. Alroy Kear, a central character in the book, was a novelist and lecturer, a social and literary snob, a careerist set upon becoming the Grand Old Man of letters. Walpole was convinced it was an unmistakable and malicious portrait of himself. Frere-Reeves, who knew Walpole well, replied that he could not see any resemblance. The next day he lunched with Walpole at the Reform Club together with H. G. Wells, Arnold Bennett, and J. B. Priestley, who had also read the proofs as a Book Society selector. Priestley then went back to Great Russell Street with Frere-Reeves and suggested they ought to try to persuade Walpole that Kear was not him but a portrait of John Drinkwater. With this intention he telephoned Walpole, who was by no means convinced, for he wrote in his diary that he was still '"dreadfully upset . . . he [Priestley] says that Maugham absolutely denies that it is me. But how can he, when there are in one conversation the very accents of my voice?"' Later he noted that he was '"still brooding over the Maugham book. It is the stab in the back that hurts me so. He has used so many little friendly things and twisted them round. Anyway it's a caddish book."'[35]

After receiving a letter of protest from Walpole, Maugham replied:

'My dear Hugh,

'I am really very unlucky. As you may have seen I have been attacked in the papers because they think my old man is intended to be a portrait of Hardy. It is absurd. The only grounds are that both died old, received the O.M. and were married twice. *You* know that for my story I needed this and there is nothing of Hardy in my character. Now I have your letter. I cannot say I was surprised to receive it because I had heard from Charley Evans that Priestley and Clemence Dane had talked to him about it. He told them that it had never occurred to him that there was any resemblance between the Alroy Kear of my novel and you; and when he spoke to me about it I was able very honestly to assure him that nothing had been further from my thoughts than to describe you. I can only repeat this. I do not see any likeness. My man is an athlete and a sportsman, who tries to be as little like a man of letters as he can. Can you really recognize yourself in this? Surely no one is the more complete man of letters than you are and really you cannot think of yourself as a famous golfer and a fervid fox-hunter. Nor is the appearance described anything like yours. Nor so far as I have ever seen do you frequent smart society. Frankau or E. F. Benson might just as well think themselves aimed at and Stephen McKenna much more. The only thing you can go on is the fact that you are also a lecturer. I admit that if I had thought twice of it I would have omitted this. But after all you are not the only English man of letters who lectures, but only the best known; and it is hard to expect a writer, describing such a character as I have, to leave out such a telling detail. The loud laugh is nothing. All big men with the sort of heartiness I have described have a loud laugh. The conversation you mention in California has entirely slipped my memory and I cannot place it in the book. I certainly was not conscious of repeating it. Really I should not have been such a fool. I

certainly never intended Alroy Kear to be a portrait of you. He is
made up of a dozen people and the greater part of him is myself.
There is more of me in him than of any writer I know. I suggest that if
there is anything in him that you recognize it is because to a greater or
less extent we are all the same. Certain characteristics we all have and
I gave them to Alroy Kear because I found them in myself. They do
not seem to me less absurd because I have them.

'I do not think for an instant that there will be any reference to this
business in the papers, but if there is I promise you that I will
immediately write, protest and vehemently deny that there has ever
been in my mind any thought of portraying you.

'Yours always,
'W. S. MAUGHAM'

Walpole replied briefly, signing himself 'Alroy Somerset Walpole', but
he was never really reassured and was 'upset all over again by a very
favourable review in *The Times Literary Supplement*. "People really do like
malice and cruelty in their literature these days. I cannot see it is a good
book, or in any way convincing, but I, of all people, am in this case
prejudiced!"'[36] *Cakes and Ale* is generally considered to be Maugham's
finest novel, though years after Walpole's death he was justified in his
protest because Maugham in an introduction to a new edition admitted
that he had Walpole in mind when he created Alroy Kear but, not wishing
to hurt Walpole's feelings, did all he could to cover up his tracks.[37]

Less than a year after the publication of *Cakes and Ale* a book called *Gin
and Bitters* came out in America under the obvious pseudonym A. Riposte
who was actually May Wiehe, though she normally wrote as Elinor
Mordaunt. Ironically it was a malevolent and barely veiled attack on
Somerset Maugham, and inevitably the word went round that Walpole
had penned it in revenge, but he immediately wrote to the Villa Mauresque to deny this and Maugham accepted his words. Meanwhile the
British rights in this vicious book had been offered to Heinemann and
Walpole urged them not to take it, but Frere-Reeves replied that half-a-
dozen English publishers were after it and, after failing to persuade
Maugham to get an injunction against its publication, they had decided
that all in all it was better that Heinemann should publish it rather than
anyone else. 'As much as you I would like to see that book stopped. We
suggested it to Willie, but it is his decision and desire that we should do it.

Quite obviously if it *is* published, it is better with us than being boomed and stunted in someone else's list. Several people, as well as ourselves, have been urging Willie to try and stop it. I think a line from you on the subject might help. Meanwhile the mud is properly stirred in New York and the story has already got into the English papers. It is a dirty, loathsome and mucky business and I hate it like hell. Why can't authors behave like grown-ups – even if they can't manage to be gentlemen?!'[38] Walpole wrote again to Maugham, pleading for an injunction, but he still refused. In the end the book was not published by Heinemann but by Martin Secker, who was forced to withdraw it when Maugham sued him for libel. It also appeared in the United States.

11

A List of Many Talents

In *The Summing Up* (1938) Maugham writes of the ephemeral nature of most books, specially novels, and that authors should seek consolation not in how a book is received by the public but by the realization that 'artistic creation is a specific activity that is satisfied by its own exercise. . . . The publishers will tell you that the average life of a novel is ninety days. It is hard to reconcile yourself to the fact that a book into which you have put, besides your whole self, several months of anxious toil, should be read in three or four hours and after so short a period forgotten. Though it will do him no good, there is no author so small-minded as not to have a secret hope that some part at least of his work will survive him for a generation or two. The belief in posthumous fame is a harmless vanity which often reconciles the artist to the disappointments and failure of his life. How unlikely he is to attain it we see when we look back on the writers who only twenty years ago seemed assured of immortality. Where are their readers now? And with the mass of books that are constantly produced and the ceaseless competition of those that have lived on, how small is the likelihood that work that has been once forgotten will ever be remembered!'[1]

This states precisely my problem, referred to earlier, of how to select who, among the thousands of authors and a total reckoned at being some fifty thousand titles published during close on a century, merit inclusion in this history – though 'merit' is perhaps the wrong word, because other considerations are also operative such as timing, notoriety, uniqueness of subject matter, peculiarity, and other factors. Who am I to attempt to grade them, particularly when critical criteria changed so dramatically from decade to decade? – not that this book has serious pretensions to be a work of literary criticism. Inevitably some critical signposts are necessary, and yet the selection of authors and titles has to be, in part at least, subjective. As we have seen, the big names of course select themselves; most of the authors who were limited to two or three *apparently* undistinguished,

[219]

virtually forgotten books, likewise eliminate themselves, even though they may include not a few unrecognized masterpieces; but how to discriminate between the large group in the middle, mostly novelists with ten or more titles to their credit but many of whose names may mean little to anyone other than our grandparents or great-grandparents? The somewhat less obvious (at least to me) yet still familiar names brought briefly to life in this and other chapters have emerged from this very unsatisfactory selection process. Other even less obvious authors, together with a few of their titles, appear in the Appendix at the end of the volume. There are still hundreds of others who appear nowhere, for if they did this history would degenerate into an immensely long bibliography.

Several authors again present difficulties of a different sort in that their writing took a variety of forms. John Masefield's prolific output, for example, was even more diverse than in the earlier period and included poetry and verse; plays in verse and prose; history; essays; literary criticism; autobiography; stories for children; and many novels. So far as possible I have tried to avoid fragmenting an author's output, but with some like Masefield this becomes illogical and in this section of this history he appears under more than one category as well as decade. As this chapter is concerned very much with fiction it is an apposite place to mention that during the 1920s and '30s Heinemann published seventeen of Masefield's novels and other works of prose. The talented story-teller was still loved, particularly for his straightforward narratives of life and adventure at sea. Among his best known books were *Sard Harker* (1924), *Odtaa* (1926) – an acronym from 'one damn thing after another' – and *The Bird of Dawning* (1933), about China clippers and shipwreck.

Some authors qualify for the prime self-selecting category even though they either left or joined Heinemann in mid-career. Storm Jameson is an undoubted example of this group, as eight of her novels were published between 1920 and 1932 when she decided to move to Cassell, Nicholson & Watson, and others. Her first novel had been published by Michael Sadleir at Constable's, but he did not like her second one and she sent it to Charley Evans. It was reported on favourably by Galsworthy: 'I've finished *The Happy Highways* and congratulate you on your choice. This authoress has done what none of the other torrential novelists of the last ten years has achieved – given us a convincing (if not picture, at least) summary of the effervescence, discontent, revolt, and unrest of youth; the heartache and the beating of wings. I should like to meet her. She must have seen and felt things. . . . To an old-fashioned brute like me, of course, the lack of form and line and the plethora of talk and philosophy pass a little stubbornly down the throat and stick a little in the gizzard; but the stuff is undeniable, and does not give me the hollow windy feeling I get from a German novel – say; nor do I feel suffocated by the crude ego that stalks through most of their novels.'[2]

Published in 1920, it did quite well, but not being tethered by an option clause she decided to return to Constable's. 'I wrote to tell Charles Evans what I was doing: it says everything for his patient kindness that he later took me back into Heinemann's bosom, without reproaches. He was a good man, and my friend. He would never, as did an elderly director of his firm, Mr Pawling, have taken me out to lunch and lectured me solemnly on the duty of a young writer. This was, if you believe me, to live for art, not money. It was too much for my – at the time – famished stomach.'[3] It was when Constable were not too keen about the first of a trilogy that she returned to Heinemann. Evans accepted it unseen for an advance of £400. It was *The Lovely Ship* (1927), which was followed by *The Voyage Home* (1930) and *A Richer Dust* (1931). The trilogy was about Whitby, the small port in Yorkshire where she had grown up, and centred on the life of Mary Hansyke from her birth in 1841 to her death in 1923 against a background of shipbuilding from sail to steam to turbines.

Having personal experience of working for the American publisher Knopf, Storm Jameson understood far better than most authors the difficulties and risks faced by publishers, though in an article for *The Bookseller* in October 1933 she admitted that she would rather be a publisher than a writer. 'It is not likely that he went into publishing with no thought but that of making money, since there are many ways in which so much energy and finesse could be more profitably used. Be that as it may, sooner or later, the question of profits becomes all important. When he reads a manuscript by an unknown writer he has two thoughts in his mind. Is this good? Will it pay for itself? That law which says that bad money drives good out of circulation holds good for other currencies than gold. In the end the second question leaves less and less room for the first. Experience does not encourage a publisher to run risks for the sake of good (but commercially dubious) books. If he varies the question "Will it pay?" to "Has this author a possible future which will repay me for losing money on his first, second or third book?" it is more than possible that his dealings with the author in question will be confined to the three unprofitable books. The fourth, and successful one, will be published by a more cautious or hard-hearted rival. It is natural. The writer, poor man, cannot but feel that three times unlucky and unsuccessful is enough, and wish to try his luck elsewhere. The publisher, poor man, learns another lesson. His experience is in any event less tragic than that of the serious writer who has never had any kind of success. Every publisher has had the experience of saying "X is a good writer. It's true he doesn't sell, but I'm going to try to sell him" – and of sadly giving X up after a repeated failure. The case of X is hopeless and dreadful. Nothing can be done for him by a society which allows no man to live without earning money unless he has inherited it.'[4]

Charles Evans's success was the result of being adept at making such calculations with uncanny skill, of knowing which authors to back – and even he made mistakes – but of course he was also very conscious that every book must at the very least pay its way by contributing to profits and not merely break even. No publisher can escape from the need to strike a balance between profitability and quality. It used to be said that if the individuals in the editorial department personally enjoyed a manuscript it was likely to flop! – or, in other words, what Q. D. Leavis, writing in 1932, called the 'curiously inverse relation existing between esteem and popularity'[5]. What makes a book sell even moderately well, let alone become a bestseller, was as much a mystery in the 1930s as it is today.

Another Heinemann author, Gerald Bullett – *The Panther* (1926), *The Pandervils* (1930) and ten other Heinemann titles – maintained in an article written in 1934 that the relationship between a bestseller and quality – or lack of it – was very complex, but that success could be explained in one word: 'Talk. It is talk that sells a book. A book that is talked about becomes the fashion, and a fashion is irresistible to about ninety per cent of the reading public, though repellent to the rest. But . . . what gets a book talked about? Not so long ago the superstition was current that the outstanding characteristic of the so-called bestseller was a total absence of literary merit. Publishers, in particular, eagerly embraced this notion and translated it into terms of policy. . . . This ingenuous point of view is still held in many quarters, and publishers continue to ruin themselves by publishing "popular" books that stand no chance of being popular. They are martyrs to a false religion, incapable of learning that no book, however "low-brow" can hope to achieve big sales if it lacks a certain degree of sincerity and good workmanship. That the bestseller necessarily lacks the higher literary qualities is a doctrine that will not stand examination. . . . Good books fail, bad books fail. Good books succeed, bad books succeed. Between popularity and literary merit (apart from competent workmanship) there is no sort of connection. The ultimate question – what sells a book? – is still unanswered and must remain so.'[6]

Evans, as we have seen, was more than most publishers an initiate of this mystery, but there is also no doubt that under his direction the list became more obviously commercial. The more recondite type of proposal with an unambiguously restricted market which so often took William's fancy was more likely to be rejected – perhaps Evans personally was less likely to be tempted? To what extent was Evans in tune with the mood, with the intellectual growing-points of his own period? Literary historians write at length about the 'ethos of a period', 'prevailing trends', 'socio-economic influences'; and, while the firm's authors must have come under and reflected these forces, it is tempting to wonder sceptically to what extent Evans and Frere-Reeves or their literary advisers were *conscious* of shaping or even following a trend or of being the instrument through which the period's ethos was mediated. No records survive to tell us.

Stage Business:
Masefield, Coward, and others

A rewarding example of Charles Evans's nose for a bestselling author was Margaret Kennedy. After her *Ladies of Lyndon* (1923), which sold only 1,200 copies, she wrote *The Constant Nymph* (1924), which was a sensational success. With the sprawling Sanger family and their house in the Austrian Tyrol, the eccentric musician father – said to be based on Augustus John – and his daughter Tessa, the constant nymph whose love affair supplies the book's tragic climax, it depicted just the kind of clash between convention and the conventional view of 'Bohemia' which tickled the palates of library readers. After a first print of 1,900 copies it quickly reprinted four times and altogether there have been twenty-seven reprints and it is still in print. It was dramatized in collaboration with Basil Dean, with Noël Coward in the lead. Later Margaret Kennedy wrote the long-running *Escape Me Never* (1934) for Elisabeth Bergner, which Heinemann also published, as well as eight more of her books. None repeated her earlier success and she moved to Cassell. Heinemann published a biography of Margaret Kennedy, *The Constant Novelist* by Violet Powell in 1983.

Despite doubts over their commercial viability, between the wars plays together with books about the theatre continued William's pioneering policy. As well as drama by Priestley, Maugham, and other established novelists, there were seven more plays by John Masefield, in verse as well as prose, enlivened by his passion for the spoken word rather than 'written' poetic language; they included *Melloney Hotspur* (1922), *The Trial of Jesus* (1925), and *The Coming of Christ* (1928), the last being performed with music at Canterbury Cathedral. Published posthumously were two plays by James Elroy Flecker (who had died in 1915): *Hassan* (1922), for which he is perhaps best remembered, and *Don Juan* (1925). The firm also published his *Collected Letters* (1922) and *Some Letters from Abroad* (1930) from the Near East and Switzerland which also contained a long biographical essay by his wife. Flecker's nephew John Sherwood wrote a biography of his uncle, *No Golden Journey*, which the firm published in 1973.

There were also Max Beerbohm's *Around Theatres, I and II* (1924); C. B. Cochran's racy *Secrets of a Showman* (1925); and two plays by a skilful new playwright, Emlyn Williams: the now unfortunately titled *He was Born Gay* (1937) and *The Corn is Green* (1938). The two most important contributors to the theatrical list were almost certainly Clemence Dane and Noël Coward. Both were literary all-rounders and Clemence was also an actress, a talented painter, potter, and sculptor – she modelled a dignified head of Charles Evans. Among her ten plays published between the wars, perhaps the most successful were *A Bill of Divorcement* (1921), *Naboth's Vineyard* (1925), and *Will Shakespeare* (1921), written in verse and a 'distinguished' failure, though Evans, twenty years later, told her that it was the 'flower of your poetic genius' which will be here 'as a piece of literature long after I – and future generations – have gone'[7]. Among her various novels was *Broome Stages* (1931), a gigantic saga of a theatrical family, its actor managers and playwrights as well as performers, which spanned a century-and-a-half from strolling players to film stars. It was told with vivid, unsentimental skill, based on her personal experience and love of the theatre. Acclaimed by the critics, it continued to sell for many years.

In a somewhat scathing review of Noël Coward's first volume of autobiography *Present Indicative* (1937) for the *New Statesman*, Cyril Connolly argued that 'this book reveals a terrible predicament, that of a young man with the Midas touch, with a gift that does not creep and blanch and flower, but which turns everything it touches into immediate gold. And this gold melts, too.'[8] Coward's outpouring of successful plays certainly amounted to a Midas touch for Heinemann. In the 1930s they published seven of his plays plus the first two volumes of *Play Parade* (1934) which included seven more and the three volumes of *Tonight at 8.30* (1934) with nine more, making a total of twenty-three for the decade – though two had been actually staged during the 1920s. There was also his first volume of short stories. The plays in these volumes included *The Vortex*, his first real success, which shocked the public because it dealt frankly with drug addiction and dissipated young people; the comedies *Private Lives* and *Hay Fever*, full of urbane and delicate malice; among the shorter plays were *Fumed Oak* and *Red Peppers*; then *Bitter Sweet*, effervescent and unashamedly sentimental; and the equally sentimental but patriotic *Cavalcade* (1932). Though said to be lacking in social conscience, in their unique, often flippant manner Coward's plays could certainly be said to reflect the changing ethos of English society. He mocked its institutions and yet he also adored them. He was continuously and effortlessly funny and that is probably the main reason why his plays succeeded on the printed page as well as on the stage. He offered the reader more than, as he put it, 'a talent to amuse'.

Frere-Reeves told me that he had known Noël in the early 1920s when he was still playing small parts and they used to go together to a nightclub called The Hambone, whose proprietor, George Wood, gave them a free dinner and drinks in return for their providing what was termed 'local colour' by wearing tweed jackets and flannel 'Oxford bags' which in those dinner-jacketed days were revolutionary. It followed that Frere-Reeves was Coward's regular contact in the firm, though at one moment he asked tactfully if he could deal with someone else because he found Frere-Reeves 'so unreliable'. One of his editors was probably nearer the truth when he said the two got on so well because they had the same sense of humour, bitchy. Frere-Reeves also recalled how, arriving at a memorial service, Noël had embraced him on both cheeks like a Frenchman, his normal custom. A reporter spotted this.

'Noël . . . I mean, Mr Coward, sir. Who have you just been kissing?'

'My publisher.'

'Do you always kiss your publisher?'

'If you were my publisher', Noël looked him straight in the eye, 'the answer is no.'

Fiction from
America and Australasia

The connection with Doubleday and regular visits by liner to America by Byard and Evans fostered the continuation of William's policy of having a strong American contingent in his list. Seven authors will have to suffice to mark their contribution between the wars.

First, Willa Cather. Following a couple published by William there were seven more of her books. Small quantities (*c.* 1,500) of printed sheets of each were imported and their sales were unremarkable with the exception of *A Lost Lady* (1924) and especially *Death Comes to the Archbishop* (1927). This powerful novel, based on contemporary letters, about two French priests who were missionaries in the desert territory of New Mexico, with its hardships and accidents, recaptures some of the joyful energy that kept them going. This masterpiece was reprinted several times and reissued in 1948. Virago has also reissued it in paperback.

Christopher Morley was actually a member of Doubleday's staff when Heinemann published thirteen of his books during the 1920s. He was versatile and, if I were to adhere rigidly to categories, he would belong to a later chapter. He turned out novels, short plays, belles lettres, poetry, and anthologies. His like no longer exists. With affinities with James Barrie, he was described as being whimsically humorous, discreetly sentimental, witty, satirical, fanciful, delicately and discursively sympathetic – though he was 'threatened by a too conscious charm, a too practised wistfulness'.

His best-known and the three most saleable books in Britain were *Thunder on the Left* (1925), not a piece of agit-prop but a 'fantasy of childhood translated to a grown-up world that was delightfully contrived as a comedy of sentiment'[9]; *Parnassus on Wheels* (1921) about a girl who buys a travelling library and tours the country pursued by its former owner; and *Where the Blue Begins* (1923) about a well-to-do dog with an income of one thousand bones a year who adopts three puppies, goes into business, tries to enter the Church, and much else. It was meant for grown-ups and was described as being on a level with *Gulliver's Travels*.

Edna Ferber came straight from the Doubleday stable in 1922. Heinemann were to publish altogether fourteen of her novels, plays, and volumes of short stories. Her writing may not be profound but her characters show that she understood the ordinary folk of America: department store clerks, madams seeking to become respectable, a truck driver whose conversation she found more stimulating than that of the owner of a Cadillac. Her novels span the United States: *So Big* (1924), which won a Pulitzer Prize, was set in Illinois; *Show Boat* (1926), which was made into a musical with Paul Robeson, was in the Deep South; then there was *Cimarron* (1930) – Oklahoma; *American Beauty* (1931) – Connecticut; *Saratoga Trunk* (1942) – New York. Edna Ferber's departure for Gollancz in 1952 exemplifies the need for a close, continuing relationship with someone in the firm. In a letter to Frere-Reeves she said that 'since the death of my friend Charles Evans I have been, as you know, almost completely out of touch with Heinemann's. He was indefatigable in his help regarding three refugee children with whom I was involved and who were at school in Surrey. This kindness I never shall forget and if he were alive today I would not and could not sever my relations with the company.'[10] It was too late for Frere-Reeves to put things right.

A pair of solid but popular authors from the heart of America who added reliable turnover to the inter-wars list were Joseph Hergesheimer (15 titles) and Booth Tarkington (21 titles). The former wrote, for example, about the rise and fall of a family in the Pennsylvania iron belt – *The Three Black Pennys* (1918); about newly rich Virginians – *Mountain Blood* (1929); and the results of miscegenation in historic New England – *Java Head* (1919). There were also his more romantic novels such as *The Bright Shawl* (1923), set in the West Indies, and *Tampico* (1927), in Mexico.

The earlier novels of Booth Tarkington, including winners of two Pulitzer Prizes, were published by John Murray and Hodder & Stoughton, but the trilogy *Growth* (1927), which included *The Magnificent Ambersons*, was completed by Heinemann with *The Midlander* (1924). *The Plutocrat* (1927) was a powerful study of a self-made businessman travelling abroad and *The Heritage of Hatcher Ide* (1941) recreated the Great Depression in a Midwest city. Tarkington was also noted for his stories for boys such as *Penrod Jasper* (1929). With good reason Heinemann has never worried about being Cocacolonized.

Then there was Mary Borden. She came from Chicago and her writing retained something distinctively American, although she spent most of her life in Europe and was deeply involved in English and French society as the wife of Major-General Sir Edward Spears, the outspoken Conservative MP and head of the British Military Mission in Paris. She was very accomplished, but many of her books were confined to the modish and wealthy reaches of society, those she knew best. Her first book in Britain and for Heinemann, *Jane – Our Stranger* (1923), about a rich Mid-Western woman in France, was an immediate success. Numerous others followed during the next thirty years, the best-known perhaps being *A Woman with White Eyes* (1930); *Jehovah's Day* (1928) which dealt with the biological, antediluvian origins of the human species; and a bestselling *Mary of Nazareth* (1933). Later books were concerned with events in Europe, such as *Passport for a Girl* (1939) about Austria after the Nazi occupation.

There were also writers from Australia. The name of Henry Handel Richardson disguised another permanent literary immigrant, Mrs J. G. Robertson, who had left Australia at the age of eighteen and yet retained so much of her distinctive 'down-under' flavour that she was considered at the time of her death in 1946 to be the most eminent of Australian novelists. Somerset Maugham said of her novels that they were great 'in the way that Tolstoy's novels were great'. So many Heinemann novelists must inevitably fall into the category of middle-range and middle-brow, readable, entertaining, money-spinners, but Henry Handel Richardson beyond any doubt deserves to be assessed by far more rigorous criteria. Her ability was slow to be recognized and she wrote comparatively little, and it is fair to say that William (who published her first three) and Evans (who published the next five) must have been motivated by her sheer quality rather than her sales potential, though gratifying reprints and American sales came in due course. But how many are familiar with her work today? After reading her first novel, *Maurice Guest* (1908), William is reported to have said that 'this book will be here when we are all under the sod' – it still is here, as Virago brought out an edition with the original pagination in 1981. Based on a period in Leipzig, where as a girl she studied music, it is a vigorously imagined story of a man's overwhelming passion for an Australian girl, already the mistress of a composer, that leads eventually to his suicide. The book was rapidly forgotten, though it maintained an almost cult-value among some writers and it was republished in 1922 with a preface by Hugh Walpole and again in 1950. *The Getting of Wisdom* (1910), which stemmed from her experience at a girls' school in Melbourne, was thought to lack her first novel's remarkable maturity, but then came her great trilogy *The Fortunes of Richard Mahony* which follows the life of an egocentric but likeable doctor during the first Australian gold rush in the 1850s; secondly, when he visits England of the late 1860s to taste the pleasures of European civilization; and finally, in the third volume, his return to Australia where he suffers increasing mania leading to his death. The first volume, *Australia Felix*, had appeared in 1917 in the very darkest days of World War I and it was not surprising that it failed to attract much notice. Arnold Gyde, who had just joined the firm when the second volume, *The Way Home*, arrived, recalls how 'the chief reader had gone to America, and nothing had been done about it until I was asked to lay all the manuscripts on the floor of the editorial office – first novels in one pile, manuscripts of known writers in another, biographies here, verse there. Amongst those of known authors was of course Henry Handel Richardson's novel and we proceeded to hurry on with its publication. No great success attended the venture when the book appeared in 1925. Few had read the predecessor, and none knew what was to follow. This is often the way with the middle volume of trilogies. But I had noticed that the critic Gerald Gould, who wrote of books in *The Observer* and the *Daily News*, was interested in the work and I sent him proofs of the final volume, *Ultima Thule* (1929), shortly before publication. He did not acknowledge the parcel; I did not even know if he had read the work. Thus that dreadful fortnight between the issue of review copies and publication date passed slowly by. Judge of my delight when I opened *The Observer* on the Sunday before publication date! For Gould wrote: "The book is a masterpiece, worthy to rank with the greatest and saddest masterpieces of our day." A few days later Gould wrote in the *Daily News*, calling it "not only a work of genius, but a work of genius assured and triumphant." Other critics followed suit, and Ernest Newman stated that *Mahony* moved him as passages of Beethoven's symphonies did.'[11] Frank Swinnerton, another of her many admirers, sums up her outstanding virtues as 'steadiness of vision and sobriety of judgment allied to very exceptional imaginative power. The method is so quiet that its merit, and in fact the essential imaginativeness of the work, may be missed by those eager for display; a little formal as to style, it has not the pace and brilliance of the best very modern exhibitions of life. But the touch is unerring.'[12]

Two other Australian women writers published in this period deserve mention: among five novels by Mary Mitchell was *A Warning to Wantons* (1934), a romp with a difference about a minx from Paris who comes to a sticky end in the Carpathians; it was a minor bestseller. The second Australian was Helen Simpson with eleven novels, the best remembered being *Boomerang* (1932), *Saraband for Dead Lovers* (1935) and *Under Capricorn* (1937), the last two being turned into successful films. According to another publisher, Walter Harrap, she felt under a particular obligation to Heinemann: 'Her first novel', he wrote in a letter to *The Times*, 'was published by Heinemann and was a failure. She expected her second novel to be rejected, but again Heinemann backed their judgment and their faith in an author and again failure was their reward. So the story went on until *Boomerang* was ready. It was submitted in a spirit of hope but with no great belief in charity. Once again Heinemann was the publisher and that book justified their faith and established its author. . . . Summing up her experiences, Helen Simpson said: "But for their belief in me *Boomerang* might never have been written. I so recognize my indebtedness to their courage and support that while Heinemann want me as an author I am theirs to command." '[13]

This group of American and Australian titles ends with three general authors. Franklin D. Roosevelt's *Looking Forward* (1933); Ray Stannard Baker's eight-volume *Woodrow Wilson: Life and Letters* (1927–39); and, even though he once declared that 'history is bunk', perhaps not unfittingly with Henry Ford's *My Life and Work* (1922).

Selling and Promoting:
Home and Overseas –
Libraries

As on the day when William first met Pawling at Mudie's, the kind of list generated by Heinemann between the wars, dominated as it was by fiction, was equally dependent for much of its success on the libraries – particularly the circulating libraries, though increasingly the free public libraries as well. Many more readers borrowed books than bought them. Just over half of W. H. Smith's 1,250 branches offered a library service, though the stocks of many of them were pretty small. Then there were the 'twopenny libraries' which charged this sum per volume per week. Boots libraries were probably the most important for Heinemann with four hundred branches and half a million subscribers at 42s. a year to get any book 'on demand'; 17s.6d. allowed you to choose from all books currently in circulation; and 10s.6d. gave you what was called the 'ordinary service'. More exclusive libraries in London such as Mudie's, Day's, *The Times* Book Club, or Harrods (who delivered to the country) were more expensive.

Although their censoring grip was not as powerful as that of the Victorian circulating libraries, Queenie Leavis could comment scathingly in 1932: 'Undoubtedly there are subscribers who use the circulating libraries to supplement and direct their book-buying. But no one who has made a point of frequenting London and provincial branches of the book-clubs [she must have meant circulating libraries] for the past few years can avoid concluding that the book-borrowing public has acquired the reading habit while somehow failing to exercise any critical intelligence about its reading. It is significant that the proportion of fiction to non-fiction borrowed is overwhelmingly great, that women rather than men change the books (that is, determine the family reading), and that many subscribers call daily to change their novels.'[14]

It was however the libraries even more than their subscribers that influenced what kind of fiction was published and tended to standardize the taste of the large middle-brow reading public. How this happened is made clear by one of Heinemann's own authors, Denis Mackail, when in his novel *Greenery Street* (1925) Felicity visits her local circulating library: 'Twice, sometimes three times a week, she sets out with a bundle of books under her arm, goes up in one of Andrew Brown's lifts, presents herself at the desk which is labelled "FAB to KYT" and smiles at the young lady who sits behind it. In Felicity's case the young lady always returns this smile and the following dialogue then takes place:

Felicity: "I've brought two books back, and here's my new list. Have you got the first volume of *Indiscreet Reminiscences* yet?"

Attendant: "I'm afraid they're all out still. But can I give you the second?"

Felicity: "No, thank you. We've had that. Oh – I say – have you got *Spate*? No? Well, have you got *That the Swine Did Eat*? Oh, aren't you taking it? I see. Well, have you got *The Gutter*? Oh, but I'm *sure* it's published. I saw a long review of it – Oh, yes; perhaps it was an advertisement. Well, have you got *The Braxingfield Mystery*? My husband is *always* asking for it. Oh; I see. Well, have you got anything on my list? And nothing on the old list either? Well, what *have* you got, then?"

(The Attendant, who has been waiting for this moment, dives under the desk and fetches up about half a dozen novels, which she offers for Felicity's inspection.)

Attendant: "Here are some of the latest, Mrs Foster."

(Felicity looks at the backs of these works, and fails to recognize either their titles or their authors.)

Felicity (politely, but disparagingly): "I don't think I –"

Attendant (briskly): "*Prendergast's Property* – that's a very pretty story."

Felicity (doubtfully): "Oh . . . I never seem to like books where the people are called Prendergast."

Attendant: "Well, what about *The Transept*? It's going very well, you know."

Felicity (suspiciously): "Is it religious?"

Attendant (surprisingly): "Oh, no. It's about Rhodesia."

Felicity (with conviction): "I always hate that."

(By this time, however, a small queue has formed behind her, which has the effect of weakening her critical judgment. The Attendant realizes this, and goes quickly ahead.)

Attendant: "I think you'd like this, Mrs Foster. *Illumination*."
(Felicity picks up *Illumination* and opens it. Nice short
paragraphs, anyhow; and quite large print.)
Felicity: "All right. That'll do for one." (The queue shows fresh
signs of impatience.) "And – oh, very well. I'll take *The Transept*
for the other. Perhaps my husband will like it."
Attendant (more briskly than ever): "Oh, he's sure to, Mrs Foster."
Felicity: "Well, thank you very much. Good morning." *Exit*.'[15]

This may be a storyteller's exaggeration, but it probably represented a
common enough happening, one for which many of Heinemann's titles
were tailored. The middle classes still tended to look upon the public
libraries run by local authorities as meant only for the improvement of the
working classes and believed that their much handled volumes were to be
avoided lest you 'catch something', but the public libraries became
increasingly important outlets for the firm's books – and even more
important than the circulating libraries in the case of non-fiction. The
Public Libraries Act of 1919, which marked the end of the maximum
penny rate spent on libraries and the beginning of the county as well as the
urban library service, led to their expansion. Despite the check caused by
the economic depression, by 1934–35, for example, 165.67 million books
were loaned compared with 54.51 million in 1913–14 and the public
libraries had 26.43 million volumes in stock compared with 11.40
million.[16] By 1924, 96.3 per cent of the population of England and Wales
lived within the area of a library authority, though the coverage was by no
means uniform. Paradoxically, the Depression triggered an increase in
demand, particularly for light fiction. The expansion of the public
libraries reflected the increase in leisure for the employed and the spread
of education, helped by the 1918 Education Act, which raised the school
leaving age to fourteen without exception.

The circulating libraries purchased their books straight from publishers and received the same discount as booksellers – often they were
booksellers as well. The public libraries purchased from booksellers or
library suppliers and received no discount; which, as major customers,
they naturally resented. After a year of agitation the Publishers' and
Libraries' Associations signed an agreement in 1929 giving the libraries
ten per cent discount, though this had to come out of the booksellers'
discount and was not at the expense of the publishers, except that the

latter agreed to give better terms on single copies ordered for resale to libraries.

Promoting books to both types of libraries was of course a priority for the firm's sales and publicity departments, but modern-style 'marketing' as opposed to selling had yet to be invented. Publishing was still on a relatively small scale (a total of 8,738 new books were issued by UK publishers in 1920; 9,977 in 1925; 11,856 in 1930; 11,410 in 1935) and competition was not so fierce as it is today. Books had a much better chance of being reviewed. The firm's bookshop representatives had, however, been increased by 1931 from four to seven. In 1929 Leslie Munro had been made sales manager in place of G. E. Reeves who had been obliged to retire because of ill health. After years on the road himself, Munro continually stressed the importance not only of sending out advance information in good time, but also of maintaining close personal relationships with the trade buyers. Presiding over the 1932 annual dinner of the Book Publishers' Representatives Association, he told the guests that the 'publisher's representative may be regarded as the shock absorber, which makes the great machinery for the dissemination of literature run smoothly. He it is who has to withstand the shocks handed out to him by the bookseller, and he it is who has to withstand the shocks handed out on his return to the office. Give him, then, all the support you can. Feed him with early information, feed him with advance copies rather than with letters full of grouses, which serve only to disturb and discourage.'[17] The reps' job is a very lonely one and requires great reserves of self-reliance. Over the years Heinemann has been well served by its front line in the bookshops.

'"It's all a question of a certain patter"', according to Michael Mont, the publisher in *The White Monkey* (1924) by Galsworthy who had used Charles Evans as a source of inside knowledge of publishing. '"What you would have to do", Mont told young Butterfield, applying for a job as a rep., "is to impress on the poor brutes who sell the books that every one on your list – say about thirty-five – is necessary in large numbers to his business. It's lucky you've chucked your conscience, because as a matter of fact most of them won't be. . . . Only one book in twenty is a necessity really, the rest are luxuries. Your stunt will be to make them believe the nineteen are necessaries, and the twentieth a luxury that they need. It's like food or clothes, or anything else in civilization."'[18]

As well as the standard Spring and Autumn lists, review copies and

[234]

leaflets, relatively more was spent on Press advertising than it is today. In a sample thirteen-week period (December 1934–February 1935) the firm spent £2,027 for space in seven publications which were used regularly. Of this 96 per cent went on advertisements in *The Sunday Times* (£865) and *The Observer* (£1,082). An unusual offer appeared in an advertisement in *The Daily Telegraph* in connection with *What Happened to the Corbetts* (1939), Heinemann's first novel by Nevil Shute, about a surprise air attack on Britain. The book was offered free to ARP workers and others interested in the National Defence. The copy read: 'It is a novel; but so realistic is the narrative, and so important is its message today, that the publishers feel bound to bring it as urgently as possible to the widest official notice. Everyone should read it, and no one having done so will fail to take thought as to his or her own position should war come. The publishers have therefore prepared a special but strictly limited edition and will present one copy FREE (and post free) until the edition is exhausted, to applicants in rotation. FILL UP THIS COUPON NOW, AND POST IT.' With hindsight the firm's generosity must have been seen to be unnecessary!

Arnold Gyde, responsible for publicity, was not lax in buttering up his Fleet Street contacts and his publicity budget included the cost of some lavish parties in the panelled splendours of 99 Great Russell Street and on the manicured lawns of Kingswood. In 1933 the firm's annual garden party was described in *The Publisher and Bookseller* as having 'now developed into one of the season's social affairs, for the well-known band of authors connected with this publishing house are always amply supplemented by bearers of famous names from the world of society, music and the theatre. The rain luckily ceased in time for the early afternoon's sun to dry the turf and freshen the beds of many coloured flowers. Mr and Mrs C. S. Evans received the guests on behalf of the directors of the firm, and Mr Doubleday, still unfortunately confined to his Daimler parked beneath the trees, had a handshake and a word for most of the distinguished guests present.'[19] Two years later the trade journal reported that the rooms at 99 Great Russell Street with their 'lovely panelling were crowded with many authors of repute. . . . Here, for instance, was Somerset Maugham, who in a few hours was due to sail for America. Here also was Michael Arlen, admitting that the right title for the novel on which he had been working for two years still eluded him with diabolical cunning. Authors had come from near and far to be present at the gathering. Radclyffe Hall, whose profile more than her ruffles and diamond studs make her the most easily recognized of all British authors, had just arrived from Italy . . . Violet Trefusis . . . Tschiffely . . . Hamish Hamilton . . . H. G. Wells . . . Cecil Roberts. . . . A journalist with a mathematical trend of mind computed that the people in one room at one given moment had been responsible for the printing of no less than three million words since Christmas.'[20] It must have been some party!

Exports of British books between the wars were relatively of less importance than they are today and Heinemann had no overseas branches, relying on local agents and/or the services of other UK publishers more firmly established overseas and who sold on commission (e.g., the Oxford University Press in Australia). The foundations of what was known as 'imperial publishing' were, however, already well laid, though Canada was often, as it is today, a subject of dispute when US rights were sold. Most orders from booksellers in the British Empire were serviced direct from the newly built warehouse at Kingswood, but in the case of many novels there were still also 'colonial' editions produced for sale overseas at a lower price than the home edition on the assumption that in the Dominions books were to a much greater extent bought rather than borrowed. This complex situation is encapsulated in a letter written by Charles Evans in November 1929 about the overseas sales of *The Good Companions*: 'We rarely have Canadian rights of any books which are published in the USA. In Australasia we sold the book through our agent, Bartholomew, and in South Africa through the medium of the London Export Houses, as there we have no special agent. In the case of *The Good Companions* and also of two or three other novels which we have published at 15s. or 10s.6d. we did not make a special colonial edition. We sold the ordinary edition at half the English published price, having made provision in the agreements with the author that the royalty on copies so sold to the Colonies should be 10 per cent of 5s.3d., which is about 6½d. a copy. The difference between this royalty and the royalty paid on the home edition gives us a good enough margin to make the colonial sales profitable.'[21]

Whenever a publisher solicits sales direct from the public, booksellers understandably object and even make threats to refuse to continue to trade with the offender; and yet in 1925 under Effendi's guidance a direct-mail organization, called the Associated Bookbuyers Company, was set up under Frere-Reeves's control. Flagrantly, by means of circulars and press advertisements it offered Heinemann books for sale, concentrating on certain titles but including the Loeb Classical Library and Galsworthy's collected works (about which under the ABC's imprint an introductory booklet was issued). Large-scale direct mail shots were dispatched and orders poured in, though the overheads were heavy (e.g., 75.5 per cent in 1926; 79.4 per cent in 1927) and shipping costs and other problems made the venture difficult overseas, especially in India, where, as Frere-Reeves wrote to Effendi in February 1928, 'we have tried both circularizing and direct advertising, and in neither case have we met with any success. The country is badly organized, difficult to get at, and operations are always handicapped by the millions of half-educated babus they have there, who will write for anything without the faintest intention of paying for it. What we have done, which may interest you, is to write to secretaries of all the white stations in India, suggesting that we should supply them with books at regular intervals and on regular terms.'[22]

While a certain amount of direct-mail selling was to be successfully attempted some decades later, it was not through the Associated Book-buyers Company, whose activities by the end of the 1930s appeared to have lapsed, though the exact reasons for this are not clear. It did, however, achieve a large number of sales from people who would not normally have entered a bookshop. Particularly successful were Lady Troubridge's *The Book of Etiquette* (1926) and T. H. Van der Velde's *Ideal Marriage; its Physiology and Technique* (1928) which, obtainable in a plain envelope from an address in Kingswood, Surrey, gave for its day remarkably sensible advice to married (and presumably unmarried) couples on how to achieve mutual satisfaction, the techniques being explained by means of skilful graphs that illuminated the difference between *coitus interruptus* and premature ejaculation. A revised edition was issued as late as 1965.

Although they really belong to the next section, this is a convenient moment to record that several books by Havelock Ellis were published in the 1930s. The first was *Psychology of Sex* (1933), which was followed by *Man and Woman* (1934), a revised edition of a work that originally appeared in 1894; *Sex in Relation to Society* (1937); and his autobiography, *My Life* (1940).

Boulestin, Wells, Tschiffely, and other non-fiction

Under Evans's guidance the main strength of the list in the 1920s and '30s was more than ever fiction; compared with other leading publishers, Heinemann published relatively few general books, but several of them demand inclusion in any record of the period, for example Emile Coué's fashionable work on autosuggestion, *My Method* (1923) – 'Day by day and in every way I am getting better and better'; Paul Gauguin's *Intimate Journals* (1923); and David Lloyd George's *The Truth about Reparations and War Debts* (1932). H. G. Wells had come back into the list with *The Autocracy of Mr Parham* (1930), a comic novel with a contemporary political theme and cartoons by David Low. It was followed by no less than 850 pages on *The Work, Wealth, and Happiness of Mankind* (1934).

Equally influential in a somewhat different manner was the series on cookery and wine by Xavier Marcel Boulestin, which did so much to rescue British life from soggy cabbage and Brown Windsor soup. Boulestin started his working life in France as a drama and music critic and was for a while secretary to the husband of Colette. Settling in London, he revelled in the luxury and wealth of Edwardian society. After war service in France he returned to London and reopened a decorating business and acted as agent for various French artists. It was while he was showing some etchings to Theodore Byard that a deal was made for him to try his hand at a French cookery book. Byard is reported to have produced a contract on the spot and an advance of £10. J. E. Labourer, who made the etchings, also provided a frontispiece to this first book, *Simple French Cooking for English Homes* (1923) which was followed by ten others up to World War II when Boulestin returned to France, was cut off in the German-occupied zone, where he died in 1943. They included *The Conduct of the Kitchen* (1925), *A Second Helping* (1925), *What Shall We Have to Drink?* (1933), *101 Ways of Cooking Potatoes* (1932). On the strength of the books he also opened the Restaurant Boulestin in Covent Garden which still flourishes. Boulestin was not, as one of the firm's blurbs declared, a 'world famous chef'. He was essentially an interpreter of French regional cooking and not interested in *haute cuisine*. He distrusted rigid quantities and, instead, believed that one cannot provide the reader with an exact recipe. It is up to each cook to work intelligently. Heinemann also published his *Having Crossed the Channel* (1934), a record of a journey back to his native Périgord and to small country inns with the kind of menus that have largely vanished with so much of rural French life. A collection of his recipes was republished in *The Best of Boulestin* (1971).

Heinemann's extensive list of travel books was augmented between the wars, though it gradually shrank in size. There was Alexandra David-Neel's sensational *My Journey to Lhasa* (1927), billed as 'the personal story of the only white woman who succeeded in entering the forbidden city'. There was an expensive, copiously illustrated account of *HRH The Prince of Wales's Sport in India* (1925) by Bernard C. Ellison, who was described as 'naturalist to the shoots', a book to dismay HRH's great-nephew; and, somewhat surprisingly, *A Three-Legged Tour in Greece* (1927) by Dame Ethel Smyth, the composer who appeared to have 'revelled in the primitive conditions of modern Greece'. Four books came from Ralph Stocks, including the bestselling *The Cruise of the Dreamship* (1921). In 1933 appeared the celebrated *Tschiffely's Ride* (originally called *From Southern Cross to Pole Star*), being the account of 10,000 miles in the saddle in the Americas from Argentina to Washington. T. F. Tschiffely used two Argentine mustang horses and it took him two years of fighting his way over the Andes, through rivers, mosquito-ridden swamps, and sometimes regions infested with bandits. It was no wonder that by 1949 it had sold 57,000 copies, even though the production of the later editions was scrappy. At one point Tschiffely was earning a 25 per cent royalty. He followed up his classic with books about other excursions on horseback, from the *Bridle Paths* (1936) of England to *The Way Southward* (1940) in Patagonia and Tierra del Fuego. He also wrote *Don Roberto* (1937) which dealt with the life and works of another Heinemann author, R. B. Cunninghame Graham, most of whose books belong as well in this chapter as anywhere else.

South America and horses are at the heart of most of the books published for Graham, but he also wrote about Morocco, Scotland, and much else in volumes of history, stories, biographies, sketches and essays as well as travel. This extraordinary, picturesque man, partly Scottish and partly Spanish, was described as an 'aristocratic socialist', a 'hidalgo', and a 'cowboy dandy'; he was ranching in Argentina at sixteen; he enlisted in the Uruguayan army; he was a Liberal/Socialist MP for North West

Lanarkshire, a devotee of William Morris and a comrade of H. M. Hyndman; he was an early Scottish Home Ruler and was imprisoned in Pentonville together with John Burns, MP as a ringleader of riots on 'Bloody Sunday' in Trafalgar Square on 13 November 1887.

Around the turn of the century he had written four books for Heinemann, including the celebrated *Mogreb-el-Acksa* (1898), which describes his attempt to journey beyond the Atlas disguised as a Turkish doctor, Sheikh Mohammed el Fasi; he was arrested and locked up for some days in a local Cadi's goal. After a break he wrote fifteen more books for the firm between 1920 and his death in 1936. They dealt with the Conquistadores; a Brazilian mystic who worked miracles, Antonio Conselheiro; horses and horsemanship. Cunninghame Graham was, first, a man of action who wrote down no more than what pleased, interested, or amused him. Not a bad recipe!

Several important general books appeared late in the 1930s. There was Herbert Read's influential *Art and Society* (1937); the firm having previously published his *The Green Child* (1935), described as a 'romance', and a book of essays. The firm's catholic taste was displayed by books on Chinese thought and philosophy and also on Christianity. The former was represented by Lin Yutang's *My Country and my People* (1936) and *The Importance of Living* (1938), which was reprinted many times and for at least one generation penetrated the bamboo curtain with urbane wisdom; it was to be followed by nineteen of his further titles, including fiction. Christianity was represented by A. R. Vidler's *A Plain Man's Guide to Christianity* (1936), written from a liberal Catholic point of view, and E. Sutherland's Bates's *The Bible Designed to be Read as Literature* (1937). Set in Eric Gill's new Perpetua, the design was elegant – which could not be said of many of the books printed at the Windmill Press – and its purpose was to eliminate many of the features of the traditional bible which created barriers to its nonpareil prose and poetry; these included printing most of the poetry as if it were prose and breaking up the paragraphs of prose as if it were verse; the narrow double columns divided by a columnar flood of references and cross-references; the cumbersome punctuation; and, above all, the repetitions and illogical arrangement of both the Old and New Testaments, the interspersion of genealogies, legal codes, census reports; the divergencies between the four gospels; and much else. The attempt to provide a more coherent bible was summarized by E. Sutherland Bates, as rearranger and editor: 'To afford a consecutive narrative from the creation to the exile, supplementing this by a selection from the Apocryphal I Maccabees (taken like the rest from the Authorized version) in order to complete the story down to the time of Jesus; to emphasize the greatness of the Prophets and minimize the others; to rearrange the drama, poetry, and fiction, adding to the latter the world-famous tales of Judith, Tobit, and Susanna and the Elders together with selections from Ecclesiastes and the Wisdom of Solomon (all in the Authorized translation of the Apocrypha); to give the basic biography of Jesus found in the Gospel according to Mark, the earliest and most authoritative, supplemented by those incidents and teachings not found in Mark but in the other Gospels; to restrict the utterances of Paul to those only that have immortal value and to omit entirely the unimportant pseudonymous epistles; and, so far as sequence of contents permits, to print all the works in their order of composition: these liberties are necessary if one seeks to put out a Bible that can be read as literature'. There was no doubt that he was successful. The first printing of 25,000 was sold in two weeks and a reprint of 50,000 was put in hand immediately.

In at the Birth of the Book Club

The inter-wars years saw two important innovations: the introduction of book tokens in 1932 and the birth of the first British book club, the Book Society, in 1929. Heinemann, and particularly Frere-Reeves, were closely involved with the latter from the outset. It was inspired by the success of the American Book of the Month club, though credit for first suggesting something of the kind for Britain goes to Arnold Bennett, with whom Frere-Reeves began to formulate a plan. Bennett was willing to lend his name and prestige to the venture, but things had not progressed far before there was a serious misunderstanding. In the words of Reginald Pound, who wrote a biography of Arnold Bennett (which Heinemann published in 1952), he 'had conducted himself not entirely becomingly in negotiations for the founding of a book club in Britain. . . . Taking him at his word, which included a promise to sponsor the scheme generally,

Frere-Reeves went to a great deal of trouble to secure backing. Having finally got it, he heard that Bennett was in touch with the *Daily Express* about a similar scheme. It seemed important to lose no time. Frere-Reeves promptly registered several likely book club names, secured the interest of Hugh Walpole and J. B. Priestley, and started what became the Book Society, which has had a successful history over many years. When he next saw Arnold Bennett there was a sharp exchange between them, Bennett protesting that Frere-Reeves had used *his* idea. Taxed then with having gone back on his word, Bennett said with a lift of his crumpled chin: "I suppose I am at liberty to change my mind if I wish to do so." If this was a wilful deviation from his high standard of personal rectitude one feels that its originating impulse was beyond his control.'[23]

Hugh Walpole was, however, glad to become chairman of the first selection committee which, in addition to Priestley, consisted of Clemence Dane, Sylvia Lynd, and George Gordon. Finance came through a Heinemann author, Alan Bott – who later put together *Our Fathers: 1870–1900* (1931), an entertaining assembly of engravings from the *Graphic* and other Victorian journals. Arthur Barker from Heinemann's editorial department was made manager, but he soon left to found his own imprint, being succeeded by another Heinemann employee, Rupert Hart-Davis. Despite the connections with Heinemann people, The Book Society prided itself on being genuinely independent of any publisher and, once it was established, Effendi told Frere-Reeves to loosen his contact because he believed that one could not be a successful publisher and run a book club at the same time – though not long afterward Doubleday Doran was to own the American Literary Guild!

The Book Society soon flourished, though Priestley was unhappy as a selector and resigned because, as he told Hart-Davis: 'The trouble is that Walpole wants to choose every book we are sent; I want to choose no book at all; Sylvia Lynd wants to choose books by the people she has been out to dinner with; and Clemence Dane has a pre-Caxton view of books – the sight of print on a page excites her to madness.' Members received the month's choice by post on the day of publication, paying the full published price, though as membership grew the publishers charged the club less because the increased print run reduced costs. The Fiction Group of the Publishers' Association agreed to a scale of discounts which enabled the publishers to supply copies of a novel at 4s.9d. or 3s.3d. according to the quantity ordered. If members felt that the selected book was not *their* kind

'Triennial Negotiations between Mr Heinemann and Mr Hall Caine'
by Max Beerbohm, 1909

James Loeb, Ph.D, LL.D

of book, they could return it within five days and choose an alternative title from a supplementary list. Although it opened up an important new market for books and clearly met a need, academic critics such as Queenie Leavis believed the Book Society and other book clubs that were soon to follow were leading to a yet further standardization of literary taste and exercised an unhealthy influence on publishers who were more likely to issue bland, sapless, second-rate novels or those which were smartly fashionable.[24]

Writing with hindsight in 1971, Malcolm Bradbury is equally adversely critical of the influence of the early book clubs and of much that was published in the 1930s by big fiction houses like Heinemann: 'This concern with the growing standardization of taste is very much a topic of the thirties, and the "worsening" of the situation may well have been exaggerated. But the assessment partly results from the increasingly effective usages of the producers of mass media generally. The seamless, undemanding and above all standardized quality of this writing, designed to appeal to a wide spectrum of people at the lowest common denominator of interest, and tricked out with sensational and gaudy appeals both of packaging and content, showed that the book was being drawn even more into the expanding universe of the mass media. And in the presence of this broad pattern of development, it became extremely difficult to conceive of the idea of "literature" at all. It seemed a minority function on the edge of taste both lowbrow and middlebrow; for these two tended to cohere, leaving the serious author and a minority of critical readers isolated from the large mass.'[25] While much of Heinemann's list between the wars may be said to have shifted towards the unadventurous centre of middlebrow taste, it is important to stress that the firm still issued many books which have withstood the critical assessment of posterity.

Another club, the Book Guild, was blatantly middlebrow, even Philistine. Its explanatory literature assured potential members that 'One of its chief aims is to avoid indulging in the deplorable affectation of recommending as a work of "genius" the sort of thing which is dubbed clever simply because it is mainly unintelligible and written in an obscure manner, or boosting some foreign work simply because it is foreign, and the author's name difficult to pronounce.' It also wrote about the 'sheep-like crowd who follow the dictates of highbrow literary critics'. Charles Evans seemed to have heartily disliked the Book Guild and led an attack in the columns of *The Bookseller* on the anonymity of its ownership and selection committee: '. . . this organization has always been as much of a mystery to me. I find that they have conducted a lively if somewhat one-sided correspondence with my firm, mostly to express regrets that we neither advertise their "choices" nor "recommends", nor band our books with their hallmark. They have regretted that their "committee" should be thus disappointed in us, but so far have neglected to state who their committee are. Moreover, they write from an accommodating Monomark address and Mr John Stafford is apparently in the habit of signing his letters with a rubber stamp. While the more sophisticated may admire the pertinacity with which the activities of this Book Guild are conducted, I cannot doubt that the aegis of their choices and recommendations would be strengthened if they would tell us who they are.'[26]

In 1939 Alan Bott – whose relationship with Frere-Reeves alternated between great mutual respect and violent quarrels – also became managing director of a new club, the Reprint Society (later World Books) which had been set up by five top publishers – Cape, Macmillan, Collins, Chatto & Windus, and Heinemann, who were represented on its board by A. Dwye Evans, Charles's eldest son. By then, with some dozen clubs in existence it was more widely accepted that they were reaching new markets; booksellers' fears about being undercut had to some extent been resolved, so that the monthly choice of the Reprint Society cost only 2s.6d. on which authors received a royalty of 2d. a copy, paid as a lump sum on publication. While books from other publishers were considered, those issued by the five controlling publishers were given preference.

Fired presumably by the runaway success of Gollancz's Left Book Club, Frere-Reeves and Arnold Gyde together thought up the idea of a Right Book Club, though this was eventually started by Foyles. Gyde's journal entry explains why the Heinemann plan foundered: 'I never came across such chumps as the men on the formation committee. First came Sir Waldron Smithers MP. He let it be known that he was very much in with "S.B." as they all called him. Actually he had a stockbroker's business in the City and knew as much about Stanley Baldwin as I knew about the President of the French Republic. He was a boaster of the type which says "If only I were free to tell you –" This book club would have been a marvellous advertisement for him. He already saw himself blabbing away in the Lobby of the House and using its success as a lever to his own preferment in politics. He was a boyish chap . . . all leadership and no capacity for original thought, a terrific expender of physical energy refreshed with great draughts of liquor and hearty eating. Then there was Sir Home Gordon, a tiny little chap, dark, dexterous of gesture, old-fashioned in the cut of his tight little trousers . . . who practically lived in the Garrick. . . . There was another beauty but I forget his name and almost everything about him except that he had been for a year or two in the Brigade of Guards. I think he was connected financially and aestheti-cally with the brewing industry. . . . After each meeting Sir Waldron and Sir Home took Frere-Reeves or me aside to explain that the other was an idiot [but] that one just had to put up with him. . . . The only person who gave us money straight away was Lord Derby. He sent Sir Waldron £100. But the real trouble with us was that we feared striking quickly, whereas Christina [Foyle] who had a clear idea of how to win battles made a start by just starting.'[27]

At Heinemann's whenever someone had introduced a flop, a colleague would usually utter the comforting words: 'Never mind, old boy. You can't win 'em all.' It was perhaps as well that Heinemann failed to win this one.

Galsworthy: Flagship of the List

A superb and in every sense rewarding examples of Evans's commercial as well as literary judgment was his invention of the literary vehicle known as *The Forsyte Saga* (1922), the first of John Galsworthy's three trilogies about this complex, upper-middle-class family in which the new *In Chancery* (1920) and *To Let* (1921) were combined with the much earlier *Man of Property* (1906), linked with the 'interludes' of *Indian Summer of a Forsyte* and *Awakening*. It was a bold commercial innovation, as effective as William's abolition of the three-volume novel. Almost overnight it turned Galsworthy from a respected, established writer into a bestselling one of the first magnitude. In its first year the *Saga* sold 10,899 copies. It went on selling regularly until the early 1970s when a twenty-six week BBC television series based on the first two trilogies stimulated 200,000 sales in hardback. The hardback total approaches 690,000 copies and the Penguin editions 1.5 million.

The conflict described in the original *Saga*, played out by Soames Forsyte and his rebellious and eventually lost wife Irene, has often been summed up as being between the desire of possession and the 'instinct for beauty'. It also traces the decline of the Victorian upper-middle-class: 'Here', in Galsworthy's own words, 'pickled in these pages, it lies under glass for strollers in the wide and ill-arranged museum of letters, there it rests, preserved in its own juice, the sense of Property'[28]. The affairs of the Forsytes and their marital connections were carried on during the 1920s and '30s in two further mammoth trilogies, though Galsworthy was now writing about the contemporary world: first, *A Modern Comedy* (1929), comprising *The White Monkey* (1924), *The Silver Spoon* (1926), and *Swan Song* (1928) with the interludes *A Silent Wooing* and *Passers By*; the central figure of Soames died with *Swan Song* but the *Saga* is continued through his daughter Fleur in the third trilogy, *The End of the Chapter* (1935), comprising *Maid in Waiting* (1931), *Flowering Wilderness* (1932) and *Over the River* (1935).

Already blessed with considerable inherited wealth, Galsworthy became even richer, though he is reported to have given at least half his income away. His literary agent was Pinker, who at that time had particularly annoyed Evans because he had signed up with Chatto & Windus another successful Heinemann author, Crosbie Garstin, without a word of warning. As Evans confided in David Higham, '"He'd never said a word to me, not even that Crosbie didn't want to go on. Just went behind my back."

'"That's bad", I said. It was.

'"Yes. But d'you know what happened after that?"

'"No."

'"Well, we keep all John Galsworthy's money here for him until he says he wants it. He rang me and said, 'Charles, may I have £6,000 please?' 'Of course', I said." (This was in full Forsyte days and there would have been plenty in hand.) Charles paused. Then he said: "And d'you know what happened then?"

'"No."

'"Pinker is Galsworthy's agent, so the cheque should have gone to him. But there was a mistake and the cheque was made out and sent to John instead. He had to send Pinker a cheque for £600. John doesn't like writing cheques like that. So he has made his new agreement direct with us".[29].

Galsworthy's *oeuvre*, including volumes of his short stories and other works, was for over a decade equivalent to the flagship of the firm's solid, readable, competent fleet of novels which so satisfied the middle-class readers who as well as purchasing copies were, as we have seen, the backbone of the circulating libraries. Although burdened with a strong social conscience, expressed particularly in his plays such as *Strife* and *Justice*, Galsworthy denied that his writing amounted to social criticism. He would have liked to see the world become a much better place – and yet not a very different one. His books were not manifestos. He was no revolutionary. If he had been, his books would not have given so much pleasure and satisfaction to 'people who mattered', even though they must often have seen themselves mirrored in his characters – or, more often perhaps, imagined that they did! A *Times* leader on the day after his death, a rare honour, with inimitable acuity, explains his popularity: 'But in nothing was he more fortunate than in this – that his opinions were not (as are those of many an artist in literature) so unlike the generally accepted opinions as to rouse horror or derision in the general reader or playgoer . . . to disagree with him was not to feel outraged. To some robuster minds his pity for the underdog, for the square peg in the round hole of civilization, for the undervalued woman and the ill-treated animal seemed, no doubt, sentimental. . . . But in all this there was nothing to rage at, and his influence was all the greater for his moderation. So it was with his artistic form. Neither in novel nor in play had he any particular tricks, any discomforting theories about style or method.'[30]

Shortly after his death an influential committee was formed by Leon M. Lion to mount a Galsworthy Festival, at which his plays would be performed at the Playhouse theatre. Its membership included not only celebrated names of literature and stage but also the Prime Minister, ambassadors and high commissioners. Heinemann did not publish the plays, but in a foreword to the programme Charles Evans wrote that: 'It is not merely as a social and intellectual force that Galsworthy is supreme; it is because, both as dramatist and novelist, he has expressed supremely the spiritual significance (if one may call it so) of the problem of modern life – the contagious conflict, never more apparent than it is today, between the desire for material and the necessity for spiritual well-being – the urgent striving after the things which do not ultimately matter and the neglect of things which matter most of all, "the beauty and the loving of the World". . . . Galsworthy stands in this present age for all that is best and sanest in the idealism which brings the vision of a better world. He stands for cleanness of view and for courageous expression. He speaks for those who cannot speak for themselves, and if, sometimes, he disturbs our easy complacency, that in itself is one of his greatest virtues.'[31]

Evans undoubtedly meant this sincerely, though, as with Maugham, the more recondite critics failed to join in the general adulation, especially the 'Bloomsberries'. Galsworthy, they declared, had become the complacent president of the literary Establishment. Edward Garnett, who had given him so much help and advice in the early days, thought that his later work was relatively poor. In her famous essay *Mr Bennett and Mrs Brown* Virginia Woolf disparaged Galsworthy as one of those novelists who 'write of unimportant things . . . spend immense skill and immense industry making the trivial and the transitory appear the true and the enduring'[32]. Lumping him with Wells and Bennett, he was 'her natural antagonist . . . while her natural allies were (not without some reservations) E. M. Forster, D. H. Lawrence, T. S. Eliot, James Joyce, and Lytton Strachey. It was possible, in 1924, to see the party warfare of literature in those terms.'[33]

This literary warfare – between what may be approximately termed neo-realism and experimentalism – could be felt at Great Russell Street and Kingswood. Galsworthy, who disapproved of D. H. Lawrence, also disapproved of Frere-Reeves, who was involved in helping to distribute through The World's Work company an *avant-garde* literary review published in Paris, called *This Quarter*. It was edited by Edward Titus, husband of Helena Rubinstein, and its contributors included Lawrence, Hemingway, Ezra Pound, Samuel Beckett, and Richard Aldington. Frere-Reeves also put himself in the wrong by telling people at a cocktail party that the trouble with Galsworthy was that he went about the countryside erecting stiles in order to help lame dogs over them. This got back to the great man, who demanded that any member of the firm who spoke so disparagingly in public of its principal author should be dismissed. To his credit Evans did nothing and his own happy relationship remained untarnished. It must have been a worrying moment, but Galsworthy's bond with the firm was too long established to be easily severed. 'I believe in an author finding a publisher to his taste, and sticking to him', he wrote in *The Author*; '. . . the more confidence there is between a writer and his publisher the better for both. When authors persist in treating publishers as if they were natural enemies – seeking to get as much out of them as possible – and publishers try to steal marches on experienced authors, the whole fine effort of book making suffers. We do want co-operation, and again co-operation.'[34]

Towards the end of his life Galsworthy was showered with honours: doctorates, the Order of Merit, and the Nobel Prize for Literature – he accepted the last when he was virtually on his death-bed. The accompanying prize money, over £9,000, became a trust fund for the benefit of the PEN Club, of which he had been President since its foundation, believing since World War I that the cause of international understanding must be his first priority. His death on 31st January 1933 by coincidence also marked the end of another major phase in the company's history. Various events, mostly unexpected and some tragic, including the decision by Doubledays to dispose of their Heinemann shares, resulted in an almost complete change in its control and ownership.

Two studies of Galsworthy were issued by the firm: *The Life and Letters of John Galsworthy* (1935) by H. V. Marrot which was a comprehensive biography and included many of his letters; and *The Man of Principle* (1963) by Dudley Barker, an account of his life against a background of the society in which he lived.

End of the Doubleday Era:
a British Firm Again

Several and disparate factors must have influenced Doubleday's decision to relinquish the ownership of their English company. The surviving correspondence and records in America as well as England give us no clues. It seems certain, however, that it had nothing whatsoever to do with the soundness of the company's finances or its future prospects – unless, that is, these would guarantee them a good price. Indeed, since they had taken over at the end of 1920 the company had continued to prosper and expand. Turnover had increased regularly each year from £133,000 in 1923 (the figure for 1922 cannot be traced) to £250,853 in 1930, though it declined to £205,125 in 1931 and to £186,016 in 1932 – the year they decided to sell out. Subsidiary rights remained steady around £3,000 annually, but net profits grew dramatically from £1,360 in 1921 to £33,804 in 1930. True they dropped to £10,182 and £10,838 in 1931 and 1932, which must to some extent have reflected the drop in turnover. On the other hand, as the satisfactory profits throughout the 1930s were to prove, the company's prospects were obviously very healthy. Quite apart from declared results, the company, with the help of Doubleday's capital and leadership, had been given a much more secure basis with its own printing plant and warehouse in Kingswood and palatial new offices in London. The acquisition of new bestselling authors, the real future wealth, underwrote the whole enterprise. Even more satisfactory, Doubleday's initial investment had already been written off.

The simplest and also the most likely explanation was the Wall Street Crash in 1929 and its aftermath, which meant they needed more working capital at home in the USA. The US Government required too that American overseas investments be repatriated. The dollar/pound exchange was also causing problems; they were said to be 'pulling against each other'. But there had also been changes in the Doubleday organization which may have had some effect. In 1926 Arthur Page had resigned to take a big job with the American Telephone and Telegraph Company and the next year Doubleday merged with George Doran to form a new company, Doubleday, Doran, and Co. The newcomer ran a strong list of British authors, including Somerset Maugham, and the two companies dovetailed well together, but there was soon friction with Nelson Doubleday, so that Doran left during the 1930s, though retaining his shares and leaving his name on the notepaper.

Possibly Effendi's worsening health contributed to the decision to pull out of Heinemann. He suffered from a form of sleeping sickness which affected his voice, but curiously he managed to obtain some relief while in motion and used to conduct interviews and even hold meetings while being driven in his limousine around the Surrey lanes near Kingswood. Affectionately the staff spoke of 'being taken for a ride'. In the summer of 1933, however, we know that he was well enough to be able to visit England, have luncheon with the Prime Minister, and take T. E. Lawrence to Burwash to see Kipling. Whatever the reasons, the sale took place in the most amicable manner, with Effendi hoping for the two firms still to collaborate closely.

On the British side there had also been changes, in particular the death on 23 September 1931 of Theodore Byard. Two years earlier he had undergone major surgery and had been in poor health for some time. As 'resident chairman' he was not immediately replaced, but Charles Evans as managing director was from then on the effective head of the company along with Frere-Reeves as the only other British director and B. F. Oliver as secretary, as well as being in charge of the printing works. Among the few still alive who worked under him there is a tendency to remember Byard as a pleasant, rather ineffectual man who knew little about books, but his voluminous correspondence with Effendi and, above all, the firm's achievements when it was under his charge leave no doubt that, in partnership with Evans, he laid the foundations for its growing eminence. Despite Byard's death, Effendi could feel confident that the British company was by then in capable hands and it is conceivable that as early as 1928 he had envisaged relinquishing the controlling interest because it was then that, as the capital was increased, he encouraged the staff to have their own stake in the company. A number of the ordinary staff bought Heinemann shares for as little as a shilling a week, but the top executives were able to accumulate relatively large amounts – in fact Effendi went so far as to arrange personal bank loans to enable them to do this, repaid by means of monthly deductions from their salaries which were also raised to make this less onerous! Evans had owned £1,562 of ordinary shares since 1922 and in 1928 he had been joined by Frere-Reeves with £1,500, Oliver with £468, and Hall (see later) with £312. A year later their joint ownership of ordinary shares seems to have increased to £11,000. By the time of his death Byard owned £8,000 worth of preference shares.

The transfer in ownership was facilitated by the floating of a new public company, Heinemann Holdings Ltd, with an authorized and issued capital of £225,000, in the form of 150,000 6 per cent cumulative redeemable preference shares of £1 each and 300,000 ordinary shares of 5s. each. The new company acquired the entire capital of William Heinemann Ltd (which by then had increased by stages to £175,955, including £66,000 undistributed profits) and 51 per cent of The World's Work (1913) Ltd (with a capital of £8,532). The total cost came to £198,112 and was satisfied by the issue of 125,000 paid up preference shares of £1 each and 75,000 paid up ordinary shares of 5s. each to the Doubleday interests; the British directors received 16,862 paid up preference shares and 150,000 ordinary shares. The balance, being new working capital of £15,000 plus the excess over the latter's own share-holdings in the old company, was raised from various sources by the British directors and by the issue of shares to individuals, in particular the Winterbottom Bookcloth Co. Ltd.

According to the new company's prospectus, its finances were soundly based, the assets, without taking account of the values in the World's Work company or of copyrights, goodwill, leasehold premises, or newly raised capital, were sufficient to cover the capital represented by the preference shares with a substantial margin. The available profits were sufficient to provide three-and-a-half times the annual dividend requirements on the preference shares and showed average earnings equivalent to 30 per cent on the ordinary shares. The shares were quoted on the Stock Exchange by September 1933, the 5s. ordinary shares being marked up to 7s.6d.; the £1 preference shares were marked down to 19s., but this was because there were none for sale.

Doubleday, Doran and Co., together with Effendi and members of his family, still owned the bulk of the capital and Effendi had a seat on the board of the holding company, but not of William Heinemann Ltd. In practice, however, once a public market had been created, they fairly soon disposed of their holding to a number of private investors. The bulk were sold in 1933. Altogether they must have received approximately £153,000. This meant that Heinemann was now essentially British owned, with the working directors in effective control. They strengthened their hold by pressurizing the rest of the staff to sell them their very much smaller holdings, with the threat that if the control of the company got into strange hands, all their jobs would be at risk. Most of the staff were content to receive payment for their shares at par value, which in most cases meant a total of under £5, but a minority, particularly in the bindery, resented this kind of pressure.

Charles Evans became chairman and joint managing director with Frere-Reeves of both the holding company and William Heinemann Ltd; the other directors were B. F. Oliver and H. L. Hall, who was made company secretary. Hall had joined the firm as a boy in 1912 and had taken over the financial side soon after Oliver had been put in charge of the printing works. Hall had a reputation for an uncanny facility with figures. 'Figures can't lie', he used to tell people, 'but liars certainly know how to figure!' Hall had himself written a book called *The Four Horsemen Ride* under the pseudonym of 'Trooper'. Published by Peter Davies in 1935, it described how he had joined up under age in 1914 and served throughout the war as a ranker, seeing service in the trenches at Ypres, the Somme, and Northern Italy. He was discharged after the Armistice with a badly infected arm and a fever, resulting from a wound. His book was later reissued in a popular edition by the World's Work company.

The capital invested by the Winterbottom Bookcloth Co. was represented on the two boards by Miss G. V. Woodman and Mr M. Brickhill. Chalmers Roberts, the American who ran the World's Work company, acted as an alternative director for Effendi. Charles Evans's eldest son, Dwye, acted as an alternative director for his father and in October 1933 became a director of William Heinemann Ltd. He was then only twenty-six but he had been introduced to the firm a few years earlier, gaining experience of different departments, starting with the trade counter at Bedford Street. He had also spent several months at the Garden City Press, learning Doubleday's methods and procedures. All of this would of course stand him in good stead as a future chairman, though inevitably at the time a few people resented what they felt was favouritism and they tended to be guarded in what they said in front of him. But he was genuinely liked for himself and for his easygoing attitude to everyone. An unctuous notice of his elevation was placed in *The Publisher and Bookseller*

[253]

which must have made any young man squirm: 'His promotion on account of his remarkable and proved qualifications as a publisher should be of great advantage to his firm; by reason of his popularity and charm it will be a source of gratification to his countless friends.'[1]

On 10 January 1934 Effendi died and Chalmers Roberts took his place permanently on the board of the holding company, investing some of his own money. Evans, Frere-Reeves, and the other English directors must have felt more than a gap in their lives. Effendi had been their remarkable benefactor whose belief in their abilities had given them power and the promise of wealth they could not have imagined when he first bought the company. They had no doubt that it was his vision as well as his money which had enabled them to control a firm which more than ever had to be counted among the leading British publishers. His legacy was not only the neo-Georgian splendours of Kingswood, but his manner of combining a nose for a sound book with shrewd business *nous*, of looking well ahead with a grasp of the strategy of publishing as well as its day-to-day tactics.

Early Coups by Frere-Reeves: Aldington, Wolfe, D. H. Lawrence

As joint managing director Frere-Reeves was now commissioning books without reference to Evans. 'I have always believed in a publisher being allowed to use his own judgment,' he once told me. 'I am dead against publishing by committee. Charley used to tell people that I didn't know a good book from the back of a cab. The truth is that he didn't like what he thought was my 'highbrow nonsense' just as I didn't like his trash! In fact we complemented each other very satisfactorily. It made for a balanced list.' It is impossible to gauge the strength of their mutual antagonism and it would be wrong to exaggerate it because there is much to show that on the whole they worked effectively together. Frere-Reeves also told me that he made a point of reading other publishers' books, at that time reviewing some ten books regularly for *The Sphere* magazine under the pseudonym of Oliver Way. He was already showing a talent for mixing in London society, being invited to *soirées* by the literary hostesses Lady

(Emerald) Cunard and Lady (Sibyl) Colefax. He, like Evans, became a member of the Garrick and was close friends with several authors not on the Heinemann list – Hugh Walpole, H. G. Wells, Anthony Hope, Hilaire Belloc, and particularly his old drinking pal Dikran Kuyumjian (Michael Arlen). It was Dikran who first introduced him to the intellectual Paris of the 1930s, to Edward Titus's bookshop in the Rue Delambre where young writers used to congregate, and to the famous trio of cafés in Montparnasse – the Dôme, Rotonde, and Coupole – where with luck you might find yourself sitting next to Picasso sipping his aperitif or to Hemingway having an argument. It was at the Dôme that Frere-Reeves got to know Richard Aldington and Thomas Wolfe and, as a result, became their publisher. His relationship with both shows how a publisher's professional and social lives can be inextricable, though often in his case the relationship could operate at many levels of intimacy.

Aldington provides glimpses of Frere-Reeves out of the office which help explain why his authors liked him and even relished him: 'You could tell at once that he was a flying man [Aldington is referring to his time in the Royal Flying Corps], for while he claimed he was driving a baby Austin at twenty-five miles an hour, everyone else thought it was a racing Bentley going at eighty-five. Furnished with a slightly Wellingtonian conk, indicative of aristocratic origins, Frere [as he later called himself; long before he dropped the 'Reeves' and after it people always addressed him as 'Frere' as if it were a Christian name] has quickness of wit and irreverence which seldom flourish above the perpetual snowline of the upper classes. . . . When I add that Frere is the world's (unrecognized) amateur champion in tap-dancing on café tables, you will understand how warmly such a one should be cherished. . . . Frere, who has many accomplishments denied to lesser men, for some occult reason knows and can sing large portions of the Mass. So I was not surprised early one morning when he and Tom [McGreevy, the Irish poet] began their devotions in the Bateau Ivre, a Parisian cabaret run by a melancholy White Russian. They were requested to desist, on the specious ground that it would disturb neighbours who were insensible to the sounds of a jazz band. It is a nice point of theology. Might they not perform their devotions if they chose? The hour was canonical (3 a.m.), but then there was an incongruity of place and neither was in holy orders. If they had merely said their prayers, it would be a different matter, to be defended by precedent. . . . If I had followed Wells's advice and cultivated people who habitually fed Archbishops and

Prime Ministers, I think it very probable that I should never have taken part in scenes like this and consequently should have had far less fun in life. At any rate, if I had not been so strongly attracted by Frere's many virtues, I should have been in a hole when Charles Prentice [Aldington's previous publisher at Chatto & Windus] suddenly abandoned the peace of publishing for the turmoil of archaelogy. As it was, I merely walked over to Frere's chambers in the Albany, put the matter to him, and was speedily transferred lock, stock, and barrel to Heinemanns. I knew that I could rely completely on Frere, that he would keep tabs on my various works and not allow them to go out of print, that he wouldn't want me to go on writing the same book, that if I wanted to try an experiment which turned out a plug he wouldn't complain, that if I needed advice his would be shrewd and sensible, and that he wouldn't presume to try and rewrite my books for me.'[2] This was in 1937. The more specifically publishing relationship with Aldington belongs in the main to the 1940s and '50s and will be discussed later (see pages 392–3).

The manuscript of Thomas Wolfe's first novel, *Look Homeward, Angel* (1930), which Frere-Reeves carried back from Paris, was so long and heavy that it exceeded the meagre luggage allowance prevailing on the Imperial Airways plane, so that he had to cancel his flight and return by the boat-train. Everything about the young American author, then twenty-nine, was large and shambling. He had a gargantuan appetite for life as well as food and the words flowed in exuberant, frenzied torrents, expressing by turn elation and tempestuous despair. All his five novels (two published posthumously because he died at thirty-eight) were at heart autobiographical and they were said to link up as one vast book. At first Evans, backed by a negative report from F. Tennyson Jesse, tried to get *Look Homeward, Angel* turned down, but Frere-Reeves insisted and it was published in England before America.

It was an immediate success with sensational reviews – to quote merely from two: '... I shivered with apprehension. How could I praise it adequately? As for criticising it, Heaven, save me from the impertinence! ... here, quite obviously, was a master. ... This is a new voice, asserting America with an unmistakable authority' – *Evening Standard*. 'Here we have a talent of such torrential energy as has not been seen in English literature for a long time' – *The Times*. Despite the acclaim, it reprinted but once and sold only 5,858 copies. The praise was not, however, unanimous. Frank Swinnerton's review, for instance, touched Wolfe on the raw at several points: 'Mr Wolfe has a very dangerous fluency. He is almost glib, particularly in his improvisations of bar-room scenes, domestic scenes in which a ranting father performs mechanically, and scenes of coquetry; and to my mind he is intolerable in his pages of ecstatic apostrophe. . . . The book is a great jumble of good and bad. It is laboured with adjectives and adverbs. . . . It is emotional without feeling, crowded with violences and blasphemies, and to one reader appears incoherent, not from strength or intensity, but from over-excited verbosity.'[3] In a lengthy letter to Frere-Reeves Wolfe let off some magnificent steam. 'Swinnerton uses the words "glib", "superficial", and "pretentious" in his discussion of my book, but I think he might better have applied them to his own review. I do not put much faith in the people who rely on the word "pretentious" – it is simply a curse-word, a term of abuse, a word wherewith we can ease ourselves of our prejudices; and I have noticed that it is most often used by folk who pride themselves on "the quiet note", "urbanity", "restraint" – and all the things that have no part of your magnificent literature. I have loved and honoured your great poetry since I was old enough to hold a book in my hands, but my dear Frere, I thank God it was pretentious. At the present time you have Mr Frank Swinner-ton – you have better than that, I grant you – but you *had* Dickens, you had Donne, you had Shakespeare, you had Coleridge, you had Pope, you had Chaucer, you had Sterne and Fielding and Sam Johnson. A nice bloody Goddamned lot of "quiet", "restrained", "urbane" bastards, weren't they? In the name of Jesus, where has this horrible business of "quiet-ness", "restraint" – the "steady, old man" school of literature come from? You had Smollett and Defoe and *Moll Flanders*, and now you have Squire Galsworthy with his quiet manly gulps. I don't say a word against *that* man because Perkins tells me he's a fine fellow – but Good God! Frere, where did this great English convention of *not having any emotions* come from? No people in the world use the word "sentimental" so often as your people do today, and no people in the world are so tainted with sentimentality.' This letter, found among Wolfe's papers, was not finished nor posted, because as he explained in another letter to Frere-Reeves, describing his first air flight, between Geneva and the Black Forest: 'While I was flying three thousand feet above the valley of the Rhone, I looked down and saw a little moving dot in one of the fields shovelling manure: it looked so much like a critic that I have not wanted to finish my letter since. Besides, the only thing a writer can do is to keep his mouth shut: I have discovered that once his book is published he is the target for what anyone in the world wants to say about him or his work, but I think he ought to hold his tongue and his peace.'[4]

It was five years before his next novel, *Of Time and the River* (1935), was published. The original manuscript was about twice the length of *War and Peace* and without cutting and rearrangement by Maxwell E. Perkins, his editor at Scribners, it would have been unpublishable. This process took a year with Wolfe writing additional thousands of words faster than Perkins could cut, in one two-week period sending in 50,000 more words. This epic which charted the wanderings of Eugene Gant from the Deep South to the cities of the North and eventually to Europe, driven by despair and obsessive hunger for experience, not unlike the author's, at last appeared, but again Heinemann sold only 5,010 copies and 2,000 had to be pulped. A book of short stories, *From Death to Morning* (1935) and *The Story of a Novel* (1936) came soon afterwards but sold badly and it was not until nine years after his death in 1938 that with the publication of his posthumous novel, *The Web and the Rock* (1947), his undoubted but unwieldy genius was reflected in a sale of over 11,000.

I am giving Wolfe so much space because not only was he a very important writer but because, unlike so many American writers, his English publisher played a big part in getting him into print and because his letters give a taste of the relationship between an author and his publisher, particularly one as sympathetic as Frere-Reeves. Wolfe was always grateful to him for being among the first to recognize his talent and to Pat Frere-Reeves as well for putting him up at their home in Kent, for finding him lodgings in London, introducing him to literary London, for tolerating his moods – he was certainly not an easy friend and he always seemed to be apologizing for getting drunk. His affection for them stands out in many letters such as when he wrote from Montreux in Switzerland on 2nd August 1930: 'I think it was a lucky day when I met you, and you became my publisher. I can never know the history of all you've done, but please don't think I accept all this complacently: I know your value, and I am filled with profound and enormous gratitude. I hope you will always be my friend and that you will find no strangeness to me because I am from another country and speak a different accent. Remember that I am an American and that I will open my heart to you on any thing that may belong to my vision of life and not to yours; but never remember me as a foreigner and a stranger – the real republic of this earth stretches from here to China, and just as you are closer to me and nearer to the colour of my hand and heart and spirit than most Americans, so I hope and believe, do I come closer to your thought and language than most Englishmen.'[5]

The jottings in Wolfe's series of pocket notebooks give some of the flavour of an author–publisher relationship that went far beyond professional necessity. In 1935, for example, he wrote: 'Wednesday, March 27. Up and to meet Pat [Frere-Reeves] to go for an overcoat – walked down New Bond Street and to Albany – Thence to Austin Reed's where selected and chose material and was measured for coat – the smoothness of buying clothes in England – thence back to Albany where had glass of sherry, and Frere came in, and all three of us down Piccadilly of a glorious sky day – Frere in great spirits – and greeting people all along way – the Green Park filled with people sunning themselves – so to Walpole's sumptuous flat for dinner – a delicious one – the three flunkeys – the art treasures – So left a little after three, Walpole inviting me to lunch on Saturday – so left Frere and Pat at Albany. . . .'

'Thursday, March 28. Frere called asking me to come down at ten o'clock after dinner – went down and found several guests – Sir Somebody, Ronald Squire, the two du Maurier ladies, man and woman who dropped in later – talked to du Maurier gal – very lovely, I thought – was rude to Sir Somebody and told him of 18,000 war airplanes in Peru. . . . Frere asked me to stay and I stayed when all had gone and acted badly toward Frere – was drunk – left in an atmosphere of tension – went to find something to eat – to Oddenino's – couldn't get in – finally ate at Lyons – fillets of fish, etc. – and so home drunk and miserable.

'Friday, March 29. Woke feeling very shaky and jittery after night before (at Frere's) – Frere called me at 10.30 and asked how I felt – I told him I was wearing a hair shirt and apologized for the night before – I wanted to send Pat a letter or some flowers and he said not to, it was all right – Sounded very tired, said he was on edge too, and going down to the country at once – Asked me not to forget luncheon with Walpole next day and to call him up later.'[6]

Heinemann marked Wolfe's very special talent by the publication of *Thomas Wolfe: a Critical Study* (1947) by Pamela Hansford Johnson. Her verdict was that 'Wolfe is incomparably the most significant figure in the last three decades of American literature.'

Greatly to Frere-Reeves's credit was the return in 1935 of D. H. Lawrence to the list. Since *The White Peacock* in 1911, Heinemann had only published *Pansies*, a volume of poems in 1929. The copyright in virtually all the Lawrence titles was vested in Martin Secker who, as well as being Lawrence's publisher since 1918, had taken over the earlier novels from Duckworth. Martin Secker being in financial difficulties was prepared to sell the entire *oeuvre* for £7,000. It amounted to forty-three titles and included existing stocks, sheets, and printing moulds. Though Evans, according to Frere-Reeves, opposed the deal, it proved to be an incredible bargain because even if some of the minor titles were slow sellers the rest have remained in the Heinemann list for over fifty years. As well as the standard editions, there were now thirty-three Lawrence titles in the firm's 3s.6d. Phoenix edition, including three volumes of collected poems and two of miscellaneous articles, short stories, and essays under the title *Phoenix* (1936), edited with an introduction by Edward D. McDonald. The Lawrence domain in the list was completed by three other works: Aldous Huxley edited and introduced *The Letters of D. H. Lawrence* (1932); Richard Aldington chose and arranged selections from Lawrence's prose works under the title *Spirit of Place* (1935); through Aldington Frere-Reeves had become friendly with Frieda Lawrence and this led to the publication of her memoirs: *Not I but the Wind* (1935). Three volumes of short stories and the unexpurgated version of *Lady Chatterley's Lover* were published after World War II.

Prices, Royalties, Agents

The annual number of Heinemann titles during the 1930s (including some new editions) dropped quite steeply during 1932 and 1933, but after that fluctuated around the mean for the previous decade as follows: 1930 – 212; 1931 – 238; 1932 – 157; 1933 – 103; 1934 – 188; 1935 – 226; 1936 – 222; 1937 – 147; 1938 – 179; 1939 – 143. In deciding how much and what to publish Evans, together with Frere-Reeves and particularly Hall, never let himself forget that his literary judgment must be subservient to the harsh limitations imposed by publishing economics. He understood, for example, the folly of inflating the number of copies to be printed in order to bring down the unit cost and therefore the published price to a level which its public would be prepared to pay. But he also knew that a book's price was only one of the factors with which they had to juggle. 'People do not buy books merely because they are cheap', wrote Evans in *The Author* in 1931, one of his rare, compared with other top publishers, contributions to a trade or professional journal: 'The book they want they will buy whatever its price, provided they are satisfied that not only intellectually but materially they are getting their money's worth. Proof of this is the fact that my firm has sold 125,000 copies of Mr Priestley's *The Good Companions* [published in 1929] at 10s.6d., and it still continues to sell on an average about 1,500 copies a week. On the other hand, every publisher knows that, generally speaking, if the public will not buy a new novel at 7s. 6d. they will not buy a cheaper edition of it.'[7] Discussing royalty rates in the same article, he stated that 'my experience teaches me that 15 per cent of the published price is the limit which is economically possible (that is 22½ per cent on the actual yield: the retail trade takes 33⅓ per cent, the wholesalers even more; leaving the publisher at most 44 per cent out of which to pay for the manufacture of the book, advertising, overhead charges, and to make a profit'. Even so, Heinemann's cost of sale (manufacture, royalties, stock depreciation, but no overheads) during the 1920s and '30s fluctuated between 41.2 and 48.7 per cent of turnover.

Royalties during the 1930s similarly varied between 19.82 and 24.29 per cent of basic turnover, though, as is customary, the rates were normally of course expressed in terms of a percentage of the published price for home sales and of net turnover for sales overseas. To take a few random examples, though they are not necessarily representative:

Mary Mitchell, *A Warning to Wantons* (agreement, 12 June 1933): royalty of 10 per cent of the published price to 1,500; 12½ per cent to 2,500; 15 per cent to 7,500; 20 per cent to 15,000; 25 per cent thereafter;

advance £60;

10 per cent of price received on exports;

10 per cent on published price of cheap editions (which could be the equivalent of the modern paperback).

J. B. Priestley, *The Good Companions* (23 August 1928): 20 per cent of the published price to 10,000 copies; 25 per cent thereafter;

advance £500;

10 per cent of price received on exports;

10 per cent of published price of cheap editions, but for the 1931 edition this went up to 15 per cent after the sale of 25,000 copies.

John Galsworthy, *The White Monkey* (4 September 1924): 25 per cent of the published price;

advance £500 (though three years later this increased to £1,000 for *Swan Song* with otherwise the same terms).

4*d*. per copy on exports.

W. Somerset Maugham. Royalties increased on three successive books: *The Casuarina Tree* (8 September 1926) – 15 per cent to 5,000, 20 per cent to 10,000, 25 per cent thereafter, but no advance; *Ashenden* (25 January 1928) – 20 per cent to 10,000, 25 per cent thereafter, advance of £500; *Cakes and Ale* (21 October 1929) – 25 per cent throughout, advance £500.

Francis Brett Young. After *Portrait of Clare* which paid 15 per cent to 4,000, 20 per cent to 6,000, and 25 per cent thereafter, he received 25 per cent throughout on all subsequent titles, though he does not seem to have received any advances.

It is clear that in respect of his bestselling authors Charles Evans must privately have eaten his own words, quoted above, that 15 per cent of the published price was the economically maximum limit, but his figures and arguments are convincing in terms of most authors. On the other hand average royalties were probably a good deal higher than they were in the 1980s.

What might be called the standard terms for most established authors, and also some of the inexperienced, were increasingly the result of negotiating with the leading literary agents – Watt, Pinker, and Curtis Brown now having rivals in A. D. Peters, Audrey Heath, Hughes Massie, and others. When members of Curtis Brown broke away in 1935 to form Nancy Pearn, Laurence Pollinger, and David Higham, it was Charles Evans who was reported to have remarked that 'Curtis Brown's pupped again!'

Although relationships with agents could still be chilly, Evans and Frere-Reeves realized that they were now an integral part of publishing. It was important to keep in with them, not merely in order to oil the wheels of bargaining, but also to be offered the most promising new authors and the chance to take on disgruntled established ones – not that the firm poached aggressively. It was important to keep agents informed about the kind of authors the firm needed and about any shifts in editorial policy, though agents would then, as today, direct their most promising authors to firms with the best sales force, advertising budgets, efficiency of production, and so on as well as the highest royalties and most generous advances – though at times these considerations would be overridden when a certain publisher seemed to be 'just right' for a certain kind of book.

The relationships with agents were certainly on quite a different, warmer basis than in William's day. Evans was even in the habit of recommending an agent to a new author. David Higham recalls how one day in 1929 a note from Charles Evans arrived in his office at Curtis Brown which 'read (from memory): "The bearer of this note is a young author whose first novel I have just taken and who has, I believe, a considerable future. He ought to have an agent and I should like that agent to be you." I rang reception at once. The young author who came up was Graham Greene [Greene confirms this event, see pages 292–3]. Later, when we were starting on our own, Charles sent me Ella Maillart, the girl who had just crossed China and Tibet solo with Peter Fleming. He would publish *Forbidden Journey* (1937): we should negotiate the terms on Ella's behalf. No publisher can be kinder than that. But naive or no, Charles was no fool, nor one to offend, either.'[8]

The 'Woman's Novel'

The strongest element in the list still continued to be fiction, at several levels and with sub-categories such as historical novels and detective and crime stories – by 1939 the trade order list included forty crime books in print at the popular, reduced price of 2s.6d. and there were other newer titles at 7s.6d. Two prolific crime writers predominated: Margery Allingham and Carter Dickson (pseudonym of John Dickson Carr, published by

Hamish Hamilton). A characteristic of the fiction list as a whole, however, was the large number of novels *by* women written in the main *for* women. To say this is not to disparage them. In a *A Very Great Profession*, a perceptive study of the woman's novel between 1914 and 1939, Nicola Beauman writes that 'it soon became clear that those novels which school, university and critical dogma had chosen to ignore were, to me, infinitely greater and more memorable than those which had for so long and so regularly appeared on reading lists. A novel is "good", I believe, because it moves the reader and feeds her imagination. . . . Writers and critics have frequently expressed their disgust at women novelists being restricted to a ghetto defined by sex and their reasons are perfectly understandable. But to anyone interested in the fiction written during the period between the wars it soon becomes clear that there *is* a category of fiction written for women – 'the woman's novel'[9]. Among the established women's novelists she discusses are at least eighteen published by Heinemann. Most of them belong to the category Beauman is describing when she says that 'Novelists wrote for women leading much the same kind of lives as themselves, the leisured who could perhaps still afford one or even two servants, who were beginning to enjoy the new labour-saving devices such as vacuum-cleaners and refrigerators, and who would still have been considered unusual if they tried to do anything "for themselves". Middle-class families were at this period generally small and boys were often sent early to boarding school, so it is hardly surprising that time hung heavy on many women's hands and that novel reading was one of life's chief pleasures. Since writers and readers formed a homogeneous group it is clear that the woman's novel at this period was permeated through and through with the certainty of like speaking to like. . . . The years between the wars were the heyday of fiction written by women. Novel writing was, finally, a respectable occupation. . . . Middle-class women had time, warmth, freedom from drudgery and an intelligence insullied by the relentless and wearying monotony of housework. And, as in Jane Austen's day, when her manuscript was hidden as visitors arrived, fiction was easy to pick up and put down, as well as quietly boosting the often bruised spirit.'[10] Beauman also argues convincingly that the increase in successful women writers was in part because of the slaughter of so many of their male rivals during World War I.

The problem of which of the firm's women novelists to include in this chapter is insurmountable, and those chosen must be considered representative of the rest. One cannot, for example, possibly omit Marie Belloc Lowndes, an old hand, having earned £9 from the *The Heart of Penelope*, her first novel published by William in 1904. Six more of her novels followed before 1914 and during the 1920s and '30s twelve more. Many of her novels were inspired by crime mysteries; probably her best remembered is *Letty Lynton* (1931).

Another even more typical representative of this group was Beatrice Kean Seymour, who between 1932 and 1955 gave the firm nineteen novels, almost one a year. Her books were highly professional and genuinely competent, most of them portraying English domestic life against a large social and political background. Her 'Sally' series and her histories of the Gaywood and Malling families were perhaps the best known. In an after-dinner speech in 1934 she explained frankly the approach and mechanisms which made her own – and other Heinemann authors – so successful: 'As to method, I am a traditionalist. I believe a novel should tell a story in as straightforward a manner as possible, and that it should *create character*. Despite the London aesthetes who limit the list of novelists worth considering to something less than a dozen (not one of whom has ever to my knowledge written anything which even begins to look like a novel) I believe there are a considerable number of present-day novelists who think that a novel should do these two things – should tell a story and draw character. All the novels which make incomes for their authors are the work of those who have been content to express themselves in the traditional story-telling vein, and all these novels are unusually successful and remembered from year to year. . . . I do not believe that any real novel has ever been written which does not imaginatively create character, but there are many clever young writers today who are attempting it, without knowing that they are not novelists at all but only experimenters in form, in technique. Their compositions are decorations, often of considerable merit, interest and ingenuity, but they are quite devoid of the creative impulse. What these clever young people do not know is that the conception of a novel has nothing whatever to do with the intellect; it is primarily a work of the imagination. I remember a highbrow critic once saying that a book of mine was this and that and something else, but that it wasn't a work of art. The idiocy of it! Did one ever, I wonder, sit down to produce a work of art? No, you sit down to write a story which you have imaginatively created, and to write it as well as you can. If it's a work of art when you've finished, all well and good; if not, well, at least it's what it set out to be – a novel. And that's the point.' To our ears Beatrice Kean Seymour may sound Philistine, but she was professional in knowing what made a book for her large market sell. She was also very aware of the changed and changing status of women and that this must concern her readers even if their own lives continued much as before. 'Unfortunately, whenever you speak of the relationships of men and women you discover there is a very large number of people who immediately jump to the conclusion that you mean "just sex". I don't really know what "just sex" is but, whatever it is, it is the only relationship these people can conceive of between the sexes. But apart from ladies in cathedral towns or on the horn of dilemmas, or wherever they are, I think the novel which deals very largely with love and marriage does quite frequently need a word said in its defence.'[11]

Personal problems, particularly those of young people between the wars, are a continuing theme in the novels of Sylvia Thompson. The second of her twelve Heinemann novels, *The Hounds of Spring* (1926), was a polished bestseller about the moral dilemma of a woman who, believing her lover to have been killed in the war, marries someone else, but then the lover reappears. Many of her war-bereaved women readers must have been moved by the insight with which she portrayed how women cope with their grief.

This group of women writers were of course very mixed in character and no one fits into it neatly. This was particularly true of the two Irish-born writers, Norah Hoult and Kate O'Brien. The former must have indeed shocked her library readers with her use of stark naturalism to depict the more sordid corners of life and her first book, *Poor Women* (1928), was praised even by Virginia Woolf. It contained stories about estranged wives, a prostitute on the beat outside Victoria Station, domestic servants, and faded gentlewomen. *Time, Gentlemen, Time!* (1930) broke into the pub to give a portrait of an habitual drunk. Later books were staged in her native Dublin and the American South – *Smilin' on the Vine* (1941) and *Augusta Steps Out* (1942). *There were no Windows* (1944) was about old age.

Kate O'Brien's first novel, *Without my Cloak* (1931), accepted on the strength of the first eleven chapters, announced the arrival of a major talent. Set in a Victorian Irish provincial town and about a large, wealthy, middle-class family, it gained her the Hawthornden Prize and quickly sold 50,000 copies. *The Ante-Room* (1934) dealt with the same family, but

Mary Lavelle (1936) centred on an Irish governor in Spain, a country she grew to know intimately. For *Pray for the Wanderer* (1938) she returned to Ireland to create Una, a contented and deeply fulfilled wife and mother whose life 'rose from the accident of perfect mating', but it was a domestic love which transcended sex. *The Land of Spices* (1941), the story of a nun which expressed her strong religious sense and knowledge of Roman Catholicism, was banned in Eire.

Kate O'Brien was very fond of Charles Evans, who gave her much personal help. She was often short of money and would write to him from County Galway, saying she was half-mad with worry and that this was distracting her from her writing. At one point the firm was to give her an interest free loan of £1,000. Even so, like not a few authors who have had to struggle to live off their royalties, Kate O'Brien had a grudge against the whole literary Establishment, including publishers. In an article in *The Author* (autumn 1930) she wrote of the extraordinary vitality authors needed to survive in a society where they were so obviously unwanted. 'If the young author thinks publishers are waiting to bring his works before the public he is mistaken. Publishers are not there to bring the author to the public: they are there to keep the author away from the public. Publishers do not want authors. They dislike authors. They spend their time telling authors to go away. They lease old and stately buildings with Adams fireplaces and Georgian windows and Hepplewhite furniture in which they can be Not at Home to authors. They employ large staffs to return the manuscripts to authors, so that they themselves need not handle the horrid things. . . . I have a conviction myself that the public is the author's best friend, but with so many people – publishers, editors, reviewers and library assistants – trying to keep author and public apart it is seldom that they can slip past these formidable barriers and really make one another's acquaintance. . . . Still, some authors do slip past publishers and editors and reach the public at last, I don't know how. Many of them have risen above the status of the oppressed, and have quite nice homes. In that case they often, when they get the chance, turn editor, publisher or reviewer themselves. After all, it is only human. They can then get back on other authors something of what they had to go through, in the horrible early struggles of their profession.'[12]

Kate O'Brien's irony provides a salutary reminder that while publishers take pride in building their lists and often speak as if they were largely the fruit of their own creative genius, they are no more than midwives. Over lunches at the Garrick and Savile, with a full flush of bookclub, paperback, film and American deals, it is surprisingly easy to forget that the long drawn-out labour and birth is not theirs but their authors'.

The Loeb Classical Library

Throughout the 1930s the firm's subdivisions – the Loeb Classical Library, Heinemann Medical Books, The World's Work company, the children's and educational departments – continued to produce books, though some on a relatively small scale. A potential crisis arose with the death of Dr Loeb at the age of sixty-five in May 1933, but his will provided for $300,000 (about £60,000 at par) so that the great work of translation could continue with a stated goal of about 375 volumes, though this total was in fact to be greatly exceeded. The money was entrusted to a Loeb Classical Library Foundation, though the series was in fact left to Harvard University, Dr Loeb's *alma mater*. In accordance with his will a three-member board of trustees was set up, the first chairman being Arthur Stanley Pease, the Pope Professor of Latin at Harvard, who served for thirty years until his death in 1964. David T. Pottinger, the secretary of the new foundation, came to London and after five weeks of investigations it was agreed that Heinemann should continue to manufacture the books and distribute them on commission as before, though the Harvard University Press took over distribution in America from Putnams. Loeb, whose health in recent years had improved and allowed him to take a more active interest in the series, was to the last a discriminating as well as a magnificently generous patron.

By 1939 the series had increased to over 350 volumes, administered first by Elsie Buckley (1915–26) and then Charlotte Rowan Robinson (1926–59) – both Girton classical scholars. T. E. Page, E. Capps, and W. H. D. Rouse continued as joint editors until 1936 when Page died. He was succeeded by Professor L. A. Post of Haverford College, Pennsylvania. At the London end they were joined by Professor E. H. Warmington of London University, who became a full joint editor in 1939.

Warmington has provided a description of a meeting in the Loeb office at Great Russell Street when Page was eighty-five: 'A minute before the meeting was due to begin there would be a commotion below; then slow, heavy steps would be heard climbing the stairs; and eventually the large familiar figure would struggle panting into the room and slump onto a chair. The others around the table, including Rouse, Warmington, and Mrs Robinson, carefully obeyed the rule ordained by Page himself that no one should address him for two minutes. Then, after he had recovered from his exertion, the discussion would commence. As Page's sight was by now no longer sharp, he did not always concern himself with detecting misprints in the galley-proofs; but he still wrote forthright criticisms in very black ink in the margins. Vigorous and searching indeed were his strictures; and if we saw an outburst prefixed with a large asterisk we knew that solemn things would follow. Personal relations, however, were always harmonious. Page, the old-fashioned Liberal, got on well with Rouse, an old-fashioned Tory – no doubt because your old Liberal was in most ways a conservative.'[13]

Page was most painstaking as well as a learned editor, supplying detailed criticism of each translation. The following extract from a letter Page wrote in August 1928 to T. R. Glover, the translator of Tertullian, deals with more general points but conveys an impression of his editorial role: 'Certainly in the first place my desire is that you will take Tertullian and *do what you will with him.* As to advice, I can give you none, because my ignorance of T. is great. I have taken him up several times and found him *very difficult,* partly because of his using words with which I am not acquainted. Now it seems a necessity for our library (and the fact has often rendered our translations less easy than others) that if the reader was reading Latin and could not understand it he should find it made clear in the translation. On the other hand I consider that your view of how T. should be translated is absolutely right, and I am suggesting that in cases where there was special difficulty and *the ordinary intelligent reader* might be perplexed you might put a word or two of explanation in a note.

'Anyhow, don't sacrifice the general effect. I am myself surprised how few scholars understand oratorical effect. I am just now looking over some proofs of Demosthenes – the most difficult writer I know to reproduce – and I am sure that the translator has never stood on a platform. Not so often as you, but sometimes I have had to make speeches (mostly to very critical audiences), and so I have learned something of the art of speech.

Of course all Latin later literature is meant to be declaimed, but translators utterly fail to see this. . . . Pardon my writing; it is always bad, but today the close weather makes it execrable.'[14]

Medical Company, World's Work, Children's Books

In the 1920s and '30s the medical company made progress, albeit slowly, the creative drive coming from a remarkable Quaker surgeon from Northern Ireland J. Johnston Abraham – known to all as 'Barney'. A chance meeting with C. S. Evans in the Savage Club (p. 187–8) led to his joining the medical company as part-time editorial advisor, eventually becoming chairman and managing director in 1941 – a post he held for more than twenty years. Barney was an enormously distinguished medical man, with a whole string of degrees and qualifications, in addition to the DSO and MC from the First World War; he was also author of a dozen books, the most successful of which *The Surgeon's Log* went into thirty editions, and was one of the first Penguins in 1936. A man of great wisdom and understanding, with a rich, warm Irish voice, and highly accessible in his room on the third floor of the Heinemann offices in 99, Great Russell Street, Barney was a friend to whom everyone from the chairman downwards turned for advice and support in times of trouble.

Barney's instincts were literary, so it is not surprising that his most successful publishing at this time was outside the main line of medicine. The books tended to be either serious general works, or semi-popular 'do it yourself' texts. The best-seller was Van der Velde's *Ideal Marriage*, closely followed by Grantly Dick-Read's books on natural childbirth. However, the company brought off an occasional medical coup, as in 1939, when it published an immense project *Positioning in Radiography*. Half a century later this work, now in its eleventh edition, has become a classic.

Despite all the steps taken to improve it, *The World's Work* magazine had outlived its usefulness and was losing so much money that in 1930 it was eventually closed down. The World's Work (1913) Ltd. still, however, continued as a separate company under Chalmers Roberts, who refused to give up his forty-nine per cent of the shares. The company's main activity continued to be the distribution of pulp magazines, to which were added cheap mystery and Western novels and various periodicals such as *This Quarter* and *The Bermondsey Book*. There was also the Master Thriller series. All these helped to meet overheads, though the sale of the pulp publications dwindled until in 1939, after a loss of over £600 was recorded, it was decided to give the company only one more year's trial before winding it up. They had not reckoned, however, with Phyllis Alexander who, having been his secretary, had succeeded Frere-Reeves as The World's Work company's business manager and was later to become its managing director and chairman. She determined to save the little company by publishing 'ordinary' and less disreputable books, though it was difficult to attract authors of any quality. The breakthrough came when Charles Evans suggested that she took on Dale Carnegie's *How to Win Friends and Influence People* (1938) which he felt was not a suitable companion for Masefield and Galsworthy. It was already a well-established bestseller in the States and, while it started slowly and the Australasian and Indian rights had already been bespoken elsewhere, it was to sell eventually 741,000 copies under The World's Work imprint. Even more important, it laid the foundation on which Phyllis Alexander created an entirely different kind of list based initially on American books on practical philosophy, public speaking, and other forms of self-improvement and, later, on a wide range of illustrated children's books – but most of this was to happen after World War II.

The main firm's list of books for children was small, only twenty-one authors appearing in this category in, for example, the 1937 classified catalogue. It still included, too, some of William's juvenile classics such as Frances Hodgson Burnett's *The Secret Garden*, William Nicholson's *An Alphabet*, and seven old titles by Arthur Rackham. Prominent among the newcomers were Alison Uttley, with four animal story books, and Noel Streatfeild with eight books, but not the titles for which she is most celebrated; the first of her Heinemann titles was *The Whicharts* (1931) and a book of plays to be acted by children, *The Children's Matinee* (1934).

[271]

The Birth of
Educational Publishing,
Peter Davies Ltd

C. S. Evans had a strong belief in publishing as an important factor in popular education – not surprisingly, for he had started life as an educator. Leaving school at the age of twelve to become a pupil teacher, Evans worked his way up from the grass roots by evening study; and it was his warmly human stories in the educational weekly *The Teacher's World*, written from the classroom of a Welsh elementary school, which attracted the attention of the publisher Edward Arnold – whom he joined in 1909 at the age of 26 as an educational editor. Four years later he moved to Heinemann, who now began to publish some textbooks; but the war of 1914 put paid to this initiative, and it was not until 1930 that Evans felt able to pick up the torch once more, appointing Rex Welldon Finn to start an educational list.

Finn had learnt the trade from the eccentric Bertram Christian, whose small private company, Christophers Ltd, was a seminary for many successful educational publishers. Advising Finn was the prolific Frank Sherwood Taylor, whose highly regarded science textbooks, most notably his *Inorganic and Theoretical Chemistry* (1932), were to be the foundation of the new educational list. F. S. T.'s weekly visit to the office was the event of the week, according to Alan Hill, who joined Finn as his assistant in 1936: 'though limping from his war wounds at Passchendaele, F. S. T. would come resolutely up the stairs, his pallid black-bearded features sparkling with zest. In addition to his text-books, his interest in the history of science was later to materialize in a long succession of books, which were both to earn him the directorship of the Science Museum, and to put us in business as leading publishers in the History and Philosophy of Science.'

Finn was essentially a one-man publisher, with no ambition to build up a large organization, so by 1936 he had published only around thirty books; but within his limits he was a shrewd opportunist, as Holderness and Lambert would testify. They were two chemistry masters at the Woodhouse Grammar School near Sheffield, who in 1934 compiled a small book of test questions and sought a publisher. Lambert wrote to the leading educational publishers in London asking for an appointment at the only time he could manage – after school on a Friday evening around 7.00 p.m. There were no takers. As a last resort he wrote to Heinemann, where Finn agreed at once to see him. Sherwood Taylor was also present and by 8.00 p.m. Holderness and Lambert had become Heinemann authors. Alan Hill describes this as 'a classic publishing event. In the first place, it was not luck. It was Finn's total commitment to the job that kept him in the office late on a Friday night. In the second place, his instant decision to publish was not based on any consultations with accountants or committees, but reflected his own judgement of the authors' potential. The chance came and he took it. Two years later he was rewarded by the authors' *School Certificate Chemistry*, of which a reviewer said, "with this book, no-one who can read and remember can fail to satisfy the examiners". And for the next half century, all the world over, the examiners have been satisfied. The book became the standard work at its level, and over four million copies have been sold.'

Despite this success, however, the firm's educational publishing remained on a small scale until the war. There was some Classics and rather more English, but only in chemistry was there a list of any substance, based on the works of F. S. T., Holderness and Lambert and the long-running A. J. Mee. And as Heinemann catered only for the grammar and public schools – a minority market even in those days – turnover crept up slowly, until in 1939 when the war broke out it had reached no more than £8,000.

Finn and Hill were now called up into the Forces, and the educational business effectively closed down for the duration, leaving Finn's secretary, Mary Whitehead, to arrange reprints when paper was available. For the next six years, no new books were published.

A new departure was the purchase in 1937 of a substantial holding in Peter Davies Ltd, the first of several Heinemann subsidiaries to have originated outside the group. It was made clear that it was an amalgamation, not an absorption, as Peter Davies Ltd would continue to exercise complete editorial independence. On the other hand it should benefit from a much a larger distribution machinery and have access to more working capital. It had been founded by Peter Davies in 1925 with some help from James Barrie, who had adopted Peter and his three brothers, orphaned during the 'flu epidemic that followed World War I, Barrie having been a close friend of their parents.

Some twenty books were published each year, split roughly equally between fiction and general titles. The company's finances were somewhat shaky but the attractive list included among its authors Lloyd C. Douglas (*The Robe*, etc.), Uffa Fox with his books on sailing, Rumer Godden (*The Black Narcissus*, etc.), Cecil Lewis (*Sagittarius Rising*), Josephine Tey (*The Franchise Affair* and *The Daughter of Time*), Mark Benney (*Low Company*), and *Her Privates We*, published anonymously. Peter Davies continued personally to run the company and was joined by his brother Nicholas – invariably known as 'Nico'. Evans, who was largely instrumental in arranging the purchase, had a high opinion of Davies's ability and believed it would be useful to have an extra outlet through which books of a type that would benefit from being handled by a smaller publisher could be channelled. Evans, Frere-Reeves, and Hall formed the board with the two Davies brothers. Sales were handled by Heinemann travellers, but the principle of editorial independence was strictly adhered to.

Charles S. Evans

'Effendi' – F. N. Doubleday

13

Sued by the
Duke of Windsor and
Winston Churchill

In the case of a novel and two general books published in the 1930s the firm fell foul of the libel laws. The first offence consisted of an unfortunate reference to 'Friary Ales' on a single page of a novel called *Nancy Brown* (1935) by H. P. McGraw. The brewery accepted an apology, provided that the book was withdrawn from the circulating libraries and the principal distributors. This meant that unsold copies had to be bought back and in the remaining 1,600 copies of the original edition the offending page had to be removed and reprinted, before they were issued as a cheap 3s.6d. edition. Although the author's contract stipulated that the legal and other costs should be split equally, Evans generously let McGraw off paying his share.

The next case was more serious. A fine of £100 and 100 guineas costs were imposed on the firm at Bow Street Magistrates Court for publishing what was alleged to be an obscene libel in *Bessie Cotter* (1935) by Wallace Smith, his second novel. For many years the courts followed the ruling made by Chief Justice Cockburn in 1868 which defined the test of obscenity as being whether the tendency of the matter charged as being obscene was to deprave and corrupt those whose minds were open to immoral influences and into whose hands the publication might fall. This vague, open-ended definition had for long caused anxiety and uncertainty among publishers and authors. Most, including Heinemann, were normally very cautious and issued little which an aunt might be worried about giving to her niece, but when an author wished to portray real life, let alone its seamier aspects, he was up against aesthetic rather than ethical prejudices. A passage which one reader might consider truthful and even pleasing might shock another who would find it offensive and disgusting. Judges and juries tended to lack sympathy for literature, and the opinion of eminent literary witnesses was not considered to be evidence. The Press on the other hand prudishly relished any case involving a book alleged to be smutty. In the case of *Bessie Cotter* the Attorney-General (Sir

Thomas Inskip, KC), who conducted the prosecution in person, argued that nothing could be plainer than that the book fell into the obscene category and that it could not fail to corrupt the minds of readers, especially young readers; it would soak their minds with the subject of sex in such a way as to disturb in them what was termed in medical circles 'sexual balance'. 'It is sometimes said that the frank discussion of sex is to be desired. That may be so in an appropriate place and in a proper way. But frank discussion of sex subjects is one thing and the lewd treatment of that subject in a work of fiction is another thing.'[1]

Although the firm engaged the most eminent and, presumably, very expensive counsel in Sir Patrick Hastings KC and Mr G. D. Roberts, they had no alternative in those days but to plead guilty. Certain passages were certainly frank in employing colloquialisms to describe parts of sexual anatomy and their use just could not be defended. Some 6,000 copies had been sold, but Hastings told the court that when the firm's attention had been drawn to the book's nature it had circularized every buyer and bought back every copy possible and had them destroyed. This had involved considerable expense. Heinemann, he continued, was proud of its reputation and took the view that the novel gave a brilliant picture of a sordid side of life. 'It did not in the least degree extol or advocate vice or improper habits, but made such a revolting picture of it that the tendency would be to end the ambitions of people with such inclinations.' In further mitigation Hastings spoke of a publisher's difficulty in foretelling just what the attitude of the authorities would be about any given book and he wondered whether some agency could be set up which would decide upon doubtful books in *advance* of publication. As things were, a publisher did not, could not know whether or not he was on the 'edge of a precipice'. But the Attorney-General, with sound reasons, felt that this would amount to censorship and was neither possible nor desirable.

Bessie Cotter was a depressing experience. The court's attitude flouted common sense but during a period when sexual mores were changing continually, prosecutions for obscenity were almost an occupational risk. The next case was, however, very different and could not have been anticipated. It was no less than a writ for libel served on the firm and the author, Geoffrey Dennis, by HRH the Duke of Windsor, coupled with a threat of a further writ from Winston Churchill. The alleged offending book was *Coronation Commentary* (1937) written by an eminent author, a high official at the League of Nations in Geneva who had previously written five Heinemann books including the novels *Mary Lee* (1922) and *Bloody Mary's* (1934) and was the winner of the 1931 Hawthornden Prize.

Written to coincide with the forthcoming coronation of Edward VIII and rapidly changed to include a chapter on his abdication to be in time for the coronation of his brother George VI, it was intended as an historical treatise on the monarchial system and, though some acerbic comments were made on earlier monarchs, its overall aim was to defend it. It was the additional chapter on the abdication following Edward's decision to relinquish the crown rather than Mrs Simpson that caused the trouble. Passages objected to were for the most part repetitions of rumours including: (1) that Mrs Simpson had been the Duke's mistress before their marriage – page 259; (2) that the real cause of the abdication was not the marriage but that his ministers had wanted to get rid of him for other misdeeds: 'Until this marriage was mooted they had no notion *how* to get rid of him. She, whom they pretended was a disaster, was in fact a Godsend' – page 264; (3) that the Duke at times had recourse to 'other sources of courage', a euphemism for too much to drink – page 262; (4) one passage talked of 'things left undone, in his infatuation. Duty neglected. Papers held up. Papers curiously, neo-Kaiserishly, annotated. . . . Irregular hours; irregular habits. Muddling. Fuddling. Meddling. . . .' – page 262; (5) that at the last minute the official opening of an infirmary in Aberdeen had been cancelled and the Duke of York sent instead, so that Edward could meet Mrs Simpson at the railway station – page 263; (6) that the Duke was prolonging the crisis so as to hold out for more money – page 276.

Before the writ was served the book had been selling rapidly with four reprints in April 1937, the month of publication. In the hope of a settlement out of court, the book had been stopped and over 2,000 copies returned by the trade, leaving a net sale of 9,732 out of a total print of 18,078. But it was impossible to prevent Dodd, Mead, and Co. selling their edition in America and it was this that decided the Duke's advisers to insist on the writ being issued.

Appearing before the Lord Chief Justice, the defending counsel for the firm, Mr Valentine Holmes, maintained that 'it was never their intention that any of these rumours should be taken as facts, their intention was rather to destroy and discredit them, and it is for them a matter of regret if such intentions were not throughout made manifest'. Mr J. W. Morris, KC, appearing for the author, confirmed this: 'his intention in writing the offending chapter was not to give currency to false and libellous rumours, but as a humble admirer to discredit them'.

But in law there could be no excuses. Sir William Jowitt, KC, appearing for the Duke, made clear that 'no writer giving further currency to unfounded rumours can protect himself by the mere assertion that such rumours had existed before his book was published. Neither is he entitled in his book to publish such rumours, even though he goes on to add – as the author of this book frequently does – that there is no evidence, or insufficient evidence, to support them.' Jowitt recognized that both the publisher and the author were eminent and distinguished, 'but the very fact that rumours are repeated by these responsible persons makes them the more serious, and makes it impossible to disregard them, for any repetition of them by persons in such a position inevitably lends substantial backing to what might otherwise be regarded as idle gossip'.

It was clear that no defence was possible. During the seven months between this issue of the writ and the hearing in court the lawyers on both sides had spent many expensive hours negotiating a settlement in which their own fees and substantial damages to be divided between the Duke's favourite charities were horribly entangled. The total costs including the Duke's came to £2,250 (the firm's libel insurers bore £1,500) out of which the charities received £750, though this figure was not made public. On top of this Dennis had to pay a further £900. Both publisher and author made ample and humble apologies, but this was scarcely enough to placate the Lord Chief Justice: 'In my opinion, it is remarkable that any man should have permitted himself to write, and that any publisher should have been willing to publish, the foul and cruel libels which form the subject-matter of this action. There is not even on the pleadings any attempt to allege that the libels are true in substance and in fact. It appears sometimes to be forgotten that the writing and publication of a libel may be a crime because it is calculated to provoke a breach of the peace. These particular libels, a jury might think, appear almost to invite a thoroughly efficient horse-whipping. It may well be that a criminal prosecution will follow.'[2]

Such a brutal statement from the bench has to be seen in the light of the passion and anxiety stemming from the abdication. For many, to repeat unkind things about royalty – even an ex-king – was, literally, a form of blasphemy. Fortunately the criminal prosecution never materialized, but further months of anxiety arose from the threatened writ from Winston

Churchill. It was widely known that he had supported the Duke against Baldwin and the Archbishop of Canterbury, but he had been offended in particular by Dennis's description of 'those who came out as King's champions' as an 'unprepossessing company. An unstable ambitious politician, flitter from party to party, extreme reactionary, himself the first-fruit of the first famous snob-dollar marriage; "half an alien and wholly undesirable", as long ago was said.' To rub it in, these words were then repeated: 'An unstable ambitious politician, flitter from party to party, extreme reactionary, whose wife had been the fruit of another eminent snob-dollar marriage; leader of a movement in spirit wholly alien and wholly undesirable, as some might think' – page 274. Dennis was also accused of uttering damaging innuendoes.

Before the book was published Evans had studied this passage and decided it was not libellous and undoubtedly a sound case could be made out that it was 'fair comment', but in the circumstances and following the remarks of the Lord Chief Justice it is understandable that he and Frere-Reeves eventually agreed to settle out of court, though it cost the firm another public apology and the net sum of £1,098.

But the Duke was not yet finished with Heinemann. Soon after Dennis and the firm had made their apologies the Duke's solicitors wrote to allege further libels in *Ordeal in England* (1937) by Philip Gibbs who still published most of his non-fiction through the firm. The distinguished war correspondent and successful novelist, Gibbs (later Sir Philip) protested that his work showed clearly that he had the 'deepest loyalty and sympathy for the Duke at the time of the crisis and very great admiration and devotion to him for his personal qualities'. The passages complained of were said to convey the 'distinct meaning that the friendship between His Royal Highness and Mrs Simpson before their marriage was a guilty one'. Objections were also made to references to Mrs Simpson before their marriage in connection with the mistresses of Charles II – page 110; to the suggestion that odd behaviour occurred at Fort Belvedere – page 116; and to the sentence: 'Her mother had once taken in lodgers in Baltimore, where this girl "Wallie", as they called her, had helped in the work of a poverty-stricken household. . . . The fact that her mother had taken in lodgers made her unacceptable as Queen' – page 101.[3]

Forty thousand copies had been despatched to the bookshops but, although the typescript had been approved by two lawyers, again in the prevailing atmosphere there was no alternative but to agree to withdraw the book and call in unsold copies. The total cost came to some £3,000 of which the author paid half.

Evans and Frere-Reeves can scarcely be blamed for not risking a further trial and possibly this time an actual horse-whipping. Even so these clashes with the Duke were, according to Frere-Reeves himself, to be the reason for his undergoing a further trial, sixteen years later, with even more threatening penalties.

14

The Counter-Penguin-Revolution

On 30 July 1935 Allen Lane issued the first ten Penguins at sixpence each and the 'paperback revolution' had begun. They were by no means the first cheap or even paperback series, a form of which had appeared in the nineteenth century; also the five-thousandth title from Tauchnitz was published in 1937, though this series was supposed to be limited to the Continent; and there were various other cheap, pocket-sized series, even if not bound in paper, such as Nelson's Classics and the Readers' Library which was sold at Woolworths. The dramatic success of Penguin Books can in part be explained by their attractive presentation, their high literary quality, and their bargain price, considering that many of the hardback originals were of relatively recent date. There were also Penguin's and Pelican's own originals. The whole Penguin venture rapidly won an entirely new market among people who had never before been able to own books, unless they were secondhand. It reached this new public not merely through bookshops, but via a network of new distributive channels, including Woolworths, the village shop, tobacconists, and even slot machines.

Few publishers and booksellers could at the time comprehend the scope of the changes afoot, sociological as well as commercial, but Evans foresaw only too clearly what was likely to happen commercially – and he did not like what he saw. He feared that authors and booksellers as well as publishers would find that their incomes were seriously undermined and for several years he refused to allow any Heinemann titles to become Penguins, unless their author positively forced him to do so.

The most damaging threat, he was certain, would be to Heinemann's cheap editions and collected series which, as in William's day, accounted for a substantial proportion of the turnover. Typically, with any reasonably successful novel, once the sales of the initial 7s.6d. edition were exhausted, a 3s.6d. edition would be launched and often be kept in print for many years. This was particularly true of the more successful authors. The

1938 Trade Order List, for example, included popular editions of Max Beerbohm (10 volumes), Galsworthy (20), D. H. Lawrence (30), Fiona MacLeod (8), Masefield (14), Maugham (9), Moore (20), Pinero (9), Turgenev (18). Surprisingly, no less than three collected editions of Robert Stevenson's collected works were published by the firm during 1922–26: the Vailima edition (26 volumes sold as a set for £42), published jointly with Scribners of New York; the less expensive Skerryvore edition (30 volumes at 7s.6d.); and the Tusitala edition (35 volumes at 2s.6d. cloth and 7s.6d. leather). The last two were published jointly with Cassell, Chatto & Windus, and Longmans, Green, the role of Heinemann being essentially that of sales agent, an operation which proved to be very profitable.

There were also numerous cheap library editions selling at 5s., 3s.6d., 2s.6d., and even 2s. Among Heinemann's own regular series of cheap books, offering a miscellany of authors, were the Windmill Library (3s.6d. each); Crown Library (5s); Kingswood Library (2s.6d. cloth and 1s. paper); Leather Bound Library (actually half-bound with gilt tops – 5s.). There was also, in conjunction with Cape, the Travellers' Library (3s.6d.). All these could be threatened by the upstart Penguins.

At the other end of the scale a few authors had the benefit of being issued in expensive *de luxe* editions; but it was the fate of the cheap series that worried Evans. He was under pressure from many authors to let their books appear in what they believed rightly to be the brilliantly conceived new Penguin series and he had the utmost difficulty in explaining why it would be unwise. Enid Bagnold, for example, pleaded on behalf of her very successful, horse-racing novel *National Velvet* (1935), but Evans was adamant in refusing: 'We have sold 19,655 copies of the original edition', he wrote to her in 1937, 'and we have postponed issuing it in cheaper form until we were certain that the demand for the original edition had practically ceased. It is best for everybody's sake to get the last drop of milk out of the coconut. We shall put the book into the cheap edition – either at 3s.6d. or 2s.6d. – I am not yet sure which – very shortly. So let us leave the Penguin matter over for the time being. Obviously, if the book is issued at 6d. there will be little hope of selling it at 2s.6d. or 3s.6d.'[1]

A year-and-a-half later Enid Bagnold was still pressing and he was still resisting. As his letter summarizes an attitude that was perfectly legitimate at the time but now seems curmudgeonly and wrongheaded, it justifies a long extract: 'It is my considered opinion, based on facts, figures and experience, that the sale of Penguins has done more harm to publishers and authors than any other movement for a great many years. I feel fairly certain that the majority of publishers (particularly publishers of fiction) would bear this out. As I told you the other day, at least twelve publishers are refusing, except under very great pressure from authors, and sometimes in spite of it, to let any of their books go into the Penguin series. And some of the most important agents are taking the same line. They have realized from their returns how the sales of books have been affected by these sixpennies, and quite a number of them, to my knowledge, are advising their authors against it. The same thing applies to booksellers: there are many booksellers who would tell you that since the demand for Penguins they can sell practically nothing else. Before the advent of this series there was a fairly substantial sale for cheap editions of novels after the sale of the original edition. These were first issued at 3s.6d., later at 2s., and even later at 1s. Now the 3s.6d. edition is practically dead. The same thing applies to 2s. reprints: we used to keep going a large number of titles and sold hundreds of thousands in a year. Since Penguins were issued, the sales have dropped so much that is hardly worth while putting a book into a 2s. edition.

'Not only have the sales of cheap editions been seriously affected, but there is no doubt at all that the sale of the original 7s.6d. novels have as well. This is not a matter of guesswork. It is a matter of actual observation. This firm used to be able to subscribe a minimum of 800 copies of a book by an unknown author. Today eight travellers will go all over the country and bring back a subscription which is sometimes less than 300 copies. I think you remarked to me when we were talking at the Ritz that Penguins had made the public "sixpenny book conscious". That is unfortunately a fact and also the danger. Nobody can live off sixpenny books. Nobody makes any money out of them except the Penguin publishers and possibly their printers. So long as they have open access to the novels published by everybody else they are on jam – but whatever profits they make are at the expense of writers and other publishers. If they are to continue to be allowed this open access to comparatively new fiction, there will ultimately be practically no market – at any rate, a very much reduced one – for current new books at the price at which they have to be published.'

There was a good deal more in the same vein. After demolishing the argument that a Penguin edition gave rise to publicity for the author's next new book in hardback, he reiterated that 'in the long run all authors who have given encouragement to the Penguin series are helping to cut their own throats'. His argument about the effect on her income from royalties still sounds convincing: 'The sale of 100,000 copies of a sixpenny book brings the author only £104. An author who sells 50,000 copies of an 8s.6d. book and gets a royalty of 25 per cent receives £5,312 and further amounts on subsequent sales of cheap editions.'[2]

Enid Bagnold was not, however, appeased. 'It's the reaching of a different public that is such a burning attraction. *National Velvet* is now dead. Dead as mutton. But it could have this huge second life, and I feel desperate when I think I can't have it, and *NV* can't have it. That it is shut away in a 7s.6d. coffin, decent, rich, with brass handles, and it might have sixpenny wings. . . . I can hardly bear to ask you again, because you give me every sort of generosity. Generosity of thought, of dealing, copious, generous admiration, encouragement. You have dealt always magnificently by me. But *NV* is like a child who is eating her heart out to go on the music halls.'[3]

Evans now felt bound to give in. But there is a tide in the affairs of men . . . and it was a tide which before long no publisher could withstand. Allen Lane's timing was historically perfect. Penguins were not merely a good idea, brilliantly put into operation; they were an essential element in a social force, a tool for a generation which not only was going to make publishing a book very different, but would fight an anti-Fascist war and create what at least they hoped would be a better post-war world.

The Historical Novel

Writers who were primarily historical novelists have always found a place in the list. Between the wars four names became prominent. First, there was the prolific Marjorie Bowen who, with the exception of *Wrestling Jacob* (1937), a study of the life of John Wesley, wrote all her Heinemann novels between 1932 and 1951 under one of her pseudonyms – Joseph Shearing – the best known probably being *Blanche Fury* (1939). The opening blurb of another, *Mignonette* (1949), sums up her approach: 'Here once more is that dark atmosphere of mystery and fear which readers expect to find in a work by Joseph Shearing. It casts a spell upon the reader's mind which will not be broken until long after the last page is turned. . . .' Similarly, the opening of the firm's reader's report on *To Bed at Noon* (1951) suggests the flavour: 'This is an exceedingly romantic, melodramatic tale of a woman who sets herself to ruin the man she loves. It is based on the Kentucky tragedy which took place at the beginning of the nineteenth century. The author says that 250 novels, all forgotten, have been based on the episode. But I have no doubt that she is the only one to give it a heroine who is as wicked as she is beautiful (on the *Blanche Fury* model). A very skilfully contrived story, it carries the reader along. There are some absurdities – the high-flown language, for instance, of the last dialogue between the heroine and Hosea Baylis. The book's title gives some indication of the theme. Go-to-Bed-at-Noon is the old name for the convolvulus, which dies at midday, and the heroine's life is not unlike it – full of beauty and promise, only to be early blasted. . . .'

Writers like Marjorie Bowen knew exactly how to titillate and satisfy their vast library public. In a contribution to *The Author* in 1925 she seemed to be making very much the same point as Beatrice Kean Seymour and inveighed against what she called the 'violent trend towards realism – so-called' by fashionable writers in the 1920s: '. . . this violent reaction towards depicting the sordid, the commonplace, the ugly, the usual, in itself a good thing in as far as it revolted from the academic falseness of the so-called "romantic" school (here again it is a misnomer – it was not "romance", but merely bad work) has now gone too far and will, if unchecked, kill all that has been worth while in fiction from the time of Blandello. As in painting, the revolt from David and Ingres has finally resulted in the eccentricities of Picasso or Matisse and the intelligent, balanced mind turns in disgust from both, so a sane judgment must be equally wearied by the meandering of a Lytton or the ramblings of – any of our ultra-modern novelists.'[4]

History blended with 'romance' was D. K. Broster's *forte*. Her Jacobite trilogy – *The Flight of the Heron* (1925), *The Gleam in the North* (1927), *The Dark Mile* (1929) – made excellent sellers, particularly in the firm's own 2s. edition. *Sir Isumbras at the Ford* (1926) was concerned with French Royalist opposition around 1795 to the revolutionary government and contained a love story with a happy ending. Twelve other titles had similar themes appealing to a similar public.

Pre-eminent in the genre, however, was Georgette Heyer. Her first success, *These Old Shades* (1926), which sold 190,000 in hardback, started a career with Heinemann that would lead to forty-four titles. Her main categories were straight historical books such as *An Infamous Army* (1937) about the year of Waterloo; detective stories in a more modern setting – she wrote eleven of them; and historical stories of romance and high adventure. She was equally adept in several periods: *Simon the Coldheart* (1925) was late medieval; *Beauvallet* (1929) was Elizabethan; and *Royal Escape* (1938) was Stuart. But her most characteristic period was of course the Regency. Her plots set in this period were ingenious though seldom original; they were light-hearted with plenty of rakes and Regency bucks, duels and gambling debts, dashing heroes and heroines who were apt to elope – and again they were just what a vast public lapped up. The only problem was to know whether to print 70, 80, 90, or 100,000 copies of the first edition.

She was originally handled by Charles Evans, but they fell out. Frere-Reeves told me how one day she had burst into his own room, declaring that she wouldn't go anywhere near Evans again. 'I know all about you, but I've never met you. Will you look after me instead?' Frere-Reeves agreed – 'Anything to annoy Charley!' – and she soon grew to rely on him for many things besides publishing, writing him long letters with almost the same compulsion as her novels.

Once she demanded if Frere-Reeves had ever read any of her novels and he had to admit: 'If I was tied to the stake, I don't think I could answer that question.' She was always upset that people she respected did not take her work seriously enough and that she lacked literary recognition. As with other top sellers, her lack of reviews, certainly good ones, were in inverse ratio to her enormous and continuing sales. Some of her books were of course pot-boilers but the firm knew that most were very much better. They had a reliable core of scholarship and her research into period detail was copious and meticulous.

In private life she was Mrs George Rougier, and she and her husband lived through numerous financial crises. Short of funds in 1940, she arranged for Heinemann to make an outright purchase of three of her earlier titles published by Hodder & Stoughton. This was done, though it led later to problems because the Inspector of Taxes insisted they must be regarded as taxable income and not a capital sum. According to her biographer, Jane Aiken Hodge, her relationship with Hodders 'was less happy than that with Heinemann. She had failed to achieve with that patriarchal house the personal relationship she needed with her publisher, and had found with A. S. Frere.'[5]

The detailed historical content of several of his nine books for Heinemann justifies the inclusion of H. M. Tomlinson in this section, but he could fit in equally well with books on travel and especially his first love, seafaring. Both subjects feature strongly in his first novel, *Gallions Reach* (1927), which centres on the hero's voyage to Rangoon and Malaya. The structure was thought to be somewhat formless but the narrative was vivid and compelling, so that it was awarded the Fémina-Vie-Heureuse literary prize. His second novel, *All Our Yesterdays* (1930), was part fiction, part history and amounted to an account of British society and attitudes from 1900 to 1919, based on his experience as journalist and war correspondent. In *Mars the Idiot* (1935) Tomlinson wrote an indictment of war and gave passionate expression to his belief in the supreme value of individual personality.

Belles-Lettres and the Decline of Poetry

In the lists of the 1920–30s Belles Lettres were still a thriving category, with authors contributing books of essays, verse, memoirs, novellas, etc. Sir John Squire was typical. He was founder and editor of *The London Mercury*, a periodical which from 1919 onwards offered a catholic literary selection which amounted to a distillation of the 1920s, though his own taste stopped short at T. S. Eliot's *The Waste Land*, which he failed utterly to comprehend. Heinemann published two volumes of his own poems (1926 and 1932); three volumes of reminiscences, the best known being *The Honeysuckle and the Bee* (1937) and *Water Music or a Fortnight of Bliss* (1939); there was *Sunday Mornings* (1930), articles reprinted from the *Observer; Outside Eden* (1933), a book of tales; *The Grubb Street Nights' Entertainments* (1929); and *Robin Hood* (1928), billed as a 'farcical, romantic pastoral'.

Squire was a passionate follower of cricket with his own team, 'the

Invalids'. So was Thomas Moult, President of the Poetry Society and a loyal friend of the firm. Among his books for Heinemann were a book of poems, *Down Here the Hawthorn* (1921), and *The Comely Lass* (1923), advertised as a 'tale of moorland and harbour'. Lord Dunsany was another enthusiastic cricketing poet-novelist-playwright-storyteller-critic. Among the dozen books he wrote for Heinemann were *Time and the Gods* (1906); *The Book of Wonder* (1912), described as a 'chronicle of little adventures on the edge of the world'; *The Curse of the Wise Woman* (1933); *Mr Jorkens Remembers Africa* (1934); and *Patches of Sunlight* (1938), which was autobiographical. Also in the category of Belles Lettres were Maurice Hewlett's *Last Essays* (1924); five collections of the miscellaneous writings of Lafcadio Hearn, such as *Books and Habits* (1922) and *Essays on European and Oriental Literature* (1923); and, impossible to exclude, further books from Max Beerbohm whose very name conjures up gentler exercises in writing and who contributed *Yet Again* (1927), as well as three volumes of his inimitable cartoons (1922, 1923, 1925).

Then there was Maurice Baring, thirty-three of whose books appeared under the Windmill between 1922 and 1943. His range was so wide – novels, plays, poetry, children's books, anthologies, translations, war diaries, essays, travel – that he belongs to many categories, but he can probably rest most comfortably here. A Roman Catholic, but not self-consciously so, his novels were full of doomed, romantic figures; *Cat's Cradle* (1925) and *C* (1925), for example, convey sexual obsession and passion without erotic language. Among his other books were curious collections like *Dead Letters* (1925), a parody of correspondence between literary characters that never was, but just might have been written. His knowledge of pre-revolutionary Russia and of its language led to travel writing – *What I Saw in Russia* (1927) – and to translations of its poetry and criticism. His *Have you Anything to Declare?* (1936) was the work of a true belles-lettrist, being a very personal literary anthology; its title, he explained, came about because he had dreamed that '"I had pass'd the melancholy flood with the grim Ferryman that poets write of" and that, when we reached the other side, there was a Customs House and an official who had inscribed in golden letters on his cap *Chemins de fer de l'Enfer* who said to me, "Have you anything to declare?" And he handed me a printed list on which, instead of wine, spirits tobacco, silk, lace, etc there was printed Sanskrit, Hebrew, Greek, Latin, French, Italian, German, Spanish, Scandinavian, Chinese, Arabic, and Persian, and it was explained that this list referred to the literary baggage I had travelled with during my life, and that I need only declare those things of which I had a permanent record either here in my memory or in written notebooks.'[6] There was also his *Collected Poems* (1925). As late as 1970 Heinemann published a one-volume selection of his work, *Maurice Baring Restored*, edited by Paul Horgan.

The legacy of poets inherited from William was kept alive, though by the 1930s the number of new poetry titles was beginning to decline. Foremost was John Masefield, OM, appointed poet laureate in 1930. In addition to his new novels and drama mentioned already, he was responsible for no fewer than thirteen volumes of poetry and verse between 1921 and 1939; they included two volumes of *Collected Poems* (1923 and 1926) – the first sold over 80,000 copies – and *Selected Poems* (1938). There was also Walt Whitman's *Leaves of Grass* (1924); and Robert Frost's *Selected Poems* (1923). William's legacy of the works of Swinburne was also added to in two grandiose projects: *The Complete Poetical Works of Algernon Swinburne* (1924) ran to 2,270 pages in two volumes at 15s. each – printed on bible paper, the 'volumes could be held without fatigue'. They were soon followed by the Bonchurch edition of *The Works of Algernon Swinburne* (1925–27), edited by Edmund Gosse and T. J. Wise, which included plays and prose works as well as poems; it was limited to 780 sets – half of which were sold in America – of twenty volumes at 25 guineas (£26 5s.) the set. Mention must also be made of the six anthologies of *Public School Verse* (1920–26), issued with the curious recommendation of possessing a 'definite value for all who are interested in the trend of modern poetry'.

Inherited too from William were the rebel, visionary poets Robert Graves and Siegfried Sassoon. For Graves the firm published collections of *Poems, 1914–26* (1927) and *Poems, 1926–30* (1931); he also wrote *English Poetry* (1922), described as an 'irregular approach to the psychology of the art', a group of poems entitled *Whipperginny* (1923), and (with Laura Riding) *A Survey of Modernist Poetry* (1928). For Siegfried Sassoon four more volumes were published, including *Selected Poems* (1925), *Satirical Poems* (1926), *The Heart's Journey* (1928), and *Vigils* (1935). The initial print for most of them was 2,000, but *Selected Poems* was reprinted ten times by 1940 and *The Heart's Journey* six times. Also in the list was one more volume from Laurence Binyon, *Arthur: a tragedy in verse* (1923) and Vita Sackville-West who wrote *The Land* (1926), a poem

[289]

with woodcuts by George Plank which was awarded the Hawthornden Prize and remained on the list for sixty years. The firm had also published her successful *Knole and the Sackvilles* (1922) as well as a book of stories, and a novel.

There were a few others but during the 1930s this group of poets seemed to have left one by one and, like other major publishers, Heinemann let their brilliant, promising poets go elsewhere. The mantle that was to fall on Faber might so easily, one feels, have fallen on Heinemann. Two events however lighten this sombre picture: the first, a flash-in-the-pan, was the translation by A. L. Lloyd of F. García Lorca's *Lament for the Death of a Bullfighter and Other Poems* (1937); secondly, a poet who was to become one of the largest sellers of the century, the Lebanese Kahlil Gibran whose first volume, *The Prophet*, appeared in 1926 and reprinted 22 times by 1963 when the type had to be reset, since when it has gone on from strength to strength. Sixteen other volumes by Gibran were to appear eventually, prose and drama as well as verse, some illustrated by the author. Gibran is a curious and perhaps instructive example to publishers. Ignored or, with exceptions, scorned by the pundits and critics as a purveyor of insipid religiosity, his writings, which owe much to the insights of Sufism and a subtle blend of Oriental and Occidental philosophy, have conveyed a mystical wisdom to hundreds of thousands – he is translated into at least twenty languages. His books have never been vigorously promoted by Heinemann, but like so many best-sellers they have achieved their astonishing success through the mysterious workings of words-of-mouth.

A few who 'Got Away'

It was not only celebrated poets who were somehow allowed to slip from the list, because from time to time with every category of book all publishers miss opportunities or make gross errors of judgment. If Heinemann benefited from the misjudgments of other firms, so did the latter benefit from those made by Evans, Frere-Reeves, and their advisers. No history should be a catalogue only of successes and this account of the 1920–30s needs to be balanced by recording a few of the authors who, for whatever reasons, 'got away'. Among them was Charles Morgan. After publishing *My Name is Legion* (1925) both Evans and Frere-Reeves had no difficulty for once in agreeing that they should reject *The Fountain*, which Macmillan turned into a famous bestseller. Another loss was Algernon Blackwood: after his *Strange Stories* (1929) nothing more was published.

Following Louis Golding's *Give up your Lovers* (1930), by no means his first book, they let the enormously successful *Magnolia Street* go to Gollancz, mainly as the result of an adverse report by Frank Swinnerton, though later he gave it a glowing review and this led to an almighty row with Charles Evans. C. S. Forester was lost after only two books, *The Peacemaker* (1934) and *The African Queen* (1935). C. P. Snow went after only one novel, *Death Under Sail* (1932). Three novels were published for Daphne du Maurier, but her bestselling *Rebecca* also went to Gollancz. Frere-Reeves turned down J. Paul Sartre's *La Nausée* because he 'did not think it was the kind of thing which would have any success with the English public'. The last words in this sad summary lie with Ivy Compton-Burnett. After she had begun to be well known Heinemann offered her a contract for three novels which were duly published – *Men and Women* (1931), *More Women than Men* (1933), *A House and its Head* (1935) – but she too left for Gollancz. Disappointing sales were said to be the reason. 'Years later she described being accosted at a publisher's party by a man from Heinemann who claimed that his firm had once had the honour of publishing her: "Honour?" said Ivy. "No one would have known it at the time."'[7]

John Steinbeck and Graham Greene

This chapter can, however, end on a strong and fitting note of achievement with the recruitment of John Steinbeck and the discovery of the young Graham Greene. There is less to say about the former because, important though his place has been on the Heinemann list, his novels were written and developed in America and the firm's role was merely to promote and distribute them in the UK and Commonwealth. It may be significant that in one of the few letters from him extant in the firm's archive, one written as late as 1952, he has to apologize for not knowing the chairman's Christian name. There was evidently none of the close author-publisher contact as was fostered with an American such as Thomas Wolfe. Steinbeck's normal themes, too, were American through-and-through, his greatest works being about the America of the Great Depression in the 1930s. But his appeal was universal. He expressed the plight and resistance of ordinary people such as the Joad family emigrating in their collapsing old car to California in *The Grapes of Wrath* (1939), grappling with every kind of obstacle, especially poverty itself. He became a forceful voice protesting against social oppression and injustice, though without being a doctrinaire politician. He made the moral issues obvious and unanswerable. He was also at home with the bums, drunks, and whores of *Tortilla Flat* (1935) and *Cannery Row* (1945). Post-war no less than twenty-five of his novels and books of stories were to appear before his death in 1968, among them *The Moon is Down* (1942), *East of Eden* (1952), and *The Winter of our Discontent* (1961), but his finest work was to be found in his earlier writings and undoubtedly it was for these that in 1962 he was awarded the Nobel Prize. In 1976 the firm published a collection of his letters, *Steinbeck. A Life in Letters*, edited by his widow Elaine Steinbeck and Robert Wallsten, and rounded off his life with a biography of 1,116 pages by Jackson J. Benson: *The True Adventures of John Steinbeck, Writer* (1984).

Graham Greene's first published novel, *The Man Within* (1929), was the third he had submitted to Heinemann. He had sent the typescript at the same time to The Bodley Head and told himself that if he failed this time, he would abandon the ambition to be a writer. As the firm had taken nine months to reject the previous submission, he was prepared for another long wait. After less than two weeks, however, while he lay in bed with a bad attack of flu, his wife came into the bedroom to say that a Mr Evans was on the telephone – but to use Greene's own words:

'"I don't know anyone called Evans", I said. "Tell him I'm in bed. Tell him I'm ill." Suddenly a memory came back to me: Evans was the chairman of Heinemann, and I ran to snatch the telephone.

'"I've read your novel", he said. "We'd like to publish it. Would it be possible for you to look in here at eleven?" My flu was gone in that moment and never returned.

'Nothing in a novelist's life later can equal that moment – the acceptance of his first book. Triumph is unalloyed by any doubt of the future. Mounting the wide staircase in the elegant eighteenth-century house in Great Russell Street I could have no foreboding of the failures and frustrations of the next ten years.

'Charles Evans was a remarkable publisher. With his bald head and skinny form he looked like a family solicitor lean with anxieties, but a solicitor who had taken an overdose of some invigorating vitamin. His hands and legs were never still. He did everything, from shaking hands to ringing a bell, in quick jerks. Perhaps because the flu had not entirely departed, I expected at any moment the legendary figures of Heinemann authors to enter the room behind me. Mr Galsworthy, Mr John Masefield, Mr Maugham, Mr George Moore, Mr Joseph Hergesheimer. I sat on the edge of the chair ready to leap up. The bearded ghost of Conrad rumbled on the rooftops with the rain.

'I was quite prepared to hear what I had always understood to be the invariable formula – "of course a first novel is a great risk, we shall have to begin with a small royalty" – but that was not Evans's way with a young author. Just as he had substituted the direct telephone call for the guarded letter, so now he brushed aside any ancient rite of initiation.

'"No publisher", he said, "can ever guarantee success, but all the same we have hopes. . . ." The royalty would begin at $12\frac{1}{2}$ per cent, with a fifty-pound advance, he recommended me to take an agent, for in the future there might be subsidiary rights to deal with. . . . I went out dazed into Great Russell Street. My day-dream had never continued further than a promise of publication and now my publisher (proud phrase, "my publisher") was suggesting even the possibility of success.'[8]

A few days later The Bodley Head also offered to publish this book, but Evans had been the first to recognize the promise of Greene's extraordinary talent. In a chatty letter to Florence Doubleday he enthused over his new young author and the sale of his novel's first printing within a fortnight. Altogether the first edition of *The Man Within* sold 12,594 copies, the price being reduced from 7s.6d. to 3s.6d. within a year of publication – it was not reissued until 1952. So certain was Evans about the potential of his new discovery that he guaranteed Greene an advance amounting to £600 a year for three years, persuading Doubleday who had taken him on in America to share the cost. This enabled him to leave his job on *The Times*, move to a cottage in Chipping Camden, and concentrate on more novels.

On receiving the typescript of Greene's next published novel, *The Name of Action* (1930), Evans despatched a telegram to congratulate him. 'It was a thoroughly bad book,' Greene told me on a visit to his flat in Antibes over fifty years later. 'That telegram was not at all helpful. What I should have had was severe criticism.' But according to Greene, Evans, with his reputation for discovering young writers, could not admit his mistake. The second novel was relatively a flop and so was the third, *Rumour at Nightfall* (1931), which was harshly criticized by Frank Swinnerton. 'This really showed me the error of my ways,' Greene told me. It opened his eyes, in particular, to the bad influence Conrad was having. It made him realize that he was over-concerned with style and that his was too derivative. There were too many adjectives, extravagant similes and metaphors, and too much description. The dialogue was ambiguous. 'After that bad review I made a vow to stop reading Conrad and I kept it until I visited the Congo in 1959 to see leper colonies.'

Poor sales meant that the guaranteed £600 a year advances were far from being earned. He sent Evans the typescript of a biography of the Earl of Rochester, the poet, but this was rejected. By the time *Stamboul Train* (1932) was being considered the three years were up, but Evans agreed to extend Heinemann's share for another year, though Double-days would join in for only two months. There were heavy conditions: another two-book contract and any losses suffered by the publishers had to be recovered before further royalties would be paid. But *Stamboul Train*, a book he deliberately designed to make money, justified the financial risk taken by Evans. The first edition sold 20,829 copies, including a Book Society choice amounting to some 10,000. Ironically, just prior to publication, a telegram from Evans announced that J. B. Priestley, who has seen a set of proofs sent for review, was threatening a libel action because he was convinced that Mr Savory, described in *Stamboul Train* as a novelist in the manner of Dickens and who smoked a pipe, was a take-off of himself. It was a case of Hugh Walpole and Somerset Maugham all over again. Before World War II the libel laws were even stricter and even unintentional similarities with living persons, of which Greene was unluckily culpable, could make an author liable to prosecution. Greene wanted to fight the action but Evans dismissed the

John Steinbeck and Graham Greene

idea, making it clear that if they were going to lose an author they would much prefer not to lose Priestley. Alterations to the text were agreed over the telephone and some twenty substitute pages had to be printed and inserted in the 13,000 copies already printed. Greene's share of the cost would be deducted from his royalties – or rather added to his debt.

It was not until after three more novels – *It's a Battlefield* (1934), *England Made me* (1935), *A Gun for Sale* (1936) – and his account of his travels on foot through Liberia, *A Journey Without Maps* (1936) – which had to be withdrawn with small damages because of a libel threat from a doctor Greene did not even know existed – that the royalties from *Brighton Rock* (1938) just paid off his unearned advance. Even so, although he himself thought of it as one of his best books, the first edition sold only 6,804 copies.

Brighton Rock was his first specifically Catholic novel – his conversion had been in 1926 and he says he has been forced to declare himself not a Catholic writer, but a writer who happens to be a Catholic. Although it starts as a detective story, it is generally considered to be his first major work. Its achievement was to reflect the anxieties of the threatening 1930s in the story of betrayal, murder, and revenge in the seaside underworld. This was also of course true, to various extents, of the earlier novels which dealt with strikes, political murder, armament manufacturers, and the callous power of international finance and other contemporary issues – but in his own, inimitable manner.

Greene had become the firm's ideal author. He won the respect and praise of the intellectual critics and, to boot, he commanded an increasingly large popular sale which was later to escalate dramatically – a combination that happens but rarely. He is not only a superb technician and story teller. He has always written books that people not only want to read but *need* to read.

[295]

Wartime Publishing

During the first seven years of its existence the performance of Heinemann Holding Ltd can be considered to have been very satisfactory. Annual turnover was surprisingly consistent: for William Heinemann Ltd only, which accounted for most of it, turnover amounted to:

1933	£185,363
1934	£177,035
1935	£184,221
1936	£170,464
1937	£204,458
1938	£179,121
1939	£182,382

Likewise the group's profits (after tax) were fairly consistent, as were dividends, even though as war came nearer they showed a tendency to decline. Figures were calculated to 30 November for each year:

	Net Profits	Dividend
1933	£15,422	10%
1934	£17,890	12½%
1935	£17,852	12½%
1936	£15,908	12½%
1937	£14,486	10%
1938	£14,337	10%
1939	£10,591	7½%

As a public company, shares changed hands but not frequently once the Doubleday interests had unloaded most of their holdings. The 6 per cent

£1 preference shares fetched between £1 2s.6d. (1935) and £1 0s.0d. (1939); the price of the ordinary shares ranged between 11s.5½d. (1936) and 5s. (1938), ending up at 8s.3d. (1939).

Comparative figures for the war years are surprising. Business was far from being 'as usual', as brave shopkeepers would tell their customers after their premises had been shattered in an air-raid, but Heinemann not only survived the war but prospered despite it:

Turnover

1940	£170,247
1941	£201,635
1942	£227,662
1943	£215,371
1944	£240,420
1945	£251,294

These amounts were marginally an improvement on the annual turnovers for the 1930s, despite the fall in the number of new titles, thus indicating that, as expected, a higher proportion of sales came from the backlist. Expressed in financial terms, the performance of the holding company was, apart from a drop in 1940 and 1941, equally reassuring:

	Net Profits	*Dividend*
1940	£ 5,677	Nil
1941	£ 9,880	10%
1942	£15,845	10%
1943	£11,130	10%
1944	£10,307	10%
1945	£12,934	20%

By the end of the war ordinary shares were changing hands at between 12s.4d. and 16s.6d.

Apart from continuing to make money, the war years, so far as this history is concerned, were relatively uneventful. Progress was of course arrested by the outbreak of war in 1939, but by no means as drastically as most people feared. In common with all publishers Heinemann suffered from war risks insurance, restrictions on paper supply and manpower, reduction in retail outlets, and other expected shortages and harassments but, compared with many of its competitors, the firm was extraordinarily fortunate. During the London blitz the offices and warehouses of many other London publishers were burned out and their stocks totally destroyed. The worst disaster was on the night of 29–30 December 1940, when Paternoster Row and the surrounding City streets close to St Paul's, where publishers used to congregate, were demolished. The buildings occupied by Longmans, Nelsons, Hutchinsons, Collins, Eyre & Spottiswoode, and others were flattened or gutted; Simpkin Marshall, the main book wholesalers, were a major victim. Altogether at least 20 million books were lost.

Apart from some broken windows at 99 Great Russell Street, Heinemann suffered no physical damage. The Windmill Press also escaped, though it lay on the direct route for German bomber planes; it was said that the large, isolated building set among thick woods provided a useful signpost for the enemy bomber pilots making for central London. It also happened to be situated in the centre of 'doodle-bug alley' during 1944, each day as many as twenty to thirty flying-bombs passing overhead, attacked by ack-ack and our fighters; but the press was unscathed, though there were some near-misses, on one occasion three bombs being dropped uncomfortably close. The only physical inconvenience was the requisitioning of a large section of the Kingswood building by the military authorities as a centre for the preparation and printing of the numerous maps needed for D-day. Presumably for security reasons the map-makers kept very much to themselves and the army's sector was separated off by a complex series of breeze-block walls. The firm put in a claim for compensation amounting to £1,604 a year, to include loss of profits and other items, but they were probably lucky to be granted £600 a year with the army paying its share of the rates, insurance, electricity, and expenses of removal.

Only a skeleton staff was kept at Great Russell Street, including the trade counter, the rest being evacuated to Kingswood. Book printing and publishing were not by any means reserved occupations, and as men were called up or volunteered for the Forces there were few men left younger than thirty-five, except for the physically unfit. Among the men to disappear were Dwye Evans who joined the RAF; Arnold Gyde who rejoined the Army; and Frere-Reeves who in 1940 was engaged by the Ministry of Labour and National Service as head of its public relations department, with which he had been associated during the previous year. He worked under Ernest Bevin, whom he much admired, his chief task being the important one of explaining to the public the need for the mobilization of the nation's labour force on a wartime footing. Being in London, he was not completely out of touch with the firm and received half his normal salary. Both Peter and Nico Davies rejoined the Brigade of Guards soon after the outbreak, and their offices were moved to Kingswood, where John Dettmer ran this company successfully, becoming one of its directors. Charles Evans split his time between Great Russell Street and Kingswood where Hall and Oliver, being older, were able to remain in charge.

Later, women under twenty-five were also liable to be called-up, but the disappearance of most of the men meant that female employees took their place and were given greater responsibilities, which they assumed with enthusiasm. This led, in January 1943, to Louisa Callender being made a director of William Heinemann Ltd. She had joined the firm in 1918 as secretary to Sydney Pawling and later to William himself. For many years she had looked after Charles Evans and thus had always been at the very heart of things and was on friendly terms with most of the top authors. A very large woman with a basso profundo voice and dark chestnut hair worn in a roll like a tiara, she had immense presence. She was known to be the only person able to cope with George Moore when he was at his most difficult. Similarly, in Gyde's absence Grace Cranston was put in charge of publicity. Mary Whitehead, secretary to Weldon Finn in the education department, took his place when both he and his assistant, Alan Hill, joined up; despite little experience she was made responsible for putting in hand reprints of successful textbooks, though there were virtually no new ones for the duration.

Fiction manuscripts still kept arriving and were mostly read by Maire (pronounced, and commonly written, 'Moira') Lynd. She had been introduced to the firm in 1934 fresh from the university, by J. B. Priestley, a friend of her parents Robert and Sylvia Lynd, both well-known literati and reviewers. She started at £3 a week and soon became chief reader and in many ways was the most important member of staff. Normally anything which passed through the initial sieve of the 'trash pile' would be sent to her for a synopsis and a detailed opinion, ending with a recommendation whether or not to publish – sometimes subject to the author being willing to undertake various revisions. The final decision would be taken by the chairman or managing director, but the assessment on which this was based was more likely than not to be Maire Lynd's. Normally, if she said 'no' to a manuscript, it would be rejected. The war helped to consolidate her position, though being a young mother she was excused having to traipse down every day from London to Kingswood and was able to work largely from home. Apart from another woman reader, Tegan Harris, who also worked from home and read in addition for another publisher, during much of the war there was no one else carrying on the work of the editorial department.

Maire Lynd was to remain with Heinemann throughout her working life, but this is perhaps an apposite moment to say more about her. Both she and her sister, Sheila who worked for Gollancz, were well known for being active Communists. The firm was always tolerant about people's politics, but at the time of the Munich sell-out Maire had overdone it, taking round the office staff a petition demanding an Anglo-Soviet pact which she had typed on the firm's headed notepaper. 'Mr Evans was very cross with me indeed. Stupidly I never cottoned on that I could be at fault, even though the firm had some Government contracts. But I was forgiven. They never interfered with my politics, just as I never let my politics interfere with my literary judgment. Frere was always particularly nice to me and understanding – once he even contributed to a collection I made round the office on behalf of strikers in the aircraft industry. He was also forgiving when one morning I arrived very late at work, having appeared at Bow Street for lying down in Piccadilly during a demo. against non-intervention in the Spanish Civil War. Yes, I was always very well treated, but terribly badly paid!'

Restrictions Reduce the List

As the war progressed, problems and frustrations inevitably multiplied. By far the worst was the shortage of paper. After the invasion of Norway and the ending of the phoney war the Government imposed rationing at 60 per cent of what had been a firm's total consumption during the twelve months prior to 31 August 1939. The percentage fluctuated during the war and rationing was to continue after it for several years, at one time falling as low as 37½ per cent, even for firms which had signed the Book Production War Economy Agreement. This laid down for most books complex restrictions on type-sizes; width of margins; minimum number of words on a page; quality and weight of paper; and much else. Shorter prints led to an increase in the published price for books of inferior physical quality. There were similar severe restrictions on Press advertising, the production of catalogues, leaflets and posters. By 1943 the number of column inches of advertising space in the Sunday newspapers booked by Heinemann had been reduced by 92½ per cent and there was much less room for reviews. Advertising was, however, supererogatory because with paper rationing and the enormous losses by other publishers in the blitz there were not enough books to go round. With reprints as well as new books bookshop supplies had to be rationed.

Ironically, the shortage of books coincided with an increase in demand well above peacetime levels. The blackout, a reduction in alternative forms of entertainment, the tedium of life in the armed forces meant that people were reading more, were voracious for reprints of established books, let alone the latest novel. Evans, Hall, and Oliver were faced each week with difficult decisions over the allocation of the paper quota, so as to preserve a reasonable balance between the old and the new. The annual number of new titles dropped from a yearly average of 181 in the 1930s to an average of 55, *viz*: 1940 – 98; 1941 – 63; 1942 – 53; 1943 – 36; 1944 – 38; 1945 – 45. Among books by the established stalwarts were *The Corinthian* and *The Spanish Bride* (1940) by Georgette Heyer; *The Nelson Touch* (1942) by Clemence Dane; *A Man about the House* (1942) by Francis Brett Young; *The Razor's Edge* (1944) by Somerset Maugham; *The Power and the Glory* (1940) and *The Ministry of Fear* (1943) by Graham Greene; *Blackout in Gretley* (1942) by J. B. Priestley, for whom also was published a collection of his famous wartime wireless *Postscripts* (1940).

Several noteworthy newcomers joined the list during the war, but for the moment I shall limit myself to mentioning two of them. Both wrote about wartime life. The first is Gerald Kersh who made a great reputation with *They Died with their Boots Clean* (1941), a racy, vigorous story based on his experiences as a ranker in the Coldstream Guards. This was followed by *The Nine Lives of Bill Nelson* (1942), also about the Guards, and *The Dead Look On* (1943), an awesome, graphic parable of the destruction of the Czech village of Lidice and its inhabitants. Altogether he was to write for the firm thirty-two books, over half of which were collections of short stories, before his death in 1968. In the preface to *The Best of Gerald Kersh* (1960) Simon Raven describes his stories as 'neat, dramatic, bizarre, perverse, scientific, supernatural, historical . . . there are short "novels" of perhaps 30,000 words, long short stories of 10,000 or 12,000 and a great many short stories of what one might call classical length (4,000 to 8,000). All of them, from the novels proper to the little jokes, have three things in common: they are vigorous, they are inventive (sometimes to a point near lunacy), and they can be read with the greatest of ease. . . . Kersh's people, whether squalid or not, are always on the go; cheating, drinking, cruising, fornicating, making money or spending their immortal souls, they live in a world where it is always necessary, for good or ill, to act. . . .'[1]

Kersh was known in the office to be 'difficult' and eventually became embittered with Heinemann for not advancing enough money, but he never ceased to be grateful to Evans for a loan when things were difficult for him and he was just starting as an author. In a caustic, joky piece, very typical of his style, he gives a picture of Evans which is both affectionate and wounding: 'Perhaps the last of the great British publishers, Charles Evans was quick enough on the draw with a cheque for a hundred pounds for a needy author, but when it came to picking up a bill in a restaurant, he became singularly absent-minded. He looked at the ceiling. He scrutinized the pictures on the walls. He became interested in the floor, and stared fixedly at his fingernails, as if he had never seen them before and wondered how they had got there. Then, clasping his hands – locking his fingers in a terrific grip, looking into your eyes, but not at the bill, he would go into reminiscences with a breathless rush: "Yes, yes, yes, yes, Kersh, you have got talent. Genius. Great writer. Sit down, Kersh, and write!. . . . Mark my words.' Reminiscences about other authors would continue until Kersh had paid the bill. '. . . . Two bestsellers later he invited me to lunch again. I cashed a cheque and met him at the Speranza where, to my astonishment, he ordered everything that was rare and most expensive. I felt my royalties leaking away, but he called boldly for the bill. I reached for my pocket. But he waved me aside. He borrowed a pencil from the waiter (which he later absently put in his pocket) and signed the bill "As for Mr Hall." Then it came out that his accountant, Hall, had invited him to lunch the week before, but Charley, otherwise engaged, had taken a rain-check. And on this occasion, it didn't rain – it poured. . . . That same man, when I was broke, tossed me a hundred pounds in cash, without the slightest hope of getting it back!'[2]

Edith Pargeter, the second author whose recruitment fits naturally into the war years could scarcely have been more different. After two earlier novels she joined the Wrens and from her experiences wrote *She Goes to War* (1942) and followed it with an ambitious, skilfully documented trilogy under the umbrella title *The Eighth Champion of Christendom*. The first part, *Lame Crusade* (1945), was written from the viewpoint of other ranks and recreates the days of an army private through the fighting in Belgium and France before his perilous escape back to England; the second, *Reluctant Odyssey* (1946) follows him through the desert campaigns in Libya and the horrors of the retreat in Malaya and the disastrous fall of Singapore; in the third *Warfare Accomplished* (1947), the same soldier is traced through the Normandy landings on D-Day and the fighting in the Caen–Falaise Gap. Critics expressed astonishment that a young woman could depict with such forceful realism the technicalities of tank warfare, artillery concentrations, and *maquis* ambushes. For another twenty years Edith Pargeter was to appear regularly in the spring and autumn lists. Among her novels was *The Soldier at the Door* (1954) which dealt again with the brutalities of war, particularly in Korea, but expressed her ethical doubts about conscription. There was also another trilogy set in the Middle Ages and partly in her native Shropshire.

It was fitting that the limited wartime list should have included the delicate work of the airman-author Antoine de Saint-Exupéry who was thought to have been shot down by a German fighter pilot. He was one of the first to write thoughtfully about the new perception of the world – and of Man – made possible by flying, about perspectives that had never been witnessed before. His reminiscences, *Wind, Sand and Stars* (1939), was followed by his novel, *Flight to Arras* (1942) – reissued in 1955 with illustrations by Lawrence Irving; then came *The Little Prince* (1944) with his own drawings. Finally there was *Letter to a Hostage* (1950), not much more than a fragment but a 'confession of faith' as he remembers the French refugees of 1940 and speculates on the invisible cord that holds each human being to life. Years later the firm published *Antoine de Saint-Exupéry* (1971) by Curtis Cate.

Other noteworthy newcomers who joined the list during the war will be introduced later, in Book Three.

[303]

Formation of Heinemann &
Zsolnay Ltd

In wartime even the ailing World's Work company began to prosper. With the influx of US servicemen the two surviving American magazines, *West* and *Short Stories*, found an eager market and were printed to the limits of their paper quotas. But this provided only temporary prosperity and Phyllis Alexander skilfully made use of the paper quota resulting from the pre-war Mystery and Western novels and, in particular, from *How to Win Friends and Influence People* to take on further Dale Carnegie and various other self-improvement titles. In June 1939 Chalmers Roberts had agreed to surrender his shareholding and the company became a wholly owned subsidiary. Turnover slowly grew from £1,293 in 1940 to £8,051 in 1945, so that from making a loss it started to make profits which by the end of the war increased to £4,084.

During the war another subsidiary was formed, with very much an eye to the future: Heinemann and Zsolnay Ltd. Paul Zsolnay was an Austrian refugee of Jewish origins, though his family had been Protestant for several generations and he was a Churchwarden – not that Hitler recognized such distinctions. He had been very wealthy, owning a small type of château in the suburbs of Vienna and an immense estate on the other side of the Danube in what had become Slovakia, where he was proud of his 13,000 rose bushes. Some of his income came from his own distinguished publishing house which had a balanced list of high- and middlebrow titles, including many of the German Expressionist writers and the German translations of Galsworthy, who used to stay with him. Arriving in London before the war almost penniless and with an elderly mother, he had contacted Charles Evans, whom he knew because of Galsworthy, and was offered a very modest job in charge of Heinemann's dustjackets. When the raids were at their worst he moved down to a tiny office at Kingswood. He was full of ideas and an exceedingly astute businessman, with plans to sell French translations of English books to parts of the French-speaking world which were not occupied and later to create a list of books, especially fiction, translated into German. His enthusiasm and experience led to the setting-up of Heinemann & Zsolnay

Ltd with a capital of £1,000, two-thirds owned by Heinemann and one-third by Zsolnay. Post-war this was to prove an important and rewarding venture.

Death of Charles Evans

One of Heinemann's few setbacks and in a sense its severest casualty was Charles Evans himself. The first blow came when his youngest son, David, was shot down in an early (1942) night raid over Bremen. For five months he was posted as missing before his death was confirmed. He was only twenty. Both Charley and his wife, Rose, took it very badly. Not long afterwards their London flat was blitzed and he moved into the flat at the top of 99 Great Russell Street and spent long working weekends at his small Elizabethan house at Ewhurst, Surrey, which he had bought from Philip Gibbs. Then one morning he woke up to find that the whole of the left side of his body felt numb. Dr Barney Abraham, of the medical company, reassured him that it was merely a derangement of the sympathetic nervous system. This diagnosis was confirmed by two Harley Street doctors and he was given spinal manipulation to increase the blood supply. His weight was under eight-and-a-half stone.

His health did not improve and in the spring of 1944 Frere-Reeves left the Ministry and took over the executive control of the business. Evans came into the office two or three days a week but could not do much, and when the flying-bombs started he spent most of his time at Ewhurst. Then one night a flying-bomb was shot down within fifty yards of his house, which was made uninhabitable, and Evans was taken to hospital with superficial injuries and shock. There can be no doubt that this last blow hastened his end, which came on 29 November 1944. Arnold Gyde, who had also been released from his war service, wrote about the funeral in a letter to Jessica Brett Young: 'Charley lies beneath a cherry tree on the slope of a little hill facing the Surrey hills to the west. On the summit is the old church of Ewhurst. No one could wish for a pleasanter spot. There were very few of us – just Frere-Reeves, Oliver, Hall, Louisa, Dettmer, Roberts, and at the last minute three of the travellers.

'It was such a little coffin. All his children were there, except of course Seddon, who is on the Staff in Italy. Rose on Dwye's arm. Sgt. Owen out of hospital with an all too palpably smashed jaw, with his sister Peggy. "Wiggie", the bomber ace, with a greatcoat hiding whatever other medals he has earned besides his DFC. . . .

'The organist struggled with Handel's *I Know that my Redeemer Liveth*. Then the melancholy little procession filed out into bright sunshine. Rose looked finer than I have ever seen her, with her hair now silvered. Her suffering has beautified her. I was glad it was all so quiet. If it had been peacetime there would have been fifty authors there, twenty other publishers, booksellers, as well as a fruity contingent from the Garrick.

'Then it was all over. We left Charley for the peace and rest he so seldom allowed himself in life.'[3]

BOOK III
1945–1961

Post-War Boom and Problems

The aftermath of war, with the continuation of an austerity economy and only a slow return to normality, was a frustrating time for any publisher. Frere – by then he had stopped being Frere-Reeves – was of course now chairman and optimistic plans were made for the future but, though male staff began to return, there was a shortage of labour in the printing works and bindery and paper, like many commodities, was still rationed, often severely, until 1949 – and even after this supplies were often irregular. Even deliveries of the meagre licensed allocations were often delayed. Surprisingly some paper was to be had in Holland and arrangements were made to print some books there and also in Australia, but this made little difference. Although almost any kind of book would be snapped up by bookshops, the irony was that in 1945 some 1,600 Heinemann titles in demand were out of print, including books by such as Priestley, Brett Young, Maugham, Masefield, Galsworthy, and Lawrence. Pressure was put on the Government, but in its eyes book publishing was a non-essential industry and its important export potential tended to be ignored.

With the ending of restraints at the close of the 1940s the boom years for selling ended with unexpected suddenness and the trade as a whole began to suffer for the first time in ten years from overproduction and accumulation of stocks. By 1949 there was intense competition among publishers and the annual total of new titles had returned to pre-war levels. The unfamiliar phenomenon of the public's sales resistance was hastened by large increases in the cost of manufacture. Printing in 1950 cost three to four times more than it did in 1938; paper was 10*d.* per pound compared with 1½*d.* This meant that to gain the same margin of profit a price rise of at least six times was necessary, though in practice this did not happen because of large editions, paper of poorer quality and therefore *relatively* cheaper, and the payment in some cases of lower royalties. For reprints costs had also increased because during the war the Government had called in all standing type and metal blocks that were unlikely actually to be used in the near future, and therefore type for reprints now had to be reset and blocks remade.

All this had to be explained to authors anxiously awaiting news of reprints and they had to be asked to accept reduced rates of royalty. A letter written by Frere to John Masefield in November 1949 is typical of many: 'I have tried to get out some figures which would show you how the rise of the overall cost of production of 300 per cent higher than pre-war is made up. For instance, the actual paper which we should use in two of your books under discussion now costs 275 per cent more than the same paper did in 1939. Metal, which in 1939 was £35 a ton, is now £167 a ton. The various materials used in binding are now averaged out at nearly 200 per cent above their pre-war costs. The details of the general rise in wages, selling costs, advertising rates, etc are too numerous for me to set forth in detail, but these, together with the rise in the cost of raw materials, represent the total percentage overall. . . . In 1939 I suppose it would have been possible to have issued these books at 8s.6d. The proposed price of 10s.6d., as you will see, does not represent an adequate return for the extra costs of production involved. The only other alternative is further to increase the price of the books, but there, I am afraid, we have reached a point where the booksellers advise us that the public will not respond. So that if we accept the price of 10s.6d. as the only one in the circumstances, we must face a reduction in our own returns and that, I am afraid, is why I have had to make this proposal of a reduced royalty to you.'[1]

Despite all the difficulties, the post-war 1940s and the 1950s were essentially years of continuing growth in turnover and titles for Heinemann and of development of its organization. New overseas branches were opened in Australia, New Zealand, South Africa, and Canada. The group gained added lustre by the acquisition of distinguished independent imprints. In many ways it was one of the peak periods in the firm's history, though expansion brought in its train inevitable difficulties, particularly, as will be seen, towards the end of the 1950s, when financial and administrative problems coalesced to create a dangerous crisis. The list nevertheless must have been the envy of rivals. The fiction backlist and a continued flow of new novels from several of the pre-war 'giants' provided the bedrock and each year new authors of importance and promise were added. Likewise it was in these years that the foundations were laid for a major educational list.

Augmenting the Sales Drive

As we have seen, by 1950 the book trade had largely recovered from the effects of the war. The total number of books published in the UK had not only virtually equalled the pre-war record of 17,137 in 1937 but during the ensuing decade was greatly to exceed it (the figures in brackets were new editions and reprints):

1945	6,747	(921)
1950	17,072	(5,334)
1955	19,962	(5,770)
1960	23,783	(5,989)

There were approximately 225,000 titles in print of which the normal bookseller could at most stock only 10,000. Among the new titles were some 150 paperback titles each month. The shape of the institutional market was changing. The popular circulating libraries were finding that their role was increasingly difficult, mainly because of the competition from bookclubs and paperbacks as well as from the growth of public libraries – by 1961–62 446.32 million books were loaned by public libraries annually, compared with 165.67 million in 1934–35, from a stock of 76.01 million compared with 26.43 million.[2] Mudie's had closed in 1937, W. H. Smith's last library closed in 1961 and The Times Book Club in 1962, but Boots hung on until 1966. The twopenny, fourpenny, and sixpenny shop libraries likewise faded. Fortunately the larger book-reading public formed during the war was not lost, despite the novelty of television (11 million homes having a set by 1960). The relative affluence of the 1950s after the post-war economic freeze was a great support for the trade, and the demand for books, not only textbooks, was further stimulated by the long-term effects of the Education Act of 1944.

For Heinemann these positive factors offset the increased competition from other publishers, of whom perhaps 200 out of a total of 1,458 firms (whose books were listed in *Books in Print*) could be classed as serious rivals, so that in the 1950s sales had to be fought for as never before.

Particular attention had to be given to the wholesalers, particularly W. H. Smiths and the bulk suppliers to public libraries. With the final demise of the resurrected Simpkin Marshall, so important as a single-order house, Heinemann agreed in 1958 with other leading publishers to give retail booksellers a flat 33⅓ per cent discount for all orders, though in practice it had been giving this for some time. The home sales department was augmented by Derek Priestley as sales manager; Leslie Munro had been made a director in charge of sales in 1955 and continued in this post until his retirement in November 1960. Priestley had to work from Kingswood, often under difficulties because so many of his important customers were in London and also because of growing tensions between Kingswood and Great Russell Street. He was, however, reinforced by Marjorie Macphail, who had been in the department since 1922 and was noted for her prodigious memory and her familiarity with the minutiae of the backlist. John Dettmer, who had been with the company since starting as an office boy under William, was also made a director in 1955. As well as helping to run Peter Davies Ltd, he was responsible for many of the sales to bookclubs, particularly Foyles.

The publicity department was similarly strengthened by the appointment of Douglas Baber as assistant to Arnold Gyde (who retired in 1959 and died three months later). Baber himself wrote novels for Heinemann, among them *The Slender Thread* (1950); *My Death is a Mockery* (1952); and, in particular, *Where Eagles Gather* (1954), a novel based on his own experiences after parachuting behind German lines, where he was hidden by a Belgian family until discovered by the SS; Baber was made a prisoner of war and the family sent to Dachau. Considerable advertising space continued to be booked. Its extent can be gauged from the proud full-page announcement in *The Bookseller* (June 1949) of the coverage given to two books, *I Capture the Castle* by Dodie Smith and *The Willow Cabin* by Pamela Frankau. Whether or not extensive press advertising really did sell books, it certainly pleased the authors. Peter Barnard, who had recently joined the firm and whose main job was to get jackets designed and printed, remembers how after J. B. Priestley's *Festival at Farbridge* (1951) had been heavily panned by the critics he was sent for by Frere. An irate Priestley sat grumbling about homosexual reviewers.

'To placate him Frere told me in front of Priestley to take a full page in *The TLS* and big ads in *The Sunday Times* and *The Observer*, a double-spread in *The Bookseller*, and a good deal else. Back in my own office I worked out what it was all going to cost and that afternoon reported the sum to Frere who told me: "Just book the double-spread and perhaps one other big ad. That'll keep him quiet!" A typical piece of Frere's showmanship, but his authors respected him enormously. You couldn't help being fond of him.'

While all books received a modicum of attention, the overall publicity policy seems to have been to 'reinforce success' rather than cosset relative failures. Publicity as well as deserved adulation was achieved when three hundred guests were invited to celebrate J. B. Priestley's sixtieth birthday party, at which Frere spoke of their continuing friendship over thirty-five years and Priestley's health was proposed by Sir Compton Mackenzie, Norman Collins, and Lionel Hale. An even more ambitious publicity venture was a series of short films called *Authors at Home*, with the idea of showing them on television, in schools, and elsewhere. At least two were made: one about John Steinbeck, who in an interview discussed 'everything from Ascot to Angry Young Men', and the other about Elleston Trevor, who was filmed working at his home at Roedean and pursuing his hobbies of kite flying and miniature car racing. Another imaginative innovation was Authors as Artists an exhibition of paintings and drawings by Heinemann authors held at the Army and Navy Stores in October 1956. Opened by Somerset Maugham, it included work by seventeen authors, among them Enid Bagnold, Max Beerbohm, Mary Borden, Noël Coward, Edward Gordon Craig, Johan Fabricius, Mervyn Peake, and Laurence Whistler.

A major factor in the company's post-war development was the expansion of the export department and the establishment of offices in Commonwealth countries. The first steps in opening up Europe were taken by E. Maxwell Arnot and later by Derek Priestley before he was made home sales manager, and their efforts were consolidated and expanded by Alewyn Birch, who joined the firm from Zwemmers as export sales manager in 1953 – at double his previous salary. He functioned with great gusto from Great Russell Street and was given a staff of three. At first he used to visit the main European bookshops himself, but the long absences from London led to the appointment also of John Beer who in addition worked for Paul Zsolnay. Birch claimed to be 'half Irish, half Dutch, and half Italian'; Beer originated in Czechoslovakia. Their cosmopolitan backgrounds were of great benefit to the firm, not only because of their fluency in many European languages.

[313]

They knew that Europeans hungered for books in English and that potentially Europe represented the second biggest market after America.

Before long Heinemann could boast that it controlled what was almost certainly the most effective network of European representatives. The earliest to be appointed was Raymond Conrad who from Zurich covered Switzerland and Austria and later Western Germany as well. Educated at Highgate School and Cambridge, he spoke perfect English and was a total Anglophile. Elsa, his wife, an émigrée Russian, worked with him and between them they knew personally every bookseller in their area. Next to be appointed was Graham Powell who covered Italy and France, and later Yugoslavia. In Holland coverage was provided by the firm's own subsidiary William Heinemann/Nederland NV run by Corolus Verhulst. It was set up in 1953 to distribute and travel Heinemann books on an exclusive, closed-market basis in Holland. It warehoused most titles and during the worst post-war shortages supplied some paper. For a while the existence of this company provided a useful source of local currency and helped overcome exchange problems. A Dutch representative, Frits Maurick, was taken on and when in the early 1960s there was no longer a need for a local company and warehouse, he took over the whole Benelux territory. Scandinavia was looked after by Helge Marthinsen, onetime tea-planter in Kenya, who worked from Copenhagen. When he had to retire because of poor health, he was succeeded by Sven Gade who, as well as travelling the shops, ran from his Copenhagen flat a uniquely elaborate mailing list of booksellers, librarians, and individuals. The only parts of Western Europe not covered by Heinemann's own agents were Spain and Portugal, which were looked after spasmodically by various members of staff anxious to visit there.

The network was based on close and regular contacts with booksellers, who were effectively serviced. Other publishers were impressed by this network and so Birch formed a consortium. Among the first to join were Batsford, John Murray, and the Architectural Press; eventually it serviced some two dozen firms. Once a year they were invited to a conference attended by all the Heinemann European representatives who supplied them during the year with very competent reports. Member firms were charged between 12½ and 15 per cent of the net income they received from Europe, whether or not it originated from the activities of the representatives – European booksellers were given 35 per cent trade discount, single copies included, and 90 days' credit. The representatives received about 7½ per cent on net turnover arising from their territories, out of which they had to pay all their expenses. The excess margin between what the consortium firms paid and the total commission earned by the representatives, including that on Heinemann titles, meant that the firm's European representation was totally free of cost. The consortium also enabled the number of booksellers visited to be extended. Everyone was satisfied but the system worked only because of the high quality of the representatives and the efficiency with which they were controlled and administered. There was no jealousy between the firms and no one feared they would be 'last out of the bag'. Their lists were seldom directly competitive and on the whole complemented each other. The books were presented by subject rather than by imprint. The real competitors were not each other but the Americans.

The consortium also provided the basis for joint representation at the annual Frankfurt Book Fair which was started in 1949 to replace, so far as the West was concerned, the pre-war fair in Leipzig. As well as being a marketplace for the sale of rights, the Frankfurt fair increasingly became a centre for the promotion of books to Continental booksellers and it was for this function that the joint stand was operated on behalf of the consortium. Its members' financial contributions again covered the cost of Heinemann's own appearance at the fair, apart from hotel bills.

Creation of a Commonwealth Network

Beyond Europe and omitting the United States the main outlets for British fiction and general books were the Commonwealth countries of Australia, New Zealand, South Africa, and Canada. In all these areas Heinemann offices were established between 1948 and 1955. Some years later further offices were to be opened by Heinemann Educational Books, Ltd in South East Asia, West and East Africa and the Caribbean. There was never any question of opening a full-scale branch in the United States for fiction and general books, as it was felt to be more effective and more profitable to sell (and buy) to (and from) American publishers.

[315]

Before the war ended Leslie Hall and Arnold Gyde had made a first investigatory visit to Australia. Their ship, loaded with TNT, sailed uneventfully, apart from one submarine attack, via Panama across the Pacific to Brisbane, arriving in March 1945. Heinemann was then represented in Australia by the Oxford University Press, but as well as getting the feel of the market the two emissaries made valuable visits to bookshops and arranged for a number of books to be printed locally, to make use of Australian paper, copies being shipped back to Europe. The first to be put in hand was appropriately the Australian Henry Handel Richardson's *The Fortunes of Richard Mahony*. A second trip was made the next year, taking in India as well. Their journey as fee-paying RAF passengers proved to be hazardous. The aircraft, for much of the way a seaplane, was unpressurized and they made numerous stops for fuel – the South of France, Sicily, Cairo, Habanjina (near Baghdad), Karachi, and Bombay where they disembarked with the idea of visiting Indian bookshops and seeing if representation could be improved. After a few business calls in Bombay Hall and Gyde arranged to fly by RAF Dakota to Calcutta where they found themselves more or less interned in a military camp seventy-two miles outside because it was February 1946 and India was in uproar during the birth-pangs of Independence. It was considered by the authorities too dangerous for them to enter the city. Hall wrote to Louisa Callender: 'This desert is edged with thick bush and as we go to bed (thirty-two of us in a hut and us the only two civilians) we hear the throb of the native tom-toms. To say the least of it, with a rising only seventy miles away, it is rather eerie and disturbing. However here we are with only one bag between us and no change of clothing. Black lizards, anywhere between 6 and 12 inches long, suddenly look in at the door and scuttle across the floor or up the roof struts. We get our food (awful) from the cookhouse with the troops and set to cleaning our plates and mugs and making our beds.'[3]

Back in Bombay they found that the situation had worsened. Hall's diary records: '*Tuesday*: Today the Indian Navy has gone on strike and the hooligan element is loose in the town, burning, looting, and rioting. Shops and business houses are closing. Buses are stopping. Things look ugly. *Wednesday*: The naval situation is worsening. Mobs swirl and shout. Cars, buses and lorries are set alight and columns of smoke rise from the streets. Machine-guns begin to chatter. Naval ratings have collared twenty ships and have turned the guns of those riding in the harbour on to shore installations and they threaten to send in a few broadsides. All day long rifles crack and machine-guns stutter. Below my window I hear the screaming of hysterical sailors as they go by in an overloaded bus – even on the wings they ride. *Thursday*: Today the rioting increases. Still looting, arson and shooting. Europeans, if seen, are pulled out of their taxis and treated not too pleasantly. *Friday*: The worst day in the history of Bombay so far. Over 700 casualties, 59 killed.'[4] In the middle of all this Hall was suddenly taken seriously ill with pneumonia but was nursed back to near-health by Gyde, 'assisted by a worthy barman'. They managed to get tickets for a flight to Perth in Australia. The doctor said Hall was not fit enough to travel, but Hall declared that if he stayed any longer in the humid Bombay heat, he would die, and so they left. Once they reached Sydney Hall's health improved and they had a successful visit, arranging for many thousands of books to be printed on Australian paper. They then went on to New Zealand.

In 1948 a company was formed in Australia with the idea of enlisting local authors as well as distributing titles published in the UK. Clem Christesen, a distinguished Australian literary figure, was appointed manager, but he retained the right also to continue editing *Meanjin*, the Australian literary magazine he had founded. At the outset this presented problems because, following the magazine's very critical review of Richard Aldington's *Poetry of the English Speaking World* (see pages 399–400), Christesen was 'sacked' in January 1948 – on his first day in office! The trouble, however, blew over and for a while he continued to run the office with considerable success. But Frere never forgave him for what he considered to be an insult to one of his closest friends. There were also rumours in London, originating with Paul McGuire and quite unfounded, that he was a dangerous Red.

At first Christesen operated from the premises of OUP who continued to act as Heinemann's agents, but with the growth of the business over the next three years and after a further visit by Hall in 1951, accompanied this time by Frere, it was arranged to break away from OUP, though 'in the friendliest manner'. Heinemann's first independent office and warehouse were thereupon opened in commodious premises at 317 Collins Street in the very centre of Melbourne, and trading started on 1 January 1952. Simultaneously, Christesen was demoted to handle publicity only, being replaced as manager by OUP's manager, F. T. Sambell. Understandably Christesen could not swallow this and resigned. Hall also engaged OUP's now-retired manager, E. E. Bartholomew – always known as 'Barty', a great book trade character whose father had started travelling the shops in Victoria in the early years of the century on horseback. Both Sambell and Bartholomew were strict teetotallers.

In 1953 additional offices, run by David Lemon, were opened in Sydney in order to provide better coverage of New South Wales and Queensland. These pioneering efforts attracted other UK publishers who wished to be represented, and they were welcomed. It was also planned to enlist and develop more Australian writers, Paul McGuire being appointed local talent scout and editor. When books were taken, they were still however edited and handled in London. Two years later G. W. Moore opened Heinemann's first New Zealand office in City Road, Auckland, as a branch of the Australian company.

At that period the Australasian market was relatively straightforward. Most of its population looked upon Britain as home and were eager for the kind of books published by Heinemann. British publishers enjoyed total market rights and the fiction market was not yet split with the Americans, though they were beginning to muscle in with their academic books, particularly in the universities which were increasingly following the American type of syllabus. The growing educational sector of the Heinemann list was unwisely neglected in Australia and this was later to lead to the setting up there of a separate educational branch.

British Book Services (Canada) Ltd, as its name implies, was from the outset supported by other UK publishers, soon numbering no fewer than twenty-two. Founded in 1949, the original participants included the Architectural Press, Chapman & Hall, J. & A. Churchill, Evans Brothers, Faber & Faber, Grey Walls Press, Hamish Hamilton, Methuen, George Newnes, Pan, Pilot Press, Routledge & Kegan Paul. Hall was again largely responsible for establishing this ambitious project. William Gordon, formerly export manager of Collins, Glasgow, was put in charge and a turreted Victorian mansion on Broadview Avenue, Toronto, was renamed Kingswood House and became the headquarters. In 1954, however, Gordon was succeeded by Ann Orford who had long experience as a bookseller at Simpsons.

Warehousing books on the spot had obvious advantages for members of this consortium, but it also brought problems. Too much money and effort went into selling their books and not enough into selling Heinemann's, and working capital had to be increased. For UK publishers

[318]

Canada has always been an uphill struggle. As well as the vast distances, the Press, radio and TV are dominated by the United States. The kind of support normally expected from *The Times Literary Supplement, Guardian, Spectator, New Statesman, et al.* just is not there. Even when Canadian rights are reserved by UK firms, US versions of the same titles pour across the border and librarians often find these easier to buy – on the other hand, if the deal with the American publisher is sound, neither the UK publisher nor author may suffer, except that it hits the former's Canadian based operation. Largely for this reason, if for no other, Heinemann over the years has jealously resisted releasing the Canadian rights when selling rights to American publishers. Ironically, the Americans who have a home market of 220 million often think it is scarcely worth their while to bother much about the 15 million English-speaking market across their northern border.

South Africa was tackled in a slightly different manner, a joint company being formed at the end of 1951 with Cassells, known officially as Heinemann and Cassell South Africa (Proprietary) Ltd. E. Maxwell Arnot went out as manager to Cape Town where he opened a small office with a tiny staff. Five years later they ran a warehouse and occupied seven rooms in a modern office building, employed eight staff, and represented twelve other publishers. From a branch office in Johannesburg Alexander Fullerton, a Peter Davies novelist, covered the Transvaal, East Africa, and what was then the Central African Federation of Northern and Southern Rhodesia. Large stocks were carried for the other publishers and it was eventually agreed with Cassells that the whole operation was expanding too fast and becoming unwieldy. Arnot, who was very dynamic, was against cutting down, resigned and came back to England. He was succeeded by Mendl Jacobs, who was the senior representative and had experience as a bookseller.

In the Far East Heinemann, together with other leading UK publishers, was represented by Donald Moore who operated from Singapore and Kuala Lumpur and whose coverage included Japan, Hong Kong, and Indonesia. He was very successful but eventually ran into a cash crisis brought about by wholesaling his clients' books as well as representing them. His company was rescued by the supporting publishers.

This was the culmination of the plan to provide extensive direct overseas coverage of all the most important markets in the English-speaking world. It soon had a marked effect on turnover, but just as rapidly it also began to bring severe problems. Control from London of such a widespread network was difficult and yet most of the overseas branches were neither strong nor experienced enough to function effectively without detailed guidance. They were under constant pressure from London to import excessive quantities, often of books with limited local appeal. Local speculative holdings had to be limited to potential bestsellers or to books with a strong regional appeal. In Australia and New Zealand, for example, a very few titles, maybe four or five a year, were declared to be 'closed market books' which meant that booksellers could not order from London and had to buy from the Heinemann local office. Stocks of only a fraction of other titles were held locally and with most the normal procedure was for the overseas company's representatives to collect orders from bookshops which were sent back to London, but the bookseller could order either from London or locally. If he ordered direct from London, he received 50 per cent discount for fiction and 45 per cent for non-fiction off the UK price and paid the carriage. But with a closed market book it would be only 40 per cent off the local retail price carriage paid. The overseas companies were normally supplied from Kingswood at a fixed discount of 55 per cent, but with a few very big sellers it went up eventually to as much as 60 per cent, with the idea of lowering the local published price in order to increase sales. The local mark-up could be as much as three times the UK published price. Stock was supplied by sea from the UK and this could take weeks – a minimum of ten in the case of Australia but much less to reach South Africa. Despite all these precautions, excess stocks tended to build up rapidly, particularly in Australia and Canada. This problem was to cause increasing concern in future years. The export figures might look good on paper but they were misleading unless actual sales had been achieved on the spot.

Production – Friction between Kingswood and London

Just before the close of 1948 a slap-up dinner was held in the Napoleon Room at the Café Royal to celebrate the twenty-first birthday of the Windmill Press. Staff numbering 270 from Great Russell Street as well as Kingswood enjoyed *Médaillon de Flétan Cardinal*, *Poularde Poêlée Champêtre*, and *Gâteau Glacé aux Fruits Arlequin*, and after a toast proposed by A. S. Frere and responded to by B. F. Oliver, they danced to Leon Wayne's orchestra. Frere told them and the assembled journalists that the Windmill Press had amply fulfilled the optimistic prophecies when it was opened and it was recognized as being 'among the showplaces of industrial achievement'.

In truth all was not well at Kingswood. Typesetting equipment and printing machines were tending to break down and had been deteriorating steadily throughout the war years and it had been difficult to obtain spare parts. The plant was also getting out of date. The typefaces were limited and the standard of setting and paper was very low. With exceptions the appearance of a typical post-war Heinemann book, even after wartime restrictions had been removed, was shoddy compared with the products of, say, Cape, Faber or Chatto & Windus.

All these problems became more pressing once paper supplies were back to normal (1949/50). With the return of competition between publishers it was vital to be able to produce books faster. Oliver was approaching retirement and an assistant and eventual successor was found in Peter Barnard, who hitherto had been in charge of jackets and wrote copy for and designed advertisements. He was highly thought of by Frere and Hall – 'Peter has guts and staying power.' He had no printing background but took evening classes and rapidly learned from other book printers, especially Mark Clowes and Richard Clay. After Barnard became works manager in 1950 he soon discovered that the press was allowed more or less to run itself and that output was much lower than it should have been. Various forms of petty corruption had become standard practice. The odd pound note or two would be slipped across a desk by the representatives of paper suppliers. A firm of efficiency consultants brought in by Barnard went around studying work patterns with stop-watches and this thoroughly upset the staff, particularly the compositors and binders. An incentive scheme was proposed, but this made the trade union chapels very restive. Barnard told me how he had invited Bill Keys, then an organizer from the Printers and Paperworkers Union (later SOGAT), to pay the press a visit.

'On arrival Keys said: "Leave me alone with the lads. Don't worry. We'll sort it out ... but I shall look forward to a very good lunch afterwards!" Keys told them that the incentive scheme was the best thing possible and that they should bloody well shut up. He gave them chapter and verse of what had happened at other book printing firms and how much they could expect to gain. He was proved right and so were we. The output of the composing room went up by some 40 per cent, of the bindery by 30 per cent, and the machine-room by 10 per cent – but this had been much better run before.'

When Oliver retired in 1952 (he died soon afterwards in March 1954) Barnard was put in sole charge of the press and made a director of William Heinemann Ltd; later he also joined the board of the holding company. He found himself increasingly involved in the Kingswood-London friction, though he did his best to remain neutral. There was a fundamental conflict of interests between the two halves of the business: Kingswood wanted to keep its departments running without breaks and to be profitable, whereas London, particularly Alan Hill in the education department and the three semi-independent subsidiaries, wanted to be free to choose the printer who offered the best service, a high standard of production, and a keen price. This was not necessarily the Windmill Press. Although financially the press was part of the same organization, Hall, who was in sole charge of costing, made sure that the press's margins were generous, in fact at the expense of the margins on publishing. It is significant that during the 1950s the production cost averaged 50.9 per cent of net turnover, compared with 45.0 per cent in the 1930s and 38.2 per cent in the 1940s. The (printing) tail wagged the (publishing) dog. In the 1950s this also led to unnecessary or too early reprints, rather than let the machines stand idle. For many jobs offset lithography, which was becoming increasingly available, was more suitable than the kind of old-fashioned letterpress printing which was all that Kingswood could offer. This was particularly true of books which had already been manufactured by an American publisher. The obvious and cheaper process was to have the typesetting photographed, but Hall would refuse to agree because the keyboard operators at Kingswood needed more work. Some efforts were made to get setting and printing contracts from outside customers, but this was not very successful because, rightly or wrongly, they feared they would be given second-best treatment. Understandably Hall employed maximum pressure to get as much printing as possible done at Kingswood; equally understandably London, especially the new subsidiaries, resisted. Frere seems to have played a fairly neutral role, but production was far from being his main concern and he tended as usual to side with Hall, though the two men had little in common apart from self-interest and their dislike of Dwye Evans, whose commercial judgment was almost certainly more acute than that of the other directors. Hall went so far as to scorn, in Dwye's absence, his not very apparent Welshness. I have been told that whenever his name came up at the interminable lunches in the directors' dining-room at Kingswood, Hall would chant 'Taffy was a Welshman, Taffy was a thief . . .' and look down the table for fawning looks of approval.

Even after the establishment of the editorial department at Great Russell Street there was regular confusion over the division between it and Kingswood. Despite editors in London, the detailed copy preparation was still the responsibility of Kingswood who did employ first-rate experts: G. V. Carey, who worked from home and had written an author's and printer's guide for the Cambridge University Press; and later the very learned Herbert Rees, who worked at the press. It was Kingswood rather than London which controlled the flow of production and there was insufficient forward planning. Dwye Evans was very conscious of these shortcomings and circulated a confidential memorandum to other members of the board which, among much else, underlined the weakness of the existing system: 'The average time taken to get a book out is about ten months, though in some cases we do it in six months or less; in others it is as long as eighteen months. Proofs come up five or six weeks in advance of publication, supplies of the finished book precede publication by a bare two-and-a-half weeks, on average. There is *no* chance under our present system (a) to do adequate publicity work on a new book; or (b) to handle effectively the sale of subsidiary rights – which in many cases is an adjunct to and a part of the publicity for the book.' Dwye also urged that they should 'ruthlessly prune from our list the borderline books which clutter up the press, which sell only a thousand or two, and bring us neither prestige nor profit. This is not as difficult as it sounds; any one of us could compile a list of books we need never have published and need never miss. The result of this policy decision would be to give first, more time to rewarding titles and to enable us to get finished copies in ample time of those books to which we intend to give star treatment. Secondly, to carry our present policy of "a big book a month" a stage further and to choose well in advance the books in our future list – other than the obvious ones – which merit special treatment and can be made into bestsellers.'[5]

[323]

All these criticisms resulted in the decision to create a new position, that of production manager who would, though answerable to Peter Barnard, become responsible for scheduling the annual list logically, for ensuring that books came out to time, and that the press gave the publishing side a better service all round. He would also be employed to improve the typography and the books' general appearance. This meant another major shift in power from Kingswood to London. In 1955 Hugh Williamson, then at the OUP and author of a very distinguished work *Methods of Book Design* (OUP, 1956), was appointed. He told me that he was astonished at the haphazard nature of the system – or rather lack of system.

'At the weekly meetings current sales figures would frequently put everyone in a tizzy, because whereas in some months there would be three bestsellers, during the following two months there would be none. There was no proper forward programme. I would send typescripts down to Kingswood where Renee Muller, who had been at the press since its opening and was a loyal and hard-working assistant works manager, would stack them up by a radiator. Whenever the composing room manager told her that they were ready for another typescript, she would ask "What about this one?" If it wasn't quite thick enough he would look a bit downcast and she would then offer him a thicker one. There was no question of planning or thinking out which title was due to come next. Even a Graham Greene could be mouldering under a heap of relatively piffling authors – that is until there was a panic when someone asked when the next Greene would be published.'

The long print runs on a Graham Greene, Georgette Heyer, Nevil Shute, and several others could take weeks to run off, making planning even more essential. Williamson introduced, astonishingly for the first time since the war, a reliable system of scheduling and a blank form which accompanied the typescript from department to department and showed essential information including details of royalty rates and the amount of advance; a rough estimate of wordage and the proposed number and type of illustrations, if any; type of jacket design; forecast of various quantities of sales on which manufacturing estimates should be prepared. With most books, however, the actual costs and how the published price was arrived at still remained something of a secret.

'There was a mystic formula guarded over by Hall. He would bring out a piece of paper, hold it close to his chest, and read out the decision *ex cathedra*. The only adjustment was up or down to one of the published prices then recognized by all publishers. Once I managed to glance at the magic formula over Hall's shoulder. I could see it allowed 33⅓ per cent for overheads, 10 per cent for advertising and publicity, and a simple royalty calculation. No allowance was made for the smaller turnover from export sales.'

With some projects it was agreed that rough costs, based on sales estimates and a reasonable selling price, should be discussed before a contract was issued. Williamson also managed to impose some degree of quality control over the whole production process. He changed the type faces and greatly improved the quality of paper. With Barnard's full support he introduced a system of very accurate cast-offs, so that it could be ensured that long books had even workings. Much more attention was paid to sound design and the books undoubtedly were more elegant, though it had to be admitted that this had no obvious effect on sales. Even the shoddiest books by popular Heinemann authors had sold prodigiously. The travellers reported however that better quality production did make books that much easier to subscribe and it was also thought to attract new authors to the list.

With post-war expansion, the growth of the educational department, and the additional stocks from subsidiaries, the warehouse became seriously overcrowded. Temporary buildings were erected to the south-west of the main Kingswood building and Trenwith Wills, one of the original architects, was commissioned to design two new wings so that the buildings formed a capital H instead of three sides of a square. This provided 12,500 additional square feet. Somerset Maugham performed the opening ceremony on 24 June 1952. In the course of his address he told a distinguished gathering that it was 'fifty-two years since they published my first book, and since then they have published practically everything I have written. I think, on the whole, the connection has been satisfactory both to them and to me. I have been able to keep the wolf from the door, and they have been able to erect these sumptuous buildings. I would advise every author to stick to the same publisher, as long as his publisher is prepared to stick by him. All of us authors have our ups and downs, and we are none of us always at our best. If the publisher is confident that his author will stay with him, he will naturally be more willing to take the rough with the smooth, thinking that if one book disappoints him, he may like the next one rather better. It takes all of us authors a long time to secure a public, and to a certain extent, to a great extent sometimes, it depends on our publisher to secure our public for us. It is evident that a publisher will only take the trouble to do that if he is sure that so long as he does his best by his author, the author will remain faithful to him.'

After Maugham had unveiled a memorial tablet he presented the blue-and-gold Windmill Press flag which had covered it to a member of the recently established Canadian branch of the company, a Mrs Weatherill, who took it back the next day so that it could fly over Kingswood House in Toronto. Arnold Gyde confided some jottings to his private journal which provide vignettes of such an occasion. 'The press was looking at its best basking in the sunshine, scrupulously swept, newly painted. It made me proud to see it. . . . Frere read his speech. It was silly enough in any case and sounded sillier through the microphone's amplification. Maugham spoke much better. . . . Had rather a ghastly time, trying to recognize those who thought I knew them well. No one helped me. The Heinemann people simply fade into thin air on these occasions. Frere, as the chairman should, rightly kept concentrated on the big authors and I alone know all the rest – or I should say *ought* to know them. . . . Introduced Noel-Baker as "Mr Black of the *Daily Mail*" and called Georgette Heyer "Enid Bagnold" . . . in the board room all sorts of people wedged round a bar where champagne was being served. Jack Priestley among them. "Eh, lass, doarn't give me them Janey glasses. I'll 'ave mine in mug." Terrified, the girl served him champagne in a pint glass. I thought it was time to go. Sir John Squire getting maudlin with Mrs Peter Davies. I could see that if I didn't get him away soon we'd have to carry him. . . . Heard over my left shoulder: "Eh, lass, this is French tart's drink. Top it up with right spirit". . . .'[6]

The increase in orders necessitated also the modernization of the clerical procedures. Orders had hitherto been recorded manually with indelible pencils, but soon after the end of the war typewriters were introduced and later, in 1959–60, when mechanization became essential, Hollerith machines were installed. This system was based on punched cards and worked on the same principle as a pianola. Eric Rabbets, then manager of the trade department, explained to me that it did not amount to computerization and it was labour intensive, but it automatically calculated discounts. This was a great boon when working out non-net (educational) terms of $16\frac{2}{3}$ plus 5 per cent discount and with some invoices where, for royalty purposes, each line had to be calculated separately.

A further step to rationalize the functions of Kingswood was to hive off, in 1958, the printing, binding, and warehousing sections in a new company, The Windmill Press Ltd. As a wholly owned subsidiary of the holding company, it purchased formally from William Heinemann Ltd the press, the buildings, and the freehold land. Hall was made its chairman and Barnard managing director. In a memorandum Barnard explained to all the companies in the group that they 'would have exactly the same relations with The Windmill Press Ltd as they had with any other commercial printer. The new company would not arbitrarily demand work, but it should be borne in mind that it was advantageous to the group that the press should have as much work as plant and machinery would allow.'[7] Nicely put, but the pressure was still on!

A Proper Editorial Department

The centre of power was still at Kingswood, but during the 1940s and '50s much of it shifted to Great Russell Street, where the directors, other than Hall and Oliver, and other key executives such as Alan Hill and Arnold Gyde, spent most of their time. Every Wednesday morning, however, Frere in his Bentley, driven by Mr Grey the chauffeur, and the others in less impressive vehicles would still make the long exhausting trail across 'transpontine' London for a morning of meetings at Kingswood. The directors and a few others of the Elect would continue over luncheon in the directors' private dining-room, and the London staff were lucky if they got back to their desks by teatime.

The processes by which books were selected and edited were very haphazard. Since the war Arnold Gyde had been largely engaged on publicity and there was no longer an editorial department as such. The reports by the two regular readers, Maire Lynd and Tegan Harris, always went first to Louisa Callender, who passed them on to Dwye Evans and Frere. Each would scribble their opinion at the top or foot of the report and occasionally a further opinion would be sought from Leslie Munro as sales manager. There was no routine procedure, some books being commissioned by Frere, Dwye Evans, or Louisa Callender without consultation. The three did not get on. Frere transposed his dislike for Charley Evans on to his son; when I asked him bluntly what he felt about Dwye, he lapsed for some reason into French and snapped spitefully: '*Le fils de son père!* Need I say more?' He was also increasingly at odds with Louisa Callender who, he maintained, had been a splendid secretary but once made a director she had become stubborn and stupid, possessing neither literary nor political judgment. She retired in 1954. I was told by Malcolm Muggeridge, who at that time was employed as a freelance adviser, that his meetings at Great Russell Street made him uncomfortable, because on some days Frere and Callender were barely on speaking terms and Frere's disdain for Dwye was only too obvious.

Opinions about Frere polarized between enormous liking and distrust. He seemed to win, however, the loyalty of most of the staff, who respected him for his judgment, his intelligence and, in particular, for the almost impulsive confidence he showed in them. Maybe he overdid it, but he knew how to delegate. Just as he left the commercial side of things to Hall, the 'wizard with figures', he expected more junior members of staff to act independently and to exercise full responsibility.

As the business expanded and with it the flow of manuscripts, it was decided in 1952 to make the editorial processing less haphazard and to appoint an editorial manager. Roland Gant, who since 1950 had been in charge of jackets, was an obvious choice. He was himself a writer, translator, and later novelist who had previous publishing experience at the Falcon Press and the Grey Walls Press. His French wife, Nadia Legrand, wrote a novel and two stories, *The Estrangement*, published by the firm in 1953.

Frere's method of offering the job was characteristic: 'Roland, aren't you fed up with that bloody awful job of yours? You really ought to be doing editorial work. It's time we had a proper editorial department and you, dear boy, are the chap to run it.'

Gant's appointment meant that the commissioning and editing of books became more systematic, though the actual copy preparation was still carried out at the Windmill Press. He was allowed to enlist a talented team consisting of an assistant, James Michie, who had just returned from schoolmastering in Jamaica and was later to pursue his interest in Latin classics to become renowned as a poet and translator of Catullus and Horace; and a young secretary-*cum*-general-dogsbody, Claire Delavenay who later, under her married name of Claire Tomalin, was to become well known as an author and literary editor. She was the first of a succession of highly educated women who started with the firm as secretaries. Claire told me that she was paid £5 10s. a week which went up to £6 10s. after a year.

'In those days I think I was quite ready to accept that women were automatically given advisory or service jobs in publishing, whatever their qualifications, whereas men made the decisions and became the directors. When I went for my interview, I had to walk through the room where James sat and go into Roland's little room. Half way through the interview James came in and put a piece of paper on Roland's desk discreetly. Much later they told me that it was a mark out of 10 for my looks – 7, I think it was. Very male chauvinistic stuff!'

There was also Ethel Sutton who, in Roland's words, 'must have been close to seventy and had been there for ever. She looked like Edith Sitwell and was given to wearing green brocade and chunky jewellery. She used to surround herself with a rampart of hassocks and other quaint objects, including an Art Nouveau iron stand for her coffee cup, called the "Lady Typewriter's Companion". If anyone should leave the door open, she would cry "Kindly shut that bloody door!"'

Maire Lynd and Tegan Harris would call in weekly with their reports and to pick up another batch of manuscripts. As well as authors, the editorial department's rooms on the second floor always seemed to be full of casual visitors and there was often an aroma of freshly ground coffee. Roland, a talented mimic, loved to tell anecdotes. A frequent visitor was the convivial Arnold Gyde from publicity upstairs.

'We were very fond of him', Roland recalls, 'but the trouble was that he would chat for anything up to two hours and we couldn't get through our work. That was until Ethel produced what she called the "Gyde Trap", a large, very elderly typewriter which was placed on his favourite armchair. At least this cut down the length of his visits!'

The new editorial department had considerable influence over what was commissioned. The post-war period saw the balance between literary quality and commercial potential almost certainly tip in the former's favour, though such judgments can be unreliable. Gant was however experienced enough to be aware of economic realities, particularly as competition grew fiercer after the ending of paper rationing, but with fiction particularly he believed that his department's recommendations should be founded largely on personal preference. Maire Lynd, for one, always took this view when writing reports:

When reading the manuscript of a novel, I merely consider its quality and never think too much about whether or not it will sell. I never had a concept of what a Heinemann novel should be like. I just longed for everyone to be as good as Turgenev. I just made sure that the writing was good and that what the author had to say was interesting. If I enjoyed a book maybe others would as well. But a publisher's reader must always be on her or his guard. When something comes along which is very different from the typical books then being published and to which one is attuned, there is always a danger of missing it. I can understand why William H.

rejected *Dubliners*. I think that was why I turned down *Orlando the Marmelade Cat*. I felt it would only be enjoyed by grown-ups. How wrong I was!

Roland and in fact everyone in the editorial department was encouraged to develop his or her own authors. Whether or not they had discovered them, they should as members of their individual lists nurture them and promote their interests. 'Publishing is a highly individual business and a highly personal one,' Frere told an interviewer from the *New Statesman & Nation* in April 1957. 'That's why it's so difficult to generalize about publishing – all good publishers are different. A publisher's tools are his judgement and his taste, which have to be individual and personal if they're to be any good at all. He works very largely in the field of the subjective; quite literally, when he chooses and publishes one specific book out of all the manuscripts that come in to him, he's backing his fancy. Then his relation with his authors is a personal one. It can't help but be; for he has to find them, nurse them, cherish them, and not lose them. He hasn't only to sell their books. He's got to provide them with an atmosphere in which they can flourish as creative people and which is right for them as the kind of authors they are.' Frere also emphasized the importance authors attach to an imprint – in other words what matters to them is the quality of the list as a whole, the standing of its authors, and not whether the books are profitable to the firm. In cruder, commercial language Frere might have been arguing that certain recondite or highbrow works with only modest or even poor sales can act as 'loss leaders' to attract authors of bestsellers. It is the list as a whole that counts in building a publisher's reputation. 'Why does an ambitious young novelist choose one publisher rather than another to send his manuscript to? Not because he knows anything about the abilities of the various publishers to sell books. No, one publisher out of them all represents for him the best, and the firm in question does so because it publishes what seem to the young man the best novelists and the most exciting novels of his time. He wants to appear in the company of his equals and those he aspires to equal. It's a question of standards. . . .'[1]

Roland Gant was a success, just what the firm needed, but after five years he left for a very basic reason: his salary (under £800 a year) was derisory. When Michael Joseph offered him a great deal more, he had no option as a married man with a child but to accept. Publishing salaries have always tended to be low compared with those in businesses requiring similar talents (e.g., advertising or journalism) because people have been prepared to settle for less in return for the 'privilege of working with books' and, as the ceaseless stream proves, there has never been a shortage of job applicants. In those days pensions at Heinemann seem to have been at the whim of the directors, though in 1949 a somewhat meagre non-contributory scheme was introduced which gave all employees who had reached the age of sixty-five (for men) or sixty (for women) and who had completed ten years' continuous service a pension equal to one-fifth of an employee's wages or salary, but limited to a maximum of £200 per year; plus a grant of ten shillings per year for each complete year of service. In a booklet issued to staff the following examples were given: an employee earning £10 a week and with 20 years' service would be granted a pension of £2 3s.10d. a week; earning £5 a week and with 12 years' service would mean £1 2s.4d. a week.

As with many middle-class commercial employees, Heinemann staff seldom knew what their colleagues were earning, whereas the so-called humbler ranks of printers, binders, and packers, organized in trade unions, knew this down to the rate per hour. Teachers, civil servants, and members of other professions also enjoyed clearly understood salary scales, but the discrepancies among the pay of Heinemann editors and the firm's other office workers were then often grotesque, as each of their salary rates depended largely on individual, private bargaining. When James Michie succeeded Roland Gant as editorial manager, he suspected that he was being paid very much less than the home sales manager, a job at about equivalent level. Salaries were administered by Dwye Evans, but first Michie sought advice from Frere who (it turned out) had no idea of what people were getting. 'Leave it to me,' he told Michie. 'Say no more.' Three days later he handed over a crumpled piece of paper on which was written the sales manager's salary – more than double that paid to Michie – who with this evidence went to Dwye Evans and threatened to leave at five o'clock that afternoon unless something was done. His salary was more than doubled and eventually, in 1961, he was made a director.

Though relatively inexperienced, James Michie told me that from the start he enjoyed Frere's fullest backing. '"Dear boy," he would say to me, "publish anything you like. Simply buy books you feel personally are good. Back your own judgement." Sometimes he took a look at a manuscript I'd recommended, but he never suggested the need for a further opinion unless the subject was specialized, though of course I relied greatly on the opinion of Maire and others. I merely reported to Frere what I wanted to accept and gave my reasons. Sometimes he might recommend caution, and of course it was understood that if I picked too many of the wrong books we would part – though this was unspoken. Mind you, in those days it was rather difficult to lose money in publishing. With novels, in particular, if you liked them and had a fairly promiscuous taste, the chances were that other people would like them too. I learned from Frere that this ideally is how publishing should work. He took the view that the sales department existed merely to sell your books. To provide a service. That's why he seldom consulted them. I am sure he respected them but he believed that once you bring in everybody, you are finished.'

Michie confirmed Frere's distrust of committee decisions on books. The hidden motives of its members were negative; to refuse credit to an individual and to share blame. They were incapable of taking risks. When in doubt the answer was always 'Out!' An individual may make mistakes, but he or she cannot be paralysed by doubt as a committee can.

Two instances throw light on Frere as an employer and show why his staff appreciated him. 'The trouble with you', he told Michie one morning, 'is that you do things too quickly. I'm not saying you don't do them well, but you need better timing. Slow down.' He pointed to the four trays on his desk. 'Look at these. This one here is "urgent" – which means I do something about it tomorrow. The next one is called "normal" which means I shall take a week over it. The one on the right is called "Let them wait and wonder." The last one is called "Give them enough rope and they'll hang themselves."'

The other instance was when Michie very much wanted to take three months' leave without pay, though he knew it would be inconvenient and would mean risking his job. 'When I'd managed to make my request, Frere paused for several moments, a favourite ploy – let the other chap dig his own heffalump trap. When he asked why I wanted such a long break, I told him that it might seem ridiculous but I'd never been to Greece, though I'd read Greek at the university. I also said I was thirty. . . . Eventually after an even longer pause he said: "Well, I'll see you on the third of July" – which was three months ahead. As I stammered my thanks and made for the door, he stopped me to add that if I'd said I was overworked, or in love, or about to have a nervous breakdown, he would have told me to behave more reasonably and get back to my desk. I didn't get paid for that three months, nor did I expect it. He was the sort of man who inspired loyalty.'

Developing New Talent

The growth in the post-war list is demonstrated by the annual number of new titles. Until 1950 this was restricted by shortage of paper, but after then it grew steadily, escalating towards the end of the decade to reach a peak of 249. Compared with an average of 55 during the war years and 181 in the 1930s, it increased as follows: 1946–57; 1947–96; 1948–88; 1949–80; 1950–100; 1951–122; 1952–130; 1953–128; 1954–143; 1955 –158; 1956–143; 1957–170; 1958–189; 1959–166; 1960–249; 1961– 230. Each year produced its crop of new authors, some of whom soon became bestsellers, but the whole enterprise was underpinned by the rich backlist and the established pre-war authors. Priestley, for example, contributed another six novels including *Bright Day* (1946), *Festival at Farbridge* (1951), *The Magicians* (1954), and *Low Notes on a High Level* (1954); there were also three of his plays, including *An Inspector Calls* (1947), and six volumes of essays, including one written jointly with his wife Jacquetta Hawkes – *Journey down a Rainbow* (1955); and the ambitious *Literature and Western Man* (1960). Although his books still sold well, they never reached the heights of *The Good Companions*. Priestley himself blamed this on the antagonism of many of the critics. 'In these days', he wrote to Frere, 'I am in a kind of trough between the grand old men and the up-and-coming writers, and, largely for political reasons, during the last few years I have been the target of so many ill-natured references'.[2]

Somerset Maugham, re-established in his Villa Mauresque at Cap Ferrat after his wartime sojourn in America, continued to send in his meticulous manuscripts, among them the novel *Catalina* (1948); a collection of new short stories, *Creatures of Circumstance* (1947), and three volumes of *Complete Short Stories* (1951); volumes of essays, *The Vagrant*

Mood (1952) and *Points of View* (1958); and the very successful *Ten Novels and their Authors* (1954).

His worldwide sales were believed to number well over sixty million and his eightieth birthday was treated as a national event with a large exhibition of his first editions and seven handwritten manuscripts, first night theatre programmes, film stills and his bronze bust by Jacob Epstein. There was also a gala happening at the Garrick, though Frere recalled that this 'began in a disquieting, nerve-testing way. Maugham was introduced, took a standing ovation and, when the guests had regained their seats, began his address. He spoke the customary salutations, paused for a moment and said: "There are many . . . virtues in . . . growing old." He paused, he swallowed, he wet his lips, he looked about. The pause stretched out, he looked dumbstruck. The pause became too long – far too long. He looked down, studying the tabletop. A terrible tremor of nervousness went through the room. Was he ill? Would he ever be able to get on with it? Finally he looked up and said: "I'm just . . . trying . . . to think what they are!"'[3]

Georgette Heyer continued to be prolific with seventeen books in sixteen years, mostly historical novels, but two were thrillers and there was one volume of short stories. Among the novels were *Arabella* (1949), *The Grand Sophy* (1950), *Cotillion* (1953), *Sprig Muslin* (1956), and *Venetia* (1958). She continued to sell prodigiously, though she was always adamant in refusing to take part in any personal publicity. For example, when the *Sunday Express* wanted to interview her in 1958, she told Lady Avebury, then on the Heinemann publicity staff: 'Sorry! Nothing doing. Even if I wanted to oblige that particular section of the Press, which I don't, I couldn't possibly be "interviewed". For years now I have consistently refused to see reporters and to make an exception would not only be invidious, but would lead to trouble. . . . No, thank you! If the *Sunday Express* wants to write about me, let it employ someone to write about my books, not about me – myself. I expect you are sighing in exasperation by this time, but pause and consider the case of Ethel M.Dell whose personality was wrapped in an impenetrable cloud from start to finish. I never heard that this affected her astronomical sales.'[4] This insistence on privacy or shyness, if that is what it was, seems to have been linked with her habit of self-denigration, except in respect of her more serious historical works. In a letter to Frere in 1954 about her latest manuscript – probably *Bath Tangle* (1955) – she wrote with heavy sarcasm: 'Of course, should there be any sort of trouble over this book, it must be understood that I consider it quite deathless, superb, and the sort of book any publisher should be proud to handle. That you – poor clot! – could ever hope to appreciate its excellence I am not optimistic enough to hope (for it is well known that publishers do not *start* to appreciate the books they do their best to wreck), which is why I am telling you. Pending trouble, I do not mind saying (without prejudice) that I think it stinks. And for *this* – this hurried, hackneyed nonsense! – *you* will pay me £3,000 down . . . and Joyce [Weiner, her agent] has sold the second serial rights to an Australian paper for the unprecented sum of £325! And, mark you, she has done this without showing them as much as a page of the book, and also with an embargo on publication before April. It is enough to turn one into a cynic'[5]. She was very fond of Frere and continued to rely on him for advice on numerous non-literary problems. Once she told him: 'Thank you for adding my stupid cares to your own. . . . There are two sorts of people in the world: those to whom you take your successes, and those to whom you take your failures – far less numerous. You belong to the second – and that is your misfortune, and creatures like me trade on it'[6].

The great promise shown by the early Graham Greene was now realized in full with titles such as *The Heart of the Matter* (1948), *The End of the Affair* (1951), *The Quiet American* (1955), *Our Man in Havana* (1958), and *A Burnt-out Case* (1961). There was also *Twenty-one Stories* (1954) and a volume containing two longer stories, *The Third Man* and *The Fallen Idol* (1950), both of which, like many of his novels, were made into films.

While there were of course plenty of books by other established writers, the emphasis was very much on discovering and fostering new ones. In addition to the normal cheaper editions of established titles, in 1953 'Heinemann Specials' were announced, a series of 'New Fiction at 7s.6d.! – A Successful Experiment!' It was declared that 'in the attempt to solve the problem of how to publish new works of distinction by unknown writers and obtain a worthwhile sale, Messrs. William Heinemann have decided to lower production costs to a minimum, without impairing the standard of production.' The first novel in the series was Jerzy Pietrkiewicz's *The Knotted Cord* (1953). The scheme was widely welcomed in the book trade, but the critics tended to ignore them. There was only a trickle of other 7s.6d. novels and the series seems soon to have been allowed to peter out. Once again price was found not to be the decisive factor.

Another scheme to introduce new talent was the Blue Passport Series, developed largely by Alewyn Birch. It was an ambitious attempt to break down the insularity of British readers and introduce them to translations of some of the best and most successful of contemporary foreign writers. Talent scouts were appointed in France, Italy, and Germany. As well as high quality, 'the accent will be on plots from contemporary life with a strong narrative line.' Nothing highbrow. It was hoped that the books, distinguished by a special binding and jackets, would support each other. The series was launched with novels by Alfred Andersch and Ruth Rehmann (German), Rinzo Shiina (Japanese), Marek Hlasko (Polish), Julien Green and Carlo Coccioli (French), but sadly they did not catch on and the series soon fizzled out after ten titles, whether because of the impenetrable insularity of the British, the never ceasing flood of American as well as home-grown fiction, or inadequate marketing it is impossible to assess.

Another imaginative innovation had been the launch in 1944 of an occasional literary magazine titled *The Windmill*, though strictly speaking it was a relaunch, because an earlier *Windmill* had been issued in 1923. The latter had been a stout quarto volume with coloured plates edited by the young Louisa Callender. It contained a large number of stories, essays, poems, and illustrations by authors and artists 'whose works are published at the Sign of the Windmill'. The cream of the firm's authors during its first thirty years' were represented. Much of the material was new, though there were also extracts from their books. The new *Windmill* which ran for eleven issues (1944–8) was less commemorative and included stories, articles, snatches of memoirs, and poems from a wide spectrum of the most celebrated and fashionable post-war critical and creative writers – Elizabeth Bowen, Pamela Hansford Johnson, George Orwell, Stevie Smith, A. E. Coppard, Roy Fuller, to mention just a handful. It was edited by Reginald Moore and Edward Lane (the pen-name of Kay Dick, the author of four Heinemann novels), though Moore dropped out after the fifth issue. They included features like 'Around the Galleries' and a clever series of 'Alphabets of Literary Prejudice' contributed by people such as Daniel George, Rose Macaulay, William Plomer, James Agate, Geoffrey Grigson, and others. Later issues carried book reviews. Some preference seems to have been given to Heinemann authors – though the firm complained that there were not enough of them! – and there were occasional excerpts from their forthcoming books, including Somerset Maugham's novel *Catalina*. Ten thousand copies were sold of each of the first three issues, but after that sales began to drop steeply. There could be no doubt about the excellence of the magazine and of the prestige, if unquantifiable, it brought to the firm, but it was not the only literary magazine of the period to find it difficult to survive, and after the eleventh issue the directors decided that its further subsidy could no longer be justified.

As early publishers of H. G. Wells it was fitting that Heinemann in 1954 announced a 'new and individual series' of science fiction titles. Almost apologetically advertisements declared that science fiction 'has a long and mixed history ... and a number of competent practitioners. Today it exists at many levels – a vehicle of pure escape and relaxation, of creative reverie, of social comment and reflection, of alert scientific speculation, and of excellent entertainment. It is as well written as any prose produced today.' The tone was set by Paul Capon's *Down to Earth* (1954), the concluding volume of a trilogy, the others, also published by Heinemann, being *The Other Side of the Sun* (1950) and *The Other Half of the Planet* (1952). The plot centred on a Professor Pollenport who had left Earth five years earlier and hoped to return in a spaceship built on Antigeos. There was a progressive political slant in that unscrupulous financiers gambled on the chance of exploiting planets as in the past they connived to exploit colonies. The others were *Utopia 239* (1955) by Rex Gordon and *Dark Dominion* (1955) by David Duncan. As with other innovative schemes there appear to have been only six more titles and the series had disappeared from the list by autumn 1956.

Shute, Powell, Frankau, Manning

The most successful of the newcomers, if not the most prestigious in the eyes of the critics, was almost certainly Nevil Shute, the pen-name of Commander Nevil Shute Norway. He occupied a place in the list similar to that of Hall Caine, Galsworthy, Priestley, and others in that he sold prodigiously to a large book-buying as well as borrowing public and, like

Maugham, he possessed an extraordinary talent for buttonholing the reader with his story. During the first half of his life he had been a very successful and pioneering aeronautical engineer, working under Barnes Wallis on the construction of the airship R.100, and later running the Airspeed company of plane manufacturers. These early experiences undoubtedly provided rich material for his novels such as *No Highway* (1948), about the building of airliners and metal fatigue, and his last big book, *Trustee from the Toolroom* (1960), as well as his autobiography *Slide Rule* (1954). He was said to 'engineer' and design his novels with the same meticulous care as his aircraft. Each was rewritten at least twice and some four times. His characters were often considered to be too alike and his style too flat but his books teemed with ideas and had a decidedly moral tone – even the nymphomaniac in *On the Beach* (1957), about the likely legacy from a nuclear war, never actually climbs into anyone's bed. Following a flight in his own plane by easy stages to Australia he wrote *A Town like Alice* (1950) and eventually decided to settle in the Commonwealth, running his own model farm near Melbourne. Among the twenty-five books he wrote for Heinemann were also *Pied Piper* (1942), *Round the Bend* (1951), *In the Wet* (1953), and *Requiem for a Wren* (1955).

Nearly all his books were bestsellers and he became a millionaire. Initial prints of 150,000 were the rule and several books were turned into highly successful films. He was proud of being such a popular writer and was scathing about most of the critics. Stung by a review in *The Author* (autumn 1951) of an American novel which was described as a bestseller that gave 'an idea of what is read on the periphery of literacy, the reading matter of those who have graduated from the literature of the lavatory wall to the printed word', Shute wrote a furious letter to the editor. It merits quoting at some length because it helps one to understand some of the reasons for his success: 'I have written a good many books which have sold in large numbers and, perhaps not unnaturally, I take a different view of the intelligence of the reading public. On three separate occasions. . . . I have found myself with a large public for my books and with money enough saved to keep me for ten years. On each of those occasions I have made the decision to cash in on my popularity and slam down upon my public with a book that would have real social value, accepting the probability that my sales would decline heavily in consequence because it seemed to me to be a good thing to do. On each occasion I have written this book as a work of fiction in order to get the widest public for the things I wished to say.

'On each of the three occasions that book has sold in larger numbers than anything else that I had written to that date. . . . In my opinion the readers of novels are far more intelligent than unsuccessful writers will believe. They are expert in detecting, and merciless to, the conceited author, and the insincere author, and the author with all the tools of literature at his command who has nothing to say worth reading. Most reviewers are unsuccessful practitioners of the art of creative writing or they would not be interested in the meagre fees they get for writing about other people's books, and in part their lack of success may be due to the fact that they have completely misunderstood the character and intelligence of the reading public. Young authors should accept the embittered fulminations of reviewers against that public with the greatest reserve; from the nature of their employment these people are quite unlikely to know what they are talking about.'[7]

Tough words; but nobody who has read his books could call Shute a Philistine. Gant told me that 'in manner and appearance he was totally unlike the general idea of a popular novelist. Very shy and courteous, his face was long and lugubrious and looked as if it had been put together by means of a photofit kit. Nothing quite fitted in with anything else.' He was mostly looked after by Dwye Evans of whom he was very fond. When Shute died in 1960 Dwye spoke a brief obituary on national television and later, in accordance with a request in the will, committed his ashes to the sea off Hayling Island.

The catholic nature of the fiction list was demonstrated by the recruitment of another newcomer who could scarcely be more different from Shute – Anthony Powell. He also was adept at inventive story-telling, but his style was far more polished, urbane, drily witty, superbly finished, authoritative, 'mandarin'. His settings – Eton, Balliol, Mayfair, London's Bohemia – were closely focused and his proliferation of characters, brought alive by a precise ear for speech, were themselves usually more important than what happened. Before the war he had written four novels for Duckworth and one for Cassell, all of which were reissued by Heinemann during the 1950s, starting with *Afternoon Men*. Around 1950 his wish to change publishers had been confided to Malcolm Muggeridge, who introduced him to the list. It was the start of a remarkably relaxed relationship, profitable to both sides.

The first of what was to become a series with twelve volumes called *A Dance to the Music of Time* appeared in 1951, *A Question of Upbringing*. By 1961 there had been four more: *A Buyer's Market* (1952), *The Acceptance World* (1955), *At Lady Molly's* (1957), *Casanova's Chinese Restaurant* (1960). On the second page of *A Question of Upbringing* Powell refers to '.... Poussin's scene in which the Seasons, hand in hand and facing outward, tread in rhythm to the notes of the lyre that the winged and naked greybeard plays. The image of Time brought thoughts of mortality: of human beings, facing outward like the Seasons, moving hand in hand in intricate measures: stepping slowly, methodically, sometimes a trifle awkwardly, in evolutions that take recognizable shape: or breaking into seemingly meaningless gyrations, while partners disappear only to re-appear again, once more giving pattern to the spectacle: unable to control the melody, unable, perhaps, to control the steps of the dance. ...'[8]

The *Dance to the Music of Time* books are narrated by Nicholas Jenkins, whose life is not unlike Powell's own. The series spans the period from the early 1920s to the 1970s and contains some four hundred characters. Among them there is of course the somewhat ludicrous Kenneth Widmerpool, a great intriguer; J. G. Quiggin, the reviewer of humble origin with Marxist beliefs; Lady Molly Jeavons, the kindly hostess, fond of animals, and sister of Jumbo Arglass and Katherine, Lady Warminster; Charles Stringham, married and divorced from Lady Peggy Stepney, and who takes to drink; Dicky Umfraville, Mrs Baby Wentworth, Werner Guggenbuhl, Sir Magnus Donners ... and many, many more. Their lives intersect, bickering, falling in love, suffering, striving and often failing, having great fun.

When I visited Powell and his wife, Lady Violet, at their elegant, book-lined Regency house near Frome he told me: 'A happy country is said to have no history. The same can be said about a happy relationship with one's publisher, as in my own case. Violet says that having once been a publisher myself' – he worked at Duckworth for seven years before the war – 'I am like the couple in a *New Yorker* cartoon when one of them protests: "You're always on the car's side!" I am sure that if you can avoid changing publishers it's much better, but of course it all boils down to whom you are dealing with. If he gets on your nerves, then it's no good. You have to move on.' For most of the time it was Roland Gant. 'It has been an ideal publisher-writer relationship.'

Two others automatically select themselves: Pamela Frankau and Olivia

[341]

Manning. The former had written seventeen books (for Hurst & Blackett, John Lane and others) before she joined Heinemann shortly before the war; but she reached her peak on the firm's list during the 1940s and 1950s. After *Shaken in the Wind* (1948) she wrote what many believed to be her finest novel, *The Willow Cabin* (1949). A letter to Frere written from Palo Alto in California describes its birth: 'After the dreariest autumn, making a balls of *The Island* and abandoning it, writing a very long short story that went wrong, and another great thing that was completed but hasn't worked out, I decided to give up and concentrate on liquor, evil thoughts, and housekeeping; when suddenly into my head there sprang this piece and plotted itself in a week and I have now done nearly 50,000 words. . . . It gives me no peace; it wakes me at dawn and keeps me hammering at it until midnight and has no consideration for others. I cannot believe that anything writing itself so effortlessly can be good and yet I know it is.'[9] Later she begged Frere in a typical letter to 'plug it for all you're worth, and back it as an urgent need on the library lists of the most improbable types from Thurso to Pevensey. Don't think of me as me – the at-last-matured novelist for whose maturity you'd been waiting with a lamp in the window while she indulged her "neat, little, taut, little mannerisms" – but as a person who is read by an enormous number of ex-ATS and dim educational girls and boys in technical schools and grave-diggers in Bangor and unhappily married women in Belfast.'[10] It went well, with a Book Society choice and advance sales of 33,000.

Correspondence with Frere over the final draft of *A Wreath for the Enemy* (1954) sheds light on the publisher's role in criticizing a novel's plot. He had suggested that one of the characters should die, but Pamela had bluntly refused and Frere gave in with one of his joky letters: 'It is your book. I should have failed in my duty as a publisher and a friend if I had not made my point but, having made it, I should be extremely foolish to persist in the belief that I was right and you were wrong. The publisher side of me can only pray that the customers will agree with you, and from my own heart I can only say that since you feel so deeply about it, I am glad you have stuck to your guns. Some day I will send you a pretty picture of somebody being stuck to a gun. Perhaps we could get Graham Sutherland to do it with a nice lot of spikes stuck about the place – what place? – ssh!'[11] This book also did well, selling virtually all of its print of 40,000, including 16,250 for the Book Society.

Altogether she wrote fifteen books for Heinemann, among the others being *The Offshore Light* (1952), *The Winged Horse* (1953), *The Bridge* (1957), and *Ask me No More* (1958). The last gave rise to an angry protest following her discovery on reading the proofs that her script had been dealt with too severely by the Heinemann copy-editors, particularly the punctuation with, in her view, deplorable results. Like most publishers, the firm had a policy of making everything conform to its house rules, which were approximately the same as those laid down by the Oxford University Press. The rules had nothing to do with altering the author's choice of words and/or meanings – though this was sometimes done, generally in consultation with the author, particularly where the syntax was obviously faulty or the sense might be ambiguous – but to make sure that the system of punctuation was followed logically and that there were no inconsistencies in the employment of italics, apostrophes, hyphens, spellings, and other instances which offered typographical alternatives. Throughout the aim was to ensure consistency.

Pamela Frankau's grouse turned mainly on the use of semi-colons and of single quotation marks to denote when a character was thinking aloud. Her kind of complaint was by no means infrequent and it raises the whole difficult question of how much editors should interfere with a manuscript. Most authors were grateful when their work was checked and polished, but with the establishment of a full-blown editorial department there was a tendency at times to over-edit, to forget that its role should normally be limited to acting as the manuscript's 'midwife'. Nevil Shute, for example, once sent a five-page telegram complaining about unnecessary changes and most of his book had to be reset. Similarly, Fred Hoyle refused to be bound by the uniform logic of the house rules, though he admitted that his approach was somewhat bizarre: 'The difficulty is that unless one is content with entirely formal and flat punctuation, etc. decisions depend on instinctive judgments of what is needed in each particular sentence. The formal rules really date from times when even the best writers wrote such tangled sentences that aids were needed – the question-mark for instance – in order to make meanings clear. Does one really need a question-mark if one writes: "What now?" I would say not. I doubt whether the question-mark has any formal value at all nowadays. It does acquire a value, however, in permitting emphasis – i.e., once the mark is discontinued as a formal device it becomes available to the writer as a device for indicating importance or urgency. This will perhaps go some way to explaining why question-marks are not used consistently in the book, although I cannot claim that anything more than quick judgments have been used.'[12]

Hoyle also had idiosyncratic views on hyphens. But to return to Pamela Frankau's objections. 'This damage has been done', she wrote, 'not only without my permission, but against my specific instructions. Mr Michie told me, in March, that he had been busily removing semi-colons and asked me if I objected. I did. I told him that, although I might prove to agree with some of these changes when I saw the MS in print, I would prefer to judge them myself. He therefore proposed to send down the second copy of the typescript, then in your possession; he admitted that to revise his own revisions would be a long job. (It is; I began it on Thursday and finished it tonight, Tuesday.). . . . During one of our telephone conversations Mr Michie suggested that where a character was thinking aloud in double quotes, he should alter these to single quotes, to distinguish the thoughts from the spoken dialogue. I agreed. There are, however, frequent passages where I record the thoughts of characters, deliberately, with no quotes at all. These were ringed around with single quotes, which dispose alike of the intention and the effect. . . . I need hardly remind anybody that the effect of punctuation, brackets, quotes, etc. is not only subtle and important, but a matter of the author's choice and deliberate design. In restoring the effect I intended, I have now been involved in many hours of heavy, niggling, unnecessary work. So, equally, will the printers be. . . .'[13]

Poor James Michie had to take a portion of the blame, though the printers had ignored his instructions to stet her use of the semi-colon and of three dots, but he failed to comprehend her objection to the introduction of single quotes for characters thinking aloud. It is likely that this argument was not unconnected with her decision to write *Pen to Paper* (1961) which, together with snatches of autobiography, gave her views on the craft of writing fiction and a summing-up of the manner in which a novelist should work. The manuscript was duly copy-edited by an editor, Robert Brain, with very much a mind of his own and who later became a distinguished anthropologist. Disagreeing with much of what she said about grammar, he made a good many alterations without consulting her. Of course when she received the proofs she again hit the roof and the whole book had to be reset at the firm's expense.

From the outset Olivia Manning was clearly very competent, but it took some time before it was realized that the firm had acquired a major talent.

There had been an early novel published by Cape in 1937 but her first book for Heinemann was straight history, *The Remarkable Expedition* (1947) which retold the story of Emin, the visionary 'White Pasha', Governor of the Equatorial Province of the Sudan, and of Stanley's expedition to rescue him during the Mahdi rising. *Growing Up* (1948), a volume of short stories, followed and it was not until 1949 that she wrote another novel, *Artist Among the Missing*, about a painter caught up in the war in North Africa. Next came *The School for Love* (1951), set in Jerusalem with a sixteen-year-old as the central character; this was much admired, Pamela Hansford Johnson describing it as 'among the best ten novels written by women in the past twenty-five years'[14]. But the author was depressed that her books sold so badly and wrote to Louisa Callender: 'Have my sales been so terrible that Heinemann's have lost all faith in me? I feel I have been a disappointment. . . . I really don't know what to do to make myself sell. I don't know at all. I often feel like giving up writing altogether.'[15]

She was already thinking of leaving Heinemann, an idea she was to toy with regularly during the next twenty-five years. It was true that her sales were usually less than might have been expected even when she was fully established but, rightly or wrongly, she always felt she was never given enough attention or publicity. Her approach to another publisher was blocked by Heinemann insisting on their option and the former advised her to stay where she was: 'From your point of view I know very well what your objections to Heinemann are, and to a great extent they are the objections which any author of your character would have with a large firm. It is not normally possible for a large firm to give the same individual attention to authors that a smaller one could do.' This was almost certainly true because it was always the successful authors who received the biggest share of the advertising budget; like most publishers, Heinemann believed in the military maxim of exploiting success to the full and of not reinforcing failure. This other publisher concluded his letter with an observation which proved to be prophetic. After telling her that if ever she became free, he would be very happy to take her on, he added: 'You are a most distinguished writer, but almost certainly, as I told you at lunch, not one of the easiest in the world to publish for! . . .'[16]

After two more novels – *A Different Face* (1953) and *The Doves of Venus* (1955) – the firm published a volume of her pieces from *Punch* under the title of *My Husband Cartwright* (1956). To anyone who knew him – and many people did – Cartwright was extraordinarily like Olivia's real husband, R. D. Smith (always known as 'Reggie'), a well-known drama producer at the BBC. But Cartwright was also a husband recognized by many wives, as the blurb put it: 'an enigma of pure reason, a helpful hindrance, the quintessence of kindly egoism, generous to a fault – and what a fault!' The real-life, lovable, extroverted, impulsively generous Reggie with his talent for telling stories in regional accents was the opposite to moody, introspective Olivia, though they remained securely married. Their contrasting characters are important because they both undoubtedly appear, as Guy and Harriet Pringle, central characters in Olivia's major work, the novels of the Balkan trilogy: *The Great Fortune* (1960), *The Spoilt City* (1962), *Friends and Heroes* (1965). These are based on their actual experiences during the war in Bucharest, Greece, Egypt and Jerusalem. They are vivid recreations of history, though there are of course many other characters, absurd but suffering, often poignant, such as the scrounging Russian émigré Prince Yakimov. Olivia was self-conscious of her self-portrait. In a revealing letter to another writer, Francis King, she says: 'Recently Reggie had a letter from Priestley (about a play being done by the BBC) in which he said he and his wife had read my book and, though they liked the way in which I conveyed the atmosphere of the times, they disapproved of the character of Harriet who was not what a heroine should be. Poor Harriet! If any critic has wished to attack me, he has done so through the character of Harriet. . . . I have been in despair and wonder if the only people who can tolerate her are those who have pictured her as me. To those who cannot overlay (and clarify) her by reference to me, is she merely a shadow?'[17]

The Balkan trilogy secured Olivia Manning a permanent place in this century's literary pantheon, but she still failed to sell as she should despite genuine efforts by the publicity department and the travellers. She was annoyed that she didn't receive the same attention as Kingsley Amis, Edna O'Brien, Muriel Spark. She was annoyed, again with good reason, that she was not 'Penguined' [she was eventually in 1981]. Panther did take her on until there was a libel threat from a Rumanian and this led to two of the paperback volumes being withdrawn and to her having a row with Dwye Evans when he insisted that she would have to pay her share of any libel costs. Again she wanted to leave. She probably had some justice on her side, but Olivia Manning was never an easy author to handle. But being difficult often goes with being a great writer.

Some authors who were first published by Heinemann during the 1940s and '50s, are introduced in Book IV that covers 1961–83, during which appeared the bulk of their work under the Windmill imprint – e.g., Anthony Burgess, Patricia Highsmith, Peter Ustinov, Gore Vidal, Morris West.

A Wide Spectrum –
from Lodwick to *Angélique*

As in earlier periods I am again faced with the invidious problem of how to select a very small number from the hundreds of new novelists taken on during 1945–61 – though others will be found in the Appendix. One who selects himself is John Lodwick, not only because of his talented books but also because of his extraordinary character and his love-hate relationship with his publisher. For most of his life he lived violently. He began the war by enrolling in the French Foreign Legion and after being imprisoned on a charge of mutiny and fighting for the Legion in its retreat near Paris he was captured, escaped, and arrested again as a bicycle thief. Eventually he found his way back to England and became a special agent. In all he was imprisoned over a dozen times – all this and much more was recorded in his reminiscences *Bid the Soldiers Shoot* (1958). The war over, he became involved with smuggling rackets. He had several wives who gave him several children. Latterly he lived in Barcelona, was usually having to write too fast so as to keep his creditors at bay, and there were continual crises interspersed with drinking bouts. In 1959 he died violently in early middle age as the result of a car crash in Spain.

Much of his life was reflected strongly in his novels, of which he wrote fourteen for the firm between 1948 and 1960. Among them were *Something in the Heart* (1948), *Love Bade me Welcome* (1952), *The Starless Night* (1955), *Equator* (1957), *The Moon through a Dusty Window* (1960). Michie told me that both he and Roland Gant 'admired his writing, which we felt was something special, though also remarkably careless. He never became a really important writer, maybe because of so many Spanish wine stains on the manuscript. He possessed overwhelming charm and rascality of the good sort. He once told me that he liked the wicked gleam in my spectacles.' Maugham, whom he visited, also thought Lodwick had great talent as did Rebecca West, whose report on *Somewhere a Voice is Calling* (1953) throws a percipient light both on his personality and his writing: 'This man is a distressing creature. He upset me when he came here, because he was so like one of my traitors: not that I suspect him of any treachery, it is the abstract treachery to candour, the mere doing of things furtively and against the common understanding of the world, which covers people with a Graham Greene mould. If you get rid of candour you disorient people, they go off to the wrong point of the compass with an air of infinite cunning and superiority to the people who are outside the frame, and it all means nothing. . . . The queer thing about this book is that it is spiritually homosexual. . . . He is the spinsterish female who wants a big he-man mate who rapes the other girls right and left and drinks everyone else under the table. She adores this mate, and hates the other girls who get raped, and goes and settles things with the people who are involved in his drunken scenes. Sometimes the two figures, the spinsterish female and the roaring male, coalesce. . . . All this stuff about the girls seems to be very half-baked. . . . When Thornton locks the girl up in the Ladies it is a queer male version of a spinster getting terribly excited because a lonely gentleman tries to pick her up and she swept off saying that she had never been so insulted in her life. God, I am worried about this book. It is so good in a sense. The reality of moment to moment, the reality of Thornton and Gloria, the amusingness of her comment, the Velasquez quality of the portrait of the gross Latinized Englishman, the ideal licensed Consular beachcomber, the lecher that Shakespeare hated – but why the hell give us only a single interview with him and then compromise the portrait by putting far too much weight on the sexual performances of this character, who must have been more or less interesting to women than he is represented. . . . How good the incident is with Julio. The way that Thornton in order to get Julio better treatment for his syphilis firmly leads him along a track that must end in Julio's death. . . .' Rebecca West sums up by saying: 'How much more interesting than nearly all his contemporaries. How beautifully supple his writing, he folds a sentence round a fact or a thought as the girl in the shop ties a scarf round your neck and you can't do it at home in the same way, not ever.'[18]

Lodwick wrote voluminously to Frere about his wives, his children, his moods, progress with his current novel, above all about his debts and his need for more money. To help him out the firm paid him a lump sum for each book in monthly instalments, though surprisingly by this method he actually drew out more than he would have got from normal royalties. He was very fond of Frere – 'I always think of you as my best friend, and you know very well that if you cut me off tomorrow I should still be your friend.'[19] – but he could also be very touchy. 'You once told me that were it not for my various children, you would have had no hesitation in casting me adrift. All right, God damn it, do it then. Do you really imagine that I am a less proud man than you, or any member upon your board? . . . Do you really want me to stop and write detective stories under various other names for one of your competitors? I remain loyal to the last, until people prove disloyal to me. You have always been damned decent to me like the time you walked up the road on your hobbled leg. But I can take the bad news and make other dispositions too – if you don't want me any more.'[20]

Unlike any other author he seemed to be dependent on the firm not merely to publish his books and pay him his monthly instalments, but almost as a parental institution. In a letter to Jonathan Price, a member of the editorial department, he said: 'When I was in England last year nothing impressed me more than the charm, the general *niceness* of all the young people upstairs in Heinemann. Living abroad as I do, I felt as if I were coming into my club, and I felt very proud, but also what is more natural to me, very humble. I want to be your writer. I don't like changing publishers. That is dirty procedure.'[21]

His closeness, his identification with the firm found expression in *The Butterfly Net* (1954), a novel about a writer, Adrian Dormant, who lived abroad and bore much resemblance to Lodwick himself, and his relationship with his publishers and their chairman, Mr Glenn, undoubtedly based on Frere – indeed on one page of the proofs the publisher was actually referred to as 'Frere'. This was corrected, though on the specimen copies that went to American publishers Frere himself changed it back to 'Frere', though he disclaimed any likeness. Rebecca West thought the portrait of Frere was a masterpiece. Lodwick told him that he also could not resist putting in Mr Jeeves, the Heinemann accountant, who became Mr Grieves who informs Mr Glenn that Dormant is in the red for a large sum – close to the amount in reality. To ensure accuracy he asked Frere to send him a set of old board meeting minutes. His detailed descriptions of the interior of 99 Great Russell

Street, of the waiting-room, the hall and grand panelled staircase leading to Frere's and Miss Callender's offices on the first floor is also true to reality.

'As he traversed the hall, Dormant halted beside a very fine grandfather clock. This clock had been made by Konrad in Zurich, in 1782, and apart from the actual walls of the place, was the oldest thing in the entire building, though few people judged it tactful to say so when confronted with the Jacobean panelling of the main staircase and of the more important corridors. On his last visit to his publisher, about eighteen months previously, Dormant had arrived carrying an unwrapped bottle of whisky. Bound, eventually, for a party, he had just purchased this bottle at a vintner's, two doors away. So frigid, so comminatory had been the stares of the ladies in charge of the reception desk at that epoch, that Dormant had not dared to proceed upstairs with alcohol in his hands. He had concealed his bottle in the interior of the grandfather clock. On leaving the building, he had forgotten to retrieve it. . . . Dormant now opened the grandfather clock, but only dust and the great pendant bollocks of the mechanism were to be seen.'[22]

This incident had actually happened when Lodwick visited the offices to keep an appointment with Louisa Callender. When some months afterwards the clock stopped working, the repairer discovered the bottle.

Manuscripts continued to arrive from the Dominions. Jack Cope, for example, wrote several carefully observed and deeply felt novels about life in South Africa and there were some brilliant short stories such as those collected in *The Tame Ox* (1960) and *Alley Cat* (1973). Growing up on a farm in Natal, he spoke fluent Zulu and his knowledge of the country and its various peoples was put to good use in novels such as *The Golden Oriole* (1958), whose central character is a young ambitious Zulu who soon learns painfully that his colour is against him and inevitably, though reluctantly, he gets drawn into the African political struggle. In *Albino* (1964) a white boy brought up in a poor Zulu village epitomizes the race conflict. Although *The Dawn Comes Twice* (1969) was banned by the South African censor, most of his books avoided being overtly political.

From Australia there was *Come in Spinner* (1951) by Dymphna Cusack and Florence James about the girls who work in a hotel beauty salon in wartime Sydney, their clients, their lovers. It was an instant bestseller with five reprints during its first year totalling 30,600 on top of an original print of 24,000 copies. It was bought by Pan, published in America, and was translated into eight other languages. By herself Dymphna Cusack went on to write seven more novels for Heinemann including *Say No to Death* (1951) about which Maire Lynd's report said: 'This is only the second modern novel which has recently made me understand what Aristotle meant when he said that tragedy purged the onlooker through pity and terror.' It was followed by *Heatwave in Berlin* (1961), *Picnic Races* (1962), and *The Sun is not Enough* (1967). There were also two non-fiction titles: *Holidays among the Russians* (1964) and *Illyria Reborn* (1966).

Dymphna Cusack was not the first to grumble at the considerably lower earnings from royalties on copies sold in the Dominions compared with those on sales at home or by an American publisher. The basic reason for this was that it was customary – and indeed it still is – to calculate royalties on the published price for home sales, but on the price charged to the bookseller for exported copies – i.e., on the actual monies received in the UK. As an unusually higher proportion of her sales was made in Australia she suffered more than most. She made matters very clear in a letter to *The Author* (autumn 1952) which merits quotation at some length because it was an issue on which many Heinemann authors felt strongly: 'It is not denied that the publisher makes at least the same profit on his overseas sales as on his home sales. But . . . the royalty rate of 10 per cent flat of the price at which sold to the overseas booksellers gives 5 per cent or less to the author as his return. This is palpably inequitable for the English writer, but how much more so for the Australian writer, the bulk of whose "overseas" sales are in his home market – at least one in two as against the English authors' one in four.' She then gives the example of *Come in Spinner* which sold more than 27,000 in Australia in seventeen months. 'It was published in the UK at 10*s*. 6*d*. a copy and sells in Australia at 11*s*.6*d*. We receive a royalty of 5.46*d*. on overseas sales compared with an average of 1*s*.3*d*. (approx.) on copies sold in England. . . . When my third book was accepted by my publisher I asked for a readjustment of royalties, particularly those on overseas sales. The reply was: "Concerning the rate of royalty on copies exported or sold for export this royalty (i.e., the 10 per cent on price sold to Australia) is the standard royalty paid by all publishers for overseas copies and is necessitated by the fact that we have to sell the books at half price. No matter whether one sells 5 copies or 50,000 copies, they are still supplied at half price which does not, of course, allow of the payment of royalties based on published price."'

She went on to emphasize that publishers were not compelled to give the 50 per cent overseas discount and that no other commodity was sold to Australian retailers at a depreciated price. 'It is high time that the position regarding overseas royalties, established, I understand, more than half a century ago when the Dominions were Colonies and took extremely small quantities of an edition, should be re-examined. It is not only an anachronism but an injustice.' Publishers themselves, she argued, were not affected by the high overseas discounts. Their profit was much the same whether a book was sold at home or overseas. 'My enquires for a new publisher have elicted the fact that there are at least three large publishing houses in London which are prepared to agree to a reassessment of the old and outdated "export" royalty rate, proving that a revised rate is not only equitable but profitable.'[23]

There is unfortunately no record of whether Dymphna Cusack got her way, but Heinemann remained her publishers for almost another twenty years.

There were probably relatively fewer recruits from America compared with pre-war, but they were by no means insignificant. Erskine Caldwell, for example, was already very well established, being published mainly by the Falcon Press and having made his name with *Tobacco Road* and *God's Little Acre*, the latter being reissued by Heinemann in 1955 when *Love and Money* was also published. Between then and *In the Shadow of the Steeple* (1967), mostly about his father, the firm issued twenty-three of his books, including volumes of short stories, autobiographical material, and a few reissues. Most of his writing was about blacks and poor whites in the Deep American South and of course the colour problem. Maire Lynd's report on *In Search of Bisco* (1965) gives the flavour: 'In the course of his wanderings through the Southern states he notably shows us the social and economic problems, but he also lets all kinds of people express their points of view – the fireman on the 'Frisco railroad, the cotton-picker displaced by machinery, the student at Little Rock . . . the old Gumbo yard "boy", the nigger-hating and liberal whites.' In the autobiographical *In the Shadow of the Steeple* there was also the store-owner: 'I'm a good Christian and I'd get down on my knees and wash the feet of Jesus Christ if I had the chance. But you'll never get me getting down like that in front of a black nigger and tying his shoelaces for him. But the Jews will do it because they're Jews. That's all that need be said about it.'[24] Caldwell told people: 'I work like any stenographer or book-keeper. Regular hours, and I never got beyond the two-finger typing stage. . . . I throw away more than

[352]

I keep. The more you throw away, the better the book. Writing is an individualized service. It's not a public service like garbage collecting; you are doing that for somebody else. When you write you are doing it for yourself . . . [but] you have to forget yourself and identify with your characters, and they will tell the story. . . . Writing now is like the greeting card business. It's a question of how wild you can get.'[25]

From West Virginia was Mary Lee Settle, though her earliest two novels, *The Love Eaters* (1954) and *The Kiss of Kin* (1955) were first published by Heinemann. Her having come to England to join up in the war led to *All the Brave Promises* (1966), a deflation of the glamour of war arising from her service as an Aircraftwoman, second class. She is probably best remembered, however, for her trilogy beginning with *O Beulah Land* (1956). A New Yorker, Betty Smith wrote about her native city in *A Tree Grows in Brooklyn* (1951), published in association with Penguin, but originally published by Heinemann in the UK as *A Tree in the Yard* (1944). She followed it with three more including *Maggie – Now* (1958) about girls growing up in slums. Alabama in the 1930s was the scene of Harper Lee's enduringly successful *To Kill a Mockingbird* (1960) which centred around the trial of a negro for rape. It won the Pulitzer Prize and has remained in print for thirty years.

The most prolific and most profitable new author from America was Frank Yerby, advertised somewhat condescendingly as the first negro author to write a bestseller. This was *The Foxes of Harrow* (1947), set in New Orleans and Louisiana between 1825 and the Civil War. There followed twenty-eight other fat books, mostly historical novels ranging over the centuries including biblical times – *Judas, my Brother* (1969) about the thirteenth disciple; the French Revolution – *The Devil's Laughter* (1954); tenth-century Spain – *Griffin's Way* (1963); ancient Sparta and Athens – *Goat Song* (1968); all blockbusters, opulent and crowded with characters, rich with drama, passion, violence, heat and dust. There were also novels with more contemporary settings – such as *Speak Now* (1970), about a black jazz musician in Paris and his fateful love for a white American girl, and *Tobias and the Angel* (1975), about a post-World War I veterans' psychiatric ward.

Yerby is the kind of writer who is too easily dismissed as too prolific and too popular, but he believed fervently in his craft. This becomes clear in a caustic correspondence with Dwye Evans over proposed cuts and changes in *The Odour of Sanctity* (1966): 'It seems to me that I have been the most managed writer in modern history; and that the habit of my publishers, editors, agents, *et al.* have fallen into of expecting sweet reasonableness of me, has operated to the total detriment of my literary reputation, and even, I venture to add, to a certain diminution of my sales. Nor do I exclude myself from blame: that sweet reasonableness has always been a sort of spinelessness, a cowardly disinclination to fight . . . never an unawareness that my associates, editors, publishers and agents simply were operating out of a monstrously perverted vanity which has always kept them from admitting – as I freely do – that they simply don't know which side is up as far as what makes a book worthy, worthwhile, or even saleable is concerned. This . . . is a matter of principle. . . . I don't grant you omniscience, my dear Dwye, nor, I repeat, do I claim it for myself. It is just that I am ill disposed to accept the praise or blame for a work tailored to your or anyone else's measure; since it appears above my signature, let it at least be mine. However, while establishing the limits of my knowledge, let me without vanity set forth what I *do* know. I know how to write a novel. A real novel in the old fashioned sense, rich, teeming, opulent, *slow moving* (strange that no one ever thought of telling Dostoevsky, Tolstoy, Balzac, Hugo, Thackeray, or even Dickens that a novel should be lean, stripped down, built like a race horse, and fast moving – concepts that I reject with all my revolted soul!) and alive. . . .' There was much more, but he ended: 'To a writer the reader is at best an irrelevancy; when you're really writing, he doesn't even exist, nor should he.'[26]

Yerby and Heyer were not the only successful writers of the more popular type of historical fiction. A one-off bestseller was the Austrian, Annemarie Selinko's *Désirée* (1953) – known in the trade as '*Daisy Ray*'. Tegan Harris in her report at once recognized its possibilities, though she emphasized that there was 'no sentimentality, no near-pornography . . . it is never cheap or vulgar.' It had everything this kind of book needs: a silk-manufacturer's daughter who became the fiancée of Napoleon; usurped by Josephine she is saved from drowning in the Seine by Bernadotte, one of Napoleon's greatest marshals, who married her; finally the crowned queen of Sweden and the founder of a Royal dynasty. She moves, gushed the publicity, 'like some new Cinderella through the pomp and pageantry of the Napoleonic scene, crowded as it is with gallant soldiers and beautiful women'. There were nightmarish problems with the translation from the German, the author not approving of the original attempt and the revising translator falling ill. It was also very long, but it was decided not to cut it and it was published at 15s. for 700 pages. The spring list announced that '*Désirée* is a predestined and inevitable best-seller with a long life in front of it'. It was not wrong. *Désirée* sold 7,327 in its first year, but boomed to 35,000 in its third year and totalled 65,449 copies by 1979.

The eight hundred-page *Angelique* (1959) was about another young girl in France, but this time 'with shrewd eyes and golden-red hair meeting the challenge of the riches, vices and social wrongs of the age of Louis XIV . . . an historical panorama which pulsates with action: the famous figures of the time strut or slink through scenes which range from the brilliant world of intrigue at the court of the Sun-King to the sordid oak of the slum streets of old Paris'. The author was Sergeanne Golon, a composite of Serge and Anne, a married couple. Frere had bought it in America and more or less admitted that he might have made a mistake, but being lumbered with it they had to turn it into a success. He insisted that they should print 30,000 copies. There was a costly jacket showing the apotheosis of the cleavage. There were streamers, ribbons with a *fleur-de-lys* motif, posters, and a 'moving fan' for display in the shops. There was even going to be an Angelique hairstyle. It all worked splendidly, the book selling 71,410 copies up to 1983. It was followed by eight others, including *Angelique and the King* (1960), *Angelique and the Sultan* (1961) and ending with *Angelique and the Demon* (1973).

Entertainments and/or Quality

The prosperity of the firm depended as always very largely on books which, judged by strict literary canons, might with justification be classed as 'popular' or even 'second rate'. A high percentage of the reading and particularly borrowing public craved entertainment above all, even though the literary levels of such entertainment might vary. It is not to disparage them to say that many authors went out of their way to satisfy this demand. The ten novels by Anthony Thorne, for example, might be labelled as high-level entertainment – *Cabbage Holiday* (1940), *So Long at the Fair*

(1947), *The Baby and the Battleship* (1956), *et al.* A few were flops but most did well, became paperbacks, and several were made into films. Frequently filmed and paperbacked also were the 'unbeatable, readable', novels of Max Catto, another entertainer. Heinemann published eighteen of them between *The Killing Frost* (1950) and *Sam Casanova* (1973). Catto prided himself on keeping his ear rather desperately to the ground. Writing to Dwye Evans about *Love from Venus* (1965), he emphasized that he had 'sensed from long discussions with the younger generation of readers a yearning for warmer, more effervescent reading with less hypocrisy about the existence of sex. This is not an over-sexed book. . . . We may, or may not, like TW3 [a shortening for the relatively way-out TV revue *That Was the Week that Was*], but its electrifying impact on the young and middle-aged generations speaks for itself, as do the razzle-dazzle antics of James Bond and the bawling of four young men whose unconventional coiffures have literally made history.'[27]

Perhaps the highest guarantee of entertainment could be attached to the twenty-three novels by Elleston Trevor – four of them under his pen-name, Adam Hall. He was a master of the rattling good story with fairly basic characters, plenty of suspense, the reader hooked onto the plot and never let off until the end. Among his themes were the D-day landing by a tank unit in Normandy – *The Killing Ground* (1956); the kidnapping of the ex-king of 'Slavakia' – *The V.I.P.* (1959); the world of American advertising – *The Billboard Madonna* (1960); a crash landing in the Sahara – *The Flight of the Phoenix* (1964); the disillusionment of young men fighting in World War I – *Bury him among Kings* (1970). Elleston Trevor's cool professionalism comes out clearly in correspondence with his editors as in this extract from a lengthy retort to criticisms of *The Warsaw Document* (1971), one of the 'Quiller' books under the name of Adam Hall: 'You say that half the time Quiller is in the dark. I don't want to depart from this established tradition. Actually it doesn't matter what his original plan was, does it? The interest here is that we know it's up the spout when they double the guard. The reason for this is to get us a chapter-ending and shock beginning on the cheap, at the cost of precisely three paras. Inside that short space Quiller has had to hack out an alternative operation so who cares what he originally meant to do? The value is fairly high: we've got ourselves interestingly out of a chapter and into the next and we now see that Quiller is even nearer the edge of perdition: "no hope of survival". Turning the screw, legitimate thriller technique, and I don't see it as merely an example of holding back info. Though of course there's a *lot* of info. held back, throughout. Agatha Christie does it too. . . . You once asked me about Q and women and I still say I'm agin them. When Q or any Bureau agent gets into a mission they don't just Bond around: they play it for real and there's a lot of pressure, like climbing the Matterhorn. How the hell can you go fiddling about in knickers when there's a sheer suicidal drop? The obligatory presence of women in the Q stories is an immense drag on the tension-building: there just isn't *time* to do anything except try staying alive. But we have to sell the reprint rights so I'm a whore.'[28] When once asked by Alan Hill how long he had stayed in Warsaw to capture the atmosphere and local colour so exactly, Elleston Trevor replied that he had never been there. He had invented the background with the aid of a guide-book and a street-map.

Heinemann also had a big share in the traditional 'whodunnit', mystery thriller market through the Perry Mason casebooks and other titles by Erle Stanley Gardner. Taking him over from Cassells, they published fifty-six of them plus another twenty under his pseudonym, A. A. Fair. They had titles like *The Case of the Angry Mourner* (1958), *The Case of the Cautious Coquette* (1955), *The Case of the Bigamous Spouse* (1967). . . . Gardner, himself once an attorney in California, wrote an average of three books a year. 'I am seldom far from a dictaphone. I dictate all my books and typing them back keeps five secretaries busy all the time.' From the Australian outback came Arthur Upfield with 'Bony', Detective-Inspector Bonaparte modelled on a half-Aborgine friend whom Upfield had seen making astonishing deductions from tracks in sand of the movements of animals and birds. Upfield started to write during lonely spells patrolling the 12,000 mile rabbit fence, going out for two weeks at a time with only his two camels for company. Including a few reissues, he wrote nineteen titles for Heinemann, each with a built-in Australian order for some 6,000 copies, with titles like *Death of a Lake* (1954), *Cake in the Hat Box* (1955), and *Bony and the Kelly Gang* (1960). Upfield was rare among Australian writers in his feeling for the Aborigines; indeed his books possess an anthropological value quite apart from their merits as mystery thrillers. His views on authorship were expressed in the heading on his notepaper: 'All Fame and No Bloody Money.'

In a class of his own was Eric Ambler who, already a bestseller, joined the list with *The Schirmer Inheritance* (1953). Before the war his books had pioneered a new kind of vehicle very different from the conventional detective story. They might be described as thrillers with the technique and depth of novels. Introducing Ambler before he gave a talk on 'The Writer and Films', Frere said that he was 'first and foremost a very fine storyteller. . . . His great strength is the accomplished dexterity with which he handles action and suspense and, at the same time, making his characters into people we immediately begin to know and in whose actions he catches our passionate interest. . . .' True perhaps of any sound writer but an accurate description of Ambler's relaxed skills.

Ambler was a close friend of Frere's and shortly after the war shared the cost of leasing a villa at St Jean-Cap-Ferrat just along the road from Willie Maugham, whom he also got to know. In his memoirs Ambler includes a description of a dinner party at the Freres' rooms in Albany which merits a diversion because all but one of the other guests were Heinemann authors and it conveys the atmosphere of Frere's personal/publishing circle. It also provides a vignette of Maugham at his most waspish: 'The guests were Mr Maugham, J. B. Priestley, Noël Coward, Philip Jordan of the *News Chronicle* and me. Willie and I were the early arrivals. More from the need to say something than because I thought it would interest him I mentioned that I had bought a first edition of the *The Explorer*, a bad novel of his that had been published in 1908.

'He gave me a sharp look. "How much did you have to pay for it?"

'"Three pounds." Those were still the days of the seven-and-sixpenny novel and before collecting contemporary first editions became fashionable. He may well have gathered that I thought the price excessive.

'"Wasn't it worth three pounds?" he asked.

'"Well . . ."

'He nodded bleakly and went to talk to Frere. He had had enough of me. Noël was the one who knew how to please him. He came bounding in, made straight for Willie, bobbed a curtesy, went down on one knee and said, "*Maître!*"

'Willie simpered with pleasure. They began to talk about the theatre.

'At dinner, Willie, who was at the head of the table, concentrated on his food until someone, I think it was Priestley, in saying something about the Book Society regretted Hugh Walpole's death. He had often been helpful to promising writers.

'Willie put down his knife and fork and looked up. "I knew Hugh Walpole for a great many years", he said deliberately. "I can tell you from my own knowledge that he behaved disgracefully to several talented young writers, one of whom I knew personally. Hugh Walpole ruined his life."

'He glowered at us. His meaning was plain. We all knew perfectly well that what he was really talking about was not a talented writer but a stolen boyfriend, an unrequited love and an old canker of jealousy. Only Priestley remained unimpressed.

'"You know, Willie", he said, "I've always thought that in *Cakes and Ale* you were a little unkind to poor Hugh."

'Willie began to stammer badly. Priestley waited for a moment and then went on: "There were five men in Hugh Walpole", he said, "and one of them was a very nice fellow."

'Philip Jordan muttered that one nice fellow in five didn't seem much of a percentage, but the remark was lost when Noël tried to introduce a lighter note.

'"I once travelled up from Cornwall on a train with Hugh Walpole," he said. "I was fifteen at the time. He patted my knee and gave me half-a-crown."

'Willie did not join in the amusement. He began to stammer again, and then suddenly the words came, and his anger with them.

'"I have known some odious men in my time," he said deliberately. "One of the most odious was Lord Alfred Douglas. But, odious though he was, he always remained a gentleman." His voice rose. "Hugh Walpole was a c-c-c-cad.""[29]

Authors can be as vicious about each other as can academics, though this sliver of literary table talk may be an extreme example. Ambler soon went to work in Hollywood, but he wrote three more books for Heinemann: *The Night-Comers* (1956), *Passage of Arms* (1959), *The Light of Day* (1962).

The traditional women's market was still recognizable in the post-war period, but it was not so distinct as in the 1930s and 1920s. Women readers too wanted entertainment, but usually something else as well. Among the writers whose work falls inescapably into the category of the 'woman's novel' was the prolific Barbara Goolden who between 1940 and 1974 wrote no fewer than seventy novels for Heinemann, including a few for children, an average of two books a year. She enjoyed a very faithful readership and, though no one would call her style 'mandarin', she dealt with many serious themes and was above all considered to be a thoroughly 'likeable' writer. Probably the best way of conveying the character and

[359]

quality of her books and why they continued to be popular is by means of extracts from a few of Maire Lynd's reports. *The China Pig* (1953): 'Her new novel is very much what her readers will expect, and quite good of its kind. It is a study of the difficulties of the parent-child relation when the children are growing-up, and the inevitable friction and struggle to escape, even where there is affection.' *Who is my Neighbour?* (1954): 'I like her new novel a great deal better than most of hers I have read. It is present-day social history laced with romance. Its great virtue is that in these days of gloomy novels it is essentially a happy book, even while its central theme is a serious one. . . . She sees both sides of an age-old problem with the utmost fairness and sympathy.' *Through the Sword Gates* (1957): 'She maintains her extraordinary ability to convey the small agonies of being young. . . . Pleasant, sympathetic and easy to read. Extremely suitable for the feminine library public.' *Marriages are Made in Heaven* (1963): 'Barbara Goolden at her best. She shows us three brand-new marriages in an English country town, the very different (and unexpected) problems which face them and the qualities needed by her three heroines. . . . Extremely easy to read. It deals in a human way with real human problems.' *The Little City* (1962): 'Rather less plotty than most of her novels, though it still draws a likeable picture of her charming adolescents. It borders on being a novel of ideas, but she does not venture out of her depth.' Some of the comments may be condescending but it is a publisher's reader's job to be as frank as necessary. Even when the reports were not so good her books went on selling, though not in immense numbers. She was part of the firm's bread-and-butter.

By no means all or even the majority of novels in this period could be described in this way. There were still plenty of books taken because of their literary quality with relatively little concern over their sales potential. With so many established good- and best-sellers it was still possible – or at least thought to be possible – to ignore in practice harsh business realities. The outlook of the independent gentleman publisher who liked to back his fancy still pervaded the offices of Great Russell Street.

The Rack (1958) by A. E. Ellis, a pseudonym, is an example. Almost certainly based on the author's personal experiences, it was about a young man's physical and mental ordeal during two-and-a-half years in a tuberculosis sanatorium in the French Alps. But it also blended tragedy with farce, the fluctuations of hope and despair amid the heightened relationships among the patients in the encapsulated sanatorium world.

Publishing it was not easy and meant persuading the author to cut it drastically to bring it down to 150,000 words and there were potential libel problems, but Michie was determined that it should be published and Frere readily agreed. His and Maire Lynd's judgment was justified by excellent reviews. Graham Greene wrote: 'There are certain books which we call great for want of a better term, that rise like monuments above the cemeteries of literature: *Clarissa Harlowe*, *Great Expectations*, *Ulysses*. *The Rack* to my mind is of this company.'

The books of Rhys Davies were not exactly poor sellers, but presumably he was kept in the list largely because he wrote so well. Between 1936 (*Things Men Do*) and 1975 (*Honeysuckle Girl*) there were 12 of his novels, 7 volumes of short stories, and one of reminiscences – *Print of a Hare's Foot* (1969). He is best remembered for the short stories, many of them stemming from his upbringing in the Rhondda, so that he was called the 'Welsh Chekhov'. They were a trifle old-fashioned in that they relied on a strong plot and suspense, and yet they skilfully avoided the slickness of the mechanical magazine story. There were also other serious, painstaking, skilled novelists whose sales were usually in inverse ratio to their quality, such as John Sommerfield – *The Adversaries* (1952), *The Inheritance* (1956), and others; Elizabeth Berridge with *Upon Several Occasions* (1953), *Across the Common* (1964); and the thirteen books by Hubert Nicholson, mostly novels that included *Here Where the World is Quiet* (1944), *Sunk Island* (1956), *Duckling in Capri* (1966). After the publication of his *Patterns of Three and Four* (1965) Nicholson wrote a long, gloomy letter, complaining that 'twenty years ago you were able to sell four or five times as many of my novels as this.' He was not particularly concerned about the money, though he added '. . . all that sweat and blood for what I make in five weeks at Reuters. It doesn't make sense.' Like so many authors he grumbled about the lack of advertising and promotion and ended sadly: 'I expect you think me very ungrateful to write like this. But it's all so desperately disheartening. It surely needn't yet be too late to make a real effort to get my book across? Or am I already left behind, and all the effort going into the books of next week and the week after that? Meanwhile, the American fledgling writers fly across the Atlantic to "launch" their books, and there are cocktail parties at the Savoy, and bits in all the gossip columns, and. . . . All right, cut me down to size. Who do I think I am, Saul Bellow? Daphne du Maurier? A WRITER?'[30] Roland Gant replied with a kind and courteous letter which concluded: 'Sadly, all that remains to be said is that it is now no longer enough to write a good book. Some good writers have good luck. Many bad writers have a great deal of success. In your final paragraph you ask who you are. You are a good writer who, up to now, has not had good luck and who is too good a writer to produce some cynically commercial piece of work.'[31]

A curiosity was *Madame Solario* (1956), announced as 'an anonymous novel certain to arouse speculation and discussion.' Its four hundred pages, printed on creamy laid paper with tinted end-papers, described a holiday enclave of wealthy, fashionable Edwardians and Continentals on the banks of Lake Como. The silken, atmospheric prose was heavy with allusions and innuendo that beneath the happy world of picnics on the mountainside, excursions on the lake steamers, of great ladies conversing on the hotel verandas, there lay the unclear pasts of some of the guests, worse some serious social flaws, particularly the unmentionable suspicion of incest. *Madame Solario* was well received and became a Book Society choice. At first only the editorial department knew what eventually leaked out, that the author was Gladys Huntington, an American whose husband had once run the London office of Putnams. She must have been at least seventy and was very rich. She had published only one other book and that had been forty-five years earlier. Did *Madame Solario*'s anonymity conceal that the book was autobiographical? James Michie told me that he felt she wouldn't have liked to be asked that question. 'She had probably written it years before it came to us. Maybe her life had reached the point when publication no longer mattered.'

A history is not concerned only with recording successes. As in previous periods good authors were lost as well as captured. Three losses in particular have to be recorded. It was a great coup to publish Truman Capote's first novel *Other Voices, Other Rooms* (1948) about a boy reaching adolescence in circumstances that were frightening, mysterious and perverted. He was hailed as a new, if precocious literary voice. Maire Lynd at once spotted his talent, though she had some reservations. On the radio Rose Macaulay confirmed his arrival and spoke of his novel's '. . . fantastic riot of colour, its luxuriance, its febrile beauty, its orchidacious richness.' There followed another novel, *The Grass Harp* (1952); a volume of short stories; *Local Color* (1955), evocative studies of places and people from New Orleans, Venice, and Tangier; and *The Muses are Heard* (1957) about the tour of the opera *Porgy and Bess* to Leningrad. But Capote soon seemed to be disenchanted with Heinemann and in particular wanted fatter advances and to move to Hamish Hamilton which, after considerable resistance from Frere and an apologetic letter from Hamish, he eventually did – and so it was that, despite the initial talent-spotting and investment, his later big successes like *Breakfast at Tiffany's* and *In Cold Blood* went elsewhere.

It was Graham Greene who introduced Elizabeth Montagu with what he called 'an extremely interesting, talented and promising' first novel, *Waiting for Camilla* (1953). It was well received by the critics and so was *The Small Corner* (1955) – '. . . a distinguished piece of writing. . . .' '. . . a highly intellectual novel. . . .' Frere told Michie in a note that her third, *This Side of the Truth* (1957), was 'original, perceptive, a good yarn. She gets better every time and could easily start a cult – a sort of female Waugh. If those clots at the Book Society could see this one we might easily get a choice. Put in a provisional printing of 7,000. That won't be enough.' After this she fell seriously ill and it was nine years before *Change and Other Stories* (1966) appeared and after this Heinemann published nothing else of hers. So often in publishing brilliant promise is short-lived or is lost to a rival firm.

Another disappointing loss was Audrey Erskine Lindop after she had written six novels for the firm, starting with *Soldiers' Daughters Never Cry* (1948) and ending with *The Judas Figures* (1956). Perhaps the best known, however, was *The Singer not the Song* (1953), set in Mexico with a long symbolic struggle between a town's priest and an evil Mafia-type who with his gang terrorized the population. Tegan Harris, the reader, described it as an 'original and remarkable novel, beautifully written. . . . She is a born writer and has the most extraordinary imagination of any novelist I know.' When Lindop decided to move to Collins because, like so many authors, she felt that her books had not been sufficiently promoted, Frere sounded hurt as well as angry: 'It was nice of you to write me so fully but naturally I should have preferred to have heard from you before getting it from Spencer Curtis Brown. . . . [When we first met] I think I discerned a talent which showed promise of blossoming into a successful career as a novelist and I was delighted to be able to play some part in that subsequent fulfilment. . . . Your decision to go somewhere else – and nobody has yet done me the courtesy of telling me to whom you are going – argues that you think some other publisher can do it better than we can. Frankly I think this is nonsense. No publishing firm in London can touch our record and standard of success in the publishing of fiction, and particularly of fiction of the kind which you write so supremely well. . . . There are always publishers ready to gamble over the odds in order to try to lure an author, established in someone else's list, into their own. In my long experience I have never known a case in which this sort of thing has succeeded to the benefit of the author. . . . I not only think you are wrong but I *know* you are wrong, and it grieves me more than I can tell you to have to say so.'[32] Guarding and holding on to successful authors whom you have expensively nurtured can be as taxing as discovering new ones.

An author lost through, in the circumstances, justifiable prudence was Vladimir Nabokov. After successfully publishing his novel *Pnin* (1957) and a book of thirteen stories, *Nabokov's Dozen* (1959), the firm's option on his next work would have brought the submission of *Lolita*, an account of a middle-aged man's passion for a twelve-year-old bobbysoxer. Some said it was the worst kind of filth about a pervert, and yet others, including Graham Greene, believed it to be a brilliant and seriously intended novel far removed from pornography. But after his ordeal in the dock over *The Image and the Search* (see Chapter Twenty), Frere understandably didn't want to know about it and it went to Weidenfeld & Nicolson. Thus was lost a remarkable book and a major bestseller.

18

Reluctant Acceptance
of Paperbacks

During the post-war 1940s and the 1950s there was nothing that could stop the tide of paperbacks. By 1955 Penguin was selling some 11 million copies a year; Pan 8 million; Corgi, scarcely two years old, 4 million; and there were other new paperback imprints. By 1960 there were 5,886 titles in *Whitaker's Paperbacks in Print*, though this was only a fraction of what it would amount to a few years later. Penguin paperbacks by Shaw, Wells, and D. H. Lawrence sold totals counted by the million, though the average annual sale for a Penguin was around 50,000. They were still breaking into hitherto untapped markets, but it was also true that they were taking away readers who previously would have bought the same book in hardback, especially in cheap editions. A significant sector of the new market was captured by 'egghead' paperbacks – mainly for students, a 'known' rather than a mass market – and by original and newly commissioned titles, but paperback fiction still consisted almost entirely of reprints. Their prices of course increased with inflation from the original 6*d.* to 3*s.*6*d.* and 5*s.* for more specialized titles, but they remained very much cheaper than the equally inflated prices of most hardbacks.

Describing the paperback as 'an important agent in the further demo-cratization of the book as such', Ray Bradbury has succinctly summed up what was happening: 'The general pattern in fact suggests that the paperback has enlarged audiences somewhat, but has also captured most of the old hardback purchasers as well; it has become the new book-market. If this is so, the new pattern represents an interesting mixture of change and conservation; it has produced a certain expansion and restratification of the audience, changing its mix somewhat while contain-ing many of the old stratifications and reading habits. One can read in the situation genuine signs of expanded interest in books, and of extended reading, especially among young people; one can find in it greater use of the classics and of new authors who acquire prestige or popularity. But one can also find a large growth of disposable reading of undifferentiated quality, an increase in sensational reading, and a general coarsening of the pattern of the market, partly derived from the fact that paperbacks block out in larger scale the extant patterns of the hardback market.'[1]

Heinemann was not the only traditional publisher to feel threatened. Even during the war a group of nine firms, among them Heinemann, had got together in an attempt to beat the paperback firms at their own game. Their co-operative undertaking was called The British Publishers Guild and they were frank in explaining that it had 'been born of the realization that the trade's most urgent need is to prevent the marketing of books from sliding beyond the control of the established book publishing industry. The demand today is for cheap books, and it is a demand which in the last two or three years has been supplied to an ever increasing extent by organizations which, themselves outside the established publishing trade, profess neither allegiance nor responsibility towards it. The flow of cheap books (either reprints of books which their original publishers had laboriously built up or new books by authors on whom their original publishers have spent much time and money in establishing) has wandered outside trade channels. The main object of The British Publishers Guild is to bring back the stream to the book trade's own garden.'[2] There was a wide selection of titles priced 6d., 9d., or 1s. Each member firm was responsible for manufacturing its Guild titles, but they were marketed under the Guild's imprint jointly with their own. The Guild was responsible for distribution, though it was planned that it would make use of member firms' own sales machinery, though they were in fact published from Harraps' offices and distributed through the Book Centre. Leslie Munro was one of five members of its controlling committee, of which Jonathan Cape was initially chairman and Walter Harrap secretary.

The Guild seems to have begun well and was aided by special editions for the armed forces printed on paper made available by the Authorities. In 1946, however, Dwye Evans, back from the RAF, attended a Guild committee meeting and was alarmed at their future plans. In a memorandum to Frere which might have been penned by his father he reported that he was 'very impressed by the high co-operative spirit of this body of publishers. It is obviously a flourishing and ambitious business and therein, I'm afraid, lies the danger to the book trade. In the course of the meeting the general manager remarked that if some people could know the extent of the Guild's plans – envisaging the production of some millions of paperbound books at 1s. – they would be startled. He is right. *I* was startled. I was also horrified to think that the home market in the coming years would be flooded with a spate of cheap books for sale to a public, a great many of whom have become accustomed, in the years of austerity and shortage, to pay as much for a book they wanted as they would for a seat in a theatre or one of London's grander cinemas.

'No one can, I think, quarrel with the statement that the British book trade was in the doldrums in the years before the war and I believe it to be true that in the same period Penguins reached the peak of their success. Is there no connection? I think there is: the obvious inference is that the sale of millions of sixpenny books had a very deleterious effect on the sales not only of the normal high-priced fiction and general books, but also on the 5s., 3s.6d., and 2s. reprints and series of books, and even on the libraries, fiction and public alike. Are we now to re-educate the public to buying their books at 1s. at the expense of our bread and butter? The argument that by each publisher issuing a few titles each year in the Guild they will prevent Penguin from expanding just does not hold water. There are plenty of titles to go round; the majority of the books in the Guild would not be chosen by Penguin at all. The Guild is merely another and parallel method of distributing large numbers of books in the lowest price range. There will be others. In an alarmingly short time the octopus of too-cheap books will once again be strangling the book trade.

'During the meeting some mention was made of the fact that one publisher would be receiving £6,000 as his share of the profits made by the Guild during the year. Would it be impertinent to ask how much rationed paper had been used to achieve that result and how much profit that firm could have made (to say nothing of authors and booksellers) by publishing books at from 7s.6d. to a guinea? Six times as much?'[3]

After the war the Heinemann board seems to have decided to drop out of the British Publishers Guild. They were then faced with two possibilities: either to settle for some kind of compromise or to join the enemy and start their own paperback imprint. After dithering they did both, but neither very effectively. The compromise first took the form of reprints priced at 3s.6d., which was 1s. or 2s. less than existing reprint series such as the Travellers Library. The new series, called the Vanguard Library, was launched jointly with Chatto & Windus in 1952. It was proclaimed to be a 'pioneer achievement of revolutionary importance'. They cost more than most paperbacks but, on the other hand, they were still thread-sewn

hardbacks with strong boards, embellished with gold foil blocked lettering, coloured tops, and French joints. In the publicity material emphasis
was laid on the permanent, rather than expendable, character of a
Vanguard book – 'at less than the price of a packet of cigarettes'. This
attractive looking series was by no means unsuccessful. There were some
thirty reprints of established fiction titles with print runs between 20,000
and 40,000. But ten years after its launch the Vanguard Library
disappeared from the catalogue. It just could not compete against
paperbacks, which eventually took over many of the Vanguard titles.

A step towards Heinemann starting its own paperback imprint was the
commissioning in 1956 of an investigation into the whole question by an
outside adviser, James Chesterman. This could be interpreted as a classic
delaying manoeuvre, but he produced a competent and comprehensive
report which strongly recommended the idea. He proposed starting with a
programme of backlist titles, nearly all fiction, from all the group companies (see next chapter), backed up with a series of mostly newly
commissioned 'teach yourself/improve yourself' titles, less highbrow
than Pelicans and to be called Key Books, selling at 2s.6d. With print runs
of 30–50,000, it would need an investment of £100,000. Surprisingly,
Chesterman foresaw that the immense backlist was likely to be exhausted
of suitable titles after the first hundred had been issued. The board was
divided on his proposals, Frere being in favour and Dwye Evans against
because he was worried about interfering with the claims of Pan and other
paperback firms on the backlist. A compromise proposal to proceed with
the Key Books series only was agreed to, but Chesterman, who was invited
to manage it, declined and the whole scheme was dropped.

At one stage an attempt was made to palm off any home-grown
paperbacks onto the World's Work and graft them onto its recently
launched Cedar Books (see page 378); but this was firmly resisted by
Phyllis Alexander on the grounds that Cedar lacked sufficient staff, were
already overextended, and that it would interfere with their basic publishing. One result of all these discussions emerged during the 1960s in
the form of Mercury Books, a group reprint series of egghead 'midway'
trade paperbacks, relatively highly priced between 7s.6d. and 18s, the first
being Fred Hoyle's *Frontiers of Astronomy*, followed by books by Lionel
Trilling, James Reeves, Giorgio de Santillana, George Orwell, and, by
1962, thirteen others – a few bought in from outside firms. Cheap editions
of some titles continued to be launched, but eventually the project failed

because it was used as a 'dustbin' for titles that could not be sold to an outside paperback house. Most of the editions consisted of bound-up surplus sheet stock.

The enemy had actually been embraced for the first time when in February 1952 Heinemann became a member of the consortium of five other publishers to own Pan Books. The others were Macmillan, Collins, Hodder & Stoughton, Cape, and Chatto & Windus. Heinemann bought 3,000 £1 ordinary shares and £2,437 preference shares. Started in 1944 by the enterprising Alan Bott as an independent subsidiary of the Book Society, with Aubrey Forshaw as managing director, Pan had also grown fast, though on different lines from Penguin, concentrating mainly on 'middle-of-the-road entertainment'. Their list was very much smaller: in 1955 they had 150 titles in print and sold 8 million books, compared with Penguin's 1,000 titles and 10 million sales. But Heinemann's involvement did not last long. The deep-rooted dislike of paperback publishing, allied with short-term greed and an acute shortage of cash, maybe explains why in 1961 the Pan shares were sold. The New American Library wanted to buy Pan and, with the exception of Macmillan, all the other five partaking firms were content to sell their shares at a very handsome profit. Harold Macmillan argued that it would be folly to allow an American company to control the second largest UK paperback concern and he persuaded William Collins to support him and so Collins ended up sharing Pan with Macmillan owning 51 per cent of the equity. With hindsight it is not difficult to conclude that for Heinemann, if not for the others, to have sold its shares was shortsighted and mistaken. It was a decision that had to be paid for when less than ten years later they had to buy their way back into Pan at some considerable expense. It was particularly surprising because by the late 1950s any hardback publisher could not avoid accepting that not only were paperbacks a permanent part of the publishing scene, but that the day was dawning when the sale of paperback rights was to provide an essential, major part of his revenue.

Another but relatively small-scale consortium to publish paperbacks, Star Editions, had been formed in 1946 at the instigation of Paul Zsolnay. Its purpose was to publish paperbacks in English on the continent of Europe only. Each member firm manufactured its own books in the series, but they were advertised from 99 Great Russell Street. Louisa Callender represented Heinemann on its committee; Zsolnay was the general manager. This attempt to emulate the pre-war achievements of

Tauchnitz and Albatros worked well enough for a while, but towards the end of the 1950s Star Editions too was forced to bow to the competition from the large, well organized paperback firms which had also invaded the Continent.

Secker & Warburg and
Rupert Hart-Davis
Join the Group

The 1950s witnessed further expansion through the acquisition of subsidiaries. The first (1951) was Martin Secker & Warburg. Not long after the sale of the D. H. Lawrence titles to Heinemann in 1935 Secker had again been in financial difficulties and in 1936 Fred Warburg, then thirty-five, bought the backlist and unpublished titles for £3,100 with money from his aunt Agnes and obtained a further £3,000 working capital from Roger Senhouse, who was to play an important part in the newly constructed firm's literary development. Martin Secker dropped out. After benefiting from the boom years of the 1940s, they were hit by post-war inflation and above all by lack of working capital. On the other hand they had built up – and were still building – a magnificent list. They had only recently published George Orwell's *Nineteen Eighty-Four* and among their other post-war stars were Franz Kafka, Thomas Mann, Henry Miller, Edmund Wilson, André Gide . . . to mention but a few. A most distinguished list which could dovetail impressively in with Heinemann's and, with perhaps greater though more restricted literary lustre, would complement rather than compete with it.

In the summer of 1951 their financial situation suddenly became desperate. It was David Farrer, another director and a brilliant editor, who suggested approaching Frere, whom he knew, though Senhouse was opposed to it. In the end there was no alternative and Farrer made an appointment with Frere, who, after listening carefully to their problems gave him a dusty answer. Each week things grew still worse and Warburg, deciding to make a second approach himself, rang up Dwye Evans. Warburg's own account of what happened, written over twenty years later, cannot be bettered and demands to be quoted from generously: 'Evans

The Windmill Press, Kingswood, Surrey
at the time of its opening

A view of the press in spring 1969,
showing the twin extensions added in 1952

Social activities,
sport and drama
were an important
part of after-hours
life at the
Windmill Press

took me to the first floor of the Heinemann offices in Great Russell Street, where Frere had his inner sanctum, and led me in. I was, naturally, nervous, as I realized all too clearly that, if I failed with Frere, there might be a sudden, sickening and messy end to all my hopes. I shook hands with Frere and sat down in the low armchair at the side of his desk. From it I looked up at Frere, seated in majesty. I felt like a supplicant before the great king as I waited for him to speak.

'But Frere did not speak, he looked at me coolly. It is supplicants who must speak, state their case, and beg for mercy. I had not prepared a first sentence, indeed I had not prepared my case in detail, trusting to my knowledge of the facts to make my points spontaneously. I opened my mouth, and the words came out loud and clear, "I come to see you, Frere, in two capacities – first, as the man who presides over an insolvent firm, second as the head of the most distinguished young publishing house in London." Frere smiled, not broadly but slightly and sardonically. He was himself an outspoken man, too outspoken for his own good, he often said. Probably he appreciated my opening words, for I had certainly laid the gist of my case before him in one medium-length sentence.

'This first sentence I remember accurately, even though I spoke it over twenty years ago. But what followed I do not remember, except that Frere agreed in principle to assist us with money, technical help and advice. But first I had to appear, for cross-examination as it were, before the whole Heinemann board. I had to travel down to Kingswood, Surrey, on the following Wednesday.

'Accompanied by Farrer, down I went to Kingswood. . . . We entered the Heinemann boardroom, about forty feet long and fifteen wide, with windows all along its length. At an enormous table sat the Heinemann board, with Frere at its head. On Frere's left sat H. L. Hall, the finance director who was Frere's closest confidant. I was seated on Frere's right. Including Farrer, who sat more or less opposite me, there were present Dwye Evans, Louisa Callender, B. F. Oliver, and one or two others. I felt like a heretic on trial before a court of the Inquisition, and the analogy is not too far-fetched, for – though I did not realize it on that day – I did hold views on publishing which those present at the meeting might have regarded as heretical, had I voiced them clearly.

'For nearly two hours questions were hurled at me from all sides. Most of them came, not unnaturally, from Hall, the finance man. He had no wish for a recapitalized Secker & Warburg to go bankrupt on him after a dismal year or two. But actually the questions were somewhat super-ficial. . . . Soon I began to get ruffled and a trifle angry, but apparently I did not show it, for Farrer wrote to Senhouse the next day: "the atmosphere grew more friendly and cordial as the meeting proceeded. . . . Heinemann made no effort to get better terms than we offered. . . . Above all I have been impressed by the palpable goodwill shown to us by all the Heinemann directors. Fred has certainly made a hit with Frere." In my own view it was with Hall (always addressed as H.) that I made my hit that day. Before the meeting, after Frere had told him what his plan for us was, H. must have been worried. He had, as a financial animal, the greatest mistrust of small publishers who issued books they fancied and hoped for the best, with disastrous results. Apparently he did not believe that I belonged in this category.'[4]

There followed a complicated capital reconstruction as a result of which Heinemann invested an initial £8,000 and gained control of the voting shares. They also guaranteed a bank overdraft that was to reach £100,000. Frere and Hall became directors. As well as providing finance, Heinemann took charge of all the business as opposed to the literary side of the company's activities. Fred Warburg remained as the executive head and was given complete editorial freedom to contract books without consulting Heinemann, provided the advance did not exceed £300, though this stipulation was later changed.

It was an effective division of labour and as part of the Heinemann group, Secker & Warburg's list grew to be even more illustrious. Fred Warburg asked himself what made the arrangement work so well. 'I think because Frere and I understood, not so much each other, as the true nature of the situation in which we were mutually involved.' Warburg quotes from a letter of Frere's formalizing their relationship: '"Pub-lishing has a mystique of its own, and the lean and bleak economic facts have little to do with the worth and integrity of an imprint. We may, or may not, be able to improve 'the banker's eye view' of it, but we are happy to be associated with your imprint and, in maintaining it, you may be assured of nothing but sympathetic co-operation from us." This is the letter of a publisher before all else. It is also the letter of a man who proposes to run his group, not as an empire but as head or prime minister of the most powerful publishing house in a commonwealth of publishers. Frere was as good as his word. I had nothing but minor clashes with him, and when the big clash came it was not over an internal but an external group affair.'[5]

The next most important firm to be taken over was Rupert Hart-Davis Ltd. After Hart-Davis left Heinemann he had worked for Cape but after war service in the Coldstream Guards he started his own imprint in 1946. As well as poetry, his list included commercially sound titles such as Stephen Potter's *Gamesmanship* – which gave a new word to the language – and its successors; *Elephant Bill* by J. H. Williams; *My Family and Other Animals* by Gerald Durrell; Duff Cooper's autobiography; *Son of Oscar Wilde* by Vyvyan Holland; and *Seven Years in Tibet* by Heinrich Harrer, which sold over 200,000 copies. Again, here was an attractive list and a firm with already a distinguished reputation, but it lacked capital. A similar arrangement to that made with Secker & Warburg was agreed, with Heinemann exchanging five 2s.6d. of its ordinary shares for every three 10s. ordinary shares in Rupert Hart-Davis Ltd. The capital was reorganized and increased. Frere and Hall joined its board, but Rupert Hart-Davis himself retained complete editorial control. He also retained his London traveller.

Two other much smaller firms were also taken over during the 1950s: Bancroft and Co. Ltd, publishers of children's books and an early form of pop-up books; and the Naldrett Press, which, after a very short life, had become successful publishers of sports books and issued coaching manuals, a year book and boys' annuals with big circulations on behalf of the Football Association, the MCC, and other bodies. They also published for the National Trust. It was decided that the Naldrett Press should be a subsidiary of the World's Work company. There were also serious negotiations with a view to taking over Putnams and Arthur Barker Ltd, but nothing came of them.

To reflect these acquisitions the name of the overall company was changed in 1959 from Heinemann Holdings Ltd to Heinemann Publishers Ltd. Inevitably there was talk in the trade about the 'new Heinemann empire' and plenty of jealous speculation and headshaking about 'loss of separate identities'. With some reason it could be replied that the firms taken over were not so much subsidiaries but had become part of an amalgamation under a benevolent umbrella. In interviews with the Press Frere stressed that the new Heinemann group firms enjoyed, as Peter Davies had always done, complete editorial autonomy. The only way these smaller firms could survive was to combine on the purely business side in the interests of greater efficiency in marketing and in order to keep down overheads. When discussing the analogy between a publisher and a wine merchant, Frere pointed out that: 'If the population of England suddenly stopped drinking beer and took to Burgundy instead, you'd see a remarkable change in the organization of vintners' businesses. The old-fashioned publisher was often a wonderfully good publisher; but if we are going to keep the virtues of the kind of publishing he went in for, the virtues of discrimination, concern for standards, the feeling that a book is not just a mere commodity, we'll only do so by putting the emphasis on the business side of publishing; if you like, the mechanical side. What the small firms now associated with us are benefiting from are the advantages that come from rationalization and from the efficient machinery of distribution that only a large organization can provide. Take the latter, for example. The lack of it is one reason why the small publisher is very often unable adequately to exploit the books he does publish. If a really big selling book comes his way he's often in no position to handle it, and the very effort to do so may send him under. The amount of capital needed for running a successful publishing house is beyond the resources of most individuals.'[6]

It would be too much to expect that relationships with the subsidiaries were always smooth. In the years to come there would be many problems, sometimes amounting to crises, but there was scarcely ever serious friction over editorial autonomy and, paradoxically, it first arose over Heinemann's, or more precisely, Kingswood's own administrative short-comings. Warburg was frequently critical and after a very short time Hart-Davis was disillusioned.

'At the time my own firm was taken over', he told me in 1984 when I visited him at his splendid home in Swaledale, replete with shelves of first editions from all publishers, 'I had two packers in the basement who dealt with all our orders within twenty-four hours. I was assured that on being taken over our overheads would drop like a stone and everything would be much more efficient. In practice the twenty-four-hour delivery service at once increased to three weeks. Most of my books sold in the West End of London and this delay was disastrous. The cost of the packing was trebled since Heinemann, though their packing was done in the country, was then paying London union rates. This was typical of everything that happened. Everything was slower and more expensive. Frere was always calling meetings with Hall beside him. Between them they were supposed to have everything taped.'

The mother firm undoubtedly learned from this kind of criticism and, indeed, in the early 1960s Harry Townshend, the number two at Rupert Hart-Davis, was made part-time general manager at Kingswood. The meetings Hart-Davis was referring to were almost certainly those of the group management committee set up in 1959 and attended by the heads of all the subsidiaries. Its formal terms of reference were '(1) To help bring about the centralization of certain publishing functions for the mutual benefit of all companies in the group, at the same time leaving editorial autonomy with individual companies. (2) To recommend changes of policy to the parent company, and to be the specific body through which policy changes could be implemented.'[7] Its decisions and recommendations were however subject to the ultimate control of the top group board.

It was a sensible step, but it was not until the 1970s that the administrative services at Kingswood were to function as efficiently as they should. There can be little doubt that the existing machinery was not ready or even capable of taking on so many additional titles. Considered in conjunction with the problems of controlling the new overseas offices and of the general growth in the firm's structure – especially the rapid expansion of the educational department – the subsidiaries were helping to create unfamiliar difficulties that always accompany an escalation in size. Bigness has problems of its own and is seldom 'beautiful'. At the time the problems and complications were almost certainly underestimated, but it is still perplexing to comprehend the motivation behind these take-overs. The obvious justification was increased 'throughput' resulting, it was hoped, in reduced overheads and more support for the new overseas branches. Apart from the prestige of being associated with such impressive lists, it must have been believed that with better management the subsidiaries would generate increasing group profits. But to what extent was growth welcomed for its own sake? Were there attractions in the power that would stem from controlling an even larger share of the publishing industry?

Acquisitions of a very different type were extensions of Heinemann & Zsolnay Ltd. After liberation Paul Zsolnay's plans to sell French translations of English books bore fruit in the form of Heinemann & Zsolnay SARL established in a modest office in Paris. It did good business until 1959 when it was in effect defeated by exported paperbacks and was sold for £2,000. More important was the revival of Zsolnay's imprint in Austria. Soon after the war was over Zsolnay, accompanied by Dwye

Evans still in RAF uniform, returned to Vienna to discover what had happened to his old company and if he could get it back. It had been confiscated on the personal order of Goebbels and handed over to nominees who had kept it going. Several of his exceedingly loyal staff had been able to stay on and had salvaged valuable stocks. It took some time before the company could be handed back legally, but Zsolnay got round this by starting another company called Continental Heinemann & Zsolnay Verlag and obtaining an injunction which prevented his original company from issuing books meanwhile. The new company was owned one hundred per cent by the joint Heinemann & Zsolnay company in London, Zsolnay insisting on this out of gratitude for the help Charles Evans had given him when he had arrived penniless in London just before the war. It was a remarkable gesture. In return for its modest two-thirds investment of £666 Heinemann now had access to one of the most impressive backlists in Europe. Eventually opening an office in Hamburg as well as Vienna, in place of the pre-war offices in Berlin and Leipzig, Heinemann & Zsolnay Verlag expanded rapidly and was soon publishing some thirty-five books a year, two-thirds fiction and one-third general. Its list had a strong international flavour with translations from English predominating, but about a quarter of the authors were German speaking. Among the authors were Pearl Buck, Colette, Theodore Dreiser, Albert Einstein, Rumer Godden, Graham Greene, Georgette Heyer, J. B. Priestley, and H. G. Wells. The company shared in the post-war boom and built up large reserves, so that whenever turnover declined it was still able to pay dividends. Although relatively small, Heinemann & Zsolnay never became a problem and the very small initial investment paid off regularly and handsomely. As well as receiving dividends Heinemann & Zsolnay (London) retained all the subsidiary rights in the Austrian company's titles, which provided another source of profits.

This is an apposite place to record the mutually advantageous deal made with another refugee from the Nazis, Siegfried Trebitsch. He had translated many of G. B. Shaw's works into German. In return for an annuity paid to himself and to his wife during their lifetimes, he assigned to Heinemann all the German Shaw copyrights, which brought in revenue for many years. His struggle to win recognition of Shaw in Germany and Austria is recorded, together with much about the literary life of Berlin and Vienna, in Trebitsch's autobiography, *Chronicle of a Life*, which the firm published in 1953.

The firm's experience of publishing plays led to the formation in 1952 of yet another new subsidiary, Heinemann Productions Ltd, with an authorized capital of £2,000, of which William Heinemann Ltd would own at least 51 per cent. Its purpose was to act as impresarios and financiers of dramatic projects of all kinds, including films, radio, and television. It seems to have been stillborn.

World's Work's Expansion

The pattern of this book does not cater for the histories of most of the Heinemann subsidiaries, each of which deserves its own separate volume; they are included only to the extent of their relationship with and their effect on the parent company. The World's Work (1913) Ltd, which became a wholly owned subsidiary shortly before Chalmers Roberts's death in 1949, is in a different category, having from its birth been in effect a Heinemann department, though it preserved its editorial and operating independence. Post-war it continued with cowboy and 'romance' titles, purchasing the copyrights outright from the US for £100 each and marketing them at 3s.6d., which rose to 7s.6d. in the 1950s before the disappearance of the cheap libraries killed the market. World's Work might have become another Mills and Boon, but instead it followed up the extraordinary success of Dale Carnegie's *How to Win Friends and Influence People* (1938), which went on selling steadily as it still does, so that by 1984 it had recorded a total of 741,000. It was followed by six more of his books, including *How to Stop Worrying and Start Living* (1949) – 652,000 sold; and similar self-improvement and semi-religious, 'inspirational' titles by other American authors, all of which Phyllis Alexander acquired without crossing the Atlantic by studying American book trade literature. The sales of several were also up in the hundred thousands, but most sold 10,000–50,000. There was Norman Vincent Peale, an American Protestant minister, with eleven titles such as *The Power of Positive Thinking* (1953) – 824,000 sold; Billy Graham's *Peace with God* (1954) – 322,000; sold; a series on salesmanship and public speaking for the Alfred

[377]

Tack organization; *Arthritis and Common Sense* (1957) by Dan Dale Alexander – 183,000 sold; and quite a few others.

As well as the prestigious sports books of the Naldrett Press, a trade paperback series, Cedar Books, was started by World's Work in 1953 and it still flourishes. An unexpected bedfellow was *Encounter* magazine, issued by Secker & Warburg but distributed by The World's Work in return for a fee from the Congress for Cultural Freedom, funded by the American CIA. For a short period (1957–60) World's Work also distributed *The London Magazine*, the literary quarterly edited by John Lehmann, for a generously small fee of £100 per annum and a free page of advertising in each issue. After a few years it became clear that handling magazine subscriptions did not mesh well with book publishing and both magazines were given up.

An important departure came with the publication of *The Littlest Angel* (1957), an American children's bestseller by Charles Tazewell. Learning about it from the trade press, Phyllis Alexander had found to her surprise that the UK rights were still available. With two other titles, it laid the foundation of what was to be The World's Work's highly successful children's list. Some of the stories were rather mawkish but the books were very well printed in four-colour offset litho and nothing quite like them had appeared before in the UK, though they later became commonplace. The British printing industry was so busy reprinting stocks destroyed in the war that it was slow to convert from letterpress, whereas in the US what amounted to a whole new children's publishing industry had grown up based on first-class artwork and sound litho colour printing. The World's Work's first children's books were printed in Holland from American duplicate film. They sold very well and were followed up by many others. There was a backlog of similar books in America and their publishers were only too pleased to sell the rights, together with the litho film, for quite small sums and royalties. By modern standards the print runs were short, but children's books soon became the most important part of The World's Work's turnover. By 1960 this had grown from £8,051 in 1945 to £130,017 with a profit of £56,049. Despite this, in a reorganization in 1959, The World's Work ceased to operate as a completely self-sufficient unit, twenty-four of its thirty-five staff being transferred, at least nominally, to the parent company. But it remained an independent publisher with its own policy.

Children's Department

After the war Heinemann's own children's list was revived on a modest scale with Mary Whitehead as editor. Most of the twelve or so titles a year seem to have been aimed at an audience of older, comfortably middle-class children. The production at the Windmill Press was conventional, with mostly black-and-white illustrations. Among the regular authors were Ruth Ainsworth with her *Rufty Tufty* series among others; Alison Uttley with *The Little Red Fox* series, *The Story of Fuzzypeg and the Hedgehog* (1949) and *Snug and the Chimney-Sweeper* (1953). Margaret Tempest and Katherine Wigglesworth were her main illustrators. Another regular, Elizabeth Enright, illustrated her own stories mainly for 10 to 14 year-olds; Bryan Guinness contributed stories for 4 to 7 year-olds; among James Reeves's books were verse for different ages, usually illustrated by Edward Ardizzone, such as *Prefabulous Animiles* (1957); Geoffrey Trease, who was commissioned by the Educational department to write *Tales out of School* (1948), a critical survey of juvenile fiction, went on to contribute excellent children's historical novels, such as the *Black Banner* series.

'Nowadays most stories for children are completely different,' Mary Whitehead told me. 'Before television children read more and, in my view, had better taste. Books that lasted well contained plenty of action. Typical adventures would involve running away from home or being left with a widowed mother and having to cope. In those days Heinemann's children's books were far from being "frank". Sex would be limited to an occasional holding of hands. No modern 'teenager would look at some of the books we published, unless they were mentally backward.'

Educational Department

After the war the educational department was revived, this time with Alan Hill as the manager. He had returned from the RAF in January 1946 to find a depressing situation: 'I re-started my publishing career with a table and chair, a shared telephone, a handful of pre-war books and an annual sales revenue of £15,000, most of it coming from three titles. Nothing else: no staff; not even a secretary for my first eighteen months. Certainly not a company car. I had to use my own pre-war Ford Eight, and provide my own portable typewriter. In my first year I published nothing.'

This low-key start was not unwelcome to the rest of the firm, who did not want competition for their scarce supplies of paper – which continued to be rationed for another three years. So it was not until 1949 that Hill, now joined by his two assistants Edward Thompson and Tony Beal, was able to break loose. The close partnership of these three was to continue for the next thirty years, and was to result in Heinemann's rise to a predominant position in educational publishing.

History was in fact on their side. There was a dramatic growth in the market, with the population of Britain increasing from 46 million in 1941 to 56 million in 1971. During this period, thanks also to the raising of the school-leaving age from 14 to 16, the school market nearly doubled – from 6 million pupils pre-war to over 11 million in 1977. In university and higher education the increase was to be even more dramatic – from 69,000 in 1939 to 440,000 in 1969. Faced with this tremendous opportunity, the educational department resolved to publish across the whole educational spectrum, from school to university, not excluding general trade books.

The first priority was the school list, in particular two subjects – English and Science. English fitted the high literary tradition of Heinemann and had a world-wide market. Science also was a rapidly growing subject with great overseas potential. But where were the authors to be found? According to Alan Hill: 'desperately I ransacked the country for books and authors. I would leave the office at 6.00 p.m. and would drive into the provinces, arriving late at night in Sheffield or Manchester to spend the

[380]

following day looking for talent. The books came slowly. And how slow they seemed to me then! It is difficult for the uninitiated to realize how long it takes to publish an educational book. A total of five years between signature of contract and marketing the completed book is not unusual.'

The first post-war success on the English list was James Reeves's *The Poet's World* (1948), with print runs exceeding 125,000 copies. Other English books followed, culminating in the New Windmill Series, perhaps the most influential series of works of fiction for children's reading published in this century. The series editor was Ian Serraillier, a practising teacher and well-known writer of children's poetry and fiction. In collaboration with Tony Beal, over 300 titles were published by 1986, with 20 million copies sold to schools in Britain and overseas. Thanks to the New Windmill Series, vast numbers of school children have been introduced to the works of D. H. Lawrence, Doris Lessing, George Orwell, Graham Greene, Henry James, H. G. Wells, J. B. Priestley, Roald Dahl, Camus, Hemingway, Masefield, Solzhenitsyn, and many others.

On the Science side, the pre-war authors were now blossoming out into great best-sellers. In particular, A. J. Mee (who had become Chief Science Inspector for Scotland), on the basis of the post-war revolution in science teaching, masterminded Heinemann science courses for Britain, Nigeria, Central Africa, South East Asia, and the Caribbean respectively. These were hugely successful, and were a new departure for Heinemann in that each was published in and for the country concerned. New authors now appeared, particularly the astonishing physics text-book author Michael Nelkon, whose thirty or more books have made him more famous throughout the English-speaking world than many a popular novelist – whose earnings his would comfortably surpass.

The distinction of writing Heinemann's biggest-selling book published since the war belongs to another physicist – whose arrival was unpredictable, but whose conversion into an author demanded much manipulation by the publisher, as Alan Hill has described: 'Soon after the publication of Nelkon's first book, *Light and Sound*, I happened, in an idle moment, to pick up a tray of correspondence from my secretary's desk. One particular letter caught my eye because of the colour of the ink – a bright turquoise. I took the letter out of the pile and read it. It contained a critique of *Light and Sound*, several pages long and very impressive. The writer was a master at Latymer Upper School in Hammersmith. I at once got into my old

Ford Eight and drove down to Hammersmith where I ran Arthur Abbot to earth in his laboratory. "No," he said, "I can't write a book: I am far too busy." I retired discomfited, and pondered an alternative approach. I asked Michael Nelkon if he would collaborate with Arthur Abbot, who would provide the ideas while Nelkon did the writing? Nelkon agreed, and, after an agonizing delay, so did Arthur Abbot. After completing two books, during which Abbot found he was doing a great deal of the writing himself, and enjoying it, he at last signed a contract for a book of his own. It took him seven years to write *Ordinary Level Physics*. Published in 1962, it was immediately a huge and continuing success, and has sold around five million copies throughout the world: it is the basic Physics text-book right around the globe from Singapore to Nigeria, and it has brought the author a small fortune – not to mention a modest return to the publishers.'

School books, however, represented only half the educational department's activities. During the 1930s and '40s Heinemann's publishing had become increasingly focused on fiction, to the exclusion of those more general books which had always found a place in William Heinemann's lists. Even drama had been neglected. Hill and his colleagues now set about rectifying this situation. Edward Thompson started his Drama Library in 1948, and rapidly built up a list of reprints of classical and modern plays, culminating in the publication of entirely new works by hitherto unknown authors. In 1957 he was at Brighton attending the first night of a preview of a play called *Flowering Cherry*, by an unknown author, a teacher at Millfield School. Excited, Edward approached the author's agent, Peggy Ramsay, to acquire publication rights. 'Yes, darling', she said, 'the rights are free. I'll let you see the script.' The educational department published Robert Bolt's *Flowering Cherry* in 1958 and Bolt took a year off from school to try his hand as a full-time playwright. The result was *The Tiger and the Horse* and *A Man for All Seasons* – which turned out to be a real blockbuster. It sold over two million copies in the UK version, not to mention the overseas editions. In 1960 both plays came on in the West End: *The Tiger and the Horse* with Michael Redgrave at the Queen's, and *A Man for All Seasons* (1961) with Paul Scofield at the Globe – a triumph for a teacher on sabbatical leave, and quite a coup for an educational publisher, especially when *A Man for All Seasons* became an Oscar-winning film!

Meanwhile the educational department was doing some influential general publishing. As well as theatre books by writers such as John

Gielgud or Michael Redgrave, there were works of literary criticism – Robert Gittings's first major book, *John Keats, the Living Year*, being published in 1954. The range now extended to books on popular science, politics and sociology by new, unknown authors, some of whom were destined to become world-famous, and none of whom came via literary agents. Hill has described how he recruited Fred Hoyle to the Heinemann list: 'One day in 1951, Frere sent for me: "There's an astronomer fellow called Hoyle talking on the radio – marvellous stuff all about the Universe . . . you know – what you see when you put the cat out at night. . . . Can you get a book from him?" I said I would try. Assuming that it would be a waste of time to write him a letter, I drove to Cambridge, went to Hoyle's rooms in St John's College and knocked on the door. No reply. I entered and left a note on the table saying that I would return later. Feeling that Frere had sent me on a fool's errand, I now went round to Jesus College for tea and consolation with my old friend L. A. Pars, the mathematics tutor. Pars was at that time writing a highly specialized and expensive book, *The Calculus of Variations*, which I had gladly agreed to publish. It was bread upon the waters, and the return now came far sooner than I could have thought possible. Halfway through tea the phone rang; it was a friend of Pars, whom he addressed as 'Fred'. On impulse, I wrote on a piece of paper the words 'is that Fred Hoyle?' Pars nodded and went on talking. I then wrote 'Can you please give me an introduction?' Pars rose to the occasion. He told Fred that he had his publisher with him – a most valued friend whom Fred must certainly meet – and then handed me the phone. Fred, sounding like a junior J. B. Priestley with his deep Yorkshire voice, invited me to visit him at his home that evening. I hastened back to St John's, found my note still on Fred's table unopened, destroyed it, and drove out to the Hoyle residence in a nearby village. During the evening I formed a deep regard for Fred and his wife Barbara. It was the start of a close author-publisher relationship which was to last for the next thirty years.'

Hoyle's big guide to the Universe, *Frontiers of Astronomy*, came out in 1955, to be followed by other works of scientific popularization, and no fewer than fourteen works of science fiction, of which the first and probably the best was *The Black Cloud* (1957).

The educational department's *annus mirabilis* was, in fact, 1955, for it also saw the publication of R. T. McKenzie's *British Political Parties* – the product of years of unremitting research by a Canadian student at the

London School of Economics, who was also an accomplished TV political commentator. It was written, amazingly, as a Ph.D. thesis. Realizing the importance of the book, Hill rushed it into print, thereby enabling McKenzie to reverse the normal procedure: instead of submitting a successful thesis to the publisher, he submitted the proofs of his forth-coming book to the Ph.D. examiners. One of these was Professor Sir Denis Brogan, whose examiner's report commented: 'What McKenzie has done is of the first order of importance . . . the learning, acuteness and vivacity of the author make this one of the most important works of political science written in this country.'

The book's launch, which was held in 99 Great Russell Street, astonished the rest of the firm, accustomed though they were to pres-tigious literary occasions. Among the guests were no fewer than four previous or future Prime Ministers (Attlee, Wilson, Heath, Callaghan). There were past and future Cabinet Ministers galore (Benn, Boyle, Dalton, Crossman, Crosland, Foot, Gaitskell, Roy Jenkins, Woodrow Wyatt, etc.) and a glittering array of editors and political commentators, both British and American. This mêlée provided rich pickings for a sprightly article in *The Spectator*, written under the pseudonym 'Tapir', by the fledgling Bernard Levin.

How, it may be asked, did a small educational department secure such a major work in the face of the big firms, in particular Macmillan, who had bid strenuously for the book? The answer lay in the person of the department's erudite adviser, Donald MacRae, a native of the Island of Skye, who at the age of eight had contracted the habit of reading three books a day. He had been McKenzie's supervisor at the LSE, and he continued to act as Heinemann's Social Sciences consultant for twenty years or more – a period during which the educational business published a wide range of books on sociology, social history, economics and allied subjects. With authors and editors of the calibre of H. L. Beales (one of the two founding editors of Pelican Books) and his able pupil O.R. (later Lord) McGregor – who later headed the Royal Commission on the Press – and Claus Moser who wrote the classic *Survey Methods in Social Investigation* (1958) and later became Vice Chairman of Rothschilds, the educational department was making a considerable impact in a new publishing field.

By 1955, ten years after it had restarted, the educational department was firmly established as an innovative publisher of school books in

Science and English and of general books of literary and political importance, together with works of popular science. The annual publication rate had risen to 48 titles by 1955, and turnover had gone up from £37,000 at the end of paper rationing (1950) to £124,000 (1955) – from £400,000 to £1 million at 1987 prices.

Medical Company,
Loeb

After the war, the medical company suffered a crucial reverse. One morning in 1947, the first arrivals on the third floor of 99 Great Russell Street were greeted by the firm's blockmaker. A huge man, he was standing shaken on the landing exclaiming 'Poor Mr Cavander! Poor Mr Cavander!' as he pointed to the open door of the general medical office. On the floor inside was Leslie Cavander, the company's young general manager, dead of a heart attack. He had been in the job only two years, having come up through the Heinemann trade department with a high reputation. As a publisher, he had great potential, and was clearly on his way to the top. Had he survived, the future of Heinemann could well have been different.

He was succeeded at the medical company by Dwye Evans's brother Owen, who became managing director with Barney Abraham as executive chairman. The firm moved into more commodious premises next door at 100 Great Russell Street, and the balance of the publishing changed to more specifically medical texts, as in 1947, when G. Fulton Roberts's *The Rhesus Factor* first revealed this mysterious blood-group hazard to the world. In particular Owen Evans built up a strong nursing list, with the aid of Winifred Hector, who was both author and editor.

The medical list in the years 1945–60 reflected an era before 'high-tech' medicine, when antibiotics were still a novelty. But many of its authors were undoubtedly respected. There were, for example, further titles from Grantly Dick-Read including *Introduction to Motherhood* (1950) and *Antenatal Illustrated* (1955); he also wrote *No Time for Fear* (1955), an account of the author's journey in a caravan through Africa to investigate childbirth customs in primitive communities. Heinemann published a book describing his life's work, *Doctor Courageous* (1957) by A. Noyes Thomas. The same year also saw J. Johnston Abraham's own colourful autobiography, *A Surgeon's Journey*.

After the main company moved to Mayfair (see page 613), the medical company was established, together with Peter Davies, on the ground floor of a superb Georgian House, 23 Bedford Square.

The Loeb Classical Library continued to expand. By 1961 the number of volumes totalled 431. At the close of 1958 Charlotte Rowan Robinson retired as the library's 'secretary' (administrator) after thirty-two years' service. She was succeeded by Enid Hill, the wife of Alan Hill. W. H. D. Rouse had retired as editor in 1947 and died three years later. He was not replaced, L. A. Post and E. H. Warmington continuing as joint editors until the former retired in 1967. Warmington then continued as sole editor until 1979.

Boswell again
Leads the Biographies

Fiction still continued to dominate the list, but 1945–61 saw some notable general books, especially biographies, among them the very important series arising from the sensational discovery of several caches of James Boswell's personal journals, correspondence, working papers, and other documents, amounting to tens of thousands of items. Thirteen volumes created directly from this material had appeared by 1961, since when there have been eleven others. Even before this series Heinemann had begun to create something of a corner in Johnson and Boswell: the 1930s saw a new edition of a *Journal of a Tour to the Hebrides* (1936), set from the original manuscript, one of the early rediscovered items; it was edited by Frederick A. Pottle and Charles H. Bennett. Pottle also put together a slight, elegant volume titled *Boswell and the Girl from Botany Bay* (1938) about the help Boswell gave to a young woman who had escaped from the penal colony.

Sterling Professor of English at Yale, Pottle was editor-in-chief of what became known as the *Yale Editions of the Private Papers of James Boswell*, published by McGraw-Hill in America and by Heinemann in the UK and Commonwealth. It was another American, Lieut-Colonel Ralph H. Isham, who was mainly responsible for reassembling the papers during a search lasting nearly twenty-five years. Boswell had made careful plans during his lifetime to preserve all his manuscripts and correspondence, but his family, who disapproved of his friendship with Johnson and were understandably apprehensive of the frankness with which he revealed his private life in his journals, kept quiet about their literary legacy and it lay forgotten for over a century. In 1905 it was inherited by Boswell's great-great-grandson, Lord Talbot de Malahide, who removed the papers to Malahide Castle, near Dublin. Some were preserved in an ebony cabinet but the greater part were relegated to different storing places in the rambling old castle and were again forgotten. Then in 1925 Professor Tinker of Yale, while preparing an edition of Boswell's correspondence, was shown the letters in the ebony cabinet and two years later Colonel Isham arranged to purchase them. When a further lot of papers was discovered by accident in an old croquet box at Malahide, Isham bought these as well and after a thorough search of the castle discovered and bought further bundles. Meanwhile yet another discovery took place in Scotland at the home of one of Boswell's executors, Fettercairn House, Kincardineshire. A box in the library was found to contain a few Boswell letters and, following up this clue, a search of damp lumber-filled attics and a nursery cupboard led to another large cache including Boswell's journal for the year of his first meeting with Johnson. Isham, who had purchased Lord Talbot's rights to all the papers, was determined to add the new find to his collection, but to establish ownership necessitated a law suit and the purchase of a half-interest in the papers from Cumberland Infirmary as residuary legatee of Boswell's great-granddaughter. Finally during the war the second floor of a decayed outbuilding at Malahide whose staircase had long since collapsed was found to contain yet more letters and manuscripts, which were also bought by Isham. A detailed account of the fate of the Boswell Papers and of Isham's success in rediscovering them at the cost of his near-impoverishment was published by Heinemann in *The Treasure of Auchinleck* (1975) by David Buchanan.

Long before this romantic treasure hunt was ended Heinemann had signed a contract for the publishing rights with Colonel Isham and paid him a sizeable advance, but nothing came of this. Eventually Isham, keen to keep all the papers united and available to scholars, decided to sell the whole lot to Yale, and the firm agreed to waive their rights on the return of the advance. Presumably because of their early connection with the project Heinemann were obvious candidates to be publishers in partnership with McGraw-Hill of the much larger collection. Under the skilful chairmanship of Professor Pottle a scholarly team assembled the thousands of documents into a series of immensely readable volumes. The first was *Boswell's London Journal 1762–63* (1950) which described his first year in the capital, his meetings with peers and prostitutes, the sermons he heard and how he got drunk, watched cock-fights and executions, contracted venereal disease, and first met Johnson. It was franker and even more human than Pepys and soon became a bestseller. Succeeding volumes dealt with Boswell's journeys to Holland, 1763–64, (1952) and on the Grand Tour to Germany and Switzerland, 1764

(1953), to Italy, Corsica, and France, 1765–66 (1955), and the tour of the Hebrides with Johnson, 1775 (1963); there was also a volume of documents, letters, dialogues and essays relating to Joshua Reynolds (1952); *Boswell in Search of a Wife, 1766–69* (1957); *Boswell for the Defence, 1769–74* (1960); *Boswell – the Ominous Years, 1774–76* (1963); *Boswell in Extremes, 1776–78* (1971); *Boswell, the Applause of the Jury, 1782–85* (1981); *Boswell, the English Experiment, 1785–89* (1987); and *Boswell, the Great Biographer, 1789–95* (1990). There was also one other volume in the series – *Boswell, the Laird of Auchinleck, 1778–82* – which, because of what must now be seen as a deplorable and short-sighted decision, was not published by Heinemann. It was left to McGraw-Hill to distribute it in the UK and Commonwealth.

For collectors there was a parallel series of limited editions, finely produced and containing additional material. Their sale was small and progressively got smaller. There were also volumes of what were known as the Research Edition: scholarly editions of Boswell's copious papers.

There can be no doubt that the Boswell venture marked a high point in the firm's history. It meant a substantial outlay of money and effort and, specially in its later stages, it could not have been very profitable, and yet it was the kind of venture that adds lustre to an imprint and also the goodwill which attracts new authors. It was rounded off by two other splendid works: a major biography by F. A. Pottle – *James Boswell, the Earlier Years, 1740–69* (1966) – and its continuation by Frank Brady – *James Boswell, the Later Years, 1769–95* (1984). Separately from the Yale series, another great Johnson expert, James L. Clifford, wrote a well-received biography of the *Young Samuel Johnson* (1955) followed by *Dictionary Johnson* (1982), which described the Great Cham's middle years. Heinemann also published Hesketh Pearson's *Johnson and Boswell* (1958), a racy, entertaining account of both their lives which drew particularly on the accounts left by Mrs Thrale, Fanny Burney, and other contemporaries. All in all Boswell and Johnson made a very substantial contribution to the list.

Outstanding among other post-war biographies were two volumes of autobiography by Richard Church: *Over the Bridge* (1955) and *The Golden Sovereign* (1957). Their reception by the critics was widespread and ecstatic – to quote but two: the first volume, said *The Spectator*, was '. . . a fine, well-written work that stands high as a testament of the human spirit's triumph . . . it will always remain unique of its sort, and certainly become part of our literature'; *The Times* declared that the second volume provided '. . . a wonderful revelation of a poet's mind – one of the best we have ever had – that this volume is to be most highly prized. . . . Nothing has been more heartening in our literary life than the emergence of this shy, sensitive reserved soul to bestsellerdom and fame. It is a triumph of integrity.'

In the 1950–60s biographies, particularly if they were competent, solid and readable, were fairly safe propositions for any established publisher. The libraries were usually good for orders totalling two to three thousand copies, quantities which by the 1980s would have been exceptionally high. In most years Heinemann included two or three in its list. Three competent biographies came, for example, from Reginald Pound: *Arnold Bennett* (1952); *Selfridge* (1960), the founder of the Oxford Street store; and *The Englishman: a biography of Sir Alfred Munnings* (1962) – that most Establishment of all painters, who, having defeated Augustus John for the presidency of the Royal Academy, used it as a platform for virulent attacks on 'modern art'. Pound also wrote an enjoyable history of *The Strand Magazine: 1891–1950* (1966). The prolific H. Montgomery Hyde was another source of sound biographies such as *The Life of Sir Edward Carson* (1953); *The Strange Death of Lord Castlereagh* (1959); *Sir Patrick Hastings: his Life and Cases* (1960). (The firm had already published Hastings's own autobiography in 1948, followed by two collections of his cases; and *Lord Reading: the Life of Rufus Isaacs, the first Marquess of Reading* (1967) – who among other offices had been Lord Chief Justice, Attorney-General, Viceroy of India, and Foreign Secretary.) Hyde also wrote for the firm *A History of Pornography* (1964) and *The Other Love* (1970), an historical and contemporary survey of homosexuality in Britain.

Show business could also be counted on to supply good if not best-selling biographies and autobiographies. Among them were *Sunshine and Shadow* (1956), Mary Pickford's story of her life; Richard Findlater's *Michael Redgrave* (1956); Frances Donaldson's life of her playwright father *Freddy Lonsdale* (1957); Fred Astaire's autobiographical *Steps in Time* (1960); and the rumbustious *My Wicked, Wicked Ways* (1960) by Hollywood's Errol Flynn. Considerably different but in those days far more sensational than it would be today was *Roberta Cowell's Story* (1954) in which she described in full detail how she/he changed from a married man, a Spitfire pilot and racing driver into a woman. Claire Tomalin, then editorial secretary, recalls being sent downstairs to greet her. 'A huge blonde handed me an enormous, heavy case to carry up the three flights of stairs to our office. I was quite small and pregnant and Cowell was an ex-RAF man, but I suppose determined to prove his or her femininity. It made me laugh.'

Different again was *I Married the World* (1955) by Elsa Maxwell, the society hostess who operated among the fashionable cosmopolitan celebrities in New York. Mary McCarthy belongs also in the categories of fiction, essays and criticism, and travel, but her *Memories of a Catholic Girlhood* (1957) must be mentioned here. This is not so true of three books by Henry Miller which could as easily have been categorized as travel or topography, though most of his work is essentially autobio-graphical. The first, *Big Sur and the Oranges of Hieronymus Bosch* (1958), is both about California itself and his life there and his friends in-cluding the 'Devil of Paradise'. Because of the difficulties he had experienced at the hands of censors, Miller was understandably touchy over cuts. When Jonathan Price, the Heinemann editor, felt it would be wise to cut and amend some references to the French publisher Maurice Girodias, Miller reacted fiercely: 'I must say that it rouses my ire to be presented with this sort of *fait accompli*. As in the case of the previous deletions and changes of wording, I have had no choice but to submit. All this might have been avoided had my book been read carefully in the beginning. Had I then been presented with the proper choice I would have said: "Don't print the book!" Now I can only say: "This must never happen again with any of my works!" Much as I would like to be published by a house as reputable as yours, I do not want to be published in expurgated editions. Certainly not by English or American publishers, with whom I have waged a life-long battle. Every time these "mistakes" or "accidents" occur I am obliged to answer letters from astonished or outraged readers who know that I am against this sort of thing and who wonder why I "compromised". The implication is that I did it for money. Whereas the truth is that I have literally sacrificed a fortune in order to achieve freedom of expression.

'I understand that your firm has waged an heroic fight with the powers that be to obtain greater freedom [he must have been referring to the obscene libel action described in the next chapter]. It may therefore strike you as unkind of me to make such a protest. The thought occurs to me that, in order to clear your own name as well as mine, you might insert a sticker on the title page of each copy to this effect: "We regret to inform the readers that the modifications and deletions of the original text were imposed on us in conformance with the benighted laws and regulations concerning book publication in the British Empire. We offer our apologies to author and reader alike. William Heinemann Ltd".'[1] It was agreed that a somewhat modified notice should be printed in the prelims.

Big Sur . . . was followed by *The Colossus of Maroussi* (1960 – though Secker & Warburg had published it originally in 1942), about his remarkable stay in Greece during the year when war was breaking out all over Europe. Then came *The Air-Conditioned Nightmare* (1962), his caustic view of American civilization on his return after ten years in Europe, much of it being straight travelogue full of hilarious and biting comments. It was decided, however, that it would be too risky to issue Miller's – at that time – notorious *Tropic of Cancer*. So far as Heinemann was concerned, the Henry Miller canon was rounded off with *The Best of Henry Miller* (1960), edited by Lawrence Durrell.

Among other titles that deserve mention in this section were Sir Philip Gibbs's autobiography *The Pageant of the Years* (1946); Dominic Behan's *Teems of Times and Happy Returns* (1961); and the ex-MP Peter Baker's account of his seven years in prison. Some measure of selectivity being inevitable, I feel that particular attention must be given to the two imposing biographies by Richard Aldington. The first was *Wellington* (1946). With good reason Frere sent it to Georgette Heyer for a report, on the strength of her knowledge of the Iron Duke gained in writing *An Infamous Army* and *The Spanish Bride*. She took a lot of pains and her criticisms, mostly minor, were sent to Aldington, then in Hollywood. At first he was so upset by them that he wanted the book to be postponed, but when he had studied her report carefully, he relented, though he was still bitter: 'In spite of her confident air and apparent array of facts, Miss Heyer is not to be taken seriously. . . .'[2] The whole thing is of course ridiculous, a piece of impudence on the part of a writer who wanted to do a life of Wellington herself. The book should never have been shown to her in the first place and in the second I should never have been worried by her nonsense.'[3] Aldington was obviously overreacting, but one wonders why Frere broke the normal rule of not revealing a reader's identity. The book was, however, a great success and was awarded the James Tait Black Memorial Prize by Edinburgh University for the best biography of 1946. Aldington, then in Paris, celebrated the occasion with one of his typical heavily joky letters to Frere: 'I enclose the haggis-eater's letter from whilk you will perceive he makes an ex-parte statement to the effect that the punds and bawbees are not subject to seizure or spoliation by the English King's taxes. If, without going nuts, you are able to transfer the said punds and bawbees to ane humble petitioner woning in ci-devant kingdom of France, then up wi' the bonnets of bonny Dundee. If ye canna, we must e'en dree our wierd, as the cow said when she kickit o'er the milkpail'[4].

The other Aldington biography was *Portrait of a Genius, But. . . .* (1950), a life of D. H. Lawrence. It coincided with the reprint of eleven of Lawrence's works in the Heinemann Pocket Edition, to many of which Aldington had written new introductions. Aldington, who had known Lawrence well, aimed to provide a straightforward account of his strange and vehement life, but he found it a challenge '. . . to try to win sympathy for a guy with so many lousy aspects to his character'[5]. In another letter he told Frere that 'the re-writing will not be such work as the collecting and arranging the very contradictory material. Consider how much harder Lawrence is than Wellington. For instance, if someone said: "Duke, isn't it true the Spanish generals were sometimes good soldiers?", you can absolutely depend on it that he would always reply: "Stuff! They were no such thing." But if you put the same question to Lawrence, a variety of answers would come at different times according to his mood. He might utter any of the following replies: "(1) Stuff! They were no such thing. (2) Spanish generals are the best soldiers in the world. (3) I feel in my solar plexus that Spanish generals are all obscene. (4) If you go on talking like that about Spanish generals, Richard, in a year's time you'll be in a lunatic asylum – mark my words. (5) There are no such things as Spanish generals." You see the difficulty, but it is getting solved.'[6] The biography received a record number of reviews, many of which pleased Aldington, though he wrote savagely to Frere about adverse comments: 'The only sour notes so far are from Quennell and C. Sykes – the former an Eliot bootlicker, the latter a Sitwell ditto. . . . Someone sent me a little high-bruff periodical called *Nine* with a Faber Ad. of all Tom Eliot's stuff (being a director he can keep it in print!) and I thought: How paltry, how jejune, how "lit'ry" compared with that immense vital outpouring of DHL. What the hell does it matter that there are bad and boring passages in him? How about Titus Andronicus and Leviticus?'[7]. Frere did his best to calm him down: 'I do not think anything can come of sending that blast to the Lord Rothermere who, even if he could read, which I doubt, would not know what the devil it was all about. The Lady Rothermere, who dictates the paper's policy to the point where she is known as "The Daily

Female", would be influenced by other considerations. You probably know that the gentleman in question is known around the town as "Lady Rothermere's Fan". There are other ways of dealing with him. . . ."[8]

It was only five years later that Heinemann published what was described as the 'definitive biography' of Lawrence: *The Intelligent Heart* (1955) by Harry T. Moore, a great American Lawrence authority. It was copiously documented and very thoroughly researched; a revised version was issued in 1974 under the title of *The Priest of Love*. Moore also edited and introduced a new and much expanded *The Collected Letters of D. H. Lawrence* (1962).

Establishment Publishers – War and Politics

Like most substantial publishers Heinemann published its quota of non-fiction as well as novels about the Second World War. Among the most successful were the books by C. E. Lucas Phillips who had himself served with distinction in both World Wars and was a brigadier, though he always described himself as an amateur soldier. His skill was to combine soundly researched military history, as in his pre-war *Cromwell's Captains* (1938), with a breezy style that brought alive the fear and violence, the heat and dust, as well as the excitement of warfare. The first was *Cockleshell Heroes* (1956) about the Royal Marine raid in canoes on Bordeaux in December 1942 when only two survived. It sold 24,000 copies and was followed by *The Greatest Raid of All* (1958) on St Nazaire by army commandos and RN forces in 'little ships'; and *Alamein* (1962), the major engagement in the North African desert war, in which Lucas Phillips commanded a regiment. There were four others. All his books sold well, ranging between 11,000 and 15,000 copies. There was also *Escape of the Amethyst* (1957), about the RN frigate which ran the gauntlet of Communist guns on the Yangtze. A second career as a writer stemmed from Lucas Phillips's passion for gardening. He wrote four extremely popular books about plants starting with *The Small Garden* (1952) which after successful publication as a hardback remained at the end of the 1980s a standard text in paperback.

Vivid reportage was also to be found in John Steinbeck's *Once There Was a War* (1959), a collection of despatches sent back from England, North Africa, and the landing beaches of Sicily and Italy. As was to be expected, his sympathy with the ordinary man in uniform gave this book a special edge. Very different in character were the two long volumes about the first year of the war by Major-General Sir Edward Spears, husband of Mary Borden, the author, with the overall title *Prelude to Dunkirk* (1954): *vol. I, Assignment to Catastrophe*; *vol. II, Fall of France*. Spears had earlier won a reputation as a military·historian with *Liaison 1914* (1930), which was considered a classic. The new work was written from the viewpoint of someone who had participated at the highest level, sitting day by day with Reynaud, Pétain, Weygand, and Darlan, helplessly watching France being raped. He played a major role in bringing de Gaulle to England. The same events were also covered in *Recalled to Service* (1952) by General Maxime Weygand, the French Commander-in-Chief. He gave an hour-by-hour account of his efforts, his plans, his orders, his interviews with the French cabinet and with Churchill; he also described how after the débâcle he had spent eleven unhappy weeks assisting the Vichy government and his mission to Africa in order to reorganize the French army and keep the Germans out. The book ended with his arrest by the Gestapo. There was also *The Memoirs of Lord Ismay* (1960), Churchill's staff officer and his personal representative on the Chiefs of Staff Committee.

Heinemann's publishing of Establishment memoirs extended also to America with titles such as *Crusade in Europe* (1948) by General Dwight Eisenhower, the Supreme Commander of the Allied Forces. It appears he actually wrote this himself, based on his voluminous wartime diaries, and he is certainly frank, for example over his difference with Churchill over the American plan to invade Southern France which Churchill thought would weaken the Allied forces in Italy, and in the exactness of his criticisms of his various commanders. It sold well and its success opened the way later for his Presidential memoirs, *The White House Years: vol. I, Mandate for Change* (1963); *vol. II, Waging Peace* (1966). Two biographical studies of Eisenhower were also published: *Three Years with Eisenhower* (1946) by Harry C. Butcher and *American Man of Destiny* (1952) by Kevin McCann. The American war efforts were completed by yet two more

[395]

brass-hat authors: *Decision in Germany* (1950) by General Lucius D. Clay, Commander-in-Chief of all US forces in Europe, and *MacArthur, 1941–51: Victory in the Pacific* (1956) by Major-General Charles A. Willoughby and John Chamberlain.

Not all the war books were at this exalted level. One of the most successful and dramatic was *Maquis* (1945) by George Millar. As soon as he had read it Frere wrote that 'it is a long time since I could be as enthusiastic about a manuscript'[9]. The author had been parachuted into occupied France to liaise with the French Resistance, working and fighting with several groups in the Besançon area, keeping in radio contact with London to arrange for supplies to be dropped. *Maquis* was followed by *Horned Pigeon* (1946), about Millar's earlier service with the British Desert Corps, his capture by the enemy and escape across occupied Europe. Later Millar wrote several novels, a book about the discovery of the Amazon, and two accounts of his voyages in small craft around the Mediterranean. The Battle of Arnhem and hiding with the Dutch Resistance were the subjects of *Surgeon at Arms* (1958) by Daniel Paul* (Lipmann Kessel), an orthopaedic surgeon attached to the British paratroops, an unusual and gory feature being descriptions of working on casualties in the operating theatre of a Dutch hospital which kept changing hands as the battle raged all round it.

Aspects of the enemy were studied in three books: in *The S.S. 1933–45 – Alibi of a Nation* (1956) Gerald Reitlinger debunked the excuse that it was the terror rule of the SS and the Gestapo which alone was responsible for the Nazi racial murder. With detailed documentation he showed how the entire administrative and transport machinery of the German state was organized systematically to achieve mass genocide. Similarly Reitlinger dealt with the Gestapo and its peculiar limitations and the rival competing agencies of the German military intelligence. In *Doctor Goebbels* (1960) Roger Manvell and Heinrich Fraenkel used unpublished letters and Goebbels's own diary as a Nazi agent to present him as the architect of totalitarian propaganda and possibly the most intelligent and dangerous member of the Nazi hierarchy. Insights of the Fascist mind were conveyed by *Ciano's Diaries, 1939–43* (1947). Their record of the comings and goings of the Axis leaders suggests that

---

* (Co-authored, and in fact written, by John St John) – *Editor's note.*

Mussolini's son-in-law and foreign minister was in favour of so-called Italian neutrality. Ciano may have been writing 'for the record', to avoid guilt, but he did provide a lurid, even at times entertaining, record. Goering, for example, is described wearing a great sable coat, 'something between a motorist of 1906 and a high-grade courtesan at the opera'. Above all, though, he gives a picture of the mentalities and delusions that plunge nations into war.

There was no doubt that politics played some part in shaping the list. When Lord Kemsley wanted to serialize parts of Somerset Maugham's *Ten Novels and their Authors* (1954), Willie told him that it would have to depend entirely on Heinemann's publishing plans. Reporting this to Frere, Willie wrote that Kemsley 'quite understood that, but left me with the impression that he was prepared to square you. Of course as a member of the Labour Party you must know that every man has his price. I myself think that very natural, and only wonder that people seem to value themselves at so inadequate a sum.'[10] Certainly Frere was an early supporter of CND and as he had worked closely during the war with Ernest Bevin in the Ministry and came to know the Labour leaders, Maugham was probably not making a joke. In any case Frere certainly used his Labour contacts in the interests of the firm and enrolled several members of the Labour Establishment as authors. The first book was during the war, a selection of Ernest Bevin's speeches, *The Job to be Done* (1942), accepted by Frere in the teeth of strong opposition from Charles Evans. Then Francis Williams, the Labour Party's Press expert who was also the author of three Heinemann novels, wrote *Press, Parliament and People* (1946) and *The Triple Challenge* (1948), which discussed the future of a Socialist Britain. In the same year Roy Jenkins entered Parliament and contributed *Mr Attlee: an Interim Biography* (1948) and followed it with *The Pursuit of Progress* (1953), a critical analysis of the achievement and prospect of the Labour Party, in which he called for a substantial extension of public ownership and for more careful planning, among other things, as the basis for 'a new axis of advance towards Socialism'. Jenkins also wrote *Mr Balfour's Poodle* (1954), a phrase coined by Lloyd George to describe the House of Lords and used by Jenkins as the title for a scholarly account of the struggle between the Lords and the government of Mr Asquith when Balfour was leader of the Conservative opposition.

The Left of the Labour Party was also included with a hard-hitting book by Aneurin Bevan, *In Place of Fear* (1952). He was then involved in a harsh quarrel with the leadership following the defeat of Attlee's second government. It amounted to Bevan's political testament and provided a typically coherent restatement of the radical Socialist platform. It was enriched with glimpses of his own life and experience in local government as well as a cabinet minister. When it was launched at a crowded Press conference at 99 Great Russell Street, Reuters described the book as 'hurling a challenge into the arena before the wreckage of the last battle has been cleared away and making no attempt to smooth the troubles of the British Socialists'. Known in the book trade as *In Place of Frere*, a trade paperback at 6s. was published simultaneously with the main 10s.6d. edition, an unusual step in those days.

As a counterbalance to Bevan was the modest autobiography of Clement Attlee, *As it Happened* (1954). It was clearly a great coup and the announcement in the catalogue reached new heights of encomium: ' *"Here is a great Englishman!"*. This will surely be the verdict of any reader who brings to this autobiography the semblance of a fair and open mind ... in spite of the author's modesty great qualities shine through these pages: *moral and physical courage, a determined sense of duty, tenacity of purpose, unswerving honesty, enormous capacity for work and a selfless devotion to ideals.* Such qualities are good to read about in any man, and above all in a Prime Minister of Great Britain.' The autobiography was supplemented by *A Prime Minister Remembers* (1961), collated by Francis Williams from a series of tape-recorded conversations and private papers. There was also an 'authoritative' biography of *Stafford Cripps* (1949) by an American, Eric Estorick, published at a time when Cripps exercised a key influence on the British economy, but emphasizing his role as a foremost Churchman, the effect of his pre-war expulsion from the Labour Party, and his wartime ambassadorship in Moscow. This group of books concluded with the first volume of *The Life and Times of Ernest Bevin* (1960) by Alan Bullock, a major work which in effect traced the rise of the trade union movement from the days when its leaders were regarded as irresponsible agitators to the point where Churchill invited Bevin to become a member of the war cabinet. The second volume appeared seven years later and a third, *Ernest Bevin as Foreign Secretary*, in 1983.

That Heinemann was in no danger of becoming a tool of the Left was shown by the publication of *I Believed* (1950) by Douglas Hyde, one of the most literate and moving of ex-Communist exposés. Without attempting to blacken his old colleagues he described how he had first been won over to Communist ideals and then how step by step he learned to cheat, lie, spy, confess and surrender utterly to Party direction, because the ends justified the means. After five years of battling with doubts he resigned as news-editor of the *Daily Worker* and was received into the Catholic Church. His confession did well, at one point selling more than 3,000 copies a day.

At a more philosophical level there were five political titles by Arthur M. Schlesinger, Junior. Among them were *The Politics of Freedom* (1950) and three hefty volumes of *The Age of Roosevelt* (1957, 1960, 1961).

From Poetry and Drama to Science and Sex

To prevent this chapter from degenerating into an annotated catalogue, only a relatively few further non-fiction titles will be covered, those of special interest or by new authors who were to become important additions to the list.

Few new poets were enlisted during 1945–61, but there were eight further collections of verse by John Masefield; one of verse and two of essays by Richard Church; and five more volumes by the Lebanese poet-mystic Kahlil Gibran. Richard Aldington contributed two anthologies: *The Religion of Beauty* (1950) which consisted of writings by such 'acolytes and priests of the high temple of Art' as Rossetti, Ruskin, Morris, and Pater; and a thousand pages of *Poetry of the English Speaking World* (1947) which was the subject of a devastating review by A. D. Hope, the leading Australian poet, in the Australian literary journal *Meanjin* (vol. 7, No. 2, 1948). Hope's objection was that the book, despite its title, omitted work by Australian, New Zealand, and Canadian poets. Aldington felt that the review was libellous and that both he and Heinemann had been accused of fraud. The firm's solicitors were instructed to issue a protest and demand an apology. *Meanjin's* editor was none other than Clem Christesen who was also about to become Heinemann's Australian manager (see page 317). Christesen refused to apologize, but offered

Aldington space in the next issue to refute the charges. The offer was not taken up.

Among newcomers to the poetry list were two outstanding authors published with the Educational department. First, Robert Gittings, who, as well as contributing six volumes of his own poems and plays, wrote the first of his influential studies of Keats, *John Keats: the Living Year* (1954) which concentrated on the astonishing period from September 1818 when most of the greatest poems were written; he produced new evidence to show the importance in the poet's life of the hitherto shadowy Mrs Isabella Jones. Gittings pursued his literary sleuth-work in three other books about Keats, including *The Mask of Keats* (1956). The other newcomer was James Reeves who, as well as his own poems, brought to the Educational department's list books of criticism and successful anthologies, totalling thirteen volumes by 1960; they included *The Modern Poet's World* (1957), *The Everlasting Circle* (1960), and *The Wandering Moon* (1950) for children. Reeves also played an important part in the development of the educational list and was editor of the firm's Poetry Bookshelf series. Other poets included Laurence Whistler, with four volumes including *The World's Room* (1949) with decorations by his talented brother Rex; G. Rostrevor Hamilton, one of the 'civil servant' poets with six volumes of poems as well as books of 'epigrams, satires and dramatic sketches'; and Bryan Guinness with *Reflexions* (1947) and *Collected Poems, 1927–55* (1956).

By no means the least distinguished entry on the poetry list was Sylvia Plath's first collection, *The Colossus and Other Poems* (1960). James Michie, who took her on, described her to me as 'a quiet, apple-cheeked, shy, New England girl'. In a letter to her mother and sister she tells how she had a meeting with Michie in the York Minster (the 'French pub') in Soho where she signed the contract on the counter: 'Amaze of amaze. I was so hardened to rejections that I waited till I actually signed the contract (with the usual 10 per cent royalties) before writing you. They do very few, very few poets at Heinemann and will do a nice book. . . .'[11] A few days later she wrote that 'my obliging editor at Heinemann said to tell him my birthday and he will try to get my publication as close to that as possible. The gallantry of the British! . . .'[12] (*The Colossus* actually appeared during her birthday week.) Heinemann also published her novel *The Bell Jar* (1963) written under the pseudonym of Victoria Lucas. The editorial department were quick to value her genius, but, when due to have lunch to discuss her next book, she never turned up. It was the day she committed suicide. It is depressing to record that the rights in *The Colossus* were later handed over to Fabers.

The drama list continued to flourish. Talented newcomers joined the established playwrights, among whom were the astonishingly prolific Noël Coward with ten new plays, including *Peace in Our Time* (1947), *Nude with Violin* (1957), and *Quadrille* (1952); with three more volumes of his *Play Parade* (1950, 1954, 1958) which contained nineteen plays; a further instalment of his autobiography, *Future Indefinite* (1954); four volumes of his short stories; a book of lyrics (1965); and a novel, *Pomp and Circumstance* (1960). Clemence Dane contributed two more plays – *Call Home the Heart* (1947) and *Eighty in the Shade* (1959). Seven of Somerset Maugham's short stories were issued with accompanying film scripts by R. C. Sherriff and Noel Langley – *Quartet* (1948) and *Trio* (1950). Graham Greene wrote three plays – *The Living Room* (1953), *The Potting Shed* (1958), and *The Complaisant Lover* (1959). There were half a dozen more from Emlyn Williams, including *Trespass* (1947) and *Accolade* (1951). Dodie Smith followed her pre-war *Autumn Crocus, Dear Octopus*, and other plays with *Letter from Paris* (1954), based on a Henry James novel, and *The Hundred and One Dalmatians* (1956) which was turned into a hugely successful Walt Disney film; later she wrote a number of novels and a recollection of her childhood in Manchester. Among other plays that demand mention were Enid Bagnold's *The Chalk Garden* (1956); R. C. Sherriff's *The White Carnation* (1952); Lesley Storm's *Roar Like a Dove* (1958); John Mortimer's *The Wrong Side of the Park* (1960); and the collected plays of John Whiting (1957) and William Douglas Home (1958).

There were also books about acting, production, and theatrical criticism, such as Elmer Rice's *The Living Theatre* (1960); Mander and Mitchenson's *The Artist and the Theatre* (1954); Michel Saint-Denis's *Theatre – the Rediscovery of Style* (1960), and two books by Michael Redgrave: *The Actor's Ways and Means* (1953) and *Mask or Face – Reflections in an Actor's Mirror* (1958). He also wrote a novel, *The Mountebank's Tale* (1959).

Music has never featured strongly on the Heinemann list, but here again the Educational department broke new ground when 1961 saw a sudden brief flowering with the publication of the *Harvard Dictionary of Music* compiled by Willi Apel, accompanied by a junior version, the

Harvard Brief Dictionary of Music compiled by Willi Apel and Ralph T. Daniel. Two other music books were published in the same year: *Talking About – Symphonies* by Antony Hopkins and *Henry Purcell and the Restoration Theatre* by Robert E. Moore.

By contrast the visual arts were treated proudly with the publication of three well-illustrated series: The Ars Mundi, selling at only 7*s.*6*d.* each, with at least thirteen volumes on Degas, Rodin, Brueghel, Picasso, *et al.*; secondly, The Hyperion Press Art Books at 25*s.* to 30*s.* each, with an accompanying miniature series, that included volumes on Renoir, Van Gogh, Veronese, Goya, and others; thirdly, a more sumptuous, expensive series (£5 5*s.*–£6 6*s.*) on great Italian artists such as Canaletto and Guardi. There was also *Eight European Artists* (1954), edited by Felix H. Man; Derek Hudson on *Arthur Rackham – his life and work* (1960); Fleur Cowles on *The Case for Salvador Dali* (1959), and Martin Butlin on *The Works of William Blake in the Tate Gallery* (1958). A successful attempt to revive the art of book illustration for adults was undertaken with a new edition of *The Forsyte Saga* for which Anthony Gross was commissioned to provide twelve full-page litho illustrations in six colours, twenty-four drawings in black and white, and a full complement of chapter heads and tail pieces. Similarly Graham Sutherland drew a set of lithographic decorations for a commemorative edition of *Cakes and Ale* to mark Somerset Maugham's eightieth birthday.

The number of sports books was likewise expanded. Titles inherited from Naldrett Press were taken over from the World's Work and included a series published for the Football Association: *The F.A. Year Book* and *The F.A. Book for Boys*, which came out annually for many years; also official coaching manuals by Walter Winterbottom, the England team's manager, which became bestsellers. Similar cricket books, issued on behalf of the MCC, were continually reprinted. The success of these and other titles for other sporting bodies led to the appointment of John Arlott as an adviser and a whole series of sports books such as Jack Fingleton's *Masters of Cricket* (1958); J. M. Kilburn's *Cricket Decade* (1969); Clive Gammon's *Hook, Line and Spinner* (1959); Tom Scott's *Golf with the Experts* (1959); E. W. Swanton's *West Indies Revisited* (1960); W. R. Loader's *Testament of a Runner* (1960 – reissued 1988); P. A. Ward-Thomas's *Masters of Golf* (1961); Julian Holland's *Spurs, the Double* (1961); and several reports on cricket by John Arlott himself – to mention but a few.

The Heinemann tradition of publishing travel books was well main-

J. B. Priestley, W. S. Maugham, and A. S. Frere at a Kingswood garden party

Maire Lynd at a party in 1935 at
99 Great Russell Street with J. B. Morton ('Beachcomber')

A Press launch for *In Place of Fear* by Aneurin Bevan
at 99 Great Russell Street in 1952 (A. D. Evans, the author, A. S. Frere)

tained. Thirteen books about far-away places came from Willard Price with titles such as *The Amazing Amazon* (1952), *Journey by Junk* (1954), *The Son of Heaven: the Problem of the Mikado* (1945), *Incredible Africa* (1961), *Tropic Adventure* (1949). The armchair traveller was also ably catered for by Robert Payne who wrote several books about China and elsewhere; also novels about exotic places, such as *The Great Mogul* (1959), *Singapore River* (1942), and *The Lord Comes* (1948) based on the life of Buddha. The mountaineer, Wilfrid Noyce, contributed *South Col: One Man's Adventure of the Ascent of Everest* (1954), *Climbing the Fish's Tail* (1957) also about the Himalayas, *The Climber's Fireside Book* (1964), and various other books. From Europe came Mary McCarthy's elegant *The Stones of Florence* (1959) and *Venice Observed* (1961). Ian Niall had already written three sound novels before he broke through with *The Poacher's Handbook* (1950). This long-selling title with woodcuts by Barbara Greg was described as being 'for the man with the hare-pocket and the boy with the snare'. It heralded an excellent series of his books about the remote British countryside such as *The Fowler's World* (1968), *The Gamekeeper* (1965), *Trout from the Hills* (1961), and *Wild Life of Field and Hedgeside* (1970).

Sex and marriage continued to be catered for with three books from Eustace Chesser, the best known being *Is Chastity Outmoded?* (1960); with Maxine Davis's *Sex and the Adolescent* (1959) and her two books about sexual responsibility. O. R. MacGregor wrote about *Divorce in England* (1957) and James Hemming about *Problems of Adolescent Girls* (1969).

This inevitably untidy chapter ends with an incongruous handful of authors who for a complex of reasons cannot be consigned to the Appendix. First there was William Sargant's influential *Battle for the Mind* (1957), described as a physiology of conversion and brain-washing. An orphan title came from G. M. Trevelyan, *The Seven Years of William IV* (1952), the text closely married to sixty-two cartoons by the contemporary John Doyle; a limited edition of 350 copies at £6 6s. was issued in association with the Avalon Press. The conjunction of Christmas Humphreys's classic *Zen Buddhism* (1949) with Norman Douglas's *Venus in the Kitchen* (1952), a selection of aphrodisiac recipes 'likely to revive the fading ardours of middle age', indicates the catholic taste of Heinemann's selectors; as does the series of seven titles from the American humorist S. J. Perelman, e.g., *Acres and Pains* (1948), *A Child's Garden of Curses* (1951), *The Rising Gorge* (1962).

Lastly, and perhaps fittingly, this chapter ends with H. G. Wells, who at the end of his life came back once more on to the Heinemann list with what was really a pamphlet, *Mind at the End of its Tether* (1945). Its extreme pessimism undoubtedly owed something to his final illness, but it seemed to contradict all the ebullience with which he had been popularly associated. He was convinced, it appeared, that the extinction of man was certain: '*Our* universe is not merely bankrupt; there remains no dividend at all; it has not simply liquidated, it is going clean out of existence, leaving not a wrack behind. The attempt to trace a pattern of any sort is absolutely futile.'[13] In the same year Curtis Brown, his agents, told Frere that Wells was dying but wanted to see him at his house in Hanover Terrace, Regents Park, where he had lived throughout the war. When Frere entered Wells's bedroom, he was greeted with: 'Frere, my boy, Heinemanns published my first book. I've just finished what will be my last and I want you to publish this also. For the first time in my life I don't want any advance. Will you take it unread?' Frere agreed and that was the end of the interview. This was *The Happy Turning* (1945), another pamphlet, much more benign, in which Wells used dreams to express ideas and his views on life. The narrative is frequently interrupted with morsels of autobiography, the airing of prejudices, and the outbursts of an old man's petulance. Jesus Christ makes an appearance and Wells enables even Him to let His hair down.

Obscene Libel –
Frere in the
Criminal Dock

The novel which landed Frere in the dock at the Old Bailey was *The Image and the Search* (1953) by Walter Baxter, but what triggered the criminal prosecution for obscene libel was undoubtedly a prim, moralizing leader in the *Sunday Express* (7 March 1954), of which John Gordon was then editor. It declared that the book should never have been published and that it 'appears to be dedicated wholeheartedly to a simple, well-tried proposition – that sex will always pull in the customer'. The central character, Sarah Valmont, 'for 332 pages indulges a taste for uncontrolled and squalid sexuality. Her erotic odyssey . . . is persistently described in language abhorrent to a civilized palate . . . the lesson liable to be drawn from it all by younger and more impressionable readers is plain enough. It is that sexual excess can be indulged in with a light heart and a clear conscience.' The leader ended with an attack on the firm and on Frere in person: 'But the oddest part of this strange and sordid story is the identity of the publishers – William Heinemann, one of the most distinguished firms in the country. If some fly-by-night printer trading in pornography had put out this book, there might have been cause for action but not for comment. But the Heinemann imprint decorates the books of such men as the Poet Laureate and Mr Somerset Maugham. This spring they will publish Mr Attlee's memoirs. Why has a firm of this high repute enabled such a book to enter the libraries and homes of Britain? It can only be through a gross error of judgment. Mr A. S. Frere, the chairman of Heinemann's, can make good his error by withdrawing the book at once. If he allows the sale of *The Image and the Search* to continue, British publishing will indeed appear to have fallen on contemptible and evil days.'[1]

This attack, Frere told me, was a personal vendetta by Lord Beaverbrook because 'he had wanted me to publish a scandalous book about the Duke and Duchess of Windsor and I had refused. The wretched Duke was down and I didn't want to kick him. After *Coronation Commentary* I had no intention of being caught again! Later I received a telephone call from the Bahamas during which a spokesman for Beaverbrook wanted to know if I had changed my mind. When I made clear that I hadn't and I didn't intend to, there was an unambiguous threat: "Mr Frere, if you know what's good for you, I think you will publish it." I replied: "Tell Lord Beaverbrook to fuck himself" and hung up.' Soon after this conversation Beaverbrook's *Evening Standard* started to attack various Heinemann books and then came the leader in the *Sunday Express* – also owned by Beaverbrook. Be this as it may, the firm, Frere, and Baxter were summoned at Bow Street Police Court and committed for trial at the Old Bailey, the Central Criminal Court.

It was Walter Baxter's second novel. His previous one, *Look Down in Mercy* (1951), though about a homosexual attraction between an army officer and an other-ranker, escaped prosecution and had been very well received, selling over 17,000 copies plus a Readers' Union edition of 33,000. *The Image and the Search*, despite a highly favourable notice from E. M. Forster, who called it 'serious and beautiful', received, however, a mixed press and had sold only 9,000 until the *Sunday Express* attack boosted them up to 12,000, after which on legal advice it was thought prudent to announce that for the moment it was no longer for sale, though it was made clear that this did not amount to withdrawal.

Judged by the conventions and publishing practice of the 1980s, *The Image and the Search* would certainly not be considered pornographic, but by the standards of the 1950s it was undeniably frank, though its purpose was serious and clear: to depict Sarah's degradation and ultimate re-integration after her husband Robert is reported missing during the war. To quote from the blurb: 'The image in her mind is the image of Robert – the compulsive need of humanity for the perfect fulfilment of human love. First she tries to preserve this image by a form of self-mortification and when this fails she enters on a search for human happiness through wide and promiscuous sexual experience. . . .' The dramatic conclusion makes clear that 'because she still relies solely upon her own human resources she is defeated and endures a final and catastrophic sexual humiliation. It is from this nadir that she begins to understand the happiness she seeks can only be achieved by what the mystics of every religion in every country have described as "a dying to one's self" – a realization that if it were not for the hand of God she could not exist. She realizes too that this is the most difficult task in the world, and that its importance lies not in the success of the attempt, but in the attempt itself.'

Heinemann was one of at least five publishers prosecuted in 1954 for obscene libel as part of a puritan drive by the authorities. Werner Laurie, in the case of *Julia*, pleaded guilty in order to save time and money; Hutchinson's were tried by jury and found guilty and heavily fined for publishing *September in Quinze*; Arthur Barker was acquitted by a jury in the case of *Man in Control*; and, most importantly, Secker & Warburg and Fred Warburg himself were acquitted in the case of *The Philanderer* – the summing-up by Mr Justice Stable was considered to be a classic and because of its fairness and humanity undoubtedly influenced the result.

It may have also done a little to hearten Frere and Walter Baxter when a few weeks later (18 October 1954) they left the cells beneath the court at the Old Bailey and stood as 'prisoners at the bar' before Mr Justice Devlin and heard Mr Mervyn Griffith-Jones open for the prosecution. As in similar cases, the verdict would depend on the jury's interpretation of the test of obscenity laid down by Chief Justice Cockburn in 1868, which was repeated by Mr Justice Devlin: 'Whether the tendency of the matter charged as obscenity is to deprave or corrupt those whose minds are open to such immoral influences and into whose hands a publication of this sort may fall.' Griffith-Jones did not suggest that *The Image and the Search* came into the category of a book containing a lot of filthy matter deliberately introduced for the purpose of enhancing its selling value; rather, it was what he called 'camouflaged pornography', but pornography none the less.

The jury were given copies of the book and the court adjourned while they read it. They were told to judge for themselves, though Griffith-Jones drew attention to what he considered to be the most salacious passages, particularly some near the end set in India, such as when Sarah came across a Sadhu who sat motionless covered with a swarm of wild bees: 'She began to approach, horrified, and now she could see that his body was coated with the glistening shimmer of bees, his genitals and stomach thickly covered. His chest and arms and head crawled with the insects, but the flesh showed through and streamed with sweat. She came still nearer, directly facing him, watching the bees crawl across his open eyes as he stared unblinkingly into hers. A bee was half hidden in a fleshy nostril while others pushed at the thick mouth and she imagined them, wet with slime, dragging their wings and legs down his throat.

[407]

'A breath of wind carried the scent of her body to the veranda and the heavy drone took on a sharper note. She knew that she must run and yet she could not; in front of her the Sadhu rose effortlessly to his feet and a crawling cluster fell from his stomach to the stone floor. There was a bulging mass from which a lump suddenly broke away. She stood motionless, mirroring his own motionless body, watching his ejaculation spurt from his loins. . . .' – pages 301–8.

A few pages further on Sarah attempts to seduce a young Indian in a loincloth who had followed her into a cave containing a stone phallus. 'She came to him, expecting he would put out his hand to meet her. He stood quite still, but that meant nothing; only to touch would be necessary to release him. She could see his hair like wire springing from the edge of cloth. It was like other hair on other bodies and what was about to happen had happened before. And suddenly he was at once a symbol and an adding up of every orgasm she had ever had, of every haunting moment of exquisite and egotistical lust, the only moments when she was truly conscious of being far greater than herself, of fulfilling perfectly and completely the purpose of her existence. She cupped the bulge of cloth in her hand, and, as he started back, with her other hand held him against her, pressing against the rigid muscles above his buttocks. In a moment, this moment, she would feel lust swell against her cupped hand, swelling hugely to fill the cave. And there was nothing that she would not do or that could be impure. The clouds ate the sun; the dark shadows pouring from the cave mirrored what would happen, the darkness and silence and forgetting of mouths and the swollen clinging inseparability of bodies; the smooth rupturing warmth of the buried phallus. And, as the thin saliva ran and mingled, the seminal and dragged-out cry of triumph and defeat. As her hand cupped his genitals and she tried to push her thumb beneath the band of cloth her open mouth fastened on his liver-coloured lips, her tongue forced its way through the white line of teeth, slid against the sour slime of his parched mouth. . . .' – pages 325–6.

Turning to the jury, Griffith-Jones demanded: 'When Christmas comes, would you go out and buy copies of the book and hand them round as presents to the girls in the office – and if not, why not? The answer is because it is not the type of book they ought to read.' Defending counsel, Mr Rodger Winn, countered this by agreeing that the book was 'frightening and horrific', but he drew a distinction between what revolts and disgusts and what corrupts. 'The only real criticism, and it is a grave one, is that it might tend to frighten susceptible and only partly developed minds, and make a young girl about to be a bride timid about embarking on sex.'[2] On behalf of Baxter Winn read out that: 'In writing my book my object was a serious portrayal of the vulnerability to evil of any ego-centred personality, and the disintegrating effect of sin on such a personality.'[3]

Winn also made a statement on behalf of Frere: 'I personally was alone responsible for the decision of my company to publish this book. I read it and considered that it merited publication, though its literary quality was not comparable with that of the author's first book, which was very widely read and highly praised. I regard Walter Baxter as one of the most gifted writers of this generation, whose powers are not yet fully developed. I feel that publishers owe a duty to such writers and to the public to ensure that their creative work is not stillborn, if it has value and is not deleterious to potential readers. I was and am satisfied that this book would not harm any reader.'[4]

In the course of his summing-up Mr Justice Devlin reminded the jury that 'it is enough in law if there is a part that is obscene, providing that you bear this in mind, that in considering whether any particular part is obscene you have not got to take it out and judge it by itself. You have got to judge it in the light of the book as a whole from beginning to end, and not merely those parts of it which, in particular, the prosecution may say are obscene . . . that it is quite true again to say that it does not matter whether it is intended to be obscene or not. The offence is to publish something which has the effect of corrupting the mind of the ordinary man. Whether it is intended or not does not make any difference to the crime.'[5]

The jury was out for three hours, but failed to agree on a verdict – in those days verdicts had to be unanimous. The judge sent them back to try again, but after a further hour the foreman reported that they had failed again. A retrial was arranged to take place a few weeks later (24 November 1954). It was presided over by another judge, Mr Justice Lynskey; Mr Mervyn Griffith-Jones again prosecuted, but Mr Gerald Gardiner defended. The fresh jury heard more or less the same arguments for the prosecution. At one point Griffith-Jones suggested that perhaps the jury might think it a rough-and-ready rule that the novelist should take his readers to the bedroom door and leave them there. They might perhaps think he ought to take his readers further, right up to the bed and there draw the curtains. But in this book 'here you are in the bed and under the bedclothes, again and again, are you not?' How would members of the jury like their daughters to read this book? He was not talking of daughters of fourteen, but of grown-up daughters, of the young women who formed a large part of the population. 'It's filth, members of the jury, isn't it, crude, sordid filth?'[6]

For the defence Gerald Gardiner emphasized that the jury were not present as judges of taste – here he quoted at length from Mr Justice Stable's summing-up in *The Philanderer* case – but they were asked to find the accused guilty of a serious crime. The prosecution had asked if the book did not give rise to libidinous thoughts? If that were the test, what would happen to the theatres? Many a pretty chorus girl would find herself in the dock. The jury might wonder if the book was a serious book or whether it had been turned out to make money quickly. 'Extraordinary and astounding as it is', the author's intention had been ruled irrelevant, though the prosecution had asked again and again whether it was 'necessary' to put this, that or the other passage into the book. 'We have reached a strange position in law when the prosecution can ask question after question about an author's intention, while he has to sit in the dock and can't go into the witness-box.' Literature was an art. A work of art necessarily reached different people at different levels. The jury might imagine that they would be allowed to hear what eminent authors and distinguished literary critics had to say about this book, but this was not allowed. The jury must judge unaided. Gardiner also spoke of 'this new practice of putting distinguished publishers and authors in the dock. . . . Surely in this country they now don't know whether they are standing on their heads or their heels.'[7]

Gardiner's final speech amounted to a trenchant indictment of the unsatisfactory and dubious state of the law of obscene libel. Whether it was this or the complexion of the new jury, the latter found it even more impossible to agree on a verdict. The foreman told the judge that there was no hope of agreement 'even if we stayed here for days'.

At the third trial no evidence was offered on behalf of the Director of Public Prosecutions and on the direction of the Recorder, Mr Gerald Dodson, a third jury returned a verdict of not guilty. The ordeal was over and it had ended in victory and its hero was A. S. Frere. Congratulations and support came from all sides. Between the first two trials eight eminent authors, including Priestley and Maugham, had written together to *The*

Times to express their concern over the current prosecutions of publishers and authors which threatened to 'establish something of a police censorship of literature, constituting an attack upon the freedom of the pen for which a long and sometimes bitter struggle was fought and won in the past. It is, of course, recognized by all decent authors that certain books of an entirely obscene and filthy kind should be condemned and destroyed, but it is equally recognized that that duty of the law should not be allowed to open the way to a puritanical crusade, backed by police prosecution, against authors who claim the liberty and the right of describing the realities of life, freely and fearlessly for adult minds.

'On this subject Mr Justice Stable recently gave a wise and liberal direction in which he invited a jury to recognize that novels are not written solely for adolescent minds, and that what might have been thought improper at one period of history may be considered permissible at the present time when there is greater freedom of public opinion on such subjects as sex. Unfortunately this does not seem to have influenced other judges in recent cases, and authors and publishers are at the mercy of juries who vary in their verdicts according to the level of intelligence, or their ignorance of the great masterpieces of literature and contemporary writing.

'It would be disastrous to English literature if authors had to write under the shadow of the Old Bailey if they failed to produce works suitable for the teenager, and if publishers were forced to reject books which, however serious in intent and however lit by genius, contained passages which might be blue-pencilled by a police sergeant or a common informer.'[8]

An editorial in the *Sunday Times* immediately after the Heinemann trial commented that 'to write or publish an obscene libel is, *ipso facto*, a serious offence, and it ought therefore to be as clearly provable or disprovable as, say, fraud or criminal assault. It ought not to depend on the vagaries of opinion among jurymen or the personal enlightenment of judges.' Saying that the 'evident trend' towards a more liberal attitude may be satisfactory from the point of view of the freedom of the pen, the editorial continued: 'if it exemplifies, as it does, that such freedom is bounded, not by objective considerations of public interest, but by subjective judgments by Home Office officials, chief constables, judges, stipendiaries and haphazard dozens of good men and true, then it only helps to bring the law into disrepute. And one disreputable law contaminates others.'[9]

A front page article in *The New Statesman & Nation* on the case quoted from Mr Justice Stable's summing-up in the earlier case of *The Philanderer*: '"If we drive the criminal law too far, isn't there a risk that there will be a revolt, a demand for a change in the law, so that the pendulum will swing too far the other way?" In the history of English criminal law, one of the more familiar symptoms that that stage has been reached has always been the failure of juries to come to agreement on what was presented to them by the Crown as a plain issue of fact. It is a symptom that the law-makers are bound to recognize . . . the protracted ordeal of author and publisher . . . may prove to have had great value for the cause of literary freedom.'[10]

Frere provided his own summing-up of the case in a letter to *The Times* of which the final paragraph reminds readers that 'the charge was a criminal one. Mr Walter Baxter and I were prisoners in the dock, and in no way whatsoever were we treated in any respect differently from any other alleged felon who finds himself in that place. Mr Walter Baxter and I have defended this case throughout as a matter of principle, and none of our experiences will alter our determination to do so again, if the circumstances should arise.'[11]

There is no doubt that both the Secker & Warburg and the Heinemann trials helped greatly to pave the way for the Obscene Publications Act of 1959 which abolished the crude Common Law test of obscene libel and, among other reforms, gave publishers and authors the right to appear in court and defend their books against a destruction order. The new Act also required courts to listen to the evidence of experts in order to establish (or refute) that even though a book might tend to deprave and corrupt its readers it could be justified as 'being for the public good on the ground that it is in the interests of science, literature, art, or learning, or of other objects of general concern.' It was this Act, and particularly this clause, that in October 1960 led to a phalanx of the literary Establishment coming to give evidence which enabled Penguin to issue an unexpurgated version of *Lady Chatterley's Lover* – again the contending barristers were Mervyn Griffith-Jones and Gerald Gardiner.

It was fitting that in 1955 Heinemann should publish D. H. Lawrence's *Sex, Literature, and Censorship* and later, in 1972, two earlier versions of *Lady Chatterley's Lover*: one was called *The First Lady Chatterley*, which had a preface by Frieda Lawrence, and the other *John Thomas and Lady Jane*. Both had learned introductions by Roland Gant. The same year saw the

publication of *Selected Literary Criticism* of *D. H. Lawrence* (1955) edited
by A. R. Beal. Vivian de Sola Pinto together with F. Warren Roberts
collected and introduced *The Complete Poems of D. H. Lawrence* (1963)
which contained all his critical introductions. In preparing the manuscript
for press Claire Tomalin recalls that she suggested to Frere that she
should restore the four-letter words hitherto represented by dashes. He
appeared to be taken aback at such a suggestion coming from a young
lady, but skimming through the pages suggests that she had her way.
Claire's father, Emile Delavenay, wrote two scholarly studies for the firm:
D. H. Lawrence and Edward Carpenter (1971) which explored the possible
effect upon Lawrence of the ex-curate, pioneer socialist who was influenced by Indian mysticism and the concept of 'the one great consciousness'. Delavenay followed it with *D. H. Lawrence: the Formative Years,
1885–1919* (1972).

An epilogue to the trial was the formation of a spoof 'John Gordon
Society', started by Graham Greene in defence of Vladimir Nabokov, the
author of *Lolita*, following an absurd review by John Gordon. Greene
became President; with Ian Gilmour as Vice-President; and John Sutro as
Chairman. Frere joined its committee. With its founders' tongues conspicuously in their cheeks they announced that the Society's purpose
would be to promote all those ideals of censorship which John Gordon,
the editor-in-chief of the *Sunday Express*, had come to stand for. The
annual subscription would be 10*s*.6*d*.

Greene told me how the inaugural meeting was held in a hired room in
a pub in Oxford Street. John Gordon himself was invited to dinner
beforehand. The meeting was so crowded that there was standing-room
only and people were sitting on the stairs leading up to the room.
Everything went well except that Randolph Churchill in a state of drink
stormed up to the platform and started to insult John Gordon in person.
Greene wrote a report for *The Spectator*: 'The first item on the agenda after
the election of officers was the choice of a title for the Society. The
President said he considered too much importance had been ascribed to
Mr Gordon's revelation that he had on occasion smuggled pornographic
books through the Customs; it had shown great courage on Mr Gordon's
part to admit the fact, and the President was very unwilling to see the name
of the Society changed. The meeting unanimously decided that the
Society should retain the title of John Gordon.

'During a general discussion on the aims of the Society, Miss Winick, a well-known bookseller in the City, offered a window-display representing the Society's work. Mr Frere and other publishers present offered co-operation in submitting proofs of forthcoming books to the Society and agreed to indicate by means of a band the Society's disapproval if it proved impossible for them to withdraw books after condemnation. . . . Another proposal was for a plaque to be placed by the Society on the wall of the house occupied by Mr Gordon's predecessor, the late James Douglas – famous for his statement worthy of an ancient Roman, "I would rather give poison to my daughter than place in her hands a copy of *The Well of Loneliness*".[12]

John Gordon appears to have attempted to achieve a reconciliation with Frere. His letter is not in the Heinemann archive, but there is a carbon of Frere's caustic response: 'I was glad to get your letter. Voltaire once wrote that if you have gone through life having made and kept two or more friends, you were a lucky man. You and I have known each other for – shall I call it a lifetime? Of course I accept without question what you tell me about the *Sunday Express* attack on me for *The Image and the Search*. It would have been easier if you had told me at the time. The attack was personal and vicious. It could have landed me in jail, and might have done if two juries had not thought otherwise. No such attack upon you could appear in a book published under the Heinemann imprint. So let us leave it at that.'[13]

Financial Crisis –
Taken Over by Tilling

The growth in annual turnover between 1946 and 1961 was inevitably in part the result of the steady increase in book prices, but overall it reflected the expansion of the list, the galaxy of top-selling authors and the development of sales overseas. In the immediate post-war period the growth was dramatic, William Heinemann Ltd's turnover more than doubling between 1946 and 1952, a rate of increase far outstripping price inflation (Appendix B). The easing of paper rationing enabled publishers to meet demand, including that from the libraries, which were restocking after wartime shortages; with its unrivalled backlist the firm benefited greatly from their needs, overseas as well as at home.

But as this pent-up demand became satisfied the rate of increase in turnover started to slow down. Turnover may have doubled during 1946–52, but the increase of 41 per cent over the next six years (to 1958), an average increase of 7 per cent, was illusory because it was not too far different from the current rate of general inflation. Even more ominous was the start of a decline in profit margins. In 1952 the main firm's pre-tax profits were 19.2 per cent of turnover, a ratio not far different from that prevailing in 1946. During these six years the rapid expansion of sales had been accompanied by the maintenance of profit margins, a very healthy state of affairs indeed, but in the following six years (1952–8) profit margins fell from 19.2 to 10.8 per cent. By 1961 the main firm's pre-tax margin had fallen even further to 4.2 per cent, and in the Heinemann group as a whole the margins were as low as 2 per cent, owing to losses made by the subsidiaries. British Book Services (Canada) Ltd, for example, started to incur losses in 1955 and William Heinemann Ltd's accounts for that year recorded a subvention of £19,712. In 1959 Peter Davies Ltd went into the red and losses increased, reaching a trough of £30,802 in 1961. Rupert Hart-Davis Ltd in 1960 recorded a deficit of £14,707 and by 1961 its losses had increased to £20,955.

These widespread and persistent losses were of course a serious drain on Heinemann funds. Combined with the deteriorating position within the main firm itself they were to prove disastrous. The group as a whole was not earning enough to cover dividends or to generate additional working capital for its day-to-day publishing. Even so, the ordinary share dividend never fell below 20 per cent and was even increased to 25 per cent in 1957. The shortage of working capital was aggravated by the tendency, already described in Chapter 16, to reprint the better-known titles primarily in order to keep the printing presses at Kingswood busy. To have large stocks of authors like Maugham, Shute, and Greene must have seemed like a blue chip investment, an understandable point of view, were it not that hardcover sales of even these eminent authors started to decline when the post-war boom ended and when paperback editions of the same titles became widely available.

During 1946–58 Heinemann hardcover sales did, however, increase by 180 per cent, but its income from subsidiary rights increased by 500 per cent, indicating the rapid expansion of paperbacks and bookclubs. By 1960 subsidiary rights contributed £55,000 to a total pre-tax profit of £66,000 (Appendix B). Although these sources of income made a welcome addition to profits, they reflected a shifting in the source of demand which bypassed Heinemann's own warehouse. All hardback publishers were of course similarly affected, but for Heinemann, with its own printing presses to keep occupied, these changes in the pattern of marketing presented problems which the group's management could not, or did not, resolve. As discussed later, stocks of unsaleable books continued to accumulate, leading to drastic write-downs which in turn led to heavy losses.

These unsold stocks, combined with declining profitability, were producing an acute shortage of working capital. E. C. Jeeves, then company secretary, frequently came into the directors' lunch room at Kingswood and confessed that he was worn out and despondent after a morning largely spent in fending off telephone calls from persistent and irate creditors. It was no longer possible to create new share capital as had been done in the earlier, more prosperous post-war period of 1949 when there had been an issue of 800,000 ordinary shares of 2s.6d. each and the tax free capitalization of £50,000 from a capital redemption reserve. The original 6 per cent preference shares were redeemed in 1948 – which led to the resignation of their representatives on the board, M. Brickhill and Miss G. V. Woodman – and these shares were replaced by the issue of

100,000 4½ per cent preference shares of £1 each, based on a financial scheme put up by the City merchant bankers, Helbert Wagg & Co. In 1952 and 1954 allotments and bonus issues of a further 111,104 and 1,000,000 shares followed, increasing the capital to £100,000 preference shares and £277,685 ordinary shares. Helbert Wagg & Co. were again connected with these increases of capital and the minute book records in October 1952 that the investment holding company, Thomas Tilling Ltd, agreed to subscribe for any shares not taken up.

The first appearance of Thomas Tilling's name is significant because it was Tillings who were to come to the rescue when the shortage of working capital became acute. The role of Helbert Wagg & Co. is likewise significant because the chairman of both was Lionel Fraser. Frere and Fraser knew each other well as fellow members of the Garrick and as active brother Freemasons, Frere being Grand Treasurer of the Supreme Grand Chapter of England and also Grand Superintendant of the Provincial Grand Chapter of Buckinghamshire. Lionel Fraser was by no means your typical tycoon. The son of Gordon Selfridge's butler, he had begun as a shorthand writer and rose to a position of considerable power and wealth. Six foot two with a magnificent head of silvered hair, he retained an enduring faith in Christian Science and teetotalism – though he served excellent claret to his guests. He collected contemporary abstract paintings and had a passion for books. Tilling similarly were very different from a mere investment holding company and had their own distinctive management style. Dubbed by rival publishers as 'the bus people', originally they had run a large fleet of buses but in 1948 these were sold to the British Transport Commission set up by the Labour Government; and it was with the balance of the compensation money after paying off the stockholders, together with substantial holdings in property, and four subsidiaries that were retained, together with various other investments, that Tilling were transformed into an investment conglomerate. Operating from elegant offices in early Georgian Crewe House, Mayfair, they took paternal pride in owning a 'family of firms'. Their interests included companies trading in building supplies, electrical wholesaling, engineering, glassware (Pyrex), textiles and hosiery (Pretty Polly), insurance (Cornhill), car hire (Daimler Hire), and much else.

Fraser obviously enjoyed becoming involved in the affairs of such a distinguished publishing firm whose activities and character must have been refreshingly different from his other business interests. From 1956 onwards Tilling steadily acquired Heinemann shares, mainly it would appear on the Stock Exchange, so that by November 1957 they owned 35 per cent of the equity. It was contrary to Tilling's policy not to have a majority holding and they then bought sufficient shares from Frere, Hall, and Dwye Evans and their families to give them a majority holding which was equivalent to 2.75 per cent of Tilling's total capital. The price was satisfied by 61,587 £1 ordinary Tilling shares. Heinemann had joined the 'family of firms'.

It was with Tilling's help that a lease was signed for new London premises. Although overflow offices had been taken in both the houses neighbouring on 99 Great Russell Street, the building was much too small and it was decided not to renew its lease. Frere had always wanted to move to Mayfair and by a lucky chance Tilling owned a bomb-site at 15 Queen Street, hard by their own grand offices at Crewe House, Curzon Street. It was agreed to erect purpose-built offices for Heinemann on this site and to lease them at a very favourable rent. They were ready and occupied in January 1959. Although brand new, the building was ill-conceived and soon nicknamed by the staff 'The Ministry of Fear'. It was functional in the worst sense and again much too small to house the staff of some ninety people which now included those of Peter Davies, though the trade counter was moved to 36 Soho Square, the offices of Rupert Hart-Davis. The first floor, carpeted and with very superior mahogany fittings like some kind of civic suite, housed a very large boardroom which was also Frere's office, together with separate and pleasant offices for Dwye Evans as deputy chairman; for Alan Hill, a director since 1955 and a managing director since 1959, in charge of the growing Educational department; and for Elizabeth Anderson, promoted from Dwye's secretary to be in charge of contracts and rights. All the offices on the other four floors were overcrowded, poky, and separated by movable partitions which were so thin that when gossiping or discussing anything confidential it was necessary to lower one's voice. Mrs Ella Grey, the housekeeper, the wife of Frere's chauffeur, occupied a tiny flat at the top. A well-fitted showroom shared the basement with the packing department and the toilets, and not surprisingly was seldom visited. It was eventually moved to the ground floor which was equipped with an immense shopwindow more suitable for a furniture showroom with a vast empty space which was eventually filled with more partitioned cubicles. Apart from the occupants of the first floor, no one liked a building which gave every sign of having been built on the cheap, especially the lift with old-fashioned iron-trellis gates which were continually left open, leaving the car stranded. The worst feature was perhaps the under-floor system of heating which only functioned during the night, making the cubicles unbearably hot and stuffy first thing in the morning and impossible to reheat when cooled down by opened windows. People complained endlessly of headaches and dry throats. It was a disappointing come-down after the elegance of Great Russell Street. It would certainly not impress authors.

For some time Tilling had been represented on the top Heinemann board by their managing director, J. A. Falconer, but when he retired in 1957 he was replaced by P. H. D. Ryder, who succeeded him also as Tilling's managing director. As a parent company Tilling made it a rule normally not to interfere with the day-to-day running of any of their companies but to leave it to the latter's own executives. Tilling were there to provide finance (and to maximize profits) and to tender guidance whenever it was needed. When, some twenty-five years after these events, I visited him at his home in the Isle of Man Peter Ryder explained that 'our policy was to buy companies with good management and not to interfere apart from asking for annual budgets and agreeing targets to be aimed at. We were not looking for companies with potential and a bad management which could be put right. Some people buy only to sell. We tried to buy good family firms that needed very little interference, but which we would continue to own. It didn't always work out and it certainly didn't work out with Heinemanns.'

It is not clear how soon Tilling realized that all was not well with their new offspring, that its problems were more serious than a shortage of capital, but for several years they refrained from making decisive changes, though from time to time they made loans which at least postponed what looked like turning into a major financial crisis. Tilling became increasingly uneasy as from behind the buoyant turnover, the dazzling eminence of the authors and Frere's ever-reassuring predictions, the grim outlines of reality slowly emerged. There were numerous imponderables among which sound reasons for optimism were mixed with equally pressing reasons for pessimism and even panic, but the root causes of an unhealthy diagnosis soon became apparent to the practised eyes of Tilling's own experts. With hindsight these can be summarized as: over-rapid expansion which exceeded the limits of available capital, resulting especially from the financing of the new overseas offices and the recently acquired subsidiaries – some of which were making losses; the commissioning of titles without relating their cost to the funds available; the general effects of inflation which were not sufficiently counter-balanced by increased retail book prices; the need for additional funds to replace older stock of good-selling titles printed in a cheaper period; the holding of excessive stocks of less saleable titles not only at Kingswood but also at the overseas branches, particularly of titles printed in excessive quantities to satisfy the need for continuous work by the Windmill Press.

There is plenty of telling evidence from which to deduce that the firm's extended activities were beyond the capacity and abilities of the existing management, though it could be that Hall's financial grip was weakened by a major operation he underwent in 1953. Senior members of staff have bitter memories of those years. For example, Harry Townshend, who became half-time general manager at Kingswood as well as continuing to work for Rupert Hart-Davis Ltd, told me that 'the administration at Kingswood was very lax and there was insufficient credit control. In the firm as a whole my main memory is of a very unhappy house with everyone fighting each other and of a total lack of leadership at the top. There was also a complete absence of trust between Kingswood and London, including the associated companies . . . Frere and Hall had worked together for years and Dwye Evans was always the odd man out. This added to the poison in the atmosphere.' Similarly according to David Elliot who became managing director of World's Work: 'Hall simply did not have the vision to understand what was happening. A small man in a big job. Very suspicious of everybody and wouldn't take advice.' Alewyn Birch, export sales manager: 'Before long Tilling realized that Heine-mann was absolutely broke and would go down hill if left to its own devices. Sales were quite good, but Hall was a bad manager of money. Frere was largely interested in himself and there was the continuous conflict of interests between the publishing and printing sides.' Alan Hill, head of the Educational department: 'The firm was badly run from the finance angle, Hall being inadequate for the job. He was also obsessively secretive, so that the seriousness of the financial situation was never communicated to the board – nor even, I believe, to Frere. In that period publishing was a growth industry, and how Heinemann with its magni-ficent list ran onto the rocks remains a mystery. With prudent and professional management it would never have happened.'

Such accusations were endorsed by Tilling's own financial expert, R. O. A. Keel, who was eventually put in to undertake a major reorganization. This belongs to the next section of this history, but his conclusions after a year's experience are relevant to understanding what had gone wrong. His confidential letter to Lionel Fraser included the following: 'The business was not only financially below water – it was also dangerously run down as a publishing force, both in terms of the authors it commanded and the capacity of the individuals wielding authority. Although the evidence is not wholly conclusive, it would appear that once the post-war boom had spent itself the firm's momentum perceptibly receded. This is clear from the profit record as related to funds in use and also from the increasing reliance on "old" authors and the failure to promote "new" literary figures to any significant extent. Certain parts of the business progressed because of the personalities in control. . . . The rest either stagnated or lost money as well as opportunity. Top management had lost the respect and goodwill of the majority of the staff. As a result great friction existed and there was an unwillingness to employ any other than servile and mediocre types of men and women. No efforts of any effectiveness had been adequately developed to provide management succession . . . profits in recent years – particularly 1959 and 1960 – did not bear a proper charge for stock write down.' Judging by the very considerable depreciation of stock values in 1961–62–63 this was an understatement! Keel ended by saying that 'the effect of all the above could be that Tilling have for the record paid over the odds for their investment'[1]. Keel was almost certainly too hard on the staff and over-critical of the literary quality of the 1950s' lists, though it was true that there was too much reliance on ageing pre-war authors, but his strictures on the company's financial and general management were undoubtedly justified.

The McGraw-Hill Débâcle

It is impossible to assess the extent to which and precisely when the Heinemann board – and especially Frere and Hall – comprehended the seriousness of the financial situation. The group board minutes, like most minutes, are opaque and convey little but optimism and even self-congratulation. By the end of the decade, however, things came to a head, particularly as the Tillings board was becoming restive. Fraser must have been open to criticism for not having ordered a thorough financial appraisal before acquiring a controlling interest. Apart from Ryder, there was only one other firm supporter of Heinemann among the Tilling directors, Sir John Elliot who had earlier been chairman of the Railway Executive and later of London Transport: 'I believed that the ownership of Heinemann gave Tilling an element of prestige unusual in the industrial world,' Sir John told me. 'As a banker, Lionel was obviously in a dilemma, though any loss from Heinemann was relatively small in relation to Tillings' other sources of profit. Among his critics was Sir George Briggs, an important figure in the aviation industry, a delightful companion and a very shrewd businessman. Briggs kept on asking: "How much longer, Mr Chairman, are we to go on throwing money out of the window just to satisfy this whim of being civilized? – which we are not!" Others supported him and Fraser recognized he could not hold them off much longer.'

It became clear that Fraser began to blame Frere for having misled him, to conclude that there must be something radically wrong at the top for a company to be in such an unhealthy state. According to Ryder: 'There came a point when Fraser wanted to get out, but he didn't want to be unkind to or blame an old friend. I believe he felt embarrassed. He didn't think Frere was playing the game. I suspect, to be honest, that Frere also wanted to get out. He was fed up with failure and must have thought to himself that he had better cash in now or otherwise he wouldn't get anything.'

It was then that Frere, who was not easily nonplussed, produced a *deus ex machina* in the form of a proposal to sell the entire Heinemann group to an American publisher. He had received a tentative approach from an American broking house. Fraser recognized that this could be a heaven-sent way out and wrote to Peter Ryder from Cannes that Frere, who had just been to see him, 'is madly keen, seeing a wonderful surge forward for Heinemanns, and of course cash for his shares plus a contract as chairman, etc., etc. I see the point too and I see a solution of the desperate managerial problem in this way. *But* for the Yanks it would be a fantastic bargain to have the whole world of publishing opened to them, and I said to Frere that my price would be nearer a £1 [per share] for such a sale. . . . It rids us of a boring management, touchy problem with Frere and gives us a whacking capital profit too'[2]. Ryder had rather more reservations when he replied: 'As far as the employees are concerned, I share your feelings. It would not be so bad if the purchaser was a big British publishing house. I must say I would have some regret in selling control of Heinemann to Americans, because publishing is an educational force and performs a national service to some extent'[3].

Feelers were extended. The first firm to be approached was Farrar Straus, Roger Straus being a friend of both Frere and Fraser. The price asked for Heinemann was, Straus felt, too high for him and he recommended McGraw-Hill instead who were at once very interested. The early negotiations were cloaked in secrecy, Fraser insisting that no one else must be told apart from Peter Ryder and Ben Glazebrook, then Frere's personal assistant. Glazebrook explained to me that as a merchant banker Fraser had great experience of this type of negotiation and knew that a leak could lead to unfortunate speculation in Tillings' shares.

An amalgamation – or even an absorption – with one of the most powerful, go-ahead American publishers had much to be said for it. As major academic, technical, and journal publishers geared primarily to college and professional markets in the USA and throughout the world, very different from that in the UK, and without a strong line in fiction, McGraw-Hill's list would be complementary rather than competitive. Had not America in the shape of Doubledays saved the firm in an earlier crisis? Why not allow history to repeat itself? A publisher, even an American one, might prove to be a more understanding owner than a largely industrial conglomerate. From McGraw-Hill's point-of-view Heinemann, in addition to its distinguished authors and reputation, would provide entry to the prized British Commonwealth market which in those days was virtually closed to US publishers. McGraw-Hill also could afford the asking price, having access to a multi-million dollar loan from the banking house of Lehmann Brothers. Whether or not Frere was happy about the secrecy, he seems to have assured Fraser that all his colleagues would share his own enthusiasm for the deal. He could not have been more mistaken.

The negotiations were nearly completed when a leak did take place, though there are several versions, some doubtless apocryphal, of how this was possible. A jettisoned sheet from a Heinemann duplicator was a version favoured by some; an embarrassing chance meeting with Frere in Manhattan when he was supposed to be in Cap Ferrat was another. Fred Warburg got to hear about the proposed deal from a close American publishing friend: 'The news seemed to me at first incredible, but if it were true I had no doubt that it would be a bad, perhaps even a disastrous day for the whole British publishing trade. It was not that the Americans were inefficient – far from it – nor that they were hard taskmasters – we have plenty of them over here – it was much simpler. The trouble with the Americans was . . . that they were Americans. It was my view then, and it is my view now, as I have expressed it more than once that the publication of English books and of English newspapers should be with few exceptions in English hands. . . . McGraw-Hill was a huge organization, housed in its own massive skyscraper on West 42 Street, NYC. Much of the firm was occupied with the publication of trade papers with large circulations, but it also had a substantial book section. No more unsuitable owner of the Heinemann Group, so it seemed to me, could have been chosen. There was, of course, nothing to be said against its reputation or that of its directors, those were of the highest. But it was too big, too American, too insensitive to British susceptibilities. . . .'[4]

In his opposition Warburg had two allies in particular, Rupert Hart-Davis and Alewyn Birch who, though sales manager, was not yet a Heinemann director. Hart-Davis agreed that such a deal was unthinkable. Birch told me that 'the three of us were constantly in touch during that hectic period. There wasn't a day when we didn't meet. None of us was in any sense anti-McGraw-Hill as such. They were considered to be an extremely good company, well run. Indeed we had great respect for them as a cultural organization within their own country. But we believed very passionately – and I think quite rightly – that a country's culture cannot be represented by a publisher from another country. It never works. We felt it would be very wrong that an essentially British firm such as Heinemann should fall into foreign hands.'

A message of protest was sent to Fraser in New York and he immediately broke off the negotiations and returned to London. He listened carefully to the counter-arguments and also to Ryder, who told me: 'By then I was very close to the individual publishers and knew how they felt. I, too, was dead against Heinemann being sold to an American company. I felt that ours was a traditional company, one that was very, very English. I was much persuaded by Warburg's arguments that this was a famous English house which must not be controlled from overseas. You just couldn't do it. I got really worked up about it. I think Frere was only concerned with saving his own money. Whatever the money, it just wasn't worth it. In the end Fraser saw the point, but I had to fight very hard with the Tillings board to put it across.'

In the end it was arranged that Curtis Benjamin, McGraw-Hill's chairman, accompanied by a representative of Lehmann Brothers, should come to London to convince the doubters. On a Sunday morning, 16 October 1960, they met Warburg, Hart-Davis, Townshend, and Birch in the greatest secrecy. Fraser and Ryder were also there, though Frere and all the other Heinemann directors were absent. Everyone liked the two Americans and both sides spoke frankly but politely and the discussion continued through lunch at the Dorchester and then back at Crewe House till about four o'clock when Benjamin summed up the arguments by announcing that 'if this is how you feel, gentlemen, then, speaking on behalf of McGraw Hill, I have no option but to announce that we too are not prepared to go ahead.'

In Fraser's mind the need for secrecy about the McGraw-Hill negotiations persisted even after their collapse. A year later he was quoted by 'Mammon' in *The Observer* as denying there was ever any intention of selling Heinemann[5]. This provoked a caustic riposte from Curtis Benjamin: 'If this is true, then I must ask why Mr Fraser and the then chairman of Heinemann opened negotiations for a possible sale to McGraw-Hill with me and my associates here in New York? And why was I then invited by them to brave the chill of London prejudice in pursuit of the matter? There has been in London an unsurprisingly large amount of uninformed gossip and Press comment on the abortive negotiations between Heinemann and McGraw-Hill. Much of it has been amusingly chauvinistic in tone, some of it unfair to McGraw-Hill's true position. I was sorry to see *The Observer* carry on this stale and fatuous story-line.'[6]

The truth is that the great American takeover bid had, against all the odds, been defeated by three determined people. Heinemann's problems, however, remained as severe as ever.

Frere Made President – Bodley Head Merger Founders

In April 1961, six months after this débâcle, Tilling took decisive steps to reconstruct Heinemann's management. This was against their customary policy, but if they could not sell the company, neither could they allow it to deteriorate further. Fraser called a meeting in Crewe House of all the directors of all the Heinemann companies and told them that Frere would resign as chairman and Hall as joint deputy chairman, though they would remain as directors of the group board. Peter Ryder, the managing director of Tilling, would replace Frere as chairman and R. O. A. Keel would become financial director and chairman of an 'action committee' set up to deal with the financial crisis and to make recommendations for its resolution. A new office of president was being created to accommodate Frere – he was to be given a salary of £5,000 a year, the use of his grand office at Queen Street and of his chauffeur-driven car; his role was defined loosely as being to develop connections with authors, agents, booksellers, etc. and to promote the interests of the company generally, but it was spelt out that he should act only 'in conformity with the policy laid down from time to time by the board'. Hall was similarly to be appointed as financial consultant.

Frere was furious at being 'kicked upstairs', for this is what it amounted to. He had always maintained that he was not prepared to surrender the control of Heinemanns to anyone and as late as April 1957, the year Tilling was to gain control, even boasted about it in the Press: 'When a bank takes over a farm it doesn't put a bank manager in to run it; it hires a farmer. Banks, insurance companies, investment trusts, finance houses and the rest don't think they can run the businesses they put their money into, and they know better than to try. They rely on professionals. In publishing, that means publishers. And so far as I'm concerned, if and when they come into 99 Great Russell Street they do so on my terms, not theirs'[7]. Sitting in his president's chair Frere had to eat his own words. A few months before his death at ninety-one Frere confided to me: 'Fraser had been a friend, even an intimate one, but he had ratted on me. He set up one of those horrible city takeover traps and I walked straight into it – bang like that! It was deliberate. He knew what he was doing. But I believed in him, because I needed him. He double-crossed me – and so did all those people I had helped. They all ratted on me.'

As president Frere seldom appeared in the office and spent much of his time in his villa at Cap Ferrat, but a couple of months after the showdown he became involved in a scheme that could have amounted to a partial comeback. The plan was to amalgamate with The Bodley Head. Max Reinhardt, who had recently acquired this firm, and Peter Ryder would be joint managing directors of the new grouping; Graham Greene, who was already a director of The Bodley Head, would be literary director; and Frere would remain as president. 'We had not reached the stage when the roles of the proposed directors were clearly defined,' Max Reinhardt told me, 'but as president Frere would have played more than a nominal part. He would be involved in editorial decisions, make suggestions for books, and look after authors who were his personal friends.' Frere was not, as many believed, the originator of this plan, which owed its birth to a meeting in Paris between Lionel Fraser and George Ansley of Ansbachers, also merchant bankers. Reinhardt said that he himself had been hesitant. 'I was still in the process of digesting The Bodley Head and I had plenty on my plate, including taking over Putnams, but I certainly wasn't against the idea. The two companies were already very close. Jack Priestley, as well as Graham, was a member of my board and Dwye Evans had also been one, though he had resigned a year earlier when both Heinemann and ourselves were after Charlie Chaplin's autobiography – a very hot property which Bodley Head eventually acquired. Frere had always been tremendously helpful and Heinemann had arranged for The Bodley Head to be handled by their overseas representatives. We were also, together with Priestley and Greene, very good personal friends. I had lived in Albany when Frere, Jack, and Graham still lived there.'

Several meetings took place to discuss the details, attended by Fraser, Ryder, L. A. Hart – the managing director of Ansbachers – and

Reinhardt. Though a possible sale of Heinemann to The Bodley Head and Ansbachers was mentioned during the discussions, it turned out that there was now no question of Tillings getting out of Heinemann. The Bodley Head would bring with it a very sound backlist and some particularly good children's books. There was no call for additional capital, though it was agreed that The Bodley Head's owners would have a minimum of twenty-five per cent of the new equity.

The last of these meetings was attended by R. O. A. Keel, who drew up a minute recording the details. Everyone shook hands on what they believed was an excellent deal. The next step was a meeting on a Sunday afternoon in Fraser's flat in Lowndes Square at which the proposal was put to Graham Greene that he should become literary director. He was delighted to accept and later that evening he joined Reinhardt at a party he was giving and they drank a toast to the deal. On the Monday Greene received from Fraser a copy of the proposed Press announcement and approved it.

Then on the Tuesday the plan collapsed. Fraser sent letters by hand to Reinhardt and Hart explaining that it had run into strong opposition from key people on the Heinemann board, including Dwye Evans, Fred Warburg, Rupert Hart-Davis, and Alan Hill. The plan appears to have been inadequately and too hurriedly explained, but none of them could see any reasons for such a merger. Fraser felt it necessary to visit Greene at his flat in Albany to break the news in person. Understandably Greene was very upset and, worse, took it to be a personal rebuff and rejection, though undoubtedly the opposition was not against Greene himself but against being tied up with The Bodley Head. In an exchange of letters with Fraser, he wrote: 'Feeling as I do, it would be wrong if I left you with the impression that I was content to wait like Mr Micawber until something "turned up" or that my next book would necessarily be offered to Heinemann's. . . . I must in self-protection hold myself free to consider any offers from other firms, sad though I should be to relinquish a relationship which began with my first novel thirty-two years ago.'[8]

What Greene was really thinking became clear from a letter he wrote to *The Observer* a few weeks later. After a tribute to 'an individual publisher [obviously Charles Evans] who risked his reputation by supporting through the lean years a writer whom his colleagues would perhaps have been happy to shed', Greene went on: 'The character of a publishing house can very quickly change. A whole list can veer suddenly towards vulgarity ("Enterprise", the new leader may call it, but some of the old authors may feel a little lonely among the new accents). The sense of trust between author and publisher may vanish in a season. Perhaps this change happens more frequently now when the City has begun to move in. Authors are not factory hands, nor are books to be compared as commodities with tobacco, beer, motor-cars and automatic machines. A novelist ought certainly to hesitate long before he deserts a publisher who has helped him when help was most needed, in the long years of poor sales, but does he owe loyalty to a board which changes from year to year and may, in this new phase, include directors with no experience of publishing and with little interest in books save as a "quality" commodity less liable than others to depreciate in value at a period of economic depression?"[9]

The form taken by the collapse of the merger with The Bodley Head was almost identical to that of the deal with McGraw-Hill. Why was Fraser so rash as to make a firm proposal to Graham Greene before he had consulted and won the backing of the other Heinemann directors? Frere, too, with undoubtedly good reason this time, must have felt terribly let down. The merger might have possessed merits but it was bungled in a manner that was to contribute to the disastrous events that followed.

Frere Resigns – Graham Greene Lost

After this second débâcle Frere's relationship with the firm and particularly with Fraser deteriorated further. He quarrelled, for example, with Nico Davies and threatened to report him to the Garrick Club committee for having passed on confidential gossip outside the club. Nico called on Lionel Fraser, as another Garrick member, to defend him. This led Fraser to send a letter of protest to Frere: 'Isn't this quite unnecessary, and undesirable washing of private linen in public? I do pray that you will desist. It is so contrary to the tenor of our conversation last night and can only be disturbing to the atmosphere in the group, already very delicate and sensitive, even if improving. I cannot see how your action, if it is true what I am told, can do anybody any good, least of all yourself. I should view it seriously. I sometimes despair of ever getting the situation right in Heinemanns, but until we do there can be no recovery. Why can't we build up on what is good and constructive, instead of this perpetual nagging, denigration and despising of the members of the Group? And honestly I am not saying this in a personal sense, but only because I know you could help to improve matters such a lot.'[10]

Fraser's plea did not seem to have been very effective and eventually Frere resigned his presidency. The date is not recorded in the minute book, but it was probably towards the end of 1962. 'I told him that I was walking out, that I no longer wanted the job, nor his £5,000 year, nor his car. So far as I was concerned he could stuff it! What's more, I also told him that I would take one or two people I cared about with me.' Frere undoubtedly carried out this threat. Max Reinhardt confirmed that Frere had asked him if he would be willing to take on dissentient Heinemann authors who were loyal to him. 'There was never any doubt that they were influenced by Frere, but of course they had minds of their own and were, in fact, very strong characters. Naturally I said I would be very pleased to have them.' It is believed that Frere invited several leading Heinemann authors to his Albany chambers and suggested that they would be better off if they moved to The Bodley Head. J. B. Priestley and Richard Church said they would stick to Heinemann, but others took Frere's advice.

The most serious loss was Graham Greene, though he told me he knew nothing of this meeting. In fact he had almost certainly decided to leave Heinemann before it took place. As we have seen he was very seriously upset at what he considered to be a personal rebuff when the Bodley Head merger collapsed and he had been close to leaving then, but it was not until October 1962 that he finally made the break. He told me that he had only stayed so long out of loyalty to Frere: 'When he was kicked upstairs and it became clear that he was no longer in charge, I didn't trust the people who were.' In a long letter to Frere he made this very clear: '. . . the personal rebuff could have been laughed easily off if I had not become more and more aware of the fact that I no longer had any personal contact with anyone in the firm and that – to speak frankly – I could no longer depend on you to look after my work; from my agent and the rumours circulating in the publishing world I had learned that you were no longer in a position to do so. I was therefore left as an author without any personal contact with the firm of Heinemann, apart from Alan Hill on the educational side. I have never disguised from you my lack of confidence in your managing director (on two occasions during my period at Heinemanns I very nearly left the firm because of the type of publicity he thought my books required). . . . Please believe me when I say that I am quite certain no responsibility whatever attaches to you – I have become only too aware of how powerless in the whole matter is the president of the company. Under these circumstances what was I to do? Leave myself in the hands of strangers who showed so little interest in my books? I have had many years experience of publishing and I am a director of The Bodley Head and a personal friend of Max Reinhardt, so the decision to be taken seemed an obvious one. In spite of that, after thirty-two years with Heinemann, it has taken me many months to make up my mind, but a publishing firm to an author means a personal contact, a personal sense of confidence reciprocated, and this I can no longer find in a company of whom the directors are nearly all unknown to me.'[11]

In his reply Frere tried to get him to stay his hand and he sent copies of both letters to Peter Ryder. Maybe this was just for the record and to prove that he was acting loyally, and yet this contradicts what he had told Fraser about taking a few people he cared about with him. At the time of Greene's departure he had not made his own final break, though he was on the verge of doing so.

Four years later, when The Bodley Head published *The Comedians*, Greene expressed his affection and loyalty publicly in a dedication which began 'Dear Frere, When you were the head of a great publishing firm I was one of your most devoted authors, and when you ceased to be a publisher, I, like many other writers on your list, felt it was time to find another home. This is the first novel I have written since then, and I want to offer it to you in memory of more than thirty years of association – a cold word to represent all the advice (which you never expected me to take), all the encouragement (which you never realized I needed), all the affection and fun of the years we shared.'[12]

Three other serious losses to The Bodley Head were Eric Ambler, George Millar, and Georgette Heyer who, after Derek Priestley took her out to lunch and tried to get her to change her mind, wrote back: 'You were very persuasive, but my decision wasn't reached without a great deal of thought. In fact, to be asked to think any more about it almost makes me drum with my heels. Frere has been preaching thought, consideration, and caution ever since I told him that I should leave the firm when he did. . . . A lot of very murky water has been flowing under the Heinemann bridge, and I don't like it. It can serve no useful purpose to enlarge upon what I said to you yesterday, so I will merely say that I'm sorry, but my mind is made up.'[13] According to her biographer, Georgette Heyer after she had left found Heinemann lethargic. 'Worst of all, they had failed to do anything about *An Infamous Army* for the hundred and fiftieth anniversary of the Battle of Waterloo: "Frere says they probably thought it was about a suburban station! But when I recall what a press it had, when it came out, and how it is recommended to cadets at Sandhurst, and to all schools, it made me seethe with rage".'[14]

The only evidence that Frere tried to suborn a member of Heinemann's staff comes from James Michie who told me that 'when I left Heinemanns for The Bodley Head it was because he wanted me to. He got Graham Greene to approach me. When Greene invited me to have drinks with him at Albany I remember his saying fairly early on: "Let's get this straight. I've got you here to seduce you." He explained that he would be leaving Heinemann and that I would be welcome to join the band of refugees – which I did in 1962.'

The bitterness continued down the years. Fraser never spoke to Frere again and continued to believe that he had been grossly misled. He even spoke about the need for a Board of Trade enquiry into why the firm had been run so badly. Frere, for his part, continued to believe that he had been double-crossed. 'I never regretted my decision to make a clean break, apart from having to cut myself off from some close friends such as Alan Hill. When he came over to chat with me at the Garrick, I had to warn him: "Dear boy, you're not doing yourself any good being seen talking to me, and of course he didn't really understand what I was getting at, why I had to do it."' The departure of some of Heinemann's finest authors for The Bodley Head may have seemed like a sweet revenge, but it was a very, very sad end to the career of one of his generation's most courageous and intriguing publishers.

A. S. Frere died on 3 October 1984.

BOOK IV
1961–1983

The Management Overhauled:
Pick the New Editorial Broom

Having failed to sell Heinemann or to amalgamate it with another publisher, Tilling had no alternative but to strengthen their own grip on the management. Their normal policy was to interfere in the running of their companies only when they failed to give the expected return on invested funds. In the case of Heinemann once a realistic eye had scrutinized the figures and especially the stock valuation there was no gainsaying that it was making a loss and was even technically bankrupt. The need to impose a much stricter financial control had become urgent; changes in the group's structure and administration were overdue; above all, it was essential to provide the group with a new and more effective leadership.

Some of these changes were already in train before Frere and Hall resigned in April 1961 as respectively group chairman and deputy chairman, to become president and financial consultant. R. O. A. Keel's 'action committee' met weekly and he was promoted to be group managing director under Ryder's chairmanship. Supported by loans from Tillings in order to pay long outstanding debts, especially to outside printers, and their backing of large overdrafts at the bank, the purely financial side of the business was gradually but steadily put into better shape. The printing section in the form of The Windmill Press Ltd was sold to become a direct subsidiary of Tilling and before long evacuated Kingswood to occupy new premises in Crawley, thus providing much needed extra warehouse space at Kingswood (see Chapter 23). Rupert Hart-Davis had never been happy in the group and at his instigation it was decided to relinquish Heinemann's interest in his company (see Chapter 27); on the other hand a new group company was created in the spring of 1961 when the education department, under the energetic leadership of Alan Hill, became Heinemann Educational Books Ltd (HEB), a decision which was to have far-reaching consequences (see Chapter 26); so Hill gave up his position of joint-managing director of William

Heinemann. There were also other changes which will become clear in the course of ensuing chapters. In order to consolidate their control of Heinemann and as if to express their determination that it should regain its prosperity, Tilling purchased all the outstanding preference shares and 98.8 per cent of the ordinary shares. The Stock Exchange quotation was withdrawn in November 1961, as Heinemann was by then *de facto* a wholly owned subsidiary. The group's name was changed early in 1963 from Heinemann Publishers Ltd to the Heinemann Group of Publishers Ltd.

Inevitably and necessarily changes also occurred in the management of William Heinemann Ltd itself. In June 1961 Ryder took over from Hall, who had occupied the chair since 1959 when Frere decided to concentrate all his energies on the group. Dwye Evans changed his title from deputy-chairman to managing director which he had in fact been since 1955. But Fraser felt that new blood was also needed. Several of the firm's most distinguished authors were getting on in years and with the departure of Graham Greene and others in the wake of Frere the need to recruit a powerful and experienced acquisitions director had become imperative. This led to the appointment in February 1962 of Charles Pick who after a period with Victor Gollancz, starting as a bookshop rep., in 1935 became a founder member of Michael Joseph Ltd and its sales manager. Eventually, after Joseph's death in 1959, he became joint managing director with Peter Hebdon. Quite fortuitously Pick happened to be available because Michael Joseph Ltd had recently been bought as part of a package deal by Roy (later Lord) Thomson and Pick had resigned in protest, feeling unable to work for the new set-up. In December 1961 Peter Hebdon and Roland Gant, Heinemann's one-time editorial chief and then editorial director of Michael Joseph, also resigned as a protest against the company being sold over their heads. The three became involved in a plan, together with Allen Lane, to find themselves new careers with Jonathan Cape. At the last minute this had fallen through and all three were without jobs. It was at the suggestion of Fred Warburg that Pick was approached by Lionel Fraser.

Pick told me that at first he felt uncertain but 'I agreed to visit Fraser at Crewe House for an exploratory talk. Ryder was also there. They had no hesitation in revealing the full details of Heinemann's critical state, the problems with Frere and Hall, and much else. Of course I'd had no idea of how bad things were, but I was impressed with their frankness and when

Fraser offered me the job of managing director I accepted, though I explained that there was one condition: the three of us who had resigned from Michael Joseph had agreed to stick together. Could there be jobs for them as well?'

This turned out to be no problem, because Hebdon decided to return to Michael Joseph and Gant who, though he refused to be responsible for demoting his successor and old colleague, James Michie, was offered and accepted instead the post of editorial director at Secker & Warburg – sharing the responsibility with David Farrer. Pick thus joined the Heinemann board in February 1962, first as deputy and in November as full managing director, Dwye Evans moving up to be chairman and Ryder leaving to concentrate on his role as chairman of the group.

The company had without any doubt entered upon an entirely new phase. Inevitably there were fears that with a large, even if enlightened, financial conglomerate not merely owning it, but in practical control of its day-to-day operation, Heinemann's style of publishing would never be the same again. It seemed to be the end of a large slice of traditional publishing by independent entrepreneurs, using their own judgment and risking their own money, without unimaginative accountants breathing down their necks. Even during the Doubleday period this was essentially the system under which the firm had grown and, until recently, prospered. Although in many ways things never were the same again, in fact the heart of the publishing process – the commissioning of a book on the basis of individual assessment and of the financial risks involved – remained intact, even if the character and balance of the resulting list happened, as it did, to change.

During the early 1960s Tilling imposed a good many controls, but a publisher's main expenditure – on authors' advances, printing numbers, advertising, etc. – is particularly difficult to monitor except within very broad limits. Involvement by Tilling concentrated on the administrative side of the business, where it was indeed badly needed, not with the creative, literary functions. The lists were still free to reflect the personal judgment and taste of the top executives of each of the companies in the group and of their editorial staffs, readers, and advisers. Writing in the *Guardian* about British publishing in general, Peter Ryder confirmed this approach when he emphasized the need for publishers 'to consider more vigorously the need to make the utmost use of the talent they have and to provide the organization, service and funds that such talent should command. To talk of big business as an intruder into the field is to miss the point. Unless British publishing puts itself to rights and attracts financial support and know-how, it will lose its eminent position and in due course its worldwide influence to the utter shame of our nation. . . . The impact on publishing of visionary big business brings the need for a new approach to the problems of administration and service. This is no way means holding back or repressing the individuals who are the spark of publishing, but it does mean better planning and the taking of calculated risks. By providing the personalities with a firm footing (certainly not a feather bed) and a guide as to the resources at their command, they will be all the better able to carry through their vital function. Without "inspiration" this creative trade would be dead. It is in the interests of all to see that the conditions are fertile for nurturing such inspiration.'

Reflecting no doubt his experience with Heinemann, Ryder went on to write of the mistake of freezing funds in financing too many debtors and in too much stock, and of the need to watch overheads, to improve market research. He concluded by saying that 'the great volume of books will, I am certain, be produced by the larger and the more enlightened groups. Such groups may be in paperbacks or in hardbacks or perhaps in both. Their organization and strength will make them highly competitive and will enable them to allow their individual publishing members an exceptional degree of autonomy within a mutually agreed field of activity.'[1]

Reassuring words which turned out to be a largely accurate prophecy. Tilling's primary concern was with the return on funds invested, whether in the form of capital, of loans, or backing for an overdraft. There was never any shortage of the funds themselves and, except with the occasional large-scale project such as Winston Churchill's multivolumed biography, no permission had to be sought before embarking on books or whole series of books. Overall control was exercised by means of forward budgets of expenditure, set by the firm itself, and income and targets for expected turnover and profits. These were prepared annually by the enlarged accountancy staff at Kingswood under the direction of R. O. A. Keel, the new group managing director. If necessary, the budgets could be revised during the second half of a year, but they enabled Tilling to ascertain how much funds would be needed. There was of course a tendency to underestimate turnover and profits, because no one minds if you exceed your targets, though they mind a lot if you fail to reach them.

The Management Overhauled

Although among the largest British publishers, Heinemann was one of the smallest of the Tilling family of companies, but Lionel Fraser took a personal interest in its affairs and more than once admitted to Charles Pick that he would like to change places, to have meetings with famous authors instead of with fellow bankers! It appears that the rest of the Tillings board were still sceptical over being involved in such a risky business, liable to so much subjective judgment, but Fraser, by then seriously ill, arranged for Dwye Evans and Pick to appear before them in order to justify his own and Ryder's faith in Heinemann. This meeting was successful and the board seemed to be quite impressed with their long-term plans and the steps needed to bring the firm back into considerably increased profit, including the drastic writing down of the overvalued stock – it took three years to bring it down to its true value. The future, as always, depended on the books then being commissioned. The administration was being overhauled, the sales and promotion machinery improved, margins on books were being watched carefully, but without the right books, without new authors of the right calibre the finest, slickest administration would be meaningless in terms of profit and loss.

It was a question of saleability and of quality. Pick soon came to realize that each year there were too many new books and that too many people were commissioning them. 'Often they had given no thought to how that particular book was going to be promoted and sold, or at what price, or how many copies would be printed. The result was they had little idea if they had paid the right price for it. I had to put a stop to this immediately and insist that nothing should be commissioned without my agreement. Dwye was very co-operative and stopped buying books until we had discussed them.'

After a short time the annual number of new novels fell sharply. The following totals of all new titles (excluding re-issues and new editions) need, however, interpretation because up to 1961 they included titles published by the educational department and their exclusion the following year on the formation of the separate educational company cut the totals by some 50 titles a year; on the other hand the total of non-fiction was starting to rise, particularly with the establishment of a new department to publish books on technical and management subjects (see Chapter 26): 1961 – 230; 1962 – 183; 1963 – 168; 1964 – 181; 1965 – 180; 1966 – 228; 1967 – 226; 1968 – 149; 1969 – 155; 1970 – 125.

There can be no doubt that Charles Pick was more commercially minded than his predecessors, even more so than Charles Evans. It was as if he owed it to the confidence placed in him by Tilling that he should insist that no book could be taken on unless it would justify itself in terms of a profit, though with new authors this could not always be guaranteed and occasionally there were authors such as Paul Scott whose obvious promise suggested that their earlier books had to be seen as investments in the future. Costing will be discussed in a later section but, while Pick eschewed rigid formulae, a ratio of 5:1 between the published price and the cost of manufacture was considered to be the norm. In practice seldom more than 10 per cent net profit on turnover was made on most fiction, though this category additionally earned a steady overall increase from £65,000 in 1961 to over a £1 million in 1982 from Heinemann's share of subsidiary (mainly paperback) rights. This was not unlike a nation's 'invisible' exports. Most non-fiction titles, especially educational or technical titles, were unlikely to produce much from subsidiary rights and thus were expected to and did make a much higher rate of profit from the original edition.

During the 1960s publishers took on more of the role of impresarios as subsidiary rights of all kinds were becoming more important, including the growing outlets in film, radio, and television, but especially paperback and American rights (see pages 531–3). In fact many books were not financially viable without them. Rights potential had always to be considered when deciding to commission a book, particularly when a large advance was expected, much of which could ideally be offset by the publisher's share of the advances paid for the subsidiary rights. The early 1960s were before the era of 'chequebook publishing', an advance of £250–£300 being normal, but of course all advances had to be earned and each half year Pick would personally go through the carbon copies of the royalty statements to spot any not yet earned and to find out why. Dwye Evans was equally cautious and any member of the editorial staff proposing that a book be taken had to be prepared to answer his frequent enquiry: 'If your personal money were being invested in this book, would you still be prepared to risk it?'

Tilling were able to rest assured that the combination of Evans and Pick, different though they were in many ways, ensured that their firm's money was not going to be risked on many outside chances; though the perspectives of the race course and even its jargon are never far removed from publishing. You are always having to place bets and there are not all that many favourites. Nor is it easy to formulate a clearly defined publishing policy as so much depends on what turns up – and the ability to recognize its potential and to grasp opportunities. This is of course particularly true of fiction. Ideas for non-fiction books can be first thought up in the office and authors approached to write them, though this type of creative commissioning was seldom Heinemann's *forte*, at any rate since the death of William himself. By and large Dwye Evans and Pick continued the tradition of catering first of all to a large middlebrow market eager for entertainment and/or plenty of action – Wilbur Smith and Catherine Cookson were the natural successors to Hall Caine, Francis Brett Young, Nevil Shute, and others. But provided you keep a strong control over printing numbers, publishing even a first novel is not as risky as generally believed.

'Ultimately it is the marketplace that determines the character of your list,' was one of Pick's truisms. 'If certain types of book don't sell sufficiently or make their contribution to overheads and profits, well, you just cannot afford to go on publishing them.'

This may sound crashingly obvious, but it was a very different approach from William's, who balanced his Hall Caines with decidedly risky projects, largely, one suspects, just because they took his fancy. There were exceptions, but fewer new authors now joined the list on the strength only of their literary or intellectual merits. There were now virtually no slim volumes of poetry or belles lettres, apart from the perennial reprints of Kahlil Gibran and even further Gibran titles. There continued however to be limits, somewhat indistinctly defined, to Heinemann's broad mainstream of popular fiction. There were no 'servant girl romances' and it is noteworthy that Harold Robbins's money-spinning *The Carpetbaggers* with its sexual titillation every ten pages was rejected without much hesitation. It would have damaged the firm's reputation with the book-sellers as well as scared off the respectable, older authors on whom so much still depended.

Forward with the Backlist

The older, established writers were of course still very important, particularly their immense and continuing contribution to the backlist sales, but several of the most distinguished were approaching the end of their creative years. Somerset Maugham, for example, died in 1965 at the age of ninety-one, but one of Pick's earliest deals was to sell to Penguin the paperback rights in his titles for £65,000 advance against royalties. As is well known Maugham's last years were poisoned by a dispute with his daughter over the sale in 1962 of his notable collection of paintings which went for over £500,000. She claimed that her father had previously given her nine of the pictures and she secured a court order blocking the proceeds of the auction. When it was announced that Maugham intended to adopt his private secretary, Alan Searle, she was successful in getting the court at Nice to nullify the adoption and declare that she was his legitimate daughter. This wretched quarrel was eventually resolved, but there was further trouble over Maugham's last work, a book of reminiscences entitled *Looking Back*, which included an unpleasant attack on his late wife, Syrie. In the words of Ted Morgan's major biography of Maugham, when Frere 'saw the text, he was shocked. It seemed to him like the ravings of a lunatic. Abandoning all standards of good taste and discretion, Maugham was attacking, in the most degrading terms, a woman who was dead and could not defend herself. It was as if, preparing to die, he was determined to leave the world as he had entered it, alone and friendless. He seemed embalmed in hatred. . . .' He did not have a good word to say about her. Frere decided that Heinemann could not publish *Looking Back*, and alerted Doubleday, who agreed not to publish. He went to the Villa Mauresque that summer to tell Maugham of his decision. Frere was a friend of long standing as well as Maugham's literary executor. 'You can't let a man down when he gets to the end of his life and goes raving mad', he said, explaining his decision. Maugham was furious at what he considered meddling and told Frere he no longer wanted him as executor. Another reason may have been that Frere had ceased to be an executive officer of Heinemann.[2]

Spencer Curtis Brown, although Maugham's agent only for dramatic rights, took over the executorship and also *Looking Back*. It was never published in this country in book form, but it was serialized in the *Sunday Express* during September and October 1962, accompanied by sensational headlines. It provided a very depressing coda to the life's work of one of the most celebrated of Heinemann authors, one who in the words of *The Times* obituary 'graced the world of English letters with complete and polished assurance'.

Heinemann added to the Maugham archive by publishing Robert Calder's *W. Somerset Maugham and the Quest for Freedom* (1972) which after an opening biographical chapter describing his unhappy childhood and his search for freedom from his stammer, his small stature, and his homosexuality, provided a chronological survey of most of Maugham's work, analysing it in relation to his character. In 1989 this was followed by Dr Calder's full-scale biography of Maugham, *Willie*, which presented a much more sympathetic view than is to be found in other accounts; it was twice reprinted within weeks of publication and became one of the successes of the season. The firm had also published, in conjunction with Longman, Robin Maugham's *Somerset and all the Maughams* (1966) which contained a long, moving and almost cruelly frank chapter about his uncle. This supported Frere's conclusions about the unhappy, vindictive state of the octogenarian's mind. He also quoted from his uncle's writings to show that, despite the extent of his indisputable success as a writer, despite his riches, his picture collections, his Mediterranean villa with six servants and four gardeners, he still felt that 'his life had not worked out according to his plans. In *The Summing Up*, at the age of sixty, he had written, "For my own satisfaction, for my amusement and to gratify what feels to me like an organic need, I had shaped my life in accordance with a certain design, with a beginning, a middle, and an end. . . ." He thought, then, that he was near to the end of his carefully shaped existence. And at seventy, "ten years closer to death", he felt that the end had been reached. In *A Writer's Notebook* he wrote: "When I was forty I said to myself: 'That is the end of youth.' On my fiftieth birthday I said: 'It's no good fooling myself, this is middle age and I may just as well accept it.' At sixty I said: 'Now it's time to put my affairs in order, for this is the threshold of old age and I must settle my accounts.' I decided to withdraw from the theatre and I wrote *The Summing Up*, in which I tried to review for my own comfort what I had learnt of life and literature, what I had done and what satisfaction it had brought me. But of all anniversaries I think the seventieth is the most momentous. One has reached the threescore years and ten which one is accustomed to accept as the allotted span of man, and one can but look back upon such years as remain to one as uncertain contingencies stolen while old Time with his scythe has his head turned the other way".'[3] He was not to know that in his case the 'uncertain contingencies' would last for twenty-one years.

John Masefield died in 1967 at the age of eighty-eight, a year and a half after Maugham, with over a hundred books to his name and after thirty-seven years as Poet Laureate. Another corner-stone of the list had gone, but he continued writing to the end. His last works were *Old Raiger and Other Verse* (1964); *Grace Before Ploughing* (1966), fragments of autobiography from his early years; and *In Glad Thanksgiving* (1967), his happily titled final volume containing three fables in verse and twenty-six shorter lyrics, full of wisdom and mystical awareness.

Richard Church likewise did not find that old age prevented him from continuing to write, between 1963 and his death in 1972 contributing two more novels, *Prince Albert* (1963) and *Little Miss Moffatt* (1969); four volumes of essays; a children's book; *The Burning Bush* (1967), collected poems 1958–66; and a third volume of autobiography, *The Voyage Home* (1964). He also gave the firm frequent advice on books and sometimes reported on a manuscript.

Among the younger established writers there was of course Anthony Powell. As well as contributing seven more volumes in the *Dance to the Music of Time* sequence which concluded with *Hearing Secret Harmonies* (1975), he wrote four volumes of highly entertaining memoirs: *Infants of the Spring* (1976), *Messengers of Day* (1978), *Faces in my Time* (1980), *The Strangers all are Gone* (1982). There was also *Two Plays: The Garden God; The Rest I'll Whistle* (1971). The Powell cult was such that the firm in addition published Hilary Spurling's *Handbook to Anthony Powell's Dance to the Music of Time* (1977) which consisted of a chapter-by-chapter analysis of each of the twelve books plus an annotated index of all the characters. His wife, Violet Powell, also a writer, contributed eight books, including two volumes of autobiography, *Five out of Six* (1960) and *Within the Family Circle* (1976). Most of the others can probably best be described as entertaining literary/critical biographies such as *A Substantial Ghost* (1967) about Maude ffoulkes, who earned her living by ghosting books for various royal and aristocratic ladies; *The Irish Cousins* (1970) about the books and background of Somerville and Ross; and *Flora Annie Steel, Novelist of India* (1981), one of William's early bestselling authors (see pages 38–40).

Pamela Frankau came very close to leaving as a result of Frere's departure and the rows over excessive subediting, her agent, Peter Watt, writing to say that he had been instructed to ask for her release from a two-book option, particularly as she now planned to write a trilogy. Eventually after being offered better terms she agreed to stay, subject only to remarkably stringent conditions, among them being that 'the typescript is to be sent to the printers without any alteration of word or punctuation except for any clearly recognizable mistakes in literals; the author to write her own blurb which is to be published unaltered; a specimen page and jacket design (without illustration and with plain lettering) to be submitted to the author for approval; sales figures to be supplied at the end of each week.' For an illustrious publishing house to agree to such an arrangement must have been abnormal, but the trilogy was worth a measure of humiliation. It consisted of *Sing for your Supper* (1963), *Slaves of the Lamp* (1965), and *Over the Mountains* (1967). Very sadly, soon after the last volume was published Pamela Frankau died at the premature age of fifty-nine.

After her brilliant Balkan trilogy Olivia Manning wrote *A Romantic Hero and Other Stories* (1967) and two more novels for Heinemann, *The Play Room* (1969) and *The Rain Forest* (1974). Her sales still fell short of her talent, which had always been recognized in the editorial department, as shown by Roland Gant's letter to her after first reading *The Play Room*: 'Reading this has been an experience which engaged my enthusiasm, interest and the thrill of reading a work of art in which there is not a word too much. Your evocation of the abrasive relationship between parents and children and the sureness with which you portray the separateness of the contemporary adolescent world is masterly. At the end of the book the reader has got to know unforgettably such a wide variety of people – agitated and frustrated women, elderly husbands seeking refuge from them in chores, young people engaged in entertaining themselves with a kind of detached sensuality. Every character rings true, including the truly terrifying Mrs Toplady. My congratulations on having written such an unusual and gripping novel. I shall never be able to look at any South Coast town in quite the same way again'[4].

Inevitably income is related more closely to sales than to talent, and

Olivia was still dissatisfied and wanted better royalty terms. In 1965 she was complaining that her advance was no more than £600 in respect of royalties of 12½ per cent on the first 3,000, 15 per cent on the next 7,000, and 17½ per cent thereafter. She knew of other women novelists who, she said, always started at 15 per cent. Even when the firm met all her demands and she had no excuse for moving, she remained dissatisfied, though she still hesitated. In the end she transferred to Weidenfeld who offered her a large sum and published *The Danger Tree* (1977), the first of her Levant trilogy; but later she once confessed to me that she wished she had stayed with the old firm. Olivia died in 1980.

It is not only money which keeps an author with a publisher. Also needed are adequate publicity; personal attention; a personal and continuing relationship with an editor or director; very, very often the need for reassurance – writing is a lonely profession and a seedbed for neuroses. These truisms were confirmed when Frank Yerby decided to move after twenty-nine books and after appearing in the spring or autumn lists throughout the 1960–70s. After the publication of *Hail the Conquering Hero* (1978) it was impossible to reach an agreement largely because of the next book's immense length. In a letter to Roger Smith, an editorial director, Yerby wrote that 'at least as far as I was concerned, the money involved had nothing whatsoever to do with it. But the moment some member of your staff felt free to remark to my agent that Heinemann was prepared to dispense with Frank Yerby as one of their authors, if the terms were not met, both professional and personal pride compelled me to sever all future connections with a house with whom I have always felt most comfortable. Had the matter been put on any other basis but that one, I should have accepted your offer. But, since a great many things are far more important to me than money – my self respect among them! – you left me no other way out. Believe me, I am sorry. I valued the very special relationship I *thought* I had with Heinemann. . . . But then, publishing is a *business*; isn't it?. I was labouring under the misapprehension that it was a high – and kindred – art.'[5]

Even when an established author left, the rights in his earlier work still remained with the firm. This became an important issue in the case of Graham Greene, who demanded that the copyright in all his Heinemann titles revert to him, so that, in particular, there could be one uniform edition of all his works. He was prepared to buy them back, a sum of £50,000 being mentioned. Heinemann understandably refused, maintaining that Greene was an integral part of the backlist and, money apart, the damage that would be caused by his loss was incalculable. By 1965 all but two of his books carried the Heinemann imprint and if the rights were surrendered it would mean having to destroy 91,000 books and sheet stock. The wrangle continued for several years during which Greene refused to agree to the acceptance of an offer by Penguin to publish paperbacks of a further six of his books (earlier they had published ten of them). In an attempt to break the stalemate Pick held a meeting with Max Reinhardt, who tried to act as an intermediary, but it was to no avail – Heinemann would not let go of their rights and Greene still vetoed the Penguin sale.

Pick had made several offers to meet Greene who, though he had nothing against Pick personally, always said there would be no point. Then out of the blue a telegram arrived suggesting that when Pick was next in the south of France, perhaps he would drop in for a drink or a meal. It happened that Pick was due the very next week-end to visit Paul Gallico, who was also living in Antibes. They met and talked for five hours. At first Greene reiterated his demands, but a compromise was reached when Pick proposed that a new uniform edition of all his works should be published jointly by Heinemann and The Bodley Head, both firms retaining all rights in the titles they had originally published. This was soon put into operation. With this problem settled Greene also lifted his veto on the Penguin deal for his other books which were sold for an advance of £50,000, followed by a further deal with Penguin for £430,000. Following this meeting Pick and Greene met every year or so. Greene told me that he had a great personal liking for Pick. Once again, it had been the personal relationship that mattered.

Most of the backlist authors remained faithful, among them J. B. Priestley, who, after Maugham's death, was the unrivalled doyen of the list. Almost until his own death in 1984 at eighty-nine he continued to be published regularly. The 1960–70s saw ten new novels, perhaps the most important being *Saturn over the Water* (1961), *Lost Empires* (1965), and *The Image Men* (1968). An entirely new genre appeared with *The Prince of Pleasure* (1969), a quarto-sized book with lavish illustrations produced by the 'packager' George Rainbird. It was a great success and Priestley with typical zest exploited it with similar lush volumes on *The Edwardians* (1970) and *Victoria's Heyday* (1972). There was also a steady flow of volumes of essays, memoirs, and biography. Heinemann certainly did him proud during his last years, his sixtieth, seventieth, and eightieth birthdays being marked by resplendent banquets and fulsome speeches. He was invited to open the new warehouse at Kingswood and the new London offices at Upper Grosvenor Street. In his gruff way he enjoyed it all, including getting the OM – 'They've been too long about giving it me,' he grumbled. The firm also commissioned a thorough, workmanlike study of his work by Susan Cooper: *J. B. Priestley – Portrait of an Author* (1970).

Perhaps no one summed up his life better than Jack Lambert in an obituary article in *The Sunday Times*: 'He was pre-eminent as a laureate of deprivation and disappointment – *The Good Companions* may be an escapist fairy story, but it is a feeble imagination which cannot feel the reality of pain from which the members of the little troupe are escaping, just as in *When we are Married* the high jinks hardly mask the stifling strains beneath. The tragedy of man is expressed most effectively through a comic mask; and Priestley was indeed a priest of the Comic Vision. Never more so than in his own person. Capable of startlingly disagreeable ungraciousness when required to go through his formal paces, especially on special occasions, he was in relaxation the embodiment of a delicious spirit of mischief, his little eyes glinting, his pipe-laden lower lip as expressive as his wrinkled brow, his cavernous mumble as gleefully derisive as his well of absurd similes. . . . Take him for all in all, a man not to be underrated, or a writer to be forgotten.'[6]

It was at once apparent to Pick that too much reliance was placed on the ageing established authors, but paradoxically at the same time the riches of the backlist were not being sufficiently exploited. Because of the war and paper shortages it was understandable that many books had been forgotten, but there had been no proper recording of sales and stocks in order that books going out of print automatically came up for review. Assisted by Tim Manderson, the sales director, a detailed survey of out-of-print titles was undertaken and many were brought back to life. It was found that if not too many were revived at once, it was possible for the initial subscription to cover all the production costs of a reprint. This was normally sufficient to supply anticipated demand over three years with the price being increased each year in line with general inflation. For example, fourteen of Margery Allingham's titles were out of print. After an experiment with three of them, it was found possible to republish all fourteen with prints of three to four thousand each. Another good find from the backlist was the Constance Garnett translation of *War and Peace*, which had been out of print for many years and now sold over 100,000 copies.

A dramatic and very effective way of further exploiting the backlist was the revival in 1975 of the Heinemann omnibus volume. The idea came to Charles Pick and Tom Rosenthal of Secker & Warburg one hot afternoon while stuck in a traffic block while returning from a meeting at Kingswood. Between them Heinemann and Seckers had enough popular authors to make the project feasible. The concept was to provide the equivalent of the pre-war thousand pages for 3s.6d., each volume carrying three to four full-length novels, but when estimates and dummies were prepared it was found that even with a print as high as 25,000 the lowest published price would be £12.50, which was too much.

Frustrated, Pick went round to seek advice from Paul Hamlyn of Octopus Books, who had a unique knowledge of popular book marketing. Paul was at once enthusiastic. It was the best idea to land on his desk in a year. Without hesitation he said the right price was £3.95 with a print of 50,000. He went on to explain that W. H. Smith should be the sole distributors in the UK, that the project should bypass the normal Heinemann sales machinery and travellers. It was rapidly agreed that it should become a joint Heinemann/Octopus venture, though in the trade it soon became known as the 'Pickles' venture. Profits were shared equally. The authors were offered a flat 5 per cent royalty on the published price whether copies were sold at home or overseas – which accounted for half the turnover.

The meeting with Hamlyn took place in December 1976 and the first ten titles were in the shops by the spring of 1977. The standard of printing, paper and boards was elegant and they looked what they were – extraordinarily good value for money. Heinemann supplied seven of the first authors and Seckers three. An impressive list: Orwell, Maugham, Steinbeck, D. H. Lawrence, Kafka, Galsworthy, Michener, Wilbur Smith, Nevil Shute, Erle Stanley Gardner. They were an immediate, triumphant success. In the week of publication a reprint of a further 50,000 of each title was ordered, making already a total of a million books. Other publishers were brought in and four more volumes appeared the following March: Wells, Hemingway, Graham Greene, C. S. Forester. They were followed by Waugh, Scott Fitzgerald, Morris West, Georgette Heyer, Raymond Chandler, Dennis Wheatley, and a collection of famous plays. By 1983 sixty-five Pickles titles had been published in the UK and a total of 3.68 million copies had been sold with a sales value of £7.33 million. Heinemann's half share of net profit exceeded £1 million and royalties paid were at a similar level. Not all the titles have sold equally well, but it is interesting that among the fastest sellers have been Orwell, Steinbeck, and D. H. Lawrence. The paperback firms felt threatened by the series, but their own sales of Pickles authors showed no signs of dropping. It was clear that a virtually new market had been opened up. The widespread exposure of the fat glossy volumes drew attention to their authors and this led people to buy their individual titles. Books indeed sell books.

Migrants from Michael Joseph

In the wake of Charles Pick's arrival came a number of established authors hitherto published by Michael Joseph. Their transfer did much to offset the authors who had migrated to The Bodley Head after the departure of Frere. Among the newcomers was Monica Dickens, who by 1983 had written five novels for Heinemann as well as a volume of autobiography, *An Open Book* (1978), and some very successful children's books (see page 562). She had originally made her name with two light-hearted autobiographical/documentary books – *One Pair of Hands* about her experience as a cook-general and *One Pair of Feet* as a wartime nurse. Monica Dickens was a writer who because of her early popular success paid the penalty of being underrated. The critic A. S. Byatt has made this point succinctly: 'Literary reviewing tends to create an artificial border-line between serious novelists and bestselling women writers. Yet writers on both sides of this line often produce both good books and pot-boilers. There are women writers, highly praised for contemporary relevance, who alternate the pure moan and the consoling fantasy with more complex work. Equally, there are novelists like Monica Dickens who offer in-formation, insight, and a certain kind of artistic pleasure which is unavailable elsewhere, but are never seriously discussed because they were classified some time ago as bestsellers.'[7] Like her great-grandfather

Charles Dickens, she writes her novels as a social observer and with compassion for poverty, disadvantage, and misfortune.

This approach was particularly true of her first novel for Heinemann, *Kate and Emma* (1964), in which the two girls come from very different backgrounds. Kate is a sixteen-year-old offender in need of 'care and protection'; Emma is the daughter of the magistrate and, accompanying a social worker on his calls, learns how it is that young children and adolescents can be daily subjected to brutality and neglect and can be the victims of their parents' bitterness, exhaustion, and frustration. Emma also learns that affection can work miracles. Another documentary novel, *The Listeners* (1970), is built around human crisis and suicide, the title referring to the real life Samaritans who at the end of a telephone line are there not to preach or judge, but just to listen to potential suicides, the bereaved, the sexually deviant, the old and forgotten.

Her correspondence with Pick and Gant reveals the importance of the relationship between author and publisher and her constant need for reassurance and someone with whom to discuss her problems on the current book and ideas for the next book. Here are three random extracts from her letters written from Massachusetts were she lived with her American husband: 'Dearest Charles, Thank God for you. That is just what I have been thinking all along, and just what I hoped you'd say. Can you imagine spending a year writing a Gothic novel and then finding that everything on the bestseller list was imitation Miss Read? I'm not sure I know what a Gothic novel is anyway. Now I needn't find out.'[8] 'I was so very sad that I couldn't see Roland. However, we had a good chat on the telephone and he sounded very cheery. He is so stimulating. What a marvellous man he is. He told me he'd seen Lee [Lee Barker at Doubledays, her American publisher] and Lee said he thought I was unhappy with Doubleday because I hadn't written for so long! Ye Gods, it's bad enough publishers having to nurse the authors along to keep up their morale, but now authors have to do it to publishers. Anyway, I wrote him a "beautiful letter" and he is now as happy as a clam.'[9] 'I am still seething with excitement about you liking the book. Heavens, there is nothing more marvellous than to slog and agonize for months and finally struggle up to the surface and hear someone say "It's good!"'[10]

Very different was the next migrant from Michael Joseph, the American Paul Gallico. He did not attempt realism: '"We live in a rough, cold world today. But I make a different world when I write; I make it what I think it ought to be".[11] He was prolific and before he died in 1976 he wrote nearly twenty titles for Heinemann, including some for children. Though none approached the total of his wartime bestseller *The Snow Goose*, which sold a million copies, the sales of his Heinemann titles were seldom below 30,000 and some were higher, including the first, *Coronation* (1962), which topped 100,000. He prided himself on usually being able to forecast to Heinemann his sales accurately, though he never took an unrealistic advance because 'that way I'm in the saddle'.

His books were very different from each other, though they fell into easily recognizable categories: there were adventure stories such as *The Zoo Gang* (1971) and *The Poseidon Adventure* (1969) about the passengers in a cruiseship that turns turtle, made into one of the first 'disaster' films; comic whimsical tales like the charlady *Mrs Harris, M.P.* (1965); charming cat books such as *The Silent Miaow* (1964) and *Honourable Cat* (1972); more conventional novels like *Matilda* (1970). Many of his stories conveyed a quality of naïve innocence and a tenderness that only just avoided sentimentality, but he was always in control of his material and the complete professional. He knew the immense importance of finding the right title: 'I have but one fly to deposit into your ointment', he once wrote to Pick, 'and that is that I have decided to keep my title *Love, Let me not Hunger* (1963). I put a great deal of thought into this, but more than thought I should say the instinctive feeling of a writer that he has hit upon a title which not only describes the theme of his book without giving it away, but which will also intrigue the reader. I think the most dangerous thing a book can have is a label instead of a title; one that says nothing, tells nothing, catches neither the ear nor the eye and issues no challenge.'[12]

Like most authors Gallico was always pressing for more advertising, but not merely of the conventional kind. He once told Pick that '. . . today there is simply no longer time for the word of mouth spread on which we used to depend. Things are happening too quickly upon the heels of the old, and new methods and ideas are needed to catch the potential readers and induce them to buy.'[13] After the publication of *The Boy who Invented the Bubble Gun* (1974) he wrote to tell Pick that he felt very let down: 'Even a normal effort for publicizing and promoting this book would have eventually paid off in hardcover and paperback sales. The fact that the book got on the bestseller list and stayed there with no help whatsoever from Number 15 Queen Street seemed to me to indicate that the book must have some merit. . . . I know you say that the bestseller lists are phonies but phoney or not every publisher is glad to have his books listed and I would say that publishers would be glad to keep them there.'[14] Pick sent a dignified, even affectionate reply, denying the accusations, and Heinemann remained his publisher.

Another of Pick's migrating authors was Richard Gordon (pseudonym for Dr Gordon Ostlere) who with his long series of 'Doctor' books for Michael Joseph, starting with *Doctor in the House*, had won a reputation for writing tales of inspired dottiness in the tradition of P. G. Wodehouse. The goings on in the corridors and wards of St Swithin's were carried on into the 1960–70s with familiar characters like the fearsome Sir Lancelot Spratt, the work-shy Dr Grimsdyke, and many new ones in several new 'Doctor' titles for Heinemann – e.g., *The Summer of Sir Lancelot* (1965), *Doctor on the Boil* (1970), *Doctor in the Nude* (1973), *Doctor on the Job* (1976). Again like Wodehouse Gordon was a deceptively skilful writer and he developed several new literary veins, though the background was usually but not always still medical. *The Facemaker* (1967), *Surgeon at Arms* (1968), and *The Facts of Life* (1969) were serious, but not solemn novels about doctors who are presented as convincing characters with emotions and shortcomings like the rest of us. The reader learns effortlessly a great deal about modern medicine, about new treatments and medical conservatism. *The Facts of Life* had the distinction of being banned in South Africa.

With *The Sleep of Life* (1975) Gordon turned to social and medical history with a novel that combines the adventures and loves of a young man in the 1840s with the invention of and early experiments with anaesthetics, against a background of hospitals and doctors in London, Boston, and Edinburgh. A third literary vein appeared with three biographical novels based on well-known figures, starting with *The Private Life of Florence Nightingale* (1978) and followed by private lives of *Jack the Ripper* (1980) and *Dr Crippen* (1981). Yet another departure were two hilarious, 'anthropological' guides to the habits, customs, beliefs, etc. of the suburbs – *Good Neighbours* (1976) and *Happy Families* (1978). There was also a funny but instructive guide to *Instant Fishing* (1979) for trout.

Among other authors who followed Pick from Michael Joseph were James Leasor, Richard Condon, and Robert van Gulik, who will make their appearance elsewhere in this book. Similarly, authors on Michael

Joseph's list followed Roland Gant to Secker & Warburg, including Lancelot Hogben, the Canadian Farley Mowat, and the American historian, Harrison Salisbury.

'Instant' Books and
Coronet among the Weeds

Typical of the Charles Pick style and his approach to publishing was the arrival of the occasional 'instant book'. To Heinemann at any rate this was an entirely new genre, its elements consisting of speedy production, intensive promotion of a new type and, not to put too fine a point on it, 'hype'. These books possessed intrinsic merits, but the publisher's role exceeded the traditional one of 'midwife' and played a considerable part in their success.

Scandal '63, published in September of the same year, was a good example of the genre. It was written by three members of the *Sunday Times* Insight team – Clive Irving, Ron Hall, Jeremy Wallington – who provided a shocked nation with a readable documentary account of the Profumo affair and to a large extent succeeded in putting it into perspective. The tangle of sex and national security, of politics and ambition, protocol and hypocrisy, involving the Secretary of State for War, Christine Keeler the call girl, Ivanov the Soviet naval attaché, weekend parties by the pool at Cliveden, and the events leading to Stephen Ward's trial and suicide were stitched together with skill and at breakneck speed.

The idea for the book was born shortly after the news had broken in June 1963. The research, including fifty interviews, and the writing of 80,000 words, took only eight weeks. The last pages of the typescript, all of which had to be read carefully for libel by Harold Rubinstein, were in Heinemann's hands on August 8th; the proofs were with the authors in twenty-four hours; and the first copies came off the press on August 26th – very different from the publisher's normal gestation period of nine months! It may have caused temporary dislocation in the production department, but it was a venture that showed the staff and the book world generally that a new spirit was stirring the sails of the Windmill.

Scandal '63 was published as a trade paperback at 7s.6d. and within a month had sold over 60,000 copies. The reviewers recognized the book's serious intent and its quality, despite the speed at which it had been written. Only *The Times Literary Supplement* disapproved, spoke of 'a shabby race' to get the book out, and postponed reviewing it until after the forthcoming publication of the official Denning Report on the scandal. It did however print a letter of protest from Clive Irving, one of the authors, who maintained that '*Scandal '63* must be judged, if fairly, according to its own objectives. The most important lesson it brings, regardless of its quality, is the opportunity to use the paperback as an extension of contemporary reportage, a form of journalism with a long history but which has latterly been neglected. With partisan motives this is pamphleteering. With objective motives it is intended to extend the public knowledge when it is vital that this should be done. Your contemptuous comment discloses that you do not recognize this requirement. Unless publishing is to be confined to the limits imposed by your attitude, which we hope it is not, journalism can find a fresh outlet with this kind of book. To dismiss it as shabby opportunism is less than justice.' This was followed by a letter from Dwye Evans who complained that 'it appears that you have prejudged the book on its physical appearance. . . . The implication that the authors and publisher are "cashing in" on sensationalism by joining in a "shabby race" seems to indicate an extraordinary lack of perception of the importance of the Profumo affair and the merits of this particular book.'[15]

The same year saw also the appearance of another title that exemplifies the new promotional approach, though it was autobiographical and by the twenty-year-old ex-debutante daughter of a peer, Charlotte Bingham. She called it *Coronet among the Weeds*, 'weeds' being one of the four categories into which her world divided men: 'supermen, weeds, drips, and leches.' The last three abounded in Knightsbridge and Chelsea in summer and at hunt balls in winter. Supermen were few and far between, though the author's search for her own superman provided her central theme. With what the blurb called a 'deceptive innocence' she missed little in describing her progress through the conventional upbringing of convent school, being 'finished' in Paris, cooking and typing lessons, and the round of a London season with its tea parties, cocktail parties, dinner parties, country-house weekend parties, and the dances – though she did it in 'the modern style, wearing the ladders on the inside of her stockings and patching up her shoes with tape'.

Her book's extraordinary success must have surprised everyone. It went through several printings, rapidly selling a total of almost 25,000 copies. It was serialized in the *People*, which spent £20,000 on promoting the book, including screening a 60-second TV commercial. At Frankfurt the American rights were rapidly sold and translation rights eight times, her German publisher reading the typescript overnight and making an offer over breakfast. Bill Holden, then the firm's publicity director, was particularly good at handling the high-pressure promotion needed by this kind of untraditional title: 'Charlotte was a gas, a very nice girl. She and I cooked up this thing together. It came along just at the right time, just when people were getting tired of kitchen sink dramas and the reality of life. She was pretty, young, and explained how ghastly it was to be taken round all the debs' events. In a sense you might say she was on the side of the workers and she appealed to the journalists who by and large came from working-class backgrounds and enjoyed taking the mickey out of the rich. It was easy to get her interviews on TV, though in those days it used few authors. We did a lot of crazy things, including roaring round the Midlands where, appearing at a working men's club, she got caught up in an act with a boa constrictor. Nobody could believe she was a virgin and the tougher journalists kept trying to make her in the back of taxis. But she said she was and I think she was, being a Catholic.'

Charlotte appeared to enjoy every minute of her success, including the royalties which came to a great deal even for an ex-deb in the 1960s. She followed with a novel, *Lucinda* (1966) – 'The fact that Lucinda was made to wear a liberty bodice until she was fourteen might perhaps account for her being a virgin at twenty-five' – and with *Coronet among the Grass* (1972) which dealt neatly with the state of marriage in modern swinging society. She did not find it easy, however, to repeat her first kind of success.

Two super-fast instant books came from Randolph Churchill. The first, *The Fight for the Tory Leadership* (1963), described the struggle behind the scenes to decide who was to take over the leadership from Harold Macmillan. It was commissioned on November 8th; the typescript was delivered in the first week of December; the first copies were ready by December 23rd; publication was January 13th. It rapidly sold over 14,000 copies.

It was followed in 1967 by *The Six Day War* written by Randolph

Churchill and his son Winston who combined to produce a penetrating political analysis with on-the-spot reporting of Israel's pre-emptive blitz-krieg against the allied threat from Egypt, Jordan, and Syria; the war that led to the occupation of the West Bank, the Golan Heights and, for a while, the Sinai Peninsula. Randolph supplied the opening chapters, which charted the historical background to Israel's presence in the Middle East and the events leading up to the 1967 confrontation, including the roles played by the major Western powers. Winston described the actual fighting: the surprise air strike by the Israelis which paralysed the numerically superior Egyptian Air Force; the lightning ground operations by the three Israeli armoured divisions in Sinai; the symbolic occupation of the whole of Jerusalem; the vicious fighting on the Jordanian and Syrian fronts. The on-the-spot reportage combined with political and strategic analysis amounted to a *tour de force* and was well received. Basil Liddell Hart, then the doyen of military correspondents, reported that it was 'very well written on the whole and in parts brilliantly. . . . some of the chapters can rightly be termed fine contributions to historical literature, even though they be classified as "instant history". . . .' The speed with which the book was written was matched by remarkably streamlined publishing. It was a joint operation with Penguin Books, who shared costs and profits and were solely responsible for distribution. The book was commissioned on June 9th; the final corrections to the proofs were made on August 2nd; the first printing of 75,000 copies was delivered on August 4th; copies were distributed in Fleet Street on August 5th prior to publication on August 11th. A reprint of 100,000 was ordered on publication day which started to be delivered on August 14th. The book was serialized in the *Sunday Telegraph*.

Although not an 'instant' book, James Leasor's *Green Beach* (1975) was another example of Pick's capacity for putting together a certain type of book. The idea came from Michael Klinger, the film producer, who told Charles Pick about a young radar expert who had been sent along with the British and Canadian commando raid on Dieppe in 1942. His role was to investigate the importance and accuracy of a German radar station on a cliff-top outside the town. The man chosen to do the job was Jack Nissenthall, an RAF flight sergeant from Bow in East London. Being Jewish he was given a pseudonym in case he was captured, though this was unlikely because the bodyguard of ten Canadian soldiers detailed to blast their way into the radar station also had orders to kill Nissenthall if he were wounded or capture seemed imminent – he knew too much to risk his being tortured to force him to reveal highly classified information. After surviving the heavily opposed landing the little party reached the radar post, only to find it bristling with machine-guns and they failed to enter it. He noticed however that cables leading from the radar station were nailed to surrounding trees. He cut them and when eventually he escaped back to England with only one survivor from his bodyguard he learned that cutting the cables forced the German radar operators to send their messages in clear speech by radio telephone and a great deal was learned about the strength and weaknesses of the German system. Although the original objective had not been achieved, the venture had been worth while.

Potentially it was a story which smacked of a bestseller, but Klinger knew of no one who could write it. Pick recommended James Leasor, who rapidly produced an exciting three-page synopsis. Armed only with this and a talent for conveying his own enthusiasm for a project he believed in, Pick in a couple of days at the Frankfurt Book Fair was able to sell rights in the story to the New York publishers William Morrow and translation rights to nine other publishers. This brought in $354,000; on top of this were the sale of UK and US paperback rights which brought in considerable sums, and a substantial bookclub order. The book itself was something of a disappointment, though the UK hardback edition sold 19,466 copies, but it showed what can sometimes be done with three pieces of paper at Frankfurt. It reinforces the cynical view that it is sometimes easier to make spectacular deals when there is no complete typescript for editors and advisers to get their teeth into.

Selling and P.R. in the
Swinging Sixties and After

The increase in the UK publishing industry's annual total of new books not only continued during 1961–83, the period covered by Book IV, but towards the end of the period escalated as shown below (the figures in brackets were new editions and reprints):

1961	24,893	(6,406)
1965	26,358	(5,313)
1970	33,489	(9,977)
1975	35,608	(8,361)
1980	48,158	(10,776)
1983	51,071	(12,091)

The number of competing publishers had also continued to grow so that in 1960 1,843 publishers had books listed in *Books in Print* and by 1983 it listed no fewer than 9,805 – though it depends on what is meant by 'publisher', only 229 being members of the Publishers' Association. As before, the real competition came from the ten or so leading publishers who between them accounted for some sixty per cent of the total market. Throughout the period it was a case of far too many titles chasing too few readers. Although minimum printing numbers for a title still exceeded those of pre-war years, the tendency with fiction and general books was for the print runs to fall. This led to higher unit costs and therefore of retail prices, though a bigger factor was undoubtedly not only the rapid growth in inflation generally but specific increases in the costs of book manufacture. Retail prices of books increased faster than the general cost of living, and this in turn made sales more difficult.

The quality and appeal of the books published therefore had to overcome increased market resistance, and of course special demands were made on the firm's sales and publicity departments who inevitably tended to become scapegoats if the sales of a particular title fell short of expectations. It is not always appreciated how relatively small was the UK market for books compared with other commodities – 0.4 per cent of consumer spending in 1982 or less than £10 per head a year.[1] It has been written that 'a sizeable proportion of the population – perhaps a third – are completely uninterested in books. Probably another third are genuinely interested. The middle third could well be made a target group – they could be encouraged and helped.'[2]

It has been among this middle third that the expansion in bookbuying was presumably achieved, particularly (as will be described) by the paperback houses and the bookclubs; and also by firms such as Hamlyn and Octopus (also started by Paul Hamlyn) and some of the book 'packagers' which together reached for sections of the public that normally never entered the traditional bookshop. They devised large ranges of widely popular titles, superbly illustrated and consumer-oriented in that they gave people exactly what they wanted at prices way below that of the traditional publisher. Heinemann had its share of these new markets but for the most part only indirectly through sales of titles to bookclubs and paperback houses and in the case of the 'Pickles' series through Octopus. Only very occasionally did it issue a general book that was consciously consumer-oriented and created to appeal visually and by its contents to these new markets. Of course the firm continued to cater for and indeed energetically expand series of books for specific markets such as schools, further education, and children, but for the general reader its main thrust was still through the traditional book trade and libraries. Likewise the overall pattern of its list, very rightly it may be thought, tended to be modified rather than altered. It knew for example that the book trade still looked to it in particular for a 'good read', for well written and deftly constructed fiction which did not make too many demands on the reader – and over the years the firm continued to supply it: e.g., Catherine Cookson and Wilbur Smith. Of course this is an oversimplification because there was plenty of literary fiction as well. Pick always maintained that fiction was the most stable branch of general publishing and for any novel 70–80 per cent of the first printing was usually sold in the calendar year of publication. He was disappointed if less than 60 per cent was sold ahead of publication. But there can be no doubt that in terms of turnover it was the middlebrow fiction that underwrote a considerable bulk of the overheads and profit.

It is said that in the USA one book is bought for every book borrowed, whereas in the UK one book is bought for every fifteen borrowed. Loans from public libraries grew from 446.32 million books in 1961–62 to 645.38 million in 1982–83. There can be no doubt that the public libraries continued to be a most important segment of the market – in fact for some categories of books it was crucial. In the case of a first novel with a print of, say, 2,000 copies, as much as 90 per cent went to the libraries; with an average novel with a print of, say, 3,500–4,000 the libraries would account for about 75 per cent of the sales. It is only with a print run of 8–9,000 that the library sale is not so vital. Without the libraries, much fiction could never have been published. This was equally true of many general titles, e.g., an erudite but non-academic historical biography with a potential peak sale of 3,000. Library orders amounting to about 1,800 virtually underwrote it.

There were variations from borough to borough, but public libraries placed an increasing percentage of their orders with specialized library suppliers instead of with bookshops, until some seventy per cent of library orders were supplied in this way. There were five major suppliers: Woolstons and Blunts, now absorbed in John Menzies; Askews; Holt-Jackson; W. & R. Holmes; plus a number of smaller concerns. Understandably they always received priority attention from the sales staff and were allowed an average of 40 per cent discount; in turn they gave the permitted 10 per cent to the libraries, but they also charged for servicing the books – for example, adding plastic covers. With some books Heinemann would sell additional unbound sheets which the suppliers furnished with extra strong bindings which lasted for 60–70 borrowings instead of the normal 30–35.

During the 1960s library grants were higher than for some time and this led to heavy restocking of backlist titles – defined for Heinemann's purposes as being published prior to the current calendar year. The proportion of backlist to frontlist was approximately 40 per cent back to 60 per cent front. The proportion tended to be the same during the 1970s, but from 1980 onwards backlist sales declined steeply, so that by the mid-1980s they dropped to approximately 12 per cent with 88 per cent front list. This did not apply to children's books for which the ratio remained at about 50:50 per cent. One reason for this discrepancy was that children's books were less affected – but only *less* – by the arrival of paperbacks in libraries. As long ago as the 1970s they first began to appear on library shelves, but in barely noticeable numbers. It varied from library to library but by the 1980s paperbacks were seriously encroaching on traditional territories and this particularly applied to backlist titles. In the early 1970s, for example, any backlist title by Georgette Heyer would sell 800–1,200 hardback copies per year, dependent on the popularity of the particular book, but by the mid-1980s they would sell a mere 80–150 copies. Maugham, Shute, and even D. H. Lawrence showed a similar decline.

Towards the end of the 1970s and early 1980s with the onset of the economic recession and stringent cuts in local authority and educational spending the library market began to decline alarmingly. The trend was summed up in an official report which noted that 'book funds have *not* risen at the same rate as other categories of expenditure during the 1979–80 to 1983–4 period. . . . [By 1984–5] in England and Wales the real spending power of library book funds has declined by 34.2 per cent since 1978–9. The decline has been fairly uniform across the regions of the country, down by 33.6 per cent in London, by 33.9 per cent in the English counties, by 32.8 per cent in the Metropolitan Districts, by 38.6 per cent in Wales, by 26.3 per cent in Scotland. . . . There are only seven library authorities in the United Kingdom which have managed a real increase in their book expenditure since 1978–9.'[3] It is difficult to give specific examples but these cuts came to be reflected not only in declining library turnover but also in the decline in the publication of certain kinds of books, for the most part those which lacked a wide, popular 'market-orientation' but which nonetheless were of literary and social value and which were always to be found at the heart of the Heinemann list. The publication of this kind of title increasingly moved over to the new educational company, HEB, where it was regarded as an essential complement to school books.

In 1960 Derek Priestley was succeeded as home sales manager by Alexander Fullerton, whose novels were also published by the group, Priestley becoming a director and more involved with authors and commissioning books in close association with Dwye Evans. Fullerton stayed for a relatively short time and when he left, Alewyn Birch added the home market to his existing responsibility for overseas. It didn't work out. 'After two very uncomfortable years', Birch told me, 'they came to the conclusion that two managers were needed and I went back to the export side. It caused me much chagrin because I had never been given the assistance I needed.' There was also a good deal of friction between Birch and Pick, though they remained good friends, and before long, in 1967, Birch resigned and went on to become chairman of Granada.

His successor was Tim Manderson, a personal friend of Lionel Fraser's and who had been brought in to help Hall at Kingswood. Manderson too was made a director. 'From the outset', he explained, 'my aim was to make the strongest possible personal contact with the key shops at home. As well as the big wholesalers who of course got very special attention, there were about 130 shops that were really important and I made a point of visiting them all personally as often as I could. In addition I got round to see some 20–30 other shops with smaller turnovers but which were intelligently run and were prepared to have a special go with our books.'

The task of the sales manager is shown strikingly in a survey of sales by outlet based on the returns in 1977 by twenty-two publishers: direct to retailers, 51 per cent; direct to wholesalers, 16.7; library suppliers, 15.0; educational contractors, 6.7; others (including bookclubs), 10.0. Parallel statistics indicate where the public bought their books in 1973–74: W. H. Smith, John Menzies, Boots, 34 per cent; bookshops, 25; newsagents, 11; stationers, 7; department stores, 5; bookclub/by post, 8; other/don't know, 2.[4] In the 1970s home discount terms were raised from 33⅓ to 35 per cent off the retail price. Because of the cost of handling small orders, at one stage 20p was added to every invoice for servicing it, but this was unpopular and, instead, a charge of 50p was added to every invoice under £10. This encouraged shops to group their orders, but however small the order, it still qualified for the full discount. Members of the Charter Bookselling group – i.e., which adhered to minimum amounts of floor space, stocks, window frontage, training, etc. – received an additional 2½ per cent discount. Wholesalers normally qualified for 40 per cent and the large bookselling chains like Blackwells, Pentos, and the more recent Waterstones were always in a position to press for better terms in return for large orders. This meant that the pressure on blockbusting authors was exerted at both ends – the big booksellers wanted extra discount and the author extra royalties. All books were sold firm. When, however, the subscriptions for a book that should sell well were not up to expectations, copies were sometimes sent out on a sale or return basis and, if necessary, taken back after three months, provided they were clean and undamaged. Great discrimination was needed when deciding which books and which booksellers could be treated in this way.

'All the bigger accounts', Manderson explained, 'were visited by the reps. roughly every four or five weeks. Another group was visited every three months. But of course the London shops saw us much more frequently, some of them once a week. When I took over we had nine representatives plus one who concentrated on Secker titles. Towards the end of the 1970s it dropped to a total of eight, though later it went up to eleven.'

It was essential for the sales manager to keep in constant touch with his representatives. Normally they came into the head office only twice a year, to be briefed on the new books, to chat with editors, to meet the occasional author of the moment, and to be reassured that they really did matter. It is a lonely job, usually involving long hours of motoring, and inevitably prone to disappointment. The rep. knows that when he arrives with a bagful of new books – and this is particularly true if he represents a group – he cannot possibly hope to sell copies of all of them, or even many of them. The bookjacket blurbs may make each sound indispensable, but not to your experienced professional buyer. Nor does it pay to be wildly enthusiastic about all of them. Above all the rep. needs to be trusted, not only about the character and quality of a book, but about what the firm is actually doing to promote it. It is trust, often built up over many years, that lands a sale of that difficult, but genuinely worthwhile, new book by an unknown author. The order may be for only a single copy, but a rep. has to persuade himself that at least it's a start.

Lionel Foot, experienced Heinemann representative in the South of England, has recorded what one of his Monday mornings in Brighton could be like: 'It's Monday, it's raining and today I'm visiting Brighton and Hove which have about a dozen or so bookshops and there are several well-known authors in the area. I arrive at 8.40 a.m., in time to get a parking space and breathe a sigh of relief – that's the first hurdle over. I have an appointment booked for 10.30 with one of the more difficult buyers who will never see anyone without an appointment as he is far too busy and then proceeds to spend half an hour explaining why. I decide to walk through the Lanes to a well-known children's bookshop as we have some big children's titles coming and it's always nice to get a large order under your belt with your first call. As I enter the shop I am greeted by Penny, the buyer, with the words: "Good, I'm so glad you dropped in." This sounds promising and I try not to show my excitement. "We're stocktaking next week. Can you help out with a few overstocks?" She

[464]

points to a mountain of books in the corner and suddenly I feel dizzy. We come to some arrangement and I realize that this visit is not going to get an order that covers my parking fee and, with the promise that next time will be better, I make my retreat.

'It's nearly 10.30 and Graham, the next buyer, will be waiting. I enter the book department and I see him in the far corner serving a customer. That's a relief as he is often away ill and prone to catch anything going. He comes to greet me with an apologetic look on his face. "Hullo, Lionel. Nice to see you again, but I'm afraid the bar's up. We're not buying till the Autumn. The powers that be think we're overstocked and I'm afraid that's it." My protests fall on deaf ears and, looking round the shop, I wonder how they are going to survive until the autumn with only about fifty hardbacks. By this time desperation is beginning to creep in and I decide to enter the lion's den and call on Michael, a well-known name in the trade and a professional non-buyer. By this I mean that the publisher hasn't been born who can produce a book which appeals to him. It's either too large, too small, not enough photographs, not enough colour, wrong jacket, etc., etc. He reluctantly orders two copies of the 'Big One' and I sarcastically suggest that I send him a showcard as he will obviously be doing a window display.

'It is now lunchtime and over a coffee and sandwich I work out my plan of campaign for the afternoon. An old rep. I once knew told me that whenever he'd had a bad morning he would have a good lunch and then he would view the afternoon with much more confidence. This may have worked for him, but whenever I have a bad morning, I just don't feel like eating. Anyway, I've since heard that his good lunches exceeded his good mornings by about two to one!

'After lunch, however, business takes a surprising upturn and even the weather improves. A further two small orders lead up to the *pièce de résistance* of my day. I always leave this call until last and I never fail to come away feeling I have the best list of any publisher – and of course I have! Today is no exception and after being greeted at the door by the bookshop's owner, we proceed over the next two hours to spend his money. At times it can be a lonely life on the road, but it is amazing what a large order can do to one's morale.'[5]

Bookshops and, even more so, authors expect their books to be widely advertised in the national and local Press, but Pick took an opposite view to that of the firm's founder (see pages 63–4) and believed that most of it was a waste of money and the publicity budget could be better spent in other ways: 'I have yet to hear of a book that has sold because it was well advertised. By the 1960s the costs had anyway become prohibitive. Thank goodness the days of heavy, almost compulsory advertisement started in the thirties are over, though I believe it did influence people who had "on demand" subscriptions with the circulating libraries, but not sales across the bookshop counter. The most you can say is that if a book is already selling reasonably well, a few judiciously placed advertisements can act as a reminder. Reviews, on the other hand, are important, not because they drive people into bookshops, but because they help create the first wave of readers who start to talk about a book and recommend it. It's word of mouth, more than anything else, that sells books. Writers like Nevil Shute and Wilbur Smith have seldom enjoyed plentiful or consistently good reviews, but did it matter?!'

Bill Holden, who had succeeded Gyde, was publicity manager for over ten years and became a director. He agreed that Pick introduced new methods of publicity and, especially with the 'instant' books, inspired everyone with enthusiasm. Books began to be marketed as well as merely sold. Great stress was placed on public relations, specially when they were relatively free. Holden was particularly good at arranging for authors' interviews in the Press, signing sessions in bookshops, and appearances and mentions of the book on radio and TV.

New forms of PR were also developed during the 1960–70s by the industry as a whole, such as the campaign by the Book Development Council on behalf of 'twenty best writers' and the various book prizes similar to the William Heinemann Prize, such as the Whitbread, Somerset Maugham and, in particular, the Booker Prize, skilfully master-minded by Martyn Goff of the National Book League. There might in truth be no such thing as the 'best novel of the year', but it has undoubtedly created interest in the better type of fiction. Many people seek out novels they would otherwise never have heard of. Whoever wins the prizes, they stimulate the sale of books as a whole.

Holden went out of his way to make authors realize that the firm really did care about them. His small office on the top floor at Queen Street was more like a sitting-room with a cocktail bar than an office, and authors were always welcome to drop in for a drink, to discuss their worries as well as the publicity of their next book. David Burnett, then a junior editor, recalls that 'Bill would always make them feel relaxed and important. He helped make Heinemann a happy outfit to be published by and a happy place to work in – at least at my humble level. Tim Manderson would often drop in before lunch to meet an author – unlike most sales directors, Tim actually read people's books.'

The Swinging Sixties was very much Bill Holden's scene, and he certainly got results. Among other things he initiated the *Yorkshire Post*'s literary lunches. But after a long honeymoon period his style of working eventually fell foul of Dwye Evans and Charles Pick. He told me that 'Mondays were my worst problem, because it was publication day for some writer or other with a celebration lunch after which they usually wanted to be taken off to some drinking club. I felt that it was my job to keep important authors happy and so by six in the evening I was apt to have had far too much. But on top of this I had also to keep the Press and TV people happy and they didn't start drinking until the evening. On Tuesdays particularly I woke with a hangover and couldn't get into the office when I was needed.'

By the end of the 1960s relationships were so bad that Holden was dismissed, 'though it cost them plenty of money. I was so angry.' He was soon running his own very successful bookshop and became part of the Heinemann legend. He was succeeded by Nigel Hollis who recalls that at his interview it was Pick who did most of the talking with Dwye Evans making but one intervention:

'Why, Hollis, do you want to join Heinemann?'

Hollis, thinking that this was scarcely a serious question, working as he did for a not very distinguished firm of publishers, replied: 'Well, sir, it's like a footballer who plays for a team somewhere in the lower divisions being suddenly invited to transfer to the Arsenal.'

'Not a very good reply', said Evans drily, 'since Arsenal are only fourth in the League at the moment! We happen to be official publishers to the Football Association.'

Despite this somewhat unpromising start, Hollis quickly settled in and built on many of the priorities that Bill Holden had set for the job, in particular the need for authors to feel 'loved' and that their publishing house was some kind of second home. Hollis perceived that part of his job was to be available for advice, succour, and comfort at any time; that public relations should be beamed as much at authors as the media. He also placed considerable emphasis on furthering the sense of marketing within the firm, marrying a book's publicity, pre- and post-publication, to

[467]

the efforts of the sales department and the representatives on the road. Another important function was to bolster the company's own morale and to keep everyone in all departments and branches, including overseas, informed of all that was going on, specially to tell them the good news and about reviews.

It was a period of innovation in publicity methods throughout the industry. 'No doubt', Hollis told me, 'we thought we were inventing the wheel, and no doubt we weren't. Book-signing sessions by authors in bookshops were once again in vogue. Other emphases were on placing articles and interviews all over the papers, not just on the book pages, and on using out-of-London media to a greater extent. The period coincided with the dramatic mushrooming of local radio and the increasing import-ance of local TV stations. Following the lead by the *Yorkshire Post* a network of literary luncheons sprang up in such places as Bristol, Norwich, Birmingham, Leicester, Cardiff, Reading, and elsewhere. The food was execrable but the speeches were usually good and the opportunity for authors to meet their publics was not to be missed.'

A full tour of the publicity circuit by chauffeur-driven cars with train and plane interludes could take between two and three weeks and was pretty exhausting. Hollis remembers how Peter Ustinov, looking drained and lugubrious half-way through a tough fortnight to promote *Dear Me* (1977), remarked to Michael Parkinson: 'In the old days all you used to do was to write the book. Now you have to go out and sell it as well!' – and sell it he did to the tune of 100,000 hardbound copies by Christmas. Likewise Frank Muir barnstormed *The Frank Muir Book* (1976) to number one in the bestseller lists. Towards the end of this arduous tour, when Muir was asked for the umpteenth time what his book was about, he would reply with a tired smile: 'It's about £4.95.' Other authors who were submitted to similarly vigorous promotions included Monica Dickens, Morris West, Richard Gordon, Jan Pieńkowski, and Wilbur Smith.

'Some authors were promoted in a quieter manner and, dare it be said, with rather more dignity. They included Anthony Powell, R. K. Narayan, Paul Scott, Olivia Manning, Gore Vidal, Anita Desai and, of course, J. B. Priestley, for whom the firm organized a seemingly endless series of birthday dinners at the Savoy for a hundred-and-forty or so family and friends. "Don't send me an invitation," quipped one regular; "just send a season ticket." It was reported that each spring Pick's telephone would ring and J.B.'s bluff tones would be heard complaining about some minor discrepancy in his Serbo-Croatian royalties. When that had been discussed and Pick was at a disadvantage, J.B. would make peace by saying: "You know, Charles, that was a very good party you had last year for my birthday. Very useful too. . . ." Enough had been said!' Hollis still maintains that the most bizarre occasion in a career spent attempting to match ideas to people was when, making up the seating plan for another Savoy extravaganza, he placed a prominent newspaper editor next to his current mistress without being aware that they even knew each other!

When Hollis was moved to the job of publishing director in 1979, he was succeeded as publicity manager by Steven Williams, who already worked for the company, promoting the list of books for higher education. In this capacity he had developed sophisticated uses of direct mail publicity, allied with an awareness of the possibility of increasing the sale of certain technical titles through normal trade channels. This particularly applied to the Made Simple series.

Over the years both Hollis and Williams were embroiled in the traditional conflicts with management over the size of the annual publicity budget (which in the early 1980s was never enough to carry out even a part of their plans). Compared with earlier decades there had undoubtedly been a retrenchment. There was virtually no Press advertising; and, latterly, paid-for copy even in the trade Press was minimal. There were far fewer parties to celebrate a new book and certainly none to gratify the vanity of all but the most important authors. Most of the budget went on catalogues and leaflets to be targeted at specific readerships. Much of the publicity department's time went on facilitating reviews, interviews, and general publicity of the firm's current titles and their authors. This cost relatively little, but could be satisfyingly effective.

Expansion and Problems Overseas

Overseas sales continued to make a vital contribution. The network of European representatives still proved their worth, though it was a free market and competition from American publishers who handled the same titles as did Heinemann was often fierce. The sales clocked up by the publisher who first succeeded in getting copies into Europe would be way ahead of his competitor. Heinemann continued to represent a consortium of other UK publishers in Europe and their contribution to costs was of immense value. The consortium also still virtually financed the firm's stand at the autumn book fairs in Frankfurt. When Birch left, John Beer ran the whole European operation on the understanding that, though not a director, he was on equal terms with Manderson, the overall sales director. After Beer himself left in 1977 to work for Ernest Benn, he continued to run the same team of representatives from there and later from his own organization, Books for Europe. Heinemann still made use of it, though now as a member rather than the principal of the consortium.

Meanwhile during the 1960s and '70s Heinemann Educational Books Ltd were opening new offices and warehouses in so-far-unexploited territories: West and East Africa, Malaysia and Hong Kong, the West Indies and USA, most of which turned in impressive sales figures and were a source of authors and indigenous publishing.

William Heinemann's outposts in Australia, New Zealand, South Africa, and Canada continued to provide essential outlets for sales, but they were a constant source of anxiety and friction and, when assessed as independent units, several of them lost money in many years. In some cases their throughput was too small to justify the scale and level of expertise that was needed. Then again the sheer size of the organization brought its own special difficulties. A chronic problem was the accumulation – and often over-valuation – of stocks overseas. Despite frequent visits by top executives from London, underlying all these and other shortcomings were the long lines of communication. William Heinemann was just not organized to control a global structure of this complexity.

Canada presented by far the worst headache. By the early 1960s the problems of the body established in Toronto in 1949, British Book Service, escalated to the extent of a disaster. Despite, or maybe because of, the twenty-five or more other publishers represented it was losing up to £30,000 a year, more than the whole of Heinemann's Canadian turnover, and there were vast accumulations not only of Heinemann's own stock but also of books bearing the other companies' imprints, mostly bought at 50 per cent discount. In 1964 the decision was taken to wind up British Book Services. Notice was given to the British publishers it represented and Birch was despatched to Toronto to sell the building and get rid of the stocks. Several hundred thousand books were sold to close contacts in the Canadian trade, but 2.5 million remained. Birch took three full-page advertisements proclaiming the greatest book sale to the public ever known, with everything to go at fifty per cent off. The Canadian book trade were up in arms, but they knew there was no alternative. Pretty well ninety per cent of the books were sold over two weekends, together with the building and all its equipment. Even so, the total deficit on the Canadian operation amounted that year to £55,000.

As an alternative, an arrangement was come to with Collins to handle the group's Canadian sales. It worked smoothly and adequately for many years. But HEB had made separate arrangements with its own new subsidiary company, calling it Bellhaven House Ltd, under the management of Bob Southgate, hitherto British Book Services' educational manager. However, HEB never achieved the turnover to make its company profitable. By 1973 it was decided to sell out, but fortunately a deal was made with Book Society, a Canadian educational company run by John Irwin, whereby the two lists were amalgamated and HEB's staff retained.

In the mid-1960s extensive visits were made to Australia by Hill, Birch and Pick and they reported many difficulties. As well as ever-increasing muscling-in by American publishers, the spread of paperbacks a year after the issue of the original hardback gave booksellers less time in which to sell the latter; and with the often long delays in obtaining fresh supplies from the UK this meant that Australian booksellers tended to decrease their subscriptions and not to reorder. Largely as a result of sales pressure from London, there were overvalued overstocks spread between the warehouses in Sydney and Melbourne. Reforms were initiated both in the UK and on the spot, including the closing of the warehouse in Sydney where more economical offices were rented; in Melbourne the old warehouse was given up and a new, very modern one established in what had been an old glassworks in Lonsdale Street. In 1966 F. T. Sambell retired after fourteen years' service, to be followed as manager by Dennis Wren, who was recruited in England. He was in turn replaced by John Burchall, an experienced Australian bookseller and bookman, at that time managing director of the excellent Melbourne bookshop Robertson and Mullens. Burchall believed in the Heinemann standards and remained loyal to them. In a short while he turned round the Australian company to show a healthy profit.

Another handicap was the inability of the Australian office to promote the educational list. This was a shortcoming that was not confined to Australia, and it now led to a major development throughout Heinemann's overseas organization. When William Heinemann Ltd set up its branches in Melbourne, Auckland and Cape Town, they were intended solely to sell a very strong fiction and general list – mainly in the original hard-cover editions. Many books by famous authors (such as D. H. Lawrence) were not then available in paper. In that golden age of hardback fiction, the overseas branches could hardly be expected to concern themselves with the publications of the fledgling educational department. A good novel is a good novel anywhere; but educational books are only good in so far as they fit in with the syllabus and specific needs of an educational system. Their suitability can only be ascertained by discussion with teachers (not booksellers) – and this was not within the competence of the Heinemann overseas staff.

It was to have such discussions that Alan Hill toured Australia and New Zealand for three months in 1956, and returned convinced that there was a potential, which only an educational specialist could fulfil. Nick Hudson, newly graduated from Oxford, was appointed, and after an intensive course on school publishing in the London office, went out to Melbourne in 1958, to immerse himself in the educational world as a member of William Heinemann (Australia) Pty.

This move soon bore fruit. One book which was already widely used in Australia was *The Poet's World*, an anthology compiled by James Reeves. 'It would sell much better', reported Hudson, 'if it contained some Australian poets.' 'Are there any?' enquired Reeves, when the message was passed on to him. A group of Australian teachers supplied the answer – to such effect that the amount of Australian verse in the book came to exceed all the modern verse from the whole of the rest of the English-speaking world. Sales increased but it was soon asked why did the Australian poems have to be segregated in a separate section? The final step was then taken of integrating the Australian verse chronologically throughout the book, which greatly enhanced its acceptability.

Thus early did Heinemann realize that it should be seen as an Australian publisher, at a time when the nation was becoming rapidly more confident of its own identity. This realization led to the establishment of a separate Heinemann educational company in Australia. From then on, this new company produced a wide variety of Australian textbooks, until their sales exceeded those of imported books. Moreover,

London now began to sell Australian-educational books in the UK. The traffic had become two-way.

The process culminated with the outstanding *Heinemann English Dictionary*. Conceived by Nick Hudson in the Melbourne office, this was unique in being designed specifically for 12–16 year olds, but with no upper limit. Its huge impact on Australian schools was followed by similar success in Britain, New Zealand and USA. It became a highly profitable asset world-wide, selling to both schools and bookshops (where it later appeared as a Pan paperback). The venture was unique in another respect: it was undertaken by HEB's Australian company against the strong advice of the HEB management in London – thereby emphasizing the publishing freedom which the overseas educational companies enjoyed.

In New Zealand, changes paralleled those in Australia. G. W. Moore, who in 1953 had set up the Heinemann branch office in Auckland and converted it to a full-scale company in 1955, now recruited an educational specialist, David Heap, in 1962, to visit both schools and bookshops. His interest in teaching led him to concentrate on the educational business, especially as in the late 1960s the NZ government was overhauling its curriculum, creating a need for new books. Heap sought out the best potential authors for such books and signed them up. He now pressed London to set up an educational company to handle this development. Hill agreed, and in 1969 Heinemann Educational Books (New Zealand) was formed.

During the 1970s therefore, a dual organization had become established in both Australia and New Zealand: there were the branches of William Heinemann, almost totally devoted to selling UK fiction and general books; and there were the much more independent and adventurous educational companies, who not only sold UK school books, but were increasingly substantial local educational publishers, with profit potential much greater than could arise from only selling imports.

In August 1979 Alan Hill retired as managing director of the Heinemann Group of Publishers and was succeeded by Charles Pick. Hill left the group in a strong financial situation: 1979 publishing profits were £3.5 million, while the return on average funds was about 33 per cent. The group had been a loss-making liability when Tilling rescued it in 1961. They were now able to describe Heinemann as 'the jewel in their crown'.

[473]

Tilling now decided that the new management's first priority was to improve the structure of the overseas companies. Tony Beal had succeeded to the chairmanship of all the wholly owned educational companies, including those overseas. Hill, now a consultant, remained chairman of HEB Nigeria. Although there had been good results (particularly from Asia and Nigeria) the general level of profits was not high enough. In particular there were problems in Australia, New Zealand and Southern Africa where the fiction and educational businesses were now separate companies. As has been described above (pages 472–3), this separation had its roots in history: it arose from the same logic that had dictated the separation of the fiction and educational businesses in London in 1961.

By 1980, however, Tilling decided that this duality should not continue. After many months of exchanging views and visits, in June 1981 Pick, Beal and Range (the Group financial director) visited the two countries to resolve matters.

In Melbourne they found that the excellent head of the trade company, John Burchall, was a sick man. His administrative back-up was weak. His financial director had gone on holiday and there was a shortage of statistical information – so much so that the group financial director had to count the books himself, as there appeared to be no reliable stock records. It became clear that the accounts and statistics would be far more effectively run through the computerized system of the Educational Company, whose warehouse had ample space for the comparatively small stock of the trade imprints. Burchall said that such integration would take several months to accomplish. Hudson said he could do it over a week-end – which he did. The William Heinemann company was now merged with the Educational to form Heinemann Australia, under Hudson as managing director and Beal as chairman.

In New Zealand the situation was easier. G. W. Moore had left to manage a new YMCA building, being succeeded by Maurice Dowthwaite, one of the reps. Both sides saw the sense of running a joint warehouse and accounts. Maurice Dowthwaite, on the fiction side, and David Heap had a good relationship. Dowthwaite was approaching retirement and it was agreed that the two companies should reunite as Heinemann New Zealand. Dowthwaite and Heap were joint managing directors for the first year (with Tony Beal as chairman), after which Heap took over.

In Southern Africa the basic scenario was similar to that of the

Australian companies – conflict between the two businesses, separation, followed by reunion. The joint company, Heinemann & Cassell, which handled the Heinemann business, was concerned exclusively with trade books and refused to countenance any expenditure on HEB books. So in 1968, the East African branch of Heinemann & Cassell was bought out by HEB, and became Heinemann Educational Books (East Africa) Ltd. Meanwhile, in South Africa itself, the centre of the economy and bookselling was tending to shift from Cape Town to Johannesburg, to where it was decided also to move the offices of Heinemann & Cassell Ltd.

Towards the end of 1970, Cassell decided to withdraw from its partnership with William Heinemann Ltd, who purchased Cassell's shares, so as to convert the company into Heinemann Publishers (South Africa) Ltd. Mendl Jacobs's successor as the local Heinemann managing director, Stanley Jackson, was untypical: he envisaged considerable potential in the HEB list. Tony Beal went out to see for himself, and as a result, it was decided to leave the educational business within William Heinemann in South Africa.

An 'educational research assistant' was appointed, whose findings were transmitted to London, and used for sales promotion by mail from UK. Heinemann could not of course compete with the deeply entrenched South African publishers producing books in both Afrikaans and English, and often with close links with the people who prescribed the books. However, none of these had the great range of copyright English literature, in which HEB was stronger than any other UK publisher, with its New Windmill, Drama, Poetry and African Writers Series. In 1976, two prescriptions for secondary school reading alone brought in sales of 300,000 copies.

There was now a crucial turning point. The Soweto student riots caused the government to abandon its rule that blacks had to be taught through the medium of the much disliked Afrikaans. English now became the sole compulsory medium of instruction. This was welcome news to HEB, whose publishing throughout black Africa, in particular the African Writers Series, gave it a high profile. Such leading authors as Achebe and Ngugi were reviewed and prescribed first at university and then at school level. Books in the series by Nelson Mandela, Steve Biko and others banned in South Africa, were sold in the neighbouring independent countries, and found their way into the Republic.

[475]

In that same year, 1976, Tony Beal on a visit appointed Anita Wolfe-Coote to take charge of the educational business within the William Heinemann office in Johannesburg. She needed her great energy and drive, as her induction into selling school books had largely to be done by correspondence with London, there being no expertise in the William Heinemann South African office. Andrew Stewart, the affable Scot who had succeeded Stanley Jackson, was successfully selling fiction. With a limited TV service, abundant servants and lots of leisure, there was an avid audience amongst whites for the novels of Wilbur Smith, James Michener and other best-sellers on the Secker and Heinemann lists.

The HEB view of South Africa was very different. They saw it as a much wider multi-racial society with a hunger for education. Obviously Mrs Wolfe-Coote had to spend a lot of her time making contacts and having discussions with black teachers, and potential authors.

The deep division between the aims and philosophies of the two sides of the business culminated in 1977, when Stewart quite arbitrarily dismissed Mrs Wolfe-Coote. On the educational side, there was deep relief at escape from a restrictive atmosphere. Separation had at last been forced upon HEB – who set up a separate branch under Mrs Wolfe-Coote's management. The William Heinemann business now suffered financially as a result of losing the profitable educational business. Worse was to follow as Andrew Stewart became seriously ill and died tragically young in 1982. It was thereupon decided to reunite the two businesses as Heinemann Publishers South Africa. The managing director was none other than Anita Wolfe-Coote, with Tony Beal as chairman. The new company flourished, and by 1985, sales from the UK to Southern Africa were higher than those to any other territory.

So at last in the three major areas, where William Heinemann had its overseas offices, these were now re-integrated with their flourishing educational offspring. The united company's managements, though drawn from HEB, had the interests of all sections of the group at heart. It was a happy circumstance that the chairman of the three companies (Tony Beal), and all three managing directors, had worked for William Heinemann Ltd before setting up their HEB companies.

Meanwhile, HEB found it essential to develop its own distribution and local publishing structure not only in South Africa, but more importantly in the emerging independent African countries. Throughout ex-colonial Africa the numbers of schools and pupils were growing and there were startling opportunities for the enterprising UK educational publisher. The first HEB branch was opened in 1961 in Ibadan, Nigeria, with the appointment of Daniel Fagunwa, a distinguished Yoruba author, as its manager. Until then the territory had been dominated by the Oxford University Press and Longman. Their offices were then essentially outlets for sales of UK textbooks, but Alan Hill from the outset had his mind set on finding African authors as well. The growth of HEB's African organization went hand in hand with that of the African Writers Series (see pages 519–20) and the publication of textbooks specially conceived for the African school market and often written by local teachers.

Tragically only a year after he was appointed Fagunwa was drowned while crossing the Niger in a primitive ferry. His successor was Aig Higo, formerly headmaster of an Anglican school. Hill always took immense pains in selecting staff both at home and overseas:

'In Africa we didn't want little poodles of a multinational company, but proud local citizens who were strong enough to stand on their own feet. When their HEB branches eventually became HEB companies, these ceased to be subsidiaries of the London company and became equal partners. I gave them dominion status instead of the colonial subordination preferred by some of our competitors. I could foresee that these countries would not be satisfied much longer with textbooks imported from Britain. They wanted more of their own books, locally published, and I appointed men who were capable and eager to bring this about.'

This policy bore fruit in the extraordinarily rapid expansion of the Nigerian business, despite continuing difficulties, despite the civil war, despite Nigeria's political and economic problems, despite the imprisonment of leading authors such as Wole Soyinka. By 1969 the Ibadan branch had become a fully fledged Nigerian company with Aig Higo as managing director and Hill as chairman. By 1976 its turnover had soared to £2.38 million, equally split between local publishing and imported books. The profit for 1982 amounted to £152,000, of which the Heinemann share was 40 per cent – £60,800.

In 1974 Nigerian law had decreed that 40 per cent of the shares had to be Nigerian owned, and two years later this became 60 per cent. The operation was delicately handled so that the transferred shares were placed with HEB's Nigerian directors and authors; there were no outsiders and the close interdependence with London was not weakened. Substantial profits continued to be made by the Nigerian company, but after the slump in oil prices bit into the Nigerian economy and led to a foreign exchange crisis there was a freeze on overseas payments. The accumulated profits on books imported from London and the forty per cent share of profits made by the indigenous HEB (Nigeria) could not be remitted to London. By 1980 some £1.5 million were held up and further imports of books had to depend on the grudging issue of Nigerian import licences. With each new licence the old debt was left to stagnate and eventually about 50 per cent of a £3 million debt had to be written off. The Nigerian company remained nevertheless a major overseas HEB company, with Aig Higo as chief executive and Alan Hill, after his retirement in the UK, continuing as chairman.

In Kenya the situation had been different. Because of the cooler climate there was a relatively large population of white settlers. In 1965 William Heinemann Ltd, jointly with Cassell, opened an office in Nairobi primarily to sell fiction to the whites and textbooks to the European-style secondary schools. But with Independence under Jomo Kenyatta in 1963 the publishing prospects changed and, as in West Africa, education was starting to expand impressively. There was also a parallel literary awakening, among the most prominent authors being James Ngugi, an early recruit to the African Writers Series. In the neighbouring independent countries of Tanzania and Uganda there were similar opportunities. It was therefore agreed that HEB would buy out the Heinemann/Cassell company, so that in 1968 it was reconstituted as HEB (East Africa) Ltd. The existing manager, Bob Markham, was made managing director. Although British, he was fluent in Swahili, knew the territory well, and was friendly with Kenyans from Government ministers downwards. He was well equipped to discover African authors as well as to build up HEB's distribution. He also knew his way round Kenyan politics and understood the nature of the conflict between, on the one side, HEB's author Oginga Odinga, of the Luo tribe, and, on the other side, the ruling Kikuyu group around Kenyatta (who had been published by Secker & Warburg) which stemmed not only from tribal rivalry but also from basic social and political differences.

Tanzania, Zambia, and Uganda – at least until Amin's putsch – were included in the territory. Turnover of HEB (East Africa) Ltd grew steadily, reaching £400,000 by 1977 and eventually £1.7 million in 1987. When Markham retired to England, he was succeeded in 1974 by Henry Chakava who had been running the local television programme *Voice of*

Kenya. From 1972 for two years he had worked alongside Alan Hill's son, David, to learn the business.

In the Far East William Heinemann Ltd continued to be represented by the joint organization with Donald Moore, but in 1976 it was decided to let Collins handle the relatively small amount of fiction and general titles. With newly independent Singapore and Malaysia HEB once again saw great opportunities for expansion and in 1961 recruited Leon Comber as its local representative. Comber was a colourful ex-Indian Army officer and an ex-Malay Police Commissioner in the Special Branch who spoke fluent Malay and Chinese. A full HEB branch was established in 1963 in Hong Kong with Comber in charge and it was transformed into HEB (Asia) Ltd four years later. Because of the distance from Hong Kong a manager for Singapore/Malaysia, John Watson, was sent out from London to run this territory with two locally recruited managers, Charles Cher in Singapore and Leong Fook Kung in Kuala Lumpur, where there was also a warehouse. Once more local publishing was developed alongside the distribution of books from the UK. There were more than seventy titles in the Writing in Asia series, mainly fiction and poetry, and a major integrated science course was published for Malaysian schools. Nearly half the titles were translated into Malay, as English was being increasingly relegated to the status of the second language.

With the three offices and warehouses in Hong Kong, Singapore, and Kuala Lumpur, a Chinese staff of sixty and sales by 1983 approaching £3 million, HEB (Asia) Ltd was well established. Meanwhile William Heinemann Ltd steadfastly rejected HEB's offer to handle their relatively small amount of fiction and general turnover, preferring to leave the business with Collins, whose representative visited the region from time to time, basing himself – the ultimate anomaly – in HEB's Hong Kong office!

Meanwhile the launch in 1970 of HEB's Caribbean Writers Series, which brought leading authors such as V. S. Naipaul to the list, was followed by the setting-up in Jamaica of HEB (Caribbean) Ltd in 1976, with locally born Ian Randle as managing director. His first major publication was a primary school reading course; and as this was a Jamaica Government project, HEB felt it wise to indigenize the company in 1978 by selling a majority shareholding to local interests. Ian Randle now showed considerable aptitude in the area of trade books as well as educational, and eventually became the leading publisher in the Caribbean.

The last piece in the world-wide pattern of Heinemann offices was slotted into position in 1978, when HEB set up in business in USA. John Watson after nine years in the Far East opened HEB Inc. on a very small scale in Massachusetts. He soon moved to New Hampshire, achieved a turnover of $67,000 and, five years later in 1983, made his first trading profit. It wasn't very large, but Heinemann had made its first toe hold in the world's largest book market.

The overseas development begun by William Heinemann after the war, had thus been taken over in later years by the vigorously expanding HEB – a situation which climaxed in the three-day international conference called by Tony Beal, at Stratford on Avon in October 1982. The managing directors of all the eight overseas companies (together with those of the home firms) met together for the first time. They came across as sister companies who all had business to do with one another, not as 'branches' dictated to by London.

[A table showing the turnover and profits before tax in 1982 for the group's overseas subsidiaries and associated companies will be found in Appendix H, page 646]

No Longer Printers, but Sharper Costings

The separation of the printing and binding departments at Kingswood under the new title of the Windmill Press Ltd proved to be little more than cosmetic. The equipment was too old-fashioned and too limited to meet the demands of the publishing companies. They insisted more strongly than ever that they needed to be completely free to buy printing where it was cheapest and best suited to their needs. The conflict between the two sides of the business was resolved by the establishment in May 1962 of yet another company, Bookprint Ltd, as a direct subsidiary of Tillings, which would have complete, independent control of all production processes. It was very much the brainchild of Peter Barnard, who became its managing director as well as continuing to run the presses and bindery at

Kingswood, the Windmill Press Ltd having now become technically a subsidiary of Bookprint. The name of the building was changed, it would seem quite unnecessarily, to 'The Press at Kingswood'.

The main reason for Bookprint, however, was to modernize the plant and to take advantage of revolutionary new methods of typesetting which were being developed in conjunction with two experts, Oliver Burridge and his son Nicholas, at Filmset Ltd at Crawley, in which a controlling interest had been acquired by the Heinemann group in 1960. Filmsetting was hailed as 'the greatest development in printing since Gutenberg invented movable type'. With the Monophoto machine, developed in collaboration with the Monotype Corporation, the copy was first set on a keyboard which produced a perforated paper ribbon which then transferred it to the filmsetter, which by shining a narrow beam of light through 255 apertures in a grid matrix, each housing a character, translated the perforations into photographic type images, evenly spaced to fill the required length of line. The filmsetter was much more adaptable than existing methods of composition, in that display faces, mathematical settings, variations in space between lines, etc., could be set at the same time. Type set on film was much cheaper to store and transport than conventional metal type. It seemed to be ideal for book work.

Filmset Ltd also came under the wing of Bookprint, with the Burridges remaining as directors. Under the supervision of the Tillings estate department a three-acre site was acquired at Crawley and work was begun on the construction of a new factory to house not only the filmsetting equipment but also a lithographic press. There was also a London sales office in Mayfair to win business from other publishers, though it was envisaged that seventy-five per cent of the turnover would come from Heinemann companies during 1963, after which it was hoped to be self-reliant.

The Crawley building was opened with great panache by Lord Brabazon, but these estimates turned out to be excessively optimistic. Technically also things rapidly started to go wrong. The big lithographic perfector machine was a new experimental model and caused endless trouble and was very often in pieces. There were disputes with the unions, particularly over manning. It was difficult to attract new work and to compete with the efficiency and reliability of the established presses. Tillings was losing money fast at Bookprint.

Barnard was under terrible pressure. 'With a good deal of uncertainty I had told Tillings that I didn't think the new venture would be in profit for at least two years. Just as things were getting established at Crawley I was suddenly given the option of cutting the Kingswood Press's staff of 250 by a fifth or closing it down completely. This seemed nonsensical and could not solve any of the problems, particularly as the printed sheets from Crawley were transported to Kingswood to be bound.'

Despite, or perhaps because of his vision, his enthusiasm and never failing optimism, Barnard irritated people at Queen Street. The big capital investment and the alarming early losses meant a loss of face with Tilling. At the end of 1964 Barnard decided to resign. With hindsight it can be argued that like many pioneers Barnard paid the price of being some five years too early in backing this type of quasi-mechanical film-setting because computerized filmsetting was just under the horizon. It was this that was 'the greatest development in printing since Gutenberg'.

In 1966 the evacuation of the press from Kingswood to Crawley was ordered and the huge letterpress machines were moved at enormous expense, though a year later they were sold for scrap. This completed the separation of Bookprint from Heinemann and the rest of its sad life has no place in this history but, briefly, substantial losses were made up to the end of 1969, despite the addition of further equipment. The decision to close it down was announced in April 1970. Instead, however, Tilling bought the well established Norfolk printers Cox & Wyman on condition that they would absorb Bookprint. The Crawley plant was thus transferred to the Cox & Wyman works at Fakenham.

Meanwhile in Queen Street Hugh Williamson had left the production department in 1960 to become a director of Hutchinsons at a greatly enhanced salary. Edward Young was then commissioned to write a report on the functioning of the production department, but it was not until after an interval of nearly two years, by when they were desperate to find someone who could really take charge, that Williamson was succeeded by Nigel Viney. It was agreed that he would be free to place printing wherever he wanted, though he soon found himself under pressure from Tilling to use Bookprint, who in fact did most of the non-educational printing and did it well, and later Cox & Wyman.

'Essentially,' said Viney, 'my policy was to produce decent-looking books at the best price, which wouldn't necessarily be the cheapest price. Basically I used two other printers as well as Bookprint or Cox & Wyman: Morrison and Gibb in Edinburgh and Clays in Suffolk. Their prices were more or less the same. When I started one had to adhere to the basic published price for fiction of 21*s*. or 25*s*., though in recent years prices have become more flexible.'

Viney was a great believer in forward planning – important when preparing the budgets for Tilling. He also reduced the size of many of the long reprints because they meant locking up capital unnecessarily and clogging the warehouse at Kingswood or paying to keep the stock of sheets at printers or binders, all for the sake of a very small reduction in the manufactured cost per copy.

'With *The Prophet*, for example, I discovered that instead of reprinting 50,000 copies we would be better off reprinting merely six months' supply. It is well known that it is much easier to get a printer to give a reliable service with a new book than with a reprint, but we were powerful enough to overcome this. With short reprints of a novel which was selling unexpectedly well it could be vital to have them delivered within three weeks. Often this could be done only by pushing forward another less urgent, longer-term reprint. My aim was not to reprint too many copies at a time of anything and I tried to evolve an equation which would guide one towards the optimum quantity, taking everything into account, including the cost of the money locked up as well as anticipated demand and the published price.'

With the severe inflation of the 1970s and the very high cost of money this factor became increasingly important. Two or even more reprints of a title in a year could produce a better return than one. It also became customary not to bind the whole of an edition immediately. All this called for nice balancing and time-tabling if sales were not to be lost because copies were temporarily unavailable in the bookshops.

For the Wednesday meetings, at which prices and printing numbers were still fixed, Pick designed a new form which showed the total cost of manufacturing varying quantities together with the reducing cost per copy as quantities increased. These figures were followed by a forecast of net sales income, home and export, based on a notional published price for each of the quantities. From this information it was simple to deduct overheads (then running at 40 per cent of net income) and corresponding royalties (for home and overseas), and thus arrive at the estimated profit on the edition, assuming every copy to be sold. The profit was expressed as a percentage of the cost of production. The sales of any previous books by the same author were also provided. It was always essential not to allow enthusiasm for a book to inflate the printing number in order to bring the price down to what might appear to be a more attractive level. In the chair, Dwye, like his father, or Pick were always adamant that price had little to do with whether a book would sell.

With the expansion of the bookclubs and American rights costing was often complex. The edition of a print of, say, 50,000 copies for a bookclub made of course an enormous difference to the cost per copy, though the margin on the bookclub edition was often very small and called for some careful negotiation. Equally important were the number of smaller, non-fiction orders from bookclubs, which had a dramatic effect on the cost-of-sales figure. Typesetting charges could also be shared with the publishers of an American edition and, particularly if the page size and margins were proportionate, also with a paperback firm. Leaving these important considerations aside, it cannot be emphasized too often that the manufacturing cost per copy (the unit cost) depends of course not only on the book's length, quality of paper and binding, but also on the size of the print run. This is frequently the decisive factor. It can be demonstrated by the estimates for two novels of more or less the same length. The figures are for actual books, supplied by Kate Gardiner, who succeeded Peter Ireland as production director in 1984, but let us call them Novel I and Novel II. Novel I ran to 288 pages and 1,400 copies were printed; Novel II ran to 256 pages and 70,000 were printed. The unit cost for Novel I was £3.06 and for Novel II only 79p. This was entirely due to scale. Novel II was given particularly expensive jacket artwork but it made little difference.

A comparison between the percentages of the two total manufacturing costs contributed by each of the six basic elements in production is instructive:

	Novel I	Novel II
Setting and proofing	28	3
Printing	17	10
Paper	13	28
Binding	13	43
Jacket design & printing	22.5	15
Binding brass	1	0.1
Bound proofs	5.5	0.9
Total	100 %	100 %

It is clear how the labour-related costs, such as setting, printing machine make-ready, etc, are very much increased when expressed as a percentage in the case of Novel I; and equally how the materials-related costs, such as paper and binding, are very much higher in the case of Novel II. This comparison also demonstrates why for long it has been impossible to publish a title with a short run, such as a first novel, at a price which is acceptable to most book-buyers. Frequently it has to be issued at a loss unless support is coming from a paperback, serial, or an American sale. The risk can only be justified commercially if it is judged that the author's talent and promise are such that he or she will one day be an adornment to the list. In the shorter term there is always also the hope of a reprint in which the unit cost will be sometimes very much lower because the basic costs of setting, proofing, jacket design, editorial overheads, etc. have already been absorbed.

'Over the last dozen or so years', Kate Gardiner explained, 'most production costs have kept roughly in line with inflation. Paper prices fluctuate according to the strength or weakness of the US dollar, but there is never any significant variation from the rate of inflation, taken as an average over several years. But inflation has of course been rampant during the last two decades. In 1971 the unit cost of a long novel (768 pages) with a print-run of 27,500 was 42p. and it was published at £2.75; today (1988) the same book would cost approximately £1.90 and would be published at £11.95. But the ratio of cost of manufacture to published price is virtually the same: 15 per cent in 1971, and 16 per cent in 1988. Only one element in manufacture has in recent years shown a relative drop in price: the cost of setting. This is entirely because of the recent dramatic changes in typesetting technology. When I joined the firm in 1974 it was £3–£4 per page for a novel and, despite inflation, we are paying exactly the same amount today. This is an enormous advantage to a publisher like Heinemann which issues so many books with short runs.'

Computers and Work Study
at Kingswood

It was at Kingswood that the majority of Heinemann employees, who totalled some five hundred men and women, worked: about 150 were in the press and bindery; 70 in the warehouse; 90 in the office, mostly on accounts, order-processing and stock control. There was also the editorial staff of the World's Work. Kingswood's history is inevitably complex and technical, but some key events and processes of change during the course of a quarter of a century need to be recorded.

The warehousing, dispatch, and other services provided by Kingswood were considered by Tilling not only to be too expensive, but also inefficient. Orders from booksellers were processed too slowly and their dispatch was often unnecessarily delayed. In the early 1960s Heinemann regularly occupied a place near the bottom in the Booksellers Association's league table which ranked publishers according to speed of delivery. As well as dealing with these urgent problems, Reg Keel as group managing director set in train a large number of longer-term reforms at Kingswood covering accounting methods, warehousing, order-processing, personnel management, and much else. A work-study officer was brought in to improve warehouse methods and install a productivity bonus scheme.

To aid him, further expert staff were engaged and a number of working committees were set up to oversee sales, production, promotion, planning, and accounts. Wherever possible, administrative functions were taken away from the publishing companies and integrated at Kingswood in three main divisions: group finance under C. J. Platt; publishing companies' accounts under D. L. Range, another chartered accountant; and the administration of Kingswood services under R. M. Garside. In 1960 an ICT mechanized accounting system was installed to take the place of the five existing separate accounting systems. Stock records were also mechanized, and four years later further ICT 1004 data processing equipment was introduced. By 1965 the reorganization had progressed sufficiently for a new company, Heinemann Group Services Ltd, to be set up with Keel as chairman and another newcomer, Kenneth Stephenson, as its first managing director. A large man with a forceful personality, he possessed special experience of book distribution.

By the end of that year Keel, however, decided to leave for a job in the City. Although everyone agreed that he had done an immense amount to put the company financially and commercially back on its feet, his efforts to intervene in the running of the individual publishing firms were resented and there was a good deal of friction. Not for the first or last time in this history personal incompatibilities played a key part in shaping events. There was a feeling that while Keel might be an excellent accountant, he was not cut out to be a publisher. But he had been the man for the hour and when that hour was safely past and the emphasis moved from the problems of finance and administration to those of publishing, he was no longer needed for the top job.

The warehouse as well as being badly laid out was much too small. Some one-and-a-half million books had to be stored in remote overflow rented warehouses at Wembley in North London, and Greenford, Middlesex. Packing and dispatch were housed in very unsatisfactory temporary buildings distant from the book racks. The 'forward' racks, from which orders were picked, were located partly on the first floor and partly downstairs and this involved much to-and-froing, and the lift between the floors was agonizingly slow. There was serious talk of selling Kingswood and finding more functional and larger premises elsewhere; but this idea was rejected and, when the printing department eventually moved out to Crawley in 1966, close on half the total space was made vacant and the bookracks were moved down to the ground floor. With the great increase in throughput by the end of the decade even this additional space was insufficient and in 1973 a large new warehouse (20,000 square feet) was opened by J. B. Priestley. Situated at the rear of the main building, to which it was connected so that the entire warehouse space could function as one unit, it was designed by David Cole in a functional style with curtain walling of smoked glass which reflected its neo-Georgian neighbour and the surrounding trees and shrubs. Later a further 20,000 square feet were added at the rear of the new building, making 40,000 feet in all.

In an attempt to speed up the rate of dispatching orders and to reduce costs, small accounts with booksellers were transferred in 1967 to the Book Centre in Neasden, North London – already used by 120 other publishers. These smaller accounts amounted to 80 per cent of the total, but only 20 per cent of the turnover. The Book Centre physically dispatched the books to these smaller accounts and collected the money. It also supplied monthly sales statistics.

These included data for the turnover still processed by the Kingswood warehouse which comprised all the larger accounts. It was hoped that they could now be dealt with more efficiently at a much reduced cost, but this proved to be an optimistic misconception. They produced 80 per cent of the turnover but they also gave rise to 80 per cent of the workload. In fact the Book Centre arrangement neither increased Kingswood's costs nor did it radically reduce them, though it was very much more efficient and speeded deliveries.

Another problem arose from the dramatic expansion in orders for educational books. Small accounts suddenly became large ones and could not always be serviced from the relatively small stocks held at the Book Centre. Replenishments had to be rushed over, but some accounts were brought back for service from Kingswood. As can be imagined, this two-way process led to irritating delays and confusion. By 1972 it was decided to service all orders direct from Kingswood, though the facilities offered by the Book Centre computer were retained for raising invoices. It was then that Peter Range, who had succeeded Stephenson in 1969 as managing director of the service company, put up proposals for new equipment amounting to some £100,000. Capital expenditure on this scale required prior approval from Tilling, but after a good deal of headshaking it was approved. The key feature of the plan was to make use of the Book Centre computer to aid the functioning of the warehouse operations, a procedure which today is commonplace but was then considered revolutionary. Briefly, the computer, having produced a day's invoices, broke them down into batches of thirty to forty. For each batch it then produced a combined picking list, sequenced in rack number order, so that a warehouseman could move on a computer-guided route to gather books to fulfil the thirty to forty invoices at a time rather than by following a zig-zag route to collect books for but a single invoice. This method was combined with an improved replenishment system that permitted a drastic reduction in the forward rack areas, so that the warehouseman again moved more quickly through a smaller area while gathering larger quantities of books. Another improvement was to code every bookseller according to his geographical location and the route taken by the transport supplying him, so that by the time the lorry was ready to be loaded all the parcels for, say, Lancashire were ready on the same pallet. When on the same night they reached the depot where they were reloaded onto the overnight long-distance lorries, they came off together. The effect of all these innovations was that Heinemann came third in the publishers' league table instead of near the bottom.

Around this time the Booksellers Association organized a seminar at which Heinemann was fêted as the first of the big publishing groups to achieve the standard of service which booksellers had been demanding. Range made a presentation, displaying wall-charts and explaining Heinemann's techniques of batch-picking and pre-sorting. The audience listened with interest tinged with scepticism. Was there not a danger that such an improved service would turn out to be very costly? But Range was able to prove that the faster processing of orders could also mean that operating costs were lower. Heinemann's distribution ratios had been reduced from 12 to 9 per cent of turnover.

Urgent repeat orders from London retail booksellers had always been largely supplied from the firm's trade-counter at Rupert Hart-Davis's offices in Soho Square, and before that from the basement of 99 Great Russell Street. When Hart-Davis left the group a new trade-counter was opened at Gower Mews at the rear of the building in Bedford Square, two floors of which had been taken to rehouse the medical company and Peter Davies Ltd. Ian Norrie, proprietor of the High Hill Bookshop in Hampstead, added this admiring note to the revised edition of *Mumby's Publishing and Bookselling*: 'The handful of counters remaining open was kept busy and between those who manned them and those who called there grew up a relationship which was valuable to both sides and to the book-buying public. Exemplifying the best was Heinemann in Gower Mews. . . . Here collectors were welcomed by George Chapman and Pat Morris, through a barrage of two-finger typing, with items of good-humoured badinage. . . . In Gower Mews the wide knowledge they had of the lists which they sold was ever helpful to visiting booksellers. They acted as salesmen, giving useful tips about new titles which were catching on, and about "dark horses" on the backlist. Almost certainly the last of their breed, they provided a personal, efficient service which booksellers whose careers started after their retirement will not know about.'[6]

In 1978 a shock was caused by the announcement that the Book Centre would be closing their service. Only six months' notice was given, but Range by then had been exploring together with Bernard

Browning the possibility of Heinemann's acquiring its own large-scale computer.

'I had heard from the distribution manager at Hutchinson's that they had the same idea and were already briefing a softwear firm, now called Vista, to develop a system based on the DEC PDP 11/70 computer manufactured by the Digital Computer Corporation (DEC). They had already done six months' work, but he agreed to my suggestion that we should split the development costs of what was still an unproved program. This was feasible because between publishers the form of the invoices and the sales ledger entries are virtually identical, though the type of statistics required is likely to be different. Our share of the basic program worked out at about £20,000 plus a design fee of £15,000 for setting up the program for the sales and financial statistics. This has to be compared with an alternative quote for a tailor-made system amounting to £100,000.' The computer itself was leased at some £50,000 a year, though after five years this was reduced to virtually a peppercorn rent.

Although they were up against time, the result was excellent and there were few of the normal teething problems because the system had already been debugged by Hutchinsons. When it first went live, some 2,000 orders were processed, about half a normal day's invoicing was completed, but the rate of order-entering soon speeded up and there were no disruptions. Backlogs of orders very soon disappeared. Since this pioneering joint commission with Hutchinson, Vista have sold this system to many other publishers including the Oxford University Press and Longman. Parallel and linked with the computer were banks of visual display units (VDUs) with keyboards on which the girl operators entered the orders. Instead of the cumbersome alphabetical title directories used in connection with the earlier system a simple code was employed consisting of the first and last letters of the first word of title – e.g., *The Forsyte Saga* would be coded 'FE'. Once these two letters had been pressed on the keyboard the operator had 'access' to this title, which would be immediately displayed on her screen and against which she entered the number of copies required. There was no need for the order to be encoded.

The combination of the computer and the VDU's together with batch-picking and other innovations created a service which was even more rapid and efficient. As the system's capacity exceeded the group's needs it was possible to offer it to a few other publishers. André Deutsch and John Murray, both of whom had also used the Book Centre, were the first to join and they were soon followed by Weidenfeld and Time-Life. Unlike the Book Centre system the outside publishers (with the exception of Murray) were invoiced jointly with the Heinemann companies and recorded in a combined sales ledger, the computer being programed to analyse each publisher's sales and credit them to their accounts. To save several operations and staff, the other publishers' incoming money was not paid over as soon as it was received but at agreed due dates. For the time being bad debts were ignored, though a quarter per cent on turnover was reserved against them, any differences being reconciled every six months.

Handling the other publishers' throughput led to considerable economies of scale – not only a reduction in the group's own distribution costs, but an additional profit as well. Another advantage was that the credit control department could exert greater leverage over debtors, being able to 'stop' many more titles. The percentage received from Weidenfeld was particularly attractive because many of their books were highly priced – in fact it became possible to quote them the same rates as charged internally to the group's own publishers and still make money.

During the twenty-five years following 1961 Kingswood's service charges to the group companies were reduced from 15 per cent of net turnover to 12 per cent – 9 per cent for distribution and 3 per cent for accountancy, trade counter, and other items. There was also an ingenious internal charging system which more accurately allocated distribution costs according to the 'mix' of each company's order pattern.

All these changes together with the firm hand of more professional management not unnaturally had an effect on the status, conditions of work, and welfare of the staff. At Kingswood wages were largely negotiated with the unions and followed national trends. For the administrative staff salaries continued to be negotiated individually but various anomalies were ironed out, so that salaries bore a closer relationship to responsibilities and experience. Throughout this period the emphasis was on reducing staff numbers by introducing more efficient office systems, computerization, and improved warehouse layout and equipment.

The staff, not only at Kingswood but also in London, benefited however in various ways. Normal annual holidays were increased from a fortnight to three weeks. The company magazine was revived under the editorship of Edward Thompson, though its appearance was very spasmodic. Thompson also ran a drama group and organized all-day literary seminars at Kingswood with leading authors participating. A handbook specifying conditions of employment was drafted and copies issued to all staff. Most important of all was the abolition of the existing paternalistic *ex-gratia* pension scheme which apart from being parsimonious was unfair in that it gave relatively generous benefits to some and meagre amounts to others. In its stead employees were entitled to join the Thomas Tilling contributory pension scheme which was infinitely more generous and gave a reasonable measure of financial security. Like many other schemes run by public companies, the employer put in over twice as much as the employees' monthly deductions to finance an independent trust which in return for a lifetime's work gave a pension equal to roughly two-thirds of final salary, and correspondingly smaller pensions for those with fewer years behind them. Other benefits included life assurance equal to three times annual salary for those who died before retirement; additional help was given in cases of special hardship and particularly when there were children. Widows of pensioners received half their husband's pension. Years of service with the company before 1962 counted as 'half-years' in pension calculations. A few people who were already approaching retirement were understandably entitled only to *ex-gratia* pensions, though they were at a higher rate. People already retired had their *ex-gratia* pensions increased by fifty per cent.

During 1961–83 the centre of power resided almost completely in London. With Queen Street just round the corner from Tilling's headquarters in Crewe House and with few of the directors having spent much time at Kingswood, this was natural and inevitable. In 1978, however, a major event was staged at Kingswood to celebrate the fiftieth anniversary of its foundation. The idea grew out of a discussion in New York between Alan Hill and the Doubleday directors. All the top brass were there with guests of honour Nelson Doubleday, Effendi's grandson, and five other Doubleday directors. There can have been few present who were not aware that it was Effendi's vision in creating Kingswood in such beautiful surroundings which over the half-century had made it such a pleasant and happy place in which to work. Most of the staff were among the guests including a large London contingent and many old-timers, but none with such long service as Jack Dettmer, who had joined the company in 1906 as office boy and was still a director seventy-two years later. The band played, an exhibition of first editions and other memorabilia had been organized by Sid Herbert, another stalwart, and there was a buffet supper in a marquee, followed by dancing. All those with twenty-five years' service were presented with a gold watch or, if they preferred, £75. And of course there were speeches: by Douglas Manser from Tilling and the current chairman of the group; by Charles Pick; by Peter Range; and by Alan Hill as group managing director. The past as well as the present was extolled. The warehouse had expanded so that it could house some twelve million books at the focal point of twenty-two stocking and distribution points throughout the world. Dispatch was rapid and some ten thousand invoices were handled each week. The computer and the group accountancy team provided indispensable support. It was all cost effective. . . . As is customary on such occasions, there was a spate of self-congratulation; but there would be few to say it was not justified.

Editorial Changes –
Morris West and
le Carré

Although the process of commissioning books had been considerably tightened up and ultimate decisions were controlled by Dwye Evans and Charles Pick, the main editorial department were involved not only in assessing proposals but to some extent they also discovered and developed proposals themselves. The agents and American publishers tended to approach Evans or Pick directly with major projects, but their proposals were reported on by the editorial department which also sorted and considered the flood of unsolicited manuscripts and proposals that came through the mail. The children's and the tertiary education departments enjoyed much greater independence and with them it was more a case of getting their recommendations rubber-stamped by the top management, though they operated within overall guidelines.

When James Michie moved to The Bodley Head in October 1962, he was succeeded as editorial manager by David Machin, who had joined the department in 1957. There were several other young editors who spent most of their time preparing manuscripts for press and dealing with commissioned authors, though they also wrote reports and, theoretically at any rate, they could introduce new authors themselves. With an increasing number of manuscripts on offer an opinion was sought from the sales department, Tim Manderson in effect having a second job as fiction reader, though Maire Lynd as chief reader continued to have the greatest influence; everyone, including Evans and Pick, relied greatly on her judgment.

Early in 1965 it was decided to strengthen the editorial department by the return of Roland Gant from Secker & Warburg and, as well as resuming his old position as editorial manager, he was made a director. Inevitably this meant that David Machin's prospects of promotion were blocked, though he was highly thought of, and he left to join a literary agency, becoming a partner in A. P. Watt. Later he was appointed secretary of the Society of Authors, and later still became a director of

Cape. Machin was replaced by Janice Robertson, who had previously worked in the contracts department. She was essentially an efficient editorial organizer rather than a seeker after new talent. Salaries were low – about £750 a year in the 1960s for a junior editor – but the work was pleasant and not too arduous, you met well-known authors and the experience was invaluable for any ambitious entrant to the profession. By attending the Wednesday meetings at which print numbers and retail prices were fixed, editors ceased to be literary quidnuncs and were forced to get to grips with costing and production technicalities, with the implacable realities of commerce, with the ever-present tension between literary quality and profitability.

With authors who had gained that not readily defined but recognizable plateau of being 'established' this tension happily lessened, but by the 1960s competition had become fiercer and the name of the game was to recruit more established authors to your list and to cling onto the ones you already had. Morris West was a case in point. West had previously published two novels in his native Australia, one largely autobiographical, based on his early years as a novice Christian Brother, but it was only with his first book for Heinemann, *Children of the Sun* (1957), commissioned by Dwye Evans, that he became widely known. This was essentially impassioned reportage about street urchins in the slums of Naples and the work done for them by Father Borelli. It was followed by two novels, *The Big Story* (1957) and *The Second Victory* (1958) – and also two relative potboilers published under the name of Michael East – but he first became a world bestseller with *The Devil's Advocate* (1959) of which six million copies were sold in all editions worldwide. This novel about the English priest dying of cancer who is sent by the Vatican to an Italian village to make the case against the beatification of a possible saint, and who while there finds the ability to die in grace, was compellingly readable. It won the Heinemann Award and the James Tait Black Memorial Prize; it was also made into a play and a film. Next came *Daughter of Silence* (1961) which sold a basic 37,744 copies and which he turned into another play. After its opening in America to mostly good notices he wrote to Dwye Evans: 'Most of the drive was to prove I could do it and to break through the circle of bland experts who claim that theatre is an esoteric art. . . . It is an odd feeling – almost a climacteric. I had always wanted only one thing professionally – to be proven on my own terms. This has now been done, and, for me, the last questions are answered.

[495]

Now I can work calmly within my own frame of reference for as long as I am spared to do it.'[1]

Although the UK sales were considerable, a great deal of his success came in America, and he was very critical of what he thought to be Heinemann's weak performance in Australia. Other big publishers were after him, including Collins, Longman, and Hodder & Stoughton, and Evans had to agree to quite a considerable increase in his advance. By early 1962 he was still very dissatisfied and a letter came saying that he would be placing his next book elsewhere, in fact with Collins. It was a serious blow, following so soon after the departure of Graham Greene and the others. Pick had only just started and, though he had never met West, offered to try and persuade him to change his mind. As a newcomer he might have a better chance of convincing him to relent. Dwye agreed and Pick wrote to Australia asking West to delay his decision until he next came to London. This happened to be the following week and Dwye arranged an elaborate dinner party for West at Claridges; but it achieved nothing.

'It was one of those awful round tables,' Pick recalled. 'There were too many people there and I couldn't even speak to Morris, but as we were all leaving he told me rather pointedly that as it was a fine night he felt like going window-shopping. My wife and I were driving home along Bond Street when we spotted him with his wife outside Asprey's. I opened the door and they got in without a word as if we were expected. Back in his suite at the Carlton Tower we had a lengthy dialogue during which I told him of our new plans for more vigorous promotion and much else. He must have thought a new broom was at least worth another try because at the end of two hours he said he felt we could work together. New York time being five hours behind ours he immediately rang up his American agent, Paul Reynolds, telling him that he had changed his mind and that his new book would not be going to Collins. "I don't mind what you told Billie Collins. I am giving it to Charles Pick. I happen to like him."'

Two days later Reynolds was in Pick's office negotiating a contract for what turned out to be *The Shoes of the Fisherman* (1963), about the inner workings of the Vatican, with total hardback sales of 99,918 copies. West was by then reassured and signed a three-book contract, though the terms were very tough. There were thus three more mega-titles: *The Ambassador* (1965), set against the Vietnam war; *The Tower of Babel* (1968), about the

Arab–Israeli confrontation; *The Salamander* (1973), about the Italian underworld and the high society of politics and finance.

West was another highly successful author whose sales were by no means always matched with praise from the critics. One reviewer in the *Sunday Times* described *The Tower of Babel* as 'tea-bag fiction, with an instant flavour of reality but with little after-taste of truth', though he added 'I still wish I could do it half as well myself'. West's books were certainly more than 'profitable schmaltz' and, whatever the quality of the prose, they had considerable power, at least part of which came from his absorption in and concern about his religion. He once wrote: 'In so far as any writer can speak with certainty of himself and what he is doing, or attempting to do, this I believe is the motivating force behind what I am doing and have been doing for some time: the preachment in dramatic form of compassion and human love in its broadest sense as the one unifying theme in the chaos of the 20th century.'[2] His church was the target in *Scandal in the Assembly* (1970), written with Robert Francis, which was an exposure of the Roman Catholic marriage laws and an attack on their administration by the Church tribunals.

In the early 1970s West demanded even better terms, including a bigger sum up front, more than the firm felt it could pay, and so after all he moved to Collins and later to Hodder & Stoughton, to Hutchinson . . . and eventually back to Heinemann. To lose a big author who had first known success with one's imprint is particularly galling, but his loss was symptomatic of the new phase in publishing in which money more than ever was decisive.

The case of John le Carré (David Cornwell) was different in that, following two earlier novels, Gollancz had already published his sensational bestseller *The Spy Who Came in from the Cold*. Pick's description of his first meeting with le Carré sounded like an incident in one of his novels.

'It was a very foggy afternoon and we met in an old-fashioned flat in Lowndes Square. He said he would like to join us, we shook hands, and he disappeared into the fog. A year later the manuscript arrived of what would be *The Looking-Glass War* (1965). Understandably Victor Gollancz was furious at losing him. He fought hard for his option clause, but money was not the essential factor. It was just that le Carré wanted what he called a "more energetic publisher" and to deal with someone closer to his own age.'

Le Carré was of course an incredible scoop. He was very much more than a writer of thrillers – in fact, he had invented a new *genre*, the anti-thriller which showed up the sordid side of espionage, its loneliness and ultimate futility. In his report on le Carré's second book for Heinemann, *A Small Town in Germany* (1968), Roland Gant wrote that 'it follows the style of his previous work in the use of oblique allusion rather than direct statement. Much is left to the reader in the way of judgment of the various characters. Here and there the style may be too allusive for some readers' tastes. . . . But the characters are frighteningly convincing and the diplomats of Bonn sit on their shelf like specimens preserved in jars.' In an article about the book for the American Book of the Month Club edition, C. P. Snow described it as a 'superlative narrative sparkling with realistic detail. No doubt that is how the film will be made. But that misses what, I am becoming certain, is the essence and importance of le Carré. It sounds perverse, but the truth is that – despite the consummate surface realism – he is not, in his deepest implications, a realistic writer at all. He has an exceptionally strong psychological imagination: and he uses it to project a private vision. The hunter and the hunted. Outsiders, closer to each other than the ordinary run of men. It is a powerful emblem of human imagination. . . . For a writer to find a method of embodying his private vision – and through a medium so worked-over as the spy story – is an astonishing achievement.'[3]

After only two books le Carré moved to Hodder & Stoughton. Pick recalls his shock when he received le Carré's letter announcing that he was leaving Heinemann. 'It was so completely unexpected after all the firm's hard work and enthusiasm for his books. How could I help feeling let down? I think I now knew what Victor must have felt when le Carré moved over to us.'

Money-Spinners and/or Literary Merit

Anthony Burgess (the pseudonym of John Burgess Wilson) from the outset demonstrated a major talent. He had joined the list with *Time for a Tiger* (1956), the first of a trilogy based on his own experiences as a teacher

The new management team in the boardroom at 15/16 Queen Street in 1962.
Left to right: Time Manderson, David Machin, Charles Pick, Bill Holden, Derek Priestley, Dwye Evans, Alewyn Birch

The Windmill Press at work:
Above: the Monocaster typesetting machine
Below: Making corrections in the composing room

in Malaysia. It was very funny and in effect a tragi-comedy about one of the final gasps of the imperialist set-up. It received enthusiastic notices and was reprinted several times.

His success had, however, been preceded by rejections, as he has described in his autobiographical *Little Wilson and Big God*, published by Heinemann in 1987. His first submission was called *A Vision of Battlements*: 'Roland Gant told me that he had liked reading it, and so had his assistant, the poet James Michie. It was, he said, funny. I had not, in fact, intended it to be funny, but I assumed the right posture of modesty on this revelation that I was a coming comic novelist. Unfortunately, Gant then said, it did not seem possible to publish the work as a first novel: it had too much of the quality of a second novel. Would I now go home and write a genuine first novel and submit it to Messrs Heinemann? Certainly, I said. . . . The first novel, properly my second, that I now began to write was about life in a provincial grammar school. Gant had neither praised nor condemned the mythic substructure of *A Vision of Battlements*: he had merely not seemed to notice it. I felt it would be in order to apply myth once more to a realistic novel. . . .'[4] But the main theme that emerged was Burgess's guilt as a lapsed Catholic and when he sent in the typescript, 'I foresaw the kind of response I would get with fair accuracy. Gant was "cross". My novel was a mess and I probably was too. Heinemann would certainly not publish it. If I was going to write a publishable novel at all I had better cleanse myself of Catholic guilt. I had told Gant that it was likely I would be going to Malaya. A very good thing too, he opined'.[5]

The result was *Time for a Tiger* and the trilogy was completed by the equally compelling *The Enemy in the Blanket* (1958) and *Beds in the East* (1959), though Burgess was irritated by the jackets: the writer of the blurb on the first volume, 'unable to accept that Nabby Adams, with his illiterate obscenities and drunkenness, could really be a lieutenant, demoted him to sergeant, so that I could be blamed by careless reviewers for inconsistency.'[6] The design on the jacket of the second volume 'showed a Sikh pulling a white man and woman in a jinrickshaw. I, who had always looked up to publishers, was discovering that they could be as inept as authors. The reviewers would blame me, not the cover-designer, for that blatant display of ignorance.'[7]

Burgess seemed, however, to be happy with Heinemann and when he finally returned from the East after a spell in Brunei, no fewer than eleven of his novels were published during 1960–66. He abandoned the Far East for the grey and grim realities of post-war Britain and for a hilarious visit to an imaginary caliphate in East Africa, *Devil of a State* (1961). The rejected novel about life in a provincial grammar school, *The Worm and the Ring* (1961), was resurrected and published, though it led to a libel action in which both the author and publisher were sued by a Miss Gwendoline Bustin, the secretary of Banbury Grammar School. She alleged that she had been portrayed in an unflattering light and that the novel would have an adverse effect on her official position and standing locally. The defendants had to make a public apology, to amend all unsold copies, and to pay damages together with Miss Bustin's costs. Burgess next made two astonishing forays into a frightening future: *A Clockwork Orange* (1962), about a juvenile delinquent, which was made into a celebrated film by Stanley Kubrick, and *The Wanting Seed* (1962). His remarkable gift for language was demonstrated brilliantly in *Nothing Like the Sun* (1964), a story of Shakespeare's love life. Burgess was so prolific that two of his books had to be first issued by Peter Davies Ltd under another pseudonym, Joseph Kell: *One Hand Clapping* (1961) and *Inside Mr Enderby* (1963).

Bill Holden had introduced him to the *Yorkshire Post* and *The Observer* and he began to review fiction. All went well until an excellent review of Joseph Kell's *Inside Mr Enderby* appeared in the former under the name of Anthony Burgess. He thought that everyone knew about his pseudonym, but he was sacked from both papers. His autobiography makes unhesitatingly clear that there has been a tremendous amount of rumbustious drinking in his life and he was a frequent and welcome visitor to the 'bar' in Holden's office on the top floor of the Queen Street offices. Both David Machin and David Burnett recall evenings of heavy consumption in his company. Burnett told me that as a junior editor 'it was one of my jobs to take Burgess and his then wife to drink in Soho. I was twenty-five and with a light head. Before setting out I used to swallow a wine-glassful of olive oil to line my stomach. But for me it was a lucky break because through Burgess I met lots of other writers such as William Burroughs and others I considered to be avant-garde.'

Sadly Burgess decided to move elsewhere – at the same time he also changed his agent and his American publisher. Pick told me that he was certain it had nothing to do with money. In any case in the 1980s Anthony Burgess returned to the list and was welcomed like the Prodigal Son.

Fay Weldon could with justice perhaps be described as a Prodigal Daughter, because she left for Hodder & Stoughton who offered a bigger advance after the publication of *Down Among the Women* (1971), actually her second novel, and *Female Friends* (1975), only to return twelve years later with *The Hearts and Lives of Men* (1987), but soon afterwards she left the list once more. She was very much a writer of her times, reflecting the movement for 'consciousness-raising' among women and writing about the depressing lives led by many. Her books were also entertaining with a sharp, distinctive flavour of their own. She was another to leave over money. A rival publisher was prepared to pay her a very much larger sum than Heinemann, maybe wrongly, thought she was then worth.

Fay Weldon certainly was not prepared to believe that publishers were generous and founts of wise benevolence. As chairman of the five judges who awarded the Booker Prize in 1983 (to J. M. Coetzee, a Secker author) she shocked the trade with her outspoken speech at the celebratory banquet. She may have overstated her case, but an extract from what she said may help explain why authors have become less meek and often feel they owe little loyalty to their publishers:

'Writers know well enough that they are like Atlas, bearing on their shoulders all those who depend upon them for their income, the exercise of their own skills, their status and their very jobs. Publishers, booksellers, editors, librarians, journalists, academics, festival organizers, arts councils would be nothing without writers. So, to publishers I would say this. We are the raw material of your trade. You do tend to forget it, you know. You use us, the living us, and quite frankly you don't look after your raw material very well. And as you turn into an industry, so we must turn into workers and organize. I think you'd do without us altogether if you could, if there was a way of producing a book without writers – people who can never be trusted to produce a product of consistent quality. . . .

'I will ask you if in your dealing with authors you really are being fair, honourable and right, or merely getting away with what you can? Whether the "custom and practice" you quote as a reason for this and that, in an industry changed beyond all recognition since these customs and practices arose, can really go on as they are. If you are not careful, you will kill the goose that lays the golden eggs.

'I will tell you what writers dislike. The writer dislikes your paternalism. . . . The writer dislikes the way you say: "Aren't you lucky, we're going to publish your book – actually publish your book! What a risk we're taking: how very, very lucky you are, and honoured. Just sign this, please. . . ."[8]

Authors are in fact one-man businesses – certainly for income tax purposes, when some even become limited companies – and understandably they reflect business attitudes and those of an increasingly competitive society. There are a few who might be said to nurse ambitions to be literary yuppies. But many of the established, one-book-a-year authors who earned a steady if not spectacular income as members of the Heinemann list during the 1960–70s still seemed content enough. This was doubtless true of Victor Canning, perhaps the most prolific novelist on the list with no fewer than thirty-eight new titles published between 1963 (*The Limbo Line*) and 1983 (*Raven's Wind*) as well as twenty reissues of his previous books.

'The great thing about Heinemann', he told me, 'is that, although from time to time the staff change, there is a sense of permanence. I look upon Charles as a father figure. I always feel free to pick up the phone and ask questions or make suggestions. I am made to feel wanted. I am in close touch with Tim Manderson on the sales side. Roger Smith, my main editor, couldn't be more helpful – for example, going to the London Library to get books I need for reference. He is far more learned than I am. He has an eagle eye for mistakes. Over the years he has learned how my mind works.'

Canning defies classification and he could as easily have been placed among other writers of spy and mystery stories – his were often set in exotic locations abroad; but he also wrote comic novels; animal stories such as *The Doomsday Carrier* (1976) about a chimpanzee infected with a killer germ who escapes; tales of childhood adventure such as *The Runaways* (1972) and other stories about a boy called 'Smiler'; and, latterly, historical romances including a trilogy about the coming of King Arthur, starting with *The Crimson Chalice* (1976).

Historical novels continued to be published, though on a smaller scale and somehow with less aplomb. Among those new to the list were Doris Leslie – *The Warrior King* (1977), about Richard the Lion Heart, *The Incredible Duchess* (1974), and fourteen others; then there was Juliette Benzoni, especially her series of historical tales based on the lives of two women, starting with *Catherine* (1965) and *Marianne* (1969), making twelve books in all; Tyler Whittle's *Bertie, Albert Prince of Wales* (1972) and five others; and Margaret Trouncer – *The Passion of Peter Abelard* (1965).

An ambitious series of translations of classic Dutch and Flemish literature, published in conjunction with A. W. Sithoff in Holland, was launched with Arthur van Schendel's *The Waterman* (1963) and Louis Couperus's *Old People and the Things that Pass* (1963).

Discovering and nursing new talent and, once the world recognizes it, promoting it to the full is the most satisfying – and profitable – part of publishing. Penelope Lively provides a model of what can be done. After succeeding as a children's author (see page 561) she turned also to adult fiction with *The Road to Lichfield* (1977) about an affair between two married people which circumstances and characters cannot sustain. It was short-listed for the 1977 Booker Prize. Her next two were also at once recognized by the literary Establishment: a volume of short stories, *Nothing Missing but the Samovar* (1978), won the Southern Arts Literature Award; *Treasures of Time* (1979) won the first Arts Council's National Book Award. She declares that she sees no distinction between her writing for children and for adults, and that both are essentially concerned with the operation of memory. Her novels are particularly good at relating people to their social environments. Maire Lynd started her report on *Judgement Day* (1980) by describing it as a 'fast-moving and truly lively novel about, on the face of it, a village pageant to raise money to restore a Norman church, but it is really about human nature, about the continuity of history, humanism, pity, and a good many other ideas. The people in it come most wonderfully alive.' This is an accurate summing-up of Penelope Lively, who before the end of 1983 had written also *Next to Nature, Art* (1982) and two others.

The list may in the 1960–70s have laid more emphasis on books that were likely to command a large market, but some books could still be taken largely on their literary merit alone. No one could have thought that Edward Upward would ever be a great money-spinner – which he wasn't, though he did reasonably well and was sold to Penguin – but though he had published virtually nothing since the 1930s he still enjoyed a striking reputation among intellectuals who had then been young. Christopher Isherwood ended his introduction to *In the Thirties* (1962), the first of a trilogy called *The Spiral Ascent*, by declaring that he believed 'that it may well be the first part of one of the greatest and most original novels of our time'.

Some may find this judgment remarkable because the novel was written in a flat, unembroidered style and contained long passages of dialogue which might have been copied from a Communist Party tract. Indeed when Upward first responded in 1961 to an approach from James Michie, he warned modestly: 'I wish I could hope that William Heinemann would – as you so kindly put it – be the publisher to look after me, but I am afraid that my novel would not be acceptable at the present time. It is sympathetic to Communism in the nineteen thirties and ends with the central character still an enthusiastic member of the Communist Party.'[9]

Upward seems to have captured the language and thought of people caught up in the great anti-fascist movement, when the Soviets seemed to promise hope and Franco was at the gates of Madrid. The books are obviously in part autobiographical and he spoke for other intellectuals who were politically involved and also expressed their doubts. Stephen Spender wrote that '*In the Thirties* is a novel about the involvement of a poet in the politics of that decade. It is remarkable for truth, on several levels: the endeavour of the hero to live according to the social truth which he thinks Communism to be, deepening thereby the perhaps not reconcilable truth of his poetry; the truth which lies in the purity and integrity of the writing about situations described, the poetic insights. This book . . . is of a class by itself, and is probably the most revealing novel written about the preoccupations of a decade in the present century.'[10] John Lehmann was also impressed and wrote of Upward's 'extraordinarily clear, unfussy style, an exactitude of definition, and a very unusual capacity for following the interaction of internal philosophical reflection and external sensuous experience. . . . How vividly Edward Upward presents the feelings and arguments that affected us all in the thirties! It is fascinating – and horrifying – to watch how the hero's continually reviving desire for the free "poetic life" is always squashed by his own Marxist cant and casuistry.'[11]

The second novel in the trilogy – *The Rotten Elements* (1969) – depicts the two central characters, who are dedicated Communists, becoming disillusioned because the Party line has shifted and Lenin has been betrayed; they are forced out because the Party is no longer pure. The concluding *No Home but the Struggle* (1977) completes the spiral ascent so that Alan Sebrill, the hero accepts that for the poet the contribution made to the political struggle should be made through his poetry, but his political poems must be poetically true and not propaganda in verse.

There were two volumes of his short stories – *The Railway Accident and Other Stories* (1969) and *The Night Walk* (1987) – which were also very highly thought of. Publishing writers like Edward Upward may not satisfy the accountant's parameters but it is the kind of risk that keeps a publisher great or, as Upward, an unrepentant Marxist in his eighties, might say, it puts values before what Marx termed 'the cash nexus'.

Wilbur Smith and Cookson Underwrite the Profits

By the 1970s two novelists, Wilbur Smith and Catherine Cookson, had come to dominate not only the list but also the company's finances. The hardback sales of each Wilbur Smith title progressed steadily with *Rage* (1987) selling 274,000 and *A Time to Die* (1989) 360,000 (both figures including the bookclub); on top of which were about 1,000,000 for each Pan edition and sizeable American orders. In 1982, for example, Pan sold 1,524,000 of his titles (including 658,000 of fourteen backlist titles), earning Heinemann £198,000 – this accounted for 53 per cent of the firm's 1982 co-publishing profit from Pan. Cookson's figures were equally impressive with an average of two new titles a year, each selling about 75,000 (including the bookclub) plus about 400,000 for each Corgi edition. Between them these two authors must have contributed at least 30 per cent of the firm's annual profits. Like Galsworthy, Brett Young, Priestley, Shute, and others in the past they both appealed to the large middlebrow public which goes on buying or borrowing books by authors who above all else can be guaranteed to tell a good and suspenseful story – though with writers of this calibre there is much more to it. It is as if they each knew of some secret blend of ingredients.

Starting with *When the Lion Feeds* (1964) the Rhodesian-born Wilbur Smith had seen seventeen of his novels published by 1983. Their titles indicate their character: *The Sound of Thunder* (1966), *The Diamond Hunters* (1971), *Eagle in the Sky* (1974), *The Eye of the Tiger* (1975), *The Leopard Hunts in Darkness* (1984). . . . Most of them were very long and, though clichés were not unknown and the characters larger than life, Smith nearly always exercised a remarkable narrative control. There were marvellous set pieces and he drew deeply on African history, on his thorough understanding of the current situation across Southern Africa, his personal knowledge of the country's enormous spaces, its forests and veld, its wild animals, to create big, action-packed, pulsating stories. Two of his books were banned by the South African censors, but after ten years the decisions were reversed on appeal. The first of these, *When the Lion Feeds*, was subject to three court hearings, including one at the Supreme Court in Pretoria.

Tim Manderson, who as well as being sales director read a great many of the fiction manuscripts and was expert at knowing what would and would not sell, reported for example that *A Sparrow Falls* (1977) '. . . . never flags or fails to hold one's interest . . . as usual his hunting scenes are better than those of any living writer. He brings alive the tension of the stalk, the heat of the bush, and the grace and strength of wild animals.' Throughout this novel runs the need to conserve wild animals and their habitats. Most years Wilbur and his wife made a safari by Land-Rover into the dwindling wilderness of Central Africa. He also found time to travel to other countries and yet still managed to write his marathon novel almost every year.

He was advised and sustained by Rachel Monsarrat, his Heinemann editor who continued to look after him even when she left the firm to live in France, to send him detailed comments and, when she felt it was needed, quite major criticisms. These were always constructive, though at times they could be challenging. Her report to the firm on *The Eye of the Tiger* began: 'It's action, action all the way and to be frank I feel that he has got far too carried away with his big, hairy, brutal face-punching, gut-spilling villains, and his attractive, intelligent, bronzed, sexy heroes and heroines. It is a prime adventure fairy story and if the plot is somewhat simple, the characters rather weak and the suspense not all that thrilling, individual scenes – particularly one involving a fight with a hungry shark – can be very exciting. . . .'

Wilbur Smith always took her criticism very well. In response to one of her letters he wrote: 'You will know without me telling you what high value I place on your opinion, so will know also that your letter has given me grave and serious pause. I have examined each point you make with my full attention – and I will read and study it further. . . . Naturally, I do not agree completely with everything you say – but that has been the value of our relationship. We have been able to examine specifics from the different vantage points of age, gender, and sensibilities.

'As I understand it, you are chiefly warning me against: (a) Impatience and working towards self-imposed deadlines (a book a year, for instance). (b) Sensationalism – pouring on the sexual and description of violence as an easy way of catching attention. (c) Complacence and laziness – forgetting that writing is a difficult and demanding craft, where lack of attention to detail will show in undeveloped characterization and loose description. Every one of these points are well carried, and I will not dispute them with you. More than that – I will bear them firmly in mind in the future, while still not admitting that I am guilty of any of them!!'

There was a great demand for his books in Australia, New Zealand, and Canada, as well as South Africa, and they were translated into at least fourteen other languages. At first he made slower headway in America but with each new title sales improved. Many of his books have been turned into films. At the time of writing his world sales come to well over 50 million copies. All his titles, hardback and paperback, have always been kept in print. It is understandable that Charles Pick describes him as an ideal author and as the most successful ever to appear on the Heinemann list:

'We have never advertised Wilbur's books apart from the normal announcements in *The Bookseller* and elsewhere. We have never hyped him. His huge readership, which has increased from book to book, has all come from recommendation by word of mouth. He appeals to all ages and both sexes. When people read one of his later books, they frequently go back and read his earlier ones.' Pick summed up with three basic reasons for his success. 'First, readability – his books are real "page-turners". Secondly, his great love for Africa and its wild life which appeals in a period when people are very conscious of the need for Nature conservation. Thirdly, his straightforward, unmannered way of writing, including his treatment of sex.'

All these reasons are undoubtedly valid, but no amount of literary or marketing analysis can ever explain completely what it is that puts an author into the rare class of unstoppable bestsellers.

The same is true of Catherine Cookson, though she is of course a very different type of writer. Already extremely successful, she transferred to Heinemann from Macdonald's with *The Mallen Streak* (1973), the first of a trilogy, set in rural Northumberland and Newcastle, which followed the violent and tragic lives of the Mallen family from the 1850s to the First World War. Her books are almost entirely set in her native North-East and nearly half of them are about life in Victorian and Edwardian times. The characters are firmly drawn and the stories, convincing but melodramatic, move at a fast pace. Among the others were *The Invisible Cord* (1975), which spanned 1943–71 in the South Shields area of Tyneside, where the author had grown up as the illegitimate child of a mother who drank – they were so poor that after school Catherine would go out to pick bits that fell on the road from coal-carts. Her harsh childhood depicted in *Our Kate* (her autobiography published by Macdonald) and her struggles as a young woman managing a workhouse laundry before she wrote her first novel when she was past forty, have clearly helped shape her writing. Those early years explain her sympathy and understanding of the suffering and human hope that make her characters so available to millions of readers. They may also explain why one should not be surprised to find quotations from Frederick Engels's writings on the industrial North in a novel which is compulsively read by millions. It is interesting also that Lord Chesterfield's letters to his son come into several of her novels.

With *The Gambling Man* (1975) she returned to South Shields of a century ago. *The Cinder Path* (1978) took the reader from rural Northumberland to the Western Front in World War I. After several others she produced *Tilly Trotter* (1980), the first of a trilogy about the strong-minded girl who grew up in the early Victorian North-East, worked as nursemaid and in the mines, and in the later volumes was wed and widowed.

Catherine Cookson has suffered all her life from a rare blood disease that causes internal bleeding and has meant frequent and sudden visits to hospital. Out of her vast earnings, she has distributed well over £1 million among 200 charities, much of it to Tyneside hospitals and for medical research, particularly into blood diseases. There is also the Catherine Cookson Trust to deal with her royalties when she dies. Despite her physical frailty, at eighty she was still writing at least two long novels a year. She also answers over 3,000 letters a year from readers.

'I only manage because I have such a marvellous staff,' she told me. 'There are seven of them: a first-class butler, a very good footman, a private secretary, a night and a day nurse, a housekeeper, and an ordinary typist – they are all in one man, my husband, Tom.'

Indeed Tom, a retired grammar school master, cooked the lunch and fetched and drove me back to the station when I paid them a visit in 1985 at their large house in a remote, romantic part of the upper Tyne valley.

They live simply, the only obvious signs of her relatively recent wealth being a fondness for elegant chandeliers. But she clearly enjoys her extraordinary success – by the end of 1985 she had written sixty-five novels (including six under the pseudonym of Catherine Marchant), translated into seventeen languages, with sales totalling 83 million copies.

'Very often I'm sure it isn't me who has done all this. I am still Katie McMullen from East Jarrow. Who used to fetch the beer from the pub and be sent with things to the pawnbroker. But then I pull myself together in the North Country manner and tell myself: "Well, lass, you've worked for it".'

She wrote her first sixteen books in long-hand, but she contracted writer's cramp and a frozen shoulder and now dictates them onto a tape. She is fiercely reluctant to make cuts but sensibly Heinemann employed John Foster White, who had looked after her at Macdonald's, as a freelance editor.

'We understand each other very well. John is always very tactful and only "suggests" changes. It was Charles Pick who suggested taking him on and I was delighted, though at first I thought the Heinemann people were a snooty lot and I was told that Charles was the "red carpet man"; not that I was in awe of him because I have always believed that we are all equal under our clothes, but not under our skins. After twelve years the bond with Heinemann is very strong. Charles now rings me every now and again just to see how I am. So does Roland. Tim Manderson is my number one fan. I do a lot with Tim. I also particularly liked Nigel Hollis.' She laughed. 'Oh, but I got on my hind legs with Nigel in a very short time! He phoned up to tell me they were going to put an advert. in the *Daily Express* and in the *Mirror*, because he said it would appeal to my sort of reader. If you please! But I soon put him right and explained that from the very beginning I had been reviewed in the *Times Lit.* and that Betjeman had given my books wonderful reviews. He called them a social history of the North. No, I don't just write for morons! I soon discovered that Nigel has a brother who is a priest and I used to chip him about this because I am an escaped Catholic. I was so sorry when Nigel left.'

She went on to tell me that she didn't like being called a romantic writer. 'There's a difference between a romance and a novel. A romance can be larger than life or it may be a fairy tale. You can call on your wishful thinking, but with a novel the essential element is realism. The ideas for my books come very easily. I must get the end clear first. I have to write towards it. It's no good going to Newcastle station and buying a ticket if you don't know where you're going. I pick out from memory a face or an incident and I have a story. It grows out of the characters. No, I don't believe in plots, but in putting a character into an environment, because it is the environment that makes us.' Her characters then take on lives of their own. She can see them in her mind as flesh and blood and hear them speaking. 'I act it all out in my mind. You see, I am a frustrated actress but without a visible audience. Some of the characters wear me out. In the middle of the night I can do a scene which makes me cry and laugh. It can make me very tense and so I say to my subconscious: "You work it out", and I find the next morning that it has and then I put it straight onto tape – not that it comes out exactly the same.'

I left wondering if that helps explain how bestsellers are born.

Transatlantic Talent – Salinger, Vidal, Lurie, Condon, Potok, Puzo

America continued to be an important source of novelists. A newcomer was J. D. Salinger who had already made a considerable name for himself with *Catcher in the Rye*, published by Hamish Hamilton who, despite an option, was forced by the author to release him, largely because of his dissatisfaction with the appearance of a subleased paperback version. Despite their solemn inclusion in most contracts option clauses are difficult and indeed painful to enforce if the author is determined to leave. Heinemann were of course delighted to be offered Salinger's next novel, *Franny and Zooey* (1962) by his London agent, Edmund Cork of Hughes Massie. It was in the form of two long stories about a brother and sister in New York told partly by another brother, Buddy Glass, whom Salinger calls his *alter ego*. The author described it as part of 'a long-term project, patently an ambitious one, and there is a real enough danger, I suppose, that sooner or later I'll bog down, perhaps disappear entirely, in my own methods, locutions, and mannerisms.'

It was a very sensitive *New Yorker*ish novel, but the author didn't help by refusing all forms of personal publicity, declaring that 'it is my rather subversive opinion that a writer's feelings of anonymity-obscurity are the second-most valuable property on loan to him during his working years. My wife has asked me to add, however, in a single explosion of candor, that I live in Westport with my dog.' He was also difficult in other ways: all advertisements had to be submitted via his agent for his personal approval; review quotes, whether favourable or unfavourable, must not be used; he had insisted on a meticulous production and made clear that if a comma got in where it shouldn't be, Heinemann would not be offered his next book.

Franny and Zooey was published in about three months, instead of the usual nine, and manufactured to very acceptable British standards, but when Salinger saw an advance copy, he was full of complaints, describing it as 'an unnecessarily underprivileged-looking little book' which 'looks like something any of the low-budget Iron Curtain countries might have brought out as well or better . . .'12. Worse, despite intervention by Dwye Evans who happened to be in New York, he refused to sanction it becoming a 'double' Book Society choice. It sold 38,092 hardback copies.

Despite all these difficulties Heinemann published his next book with the elaborate title of *Raise High the Roof-Beam, Carpenters, and Seymour, an Introduction* (1963). It consisted of short stories from the *New Yorker* told again by Buddy Glass about his brother Seymour's wedding, jilting, elopement, and eventual suicide. After this Salinger published very little and retired to his rural home. James Michie commented: 'Salinger was of course a wonderful writer, but sadly he was one of those who give up half-way through life. There seems to have been a tendency among American writers of certain generations either to retreat into silence or take to the bottle, if not to kill themselves.'

Gore Vidal could not have been more different – prolific, at home with the Kennedy set, cosmopolitan, his interests ranging from the ancient Classical world to modern-day politics. He wrote some twenty books for Heinemann during the 1960–70s, divided into five basic groups. More important perhaps were his scholarly but always compulsively readable fictional re-creations of the ancient world, several of them of great length, such as *Julian* (1964), the fourth-century Roman emperor who renounced Christianity; *Two Sisters* (1970), a mixture of fact and fiction which counterpointed the Roman Empire with life in the twentieth century; *Creation* (1981), told by Zoroaster's elderly grandson who recalls his experiences as Persian ambassador to the courts of India, Cathay, and

Athens, a tapestry of some quarter of a million words, bringing in Darius, Xerxes, Confucius, and the Buddha. Secondly, there were novels about American history, such as *Burr* (1974), from the days of the Revolution to the 1830s, and *1876* (1976). Thirdly, novels about the contemporary world such as *Washington D.C.* (1967), an exposé of political society and intrigues; and *The City and the Pillar* (1965), a very 'frank' novel with plenty of male homosexual encounters. Fourthly, there were collections of scintillating essays, such as *Rocking the Boat* (1963); *Reflections upon a Sinking Ship* (1969); *Pink Triangle and Yellow Star and Other Essays* (1982); and, fifthly, modern satires such as *Kalki* (1978), a parable stemming from feminism in the post-Vietnam world.

In this last category there was also *Myra Breckinridge*, a very funny satire on Hollywood whose central character is changed from a man into a woman as a result of a motor accident. It was the author himself who felt it was not right for the Heinemann imprint and it was taken over by Blond who sold it in vast numbers. Graham Watson, his agent, told me that he had advised him to stay with Heinemann because they could still offer prestige and the promise of good reviews. More money could be obtained elsewhere, but Vidal was not primarily interested in money. The successor *Myron* (1975) was said by the lawyers not to be obscene and thus appeared in the Heinemann list. Myra, once again more or less transexualized into Myron, is married and undergoes a sci-fic time shift back to 1948, almost impossible to describe. It sold 5,898 hardback copies.

A critical study of Gore Vidal's work, *The Apostate Angel* by Bernard F. Dick, was published by Heinemann in 1977. An ironical coda to *Myra*'s rejection, which Gore Vidal might relish, followed the firm's publication of *Consenting Adult* (1975) by another American, Laura Z. Hobson. It was awarded the *Gay News* 1976 Literary Award, a framed certificate being formally presented in the Heinemann boardroom. It was a pity that Frere – who had stood in the dock at the Old Bailey – was not still at Heinemann to receive it.

Although Alison Lurie had been born in Chicago and grew up in New York, her first novel, *Love and Friendship* (1962), an astringent, elegant, often humorous study of marital relations on an American campus, was bought by Heinemann before it appeared in America. After *The Nowhere City* (1965), which was centred on a campus in Los Angeles and exposed the rootlessness of Californian society, she turned to a small kooky spiritualist group in *Imaginary Friends* (1967) in order to satirize the pretensions of two sociologists who investigate it. Four more books followed, including the highly intelligent *The War Between the Tates* (1974).

Another American, Richard Condon, had come to novel-writing after twenty-two years as a publicity man for Hollywood moguls. After moving from Michael Joseph he wrote four new novels for Heinemann in the 1960s, starting with *An Infinity of Mirrors* (1964), a documentary fictional account of the horrors of living during the war in Europe under the Nazis. Condon's message was that 'when evil is fought with evil's ways, these ways become serpents which entangle, strangle and pull down.' It was followed by *Any God Will Do* (1966), an indictment of British snobbery; *The Ecstasy Business* (1967) about the making of a super-motion picture; and *Mile High* (1969), about prohibition and the world of crime and the corruption and violence it created. Condon's great sociological canvases were translated into many languages and were, in every sense of the word, big. His characters were skilfully drawn, though he had a joky habit of modelling them on people he knew. Roland Gant was sure that he and Pick had been in several of his books: 'the last time I was a circus dwarf and in an earlier one a German professor of entomology.'

Condon could be very articulate about his own motivation as a writer: 'True, if one has any slant toward insanity, this sort of work does bring it out. I had entered the quiet quadrangle of the writer as a manic-depressive type, but in my third year of novel writing I began to suspect that that jolly-sounding aberration had shifted to straight paranoia. Such a switchover is inevitable in my line of work. The three classical symptoms of paranoia are the prime tools of the novelist. First, retrospective falsification: of course, this is the very core of the trade. Retrospective falsification is what story telling is. The second symptom is megalomania: the novelist who, in actual life, feels inadequate in the face of earthquake, fire and flood, invents his own earthquake, fire and flood, which are far more horrendous; and, in society's most harmless professional delusion of grandeur, the novelist is free to save from these disasters exactly those people whom it pleases him to save. The third paranoiac symptom is a persecution complex – which is the means by which novelists conduct all their business. Even writers untrained in business, those who had been marched in their youth directly to the monastery of St Remington de Olivetti, know that their work should be advertised high above the main

thoroughfares of the principal cities on large electric signs, and furthermore that their work should be advertised more than anyone else's. The
publisher never agrees. Hence the persecution.'[13]

Two other writers will have to suffice to represent the American
contingent. They both drew their inspiration from the racial subcultures
that give New York so much of its vibrancy and help explain its contradictions. In *The Chosen* (1967) Chaim Potok, himself a rabbi, writes about
Jewish sects in Brooklyn, its central theme being the conflict between the
narrowness of the ultra-Orthodox and the pressures of the modern world
as felt by the younger generation. The six million dead in the Holocaust,
the Talmud, Zionism, Hasidic hereditary rabbis are the stuff of this very
serious novel which sold 8,198 hardback copies. It was followed by *The
Promise* (1970), with the same central characters, and three more titles.

Heinemann had already published Mario Puzo's *The Fortunate Pilgrim*
(1965), about Italian immigrants in New York, when they were offered the
same author's *The Godfather* (1969), but they very nearly lost it. On a
Friday flight to Paris Charles Pick spotted Walter Minton, then head of
Putnams in New York. As a gesture he sent him a quarter-bottle of
champagne.

'When he came down the aisle to thank me, he asked what I made of a
cable he pulled out of his pocket. "My office wants me to close with a
$400,000 paperback deal for a novel by some Italian. It's by Mario
something or other." I asked if by any chance it was by Mario Puzo.
"That's the guy." When I told him that we had an option on it, he seemed
surprised and said it was going to be sold to Cassells. Worried, I rang
Roland Gant on reaching Paris to ask him to visit the office on Saturday
and examine the contract to make sure that we really did have an option.
On returning to London on the Monday I discovered there had been a
change of agents, and it was this that led to our being forgotten.'

It was only because of Pick's chance meeting with Minton that
Heinemann kept hold of this major title about the *Cosa Nostra*, the five
families of *mafiosi* at war to control the rackets in New York and later Las
Vegas, and the gang boss, Vito Corleone, a refusal to accept whose offer of
'friendship' means death. Its sales in the States were understandably
much greater than elsewhere, but Heinemann sold 62,639 hardback
and Pan the best part of a million, and later the film doubled that
figure.

The Godfather was followed by Puzo's *The Dark Arena* (1979), actually his first book in the States and which was set in post-war Germany, and two other of his titles.

Crime and *Frissons* from Highsmith, Leasor and Others

Patricia Highsmith is also American, though having spent much of her life in England, France, and Switzerland (where she now lives), but she fits more aptly into this section, which is devoted to writers of crime fiction, thrillers, mystery and suspense. She is different from Mario Puzo or a writer like le Carré because they write 'faction' rather than fiction and are focused directly on to crime or espionage in the real world. Patricia Highsmith also possesses the best qualities of a novelist and her characters and situations are decidedly real, but the difference is that she – and the other authors in this section – are, or at least appear to be, primarily out to entertain readers, to give them *frissons*; which she does superbly, e.g., the opening story in her *Little Tales of Misogyny* (1977) which begins: 'A young man asked a father for his daughter's hand, and received it in a box – her left hand.'

Between *Deep Water* in 1958 and the end of 1983 Heinemann published twenty of her novels and three volumes of short stories. They included *A Suspension of Mercy* (1965), *The Glass Cell* (1967), *The Black House* (1981), and several about Tom Ripley, her decidedly ambiguous hero. As an *aficionado* of disquiet and menace the critics have always placed her in a class of her own. A reviewer in the *Spectator* of *Ripley's Game* (1974) wrote: 'the extraordinary power and intensity with which this sense of doom and nemesis is sustained throughout a book is the most distinguishing mark of the Highsmith creation, probably the most consistently excellent body of work of its kind produced since the war'. In a foreword to her collection of short stories, *Eleven* (1970), Graham Greene wrote that she creates 'a world of her own, a world claustrophobic and irrational, which we enter each time with a sense of personal danger'. Roger Smith, who edited her books for many years, described her as 'a great psychological suspense writer' and spoke of her stories as 'probing into the wellsprings of morality and conscience and shot through with highly individual, sometimes quirky and disturbing insights'. Her love and empathy for animals perhaps provide another key to understanding her talent. The theme of *The Animal Lover's Book of Beastly Murder* (1975) is that of animals taking mortal revenge on human beings. An elephant crushes his sadistic keeper; battery chicks swarm out of their pens and leave nothing of their oppressor but a fallen column of blood and bone; a truffle-hunting sow, denied a taste of the delicacy for herself, tramples her owner to death in the forest. . . . It is little wonder that Patricia Highsmith has earned the sobriquet of 'the latter-day Edgar Allan Poe'.

James Leasor, an immigrant from Michael Joseph, was among a group of novelists who supplied a regular flow of books which were less idiosyncratic than Highsmith's but were very competent, readable, and made reliable contributions to annual turnover. Starting with *Passport to Oblivion* (1964), he wrote eight novels around Dr Jason Love, the Somerset doctor who becomes involved in cases that have little to do with medicine but had plenty of casual killing and casual sex, and suspense. Leasor's passion for vintage cars is reflected in *They Don't Make Them Like That Any More* (1969), about a dealer in these valuable adult toys, and in two other titles. Among Leasor's other books were *Follow the Drum* (1972), about the Indian Mutiny, two about Europeans in China, and some wartime adventures such as *Boarding Party* (1978) and *Green Beach* (1975) – see pages 557–8.

Nicolas Freeling, who joined Heinemann with *What are the Bugles Blowing For?* (1975) after many books with Gollancz and Hamish Hamilton, wrote about murder, terrorism, *et al.*, mostly with a Continental background. There was usually a central investigating character such as the French police detective, Henri Castang – e.g., *The Night Lords* (1978) – or Arlette, the widow of a Dutch detective – e.g., *One Damn Thing after Another* (1981) – but his work was distinguished by his quirky, taut, compressed style. His prose had a flavour very much of his own, though in one letter to David Burnett he explained: 'I am trying to speak an English that is reasonably good, and at the same time comprehensible in Vancouver or Omaha or Cape Town or Melbourne or Zurich, and not just in the brothels round St James's Square. I feel utterly convinced that you see things in this light. I know I have my personal jargon, but this is an old tradition – what about the p.j. of Waugh or Wodehouse; or the New-York-Jewish jarg of all those schmucks who are supposed to be such good writers like Updike? I truly believe that any writer at all, who is any good, on any level, "invents his own language" to a very great extent. The pressure towards writing bland, wet, advert-copy English is one which I try to resist, and this has to be separated from my ghastly tendency to speak and write Mittel-Europa pidgin, like the technical translators at Geneva or Bruxelles: "Der cheese van New Zealand is un grand problème, Excellence, aber wir have vaincu die Kangaroo-tails in conserve. . . ."'[14] In another letter, to Roland Gant, he animadverted against the single quote mark: 'For one thing the eye slips over it too easily . . . and may easily miss it altogether. Dante (or Mr Freeling) is difficult enough already without our conspiring to prevent people from seeing where dialogue ends and narrative begins. Moreover I think the single quote is ugly in itself. It looks an ass if it comes up against a final apostrophe and it looks a thundering ass when it comes to quotes within quotes. A mimsy little pale single quote trying to enclose a fat black double quote reminds me of a negro baby whose woollies have shrunk in the wash.'[15]

The last two writers in this section are Dutch. Robert van Gulik was a distinguished diplomat, serving as Netherlands ambassador in several Far Eastern countries including Japan. He was also a great expert on all things Chinese. He employed the technique of the detective story to describe crime in Ancient China, with Judge Dee as his investigator. Murder, jealousy, sadism, robbery, with clues as tangled as noodles, are presented in a Confucian world in titles such as *The Lacquer Screen* (1964), *The Willow Pattern* (1965), and *The Phantom of the Temple* (1966). No wonder Dee was variously described as a 'Tang Dynasty Sherlock Holmes', a 'Mandarin Maigret', and an 'Oriental Perry Mason'. The younger Janwillem van de Wetering also brought an Eastern background to his stories, having for a while been a lay disciple of a Zen master in Kyoto. He made his debut, however, with *Outsider in Amsterdam* (1976) where his two detectives, Gripstra and de Gier, hunt for the clues in the Dutch canals and alleyways. Eight novels later in *The Mind Murders* (1981) the same two are still on the hunt after 'tugging at the drawer of the massive morgue refrigerator' which slid smoothly towards them to reveal 'the corpse's face, slightly twisted to the side, with an expression of furious surrender'. His books virtually sold out, though never more than 3,500 were printed, but as with most titles of this kind their publication was made possible by paperback sales to Corgi and the occasional bookclub choice.

Major Novels from Africa and India – Scott Wins the Booker

'This is a very exciting discovery: a well-written novel about the break-up of tribal life in one part of Nigeria.' So runs the opening sentence in Maire Lynd's report on Chinua Achebe's first novel, *Things Fall Apart* (1958). 'It is full of characters who really live and, once begun, it is difficult to put down. It is the first novel, I think, on this fascinating theme.' The report ends: 'Likeable, exciting, new, strongly recommended.'

Following a modest first printing of 2,000 copies, this book was later to become a classic with total sales of over three million copies, most of them as a volume in the African Writers Series. There was also a comparable sale in America. It has been translated into forty-five other languages. Achebe told me modestly: 'One of my original impulses was to preserve the local Ibo imagery and sayings that were on the verge of being lost.' Elsewhere he has explained that his ambition was to prove that 'African peoples did not hear of culture for the first time from Europeans; that their societies were not mindless but frequently had a philosophy of great depth and value and beauty, that they had poetry and, above all, they had dignity'. Achebe continued to write of the impact of European culture on his people in *No Longer at Ease* (1960) and *Arrow of God* (1964). With *A Man of the People* (1966) he turned to satire to expose the political corruption in Nigeria since it achieved independence. David Machin in accepting it wrote: 'I hope some British readers do not use it as a basis for saying "I told you so" when discussing the methods of government of newly independent African states';[16] to which he replied: 'I am deeply conscious of the fact that enemies of African independence will rejoice and that some of my own people will feel that I have let them down. But it can't be helped. The book is addressed primarily to Africa and if it makes a few people think again I shall feel justified.'[17]

On a visit to West Africa in January 1959, soon after the publication of *Things Fall Apart*, Alan Hill discovered that the cover price of 15s. was far too high for a book for African readers and that few people had even heard of it – especially as African bookshops catered only for the educational market. How was the book to get into the hands of the new generation of

African readers? It was a problem that was likely to become increasingly acute, for Hill suspected that Achebe was not an isolated phenomenon: the new African universities must be turning out other talented writers. He therefore decided to start a series of inexpensive paperbacks which could be sold mainly through the African educational book network. He recruited E. E. ('Van') Milne from Nelson, engaged Achebe as series editor, and came out with four titles in 1962: reprints of Achebe's first two books (*Things Fall Apart* and *No Longer at Ease*); the hitherto unpublished *Burning Grass* by Cyprian Ekwensi; and the specially commissioned *Zambia Shall be Free* by Kenneth Kaunda. Thus was born the African Writers Series, which was to expand rapidly to become a major Heinemann division – a pioneering development of HEB, the new educational company which originated the publishing of all new African titles.

Other African countries – French speaking as well as Anglophone – were now ransacked for authors. From East Africa came James Ngugi, whose first novel *Weep Not Child* (1964) was also to sell over a million copies. Hill recalls how he commissioned it during a long distance call from Van Milne: 'Van was speaking from Kampala in Uganda. He was very impressed with a novel by a student at Makere that had won a prize awarded by the Society for Cultural Freedom. He wanted my authority to take it on, which I at once gave him. Those were the days when one published on trust in one's advisers, combined with a feeling for the market. We didn't go into contortions with accountants or worry about bottom lines. Entrepreneurial opportunism paid off much better.'

Ten years later the African Writers Series had a hundred titles drawn from all over Africa, the great majority being new publications, and after two decades the number had increased to nearly three hundred. They included the cream of Black African writing, poetry as well as prose, from Senegal to Cape Town, from Lagos to Mozambique. In the words of Edward Blishen: 'I shall tell my grandchildren that through the African Writers Series I saw a whole new, potentially great world of literature come into being.'

As a South African Alan Scholefield logically comes in to this section, but also because he hated apartheid and was horrified to see how some Whites used it for their own gain: 'When the Group Areas Act was passed which made it impossible for Non-Whites to live in certain areas where they had existed with Whites for generations, I saw people who were professed liberals going around literally trying to frighten the Coloureds into selling them their homes cheaply. I think I realized fully then for the first time that apartheid was something more than a cruel philosophy: it was an opportunity for anyone to use other people's misery for their own profit.'[18] His earlier books had been historical adventure stories about pioneer settlers in Africa, such as *A View of Vultures* (1966), or *Great Elephant* (1967) in which a white man wanted by the Cape government is allowed to settle with his family in unexplored territory by Chaka, the cruel and savage king of the Zulus. *The Young Masters* (1971) was very different and gives a chilling picture of how young Whites are conditioned to adopt racism. Scholefield's horror of the heedless killing of wild game also comes into his novels. He also wrote a straight account of some of *The Dark Kingdoms* (1975) of Africa which existed long before the Europeans came – Congo, Dahomey, and Lesotho – which was the only one of the three to survive.

Three major novelists wrote about India. R. K. Narayan's work was introduced to Frere in 1960 by Graham Greene who wrote in an introduction to one of his early books, *The Bachelor of Arts*, that 'it was Mr Narayan . . . who first brought India, in the sense of the Indian population and the Indian way of life alive to me. . . . [His novels] increase our knowledge of the Indian character, certainly, but I prefer to think of them as contributions to English literature, contributions of remarkable maturity.'[19] Narayan moved from Methuen with *The Man-Eater of Malgudi* (1962), the invented Indian town in which all his novels and short stories were set. He once told a London audience that he 'wanted to be able to put in whatever I liked and wherever I liked, a little street here, or a school, or a temple or a bungalow or even a slum or a railway crossing at any spot I liked, and demolish them when I did not want them anymore. I wanted to be a sort of minor despot in a little world. I began to like my role and to be fascinated by Malgudi's possibilities. Its river, marketplace, far-off mountain roads and forest acquired a concrete quality which I find have imprisoned me within their own boundaries, with the result that I'm unable to escape from Malgudi even if I wanted to.'[20] Readers soon feel they know their way around Malgudi's Market Road, its snuff stalls, the Regal Haircutting Saloon . . . and they recognize as old friends the town's expert on finance; Dr Pal, the journalist; and many others.

Next came *Gods, Demons and Others* (1965) which retold stories from the *Ramayana* and the *Mahabharata*. Richard Church wrote a report:

'What is most impressive, and indeed mysterious, is the way in which all mythology, no matter how varied in detail, tends to come together on certain fundamental themes and personalities. Mr Narayan's tales bring to me the smell, the scene, the music of the villages along the approaches to the Nilgiri Hills in South India, the leisurely cattle with their decorated horns, the women drawing water from the communal wells in their brass pots, the slow rhythm of that way of life with its sudden interruptions of violence and horror, and above all, the sense of timelessness among a people whose God has lived for 300 million-million mortal years, a span which accounts for the element of patience and resignation which determines the pace of these tales. This could not be carried into English by an outsider. Mr Narayan tells them from within.'[21]

Sadly Narayan then left Heinemann for The Bodley Head, but he was back again in 1977 with *The Painter of Signs* and *Malgudi Days* (1982). Heinemann also reissued all his earlier novels and published *R. K. Narayan: a Critical Biography* (1982) by William Walsh.

The second major writer about India was Anita Desai, the daughter of a Bengali father and a German mother. Her four novels for Heinemann (and two children's books) quickly established her as not only an interpreter of India but as a writer of originality with a moth-like sensitivity. But she could also be tough and her highly elaborated, lucid sentences were never sugary. *Fire on the Mountain* (1977) and a book of short stories, *Games at Twilight* (1978), blended this toughness with a perceptive and tender poetic imagination. They also conveyed the physical reality of India, its smells and sounds.

Clear Light of Day (1980), perhaps her masterpiece, re-created the stagnant, dreamlike lives of a decaying family in Old Delhi after Independence. Among the many ecstatic reviews the *New York Times* summed it up perfectly: 'Appropriately, this is a book without apparent movement. It hangs suspended, like the family itself, while memories replay themselves and ancient joys and sorrows lazily float past. . . . Anita Desai is unexcelled at conveying an atmosphere. Whether it's the atmosphere of a parched, dying garden, or a languid evening lawn concert, or the endless summer mornings of idle children, we are fully there; the mood of the place is thick around us. And in *Clear Light of Day* it is particularly the atmosphere of deterioration that she conveys – so vividly, in fact, that the deterioration takes on a kind of motion of its own. There's a feeling of depth, of multiple layers, in her description of the cobwebbed gate of a deserted house, the river drying to a muddy trickle, the rotting fruit picked over by birds, the blackened water of the well where a cow drowned long ago, Bim's bedroom choked with filing cabinets and nests of paper, Baba's little drawer of rusty, blunt, used-up gramophone needles, and Old Delhi itself: "a great cemetery, every house a tomb. Nothing but sleeping graves." This should be depressing, but instead it's oddly exhilarating. The effect is one of richness and mystery.'

Clear Light of Day, short-listed for the Booker Prize of 1980, was believed to have been very close to winning. Anita Desai's early books centred on India's professional, academic circles and many of the characters were women, but in her next novel, *In Custody* (1984), her horizons seemed to have widened and the central character was male. This also was short-listed for the Booker Prize. To be short-listed twice is of course a remarkable honour and it had an effect on her sales, including the Penguin editions, but commercially she was yet another example where literary excellence or being classed as a 'writer's writer' is not reflected in vast sales. *Clear Light of Day*, for example, sold a total of only 2,281 hardback copies. It is, however, good to be able to record that while during the 1960–70s the Heinemann list had become more 'commercial', it still had a place for writers of the calibre of Anita Desai.

The same can be said of the third major writer on India, Paul Scott. The four lengthy constituent novels of *The Raj Quartet* have been recognized widely as masterpieces and, though after such a relatively short time such judgments are risky, they were a landmark in the history of the company. Before moving to Heinemann Paul Scott had published six novels with Eyre & Spottiswoode and two with Secker & Warburg, all of which were reissued by Heinemann. Roland Gant was an old and very close friend and when he moved back from Seckers to Heinemann, Scott followed. Each of the four Raj volumes is self-contained and can be read on its own, but the enormous cast of characters appear in a complex story or system of stories that weave in and out of the four overlapping narratives. When complete they were reissued in one volume.

The first in the quartet, *The Jewel in the Crown* (1966), begins in 1942 with the 'Quit India' riots and the last, *A Division of the Spoils* (1975), ends with the Hindu-Moslem massacres following Independence and Partition. In between come *The Day of the Scorpion* (1968) and *The Towers of Silence* (1971). In close on a million words the quartet tells of the last days of the British in India and of the lives of a dozen or so Britons, most of them still trapped in the straitjacket of Colonial racist attitudes. Also depicted are the agitation for Independence with its imprisoned leaders and those Indians caught and confused between the two sides. In the background are the cataclysmic events of the war, including the loss of Burma to the Japanese supported by the newly formed Indian National Army. Skilfully Scott remains centred on the human beings caught up in the upheaval – Sarah Layton and her parents, Hari Kumar, Daphne Manners, Ronald Merrick, Guy Perron, Barbie Batchelor, and others – people known now to millions, even if they have not read the books, from the multipart television serial.

To write the quartet Scott gave up his job as a literary agent and even so it took him ten years to finish the series and his finances were inevitably strained. The sales of each book were disappointing, but Heinemann continued to have complete faith in Paul Scott and allowed him an additional £500 a quarter to be considered as instalments of an advance on some future book as yet untitled and not contracted for. A modest amount, all of which was eventually repaid out of earned royalties, income from paperbacks or other sources ... but at the time it enabled the enormous project to be completed.

Support also came from Morrow, his American publishers. In November 1972, while still engaged on *A Division of the Spoils*, one of his letters to John C. Willey of Morrow makes clear the difficulties faced by a writer without personal means in completing such a long-drawn-out work: 'What an author in my position really needs is a major grant from some sort of charitable foundation – a fellowship of about three years' duration; but there are none such over here, and even if there were some such at your side I wouldn't qualify as a British national. But anything else is, by nature, a stop-gap: absolutely essential, but a stop-gap all the same, because what I need is time – time to finish the novel (one could say it is really one-quarter finished, but that means little, since one doesn't write at a mathematically progressive rate) and then time to readjust from what will have been a nearly ten-year stint on the same subject. The valuable thing is the time, because time will contribute to the quality of the book, and from that must stem the thing in which faith and confidence is being so encouragingly shown, both by Morrow and Heinemann: the literary and commercial value of the enterprise. But how can I really expect such massive support? It is a question of compromise, of – I suppose – stage by stage. A finger in the dyke (if you will pardon the expression). . . . Of course I expect to finish by the end of next year. But I am not going to gloss over the awful possibility that I won't, that I might suddenly throw the while thing away and start again (which, as you know, I have done in the past). This is what I mean by the unimaginability of the vote of confidence I'm asking for, because on my side I'm offering nothing more tangible than the *will* to finish the book sooner than later.'[22]

As a kind of epilogue to the quartet Scott wrote *Staying On* (1977), a much shorter book about two elderly British who stay on after Independence to live out their days in a hill station. It was this that won the Booker Prize for 1977, though many felt that recognition came too late and that it should have been awarded for one or all the volumes in the quartet. In another sense it was almost too late because Paul Scott, while in Tulsa, Oklahoma, as a visiting professor, was found to have cancer. He returned home but was too ill to attend the celebratory banquet. His daughter received the prize on his behalf. Pick told me how a few months later he had accompanied Roland Gant to see him in hospital. 'I gave him the good news that the importance of his quartet titles had been recognized in India. Also that there were various reprints in hand. Paul, very weak, gripped my wrist: "Charles, I have never had reprints before. Say it again, very slowly."'

He died a few days later.

Out of the Red –
Moves at the Top

The state of the firm's fortunes in the early 1960s was more serious than had appeared from the accounts. The decline in profitability had not been fully revealed because of the failure to provide for sufficient depreciation of stock. In 1962 William Heinemann Ltd, which until then had produced virtually the whole of the group's profits, reported a loss of £65,544 of which no less than £45,000 was attributed to exceptional stock depreciation, clearly related to earlier years. Further write-downs followed in 1963 and 1964, and indeed over the whole of this decade the new management was imbued with the need to value stocks conservatively and, more fundamentally, to reduce the need for stock depreciation. This was done in two ways: first, by smaller initial print-runs, though accepting the need to reprint quickly when some books sold faster than expected – which meant closer monitoring of the sales trends of each title; secondly, the gradual elimination of commercially peripheral publishing and of books with short print-runs, so enabling the sales department to give fuller attention to the stronger books in the list.

This policy explains the relatively slow growth of William Heinemann Ltd's turnover (see Appendix C, D). Apart from one year (1967) the annual percentage increase in sales revenue was no greater than the general rate of inflation. It also shows how the revenue from subsidiary rights continued to grow faster than that generated by the firm's own editions. This partly resulted from the growing importance of paperback and bookclub rights, but it also reflected Pick's considerable skill as a negotiator.

Indeed, under Tilling's ownership there were no demands for rapid growth, at least not in the period immediately following the 1961–2 débâcle when Heinemann's viability could not be taken for granted and the extent of the eventual recovery could hardly have been imagined. In this period of convalescence Tilling wisely put greater emphasis on profit margins and on control of working capital. Appendix D shows the main firm's remarkable progress in regaining financial viability. But 1965 net profits before tax had recovered to the extent that they were nearly 10 per cent of turnover; by 1968 it was once again earning a profit on the sale of its own books on top of the ever-increasing contribution from subsidiary rights; by 1972 its margin of pre-tax profits was 14.7 per cent of turnover – and this was after charging interest, some of which was passed upwards to Tilling, so that the true profit margin at that time was close to 18 per cent of sales. Meanwhile another source of profit came from William Heinemann Ltd's (not the group's) acquisition of a one-third interest in Pan Books (see pages 538–42). In just three years the Heinemann share of profits from this source increased from £60,000 to £152,000.

The emergence and rapid growth of Heinemann Educational Books Ltd (HEB) as the second main company in the group (see pages 547–50) led to an expansion of this type of publishing. By 1967 HEB's pre-tax profits, including its fledgling overseas companies, exceeded for the first time £100,000; by 1970 they had reached £200,000; and two years later they were over £300,000. The finances of the other subsidiaries are dealt with in Chapter 27, but from Appendix C (column 10) it can be seen that together they made a combined loss in 1962, 1963, and again in 1964. Even when they started to make money, their combined profits over the next four years were only about 4 per cent of their turnover, a long way below a viable level. It was not until 1969, eight years after Tilling took control, that these subsidiaries were together earning a profit margin better than 10 per cent. In some cases the elimination of losses was commendably rapid, but in others it was long drawn-out.

The returns of the group as a whole improved steadily. By 1972 the group profit swelled to £879,000 and the next year it was to pass the £1 million mark for the first time in its history. Tilling's jubilation at this turn-round in Heinemann's fortunes can well be imagined. In 1961 they had been forced to step in to prevent a complete collapse. Now, with the William Heinemann recovery coming together with HEB's expansion, they were soon to find that the group's profit margins and return on capital were outstripping the average performance of the other Tilling's companies. Well before the 1970s ended Tilling executives were referring to Heinemann as 'the jewel in our crown'.

As confidence grew Tilling played a decreasing part in the administration of the company and this was reflected in Peter Ryder ceasing in November 1962 to be chairman of William Heinemann Ltd, though he remained chairman of the holding company. Dwye Evans was elected chairman in his place and Charles Pick was promoted to be the managing director. When Keel left in December 1965, Dwye Evans also became managing director of the group company.

The day-to-day control of William Heinemann Ltd therefore remained in the hands of Evans and Pick and they made an effective combination, maybe because their personalities were so different. Dwye's manner was unassuming with the quiet confidence of someone who has after a short apprenticeship started near the top – apart from war service in the RAF he spent his entire working life in the firm. As he sipped the best Lapsang served from elegant porcelain brought in by Mrs Grey, the widow of Frere's chauffeur and now the office caretaker, you knew you were in the presence of the tradition of gentlemanly, not tremendously ambitious publishers. In the group he was surrounded by men with more positive, overbearing, aggressive personalities than himself. He gave the impression of hoping always to avoid a fuss, but when necessary he could be quietly firm. Like Clem Attlee he often played a neutralizing role and as a result his influence was apt to be underrated. Board meetings, at least of William Heinemann Ltd, were curiously formal, sedate events. After signing the minutes Evans would turn to the company secretary and ask him politely 'to take us through the accounts' which had been circulated beforehand. With a rare interruption from Evans or Pick their key points were intoned with the solemnity of High Mass. The formal invitation to ask questions or make comments was rarely taken up and apart from affixing the company's seal to certain documents and desultory items under AOB there was seldom discussion of anything apart from financial statistics and ratios. There was no place on the agenda for serious discussion of publishing policy or of the firm's long-term objectives. On the other hand the real day-to-day decisions about printing numbers, retail prices, overhead and production ratios were taken at the slightly less formal Wednesday meetings attended by all the heads of departments. Longer term policy was in fact generated more or less by chance at one-to-one, symbiotic conversations with either Evans or Pick in their offices, over lunch or, surprisingly often, in the Gents. It was the Gents, incidentally, which had been the cause of discomfiture when James Michie first joined the firm:

'In the middle of a meeting with Dwye out of nervousness I had to go to the lavatory. To my delight I noticed that the pan was called "Middlemarch". Hoping to ingratiate myself as a man of literary distinction, on returning I remarked on its being a most suitable name for a publisher's lavatory. Dwye looked at me blankly and asked what was so peculiar about that? To my horror I realized that not only had I made a joke he'd failed to grasp, but that he must think I was obsessed with lavatories.'

Gossip in the editorial department assumed that both Evans and Pick had decidedly middlebrow tastes in fiction – though, if true, this might be no bad thing – but Dwye certainly read a great many manuscripts and his judgment could be very acute. Unlike some of his colleagues, who seemed able to read a dozen long books a week as well as watch everything on television and go to the theatre and cinema, Dwye was always honest enough to say he had 'read *into*' a manuscript when he hadn't managed to read all of it.

Pick also read a good deal at weekends, but his manner and working methods were quite different from Dwye's. He was noted for his energy, his arrival in the office before anyone else and for being the last to leave. He was at his best when outsmarting a rival or chasing after a multi-level deal involving paperback, bookclub and American rights. When he disagreed with you, he could be alarmingly stubborn, an impression heightened by a habitual gesture of pushing with both arms an invisible object out of the way. He was always in a hurry, full of excitement about his latest success, but his office door was nearly always kept open and he made a point of being immediately available to his staff. If you had a sound proposal, he at once gave you enthusiastic support. This was particularly true of non-fiction, though if it was a novel in which he wasn't involved personally, he tended to raise every kind of difficulty. If it came in via a literary agent whom he particularly disliked it had even less chance of approval.

When Lionel Fraser died in 1965, the chairmanship of Tilling was assumed by Sir Geoffrey Eley, who as well as being a Tilling director was a considerable and experienced figure in the City, having among other posts been chairman of Richard Thomas & Baldwin. Three years later, in December 1968, Peter Ryder left Tilling and it was Eley himself who took over the chairmanship of the Heinemann group. Thanks in no small part to Ryder's skilful and imaginative support and his talent for not interfering unless driven to it, Eley, who was himself deeply interested in books, inherited a thriving subsidiary and under his guidance the relationship between Heinemann and its conglomerate benefactor remained much the same. Budgets and future plans continued to be submitted yearly, but they were seldom criticized, and only projects and problems of a major character were ever referred upwards and sometimes not even then.

In May 1973 Dwye Evans felt it was time for him to retire and typically he wished to go with the least possible fuss. As the most senior publisher Alan Hill succeeded him as group managing director and Charles Pick became chairman of William Heinemann Ltd. He also remained as managing director, Tim Manderson and Nigel Viney becoming deputy managing directors, a shrewd step as neither knew who was to be Crown Prince.

Literary Agents and Cheque-Book Publishing

With too many publishers chasing too few (worthwhile) books the influence and power of the literary agent continued to grow during the 1960–70s. It is often said that it is harder for an author to find an agent who will take him or her on than it is to be accepted by a publisher. There is some truth in this because agents don't want to be lumbered with authors whose work will be difficult to sell to a publisher and, even more, to the public. The agent acts as a sifting mechanism, though like the publisher he may well be wrong in his assessment, and publishers learn from experience which agents are likely to be offering something worth having. A good agent also often spends time with his authors in cooking up workable ideas for books they may write, though on the whole this applies only to non-fiction.

Agents and publishers understand each other's business, even if they view it from different sides of the same fence. Many agents have worked as publishers and vice-versa. They are expert in selecting the publisher best suited to their authors. According to Graham Watson, for long the head of the London branch of Curtis Brown, 'it is certainly true that the professional author who tends to produce the big seller which enables the general publisher to survive, does – as a rule – employ an agent. The power that this enables an agent to wield is certainly considerable; because an agent's job is, amongst other things, to maximize his or her author's earnings, the chosen publisher's merits and demerits are bound to be closely examined. Does he market successfully? Does he keep his books in print? Does he own a paperback imprint? Is the publisher, whose personality stamps the image of the firm, backed by a competent team who can provide continuity on his death or retirement?'[1] So far as Heinemann was concerned, Graham Watson admitted to me that in the 1960–70s he had begun to lose faith in its editorial department because of what he felt was its lack of people to take a continuing interest in an author. This impression was strengthened by the departure of senior editors like David Machin, Mark Barty-King, and David Burnett. This was one reason why he tended not to offer the firm the best manuscripts and new authors.

It may or may not be true that the publisher has become more dependent on the agent than the agent is on him, but nevertheless the majority of Heinemann's most important books came through agents. Although Charles Pick was forced to depend on agents, it was no secret that he preferred some agents to others. Nor did all the agents love Charles Pick. They found that not only was he a tough negotiator – which after all was part of his job – but he gave the impression of not really wishing to tolerate them. More than one other agent has told me that because of this Heinemann tended to be well down their list of the more important publishers to be offered a valuable property.

The mantle of distrust for agents in general seems to have been inherited from William Heinemann himself. Pick told me that 'in the last fifty years or so I have seen the role of the agent change very dramatically. In the 1930s agents were more like literary advisers to their authors. Their function was to find the right publisher for a particular author and it would not necessarily be the one who offered the most money. During the 1970–80s particularly the emphasis, with honourable exceptions, has been on "How much?". It was once considered unethical to offer a manuscript to more than one publisher at a time, whereas today multiple submissions and, in fact, auctions are perfectly normal. I have known us make good offers which have been used to induce a more gullible rival to offer even more. In recent years as soon as an author really starts to sell well, the agent is only too likely to whisk him or her away, even if it is the publisher rather than the agent who was the first to recognize the talent and has done all the hard and expensive work of building the author up.

Above: The bindery in March 1958, during filming of an ITV documentary, 'The Making of a Book' (*The Radium Woman* by Eleanor Doorly)
Below: Information-processing in 1966: the Hollerith sorter

John St John with Alan Hill

This happened for example with Alison Lurie, Fay Weldon, and several others. Frequently, too, authors' reputations run ahead of their sales and this is what the agent exploits.'

Carol Smith, who runs her own literary agency and who for a short time worked in the Heinemann contracts department, seems to some extent to agree with Pick. She insisted to me that a good agent is not only concerned with money: 'If you have a really hot property, of course you go all out for the money, if necessary you auction it. But personally I only do this if I am handling an American book with someone else agenting it in New York. Primarily as an agent I think you owe it to an author to find the right house and the right list, the very best house for him or her, where the author will get continuing care, publicity, sympathy ... what publishing is really about. Never mind if you don't get so much up front.' On the other hand she claims that she has seldom sent Heinemann new talent because she knew Pick was so against agents, but also because she felt that 'for some time there was no one there who would build up the books editorially. The books I have believed should be on the Heinemann list they have turned down. A firm should stick to the kind of books it has done well with in the past, to its editorial traditions. It should not forget its history.' Pick, on the other hand, always maintained that the books she offered were much too lightweight for the Heinemann list.

Of course it was not every author who, like Maugham and Priestley, has been content to stay with Heinemann for better or worse, for richer or poorer. During the second half of the century authors, particularly successful ones, moved round with greater frequency and, indeed, Heinemann benefited probably as much as it lost from this greater mobility. In the literary marketplace Heinemann could be as aggressive an acquirer as any of its rivals – though naked poaching was considered to be unethical – and it prided itself on getting the best possible terms for paperback and other rights.

An author's decision to move could result from different kinds of dissatisfaction, particularly lack of what he or she believed to be adequate publicity, but the biggest reason of all was the search for better royalties and, above all, advances. As a rule of thumb the size of Heinemann's advances was basically limited to a maximum of half to two-thirds of what a book might be expected to earn the author from its initial subscription. This calculation was in terms of the normal trade sale only. When anyone proposed that a book be taken Dwye Evans and/or Charles Pick would ask for a breakdown of the potential trade sale and want to know how many would be ordered by W. H. Smiths, by Hatchards in Piccadilly, by Australia . . . an optimistic 'guesstimate' of, say, 5,000 might be cut down to 3,000 or less, but advances were given against all sources of income, and very much bigger advances could be risked dependent on the potential sale of paperback, bookclub, American, and other rights which, as already made clear, had become increasingly significant.

Apart from the continuing wrangles over the size of the author's share of subsidiary rights, there was increasing rivalry over who should handle them – the publisher or the agent? Bookclub and paperback rights belonged to the publisher, but the American, serial, translation, film, TV, and other rights would normally be retained by the agent, though publisher and agent frequently consulted each other and worked in harness to make the best possible deal for the author. Only the larger agents could employ a staff comparable in size and expertise to that employed in Heinemann's rights department and the smaller agents had to work through sub-agents. The frequent buying/selling trips to New York by Dwye Evans, Pick, and Gant as well as the corresponding visits to London and Frankfurt by the Americans led to invaluable personal relationships with the principals of New York firms which were based on trust and experience, a tradition that went back to William's and Charles Evans's visits by Atlantic liners.

Graham Watson accepts that big publishers can be at least equally well equipped to market subsidiary rights, but he argues that 'in many instances an author's and a publisher's interest conflict. And where a conflict arises only a saintly publisher will put his financial gain second to that of the author. I am not denying there may be such members of the book trade but most publishers resolve such conflicts not by reference to the Holy Ghost but by pretending they don't exist and that the author's interest coincides with his. In the case of an agent this is demonstrably the case. His only reimbursement is to receive commission on what he has earned for his author. It is not demonstrably the case with a publisher.'[2] Watson goes on to give two instances of potential conflict: serial rights and American rights. 'When a serial is sold to a newspaper it is stipulated that its publication shall, so far as possible, coincide with the publication of the book. In most cases newspapers are perfectly happy to adjust their plans to any such arrangement which helps to promote the sale of the book and which is in the mutual interest of author, the publisher and, usually, the newspaper. But sometimes, perhaps for reasons of extreme topicality, a newspaper wants to publish extracts long before the book can be made available in the shops. Almost certainly the author would lose the considerable benefits which would accrue from such a sale unless he agreed to this premature publication. It may be that to a limited extent the sale of the book will be adversely affected by this early serialization. Were he to be acting for the author in such a case he would be in a dilemma. Whose interests to pursue?

'Similarly many English publishers have a loose quid pro quo arrangement with two or three American counterparts with whom they maintain a very close relationship. "You scratch my back, I'll scratch yours. You offer me your books, I'll offer you mine." It is possible for an author to suffer from such a restrictive arrangement. The benefit to the publisher is apparent. But the author may find himself on the wrong list on the wrong terms. The author's book is being used as a counter to pay for benefits which the author will not enjoy. Agents also enjoy special relationships with publishers – if they didn't they would be ineffective as agents. But they would be fools if they allowed such relationships to affect their authors' earnings. To do so would be restricting their own.'[3] Be that as it may, Heinemann's ability to market subsidiary rights can be gauged from the main firm's total share of income from all forms of rights, which grew from £69,000 in 1961 to £885,000 in 1982.

As already mentioned, a typical advance in the early 1930s for a first novel would have been £25–£75. This was in respect of a royalty calculated on the published price of 10 per cent, rising to 12½ per cent after the sale of anything between 3,000 and 5,000 copies. The author, however, could expect only 10 per cent of the actual income received by the firm from overseas sales (see also page 236). The firm's standard, printed contract provided for 80 per cent of the income from American royalties and translation rights, 50 per cent of paperback royalties (see also pages 537–8), and varying percentages for serial, film, and other rights. By the end of the 1970s the advance for a first novel had increased to £750, though the rates of royalty – calculated on much higher published prices – remained much the same. As authors got more established they could expect considerably higher advances and a somewhat more generous scale of royalties. Advances for potentially big properties have on the whole grown faster than inflation, though Pick was usually not prepared to put one of the firm's prime authors way ahead of others at the top of the list. It was only a small minority of authors – or their agents – who could command the really large sums.

Large as some of these amounts were – and the final earnings from a book could of course be very much larger – it must be stressed that only a handful of authors ever are rewarded with incomes and public recognition approaching that of a pop star – and those authors are not necessarily or even likely to be the best when judged by the most open-minded criteria of literary judgment. For this lucky minority among 'recognized' authors nothing seems to succeed like success, whereas the vast majority, by no means the flops and failures, have to be content with financial rewards which by any standard are modest. Even so, few among top-earning authors in the 1960–70s were as rich as their pre-war predecessors. Writing in January 1961, J. B. Priestley, for example, explained how his 'earning capacity had declined rapidly during the 40 years I have been a professional writer. For example, 30 years ago I was receiving a royalty of 2s.7½d. per copy for my novels, today I get 3s.'[4] He went on to ask how could he make the 3s. go as far. This reflected the failure to increase book prices to their true economic level, though Priestley, unlike many top authors, also never benefited greatly from paperback royalties.

In 1966 and 1972 the Society of Authors commissioned surveys of their members' earnings. The findings were assembled by Richard Findlater, who commented in *The Author* (Winter 1972) that in 1972 '67 per cent of the responding authors earned less than £1,000 p.a. from their books, i.e., volume publication plus subsidiary rights – compared with 63 per cent in 1965. . . . More precisely, and more grimly 56 per cent of the responding authors earned less than £500 p.a. from their books – 51 per cent in 1965'.[5] The majority of these writers were not novices nor were they hacks, but educated and experienced with a number of books to their credit, though it was believed that quite a few of the best paid authors did not fill in the questionnaire. When it came to subsidiary rights no fewer than 78 per cent of the respondents earned *nothing* from this source in 1970–72 – 71 per cent in 1963–5.[6] It is also significant that whereas in 1966 only just under half the Society of Authors' responding members reported that authorship was their sole occupation, by 1972 this fraction had dropped to less than a third, and by 1980 to less than a sixth.[7]

By no means every professional writer is a member of the Society of Authors; but these surveys indicated that, at any rate in the 1960–70s, very, very few earned their basic living from writing books. In 1980 after a long campaign it was finally decided by the government to bring in the Public Lending Act (PLR) which provided for authors to be paid something for the loaning of their books in public libraries, but for most the sums have often been described as 'piffling'. The net government funding after deducting PLR operating costs came in 1986-7 to £2,408,000. Payment is based on a sample of library loans which worked out at 1.22p. per volume. Shared between 14,635 registered authors, PLR paid out the agreed maximum of £4,990–£5,010 to only 57 authors; 468 authors received £1,000–£4,989; 508 received £500–£999; 2,603 received £100–£499; 8,624 received £1–£99; and 2,375 received nothing.

Quite a number of Heinemann authors will have had some benefit from PLR and will have contributed to the Society of Authors surveys. Few can be rich or not have to earn additional income – or the bulk of it – in other ways. It is understandable why authors feel the need for the protective shield of an agent and don't grudge him/her their commission – broadly 10 per cent, sometimes more. Authors are not necessarily equipped to cope with the avaricious literary jungle, particularly now that publishing is no longer considered to be a 'profession for gentlemen' – if it ever was! Giles Gordon, a director of the agency Anthony Sheil Associates, recently expressed the need succinctly: 'With editors moving about from publishing house to publishing house in a way not contemplated even a few years ago, with publishing houses swallowed rapaciously by larger organisms, the agent has become the only constant in many writers' professional lives.'[8]

The relationship between publisher and author is complex and difficult to define. Authors are not employees of their publishers, and yet for the most part they are at the mercy of their judgment, taste, and other subjective qualities in order to get their work accepted, let alone successfully marketed. With the minority of authors who are 'established', and particularly bestsellers, the situation is of course reversed. With them it is the author who is courted by the publisher and who can threaten to leave for another firm unless his/her advance or royalties are improved or unless he/she is given a larger share of the promotional budget. Nowadays every type of author, though, has become increasingly remote from the publisher's processes. In the words of the novelist Jonathan Raban: 'In broad Marxian terms, authors are classic victims of the division of labour which has come about with the Industrial Revolution. Once upon a time

[535]

we were not alienated from the means of production. When the publisher was a tradesman, a bookseller-cum-printer, the terms of the relationship were perfectly explicit and comprehensible on both sides. But, during the nineteenth century, with the rise of the publishing "house" as an industrial corporation, the author became increasingly distanced from the processes, themselves increasingly complex, of manufacture and distribution. His book effectively ceased to be his at the point at which it left his hands in manuscript form. The manufactured object – the colourfully jacketed slab of print in the bookshop – bore so many different industrial signatures that its author felt hardly less remote from it that the screw-driver-wielder at Dagenham might feel at the sight of a new Ford Fiesta burning round the M25. (And, like screwdriver-wielders, many authors cannot afford to actually buy what are supposed to be their own products – hardback books belong to a different economic sphere from the one the author himself inhabits.) This is exactly what Marx meant by "alienation".[9]

This may be an exaggeration but in the case of Heinemann it contained several sizeable grains of truth. It was the firm's policy, for example, not to ask the authors' advice about a book's typography or page design, unless they were very insistent; likewise they were seldom consulted over the design of the jacket, though they would normally be invited to approve the blurb; the size of the print-run, the book's advertising budget, subscription orders, and much else were not considered – perhaps understandably – to be an author's business. On the other hand, it was normal to obtain from authors suggestions about the destination of review copies and possible avenues of publicity. In all publishing offices – and Heinemann was no exception – there is a tendency for harassed, over-extended executives to overlook the actual existence of their authors and to treat them together with their books as a 'property'. They talk in terms of 'my author' as if they owned him/her.

On the other hand publisher and author are in fact partners – if not often particularly equal ones. Without the complexities of modern publishing, manufacture, distribution and marketing, the books of most authors would never reach their publics. It is also likely that few on the Heinemann list ever expected to earn their living from their books. The majority, one suspects, have had books published because they found it very satisfying – which is different from financially worthwhile. They were pleased to be recognized and taken on by the Windmill. The world didn't owe them a living, though of course the more their books earned the better. An attribute of the royalty system is that it reflects accurately the extent of a book's success, though if they or their agents, if they had one, were tough enough, authors might get a slightly more generous deal. Essentially, author and publisher are on the same side. They prosper or fail together.

Part-Owners again of Pan

The ascendancy of paperbacks is demonstrated by the rise in the totals recorded in *Whitakers Paperbacks in Print* from 7,882 titles in 1961 to 63,149 in 1983, a year in which the corresponding total of both paperbacks and hardbacks in print was 365,660. With annual sales of all books totalling £1,224.7 million, paperbacks by 1983 represented 38.6 per cent of the total book market. As well as occupying an increasing proportion of the shelves in a well-stocked bookshop they penetrated markets well beyond its reach. Quite apart from not liking to lose an increasing share of the total book market, the hardback publisher was becoming increasingly dependent on the paperback houses for fiction and popular non-fiction.

Important authors and their agents were also aware of this and insisted that the rights in their books were sold only to the best of paperback firms capable of paying the highest royalties and advances. As we have seen they were no longer prepared to put up with the traditional 50/50 split of royalties and demanded a 60/40 split in their favour. They also did not see why paperback royalties should be limited to the, again, 'traditional', 7½ per cent. Eventually paperback houses were increasingly prevailed upon to offer a sliding scale of royalties, after the sale of stated quantities. Heinemann, along with other publishers, likewise improved their split in the authors' favour, *viz.* 7½ per cent royalty (50/50 split); 10 per cent (55/45); 12½ per cent (60/40). Unless a hardback publisher could satisfy their demands he was likely rapidly to lose the power to keep his bestselling authors or to attract new ones.

Ideally he needed to be in a position to offer an attractive paperback deal from the outset and the best way of doing this was to possess his own paperback imprint or at least have a stake in another one. All this makes it almost impossible to comprehend why in 1961 Heinemann had sold its stake in Pan, though admittedly the loss was mitigated to some extent by the practice of often offering Pan the first refusal on all Heinemann titles except in cases where there was a prior agreement with another firm. In return Pan would pay a 12½ per cent royalty from the outset, of which 7½ per cent would go to the author and 5 per cent would be retained by Heinemann – or in other words a 60/40 per cent split of a higher royalty – thus, incidentally, honouring the Publishers Association's ruling.

Paperback firms were of course equally dependent on hardback ones, particularly those with long backlists like Heinemann's. Early in the 1960s Penguin paid £65,000 advance against royalties for ten Somerset Maugham titles and £50,000 for ten of Graham Greene's. Paperback originals accounted for only a fraction of the paperback firms' output, and the hardback houses were still the main originators of all titles, whether or not they possessed a potential market big enough for the large print runs needed for a paperback. Although most novels and popular non-fiction became paperbacks, it was calculated in 1973 that only 5.5 per cent of the entire William Heinemann list qualified as *mass-market* paperbacks, though they accounted for a much larger percentage of the firm's profit.

Despite the advantages of the agreement with Pan, the need for a proper foothold in a paperback house was irresistible and it was decided to approach the two owners of Pan – Collins and Macmillan – to find out if Heinemann could be readmitted as a third and equal partner. It made good sense, because Collins already had an outlet in their own successful paperback imprint of Fontana and Macmillan did not publish enough of the right kind of books and in particular of fiction, a deficiency which Heinemann could speedily remedy. Collins's reaction to the approach was immediately welcoming but Macmillan prevaricated for several months, though in the end agreed in principle. Ironically the only serious opposition came from Tillings, whose acquisition committee was opposed to any minority investment. They were adamant but Pick refused to accept their ruling and fought back with such powerful arguments which involved the whole future of Heinemann that in the end they relented.

In 1969 Heinemann was able therefore to acquire a one-third interest in Pan for £415,000, Dwye Evans and Pick joining the Pan board. As Pan expanded a further investment in 1971 increased the stake to £474,850.

By 1982 Heinemann's investment and accumulated profits amounted in Pan to £1.5 million.

If the arguments in favour of having a third share in Pan were strong, those in favour of Heinemann even now founding its own paperback imprint were *a fortiori* even more telling. Only four years after Heinemann rejoined Pan the idea had taken hold and was enthusiastically backed by the chairman Sir Geoffrey Eley. Tilling could make £2 million available. It would mean that Heinemann would have all the profits and not merely one third and it would amount almost to a return to the good old days when publishers controlled and made all the money from their own cheap editions. In time they would acquire paperback rights from other smaller publishers. They could offer all authors, when warranted, a paperback deal at the outset and could afford to pay generous royalties. At first Collins and Macmillan surprisingly raised no objections in principle and Collins offered to handle the independent Heinemann paperback imprint overseas through its existing well-established machinery, which needed more throughput to combat the growing American influence in the UK's traditional overseas markets. Ralph Vernon Hunt, who in 1970 had succeeded Aubrey Forshaw as Pan's managing director, was understandably worried by the idea, but was perhaps reassured by Heinemann's guarantee not to remove Heinemann authors already well established on the Pan list.

A public announcement was prepared; Tim Manderson was appointed managing director designate of the new company; as the period of their licences had expired the paperback rights in ninety-nine titles reverted from Penguin, including books by Maugham, Steinbeck, Wells, and others of note. On the other hand the trustees of the Orwell estate (he was published by Secker & Warburg) objected to his books being transferred to a firm that had as yet to prove itself; there were also other objections and some authors or their estates needed a lot of convincing. Then when all seemed set for the launch both Collins and Macmillan started to have second thoughts.

First Ian Chapman wrote to say that both Pan and Fontana felt that it would be a mistake for Collins to take on the new company's overseas distribution, as its titles would compete too strongly for space and time. Worse, in April 1973 a letter, addressed to Sir Geoffrey Eley, came from Harold Macmillan himself which contained what amounted to a *démarche*: 'Sir William Collins and I feel that you should be informed about the situation because what is now proposed by William Heinemann Ltd is a breach if not of the letter at any rate of the spirit into which we admitted them into a third ownership of Pan some three years ago.'[10] He drew Sir Geoffrey's attention to a letter sent to Dwye Evans by Ian Chapman of Collins but written jointly with Frank Whitehead of Macmillan. Its key sentence maintained that it was their clear understanding that Heinemann would 'support Pan not only with finance but with titles. We were much influenced by the views of the Pan management who attached considerable importance to having continued access to the Heinemann list. Had there been any suggestion that Heinemann having bought back into Pan would subsequently start their own list, neither Collins nor Macmillan would have agreed to sell. On reflection, Frank and I both regret that we did not cover this point in the agreement but we took Heinemann's good faith on trust. . . . We feel a most unhappy situation is developing, but it is not of our making and we think it better that our views are expressed to you jointly and that we meet and discuss the implications of these rather than allow matters to smoulder on to the possible detriment of Pan.'[11] At a painful meeting called by Geoffrey Eley at Crewe House, attended by Pick and both William Collins and Harold Macmillan, Collins never opened his mouth but Macmillan spoke at length, admitting that his lawyers had erred by omitting to include a clause that would stop Heinemanns from ever starting their own paperback imprint, but that nevertheless the only course for honourable people in such a situation was to dissolve their partnership. As he gathered up his papers he remarked that, however, he understood that there was a possible scheme which might resolve their disagreement.

He was referring to a suggestion made a few days previously by Charles Pick to Alan Maclean to co-publish on a book-by-book basis with Pan. It was this idea that provided a solution to the impasse. After negotiations in which Peter Range was also involved an agreement was hammered out which stated that after the payment of certain agreed acquisition costs all other costs, profits or losses would be shared 50/50 by Pan and the originating publisher, whose name would be included in a joint imprint on the title page. Each of the three firms would continue to hold a third share of the equity. It would mean that Heinemann would receive 66⅔ per cent of the profits on its titles which, while not as good as receiving 100 per cent, provided many advantages including a lower overhead structure and having access to an established world-wide sales organization including that of Collins overseas. The need to be able to offer authors and their agents immediate access to Heinemann's own paperback outlet would be satisfied.

An agreement along these lines was entered into and it proved to be of immense benefit. Heinemann greatly enriched Pan's list, contributing about 15 per cent of its titles and some 20 per cent of its turnover, and presented it with a solid backlist of top authors, including some transferred from Penguin. In round figures the joint venture scheme has been worth some £½ million profit annually to Heinemann and on top of this it has received a third of Pan's total profits, as shown in Appendix F. The other two companies also gained from the scheme though not to the same extent.

On the whole the day-to-day working with Pan went smoothly, new joint ventures being initiated by Pan themselves, particularly by Simon Master, who succeeded Vernon Hunt as managing director in 1980, and by Sonny Mehta, who took over from Clarence Paget as chief editor. Each year Pan's chairman rotated so that each of the three proprietor-companies would have an equal share of responsibility, but this did not work well because a year was not long enough to get to grips with what was happening. Surprisingly, there was little friction between the three proprietors, but there was some with the Pan executives, who remained free to acquire rights from publishers other than the three proprietors. Master and Mehta sensed, for example, that Heinemann now tended to look upon Pan as a substitute for not being able to start their own paperback imprint and to insist that Pan should be ready to take on almost any title which the Heinemann management believed had paperback potential; certainly Heinemann believed that too often Pan executives exerted their right to refuse to take on a proprietor's titles with the result that valuable books were occasionally lost: for example Peter Ustinov's *Dear Me* which went instead for £60,000 to Penguin, who got their money back before they had sold their first printing and eventually went on to sell more than 300,000 copies. Others turned down by Pan included Paul Scott, Anita Desai, and Frank Muir.

Pan, on the other hand, although it took on several Heinemann titles against its better judgment, wished to be more discriminating. Its executives were keen to initiate Pan originals, though this could lead to accusations that they were abusing their independence. There was, for instance, strong criticism from Heinemann over the continuation of the

Picador range of literary trade paperbacks, because after its first two years Picador was certainly not doing well. Another grouse was that Picador carried virtually no Heinemann titles. In contrast Master and Mehta believed that Picador reflected the way the market was moving and indeed eventually the series became a soundly established and very profitable venture.

All in all, however, the partnership between Heinemann and Pan has to be reckoned an outstanding success – for all parties concerned, including Pan itself (see Appendix F). Through the 1970s it prospered, so that by 1982 its turnover had grown from £4.9 million in 1973 to £15.9 million, although this does not allow for inflation. By then Pan commanded some 20 per cent of the total paperback market.

Bookclub Hopes Thwarted – Nationwide a Disaster

A mixture of complex and disparate factors helps to explain the further growth of bookclubs during the 1960–70s. Several of the pre-war bookclubs, such as Readers' Union and the clubs launched by Foyles, continued to flourish and there had been successful additions such as Odham's Companion Bookclub, started in the 1950s, and clubs catering for specialized interests. In the previous decade some of the main clubs had memberships of up to 400,000 and together they were selling something like three-quarters of a million books each month. Their books were cheap, but it was still significant that they were able to compete both with paperbacks and the free public libraries. They were clearly finding markets the bookshops could not reach psychologically or in some cases physically, including an ability to supply readers who lived in remote areas or without access to a reasonable bookshop. Almost certainly the most important factor was their technique of mass merchandizing. Their sales literature made a very direct personal appeal to their members. The average bookshop by comparison was a very passive channel of distribution.

By the 1960s the bonanza seemed to be largely over as, with more competition from paperbacks and the arrival of commercial television, reprint bookclubs' memberships declined, some disastrously. Charles Pick was nevertheless convinced that this form of direct mail selling for newly published books was still very important and capable of even further expansion, and he wanted Heinemann to take part in it, not merely to win selections for the firm's titles but also for its own sake, as a new source of revenue. He realized that it was only a question of time before British clubs followed the American clubs' example of publishing their books simultaneously with the publisher's first edition without waiting for the statutory twelve months; that, if necessary, the humbug of implied elected membership could deal with any question of infringement of the Net Book Agreement. Booksellers had reluctantly accepted the idea of book-clubs and admitted that a bookclub selection meant publicity that benefited also their own sales.

With no lack of support from Tilling Pick went to New York in 1965 to discuss possibilities with Doubleday. They already ran the very successful Literary Guild, but liked the idea of a transatlantic venture. Some of the selections for America and Britain might be different, but they would be selected from all publishers' lists.

Pick told me that 'Dwye was worried that the bookshops wouldn't like it. My reply was that of course they wouldn't like it at first, but they would soon realize that bookclub advertising would bring additional trade sales. We were strong enough to meet their objections and they couldn't afford to boycott our books. In any case they normally only took what they knew they could sell and the books they took on spec. were fewer with each year.'

Pick suggested that they should check out the bookshops' reaction with W. H. Smith. Maybe they would join as a third partner? A meeting was arranged with Smith's chairman who listened sympathetically. He was just about to set off on a world tour but he made a tape-recording of the interview which would be circulated to his colleagues who would make a decision, though he warned that they might consider it harmful for WHS to be associated too closely with any one publisher.

Nothing was heard for some weeks and Doubleday began to get restless. It was then thought sensible also to make an approach to Collins. There was a possibility of taking over the Reprint Society with its experience, machinery and members – Heinemann already owned part of its equity, having bought additional shares in 1963. Collins seemed very keen and it looked as if with or without Smiths the new bookclub would be born. After further very secret negotiations the documents were ready for signature, but it was not to be.

According to Pick: 'Billie Collins had one of his tantrums and at the last minute refused to sign. His younger brother Ian rang me to say that his brother was in the habit of changing his mind and there was nothing anyone could do. Doubledays retired hurt across the Atlantic, though they wrote to say that Heinemann was in no way to blame. The next thing I heard was that Doubledays had got into bed with Smiths to form Book Club Associates (BCA)! To say it was a nasty disappointment would be an understatement, but they did have the courtesy to invite us to supply the first major choice – Morris West's *The Shoes of the Fisherman*.'

From its launch in 1966 BCA was a runaway success, particularly as within two years it started to sell through its Literary Guild new titles simultaneously with their hardback originators, the trade saving everyone's face by ratifying a technical loophole in the regulations. It was the beginning of really lavish bookclub advertising, especially in the quality colour supplements, with inducements of almost free books for new members – e.g., the *Concise Oxford Dictionary* (normally £6.75 in the shops) for £1 including two other books. There was no stopping BCA and of course Heinemann like other big publishers had its share of profitable main choices. By 1982 BCA's overall membership had climbed to 1.7 million with 200,000 more overseas, a market share of 80 per cent. It comprised twenty-seven corporate clubs of various types of which the largest simultaneous club was the Literary Guild. Soon after it was founded BCA had also taken over the Reprint Society, Heinemann selling its share of the equity at a good profit. It was rechristened World Books and it remains as BCA's biggest reprint outlet.

BCA's success made Pick more determined than ever to have a slice of the bookclub action. Together with Billie Collins and Ian Chapman, also of Collins, he entered into negotiations for another possible club with the *Reader's Digest* in London, but they led nowhere. The next approach however was fruitful. Again there was a consortium of three: Collins; the Swedish firm of Albert Bonniers, a publishing house similar to Heinemann and who already had much experience of running bookclubs; and William Heinemann Ltd/Secker & Warburg, with 75 and 25 per cent of the third share respectively, the group as such not being involved.

Christened 'Nationwide Book Service', it opened for business in 1980.

There was a board on which all the partners were represented, always chaired by Olle Maberg of Bonniers. Tom Rosenthal, who was full of enthusiasm for the club, was deputed to liaise with the chief executive, Tony Gould-Davies, who had previously run BCA. After a while Patrick Janson-Smith was brought in from Corgi as chief editor.

The lavish launch featured an attractive picture of Peter Ustinov and a four-colour brochure with a tempting spread of premium offers. The main choices were accompanied by offers of 150–200 other books including plenty of quality fiction at concessional prices. Though there was a 'negative option' clause which had to be posted back by 'members' if the next choice was not wanted, the club was primarily a direct-mail, multi-choice bookselling operation.

The advantages of this approach were argued forcefully by Gould-Davies, but in fact it was to some extent forced on the club because of its failure to attract sufficient top-line popular authors. BCA was not prepared to let go of their best authors, even Heinemann and Collins authors; and nor were their agents, who could see no reason why their clients should sell only to the infinitely smaller membership of a club that had yet to prove itself. With a major choice this would have meant foregoing, say, 7½ per cent on the bookclub price for a book offered to over half-a-million members compared with one offered to only 150,000–200,000 members of Nationwide. Other authors usually received a mere 10 per cent on the actual price received by the publisher from the club.

The failure to recruit enough top authors was no more than a major factor among others which explain why Nationwide failed to establish itself. Its launch coincided with a consumer recession during which even BCA was losing members. There was also some competition from Leisure Circle, the club then recently formed by the German media group Bertelsmann. The preliminary 'dry test' sent to some 20,000 potential members was not given sufficient time to justify the rapid escalation of publicity during the early months. There was constant trouble with the club's computer, which at one point erased irretrievably the names and addresses of many of the soundest members. The decision to make Nationwide a 'multi-book choice' club greatly increased the basic investment needed and the demands on warehouse space. Specialized packing expertise was non-existent and the dispatching programme was beyond Kingswood's capacity so that finally it had to be switched to the warehouse near Glasgow belonging to Collins. There was lack of communication between the club's office in London, the fulfilment centre in Brighton, and the main dispatching point in Scotland. The mails bulged with complaints from dissatisfied members.

At the monthly meetings in London or Stockholm between the partners there was increasing tension. Gould-Davies was criticized for making too many mistakes. People were getting tired of his computerized projections which no one else really understood. In the end Bonniers insisted that he left – and this proved expensive. He was replaced by Michael Pateman who seemed to be very efficient, but it was too late. At one time the membership had reached 180,000, but by 1982 it had dropped to 150,000. It had always been envisaged that substantial outlays and losses could occur in the early years. Inevitably a new club has to ensure that it possesses the capacity to service a large demand before that demand has been created. But by 1981 it became evident that Nationwide's revenues and costs were still not moving sufficiently fast in the right direction. Overheads were still outstripping income to an alarming extent and it was clear that even larger outlays would be needed to establish it as a major and viable club, contending in the same league as BCA. Even so, given, say, two more years' growth, the club might still have succeeded.

Collins were the first to decide that it was time for them to withdraw and cut their losses. Heinemann and Bonniers were willing to continue but, without Collins, the Swedes in the end decided that closure was the sensible course. In June 1982 the club was sold complete with its quite considerable stock of books to Readers' Union, owned by David & Charles Ltd, which also needed Nationwide's membership list for their own bookclub. When the numbers proved to be not quite so good as they had thought, there had to be a slight reduction in the price, but they paid £1.45 million, largely by taking over a bank overdraft. The three partners had between them to write off a total loss of approaching £5 million. To have to write off such a sum was of course a disaster, but the Heinemann Group's profits were large enough to stand it. Even after Collins's withdrawal Tilling were prepared to go on financing the club for another year or two. With sound reasons they had unshakeable faith in anything Heinemann did, but it was rash of them to have allowed things to go so far and so fast without asking the more obvious pertinent questions.

26

The Educational Department
Becomes HEB

After the dust of the Tilling take-over had settled, it was decided to hive off the Educational Department into a separate company, Heinemann Educational Books Ltd. Hill and his team had for some time been restive. They wanted much more say in the destiny of their business – now approaching in size the rest of William Heinemann Ltd. Tilling listened to Hill's arguments; and the new company was set up on July 1st 1961 with the following resounding prospectus: 'The emergence of Heinemann Educational Books Ltd, clears the way for an entirely new Group structure, with separate markets, different publishing and its own distinctive sales organisation – home and overseas. . . . During the next decade, we hope increasingly to rival Longman. Above all it is our ambition to build up a long-life business – one which will be a household name when other firms have become merely memories.'

The story of how market-leaders Longman were overtaken during the next quarter of a century is fully told in Alan Hill's *In Pursuit of Publishing* (John Murray 1988), and is not strictly part of the history of William Heinemann Ltd. Nevertheless, the growth of Heinemann Educational Books had a considerable impact on William Heinemann, especially in its overseas developments, and so it deserves some mention.

HEB was born in a period of great educational expansion. Thanks to the post-war baby-boom, the population rose from 51 million (1956) to 54.5 million (1966), causing a corresponding escalation in pupil numbers. The raising of the school leaving age to 16 in 1963 still further increased the school population. Meanwhile the publication of the Robbins Report in 1963, recommending the doubling of numbers of students in Higher Education, heralded the establishment of some twenty new universities.

The consequent growth in the market for books was a great opportunity for the educational publisher. Moreover, the democratisation of education – consequent on the Comprehensive School system and the new Certificate of Secondary Education for average and less able pupils – was accompanied by curriculum reform. Many new publications were demanded. Hill, Beal, and Thompson had been running the business for more than a decade, with turnover doubling (in real terms) every three or four years, to reach £420,000 by 1961 (£3.5 million by 1989 values). As the trio were now publishing almost seventy new books a year, the load was heavy, and they decided to create a new generation of publishers, by appointing and training suitable beginners. Their first recruit was Hamish MacGibbon, to handle Science and Mathematics. His energy and entrepreneurial capacity were to make him one of the country's most successful educational publishers. He was followed by Keith Nettle (English and Languages) and Paul Richardson (Social Studies), to form a new publishing team for the home market for the next two decades.

During the 1960s this expanded HEB team produced 1,300 new books in ten years, with a turnover reaching £2 million in 1970, and a profit of £260,000 (£11.5 million and £1.5 million respectively by 1989 values). This was the work of a team which made up in motivation what it lacked in numbers: for the entire executive staff, including all directors, editors, production and sales managers, increased from seven to only ten during the decade. It was the new independent status of HEB which triggered this outburst of creativity. It was spurred on by the complete absence of outside interference, whether from the Heinemann Group or from Thomas Tilling; and it was greatly helped by its management style, which was free from personal rivalry and office politics. This was because career growth and professional advancement, not to mention personal satisfaction, could be achieved within the unhindered expansion of the firm rather than at the expense of one's colleagues in a personally competitive situation.

Probably the most significant development came about as a result of bad luck. The Nuffield Foundation Science Teaching Project began in 1962, and invited tenders to publish the new textbooks it was developing. MacGibbon and Hill produced what they confidently expected would be the winning tender. How could they fail? They were after all the leading publishers of secondary science books. In Hill's own words:

'Like optimistic punters before a fruit machine, we cupped our hands and waited for the clanging spill of the jackpot. But it was not to be. One morning Hamish came into my office with a copy of *The Times*: to our dismay the Nuffield contract had been awarded to a consortium of Penguin and Longman. This spelt disaster. A whole new generation of science books, likely to drive our best sellers off the market, had been handed to our principal rival. We looked at each other in silence, deeply dejected. The end seemed to be in sight.

'Within days of this calamity, however, salvation appeared. Following the great Heinemann tradition, we had always treated our authors as if they belonged to the family. One of them was A. J. Mee, whose classic chemistry text we had kept in print during the dark days of the war. Our grateful author was now Chief Science Inspector for Scotland; and the week after the shattering blow from Nuffield, he arrived in my office to say that a similar project was underway in Scotland, physics being farthest advanced. Within hours, Hamish was in Edinburgh signing up that talented physics teacher Jim Jardine; and in 1964 began publishing an epoch-making series 'Physics is Fun'. So began our long involvement with the Scottish Science curriculum developments which were to lead to a cornucopia of books and series over the next twenty years.'

Not only did the stream of books culminate in one of the world's greatest educational sellers of all time – the Scottish Primary Mathematics Group series, whose sales were to escalate to over £5 million per annum – but the Scottish textbook style proved uniquely suitable for overseas schools, and was a key factor in the development of HEB's overseas empire. For it was during the 1960s that HEB set up its network of overseas offices that was in later years to take over the export business of William Heinemann Ltd in several markets.

It started in Australia in 1958, when the ebullient Nick Hudson went out to start the HEB business. Over the next twenty-eight years he built up a flourishing educational list, and HEB Australia was later (1981) able to take over William Heinemann's failing Australian subsidiary – whose turnover depended on books imported from London rather than locally published titles. Reliance on local publishing was indeed the crucial difference between the two companies. The same pattern was repeated in New Zealand, where HEB started its branch in 1964 under David Heap. As in Australia, it became a successful local publishing company, and was able to absorb the William Heinemann subsidiary in 1981. Meanwhile in Africa, HEB had similarly absorbed the William Heinemann East Africa Company in 1968, to be followed later by South Africa. (see pp. 471–6.)

Other HEB companies to be set up in the 1960s and early '70s included Nigeria, Hong Kong, Singapore, Malaysia, Canada, USA and the Caribbean. In the brief space of fifteen years there had sprung up a world-wide network of eleven educational companies, now grouped under the banner of 'HEB International Ltd' – with a combined turnover in 1979 of £20 million by 1989 values (see pp. 476–9.)

In the following year, 1980, the parent of all these companies, Heinemann Educational Books Ltd (UK), completed its second decade as a separate firm with a turnover of £8.7 million – £14.8 million by 1989 values. (This did not include the sales of the highly successful firm of Ginn, which HEB had acquired in 1977 at the request of that company's management.) The same team had now run HEB since its start in 1961, pursuing the same policy of publishing trade books as well as schoolbooks.

These years saw a flowering of HEB's general publishing, with the growth of Edward Thompson's drama list, and outstanding works of literary criticism, several of which came from Robert Gittings – in particular *Young Thomas Hardy* (1975) and its superb sequel *The Older Hardy* (1978), both receiving great critical acclaim. Popular science included several new books from Fred Hoyle, ranging from *Commonsense in Nuclear Energy* to a study of Stonehenge as a sophisticated mathematical tool. The African Writers Series, with over two hundred titles – fiction, poetry, drama – was accepted as the main repository for a new world literature. The social sciences at University level were assiduously cultivated, and Mr William Heinemann's early enthusiasm for criminology was revived by a new series edited by the famous Professor Sir Leon Radzinowicz.

What then was the impact on William Heinemann Ltd of its educational offspring – which grew during twenty years to be far larger than its parent? HEB's influence can be said to be beneficial in at least three ways. First, there was the strengthening of the group's financial structure and its common services – accountancy, warehousing and dispatch, etc, by HEB's massive contribution. Secondly, William Heinemann's list was now supplemented by HEB's vigorous trade publishing in the fields of drama, literary criticism, the social sciences and, especially, Africana – where the world's leading list carried the Heinemann name. Finally, William Heinemann's overseas subsidiaries in the white dominions were glad to merge with those of HEB, to form viable combined companies. In retrospect, the formation of HEB must be reckoned a powerful support to William Heinemann Ltd.

A New Department
to Publish Books
for Higher Education

Although some excellent general books were being published, fiction was still Heinemann's *forte* during 1961–83. The establishment of the educational department as a separate company (HEB) meant the loss of important trade titles from the main company's non-fiction list, but this was strengthened in 1961 by the setting-up of a new department to publish books on technical and professional subjects. The idea came from and was carried out by a Heinemann author who was also at the time a part-time editor.* Most of the titles catered for the tertiary level of education, but many turned out to be not merely student manuals or textbooks, but also works of interest to practising executives, to general as well as educational libraries, and in some cases of interest to the general reader.

The gradual establishment of this new section of the list filled a major gap in the categories covered by the Heinemann Group. Its timing was fortunate in that it coincided with the publication of the Robbins Report in 1963 which recommended increasing the numbers in higher education and led to the rapid expansion of universities, polytechnics, and technical colleges. The post-war 'baby boom' also swelled student numbers.

It may appear surprising that this new venture was from the outset not placed under the umbrella of HEB, particularly as the latter's series in the social sciences was growing fast. Indeed Alan Hill was later to regret that he had not insisted more strongly that this was the logical course. When a few years later Dwye Evans proposed that a new company should be formed to combine the tertiary lists of both companies Hill opposed this as he did not wish to lose either control or the turnover of HEB's own tertiary books. Likewise Charles Pick opposed the plan for the same reason. Instead of a new company it was agreed that certain engineering titles and those whose market was primarily to be found in schools rather than in universities, polytechnics, or colleges of further education should, after

*This unnamed founder is of course the author of this book, John St John. – *See p. 595* – *Editor.*

commissioning and acceptance, be handed over for publication by HEB. This led to new categories in HEB's list such as catering – Mary Foster's *Learning to Cook* (1966) was an early bestseller; mechanical, electrical, and chemical engineering; computer languages (in conjunction with ICL); book-keeping and secretarial subjects including a revolutionary new system of shorthand called *Teeline* invented by James Hill, who sadly died before it began to win its share of the market. *Teeline* subsequently became a great success and in many colleges replaced the Pitman system. Like most compromises this division of further education subject areas worked only moderately well. In practice the boundary could not be very clear cut, so that the two companies were apt to compete with each other and publish books on similar and sometimes identical subjects.

In earlier years the only Heinemann title that fitted into this new category had been Peter Drucker's *The Practice of Management* (1955). Creating what amounted to a new, self-contained list within the womb of an existing one was easier than establishing a brand new imprint, and yet it took some years and the publication of many books before academic authors in the relevant disciplines readily considered Heinemann among firms that might be approached with a new manuscript. The Windmill imprint might be renowned as symbolizing the publishers of Galsworthy, Somerset Maugham, Graham Greene, and of textbooks such as Holderness and Lambert's classic on school chemistry or Nelkon's on physics, but what did Heinemann know about handling and marketing a book on, say, quality control or commercial statistics or personnel management? The answer, in 1961, was very little; but experience was being rapidly gained and ways were found of closing the credibility gap in the potential academic author's mind, the most effective being a questionnaire which was a cross between market research and an unambiguous appeal for manuscripts.

This was something entirely new in Heinemann's history. Sent individually to every professor and lecturer in the country's technical colleges, polytechnics and, later, to those in relevant faculties in universities, it was headed 'An Invitation' and the text was surrounded by a tasteful border of printers' 'flowers'. It declared boldly that 'during the 1960s this gap in the Heinemann list of publications will be closed. In tune with the authorities' ambitious plans to satisfy industry's need for trained experts, we hope to develop a comprehensive selection of books covering all the main branches of technical education and industry – and some of the more

INVITATION

To Members of Technical, Scientific, and Medical departments in the Universities

A publisher of textbooks and advanced treatises needs to keep his ear to the ground. Without the suggestions and advice of lecturers, teachers, educationists, and other specialists he cannot hope to provide the kinds of books that are wanted. The more advanced and specialised the subject, the closer the connection with the reader has to be—particularly as among them he always hopes to discover a new author.

The imprint 'Heinemann' has for many years been familiar in universities and schools, and during the 1960s we mean to add considerably to our list of books on mathematics, all branches of the physical sciences, engineering and allied subjects, medicine, surgery, and pharmaceutics. We are also planning a comprehensive series on management and industrial administration.

We shall cater for all levels of study. Some of the books will be directly geared to the syllabus for a course, while others will cater directly for the specialist. Long experience in publishing has taught us that quality must take precedence over quantity—it is a case of 'few but roses'. Our selection policy therefore is rooted in (1) the sternest tests of ability and (2) an equally stern market analysis. If you agree with this approach we invite you to tell us on the questionnaire that you will find attached to this leaflet:

WHAT new books are required

WHICH books you would consider writing yourself

Books that deserve to be translated from other languages

The names of other potential authors

Writing a book on a technical or scientific subject is inevitably a lengthy and demanding undertaking (though in certain cases the strain can be eased if a book is written in conjunction with a colleague or even as a joint project of a university department or faculty). It is commonly believed, too, that the financial rewards to the authors are seldom sufficient; much of course depends on the particular subject and the estimated market, yet frequently the author's pessimism proves to be unjustified. At Heinemann's we have built up a book sales organization that is world-wide and second to none. We also have excellent facilities for handling, if the author wishes, U.S.A. publication rights, and we arrange translations of many of our scientific books into European and other foreign languages. We are able to offer good rates of royalty and advances for the right book.

Special attention is paid to standards of book production and clarity of presentation. To assist authors in the preparation of diagrams and charts, we are able to provide comprehensive studio facilities.

Our normal procedure is to ask authors to send us a brief synopsis, and in some cases specimen chapters, of the projected work and on the basis of this to issue a firm contract for the book to be written. Plenty of time can be allowed for the book to be completed. We are ready to wait quite a while, to think in terms of years rather than of months, so as to achieve the standards of writing and presentation that are necessary.

We invite you, therefore, to complete all or part of the attached questionnaire and post it to us. It is already addressed on the back and, if posted in the United Kingdom, it does not need a stamp.

Books accepted will be published by

William Heinemann Ltd

or Heinemann Educational Books Ltd

or William Heinemann Medical Books Ltd

HEINEMANN PUBLISHERS Ltd.
15/16 Queen Street, Mayfair, London, W.1.   HYDe Park 4141

Heinemann presents a

PROGRESS REPORT

*to all lecturers engaged in technical,
scientific, and medical education*

Four years ago the Heinemann group of publishing companies announced the setting-up of a new department and issued a questionnaire asking lecturers to make suggestions for books on technical and scientific subjects; we also invited them to offer their services as possible authors or to recommend others. The response exceeded our most optimistic anticipations. Hundreds (literally!) of suggestions, synopses, specimen chapters, and manuscripts flooded into our office. All were read and reported on by our team of expert readers. Inevitably a high percentage had to be rejected—sometimes because we felt that the particular market was already catered for; sometimes because the proposed book was not a viable commercial proposition; and sometimes (in fact, quite often) because the standard achieved by the author just was not good enough. We apologise once again to all who came into these (particularly the last) categories and we know that on occasions our judgement may have been mistaken, but we are determined to be guided by the most rigorous standards, in the belief that it is wiser for a publisher to issue *one* really excellent book than ten which are mediocre. As stated earlier, our slogan is: 'Few but roses'.

Despite the heavy rate of casualties, well over a hundred books have now been commissioned by our new technical and scientific department—usually on the basis of a synopsis and two or three specimen chapters. As can be seen from the accompanying list close on a hundred are already in the bookshops and some fifty are in various stages of preparation. Intentionally we cast our net wide. Some titles are directly geared to the syllabus of a course; others are aimed at the specialist. Our list includes publications suitable for every industrial and academic level—operative, craft apprentice, technician, technologist, national certificate or diploma, degree, management, post-graduate; it covers subjects ranging from basic mechanical and electrical engineering to cookery, aeronautics, liberal studies, wigmaking, book-keeping, and foremanship.

There are still—and always will be—many gaps in our list and having, so to speak, got our second wind we are once more inviting ideas for new books and offers of author-ship. We hope that those to whom we were unable to offer a contract will not think too badly of us and will try us again. We hope that others who have from time to time contemplated writing a book will decide that this is the moment to make a start. We invite you, therefore, to tell us on the attached form:

WHAT new books are required (not merely in the subject categories already shown in our list)

WHICH books you could consider writing yourself (or possibly in conjunction with a colleague)

Eventually, before issuing a contract, we shall need to have (either in stages or altogether) the following:

Synopsis of chapters.

Estimates of the total number of words and also of diagrams, graphs, and/or photographs.

Short description of the student (and general) market aimed at.

Two or three specimen chapters—not necessarily the first two.

For our part we guarantee:

To read your manuscript as quickly as possible—with a few exceptions, our record here is pretty good!

To pass on constructive comments from our experts and, where possible, give the reasons if a manuscript has to be turned down.

To give as much help as is necessary in the preparation of diagrams and graphs.

To publish your book as speedily as possible.

To offer good rates of royalties.

We can also make available our elaborate and far-reaching sales and promotion organization—not only here but overseas, where we sell 40 per cent of our annual turnover through our own offices and warehouses in Australia; New Zealand; Canada; South, East, and West Africa; Singapore; Hong Kong; and a network of Heinemann agents elsewhere. Judging by many recent successes there is also a good chance that we shall succeed in placing the right type of book with a publisher in the United States or in Europe

Please complete all or part of the attached questionnaire and post it to us. It is already addressed on the back and, if posted in the United Kingdom, it does not need a stamp.

Books will be published by:
William Heinemann Ltd
or Heinemann Educational Books Ltd
or William Heinemann Medical Books Ltd

HEINEMANN PUBLISHERS Ltd.
15-16 Queen Street, Mayfair, London W1   HYDe Park 4141

esoteric ones as well. The term "technical book" will be interpreted widely and as well as books on engineering, applied physics and chemistry, etc., it is hoped to include books on factory and office management, accountancy, business administration and allied subjects. We shall cater for all levels of study – from the craftsman and technician to the National Certificate and Dip. Tech. candidates and the post-graduate.

'Some of the books will be directly geared to the syllabus for a course – though we shall eschew the kind of textbook that is little more than magnified lecturer's notes and only promote books that are educational in the true sense. Other titles will cater more directly for the specialist or serve the needs of a particular section of industry. . . .' The questionnaire itself asked three main questions: 'What new books are required? Which books could you consider writing yourself? The names of any other potential authors?'

The response exceeded the most optimistic anticipations. Literally hundreds of suggestions, synopses, specimen chapters, and complete typescripts were submitted – though a number of these had obviously been previously rejected by other publishers. Later all lecturers received a 'Progress Report' accompanied by a follow-up questionnaire and a list of books so far issued or in the pipeline. This explained with bland frankness that all submissions 'were read and reported on by our team of expert readers. Inevitably a high percentage had to be rejected' – at least ninety-five per cent – 'sometimes because we felt that the particular market was already catered for; sometimes because the proposed book was not a viable commercial proposition; and sometimes [in fact, quite often] because the standard achieved by the author just was not good enough. We apologize once again to all who came into these (particularly the last) categories and we know that on occasions our judgment may have been mistaken, but we are determined to be guided by the most rigorous standards, in the belief that it is wiser for a publisher to issue *one* really excellent book than ten which are mediocre. As stated earlier, our slogan is "Few but Roses". Despite the heavy rate of casualties, well over a hundred books have now been commissioned. . . .'

The questionnaires were effective because they acted like a trawl net which among a great deal of seaweed and jetsam brought up a satisfactory number of plump fish – particularly manuscripts from youngish, ambitious lecturers so far without a publisher but with a few years' experience under their belt who were thinking it was about time they

[557]

wrote a book. Their incentive was seldom primarily financial – they could earn much more from spare-time consultancies and even research – but a published book bestowed professional gravitas and could be a valuable 'visiting card' and an aid towards promotion or a better post.

As well as the questionnaires there were extensive visits to colleges and universities to meet the respondents, to seek further authors, and learn more about syllabuses which lacked up-to-date textbooks. Advisers were also enlisted, mainly heads of departments or professors, and very occasionally an editor of a series, among the most notable being Dr J. Batty, who developed a series on accountancy and allied subjects, and Professor Rik Medlik who introduced books on hotel management and tourism.

During the 1960–70s an increasingly comprehensive list emerged under a somewhat curious assembly of subject areas, most of which arose fortuitously following the successful publication of an initial title which acted as a magnet for others in the same discipline: thus one of the earliest books, *The Chef's Compendium of Professional Recipes* (1963) by John Fuller and Edward Renold – which is still in print after nine reprints and a new edition – led to other catering texts such as *Pâtisserie* (1971) by L. J. Hanneman and *Food Commodities* (1976) by B. Davis. The success of this series also led to the decision to metricate and retranslate Escoffier's masterpiece first published by William in 1907 and in print ever since. The new version contained no fewer than 2,000 additional recipes not to be found in the 1907 edition, making a total of 5,012, and it was sold in large numbers to the general public as well as to professionals under the title of *The Complete Guide to the Art of Modern Cookery* (1979), translated by H. L. Cracknell and R. J. Kaufmann. In the same manner J. R. S. Beavis and S. Medlik's *A Manual of Hotel Reception* (1967) was the kernel around which grew a lively series on hotel management and tourism. Similarly D. J. Eyres's *Ship Construction* (1972) opened the way for a group of books on maritime studies and O. F. G. Kilgour and Margeurite McGarry's *An Introduction to Science and Hygiene for Hairdressers* (1964) pioneered a series for professionals with such exotic titles as *The Manual of Wigmaking* (1964) by Mary Botham and L. Sharrad, *Body Massage for the Beauty Therapist* (1972) by Audrey Goldberg, and *Cutting Hair the Vidal Sassoon Way* (1978). All these titles are still in print.

By far the largest group of tertiary books dealt with business management, economics, accountancy, business statistics, and allied subjects.

Doyen of this section was the prolific 'management guru' Peter Drucker, whose books sold world wide, being sought by executives as well as students. Earlier the firm had published his *The End of Economic Man* (1939) as well as his famous *The Practice of Management*. Among the best-known and bestselling titles which now followed were *Managing for Results* (1964), *The Effective Executive* (1967), and *Management: Tasks, Responsibilities, Practices* (1974). He supplemented his technical works with a candid and witty book of memoirs about people he had known, *Adventures of a Bystander* (1979), and with two novels. It is invidious to have to select from among the many authors in this section, but mention should be made of a handful to show the type and extent of the coverage, such as J. Batty's *Accountancy for Managers* (1971); Mark Houlton's *An Introduction to Cost and Management Accounting* (1973); Bernard Edwards's *Sources of Economic and Business Statistics* (1972); Meredith R. Belbin's *Management Teams* (1981); Maurice W. Cuming's *The Theory and Practice of Personnel Management* (1968); and E. R. Shaw's *The London Money Market* (1975). Inevitably these titles may sound dryasdust, but they helped place Heinemann among the most important publishers of books on business management and administration, a status which can be said to have been recognized in the firm's selection by the world-famous *Harvard Business Review* to distribute its ninety-four volume library – total price £1,528 in 1987 – to all parts of the world outside the Americas.

As the new list became recognized contracts were entered into with various professional bodies which added their imprimatur to series on their special subjects, thus providing useful specialized audiences. They included the Institute of Cost and Management Accountants, the Institute of Actuaries, the Institute of Quality Assurance, the CAM Foundation and the Institute of Marketing with a list of over fifty titles. Two generously illustrated works were published for the Landscape Institute: *Landscape Design with Plants* (1977), edited by Brian Clouston, and *Landscape Techniques* (1979), edited by A. E. Weddle. The first technical book to be published under the auspices of an official body was in fact *The Practice of Journalism* (1963) edited by J. D. Dodge and G. Viner for the National Council for the Training of Journalists, from whom several more titles sprang including the five-volume series on *Editing and Design* (1972–8) by Harold Evans, then editor of the *Sunday Times*. One of these, *Pictures on a Page* – about photo-journalism, graphics, picture editing – carried over five hundred photographs and drawings of such quality that it sold well also to the general public; there was a bookclub order and a substantial edition in America.

Each new subject area successfully published gave the lie to the frequently heard objection that it 'didn't fit comfortably under the Heinemann imprint'. It was proved that there need be no limitations provided the book was soundly written and had been assessed by the most rigorous criteria. Great reliance was of course placed on the confidential reports from expert advisers, though these were often too narrowly focused, so it was the publisher who in the last resort had to make the yes-or-no decision. As well as catering for the syllabus(es) a textbook had to be written at the right level. Some books, particularly those catering for lower levels of students, could be too good for their market or ahead of their time – or ahead even of the lecturers who were asked to recommend them. Despite what was said above about the need for quality it has to be admitted that sometimes a rather mediocre book would sell well, maybe because it appealed to mediocre lecturers instructing mediocre students! Price could be, but was not always, important, an attractive price for students being achieved by issuing simultaneously two editions: a hardback with an enhanced price for libraries and a trade paperback (i.e., with the same text, paper, and format) for students at a correspondingly reduced price.

Though expert in their own disciplines, many academics could have an amateurish prose style. In any case handling these textbooks and manuals, which were often complex in arrangement and carried numerous diagrams and much tabular setting, called for rigorous editorial and production skills hitherto seldom needed in the main editorial department. Excessive editing was avoided however by issuing each new author with a thirty-two page *Notes for Authors* (first printed in 1966). These gave advice on the presentation of the text; handling of diagrams, tables, and photographs; house style, including punctuation and use of capitals; notation and abbreviation of units; making an index; correcting proofs; and much else.

Sales and promotion methods caused worse headaches, particularly while the tertiary list was still small. The William Heinemann Ltd sales department concentrated on fiction and bestsellers and was incapable of doing much more than the initial subscribing of new titles from the new department; it suffered from the same shortcomings, particularly overseas, that led to the separation of HEB and its need to set up parallel distribution and sales networks in the Commonwealth. Attempts to arrange for these to handle William Heinemann Ltd's tertiary titles were largely stillborn. To save costs, some joint leaflets and specialized catalogues were cobbled together and for a short while the two companies shared a college sales representative-cum-peripatetic talent scout, but the division of the tertiary list into two halves was too fundamental. It was thus proved once again that the lack of a close link between commissioning editors and the promotional/sales force always leads to weakness.

Before long it became inevitable that the new department had to set up its own publicity apparatus, most of its budget being spent on direct mail shots to college and university lecturers, offering specimen copies. So as to avoid annoying booksellers, the order form on every leaflet carried the legend: 'Obtainable from any good bookshop or, in case of difficulty, direct from the publisher.' Inescapably students experienced plenty of difficulties and over the years 'miscellaneous direct sales' became one of the firm's largest customers.

The tertiary department inevitably felt the cold pressures of the recession of the late 1970s, though perhaps less than other sections of the list. Because of the necessity not to lock up too much capital in stock, print runs, including reprints, had to be curtailed drastically and as a result retail prices increased just at a time when students were spending even less than they normally did on books and when educational library grants were being slashed. By 1983, however, the tertiary education department was very solidly based and making a vital and, above all, reliable contribution to turnover. It had also created its own backlist, many of the books commissioned during the first five years still selling in revised and/or new editions. Some two hundred backlist titles appeared in the 1983 classified catalogue, e.g., Business Management, 123 titles; Technical, 54; Catering, 13; Hairdressing and Beauty Culture, 10.

In 1981 a major addition was made to the list by the purchase from W. H. Allen Ltd after negotiation with Doubleday, the owners of the series, of the entire Made Simple series for close on £1 million, including £687,000 for their goodwill. At a time when public libraries were decreasing purchases, particularly of standard fiction, the acquisition of these seventy-four titles helped to fill the gap in turnover. Robert Postema continued to edit the series as a full member of the Heinemann editorial staff and became a William Heinemann director.

Pop-ups and New Directions
in Children's Books

The 1960–70s saw a remarkable expansion in the firm's children's publishing, especially during the later years and spilling over into the 1980s. Not only were there more titles and much longer print runs, but many of them were of a very different type and there was a plentiful use of colour. It was a period during which the children's department became one of the pillars of the list, responsible for some 20 per cent of William Heinemann's turnover.

To begin with, Mary Whitehead's policy remained essentially the same, with a dozen or so titles a year by her established authors such as Elizabeth Enright, James Reeves, Geoffrey Trease, Ruth Ainsworth, and others. There were also children's stories from several of the firm's regular novelists, including two of the migrants from Michael Joseph, e.g., Paul Gallico's *The Day the Guinea-Pig Talked* (1963) and *The Day Jean-Pierre Went Round the World* (1966); and Monica Dickens's *World's End* series of children's novels and her *Follyfoot Farm* books with a useful tie-in with Yorkshire TV. Shortly before Mary Whitehead retired in 1971, an illustrator and a writer were enlisted, both of whom were to become important stars on the list. The first was Helen Oxenbury who made her name with *Numbers of Things* (1967) and her elaborate, vivacious drawings for Edward Lear's *The Quangle Wangle's Hat* (1969) and followed with others including Lewis Carroll's *The Hunting of the Snark* (1970) and *The ABC of Things* (1971). Oxenbury's were almost the first juvenile books that relied entirely on illustrations, though a start with books printed in colour was made possible by a partnership with the American publishers, Franklin Watts, who regularly took 5–10,000 sheets of certain titles. The other star was Penelope Lively, who began with *Astercote* (1970) and went on from strength to strength with others including *The House in Norham Gardens* (1974) and *The Ghost of Thomas Kemp* (1973), which won the prestigious Carnegie Medal.

Typical of the list in the 1960s were the Pyramid series of novels for the 'reluctant' teenager, each with 96 pages and a print of 5,000. They were taken very largely by the public libraries, which indeed in those days absorbed some ninety per cent of the children's list. There was little faith that it could be sold through the bookshops. This attitude was changed radically by the new children's editor, Judith Elliott, who came in 1970 after experience with Chatto & Windus and in New York with World Publishing and took over from Mary Whitehead a year later. Her first innovative breakthrough was with the *Meg and Mog* (1972 . . .) series, by Helen Nicoll, very simple, very funny little books for small children learning to read. They were illustrated by Jan Pieńkowski. Judith Elliott told me that she had a fight to get the series launched in the way she wanted:

'There were endless goings-on. It was said that we couldn't afford full colour. The libraries wouldn't take them. They shouldn't have speech balloons. Eventually I convinced people, particularly the sales staff, and it was the start of an important series which began in a small way but grew and grew until it became one of our most valuable properties.'

Until the middle of the 1970s children's publishing followed a secure pattern and Heinemann's list steadily expanded with some forty new titles a year, though it could not yet be considered among the best. A turning-point came in 1978–9, the year of the first great library cuts – some thirty-five per cent across the board for children's books. It was decided that the juvenile list must be cut back to match, but this crisis reinforced Elliott's plea that the future must lie with skilfully illustrated books designed to be sold mainly in the bookshops. Most fortunately it coincided with the arrival of Jan Pieńkowski's *Haunted House* (1979), the first of Heinemann's celebrated, literally fabulous pop-up books.

A revival and elaboration of a Victorian idea, pop-up books depend on 'paper engineering' which employs pull-out tabs, ingenious folding of items glued to the page, and the mechanical energy from turning the pages, all of which combine to produce three-dimensional, mobile effects. In *Haunted House* ghosts, insects, and other creatures appear from nowhere and also disappear. In its bathroom, for example, a giant three-dimensional monster rises as the page is opened; its mouth chews as the pages are moved, each of its spiral antennae being over a foot long; pulling a tab causes an alligator with jaws opening to come out of the stand-out bath; lifting the toilet seat reveals the eyes of a cat, causing mice to run for cover beneath the radiator. Altogether the book had over seventy moving parts. After Judith Elliott first suggested the idea to Jan Pieńkowski he produced a dummy, but this was not considered to be practical and so help was called in from Waldo Hunt in Los Angeles, an international expert with his own company, Intervisual Communications Inc. Peter Ireland, then Heinemann's production director, also played a key part and eventually after much experimenting and several crises a start was made on the complex four-colour printing, die-stamping, and the assembly of the many parts. The work was carried out in, of all places, the small town of Cali in Colombia because this was one of the few places which has the necessary plant and inexpensive labour force. Over 100,000 copies were manufactured, 40,000 for Heinemann and 40,000 for Dutton in New York, and the rest elsewhere. It was an anxious moment, but after a fairly slow start it built up a sale of well over 150,000 in the UK and over 700,000 worldwide. It had been feared that the libraries would be scared of such a project, but they loved it and it was awarded the Kate Greenaway medal.

It was followed by *Robot* (1981), also by Jan Pieńkowski. 'This was even more elaborate', Judith Elliott said, 'and it didn't do quite so well, but the important thing was that we had proved that there was nothing sacred about the traditional picture-book formula with its 32-pages, with nothing to go on the end-papers because of the library withdrawal form, and a number of other shibboleths. It also finally confirmed that the bookshops were by far the most important outlet – in fact, we were the first of the up-market publishers to really go for them.'

The next big event was *Where's Spot?* (1980 . . .), by Eric Hill who created a puppy which featured in a long series of books for the under-fives. He came in via Ventura, a 'packager' run by Robin Ellis. The format was superbly simple but very original. Judith Elliott bought it in twenty-four hours. It was not a pop-up but a lift-the-flap book. Spot opened up the under-fives market which culminated in the concept of 'Books for Babies'.

In 1971 the department had adopted the title of Heinemann Young Books together with its own colophon. It continued to build a stable of big-name artists, producing titles that sold in large quantities in book-shops, so that Heinemann could claim to be at the forefront of children's publishing. In addition to the names already mentioned, among these artist/authors were Janet and Allan Ahlberg, author and illustrator of many bestselling children's books and of the *Daisychains* (1984 . . .) which are not really books but decorated paper concertinas; Faith Jaques, perhaps the doyen of contemporary British illustrators, whose *Little Grey*

Rabbit's House (1982) with the text by Alison Uttley was a major success; Michelle Cartlidge, whose mice and bears made her very popular; and Satomi Ichikawa, a Japanese artist whose books, originated by Heinemann, sold in many countries. Highly illustrated, four-colour projects obviously need long print runs, and this means co-editions with publishers in America and other countries. Many of these deals were made, or in many cases confirmed, at the annual Bologna Book Fair, most of them having been originated by Heinemann.

With the arrival of non-stop television in so many homes, in a period when library and school library shelves were being denuded, when surveys showed that children's memory spans were shrinking, it is not surprising that books which were predominantly visual rather than verbal were so successful. On the other hand Heinemann Young Books by no means neglected books which did not rely mainly on illustrations.

In Judith Elliott's view 'sales of fiction were reduced drastically by the library cuts, but on the other hand new kinds of fiction emerged in response to the needs of a changing and multicultural society: books such as *Hal* (1974) by Jean MacGibbon, who wrote very well about a West Indian girl at a comprehensive.' There were also the novels by Judy Blume, an American whose children's books sold in millions in the United States and who dealt with present-day problems of growing up and learning about sex. After her books had been turned down by several UK publishers because they were too controversial, Heinemann in conjunction with Pan entered on a five-book contract. A publicity tour by Judy Blume brought wide coverage and, though opinions were split among librarians and teachers, her books were immediately popular with British children and went on to become an important part of the list.

An imaginative and innovative breakthrough was made by the Banana Books, an attempt to reach the neglected 7–10 year olds with stories designed to bridge the gap between picture books and straight fiction. Launched with six titles in 1984 by established authors such as Emma Tennant and Penelope Lively, each pocket-sized, hardback volume had 48 pages, full-colour illustrations, a run of 20,000, and sold at the very low price of £1.95. The series was to become another continuing success.

Keen costing combined with high quality production were essential for the achievements of Heinemann Young Books and in turn this called for the closest possible, everyday liaison between Judith Elliott and Peter Ireland of the production department.

A Prosperous Decade
Despite the Recession

During the 1970s the publishing industry continued to expand fast, the annual number of new titles growing from 33,489 in 1970 (of which 9,977 were new editions and reprints) to 51,071 (12,091) in 1983. New Heinemann titles amounted to; 1970 – 125; 1971 – 137; 1972 – 151; 1973 – 127; 1974 – 134; 1975 – 134; 1976 – 149; 1977 – 131; 1978 – 137; 1979 – 111; 1980 – 122; 1981 – 92; 1982 – 120; 1983 – 130. The firm's steady growth was, however, impeded by two events affecting the economy as a whole: first, the three-day week and the fuel crisis in the winter of 1973 which slowed everything down, the offices being without electric light or heating for two days a week. It also meant that deliveries from printers were badly delayed. As an emergency measure Nigel Viney, the production director, was dispatched to Otava, the Finnish publishers, in order to replenish stocks of a few fast-selling titles: for instance, 100,000 copies of Gibran's *The Prophet* and 5,000 of each of Wilbur Smith's novels. Unfortunately the lorry loaded with *The Prophet* skidded into a Finnish lake and the whole consignment was lost, but it was immediately reprinted without Heinemann being told and everything was delivered on time.

Far more serious and long lasting than the fuel crisis was the economic recession at the end of the decade which, though, despite foreboding, had no significant affect on turnover, but led to high interest rates. There was a sudden drop in new titles in 1981 and as a precautionary step printing numbers were cut wherever possible so as not to lock up too much capital, a measure which in particular affected reprints of long-selling titles, leading to inevitable price increases.

The 1970s, particularly the years 1976–8, can in retrospect be regarded as the apogee of Heinemann's financial recovery and post-war expansion (see Appendices E, F, and G). Group turnover increased at an average 33 per cent per annum over the seven years 1973–9. This was partly the consequence of inflation (the Retail Price Index registered a compound annual increase of 21 per cent over the same period) but there was also clearly an element of genuine expansion, much of which occurred overseas.

Key financial ratios reached their best levels ever. Return on funds reached a peak of 32.6 per cent in 1976 and in that same year the pre-tax profit percentage touched a peak of 19.8 per cent. HEB's sales to, and within Nigeria, were exceptionally high in 1976 but these were to fluctuate considerably in subsequent years. The 1978 results, which marked the culmination of sixteen successive years of record profits, owed relatively little to sales within Nigeria since it was the year when majority ownership of HEB (Nigeria) passed to local shareholders. William Heinemann Ltd produced an impressive £1.2 million profit (the highly successful 'Pickles' joint venture with Octopus being then in full swing). HEB's UK profit of £914,000 was a record and its overseas companies together contributed a further £200,000.

The development of HEB's overseas companies was now indeed proceeding rapidly. In 1972 their combined turnover was just over £1 million (sterling equivalent) and by 1979 this had grown to over £4.5 million. On the other hand their combined profit, which in 1972 had been virtually nil, by 1979 grew nevertheless to over £200,000 and in subsequent years this figure was to increase many times over. HEB's overseas companies were no longer predominantly redistribution points for imports from the UK; each was now originating its own publishing lists to meet the requirements of the changing educational syllabuses in their own regions, and it was this local publishing which provided the dynamic component in the growth of overseas profits. There was an important contribution to HEB from Ginn & Co. in their first year in the group, amply justifying the substantial premium expended to acquire this company. Secker & Warburg and The World's Work also had good results in 1978.

The record 1978 group profit was thus widely and solidly based, but the long string of record results was broken in 1979 when group profits fell by over £800,000. HEB's profits had been reduced by the need to reserve against unpaid and overdue Nigerian debts and William Heinemann Ltd's profits were also down, partly as a result of reduced revenues from Pan and the Octopus joint venture. World's Work's profits also declined sharply. Nonetheless, helped by improved results from Ginn and Seckers, the group's total profits were still a respectable £2.8 million and it was not until the following year, 1980, that a serious decline in profitability occurred (but see page 616 to note the recovery in profits from 1981).

Overall the results must have been gratifying to Tilling, and indeed, though relatively small, Heinemann became one of their most profitable subsidiaries when results were expressed in terms of return on funds invested (Appendix G). In 1976 Sir Geoffrey Eley retired as chairman of Tilling and therefore also of the Heinemann Group, his place being taken by Douglas Manser, an experienced accountant on the Tillings board. A dominating and helpful influence in the background was Patrick (later Sir Patrick) Meaney, who was Tilling's managing director and chief executive.

The group as a whole can be said to have done well, except that in the stricter sense it was becoming less and less of a group, the two Heinemann companies operating, except for shared Kingswood services, independently of each other. Once again there was rivalry leading to antagonism between individuals at the top – this time between Pick and Hill. The latter told me that their relationship which had been excellent for a decade deteriorated after Hill became group managing director. And this led Hill to a policy of non-interference. Worse, it also interfered with the smooth running of the group. Hill was hampered in his role of fully effective group managing director. Another result was the continued existence of double offices in Australia and New Zealand, neither of them by themselves being economically viable. There were also other ways in which the rift between the two senior executives filtered down through both organizations with harmful results, leading to what amounted to inter-company chauvinism. Tilling, who should have been aware of what was going on, can be fairly criticized for not stepping in more decisively, but on the other hand both companies were doing so well that they probably decided not to intervene. As with the running conflicts of earlier generations, Heinemann appeared to thrive almost because of, rather than in spite of, antagonism at the top.

Rosenthal Succeeds Warburg at Seckers

During the 1960–70s the other group companies continued to make impressive contributions to the group's output, though they also brought problems and, as can be seen from Appendix C, for some years they added more prestige than profits. As already mentioned, Rupert Hart-Davis decided to remove his company: a sad loss from a literary point of view, though their departure was financially a relief, losses of £14,707 being recorded in 1961 and £20,955 in 1962. Heinemann's interest was sold on 1 January 1962 to Harcourt Brace Inc. of New York at a price based on the value of the net assets plus a notional £5,000 for goodwill. Of the rest, Martin Secker & Warburg was undoubtedly the most celebrated and it continued to lend lustre with the quality and originality of its books and with authors such as Angus Wilson, Alberto Moravia, John Wain, James A. Michener, Malcolm Bradbury, Gunter Grass, and many others of note – not to mention its great backlist. During the 1960s Secker & Warburg's finances were, however, a continual worry because not only did it make losses for several years, but it also needed further loans from Tillings. No publisher has provided a more telling demonstration that there is no automatic conjunction between literary excellence and profits; on the contrary, its history seems to prove a Gresham's law in publishing to the effect that good books often drive profits out.

'Seckers', to give the company the name by which it is always known, moved in 1961 to 14 Carlisle Street, Soho. Apart from its finances, warehousing, accountancy, and other services provided by the group from Kingswood, it still operated largely as an independent company under the chairmanship of Fred Warburg. Roger Senhouse resigned in 1962, but David Farrer continued as senior editorial director together with Roland Gant until the latter returned to William Heinemann Ltd in 1965 after just under three years (see page 494). The board was strengthened by two younger men: James Price, who among other projects initiated the firm's cinema series; and Maurice Temple Smith who it was always understood was heir-apparent to Warburg, who was well past the normal retirement age of sixty-five. In April 1968 Temple Smith in fact became managing director. An unusual arrangement was entered into with Barley Alison, who had won a high reputation as a senior editor with Weidenfeld & Nicolson, whereby she was to introduce authors, mainly novelists, who would be published by a new imprint, the Alison Press, though Seckers would pay production and publishing costs, including advances and royalties. Barley Alison would receive no salary but a substantial share of any profits. It was an imaginative scheme and it worked out very well, Barley's discriminating taste enlisting authors of special quality. Later a similar arrangement was entered into with Leo Cooper, publisher of military histories.

Despite the infusion of editorial talent, the company was still making persistent losses out of all proportion to its size. Understandably Tilling insisted that radical steps must be taken to put things right. It was pointed out that the 'local' overheads were too high in relation to turnover – 39.5 per cent compared with 29.0 per cent for William Heinemann Ltd. Another grouse was that because Tilling owned only 29 per cent of the ordinary shares and 80 per cent of the preference shares, they were entitled to no more than 60 per cent of distributed profits, when and if earned, even though, including loans, they were putting up 93 per cent of the working capital. Dwye Evans argued that the solution was to reduce overheads radically and to publish fewer books; Warburg on the other hand believed they should publish *more* books, which he was confident could be done without increasing basic overheads.

After much discussion Warburg inescapably had to agree to make economies, which were partly achieved by William Heinemann Ltd completely absorbing Seckers' sales effort – apart from Seckers' London traveller – and putting it under the control of T. R. Manderson. Later, in 1968, Seckers' production and publicity departments were also absorbed and, at Tilling's insistence, Charles Pick joined the Secker's board and started to attend their fortnightly meetings when the key publishing decisions were taken. There was no doubt that Pick could (and did) exercise a power of veto and that no books could be bought without first 'consulting' him or, in his absence, Dwye Evans.

Not surprisingly Warburg resisted this degree of supervision and the destruction of his firm's infrastructure, but he was reassured that there would be no real interference with Seckers' editorial character and the scheme made such good economic sense that eventually he seemed prepared to accept it, though two of his colleagues were more intransigent. There had already been friction between Warburg and his heir-apparent and in September 1968 Temple Smith together with James Price wrote to Peter Ryder, protesting at the prospect of Seckers being reduced to an 'editorial function'. Further, they declared that they would like to buy Seckers themselves. In a curt reply Ryder told them that they should have first discussed their proposals with Warburg himself and added that the Heinemann Group had no intention of selling the firm. Temple Smith was also asked to resign. The dispute headed *The Times* Diary which reported that 'Warburg is simply more optimistic than Temple Smith that the firm can maintain its independence. "If there should be a threat to the editorial and general independence of the firm, it would be disastrous for the publishing trade," he says. He believes that the firm's financial arrangements with Heinemann have proved advantageous, and that it would be difficult for a medium-sized publishing house to survive on its own.'[1]

Temple Smith had to resign and James Price followed him. It seems that they had misjudged the strength and mood of the forces opposed to a sell-out, and yet a few days later, on the same day as Warburg formally accepted the streamlining proposals, though he resisted the idea that he should become president without executive powers, he himself wrote another letter to Dwye Evans, as group managing director, floating the idea of a sell-out: 'I have strong reasons for believing that Secker & Warburg can be sold to a reputable buyer at a price that Tillings would regard as a favourable one.' He asked for three months in which to explore possibilities, adding that 'the stock is written down to an extremely modest level, the backlist is around £70,000, a big asset, the future contracts are numerous and in most cases worthwhile, and among the assets which might be valued by a buyer more highly than it is in the group would be my own active exercise of power as chief executive.'[2]

Warburg had talks with Graham C. Greene, joint managing director of Jonathan Cape, having first entered publishing under Warburg, spending five years at Seckers. He reported the approach to Dwye Evans and serious negotiations were begun, balance sheets were exchanged, and an offer was made. When Pick, who was in Australia at the time, heard of the proposed deal, he was bitterly opposed to it.

'My case was that with the loss of Seckers the balance of the whole group would be upset. William Heinemann Ltd was essentially a middlebrow imprint which was nicely complemented by Seckers' higherbrowed list. In every way it would be disastrous to let them go.' While the argument was going on, Warburg told *The Times*, somewhat naïvely: 'I am not a principal in these discussions, though I have heard about them from various people. I am only a commodity being thrown about in the middle.'[3] The conflict, essentially between Dwye Evans and Pick, with other members of the group board, including Warburg himself, backing one or the other or changing sides, bore similarities to the earlier conflict over Frere's proposed 'sell-out' to McGraw-Hill. In the end Pick prevailed and the sell-out of Seckers to Cape also fell through.

[571]

As it happened, the figures for 1968 were much more encouraging. The economies were beginning to tell and there were some good new books, but Fred Warburg was now in his seventy-second year, and the need to find a successor had become urgent. For once, luck was with the company. It so happened that Thomas Tilling were at this time urging Heinemann to acquire other companies; prominent on the target list were leading art-book publishers Thames & Hudson. Alan Hill was friendly with the forceful young managing director of Thames & Hudson International, Tom Rosenthal, and so he decided to try the temperature of the water by inviting Rosenthal to lunch at the Garrick Club. It so happened that Rosenthal had been chairman of the Society of Young Publishers; so towards the end of the meal, before broaching his carefully rehearsed proposal for the purchase of Thames & Hudson, Hill asked Rosenthal if he knew any bright young people who might be suitable for Fred Warburg's job.

'Well, Alan,' replied Tom, 'if what you are saying is, would I like the job of running Secker & Warburg, the answer is yes, subject to one or two conditions. . . .'

Hill was dumbfounded. This was not at all what he was saying. Nobody had thought of Rosenthal for the job. Hill took a long swill of hot coffee, fighting for time to readjust to this astonishing new situation. As he himself put it 'like Paul on the road to Damascus, I was now struck with a blinding light. Recovering fast I replied: "Well, yes, Tom, now you mention it, that is exactly what I have in mind. . . ."'

Back in the office Dwye Evans was equally surprised. As Secker's Barley Alison commented, 'I was largely responsible for persuading Dwye that we needed a separate MD and not Charles Pick for both companies, and Tom's name was NOT on the short list . . . I had never even heard of him'. Pick, however, had noticed Rosenthal when at the long table in the Savile Club dining-room he publicly criticized Priestley's *Prince of Pleasure*, declaring that he was surprised that 'such a distinguished house as Heinemann was prepared to cobble up such a poor compilation'. Whether or not the criticism was justified, Pick could not but be impressed by this articulate, on occasion pompous young man's forthrightness and quite exceptional self-assurance. Dwye Evans now met Rosenthal and was likewise impressed. Though Rosenthal's publishing experience had been limited to art books, he was a diligent writer and critic, he read widely including American and European fiction, and he was fluent in four languages. He seemed to be just what Secker needed.

First, however, his two conditions had to be satisfied. One was that he should at once become chairman and managing director and another was that he must be allowed to buy some of Secker's shares. Both conditions caused difficulty because Sir Geoffrey Eley, who as Tilling's chairman had interviewed Rosenthal and approved him, did not want him to be chairman and therefore automatically on the Heinemann group board until he had proved himself. He also was adamant in maintaining that it was Tilling's policy that no chief executive could hold shares in the company they were responsible for. Pick was, however, so convinced that Seckers needed Rosenthal that eventually he got Eley to relent, subject to Pick taking full responsibility for the decision. His case was made easier by the existing minority holdings of Warburg, Farrer, and a few others who were only too pleased to sell their shares, which until then had been considered worthless. There was therefore no question of Tilling having to reduce their holding: in fact, once the minority were bought out Tilling's holding increased, so that they owned 80 per cent of the equity and Rosenthal 20 per cent; he bought his shares at par at a cost of some £15,000. In return he had to be content with not being chairman for the time being (he took over formally from Pick in 1980) but, as will be seen later, his personal acquisition was not only an indication of the force of Rosenthal's character but it was to play a role in the group's future reorganization.

Tom Rosenthal's forthcoming appointment was ratified in September 1970 and in the following April Warburg retired. The firm which he more than anyone had created was not only going to survive but to enter on what was to be the most prosperous period of its existence. In a profile interview with *The Times* he remarked: 'I was the first publisher of note to join a group and survive in full fig. Any publishing house lucky enough to be bankrupt twice with the backlist surviving the bankruptcies is then in a very strong position.' He also revealed some of his thinking about building a list: 'The ideal publishing house has no doubt one title which sells five million a year. But the real answer is that if you cut your list of novels from twenty-five to six, it is virtually impossible to decide which six and, secondly, to get brilliant new authors and keep old ones, you have to have a certain variety within which novelists will feel they can come and move. It would be difficult to take too many "blockbuster" authors without losing

[573]

more than we gained. The imprint cannot go far from its central, mapped out course without destroying itself. . . . I ask "is it a first rate book of its kind?"' His answer as to how he came by his reputation as a subtly dominant publishing figure was: 'By knowing what I want to publish, what I can give my heart and mind to, and by not whoring after what would be, for me, false gods.'[4] Fred Warburg died on 25 May 1981.

Although by the time of Rosenthal's arrival Seckers were again profitable, the effect of his management is shown by the mounting turnover (from £390,020 in 1971 to £1,840,751 in 1981) and by profits which increased tenfold. Even when inflation is allowed for, these increases are impressive. The backlist was fully exploited and there were many successful books by authors already on the list as well as by new ones acquired under Rosenthal's guidance. Among them were Tom Sharpe, Erica Jong, David Lodge, Carlos Fuentes, Germaine Greer, Italo Calvino, George V. Higgins, Paul Erdman, Dan Jacobson, J. M. Coetzee, Umberto Eco; via the Alison Press imprint were Piers Paul Read, Dudley Pope, and Saul Bellow – the last Nobel prizewinner; there was also Anthony Thwaite, who started a new poetry series; and of course many others, to make Seckers one of the most, if not the most distinguished list in London – and, to boot, it was very profitable.

New premises were found in 1978 around the corner at 54 Poland Street, Soho. In 1980 the staff was strengthened by Peter Grose, who left Curtis Brown, the literary agents, to become publishing director. This proved to be a necessary appointment because the next year Tom Rosenthal took on the additional duties of being managing director of the newly formed Heinemann International Ltd, part of the pyramidal structure introduced by Tilling (see pages 613–16), and at the same time chairman of William Heinemann Ltd. From then on he usually spent his mornings at Upper Grosvenor Street, wearing his Heinemann hat, and the afternoons at Seckers in Poland Street. Most men would have found the strain intolerable, but Rosenthal assured me that it didn't worry him.

'I had only one brain and it worked just as well, or just as badly, no matter where I was sitting. I had a secretary and a separate diary in each office, and I thrived.' He added, though, thoughtfully: 'There was never any question of not taking on that extra job. In a big corporate set-up like Tillings, if you refuse a promotion, you're finished. Despite what was rumoured, I continued also to be the effective chief executive at Seckers.'

Rosenthal agreed that as things turned out taking that job was surprisingly to his great financial advantage. 'But in terms of my own psychology it was to prove a disaster. At the time I just did not realize how hostile and inimical to me was the whole concept of Big Business.'

The World's Work Absorbs Kaye & Ward and is in Turn Absorbed

Durng the 1960s The World's Work switched very largely to lavish and highly coloured children's books, most of them originated in America and relying heavily on library sales. There were also other juvenile lines, catering for different age levels and directed at schools as well as parents. They included the I Can Read series, arts and crafts books, and junior science books. In Michael Percival World's Work retained their own London traveller, but otherwise it made good sense for their books to be marketed on a commission basis by William Heinemann Ltd, both at home and overseas. On the whole they were different from the William Heinemann children's books and in fact complemented them.

Phyllis Alexander, who had become chairman in 1962 as well as managing director since 1955, retired at the end of 1964. She had been one of the great post-war successes, having built up The World's Work to a stable and highly profitable level. She was succeeded by David Elliot, who had for many years played an important part in creating the list, particularly as production director, a position now taken over by Robert Aspinall. This small company continued to prosper with turnover rising from £116,840 in 1961 to £1,272,892 in 1982, but these figures are illusory because in the mid-1970s things began to get difficult, mainly because of the cuts in public library spending, combined with inflated costs of manufacture. In 1979 David Elliot left and handed over to Chris Forster, sales director and also a director of William Heinemann Ltd, who rapidly altered the firm's character. So as not to be so dependent on the public libraries, he went in for original publishing with a strong emphasis on books about sport and leisure activities. This meant an escalation of capital investment and in overheads and, though there were some good books and turnover increased, there were for the first time in many years grave losses – £187,722 (1980); £37,441 (1981).

One solution was the acquisition in 1980 of Kaye & Ward Ltd, a small company with a similar but complementary list, including the best-selling *Thomas the Tank Engine* books and other well-established retail lines. The imprint was preserved but in practice Kaye & Ward was merged with The World's Work, only two of the former's staff eventually being retained, resulting in an annual saving of £80,000 a year of overheads. But Kaye & Ward's books were underpriced and its stock insufficiently written down; it recorded losses of £81,491 in 1980 and £166,006 in 1981. Though profits were again made by the two companies, there were still serious difficulties and differences arose as to what should be done with them, exacerbating personal relationships on the group board. Rosenthal, who supported the continuation of the World's Work expansion, found himself outvoted; so eventually in 1984 the painful decision was taken to absorb them both in William Heinemann Ltd.

The Medical Company Expands

In 1962 Owen Evans became sole managing director of Heinemann Medical Books and in August the next year J. Johnston Abraham died. Shortly before his death two high-level medical advisers had been appointed and later were to follow each other as the company's chairmen: the first was Raymond Greene, a well-known endocrinologist, mountaineer, and brother of Graham; the other was Selwyn Taylor, a surgeon and Dean of the Royal Post-Graduate Medical School. The team was strengthened in 1967 by Richard Emery, ex-Butterworths.

Although books which were not strictly in the main line of medical publishing continued to be published, including a mammoth, 1,059 page *Encyclopaedia of Sexual Behaviour* (1961) by Albert Ellis and Albert Abarbanel, the list began to be reshaped under the influence of the two new advisers to reflect the change in the profession's attitudes which were placing more emphasis on science than medical art and 'tea and sympathy'. There was for example a series of monographs on specialist subjects aimed at general practitioners which proved difficult to market, but then came the highly successful *Scientific Foundations of Surgery* (1967) by C. Wells and J. Kyle. This was followed by several in the same series, including *The Scientific Foundations of Obstetrics and Gynaecology* (1970) by E. Phillip, J. Barnes, and M. Newton; of *Anaesthaesia* (1970) by C. Scurr and S. Feldman; of *Oncology* (1976) by T. Symington and R. L. Carter; and other titles.

Apart from the continued series of books on nursing, veterinary science, pharmacology, physiotherapy, radiography, and other specialities, the most successful titles in the 1960–70s tended to be on specialized subjects tied in with study required for postgraduate qualifications, such as in neurology, cardiology, urology, and paediatrics. Among the most successful, rapidly established titles first issued during the 1970s were *Medical Emergencies, Diagnosis and Treatment* (1970) by Richard Robinson and Robin Stott and *The Use of Antibiotics* (1972) by A. Kucers and N. Mick Bennett. Well timed to reflect the growing interest in 'complementary' medicine were four books on acupuncture by Felix Man, starting with *Acupuncture: the Ancient Art of Healing* (1962), all of which reprinted regularly and became standard works. There were also important, pioneering books on hemiplegia by Berta and Karel Bobarth. In the early 1980s the list was complemented by a carefully planned Integrated Clinical Study series for undergraduates, starting with J. R. Hampton's *Cardiovascular Disease* (1983).

The change of emphases in the list's character opened up important markets overseas, particularly in America. This side of the business was developed by Richard Emery, in particular, who became managing director when Owen Evans retired in 1975.

In 1980, Selwyn Taylor succeeded Raymond Greene as chairman. Like his two predecessors, he was highly distinguished, being Senior Vice-President of the Royal College of Surgeons. With such highly qualified professional management at publishing level, and a policy of greater expansion, it was now felt that the supporting functions (sales, accounting, distribution, etc.) would be best handled by a larger organization. As Heinemann Educational Books had now moved to offices next door in Bedford Square, the medical company became a member firm of Heinemann Educational Books International. In 1983 Richard Emery retired, to be succeeded by Richard Barling – himself a doctor.

[577]

The Decline of
Peter Davies Ltd

Peter Davies died tragically in 1960, but the company carried on under his brother Nico, aided by the evergreen Joan Waldegrave, Jack Dettmer, and for a short while by Sandy Fullerton and various others. In the same year they together with the medical company moved to new premises at 23 Bedford Square, to the rear of which was the new trade counter in Gower Mews. They continued to publish the same of kind of small but well-thought-out list, in particular history, religion, and biography as well as fiction, aimed in the main at a middlebrow, middle-class readership. Some of the titles were striking, but most years they lost money; 1961 and 1962 were particularly bad years, going in the red to the extent of £30,802 and £27,507 respectively. Tillings decided to urge drastic steps: Nico Davies's minority shareholding was bought out and Peter Davies Ltd was largely absorbed into William Heinemann Ltd and became no more than an imprint – just what had been feared might have happened to Secker & Warburg; there was no public announcement of the change and its own spring and autumn lists were maintained, but William Heinemann Ltd had the right to veto contracts; sales, publicity, and production were absorbed into William Heinemann's own departments and in 1964 'PD' moved to two small rooms in Queen Street. In 1964 Fullerton left and Derek Priestley was transferred from the main firm to become managing director.

Priestley considered this to be a demotion, but he liked working with Nico Davies and threw himself with energy into his new task. Trading soon improved and modest profits were recorded, reaching a peak of £17,654 in 1973. There were also some very attractive authors and books such as Norah Lofts (*Hester's Room*); Catherine Marshall (*A Man Called Peter*); Margaret Powell (*Below Stairs*); Mary Stocks (*My Commonplace Book*); and others, including fifteen novels from Elizabeth Kyle, ten from Jane Lane, and forty from Robert Standish.

Nico Davies retired as chairman in 1968. His company continued to publish some 25–30 titles a year, but it was still very much a poor relation of the main firm and, with reason, Priestley complained that Peter Davies's advance copies were always at the bottom of the travellers' bags. By 1975, although annual turnover had grown for the first time to over

£200,000, profits suddenly dropped and were little better the next year. It was the beginning of the end. What subsidiary publishing firms always feared was about to happen. From January 1977 Peter Davies Ltd ceased to be even an 'editorial function' and its stocks and what was left of its assets disappeared within its by then disenchanted parent. A melancholy end to a list of some considerable distinction.

The severing of Heinemann's link with the children's publishers Bancroft & Co. Ltd, seemed preordained after a much shorter period of ownership and losses of £41,670 in 1967 and £60,632 the following year. In 1970 the British Printing Corporation absorbed this company for a basic, all-in price of £210,000.

Despite the problems they brought, an ever-open eye was kept for further acquisitions of subsidiaries. Kaye & Ward was bought in 1980 (see page 576) and the Made Simple series in the same year (see page 561). Negotiations were far advanced for the purchase of Mills & Boon, the leading publishers of romantic fiction, for a sum in the neighbourhood of £1 million, and in July 1971 this was recommended to the Tilling board. It was very much Dwye Evans's idea, but Pick was concerned that the acquisition would be too much out of keeping with the group's publishing style – despite its large commercial advantages. At the eleventh hour Pick, supported at this time by Hill, persuaded Dwye Evans to drop the proposal. Tilling had remained neutral throughout this affair and, not for the last time, failed to support the group's managing director. With hindsight it may be thought that the fears were exaggerated, especially considering Mills & Boon's highly profitable expansion and the eminence of John Boon himself, who shortly afterwards became president of the International Publishers Association.

Paul Zsolnay died in 1961, leaving his one-third share to his daughter. John Beer then became managing director of the holding company in which Heinemann owned the other two-thirds of the equity and Hans Polak, who had been with the company since 1953, continued to run Heinemann & Zsolnay in Vienna. Inevitably it was a virtually autonomous venture and Vienna resisted pressure from Tilling to make prompter financial returns and to put their administration in neater order. But apart from three poor years in the 1960s, they made money until the end of the 1970s, when things became suddenly difficult. Turnover fluctuated between £145,585 (1967) and £1,375,825 (1977), while net profits reached a peak of £84,525 in 1966.

Editorial Managers, Salaries, and Training

The turnover among the editorial staff was larger than in other departments. People left for a number of different reasons, more money and a more senior position elsewhere being the most obvious. Anyone with a few years' experience at Heinemanns had a plum item for their *curriculum vitae.* A hard core of staff remained, including Roland Gant who together with Maire Lynd exercised the most influence on what was commissioned or rejected; he also looked after and edited several of the most important writers. Another long-stayer was Roger Smith, erudite, painstaking, unassuming, the kind of backroom rock on which every publisher depends. But of the five editorial managers who left during the 1960–70s at least two resigned because they felt their careers were being frustrated, and several obtained good jobs elsewhere. Every publisher is apt to lose talented, ambitious men and women for this sort of reason, but this history would be incomplete without mentioning them, particularly as it is the individuals, particularly editors, who contribute most to shaping the list and keeping successful authors.

Mark Barty-King, who was with the firm for eight years, three-and-a-half of them with Peter Davies, told me that he left for two basic reasons: he was not allowed to go on the firm's behalf to New York where he had many contacts and felt he could initiate some valuable deals; secondly, because he was very keen to get into paperbacks and when there was a chance of becoming editorial director at Granada with a big increase in salary, he jumped at it.

'Leaving was a traumatic experience and I was made to feel dreadful. I was letting down the side. I was made to work out my statutory six months notice. I had been much happier working at Peter Davies with Derek Priestley. There was something terribly oppressive about Heinemanns at that time. The atmosphere was curiously claustrophobic. It wasn't a lively, open sort of place. I suffered a good deal of frustration, not that I ever felt undermined. Roland and Charles were very supportive when I wanted to take on an author.' Mark Barty-King later went on to head the hardback division of Bantam Press.

His successor as editorial manager, David Burnett, felt very differently and considered that he was not allowed enough freedom to commission books and that his authority was undermined when dealing with authors and in particular with literary agents. Earlier, after a spell with Heinemann as a junior editor, he had left to become the buying editor at Book Club Associates. With this valuable experience under his belt, he was pleased in 1973 to be invited by Charles Pick to rejoin Heinemann and become editorial manager.

'I was completely accustomed to making decisions on my own and it was frustrating to have to refer everything back to Charles. At that time, though Heinemann was very successful, it was agreed that there was a need for more editorial initiatives. Charles was prepared in principle to have acquiring editors, but he didn't like the reality, particularly when it came to fiction, which was his special concern. As soon as I arrived back all the agents, most of whom I knew well, wanted to see me. "Thank God there's someone else we can talk to. Hope you've got your cheque-book with you." Within a few days Carol Smith offered me a book by Peter Straub, a horror writer of considerable promise. I liked it very much, met the author and the contract was drawn up. Charles agreed we should do it, though he was not very keen and he was not prepared to pay the author a 7½ per cent royalty for a paperback. Charles refused to budge. The book was eventually sold to Cape for £17,500, then a great sum. Even if Charles was right, the buzz soon went around that it was no good sending me anything. Everything I said had to be rubberstamped by Pick. I couldn't negotiate, couldn't take real risks. In practice I could only buy books for money he would agree to, provided there wasn't an agent – unless it was one of the few of whom he approved. No wonder most of the top agents were not in a hurry to offer us their best stuff.'

Quite independently, Carol Smith, Straub's agent, told me of the same incident: 'At that time Peter Straub had only written one, not very successful novel and needed money rather badly. I proposed he should write something more commercial and suggested a modern Gothic novel, a contemporary form of ghost story. He did this and the first person I offered it to was David Burnett who had just rejoined Heinemann. David loved it. I was invited to have tea in Charles's office with David there. They agreed to the advance and ordinary royalties. They had an

[581]

enthusiastic Pan behind them, but then Charles refused to offer more than 6½ per cent on the paperback split. I wanted 7½ per cent which everyone else was then giving. I stuck to my guns and, instead, sold the book to (ex-Heinemann) David Machin at Cape's. Peter Straub went on to become a huge international bestseller and a multi-millionaire. He was the biggest author I have so far worked with and Heinemann had first bite of him, but Charles lost him for the sake of one per cent.'

Although there might at times be acute differences between Pick and his editors, he of course had the ultimate responsibility for deciding which books were commissioned. In the case of Straub's royalty he knew only too well that if he were to give away that extra one per cent, it could have a domino effect on the firm's entire royalty strategy.

'As I understood it', Carol Smith however insisted, 'Charles's attitude to agents was that he hated them, didn't want to deal with them, and felt that he could always outwit them. In many cases he was right, but he could be short-sighted and in this particular case he was wrong. I sometimes think that Charles should have been an agent himself instead of a publisher!' Carol Smith paused before adding: 'But I also think Charles is one of the most charismatic men I have ever met. He is clever, wily, fun to talk to because he is always one jump ahead.'

Burnett, too, had a great respect for Pick's abilities. 'He was an excellent businessman, a brilliant salesman, particularly when we had world rights. I admired the way he supported Paul Scott. But deep down he didn't want me to be an entrepreneur, though later when out of the blue Gollancz asked me to come to them as their deputy managing director, Pick wanted me to stay and offered far more than Gollancz, but I knew I would stifle if I stayed.'

Other senior editors, particularly those responsible for books for children or higher education, had an entirely different experience and received nothing but encouragement. They were certainly free to be entrepreneurs. Janice Robertson also resigned, but on a question of principle. A member of her staff was not given the pay rise that Janice felt she was entitled to – that was Kathryn Court, who left to become eventually senior vice-president of Viking-Penguin in America.

In every department salaries were of course a biennial reason for discontent, particularly during the years of the official wage freeze in the 1970s, when more than a small stated percentage increase could be given only when one's job altered completely. This was another incentive to move to another firm. Pick did a great deal to rationalize the salary structure and to remove what amounted to grotesque differentials between people doing almost identical work and with the same seniority. This, together with the Tillings pension scheme, did much to improve earnings, but a minority of staff were keen to be represented by a trade union, particularly as the staff of HEB were well organized in the National Union of Journalists and of course manual workers and others at Kingswood had been organized collectively for years. The board, or at least a majority of it, were alarmed and instead proposed the establishment of a staff association, independent of any outside bodies. It was left to the staff to choose between this and a trade union, and it was agreed that representatives of the NUJ and ASTMS (Association of Scientific, Technical, and Managerial Staffs) should first address a meeting of any staff willing to attend. Not a great many turned up and when it came to a ballot, a majority opted for the independent staff association which was duly set up with elected officers. Because of the individuals who troubled to take an active part it proved to have surprisingly sharp teeth and was probably as effective as a trade union. In particular it got the management to agree to a system of grades with proper job descriptions which were linked with salary levels and offered recognized paths of promotion.

Publishing does not readily lend itself to staff training, except in the most general terms, and in any case most of the secretaries as well as editors, though not the directors, already had university degrees. It was a case of learning on the job or, as training officers put it, 'learning next to Nellie' – particularly at the meetings when printing numbers and prices were discussed and agreed. When, however, a relevant training board was set up with power to levy one per cent of the salaries bill, it was decided to appoint a training officer, Maureen Maynard (also for HEB). In addition she acted as personnel manager and dealt with staff vacancies, particularly for secretaries, most of whom were ceaselessly on the move. Directors and heads of departments contributed to an annual series of induction lectures for new staff and occasionally someone would be granted a week's paid leave to attend one of the training courses staged by the Publishers Association. In these ways most, if not all, the training levy was recouped.

There was never any shortage of applicants for jobs, the majority wanting to work in the editorial department. Publishing always attracts people with Arts degrees who don't know what to do with their lives. It still has a modicum of glamour and sounds so much more attractive than working in manufacturing industry or retailing. But publishing still has its longueurs, particularly reading proofs or ploughing through the daily 'trash pile' of unsolicited manuscripts. Literary taste and publishing 'flair', much preached by those who feel sure they possess it, are undoubtedly desirable qualities, particularly if they are combined with a hard nose for what makes commercial sense.

Doomwatching, Art, Royals, Sex, Parapsychology, Travel, Eastern Religions, Fun

Considering the size of the overall list, surprisingly few non-fiction titles of the traditional type were published during the twenty-two years (1961–83) outside the categories of biography, history, and education. The rest of the titles tended to be 'orphans' in that they do not readily coalesce into neat categories, though a few formed small subject groups. As already mentioned there was next to no original poetry. Music was neglected and the Drama Library and most other theatrical titles were published by HEB, because their editor and inspirer, Edward Thompson, was one of its founder directors (but see page 401). There were however collections of plays by Enid Bagnold, Peter Ustinov, Gore Vidal, and other regular Heinemann authors in the main company's list, and several solid theatrical biographies (see pages 382–3). There were also two important books about acting and directing by John Gielgud, a personal friend of Edward Thompson: *Stage Directions* (1963) and *Distinguished Company* (1972).

The number of books dealing with the fine arts tended to decline, though mention should be made of an authoritative, generously illustrated work *Turner* (1964) by Sir John Rothenstein and Martin Butlin. Another venture was a facsimile reproduction of *The Blake-Varley Sketchbook* (1969) containing pencil drawings by Blake and his friend John Varley – two volumes in a slipcase sold at the then high price of £15.75. Three books were published on behalf of the Royal Photographic Society. The first was a *Directory of British Photographic Collections* (1977) which gave details of over 1,500 collections under thirteen headings including their major subjects, period covered, principal photographers, etc. An exhaustive system of classification made it a useful tool for picture researchers, editors, and others. It was followed by two volumes which were finely produced to the highest standards: *The Linked Ring* (1979) by Margaret Harker, an account of the 'brotherhood' of Victorian photographers who in 1892–1910 transformed photography from a mechanistic exercise into an art form in its own right. For the other, *Treasures of The Royal Photographic Society* (1980), Sir Tom Hopkinson selected and introduced some of the finest, though often relatively unknown, examples from the RPS's archive of 25,000 photographs.

The physical appearance of Heinemann books had certainly improved very considerably and, when needed, the production department was capable of arranging for elegant designs and high-class printing. Though in fact introduced and designed by a packager, the late Charles Stainsby, this was true of the two popular volumes by Eric Trimmer: *Having a Baby* (1974) and *The First Seven Years* (1978) – the latter written in association with Elinor Goldschmied. Apart from children's books, they were a rare example of the firm initiating what was essentially a mass-market project dependent on international co-editions. The continuing demand for books on sex education was satisfied by the blockbusting *Encyclopaedia of Sexual Behaviour* (1961), edited by Albert Ellis and Albert Abarbanel with ninety-seven contributors – including some 'from the Orient' – filling two volumes of 592 pages each. In the health field there was Danaë Brook's *Naturebirth* (1976) which questioned some of the methods of 'high tech.' medicine and helped to reinforce the ideas and practices of Grantly Dick-Read (see page 386) in relation to the development of medical technology and drugs; there was also Marie Joseph's *One Step at a Time* (1976) in which she conveyed her struggle to bring up a family, though plagued with rheumatoid arthritis; Gunnar Mattsson's *The Princess* (1969) which told of his wife's leukaemia which was defied by her pregnancy; and Pat Seed's two courageous books about her struggle against cancer: *One Day at a Time* (1979) and *Another Day* (1983). A somewhat less praiseworthy contribution to physical health and well-being was Herman Taller's *Calories don't Count* (1962) which presented a 'revolutionary way in which to lose weight . . . based on years of research in laboratories and on patients.' Dr Taller's regime stemmed from a 'single principle of astounding simplicity: to grow thin we must eat fat.' It was not the calories which counted but what was in the calories. '. . . a high-fat diet reduces fat steadily and for ever'. Admittedly the book had sold over 850,000 copies in America, until its further sale was stopped by order of the Food and Drug Administration because the author was alleged to have a financial interest in the ideas advanced in the book.

New titles were still being added to the Loeb Classical Library, so that by 1983 there were no fewer than 464 volumes. E. H. Warmington retired as editor in 1974 and was succeeded by G. P. Goold. Books on science, sociology, and related disciplines were largely taken over by HEB, but a few important titles appeared on the William Heinemann Ltd list. William Sargant followed his earlier books *Battle for the Mind* (1957) and *The Unquiet Mind* (1967) with *The Mind Possessed* (1973) a study of the physiology of possession, mysticism, and faith healing, based largely on his personal observations of these phenomena in Africa and the Americas. Among much else he dealt with the drug-induced reliving of battle experiences, trance dancing of primitive tribes, the techniques of witch doctors, and the casting out of spirits. Sargant questioned the reality of such techniques and the existence of gods in so many forms. His earlier work, *The Unquiet Mind*, had been an account of his own struggle against traditional and often inhuman treatment of the mentally ill. A weighty newcomer to the list was Lancelot Hogben, the celebrated interpreter and popularizer of science and mathematics. After *The Vocabulary of Science* (1969), which amounted to a crash course in the Latin and Greek roots of technical terms, he wrote four books on the beginnings of science which appealed to adults as well as children. The first, *Beginnings and Blunders* (1970), dealt with prehistory and archaeology; the others discussed early astronomy, navigation; maps, mirrors, and mechanics; Columbus, cannon balls and the common pump. Warnings about the threat to the earth arising from man's ingenuity are no new thing and in 1962 Heinemann published *Man's Means to his End* in which Sir Robert Watson-Watt, the inventor of radar, depicted the threat that came not only from the bomb, chemical and biological warfare, but also from breakdown in communication and the destruction of social structures. Another able writer on science and society was Ritchie Calder, who joined the list with *The Inheritors* (1961), an optimistic history of how man has mastered his environment by his own ingenuity. 'The frontiers are no longer physical or climatic but those of knowledge or intention.' But Calder also warned that while the deserts might be made to bloom, man could be too clever and turn the world into a desert. Next came his *Two-Way Passage* (1964) on the importance of international economic aid in a shrinking world. In *Leonardo and the Age of the Eye* (1970) Calder explored the mind of the Renaissance inventor and investigator rather than the artist and showed how Leonardo, in contemplating the destiny of man and his own projected mechanical devices, was filled with foreboding for the future.

Contemporary society and its problems were covered by several books, among them *The Police and the Public* (1962), a symposium assembled by C. H. Rolph which demonstrated how radically the viewpoints of police and public can diverge. Then there was a book by another American president, Lyndon B. Johnson's *My Hope for America* (1964), and Geoffrey Ashe's study of *Gandhi* (1968). In his lengthy, thoroughly documented *The Reality of Monarchy* (1970) Andrew Duncan followed the Queen on all her numerous public engagements in South America as well as at home. He also talked to many people surrounding her, including Earl Mountbatten, Prince Philip, Princess Margaret, politicians, and many Court officials. The result was an objective assessment of the modern monarchical system, its cost, and its continuing and changing impact on society, written without sycophancy or knocking or Crawfie-style gossip. A very topical, scholarly, and yet provocative work was Enid Lakeman's *Power to Elect* (1982) which argued with copious supporting evidence from other countries the case for proportional representation. The concept of a shrinking globe was returned to in *A Bridge of People* (1983) in which Ben Whitaker travelled round the world to survey the first forty years of Oxfam.

A much thinned-down sports list included three successful books on improving your golf by Jack Nicklaus, starting with *Golf my Way* (1974) and two books on athletics: *Athletics – How to Win* (1963) by Peter Hildreth and *Brendan Foster* (1978) written by himself and Cliff Temple. There were also fewer books on travel, though a major new writer was discovered in Colin Thubron. Very much the lone traveller, often on foot, he not only penetrated the less obvious places and segments of life, but his scholarship and prose could be enjoyed for their own intrinsic qualities. His first four were about the Middle East: *Mirror to Damascus* (1967); *The Hills of Adonis – A Quest in Lebanon* (1968); *Jerusalem* (1969); and *Journey into Cyprus* (1975). Jan Morris summed up his talent when she wrote: 'In my opinion there is no travel writer working today in English who possesses such a remarkable combination of the observant and lyric gifts.' More recently Thubron has spent time *Among the Russians* (1983) on a 10,000 mile drive from the Baltic to the Caucasus and he has also started to write fiction, including *The God in the Mountain* (1977). He has himself contrasted the two modes: 'The mechanics of writing about something you have actually experienced is completely different. In a travel book you devote your energies to expressing that which already exists, to re-membering the quality of a city, the texture of a wall. In a novel there are no parameters. You create the wall. The same curiosity that is projected outwards in travelling is turned inwards in fiction. The one is a great delight at what is over the horizon, the other is an excavation of one's own inner guts.'[1]

Religion has only seldom appeared in Heinemann lists, but a small group of books about Eastern beliefs and practices, contemporary cults, and alternative styles of thinking made their appearance in the 1970s. The first was Anne Bancroft's well illustrated *Religions of the East* (1974) which she followed up with *Twentieth Century Mystics and Sages* (1976), who included Aldous Huxley, the Maharishi, Mother Teresa, Martin Buber, and thirteen others. In *Mindpower* (1976) Nona Coxhead surveyed current research in orthodox science as well as in parapsychology, non-medical healing, bio-feedback, and other fields in order to evaluate, in particular, altered states of consciousness. *The Thousand-Petalled Lotus* (1976) by Sangharakshita described the spiritual odyssey shortly after the war of an English Buddhist on foot with a begging bowl from the southernmost tip of India to the Himalayas. As well as conveying a profound religious experience, it gave a close-up view of small town and village life in the remoter parts of rural India. In 1982 a series of five books, edited by Brian Inglis, was issued to mark the centenary of the formation of the Society for Psychical Research. Between them they gave the history and an account of the latest developments in the main areas of research: *Hauntings and Apparitions* by Andrew MacKenzie; *Beyond the Body*, an investigation of out-of-the-body experiences by Susan Black-more; *Mediumship and Survival* by Alan Gauld; *Through the Time-Barrier*, a study of precognition and modern physics by Danah Zohar; and *A Glossary of Terms used in Parapsychology* compiled by Michael Thalbourne. The approach of all the authors was rigorous in keeping with the traditions of the SPR. As Inglis pointed out in his introduction, 'many of the most assiduous and skilled researchers have originally been prompted by *dis*belief – by a desire, say, to expose a medium as a fraud. It has to be remembered, too, that many, probably the great majority of the members have been and still are desirous of showing that paranormal manifestations are *natural* and can be explained scientifically – though admittedly not in the narrow terms of materialist science, which in any case the nuclear physicists have shown to be fallacious.'

The serious, intellectual content of most of the books in this section of the list was balanced by the occasional book which was merely funny and entertaining. Among them were Ronald Searle's sly look at and devastating drawings of America in *From Frozen North to Filthy Lucre* (1964) which had an introduction by Groucho Marx. Then there were two volumes from Stephen Potter, the inventor of gamesmanship: *Anti-Woo* (1965) which offered invaluable strategic advice on the battle of the sexes; and *The Complete Golf Gamesmanship* (1968). Lastly there were two smash-hit sellers: *The Frank Muir Book* (1976), 'his irreverent companion to social history', a quirky, skilfully annotated anthology which sold 71,842 copies. It was followed by Muir's *A Book at Bathtime* (1982), 'a social history of bathing and other bathroom activities'. It was announced that the publishers 'have co-operated by making use of new techniques and materials to produce a book which is totally new, totally washable, totally readable. At last! A book for all "wets"!'

From Nazi Genocide and Apartheid to Victorian Prostitution and the Twenties

World War II and the events leading up to and following it continued to be a source of straight books as well as of fiction. The curtain-raiser of the Spanish Civil War was the setting of Vincent Brome's *The International Brigades: Spain 1936–39* (1965). Drawn from first-hand sources, it described how men of many different nationalities were drawn to Spain to risk their lives, and in many cases lose them, in order to resist fascism. In *The Collapse of the Third Republic* (1970, published jointly with Secker & Warburg) the American journalist William Shirer examined in 1072 pages the origins of the sickness that overtook French society after the defeat of 1871 in the Franco-Prussian war; the generals' contempt for the republic and the antisemitism that culminated in the Dreyfus affair; the rise and fall of governments between the world wars, the financial scandals, and the drift through appeasement to the disastrous defeat of 1940. The bitter events were retold with immense narrative power, but the book's success was impeded by a troublesome libel action by two Frenchmen over events immediately following the collapse of France. This meant that copies had to be withdrawn temporarily from circulation, pages reprinted, that the Pan edition was delayed, a public apology made and damages paid, a proportion being paid by Heinemann.

Three thoroughly documented accounts of the lives and deaths of three top Nazis were written by Roger Manvell and Heinrich Fraenkel: *Doctor Goebbels* (1960); *Hermann Goering* (1962); *Heinrich Himmler* (1965). The same authors wrote three other accompanying volumes: *The July Plot* (1964) about the attempt on Hitler's life in 1944 and the men behind it; *The Incomparable Crime* (1967) examined the Nazi policy of genocide; and *The Canaris Conspiracy* (1969), a further study of the several other internal German plots against the Nazis as well as that of July 1944 and the terrible fate of the conspirators. Also published was Lord Russell of Liverpool's very full account of *The Trial of Adolph Eichmann* (1962), the Nazi war criminal tried and put to death in Israel. The same year saw the publication of *The Nuremberg Trials* (1962) by J. J. Heydecker and J. Leeb, who examined the argument for and against the trials and also made a dramatic reconstruction of the background and the course of the trials up to the execution of the condemned. An unusual view of the war was to be found in *Tatiana* (1976) by the White Russian Princess Tatiana Metternich. She lived with her husband, Prince Paul Metternich, in Berlin during the final collapse of the Third Reich and gave an amazing account of the air-raids and other hardships. She was privy to the 20 July plot against Hitler. In 1945 she fled across Germany in a farm cart.

Although books about Africa were now for the most part being published by HEB through the highly successful African Writers Series and other ventures, the main firm did not neglect it entirely. Hilda Bernstein in *The World that Was Ours* (1967) described how she and her husband, both courageous fighters against apartheid, had lived under extreme tension and danger – a story of arrest, house arrest, trial and eventual escape across the frontier after a period as fugitives being passed by friends from one hiding-place to another. It included a full account of the notorious Rivonia trial and excerpts from Mandela's five-hour statement from the dock. Naomi Mitchison in *Return to Fairy Hill* (1966) told what it was like to be adopted by and live as a member of the Bakgatla tribe in what was then Bechuanaland (now Botswana). Life in Rhodesia before it became independent occupied two books by Lawrence Vambe: in the first, *An Ill-Fated People* (1972) he provided the first written history – hitherto largely recorded orally – of several centuries of migration, empire building and trading in a flourishing civilization that collapsed with the arrival of the Rhodes Pioneers in 1890. He took the story up to the 1920s and followed it with *From Rhodesia to Zimbabwe* (1976), which by means of autobiographical anecdotes and social observation as well as political analysis illuminated the forces at work to turn Rhodesia into Zimbabwe. A telling picture of well-to-do whites in Kenya emerged from Errol Trzebinski's *Silence Will Speak* (1977), a study of the life of Denys Finch-Hatton and his relationship with Karen Blixen. It added valuable material to that in her own book, *Out of Africa*, and was a main source of the film of that name.

Social history at home was brilliantly and amusingly covered by three linked books from Alan Jenkins: *The Twenties* (1974); *The Thirties* (1976); *The Forties* (1976). George Rainbird Ltd, the packagers, were brought in to help with the picture research and design and the result was three sparkling, colourful quarto volumes each of which resonated with the distinctive style of its period. They were followed by *The Fifties* (1978) by Peter Lewis in a different format. Victorian attitudes to sex and the sexes were scrutinized by Eric Trudgill in *Madonnas and Magdalens* (1976). The former, the eulogized women on their pedestals, were contrasted with the latter, the vast number of prostitutes in London and other cities. He demonstrated that many present-day notions about the Victorians are misconceived and that generalizations about their notorious prudery and sexual hypocrisy can be too sweeping and do not allow for social diversity.

The very few books on general history were wide-ranging in their coverage. Jacquetta Hawkes edited a major *Atlas of Ancient Archaeology* (1974), which traced the patterns of cultures up to the start of the Classical age; as well as maps there were introductions to each geographical region and plans and reconstructions of their main sites. Tyler Whittle contributed four short books, mainly for a junior audience, on the ancient world starting with *The Birth of Greece* (1971) and ending with *Imperial Rome* (1973). He also wrote a very attractive study of *The Plant Hunters*

(1970) from the first recorded plant-seeking expedition mounted by the Queen of Egypt in 1482 BC to our own times; there were appendices on plant distribution throughout the world, on the techniques of collecting and preservation, and the principles of classification. J. M. Scott, who had also written novels for the firm including *Sea-Wyf and Biscuit* (1955), recorded two byways of history: *The Tea Story* (1964) and *The White Poppy* (1969), the latter tracing the social influence of opium and how it has affected medicine, art, and crime.

This somewhat random section concludes with two equally disparate subjects: a one-time British ambassador in Tehran, Sir Denis Wright, wrote *The English Amongst the Persians* (1977), which covered the period of the Qajar shahs, 1787–1921, when there was intense Anglo-Russian rivalry over the control of the routes leading to India. This was followed by *Twentieth Century Iran* (1977), a symposium edited by Hossein Amirsadeghi on the eve of the Shah's overthrow. The other subject was Scotland. Eric Linklater joined the list to write its turbulent history from Roman times to the present day: *The Survival of Scotland* (1968) – the kind of readable, useful, vigorous book that adds backbone to any list.

Commercial Patronage without Puffs

In previous years Heinemann had never gone out of its way to find sponsors for books, though if an organization as opposed to an author offered to take a bulk order, it was not spurned, provided the book was in all other respects worth publishing. But such bonuses happened very seldom and in the 1960s it was agreed that there would be no harm in seeking out sponsored books, subject to certain stringent conditions. There could be no question of 'vanity' publishing or being bribed by authors to take books which were otherwise not acceptable. Books which were no more than disguised puffs for a sponsor's goods or services must likewise be eschewed. Any sponsored book would need to have consider-able merit of its own and be the kind of title the firm would be glad to include in its catalogue without a subsidy. Even a company history must be readable and not merely one of those eulogizing volumes that never gets looked at, unless it be to seek one's name in the index. If there were any risk of prostituting the Windmill imprint the proposal must be rejected.

It was felt, however, that there could be a positive role for the literary patron in an age when big business patronized art exhibitions and other cultural events, not to mention the Booker Prize. Subsidies could make possible the publication of certain worthwhile but uneconomic books, particularly those with many illustrations and a small print run. The advantages to the sponsor could be very valuable, though often somewhat intangible, as is true of so much public relations, but for the publisher they were so tempting that they gave rise to much guilty hesitation. It meant publishing without any risks at all – and this conflicted with the Protestant work ethic. At worst the risks were considerably reduced. There was virtually no lock-up of capital, a major consideration when interest rates were running high as they did in the later 1970s.

With experience it was found that the most workable and acceptable arrangement to both parties was for the sponsor merely to agree to guarantee to purchase a stated number of copies at a discount starting at 40 per cent but increasing quite considerably for large quantities. (The smallest received was for 2,000 copies and the largest 104,000.) The author was mutually agreed and often suggested by Heinemann. He or she received a fee from the sponsor, who in turn received normal royalties on all copies of the trade edition sold by Heinemann. In every other respect the book was treated like any other title, being included in all catalogues, in advertisements, and in the month's dispatch of review copies. It was also handled by the overseas offices. It was only on the rare occasions when the sponsor had no outlet for his own copies that a cash subsidy was paid. Sponsorship was normally not disguised and sometimes appeared in the book's title, though it was a rule that there should be no puff for the sponsor's products in the text.

During 1961–83 nearly forty books were sponsored, and with hindsight there were at most two which might have been thought to have come close to overt advertising or given rise to any qualms in even the most delicate of publishing consciences. The types of book fell into fairly clearly defined categories. There were company or institutional histories such as *Girdle Round the Earth* (1980) by Hugh Barty-King (Cable and Wireless); *Fifty Years of Unilever* (1980) and *Metal Box* (1976), both by W. J. Reader; *The Stock Exchange Story* (1973) and for Taylor Woodrow

On Site (1971), both by Alan Jenkins; *White Collar Union* (1967) by Alex Spoor (NALGO); *University College Hospital and its Medical School* (1976) by W. R. Merrington; *Organization Woman* (1978) by Mary Stott (Townswomen's Guilds), and others.

Some of the sponsored books described the activities of an organization rather than its history, as in *Red for Remembrance* (1971) for the British Legion and for the RSPCA *Who Cares for Animals?* (1974), both by Antony Brown; *Milk to Market* (1973) by Stanley J. Baker (Milk Marketing Board); *North Sea Oil – the Great Gamble* (1966) by T. F. Gaskell and Brian Cooper (British Petroleum). Others were largely biographical, including *From Pills to Penicillin* (1976) by H. G. Lazell (Beechams) and *George Williams of the YMCA* (1973) by Clyde Binfield. Then there were books aimed at the consumer, such as *Carter's Book for Gardeners* (1970) and *The Dobies Book of Greenhouses* (1981), both by Arthur Hellyer; *Growing for the Kitchen* (1978) by D. B. Clay Jones and J. Audrey Ellison (for Dobies); and *The Independent Traveller's Handbook* (1980) edited by Ingrid Cranfield and Richard Harrington (for WEXAS).

Harder to pigeonhole were *Stone for Building* (1965) by Hugh O'Neill (British Stone Federation); *Arabian Time Machine: self-portrait of an oil state* (1978) by Helga Graham; *Honey* (1975) edited by Eva Crane; *Reuters Glossary of Economic and Financial Terms* (1983); *A–Z of Trade Unionism* (1982) by Jack Jones and Max Morris; and two books for the Wine and Spirit Education Trust: *Wine Regions of the World* (1979) and *The New Wine Companion* (1980), both by David Burroughs and Norman Bezzant.

With or without subsidies such a list needs no excuses and must by any standards be considered very presentable. Even Dr Johnson, that great despiser of patrons, would surely have approved.

EDITOR'S NOTE: John St John himself was the architect of this policy of introducing sponsored books to Heinemann during this period; all the books mentioned in this section were published under his aegis.

Churchill in Eight plus
Fifteen Volumes

What was announced proudly as 'probably the most important contract signed in the history of the firm' was the official biography of Sir Winston Churchill by his son Randolph. It was also without much doubt the most expensive as it commanded an advance of £150,000 payable in instalments, an enormous sum in those days (January 1963). It would run to five volumes with additional companion volumes of letters and other source material, making at least twelve volumes in all. Exclusive use would be made of over 300,000 of Churchill's letters, memoranda, correspondence, and other documents. The books would be serialized in the *Sunday Telegraph*; Lord Hartwell, head of the Berry family who owned the *Telegraph*, being in charge of a shell company, C. & T. Ltd (Churchill & *Telegraph*), which controlled the literary property on behalf of the Churchill family and the Chartwell Trust. The American book rights were sold to Houghton Mifflin.

The scheme was first mooted to Randolph Churchill by Frere, both being members of White's, though the story went that on one occasion Randolph, full of drink, had quarrelled with him and seized Frere by the lapels and shaken him so hard that they had to be separated. As is well known, Randolph easily took a dislike to people. He had no time for the unfortunate Dwye Evans, whom he rudely dismissed as that 'Welsh bus driver' – because of the Tilling connection. It was, however, the ex-bus company which made the biography financially possible. Because of Heinemann's still parlous state, it was felt necessary to seek additional backing from Tilling and a special loan, to be repaid over five years, was arranged to help meet the instalments on the advance. At first they had prevaricated until by chance Lionel Fraser ran into Randolph in his club.

'I got a good impression of him,' Fraser wrote to Pick. 'I feel we should go ahead, provided all conditions are satisfactory. He was restive at the delays of the lawyers in the signing of the contract, but said that a bad bargain had been done ... and that he would negotiate on a much more favourable basis elsewhere if we were hesitant. Understandably, Randolph was extremely optimistic about the book and I must say that as he described its possibilities and assessed the enormous popularity of his father, I felt we would be on a good wicket and should NOT try to wheedle out of our bargain.'[2]

Randolph's irascibility was legendary, but Heinemanns already had experience of publishing him with his life of the seventh *Lord Derby: King of Lancashire* (1959). He had written this in order to show his father that he was capable of tackling the Churchill biography. He had originally contracted to write the Derby volume for Longmans, but when it was already in galley he had a blazing row with Mark Longman, after which Frere agreed to take it on. David Machin, who was relatively new in the editorial department, was appointed his editor:

'As it was already in galley I didn't anticipate having much to do, but when I went down to Randolph's house in East Bergholt, Suffolk, to discuss the illustrations he was upset because we had been what he called "weak-kneed" about a potential libel, but which was actually a very real risk. He was furious, too, because we had sent the manuscript to the Cabinet Office to be vetted. This had been at the suggestion of one of Randolph's own advisers. He strode up and down the very long drawing-room, reading out passages from the book and declaring that the Cabinet Office would tear it to pieces. I kept very quiet sipping my orange juice – later I heard he also disapproved of this! – but over lunch at which we were joined by a woman friend his mood altered. He was charming, told good stories about his father, and treated me as an equal. But he was drinking heavily and the meal ended with a quarrel with his friend.'

There was no doubt about Randolph's ability as an author. To prepare for the biography the entire top floor at East Bergholt had been cleared to accommodate a staff of up to four research assistants, led by Michael Wolff, to whom Randolph had turned at the start of the work. Also in 'the team', as it was known, were one archivist, Eileen Harryman, and two secretaries. The documents were kept in fireproof filing cabinets housed in a muniment room built as an annexe to the house with a Chubb steel door. Each researcher was allotted a volume or part of a volume. According to Wolff, 'regular discussions are held on the progress of the research. When writing is actually done the researcher in charge of the period comes down armed with all the relevant information and documentation and sits by while Randolph dictates to a secretary.'[3]

There was no doubt that, even if he did not write every word personally, the actual writing was basically carried out by Randolph, at any rate of the first volume. When anyone suggested that it was difficult for any son to write about his father, Randolph retorted by referring to Heinemann's publication of Edmund Gosse's celebrated *Father and Son* and to Winston's life of his own father, Lord Randolph Churchill.

The first volume covered Winston's childhood and youth, but when the first fifty or so sample pages were received both Pick and Gant were very worried, because it seemed to be little more than a selection of Winston's early letters connected by brief passages of annotation.

'It fell far short of being a biography,' Pick told me. 'Randolph was then recuperating in Marrakesh following an operation, but I felt I must write to explain our concern and this upset him so much that Roland and I flew out to Marrakesh to talk it over. After a terrible flight and being held up at Tangier by a storm we were very late landing at Casablanca and by the time we had driven to Marrakesh it was one o'clock in the morning. Randolph was waiting to have dinner with us in the Mamounia Hotel. Otherwise the dining-room was empty of guests and waiters were starting to put chairs upside down on tables. Randolph, well on the way, grumpily said it must be some Arab game. Roland and I were almost too exhausted to eat and it was agreed that we should meet at eight the next morning.

'Over breakfast Randolph could not have been more charming or reasonable. After a long talk he was able to reassure us that he was working along the right lines and that as far as possible the biography would be written in Winston's own words, together with those of his contemporaries. It would be particularly wrong for him to add much about the years before he himself was born.'

'We drove up into the Atlas Mountains for lunch with of course some very heavy drinking. All went well until about five o'clock when Randolph started to bully and hector. He seemed to pick on poor Roland. "I just don't understand it, Pick, why you bring along Mr Gant. What has he written? What are his credentials to be a so-called literary director?" Roland was wonderfully calm, though he of course had published novels under his own name and was vastly experienced. As Randolph became more abusive, I complained half-jokingly of being accused of getting Roland from some literary Moss Bros, of having hired a literary director for the weekend. At this there were guffaws all round and drink overtook the rest of the conversation and he kept us up until four a.m. The next morning he was again in splendid form and very co-operative, but by five o'clock he again became difficult.' Pick added that while Randolph could be infuriating and their relationship was sometimes stormy he grew very fond of him and learned that there were also tender sides to his character. 'His intelligence was quite remarkable. I think it was this that made him feel so frustrated.'

They had little choice but to agree with Randolph's justification of his method of writing and when in 1966 the first volume, *Youth: 1874–1900* appeared, it turned out to be a major success, helped by a massive *Sunday Telegraph* advertising campaign, selling over 100,000 copies – nearly half by mail order by arrangement with W. H. Smith's, Odham's, and Leisure Arts.

The second volume, *The Young Statesman: 1901–14* appeared in 1967 with 804 pages and 56 photographs. It was again well received and among other publicity events Randolph and Pick were invited by the Swedish publishers Bonnier to Stockholm for the launching of their first volume. It was a visit Pick is never likely to forget:

'On the tarmac we were received by the head of Bonniers, the head of Scandinavian Airlines, and the editor-in-chief of the *Dagens Nyheter*. Photographs were taken, but Randolph complained that nobody had given them permission. As we drove in a three-car procession into Stockholm our hosts told him that he could choose between a simple dinner party with just the directors of Bonniers or a bigger event with thirty guests. Randolph appeared not to hear and as soon as we arrived at the Grand Hotel he merely asked for the key to his room and disappeared. Of course I explained that he was ill and tired and that they must make allowances. I even offered to stand in for him at the bigger event.

'As there was no sign of him, I had to do this, but imagine my distress when two-thirds of the way through the meal who should walk into the dining-room but Randolph with a woman friend who had come over with us. They sat at a table for two not far away, but the Swedes were polite enough to pretend not to notice, though I could scarcely swallow my food. It wasn't long before a waiter came over with a note from Randolph, telling me to hurry with my dinner. He had something important to tell me. There is nothing you can do to hasten the end of a formal Swedish dinner and it was one o'clock before I was free to go over to Randolph's table.

'After grumbling that I had taken too long, he led me up to his room. It was then that he told me that the doctors had given him only a year to live. When I made the usual protestations, he replied that he could trust his doctors and that he would pray me to do the same. We went on to discuss his successor as biographer. "I have no legal right to nominate anyone, but I am appealing to you, Charles, to reject the numerous people who will be only too anxious to step into my shoes. I want my son, Winston, to complete it. I have asked him three times but he still refuses." If he was unsuccessful in getting Winston to change his mind, then he wanted me to invite Martin Gilbert, a member of the research team for whom he had the utmost regard. Randolph planned to devote most of his remaining year to instructing him how to carry on.'

Just over a year later, in June 1968, the young Winston rang Pick to tell him that his father had died during the night. 'When we spoke again a few hours later, he declared that he had not realized the seriousness of his father's illness. On the other hand he had been planning to tell him that he would after all like to take the job on.' The decision now rested however with Lord Hartwell and the C & T company and they had someone else in mind, Hartwell's brother-in-law, the second Earl of Birkenhead, who was also an historian. 'When I went to see Hartwell and told him of Randolph's wish, he was adamant that Winston was too young and inexperienced. I then played my second card and suggested Martin Gilbert. Hartwell said he had never heard of him and so I sent round a parcel of his books. But on my next visit I noticed they were still unopened.'

There was deadlock. Heinemann was not in a position to decide on Randolph's successor and possessed only a power of veto. There was no particular objection to Birkenhead except that he had not so far been involved in the project and that at sixty he was probably too old to complete the remaining volumes. It took several months of negotiation, but with the support of Paul Brooks of Houghton Mifflin Pick eventually got his way and Martin Gilbert was appointed. As part of the compromise Birkenhead was commissioned to write a one-volume biography, for which he would have access to the Chartwell papers. (Birkenhead died before it was half done.) Winston was naturally disappointed, but he also thought highly of Gilbert, whose credentials were certainly excellent. As well as being a member of Randolph's research team, he was a Junior Fellow of Merton College and the author or editor of several books on contemporary history, including a shorter biography of Winston Churchill for schools.

The papers were moved to the safety of the Bodleian Library and Gilbert with a research team reduced by financial necessity to a single helper got down to work on the third volume. An extract from his progress report gives some idea of the complexity and extent of the work, particularly as it shows that the research was not limited to the family's papers: 'I have continued my policy of searching for unpublished material in a wide range of official and private archives. The most important new material since last August has come from the Foreign Office and War Office papers, both of which are at the Public Record Office, and from the papers of Sir Edward Grey and Lord Kitchener, also at the Public Record Office. A scrutiny of nearly four thousand files of this material has proved rich in incidents of importance for which no other source seems to survive. General Sir Edward Louis Spears has kindly given me full access to his unpublished diaries for the First World War, and Lord Birkenhead has put his father's papers at my disposal. Both these sources have proved of great value.

'I have continued to talk to those who knew Churchill during the First World War and to correspond with people with reminscences of his six months in the trenches. Two weeks ago I returned from ten days' research on the Western Front, with my secretary and research assistant, locating the places where Churchill served, first with the Grenadier Guards, and then with the 6th Royal Scots Fusiliers: Ebenezer Farm near Laventie, Laurence Farm at Ploegstreert, and the many other farms and places mentioned in his letters home. As a result of this visit we learned a great deal about the areas in which he fought, and are now able to dispel several myths. Jock McDavid, Churchill's acting adjutant in the 6th Royal Scots Fusiliers, is coming to spend a few days here in May. . . . A four-day excursion to Chartwell, Birch Grove (Harold Macmillan), Broadwater House (the young Winston), Hove (Sir Shane Leslie), Midhurst (Paul Maze), Churt (Lady Lloyd-George), Isington (Field-Marshal Montgomery), and Stype (Charles Clore) yielded much of value.'[4] It was at Stype that Gilbert located the first painting ever done by Churchill, at Hoe Farm in the summer of 1915.

Volume III: 1914–16 appeared in 1971 and the rest followed at irregular intervals, interspersed with substantial companion volumes of letters and other source material – the shortest ran to 1,300 pages: *Volume IV: 1917–22* in 1975; *Volume V: 1922–39* in 1976. The next three were given separate titles: *Finest Hour, Volume VI: 1939–41* in 1983; *Road to Victory, Volume VII: 1941–45* in 1986; and *Never Despair, Volume VIII: 1945–65* in 1988. This was three more volumes than the original plan, and far larger volumes at that (the last six averaged 1,200 pages as opposed to the 600 pages intended). Together with the companion volumes the whole project totalled 9,283,380 words on 19,866 pages. This change of scale began with the introduction of the thirty-year rule for public archives. Before then fifty years was the period of closure (so that, even in 1988, the archives of the Second World War would have been unavailable). First Randolph, and then Gilbert had access under this new rule (for which Harold Wilson was responsible) to the whole secret workings of every government department of which Churchill had been the head: a mass of material which was not part of the Churchill papers on which the biography had originally been based. Thus Heinemann became the first publishers who were in a position to make major use of this Aladdin's cave of documentation.

Judging by the reviews and the general acclaim which met each new volume, the choice of Martin Gilbert as author was more than justified. The sales varied, however, considerably from volume to volume: the highest was 125,570 copies for Volume I, followed by 61,208 for Volume II; by Volumes III, IV and V the sales had dropped to 21,797, 9,382, and 12,307 respectively. But a sales revival came with Volumes VI, VII, and VIII, which were each published more aggressively in a trade edition with a pictorial jacket and a lower price alongside the continuing uniform edition. This sales pattern was paralleled by those of the companion volumes of documents: the first two sold 11,193 and 7,602 but the next two dropped to 2,322 and 1,894 respectively. Overall, including the repayments to Tillings of the special loan, the whole project did rather more than break even; from the long-term point-of-view of the firm it was a major, unimpeachable success, the kind of venture on which a publisher's reputation is built. Within the firm much of the credit belongs to Nigel Viney and Roger Smith, Gilbert's editor. According to the *Guinness Book of Records* this is the longest biography ever published. Its quality was also of the highest.

Martin Gilbert also compiled for Heinemann *Churchill: a Photographic Portrait* (1974, reissued 1988) with 365 photographs and cartoons, nearly half of them coming from Sir Winston's own albums. Gilbert also wrote for Heinemann a life of the long-serving diplomat, *Sir Horace Rumbold* (1973); and in 1988 he undertook a final volume, a single volume life of Churchill.

Lytton Strachey, a Hoax,
and the Beatles

The Churchill biography was of course a unique publishing event, but it was by no means the only major biography to come from Heinemann during 1961–83. After fiction, biographies provided the strongest part of the list and there were a few which by any count were outstanding. Among these was the work of a young writer, Michael Holroyd, whose monumental, two-volume life and study of the writings of *Lytton Strachey* (1967–8) was at once acclaimed on all sides as displaying an extraordinary talent – as Nigel Dennis in the *Sunday Telegraph* put it: 'Never before, perhaps, has so frail and shy a talent found itself the centre of such devoted attention.'

Holroyd's only previous book was *A Critical Biography of Hugh Kingsmill* published by the Unicorn Press for the legendary Martin Secker, then approaching eighty. In a preface to a one-volume revised edition of the biography of Lytton Strachey in 1973, Holroyd described how he came to choose him as a subject and Heinemann as publisher: 'The first of sixteen publishers to whom I had submitted my Kingsmill manuscript was Heinemann. Fortunately it had fallen into the hands of James Michie, the poet and translator of the *Odes of Horace.* He had liked it, had sent for me, and gently explained that were his firm to make a practice of bringing out books about almost unknown writers by totally unknown authors, it would very soon be bankrupt. However, I might become better known myself were I to choose a less obscure subject. Had I any ideas?

'This was just the opportunity for which I was looking.' Holroyd went on to explain that in researching his book on Kingsmill he had come to examine the Strachey books in some detail. 'To my surprise I found there was no biography of him, and no wholly satisfactory critical study of his work. Here, it seemed to me, there existed the real need for a book. James Michie agreed, and a contract was drawn up in which I undertook to make a revaluation of Strachey's place as a serious historian. It would be about seventy thousand words long and take me, I estimated, at least a year.'[5]

When the year was up Holroyd had produced an almost complete manuscript but he was far from being satisfied with it. It needed at least some biographical commentary which in turn needed access to unpublished sources. The bulk of Lytton's letters, diaries, and papers were in the charge of his younger brother and literary executor, James Strachey. After a curious and tense visit to James's house to view the collection it was agreed, to Holroyd's surprise, that subject to certain conditions he could have free access to it. 'Very soon I realized that I had stumbled upon what must be reckoned one of the major caches of literary papers in modern times. Lytton was never an eloquent conversationalist and had been allergic to the telephone. But he had loved to write and to receive letters: he was one of the last great correspondents. Here, in holograph, type-script and microfilm, were nearly all his letters, preserved since the age of six, and the letters from his friends, many of them internationally famous as painters, philosophers, novelists, and economists. All this was tremendously exciting. But it posed for me equally tremendous problems – problems of how to treat this colossal quantity of published documents and of how to organize my life around it. Near the very outset I had to make the difficult decision that the subject was worth several years of uninterrupted labour and a coverage of about half-a-million words. And I had to persuade my publisher that I had made the right decision. James Michie had left Heinemann, but I was fortunate in that David Machin, his successor, was equally sympathetic.'[6]

Others in the firm were of course involved in processing a work of some two thousand pages, especially Maire Lynd, whose long reports were replete with informed notes and comments as well as wise suggestions, Roger Smith, who checked and prepared the typescript, and Herbert Rees, who read the proofs. Eventually, five years after Holroyd had first set eyes on all those papers, his work appeared in two volumes. *I. The Unknown Years, 1880–1910*, described how after an unhappy child-hood, dogged by imperfect health, the world opened up for Strachey once he reached Trinity College, Cambridge. In the company of 'The Apostles', the élite society of bright young men who included Clive Bell, Leonard Woolf, and Maynard Keynes, he became the exponent of an exotic and free-thinking way of life. After Cambridge he wrote brilliantly for *The Spectator* and found some happiness in the Bloomsbury homes of the Stephen sisters, Vanessa and Virginia. This gave Holroyd the chance to compare the legend of the Bloomsbury Group with the facts shown in Lytton's correspondence. During the years covered by the second volume, *II. The Years of Achievement, 1910–32*, the publication of *Eminent*

Victorians, *Queen Victoria*, and *Elizabeth and Essex* had made Lytton internationally famous. As the blurb claimed, 'A critical assessment of these works and others less well known shows how, to an astonishing degree, a full appreciation of them is inseparable from the emotional and psychological complexities of their author's life.' These Holroyd supplied in full measure, including the comic appearance before a conscientious objectors' tribunal; his bizarre Continental holidays; his final illnesses lovingly cared for by Dora Carrington, the Bloomsbury painter; and, above all, his intimate circle, including his unhappy infatuations with handsome young men, several of whom later became famous.

Holroyd was able to interview many of the, by then elderly, survivors. Lytton himself had once said that 'discretion is not the better part of biography' and Holroyd in what was described as the 'first post-Wolfenden biography', wrote about these affairs in detail and with candour. Needless to say, every line of the typescript was scrutinized in detail by Harold Rubinstein, one of the firm's libel advisers, and various changes were made. After publication only one person made a fuss, and the others seem to have given Holroyd full support. He states that his 'plan depended for its practicability on the co-operation of a band of mercurial octogenarians. It was for all of us a daunting prospect. "Shall I be arrested?" one of them asked after reading through my typescript. And another, with deep pathos, exclaimed: "When this comes out, they will never allow me into Lord's." In particular, it says much for the courage, candour and integrity of Duncan Grant and Roger Senhouse that, despite the shock of the unexpectedness, they did not object to what I had written. Each of them had been central to the understanding of Lytton's life.'[7]

Lytton Strachey was serialized in the *Sunday Times*, became a Penguin, and was published in America, but despite the eulogies of the reviewers, it was not an overwhelming sales success. It was followed by *Lytton Strachey by Himself* (1971), described as a self-portrait edited and introduced by Michael Holroyd, which consisted of extracts from Lytton's diaries and other writings to form 'an intermittent but not disconnected autobiography'.

Holroyd also wrote a collection of his own essays, reviews, and other items – *Unreceived Opinions* (1973) – and a novel published only in America because of threats of libel; but his next major work was another two-volume biography, this time of *Augustus John: I. The Years of Innocence* (1974); *II. The Years of Experience* (1975). Again there was the mass of detail, the re-creation of vanished artists' milieus in London and Paris which made it so much more than a biography. John's romantic physical appearance, his bravura, his friendship with gypsies, the long-suffering Dorelia, his numerous mistresses, his children, the drinking bouts, and of course the masterful handling of pencil and paint. . . . Holroyd's pains-taking, invisible craftsmanship reincarnated it all splendidly. It was also a study of a life that gradually lost momentum, whose last years were diminished by melancholy and dissatisfaction with his work, though until the end he could still produce great paintings such as his portrait of Matthew Smith.

As it happened Holroyd wrote a report on the autobiography of an earlier great professional biographer: *Hesketh Pearson by Himself* (1965), published in the year after his death. Holroyd praised 'the wonderful narrative flow, the readability and abundance of vitality. It's a splendid achievement. . . . The whole thing palpitates with life, with Hesketh's love of life. His straightforward style holds the secret of never boring the reader – it goes directly and unerringly to the salient points. But there is more to it than this. The good sense, the wit and humour are all amply displayed. . . . I do not know when the diversity of Hesketh's literary gifts have all been so well and fully exhibited.'[8] As well as his autobiography and his book about Dr Johnson and Boswell referred to earlier (page 389) Hesketh Pearson wrote five other biographical works for Heinemann: *Charles II* (1960), *The Pilgrim Daughters* (1961), *Lives of the Wits* (1962), *Henry of Navarre* (1963), and *Extraordinary People* (1965) who included Henry Fielding, Dr Erasmus Darwin, Wilkie Collins, and Frank Harris.

Among other historical biographies which call out for mention were Hubert Cole's *Josephine* (1962) and his *First Gentleman of the Bedchamber* (1965) about the eighteenth century Louis-François-Armand, maréchal duc de Richelieu, enriched with elegant correspondence with his mis-tresses. Cole also wrote a biography of *Pierre Laval* (1963) and among others a history of the resurrection men, *Things for the Surgeon* (1964). A lengthy life of *Livingstone* (1973) by Tim Jeal debunked much of the Victorian legend – he was revealed as having failed as a missionary who only made one convert; also he failed to find the source of the Nile . . . but Jeal depicted him as a 'complex and paradoxical figure: a man capable of self-sacrifice and ruthless cruelty, dogged throughout his life by self-doubts, contradictions and failure'. Jeal argued that Livingstone's greatest and hitherto unrecognized historical impact was in the field of colonial politics and that his ideals and influence were important in establishing British imperial power in Africa. Another reassessment of an archetypal Victorian was Peter Brent's *Charles Darwin* (1981), based on newly released letters and notebooks and subtitled 'A man of enlarged curiosity'. Victoria herself figured in two books: Daphne Bennett's study of the Prince Consort, *King Without a Crown* (1977), and Richard Hough's selection and commentary on the Queen's letters to her favourite grand-daughter, Princess Victoria of Hesse, *Advice to a Grand-daughter* (1975) – permission to use the letters had to be sought from Queen Elizabeth II who owned the copyright in perpetuity. Hough also wrote about his wartime RAF experiences in *One Boy's War* (1975). Thorough, competent (but in the best sense), and obvious purchases by librarians were Vincent Brome's *Freud and his Early Circle* (1965); and *The Sassoons* (1968) and *The Great Barnato* (1970) by Stanley Jackson.

To describe even a few of the *auto*biographies published in the 1960–70s, whether of famous or not quite so famous people, would make this chapter read like a reference book. The mention of half-a-dozen will have to suffice for the purpose of this chapter. Lionel Fraser might be the head of Tilling, but it is doubtful if it was merely sycophancy that induced Heinemann to take on his autobiography, *All to the Good* (1963). Nor was it as trite as it sounds, though it was a straightforward account of a banker's rise from humble origins by dint of hard work and intelligence. As a leading figure in City banking circles he was certainly in a position to give the lowdown on many big deals and mergers and bring to life the people involved. The picture which emerged, however, was of the more 'accept-able face of capitalism'. There could be no doubt about Fraser's own belief in the old-fashioned virtues of honesty, integrity, and love of one's fellows. With his passion for modern painting, his unswerving faith in Christian Science, he was by no means typical. Besides, everyone in the firm who dealt with him seems to have liked as well as respected him. The more acceptable face of politics at the top of the Liberal Party could be found in Jo Grimond's *Memoirs* (1979). From another unique vantage point the US General Douglas MacArthur was able in his *Reminiscences* (1965) to view modern conflicts, as the blurb declared, 'decade by decade, battlefield by battlefield'. Then there was Christopher Hollis looking back over seventy years of literature, of politics as a Tory MP, and Roman Catholicism in *The Seven Ages* (1974); Raymond Greene, Graham's elder brother and, as a physician, chairman of Heinemann Medical Books, in

Moments of Being (1974) writing particularly about mountaineering – he was medical member of the 1933 Everest team; and lastly an astonishingly frank book by Beverley Nichols, *Father Figure* (1972), which centred on murderous thoughts directed towards his own father.

Space must also be found to include a major biography that was commissioned by McGraw-Hill in the USA and written but which was never published or even read in manuscript! The author was Clifford Irving, for whom three earlier novels had been published, followed by *Fake* (1970), as it happened an uncannily prophetic title. It was the story of Elmyr de Hory who went to gaol after twenty-two brilliantly successful and prolific years as an art forger. A spate of Matisses, Picassos, Braques, Derains, Bonnards, Degas, Vlamincks, Modiglianis and Renoirs enabled him to live it up among the international jet set until he over-reached himself. Various charges were laid against him; the FBI were on his track; the French tried for his extradition, but he eventually was able to settle in Ibiza. The book was selling well both here and for McGraw-Hill in the States, when one of de Hory's alleged collaborators in marketing the forgeries denied that he had ever been involved and sued de Hory, Irving, McGraw-Hill and Heinemann for defamatory libel. The case dragged on for some years, during which copies had to be withdrawn from sale. Then the plaintiff was arrested and imprisoned on quite a different charge, but the matter still could not be settled.

The case was however overtaken by more dramatic events, Irving having arranged to write an autobiography of Howard Hughes, the eccentric multi-millionaire recluse. Dwye Evans felt that with such an American topic it would be better if it were handled by a New York publisher and so Irving signed a contract with McGraw-Hill on the understanding that Heinemann had the first option on the British rights. It was a great coup because the mysterious Hughes, who was noted for his earlier film making, aircraft engineering, and his design of a cantilevered brassière for Jane Russell, then lived, surrounded by a close-knit entourage, incommunicado in hotel suites and elsewhere in different cities, including a stay in London, and had not spoken publicly for fourteen years.

The project was considered so important that when the manuscript was finished McGraw-Hill said it was too valuable to send across the Atlantic, and so Charles Pick flew to New York to read it in their offices under a security guard. Pick recalls attending a dinner party on his first night together with people from the Literary Guild, Dell, and *Time-Life*, who were buying bookclub, paperback, and serial rights.

'I felt a bit out of things because I hadn't yet been able to read it. I asked some obvious questions such as how many times had Irving seen Hughes, how had he managed to get him to agree to co-operate, but somehow I always seemed to be given an evasive answer. I sensed that something fishy was going on. The next day Frank Taylor, McGraw-Hill's editor-in-chief on the trade side, gave me lunch, but in the middle he was called away to an urgent telephone call. He said it was nothing. "Just a little legal problem with this Irving book. Nothing to worry about".'

Pick never saw the manuscript because almost at once the news broke that the book was a complete literary hoax. Irving had never got in to see Hughes and the book was the product of news cuttings, invention and other people's research, skilfully and imaginatively woven together by Irving and a collaborator, Richard Suskind. Hughes himself broke his fourteen years' silence to denounce Irving and his 'autobiography':

'I don't know him. I never saw him. I had never even heard of him until a matter of days ago when this first came to my attention.'

McGraw-Hill issued a curiously cautious press statement concerning a 'possible source of the material' but added that they had informed the US Attorney and the New York District Attorney. *Time* magazine ran a story about the hoax on its stable-mate with 'Con Man of the Year' on its front cover. As the elaborate series of deceptions were unfolded it was learned that Irving had received cheques from McGraw-Hill for at least $750,000 made out in favour of Hughes but that they had been paid in fraudulently by Irving's wife into a Zurich bank account under a false name. The handwriting experts who had earlier confirmed that Howard's signature on a letter to McGraw-Hill was genuine changed their minds. It was also revealed that Irving had 'borrowed' a batch of Heinemann notepaper on a visit to Queen Street and had used it to approach various organizations connected with Hughes, each time forging Dwye Evans's signature. Detective work by Roland Gant indicated that Irving had typed the letters on Gant's secretary's typewriter during her lunch hour.

At his trial Irving pleaded guilty and was sentenced to two-and-a-half years' imprisonment. Suskind got six months. Irving's wife got two years with all but two months suspended, but she was given an additional two years by a Swiss tribunal in Zurich. Later Irving and Suskind wrote an astonishingly frank book about their complex deceptions, called *Project*

Octavio. It was published by Alison & Busby, Heinemann having had their fill of him.

Theatrical biographies still featured prominently in the list. It was no surprise that Peter Ustinov's autobiographical *Dear Me* (1977) at once became a dramatic bestseller. Claiming French and Ethiopian blood to add to his Russian origin, with a father who fought in World War I as an officer in the German army and a mother, Nadia Benois, who was a skilled painter, his account of his bizarre background went some way to explaining his extraordinary gift for mimicry and his other multiple talents. These found expression also in published plays – *Photo Finish* (1962), *Five Plays* (1965), and *The Unknown Soldier and his Wife* (1968); in novels – *The Loser* (1961), *Krumnagel* (1971); in short stories – *Add a Dash of Pity* (1959), *Frontiers of the Sea* (1966); and even in cartoons – *We Were Only Human* (1961).

Following the successful publication of the actor Robert Morley's autobiography – *Robert Morley: Responsible Gentleman* (1966) written with Sewell Stokes – his son, Sheridan Morley, wanted to write a biography of Noël Coward, his godfather. Pick was at first doubtful about such a young, inexperienced author taking on such an assignment, but he agreed provided only that Noël approved and would co-operate. Within three days Sheridan was back with a letter from Noël, saying 'I have sixty-four godchildren, but only one – you, my dear Sheridan – has suggested writing my biography. I shall be delighted.' *A Talent to Amuse* (1969) was a very careful survey of everything Coward had written or played in. It was a lasting success and was followed by Sheridan's biography of his grandmother, *Gladys Cooper* (1979). The last in the firm's numerous Noël Coward books was *Cowardy Custard* (1973), an illustrated collection, edited by John Hadfield, of his lyrics, poems, snatches of dialogue from his plays and passages of autobiography.

The title, *The Beatles: the Authorised Biography* (1968), may sound pretentious but Hunter Davies's meticulous study of the four lads from Liverpool whose 'Mersey sound' and showmanship rapidly made them millionaires was not in the least. Eschewing pseudo-sociology and attempts to explain pop culture and analyse their success, he told their story in the best documentary style of investigative journalism. He interviewed John, Paul, George, and Ringo, their families, friends and associates in depth and made good use of their verbatim speech. The young musicians emerge as real people, interesting, fallible, with their own warts and hang-ups. There are no value judgments. It wasn't intended as a book for fans, though the author was one himself, and almost certainly it must have sold to fans as well as middle-class, middle-aged book buyers and borrowers. It was just the kind of project that the revamped Heinemann sales/promotion team could get behind – 57,869 copies were sold in hardback alone.

Very different of course were J. C. Trewin's biography of *Robert Donat* (1968) and the stage biographies of *Ellen Terry* (1968) and *Sarah Siddons* (1970) by Roger Manvell, though they were equally well researched and written. The editor at Putnams who handled the American editions summed them up in a letter to Manvell: 'You have the rare ability to make these superb women emerge in all their fire, magnificence, and yet simple humanity; not only do you recreate your central character, but her whole world – the times in which she lived, the influences that affected her life.'[9] Belonging also to this sub-section is a book by an old Heinemann employee, Arnold Haskell (see pages 197–200) who had left to devote most of his life to writing about the ballet. In *Balletomane at Large* (1972), he once again combined autobiography mingled with a way of writing about dancers which was very much his own.

Several chapters in Enid Bagnold's *Autobiography* (1969) were about her plays and the theatre, but after eighty years and several different lives there was much more besides: Chelsea in 1912, where she was sculpted by Gaudier-Brzeska and drawn by Walter Sickert; seduced at eighteen by Frank Harris; her first big success as a writer with *A Diary Without Dates* (see page 159); married to the head of Reuters . . . it was a marvellous book and somehow part of the whole Heinemann story. In 1978 *The Poems of Enid Bagnold* were published in conjunction with the Whittington Press, a high quality private press started by Leslie Randle, who had been production manager at HEB for several years. He produced work of the finest standard on grained handmade paper, including books by several Heinemann authors and a second joint title by Enid Bagnold – *Letters to Frank Harris and Other Friends* (1980).

Her letters were indeed memorable, as was one written to Dwye Evans in 1964 which was as trenchant as those she wrote to his father about selling her novel to Penguin (see page 284). This one was in reply to Dwye's offer to publish her play *The Chinese Prime Minister* (1964), though he was unwilling to publish another play to accompany it in the same volume. He had told her that he thought she was being 'a tiny bit difficult'.[10] Her reply is as much about publishing as about the question at issue: 'Have I been difficult? Perhaps so. But when someone is difficult there is usually a point of view. And when the point of view has been understood the difficulty also is partly understood. Even if the point of view isn't agreed with. There *are* other things than money. Even for a *firm*. There is quality. Integrity. Skill. There is also reputation – founded on these. I have been with Heinemanns as a writer since I was 22. I am now 74. . . . It's not difficult, as you know, to fail in the theatre. One may write a good play and yet fail. . . That you should weigh whether or not you will publish a play of mine entirely on whether or not it succeeds does seem to me short-sighted. You always talk and write of money: but there are other factors in publishing. . . .'[11] This has been true at every stage of Heinemann's history.

Managerial Reshuffle:
a Cumbersome Pyramid

The move in 1979 by William Heinemann Ltd to new offices at 10 Upper Grosvenor Street, Mayfair, was widely welcomed. The spacious white stucco and porticoed early Victorian building still had the feel of a private house. There was an elegant boardroom which could be used for parties, including the celebratory opening by a very old J. B. Priestley, and the whole building suitably reflected the image most people expect of a great publisher, steeped in tradition and untarnished by too much commerce. But the move occurred at the height of the economic recession and marked the start of a period of profound, often painful changes in the company's affairs.

Before he retired as group managing director in August 1979 Alan Hill attempted to persuade Patrick Meaney (now Sir Patrick) that the separation of the group's two divisions – fiction and general on the one hand and educational on the other – should be formally recognized and the group restructured into two parallel pyramids, each reporting to Tilling and with the service company at Kingswood under their dual control. With one significant exception this plan was adopted and in fact carried to extremes with the creation of a most elaborate structure. HEB already operated its own holding company, HEB International Ltd, to control all the educational companies both overseas and in the UK, including Ginn. William Heinemann International Ltd was now set up as a sort of mirror image, to control William Heinemann Ltd itself and its overseas subsidiaries: Secker & Warburg; World's Work; Peter Davies; and Heinemann & Zsolnay.

Hill's plan would have virtually eliminated the job of group managing director, but this Tillings would not countenance. They were determined to make the group managing directorship a reality, so that its occupant would no longer concentrate on his own particular company, only paying lip service to the interests of the group as a whole. It followed that the new group managing director, Charles Pick – the obvious choice as

Hill's successor – was made chairman of both the international holding companies, but was not on the board of any of the publishing companies. Beneath him Tony Beal became managing director of HEB International and Tom Rosenthal of WH International. At the third echelon these two had a dual role as chairmen of the actual publishing companies. In practice this meant that Rosenthal was destined to become effective executive head of both Secker & Warburg *and* of William Heinemann Ltd. In addition there was a service company, headed by Peter Hart. Peter Range became group finance director. Overall was the group chairman, a Tillings official. Douglas Manser having retired a few months before Hill, the new chairman was Michael Kettle, an accountant with considerable experience as an official receiver!

This elaborate structure achieved its first objective of freeing Charles Pick to exercise unhampered control of all sections of the group, but otherwise it was soon seen to be altogether too cumbersome. In addition, many months were to elapse before Rosenthal was able to take on his new dual (actually triple) role, because a condition of his appointment insisted upon by Tilling was that he would have to surrender his twenty per cent holding of Seckers' shares, so that there could be no possible conflict of interests. Rosenthal agreed with me that this condition was perfectly reasonable:

'On the other hand a twenty per cent holding in an unquoted subsidiary of another wholly owned unquoted subsidiary was strictly non-negotiable. There was no one to whom I could sell it except them. I was then about forty-three. I had done reasonably well but I had no actual money to show for it. If I were to die in a transatlantic crash, the nice chaps in grey suits from Tillings would after a suitable interval visit my wife and say how very sorry they were, that Tom was a "wonderful publisher, in fact perhaps the best publisher in England, maybe the greatest publisher the world has ever known!" But she must understand therefore that without him at the helm Seckers was worth five shillings and ninepence and this is what they would give her for the shares.'

Rosenthal therefore held out for a sizeable sum and after seven months of bargaining he got his way and exchanged his holding for a block of Tillings shares which were of course negotiable on the Stock Exchange. They were worth many times his original investment of £15,000, but he had taken a calculated risk and it had come off; psychologically, on the other hand, his move was, as already mentioned, for him a disastrous step and, apart from the strain (which in truth he relished) of running the two companies with two different offices, he soon found himself in the midst of uncertainty and dissension at Upper Grosvenor Street. His appointment meant that the two deputy managing directors, Tim Manderson and Nigel Viney, had been passed over. Each told me that at one time or another they had been promised the succession, though latterly Viney, who for some time had handed over the day-to-day running of the production department to Peter Ireland, was considered by everyone in the office to be the front runner.

'Everyone at the top', Viney told me, 'had to nominate for Tillings whom they thought should succeed them if they were run over by the proverbial bus. I was definitely told that I would succeed Charles, but when I was invited to become a director of the ridiculous international company, I began to get the message. It was to clear the way for Tom to take over.' Viney had no alternative but to agree to join the new board, but he told me that two years later, in July 1981, he began to realize he was no longer wanted in the firm and Pick, when faced with this possibility, was unable to reassure him. Viney went. 'I was never told why. At fifty-eight, after nineteen years' service, a year's salary and a much reduced pension was not much compensation.'

The pyramidal structure allowed for a managing director to be appointed to the two main publishing firms: Hamish MacGibbon took over HEB and for William Heinemann Ltd a not unexpected choice was Nigel Hollis, who had been an excellent publicity director and was immensely popular with the staff. Unfortunately he had made a bad impression on Meaney and Kettle at Tilling and had to be content, for a probationary period, with being 'publishing director' only. This meant that all but minor decisions had to be referred to Pick and that from the outset Hollis's authority was undermined.

After Rosenthal's eventual installation at Upper Grosvenor Street he rapidly changed from being a staunch ally of Pick's and found himself in conflict with him over publishing policy and much else. The schism between the two main Heinemann companies had, however, at least been healed and Charles Pick began to take a real interest in HEB and its overseas subsidiaries, agreeing to end the dichotomy in Australia, New Zealand, and South Africa (see pages 473–6); but the discord at Upper Grosvenor Street was known throughout the book trade and *Private Eye* wrote a savage but not completely inaccurate piece, telling the world that 'the venerable publishing house of William Heinemann is once again buzzing with dissension, a familiar situation in its ninety-two year history.' It ended: 'Tillings are learning the hard way, if at other people's expense, that good managers are lousy publishers. Meanwhile, Pick and Rosenthal have no one to quarrel with except themselves. . . .'[1]

New blood was needed and a firm of head-hunters was employed to find the right person. They came up with Brian Perman, then managing director of the general trade division of Hutchinsons. He was appointed managing director as from July 1982. This made Nigel Hollis's position untenable and soon afterwards he left for another post, at David & Charles. The editorial department was also in need of regeneration, Roland Gant and others being near retirement. One of Perman's first actions was to appoint a new acquisitions editor in the person of David Godwin, hitherto at Routledge. He was young and possessed the whizzkid qualities the firm seemed to lack.

Meanwhile the group was coping with the economic recession, the high cost of money causing cash flow problems, but a tight control was maintained over printing numbers and there was a slowdown in the purchase of new books. The decline in profits which had started in 1979 continued more precipitously in 1980 when the group profit fell by £1.6 million (see Appendix E, F, and G). The major cause was the launch of the Nationwide Bookclub (see pages 544–6), but there was also an unexpected downswing in the results of World's Work (see page 576).

In 1982, however, group profits recovered to the levels established in 1978, but the sources of these profits had changed significantly. William Heinemann Ltd's profit of £744,000 was little more than half its best levels in 1978, even less considering that its figures now included a contribution from the recently acquired Made Simple series. Likewise, HEB's profits were heavily depressed by reserves against increasingly overdue Nigerian debts, but collectively HEB's overseas companies were by 1982 making a major contribution, approaching £800,000 pre-tax. Most important of all, Ginn & Co. emerged as a major force, its 1982 profit of £1.4 million being the largest individual company profit of the year. So, with Nationwide and the World's Work's losses now eliminated, the Heinemann group with a turnover of £30.47 million made a record contribution of £3.8 million to the results of their owners, Thomas Tilling. It was a far cry from when Tilling took over Heinemann with a group loss in 1962 of £87,000.

Tilling Taken Over – New Masters

Among historians there is a continuing debate over the relative import-ance of, on the one hand, economic, social, demographic, and similar seismic processes and, on the other, the role played by the individual, be it a Napoleon or a Gladstone. There are, however, other events harder to classify and ones which by their nature could not have been expected but which also have had a profound effect – e.g., the Black Death or the discovery of gold or oil. In April 1983 the main course of Heinemann's history (all allowance made for the difference in scale!) was disturbed by such an unexpected happening. Just when its major reorganization had been completed and the prospects of further expansion and profits seemed to be set fair, Tilling itself, Heinemann's support and benefactor for over twenty years, were threatened by a sudden takeover.

On 5th April a 'dawn raid' on the Stock Exchange to acquire 14.99 per cent of Tilling's equity had been unsuccessful, but it was followed by a full takeover bid, offering a share swap worth 197p. per Tillings share or a cash alternative of 185p, giving Tilling a value of £573 million. The predators were BTR Ltd, led by the energetic Sir Owen Green, a rapidly growing group originally with interests in rubber, but expanded to include everything from toy balls to submarine escape suits. The occasion for the bid was Tilling's poor 1982 results, due to a dramatic downturn in their American investments which accounted for about two-fifths of their holdings. Their other interests were healthy enough, but City analysts believed that BTR's style of management was much more aggressive and made its assets work much harder for it than did Tilling. Owen Green declared that they would put BTR management into Tilling companies to improve their performance.

Tilling put up an indignant defence. A document rushed to all shareholders declared that the bid was 'unwelcome, unacceptable, and inadequate . . . it was an opportunistic bid to get Tilling on the cheap . . . 1983 would be a year of recovery and profits will be of the order of £95 million, a new record. . . .' The chief executives of all the Tilling com-panies, including Charles Pick, were summoned by Sir Patrick Meaney to emergency meetings at Crewe House and urged to rally all possible support in the City and elsewhere. Pick, inevitably deeply concerned about what a BTR takeover could mean to Heinemann, was reported to have exerted a powerful and loyal influence.

The takeover threat raged on the financial pages of the Press, with each side taking enormous advertisements. BTR boasted the sixteenth consecutive year of growth in earnings per share and compared its growth indices from 100 (1978) to 236 (1982) with a Tilling decline from 100 (1978) to 36 (1982). Another display page compared the two conglomerates' profits – BTR: £40.1 million (1978) and £106.7 million (1982); Tillings: £64.9 million (1978) and £43.7 million (1982). Steadily BTR increased their holding of Tilling shares to 22 per cent of the total and on 17 May increased their bid to £664 million, making it the biggest takeover bid in Britain ever: 11 BTR shares were offered for every 20 Tilling shares, giving a value of about 234p, or a cash alternative raised to 225p. per share.

Tilling still fought back with giant headlines in all the national daily newspapers: 'DON'T SELL YOUR TILLING SHARES! . . . DON'T BE TAKEN IN BY BTR! . . . DON'T SELL TILLING SHORT! – DON'T SELL TILLING AT ALL!' A further defence statement claimed that 'BTR are trying to panic Tilling shareholders into selling. . . . That's because they know . . . that the companies are worth far more than the latest BTR offer. BTR know a good company when they see one. But they shouldn't profit from Tilling – YOU SHOULD!'

By mid-June it was all over. BTR's final bid proved irresistible, especially to the large institutional stockholders. The Tilling board advised shareholders who had not accepted the bid that they should now do so. Tilling who had taken over so many companies had itself been taken over, devoured by an even more powerful conglomerate. There were rumours that some of the Tilling companies, such as Cornhill Insurance and Heinemann, however successful, would be sold off because they did not fit into BTR's overall industrial pattern, but this was rapidly denied. In discussions with BTR's finance director, Norman Ireland, Charles Pick was told that BTR had no immediate plans for selling any of the companies: 'Any profitable company will always be a good fit with BTR.'

Heinemann – its authors, its staff, its values – was therefore suddenly forced to face a future with an entirely new, entirely unknown owner.

Ninety-three years after William had put up his plate in Bedford Street, it was about to enter what in every meaning of the word would be a new chapter, if not a new volume of its history.

POSTSCRIPT (1983–1989)

The nearer this account approaches the present moment, the greater the danger (as John St John himself foresaw) of its losing all semblance of history and of becoming a diary of current events. Therefore this postscript must be no more than a brief summary of the main events that have affected the firm of William Heinemann in the immediate past.

Tom Rosenthal, chairman of William Heinemann Ltd since the beginning of 1981, resigned in September 1984. Charles Pick agreed to resume the chair temporarily while a successor was recruited. The person chosen was a publisher of long editorial and managerial experience gained at Weidenfeld and Nicolson and at Pitman, Nicolas Thompson, who took up his new office in February 1985.

During the BTR era the acquisition of new books was aggressive, generally expressing a healthy balance of imagination and commercial realism. The staples of the adult fiction list remained Wilbur Smith and Catherine Cookson, soon seconded by Clare Francis and Douglas Reeman; literary fiction came from such established Heinemann authors as R. K. Narayan, Anthony Powell, Patricia Highsmith, Colin Thubron, Gore Vidal, Anita Desai, and Penelope Lively; and there were some striking new recruits such as Graham Swift, Christopher Hope, and Shena Mackay. Non-fiction continued strongly with Volume VI (*Finest Hour*) of the Churchill biography by Martin Gilbert, *The Anglo-Saxon Chronicles* by Anne Savage (a splendid illustrated compilation published with Phoebe Phillips), *Ernest Bevin as Foreign Secretary*, the third and final volume of Alan Bullock's great biography begun in the 1950s, *Secret Service* by Christopher Andrew, and other books of lasting worth.

In the summer of 1985, after two years of ownership, BTR agreed to a takeover of the Heinemann Group by the Octopus Publishing Group, founded and headed by Paul Hamlyn, with which William Heinemann had had close trading relationships for several years. Octopus paid just over £100 million in shares and BTR agreed to stay as an important

[619]

shareholder, with 35 per cent of the enlarged Octopus Group. On the completion of this agreement in September the ultimate owners of Heinemann were again publishers, for the first time since Tilling had bought a controlling interest thirty years before. Paul Hamlyn remained as chairman of the enlarged Octopus Group and Ian Irvine, formerly managing director of Fleet Holdings, owners of Express Newspapers and the Morgan Grampian Magazine Group, became chief executive in January 1986.

At the time of the takeover the main offices of the group were widely dispersed. The Octopus HQ itself, a pair of elegant Georgian houses in Grosvenor Street, Mayfair, were indeed a mere quarter of a mile from the William Heinemann offices in Upper Grosvenor Street; but Secker was in Poland Street, Soho, and HEB and Medical Books in Bedford Square, Bloomsbury. There was a strong case for rationalizing the various divisions of the group in both location and structure. The aim of Octopus management now became to re-allocate resources effectively and to establish a sense of common purpose and identity without destroying the individuality of the historic imprints. The implementation of this strategy has been a major theme of the Octopus story including William Heinemann since 1985.

One of the most urgent needs was to rationalize the warehouse and distribution system. Kingswood was antiquated, having hardly changed within the previous twenty years. Neither its service nor its computer facility had a place in group plans. In the spring of 1986 it was decided to sell Kingswood and to concentrate the group trade services at the extended and upgraded existing Hamlyn Books warehouse and distribution centre on a modern trading estate at Rushden, near Wellingborough, Northamptonshire.

One year after the move to Rushden, William Heinemann and the other trade houses, Secker & Warburg, Methuen (acquired in January 1987), Octopus Books and Hamlyn moved their London offices into superb, newly renovated Michelin House, 81 Fulham Road, South Kensington.

The same strategy of renewed publishing focus now demanded that the existing publishing divisions which had grown up over many years within the component companies of the group be grouped together according to their specializations. When Brian Perman left Heinemann in autumn 1987, Helen Fraser, previously editorial director at Collins, took over as

Publisher of William Heinemann, the trade publishing part of the group. Meanwhile the technical, adult educational and business books division, renamed Heinemann Professional Publishing and now headed by a recent recruit to the William Heinemann board, Douglas Fox, was hived off with Heinemann Medical Books (then still in Bedford Square but soon to move together with HEB to new premises in Oxford). For HEB itself the mid 1980s had marked the end of an era, with the dispersal of the team which had built it up over the previous two decades. With a fresh team under David Fothergill and Bob Osborne, a new publishing list was created, which has re-established HEB in its foremost position among educational publishers. Similarly Heinemann Young Books under Ingrid Selberg moved with William Heinemann to Michelin House, until one year later they, with Methuen's and the other children's imprints of the group, were installed at Hans Crescent, near Harrods. The Kingswood Press, the division concerned with sports and leisure-interest books, which Heinemann had launched in September 1985, was transferred to Methuen (also in Michelin House). This process of concentrating on publisher-led imprints was not only logical but also necessary to re-emphasize the publishing ethos of previous decades.

In the middle of 1987 another change of ownership occurred. On 2 July Paul Hamlyn announced that in order to ensure that the Octopus Group had the financial resources to continue to grow securely in the field of international publishing it had merged with Reed International, thus creating one of the world's largest and most powerful publishing groups. Paul Hamlyn and Ian Irvine joined the board of Reed.

The change of ownership had one very important consequence for Octopus and in particular for its trade publishing: the enforced sale of its half share in the ownership of Pan Books to the co-proprietor, Macmillan. Although this made the acquisition of rights in major new trade books more difficult, it led directly to the formation of, and significant investment in, the new, wholly Octopus-owned mass-market paperback imprint, Mandarin Books. On 14 June 1988, just a few weeks after the move to Michelin House, Paul Hamlyn announced the launch of the new imprint, to issue its first titles in spring 1989, under the direction of Richard Charkin, who was joining the Octopus board from Oxford University Press. He was subsequently promoted to executive director of the newly formed trade division of Octopus, but before delegating the direct management of the paperback arm to its former sales director, now appointed publisher, John Potter, Charkin had worked to such powerful effect that the new paperback house, with its own editorial, publicity, and sales force had convincingly come into existence under its tripartite imprint: Mandarin (popular adult fiction and non-fiction), Minerva (more literary adult fiction and special-interest books), and Mammoth (children's books). A programme of buying rights and reverting existing paperback licences for books on the Heinemann (and Secker and Methuen) backlists was set in motion and both trade and public have been made aware that Mandarin is conspicuously a major new force in paperback publishing.

It is time to take leave of Heinemann as it prepares to embark on its second century. During those ten decades obviously much has changed – the buildings, the staff, and most of the authors – but change in publishing is a condition of life. Today as at the beginning of the century authors are won and lost and publishing resources are redeployed in response to cultural and economic trends. Within William Heinemann there is a vigorous commitment to publishing good books better – witness the questing acquisitions policy, the more creative marketing of new books, and the imaginative and stylish new cover designs for the reissues of scores of classics from the backlist, Georgette Heyer, Patricia Highsmith, Alison Lurie, Maugham, Steinbeck, Josephine Tey. And the new fiction list as a whole has gained strength in depth through the acquisition or re-acquisition of such valuable authors as Douglas Adams, Jackie Collins, Jack Higgins, Ed McBain, Mickey Spillane, Morris West, and many others.

For – as at the beginning – books and authors remain at the heart of the business. In his early years as a publisher the founder had chosen as his colophon (see pp. 64–5) a W H monogram enclosed by a band bearing the motto SCRIPTA MANENT, 'written words remain'. In the final analysis nothing else can count for a publishing house and there is nothing else that it can ask to be judged by than the enduring quality of the books it has published.

Index of
Selected Authors

This consists of (a) authors whose work is discussed or mentioned in the text (shown in **heavy** type); (b) a selection of authors who have not been included together with some of their representative titles. Among those listed in (b) are some whose names are unquestionably established but whose contribution to the Heinemann list has been minimal, in some instances limited to only one title.

Abarbanel, Albert
Abraham, J. Johnston
Achebe, Chinua
Adam, Juliette L.
Adema, Pierre Marcel
   Guillame Apollinaire (1954)
Ahlberg, Janet and Allan
Ainsworth, Ruth
Aldin, Cecil
Aldington, Richard
Allen, Hervey
   The Forest and the Fort (1943)
   Bedford Village (1944)
Allingham, Margery
Ambler, Eric
Amirsadeghi, Hossein
Andersch, Alfred
Angell, Norman
Anon (W. B. C. W. Forester)
Anon (Gladys Huntington)
Apel, Willi
Archer, William
Arlen, Michael
Arlott, John
Arnold, Ralph

House with the Magnolias (1931)
   Death of a Sinner (1933)
   Jenkin's Green (1953)
Ashe, Geoffrey
Astaire, Fred
Astor, Nancy
   My Two Countries (1923)
Attlee, C. R.
Aumonier, Stacy
   Odd Fish (1923)
   The Baby Grand and Other Stories
    (1926)
   Little Windows (1931)

Baber, Douglas
Bagnold, Enid
Baker, Peter
   Time Out of Life (1961)
Baker, Stanley J.
Balestier, Charles
Bancroft, Anne
Baring, Maurice
Barnes, J.
Barty-King, Hugh
Bates, E. Sutherland

Batiffo, L.
Batty, J.
Bax, Clifford
　Inland Far (1925)
　Many a Green Isle (1927)
Baxter, Walter
Beal, A. R.
Beaverbrook, Lord
　The Divine Propagandist (1962)
Beavis, J. R. S.
Bedell Smith, General W.
　Moscow Mission, 1946–49 (1950)
Beerbohm, Max
Behan, Dominic
　Teems of Times and Happy Returns
　　(1961)
Behn, Aphra
　The Works of Aphra Behn, edited by
　　Montague Summers (1915)
Belbin, Meredith R.
Bell, Gertrude
Benét, Stephen Vincent
　John Brown's Body (1928)
　Tales before Midnight (1940)
　America (1945)
Bennett, Daphne
Bennett, N. Mick
Benson, A. C.
　Essays (1896)
　The Canon (1926)
　Cressage (1927)
Benson, E. F.
Benzoni, Juliette
Beresford, J. D.
Bernhardt, Sarah
Bernstein, Hilda
Berridge, Elizabeth
Bevan, Aneurin
Bevin, Ernest
Bezzant, Norman
Bibesco, Princess Marthe

Isvor (1924)
　Alexander of Asia (1935)
　Carlota (1956)
Billington, Rachel
　All Things Nice (1969)
　The Big Dipper (1970)
　Beautiful (1974)
　A Painted Devil (1975)
Binfield, Clyde
Bingham, Charlotte
Binyon, Laurence
Björnson, Björnstjerne
Blackmore, Susan
Blackwood, Algernon
Bland, J. O. P.
Blume, Judy
Bobarth, Berta
Bobarth, Karel
Boland, Bridget
　The Wild Geese (1938)
　Portrait of a Lady (1942)
Bolitho, William
　Twelve Against the Gods (1930)
　Camera Obscura (1931)
Bolt, Robert
Borden, Mary
Boswell, James
Botham, Mary
Bott, Alan
Boulestin, Xavier Marcel
Bowen, Marjorie
Boyesen, H. H.
Braddon, Russell
　The Year of the Angry Rabbit (1964)
　The Committal Chamber (1966)
Brady, Frank
Brailsford, H. N.
　The Broom of the War God (1898)
Brandes, Georg
Brent, Peter
Bridges, Robert

Brome, Vincent
Bronowski, Jacob
Brook, Danaë
Brophy, John
   The Front Door Key (1960)
Broster, D. K.
Brown, Antony
Buchanan, David
Buchanan, R. D.
   The Moment After (1890)
   Come Live with me and be my Love
     (1891)
Buchwald, Art
   How Much is that in Dollars? (1962)
   Is it Safe to Drink the Water? (1963)
Bullett, Gerald
Bullock, Alan
Burgess, Anthony
Burnett, Frances Hodgson
Burroughs, David
Butlin, Martin
Buttery, John A.
Byron, Lord

Caine, Hall
Calder, Ritchie
Calder, Robert L.
Caldwell, Erskine
Callow, Philip
   Common People (1958)
   Turning Point (1964)
Campbell, Michael
   Peter Perry (1956)
   The Princess in England (1964)
   Lord Dismiss Us (1967)
Cannan, Gilbert
   Peter Homunculus (1909)
   Little Brother (1912)
Canning, Victor
Capon, Paul
Capote, Truman

Carli, Enzo
   Ornaments in Gold (1958)
Carter, Angela
   Shadow Dance (1966)
   The Magic Toyshop (1967)
   Heroes and Villains (1969)
Carter, R. L.
Cartlidge, Michelle
Cate, Curtis
Cather, Willa
Catto, Max
Chamberlain, John
Chassevant, Marie
Chekhov, Anton
Chesser, Eustace
Christiansen, Arthur
   Headlines all my Life (1961)
Church, Richard
Churchill, Consuelo Spencer
   (Duchess of Marlborough)
   The Glitter and the Gold (1952)
Churchill, Randolph
Ciano, Count
Clark, K. C.
Clark, Ronald W.
   The Huxleys (1968)
Clay, Lucius
Clifford, James L.
Clouston, Brian
Coates, Eric
   Suite in Four Movements (1953)
Coccioli, Carlo
Cochran, C. B.
Cole, Hubert
Coleridge, Samuel Taylor
   Letters of S. T. Coleridge (1895)
Comley, John
   A Light in the Sky (1959)
   The Border Men (1961)
Compton-Burnett, Ivy
Comyns, Barbara

The Vet's Daughter (1959)
The Skin Chairs (1962)
A Touch of Mistletoe (1967)
Condon, Richard
Conrad, Joseph
Cook, H. Caldwell
Cookson, Catherine
Cooper, Brian
  When the Fresh Grass Grows (1955)
  The Van Langeren Girl (1960)
  Genesis 38 (1964)
Cooper, Bryan
Cooper, Susan
Cope, Jack
Coppard, Audrey
Copper, Bob
  A Song for Every Season (1975)
  Early to Rise (1976)
Coué, Emile
Couperus, Louis
Cousteau, Jacques
  World Without Sun (1965)
Coward, Noël
Cowell, Roberta
Cowles, Fleur
Coxhead, Nona
Crackanthorpe, Hubert
Cracknell, H. L.
Craig, Edward Gordon
Crane, Eva
Crane, Stephen
Cranfield, Ingrid
Creagh, Patrick
  A Row of Pharaohs (1962)
  Dragon Jack-knifed (1966)
Croce, Benedetto
Crone, Anne
  Bridie Steen (1949)
  My Heart and I (1955)
Cronin, A. J.
  A Song of Sixpence (1964)

  A Pocketful of Rye (1969)
Cuming, W.
Curie, Eve
  Journey Among Warriors (1943)
Curle, Richard
  Characters of Dostoevsky (1950)
  Joseph Conrad and his Characters
    (1957)
Cusack, Dymphna

Danby, Frank
  Pigs in Clover (1903)
  The Sphinx's Lawyer (1906)
Dane, Clemence
D'Annunzio, Gabriele
Daudet, Alphonse
David-Neel, Louise Alexandra
Davies, Hunter
Davies, Rhys
Davis, B.
Davis, Maxine
Dawson, Coningsby
Dawson Scott, C. Amy
De Bosschere, Jean
De Casalis, Jeanne de
  Mrs Feather's Diary (1936)
  Things I don't Remember (1953)
De Goncourt, Edmond and Jules
Dehan, Richard
Delafield, E. M.
Delavenay, Emile
De Maupassant, Guy
De Morgan, William
De Nerval, Gérald
Dennis, Geoffrey
De Polnay
  The World of Maurice Utrillo (1967)
De Quincey, Thomas
Desai, Anita
Dick, Bernard
Dick, Kay

Appendix A

Dickens, Monica
Dick-Read, Grantly
Dickson, Carter
Dobson, Henry Austin
   William Hogarth (1907)
Dodge, J. D.
Donaldson, Frances
Doorly, Eleanor
   The Radium Woman (1939)
Dostoevsky, Fyodor
Douglas, Norman
Dreiser, Theodore
   Sister Carrie (1901)
Drucker, Peter
Drysdale, B. I.
   Labour Troubles and Birth Control
    (1920)
Dudeney, Mrs Henry
Duhamel, Georges
   The New Book of Martyrs (1918)
Du Maurier, Daphne
Duncan, Andrew
Duncan, David
Dunsany, Lord

East, Michael
Edwards, Bernard
Eisenhower, General Dwight
Ekwensi, Cyprian
Elizabeth (Countess Russell)
   The Jasmine Farm (1934)
   All the Days of my Life (1936)
   Mr Skeffington (1940)
Ellesmere, Earl of
   Jem Carruthers (1900)
   The Standertons (1908)
Ellis, A. E.
Ellis, Albert
Ellis, Havelock
Ellison, J. Audrey
Elvin, Harold

The Incredible Mile (1970)
Enright, Elizabeth
Ervine, St John
   God's Soldier: General William Booth
    (1934)
Escoffier, Georges Auguste
Estorick, Eric
Evans, C. S.
Evans, Harold
Ewart, Gavin
   Londoners (1964)
Exupéry, A. de St-
Eyles, Leonora
   Captivity (1922)
   Hidden Lives (1922)
Eyres, D. J.

Fabricius, Johan
   A Malayan Tragedy (1942)
   Night over Java (1944)
   A Dutchman at Large (1952)
Fair, A. A.
Fauré, Gabriel
   Wanderings in Italy (1919)
Feldman, S.
Feldmann, Constantine
Ferber, Edna
Ferrero, Guglielmo
Findlater, Richard
Fingleton, Jack
Fitzpatrick, J. P.
Flatter, Richard
   Shakespeare's Producing Hand (1948)
   The Moor of Venice (1950)
Flaubert, Gustave
Flecker, James Elroy
Flynn, Errol
Ford, Ford Madox
Ford, Henry
Foreman, Russell
   Long Pig (1959)

Sandalwood Island (1961)
Forester, C. S.
Foster, Brendan
Foster, Mary
Fraenkel, Heinrich
Frankau, Pamela
Fraser, Lionel
Frederic, Harold
  In the Valley (1890)
  Gloria Mundi (1898)
  Pomps and Varieties (1913)
Freeling, Nicolas
Freud, Sigmund
Frost, David
  The Americans
Fuller, John
Funck-Brentano, F.

Gadney, Reg
  Drawn Blanc (1970)
  The Last Hours before Dawn (1975)
Gallico, Paul
Galsworthy, John
Gammon, Clive
Gardner, Erle Stanley
Garfield, Leon
Garnett, Constance
Garnett, Richard
Garstin, Crosbie
  The Owls' House (1923)
  High Noon (1923)
  West Wind (1936)
Gaskell, T. F.
Gauguin, Paul
Gauld, Alan
Ghisalberti, Mario
  Christopher Columbus (1949)
  Flying Fish (1950)
Gibbs, Philip
Gibbs-Smith, C. H.
  Operation Caroline (1953)

Gibran, Kahlil
Gielgud, John
Gilbert, Martin
Gittings, Robert
Glasgow, Ellen
  Phases of an Inferior Planet (1898)
  The Sheltered Life (1933)
Gobineau, Arthur Count
Godwin, Gail
  A Mother and Two Daughters (1982)
Goethe, Johann Wolfgang von
Goldberg, Audrey
Golding, Louis
Golon, Sergeanne
Goncharov, Ivan
Goolden, Barbara
Gordon, Rex
Gordon, Richard
Gorky, Maxim
Gosse, Edmund
Graham, R. B. Cunninghame
Grand, Sarah
Grant Richards
  Memoirs of a Misspent Youth (1932)
Graves, Charles
  Royal Riviera (1957)
Graves, Robert
Green, Julien
Greene, Graham
Greene, Raymond
Grimond, Jo
Gross, Anthony
Grossman, Alfred
  Acrobat Admits (1960)
  The Do-Gooders (1968)
Guinness, Bryan
Gyde, Arnold

Hadfield, John
Haines, Pamela
  Tea at Gunter's (1974)

Hall, Radclyffe
  Miss Ogilvy Finds Herself (1934)
  The Sixth Beatitude (1936)
Hall, Ron
Hamilton, Cosmo
  Duke's Son (1905)
Hamilton, G. Rostrevor
Hampton, J. R.
Hanneman, L. J.
Hare, Martin
  Describe a Circle (1933)
  Polonaise (1939)
Harker, Margaret
Harland, Henry
Harrington, Richard
Harris, Frank
  How to Beat the Boer (1900)
  Elder Conklin and Other Stories
   (1894)
Hašek, Jaroslav
Haskell, Arnold
Hassall, Arthur
Hassall, Christopher
  Devils' Dyke (1936)
  Penthespoon (1938)
Hastings, Patrick
Hauptmann, Gerhart
Hawkes, Jacquetta
Hearn, Lafcadio
Heaven, Constance
  The House of Kuragin (1972)
  The Astrov Inheritance (1973)
  Lord of Ravensley (1978)
Hector, Winifred
Heine, Heinrich
Hellyer, Arthur
Helmolt, H. F.
Hemming, James
Henley, W. E.
Henriques, Robert
  The Journey Home (1944)

The Commander (1967)
Heppenstall, Rayner
Herbert, A. P.
  The Man About Town (1923)
  A.P.H: his Life and Times
   (1970)
Hergesheimer, Joseph
Herling, Gustav
  A World Apart (1951)
Herzog, Arthur
  The Swarm (1974)
  Aries Rising (1981)
Hewlett, Maurice
Heydecker, J. J.
Heyer, Georgette
Hichens, Robert
Highsmith, Patricia
Hildreth, Peter
Hill, Eric
Hill, James
Hillcourt, William
  Baden-Powell (1964)
Hlasko, Marek
Hobson, Laura
Hoff, Harry
  Trina (1934)
  Three Marriages (1946)
Hogben, Lancelot
Holland, James
Hollis, Christopher
Holroyd, Michael
Holstius, Edward
  Angel's Flight (1947)
Home, W. Douglas
Hope, Laurence
Hopkins, Antony
Hopkinson, Tom
Hough, Richard
Hoult, Norah
Houlton, Mark
Housman, Laurence

The Heart of Peace and Other Poems
  (1918)
Hovey, Carl
Howard, Peter
  Fighters Forever (1941)
  Frank Buchman's Secret (1961)
Howells, W. D.
  Italian Journeys (1901)
Hoyle, Fred
Hudson, Derek
Hugo, Victor
Hume, Martin S.
Humes, H. L.
  The Underground City (1958)
Humphreys, Christmas
Hunt, Violet
Hunter, Robert
  To Save a Whale (1978)
Hutten, Baroness von
  Pam (1904)
  Mrs Drummond's Vocation (1913)
Hyde, Douglas
Hyde, H. Montgomery

Ibsen, Henrik
Ichikawa, Satomi
Irving, Clifford
Irving, Clive
Irving, Henry Brodribb
Irwin, Margaret
Ismay, Lord

Jackson, Stanley
Jaeger, H.
James, Florence
James, Henry
Jameson, Storm
Jaques, Faith
Jeal, Tim
Jenkins, Alan
Jenkins, Roy

Jesse, F. Tennyson
John, Evan
  Lofoten Letter (1941)
  The Network (1948)
  The Darkness (1955)
Johnson, Lyndon B.
Jolly, Cyril
  The Vengeance of Private Pooley
    (1956)
Jones, D. B. Clay
Jones, Jack
Jordan, Philip
  Say that she were Gone (1940)
Joseph, Marie

Karsavina, Tamara
Kaufmann, R. J.
Kaunda, Kenneth
Kavanagh, P. J.
  One and One (1959)
Keating, H. R. F.
  The Strong Man (1971)
Kennedy, Margaret
Kersh, Gerald
Kilgour, O. F. G.
King, Alexander
  Mine Enemy Grows Older (1959)
  May this House be Safe from Tigers
    (1960)
Kipling, Rudyard
Kropotkin, Prince Peter
Kucers, A.
Kyle, Elizabeth
  The Stilt Walkers (1972)
Kyle, J.

Lakeman, Enid
Landon, Christopher
  A Flag in the City (1953)
  Hornets' Nest (1956)
  Ice-Cold in Alex (1957)

Dead Men Rise Up Never (1963)
Lane, Margaret
   Faith, Hope, no Charity (1935)
   Walk into my Parlour (1941)
   A Crown of Convolvulus (1954)
Langley, Lee
   The Only Person (1972)
   From the Broken Tree (1979)
Langley Moore, Doris
   A Winter's Passion (1932)
Lassaigne, Jacques
Laver, James
   Nymph Errant (1932)
   Background for Venus (1934)
   Modesty in Dress (1969)
Lawrence, D. H.
Lazell, H. G.
Leasor, James
Le Caron, Henri
Le Carré, John
Lee, Harper
Leeb, J.
Legrand, Nadia
Lenôtre, G.
Leslie, Doris
Lewis, Caroline
Lewis, D. B. Wyndham
   King Spider (1930)
Lewis, Norman
   Every Man's Brother (1967)
Lewis, Peter
Lewis, Sinclair
   The God-Seeker (1949)
   World So Wide (1951)
Lin Yutang
Lindop, Audrey Erskine
Linford, M.
Linklater, Eric
Littmann, Enno
   *An American Archaeological
    Expedition to Syria* (1903)

Litvinoff, Emanuel
   The Lost Europeans (1960)
Lively, Penelope
Lloyd George, David
Loader, W. R.
Locke, W. J.
   At the Gate of Samaria
Lodwick, John
Lombroso, Cesare
London, Jack
Lorca, F. Garcia
Lowndes, Mrs Belloc
Ludovici, Anthony M.
   Man's Descent from the Gods (1921)
Lurie, Alison
Lytton, Lady Constance

Macarthur, Douglas
McCarthy, Mary
McCarthy, Mary Josefa
   A Nineteenth Century Childhood
    (1924)
McConkey, James
   A Journey to Sahalin (1972)
McGarry, Marguerite
MacGibbon, Jean
McGraw, Hugh
MacGregor, O. R.
Mackail, Denis
Mackenzie, Andrew
Mackenzie, Robert
Macleod, Fiona
Mac Liammóir, Micheál
   An Oscar of No Importance (1968)
Madelin, Louis
Maeterlinck, Maurice
Maillart, Ella K.
   The Cruel Way (1946)
Man, Felix H.
Mander, Raymond
Manning, Olivia

Manvell, Roger
Marchant, Catherine
Marsh, Edward
Marshall, Bruce
  Father Malachy's Miracle (1930)
  Delilah Upside Down (1941)
Masefield, John
Matthews, H. L.
  The Yoke and the Arrows (1958)
Mattsson, Gunnar
Maugham, Frederick
  The Case of Jean Calas (1928)
  At the End of the Day (1954)
Maugham, Robin
  The Servant (1964)
  The Second Window
Maugham, W. Somerset
Mauriac, François
  The Kiss to the Leper (1923)
Maurois, André
  The Country of Thirty-Six Thousand
    Wishes (1930)
Mawson, Douglas
Maxwell, Elsa
Mayo, James
  Rebound (1961)
  Asking for it (1971)
Mayreder, Rosa
Medlik, S.
Merrington, W. R.
Metchnikoff, Elie
Metternich, Princess Tatiana
Meynell, Alice
  The Work of John Sargent (1903)
Millar, George
Miller, Henry
Miller, Merle
  Reunion (1955)
  A Gay and Melancholy Sound (1961)
Millin, S. Gertrude
  Herr Witchdoctor (1941)

King of the Bastards (1950)
Mitchell, James Leslie
  Gay Hunter (1934)
Mitchell, Mary
Mitchell, P. Chalmers
Mitchell, Yvonne
  Cathy Away (1964)
  The Family (1967)
Mitchenson, Joe
Mitchison, Naomi
Mizener, Arthur
  The Far Side of Paradise (1969)
Moiseiwitsch, Maurice
  She, the Accused (1956)
Montagu, Elizabeth
Montessorri, Maria
Moore, George
Moore, Harry T.
Moore, Robert E.
Moraes, Dom
  Gone Away, an Indian Journal
    (1960)
Mordaunt, Eleanor
  A Ship of Solace (1911)
  The Garden of Contentment (1913)
Morgan, Charles
Morley, Christopher
Morley, Robert
Morley, Sheridan
Morris, Ira J.
  A Kingdom for a Song (1963)
  The Troika Belle (1967)
Morris, Max
Mortimer, John
Moult, Thomas
Muir, Frank
Murray, Gilbert

Nabokov, Vladimir
Naidu, S.
Nansen, Fridtjof

Narayan, R. K.
Nash, Paul
   Places (1922)
Newton, M.
Ngugi, James
Niall, Ian
Nichols, Beverley
Nicholson, Hubert
Nicholson, William
Nicklaus, Jack
Nkrumah, Kwame
Noble, Barbara
   The Wave Breaks (1932)
   The House Opposite (1943)
   Another Man's Life (1952)
Nordau, Max
Nott, Kathleen
   The Emperor's Clothes (1953)
   A Clean Well-Lighted Place
    (1961)
Noyce, Wilfrid

O'Brien, Kate
O'Brien, Pat
Oldenbourg, Zoë
   Catherine the Great (1965)
Oliver, Anthony
   The Victorian Staffordshire Figure
    (1971)
   The Pew Group (1980)
Ollivant, Alfred
   Devil Dare (1923)
   Owd Bob (1924)
O'Neill, Hugh
Onions, Oliver
   The Painted Face (1929)
   A Certain Man (1931)
Osbourne, Lloyd
   Love, the Fiddler (1903)
   The Adventurer (1908)
   Peril (1929)

Ouida
Oxenbury, Helen

Pargeter, Edith
Parker, Gilbert
   The Lane that had no Turning (1900)
   A Ladder of Swords (1904)
   The World for Sale (1916)
Paul, Phyllis
   Camilla (1949)
   A Cage for the Nightingale (1957)
   An Invisible Darkness (1967)
Payne, Robert
Pearson, Hesketh
Pennell, Joseph and Elizabeth
Perelman, S. J.
Pertwee, Roland
   Fish are Such Liars! (1931)
   A Prince of Romance (1932)
Perutz, Kathrin
   The Garden (1962)
   Mother is a Country (1968)
Phelan, Jim
   Turf-fire Tales (1947)
Philips, G. P. A.
Phillips, C. E. Lucas
Phillip, E.
Phillpotts, Eden
Piaget, Jean
   Play, Dreams, and Imitation in
    Childhood (1951)
Pickford, Mary
Pieńkowski, Jan
Pietrkiewicz, Jerzy
Pinero, Arthur W.
Pinto, Vivien de Sola
Piper, Anne
   The Hot Year (1955)
   Yes, Giorgio (1961)
Plath, Sylvia
Potok, Chaim

Potter, Stephen
Pottle, Frederick A.
Pound, Reginald
Powell, Anthony
Powell, E. Alexander
Powell, Violet
Powys, John Cooper
   Wood and Stone (1916)
   Ducdame (1925)
Pozner, Vladimir
   The Edge of the Sword (1943)
Pressburger, Emeric
   The Glass Pearls (1966)
Price, Willard
Priestley, J. B.
Pritchett, V. S.
   London Perceived (1965)
Puzo, Mario

Rackham, Arthur
Read, Herbert
Reader, W. J.
Redgrave, Michael
Reeves, James
Rehmann, Ruth
Reitlinger, Gerald
Renan, Ernest
Renold, Edward
Reuters
Reynolds, Quentin
   By Quentin Reynolds: an
    Autobiography (1964)
Rice, Elmer
Richardson, Henry Handel
Richet, Charles
Richter, Dr
Rickword, Edgell
   Rimbaud, the Boy and the Poet (1924)
Roberts, Cecil
   A Tale of Young Lovers (1922)
   Scissors (1923)

Indiana Jane (1929)
Robins, Elizabeth
Roberts, F. Warren
Robinson, Derek
   Goshawk Squadron (1971)
Robinson, Richard
Rockefeller, John D.
Rolland, Romain
Rolph, C. H.
Roosevelt, F. D.
Rostand, Edmond
Rostand, Jean
Rothenstein, J.
Russell of Liverpool, Lord

Sackville-West, Edward
   Piano Quintet (1925)
   The Ruin: a Gothic Novel
    (1926)
   Simpson (1931)
Sackville-West, Victoria
Saint-Denis, Michel
Saintsbury, George
   Corrected Impressions (1895)
Salinger, J. D.
Sampson, Anthony
Sangharakshita
Sargant, William
Sargent, Tom
Sassoon, Siegfried
Sassoon, Vidal
Scarfe, Francis
Schiller, Johann von
Schlesinger, Arthur M.
Scholefield, Alan
Scott, J. M.
Scott, Paul
Scott, Tom
Scurr, C.
Searle, Ronald
Seed, Pat

Selinko, Annemarie
Settle, Mary Lee
Seymour, Beatrice Kean
Shackleton, Ernest
Shakespeare, William
Sharp, Margery
  The Sun in Scorpio (1965)
  The Magical Cockatoo (1974)
  Bernard into Brave (1976)
Sharrad, L.
Shaw, E. R.
Shearing, Joseph
Sherriff, R. C.
Shiina, Rinzo
Shirer, W. L.
Shute, Nevil
Simpson, Helen
Sinclair, Upton
Sitwell, Osbert
  Three-quarter Length Portrait of
    Michael Arlen (1931)
Smith, Betty
Smith, Dodie
Smith, Paul
  The Countrywoman (1962)
Smith, Wilbur
Snow, C. P.
Somerville, Edith
  The Big House (1925)
Somerville, Edith, and Ross, Violet
    Martin
  French Leave (1928)
Sommerfield, John
Spears, General Edward
Spoor, Alec
Sprigge, Elizabeth
  1933 The Old Man Dies (1933)
  Castle in Andalusia (1935)
Spurling, Hilary
Squire, J. C.
Stacpoole, H. de Vere

The Rapin (1899)
Stapledon, Olaf
  Saints and Revolutionaries (1939)
Steed, H. Wickham
  Through Thirty Years (1924)
Steel, Flora Annie
Steffens, Lincoln
  The Shame of the Cities (1904)
Stein, Gertrude
  Everybody's Autobiography (1938)
Steinbeck, John
Stendhal
Stern, G. B.
  The Shortest Night (1931)
  Shining and Free (1935)
  Pelican Walking (1934)
Stevenson, R. L.
Stock, Ralph
Stoker, Bram
Stokes, Sewell
Stopes, Marie C.
  Plays of Old Japan (1913)
  Love Songs for Young Lovers (1939)
Storm, Lesley
Stott, Mary
Stott, Robin
Streatfeild, Noel
Stribling, Noel
  Strange Moon (1929)
  The Forge (1931)
  Unfinished Cathedral (1934)
Summerskill, Edith
  The Ignoble Art (1956)
  Letters to my Daughter (1957)
Swann, Duncan
  The Book of a Bachelor (1910)
  Molyneux of Mayfair (1914)
Swanton, E. W.
Swinburne, Algernon
Swinnerton, Frank
  The Georgian Literary Scene (1935)

Symington, T.
Symons, Arthur

Tadema, L. Alma
 The Wings of Icarus (1894)
Talbot, F. A.
Taller, Herman
Tarkington, Booth
Taylor, F. Sherwood
Taylor, Gordon Rattray
 The Angel-Makers (1958)
Temple, Cliff
Tennant, Emma
Tennyson, Alfred Browning Stanley
 A Portentous History (1911)
 Old Persia and Other Poems (1912)
Thalbourne, Michael A.
Thomas, A. Noyes
Thomas, Lowell
 Count von Luckner: the Sea Devil
  (1928)
 Raiders of the Deep (1929)
Thompson, Edward
 Night Falls on Siva's Hill (1929)
Thompson, Sylvia
Thorne, Anthony
Thubron, Colin
Thurber, James, and White, E.
 Is Sex Necessary? (1930)
Tickell, Jerrard
 See How they Run (1936)
 Silk Purse (1937)
Tolstoy, Leo
Tomkies, Mike
 Between Earth and Paradise (1981)
Tomlinson, H. M.
Toye, Francis
 For What we have Received (1950)
Trease, Geoffrey
Trebitsch, Siegfried
Tree, Herbert Beerbohm

Trefusis, Violet
 Tandem (1933)
 Hunt the Slipper (1937)
Trevelyan, G. M.
Trevor, Elleston
Trewin, J. C.
Trimmer, Eric
Trocchi, Alexander
 Young Adam (1961)
Troubridge, Lady
Trouncer, Margaret
Trudgill, Eric
Trzebinski, Errol
Tschiffely, A. F.
Turgenev, Ivan
Turley, Charles

Underhill, Evelyn
 The Grey World (1904)
 The Lost Word (1907)
Unwin, Philip
 The Publishing Unwins (1972)
Upfield, Arthur
Upward, Edward
Uris, Leon
 Mila 18 (1961)
 In the Steps of Exodus (1962)
Ustinov, Peter
Uttley, Alison

Vambe, Lawrence
Van de Wetering, Janwillem
Van de Velde, T. H.
Van Gulik, Robert Hans
Van Schendel, Arthur
Van Slyke, Helen
 A Necessary Woman (1979)
 Public Smiles, Private Tears (1982)
Vaughan, Hilda
 The Battle of the Weak (1925)
 Her Father's House (1930)

Vidal, Gore
Vidler, A. R.
Viner, G.
Vivaria, Kassandra
Voynich, E. L.

Waliszewski, Kazimierz
Wall, John
Wallington, Jeremy
Walsh, William
Ward-Thomas, P. A.
Watson-Watt, Robert
Waugh, Arthur
   Alfred, Lord Tennyson (1892)
Weddle, A. E.
Weldon, Fay
Wells, C.
Wells, H. G.
West, Morris
Weygand, General Maxime
Whibley, Charles
   A Book of Scoundrels (1897)
   Studies in Frankness (1898)
Whistler, J. McNeill
Whistler, Laurence
Whitaker, Ben
White, E. and Thurber, James
   Is Sex Necessary? (1930)
White, James Dillon
   The Edge of the Forest (1952)
   The Quiet River (1953)
   Night on the Bare Mountain (1957)
White, Percy

Corruption (1895)
Whiting, John
Whitlock, Brand
Whitman, Sidney
   The Realm of the Habsburgs (1893)
Whitney, Phyllis
   Hunters' Green (1969)
   The Turquoise Mask (1975)
   Domino (1980)
Whittle, Tyler
Williams, Emlyn
Williams, Francis
Willoughby, Major-General
   Charles
Winterbottom, Walter
Wolfe, Humbert
   Kensington Gardens in Wartime
   (1940)
Wolfe, Thomas
Wormeley, Katharine Prescott
Wragg, Arthur
   Seven Words (1939)
Wright, Denis

Yerby, Frank
Young, Francis Brett
Young, Jessica Brett

Zangwill, Israel
Zohar, Donah
Zola, Emile
Zweig, Arnold
   De Vriendt Goes Home (1934)

WILLIAM HEINEMANN LTD
Sales and Profits 1945–61

	Wm Heinemann Limited			Heinemann Holdings Ltd.
	Sales	*Subsidiary Rights*	*Profit before Tax*	*Consolidated Profit before Tax*
	£000	£000	£000	£000
1945	251	3	104	104
1946	308	6		
1947	380	10	128	170
1948	394	11	115	149
1949	418	12	126	173
1950	480	12	115	119
1951	559	18	108	137
1952	609	28	122	135
1953	596	21	89	124
1954	629	18	81	113
1955	713	22	92	138
1956	773	29	93	123
1957	782	31	64	112
1958	863	38	97	139
1959	840	45	13	77
1960	1098	55	66	144
1961	671	65	19	4

NOTE: The difference between the pre-tax profits of William Heinemann Ltd. and that of Heinemann Holdings is prima-facie attributable to profits earned by other companies in the group. Since we have no information on inter-company adjustments, subventions, etc. we have to be cautious in so interpreting these figures; but what can be reasonably inferred is that Heinemann accounted for the major part of total profit in these years.

APPENDIX C

THE HEINEMANN GROUP OF PUBLISHERS
Sales and Profits 1962–72

	HEINEMANN GROUP CONSOLIDATED ACCOUNTS				WILLIAM HEINEMANN LTD (UK only)		HEINEMANN EDUCATIONAL BOOKS LTD (UK only)		THE REST OF THE GROUP (see note below)	
	Sales	Profit before Tax	Sales Increase on Previous Year	Profit % on Sales	Sales	Profit before Tax	Sales	Profit before Tax	Sales	Profit before Tax
	£000	£000	%	%	£000	£000	£000	£000	£000	£000
1962	not given	Loss (87)	—	—	not given	Loss (66)	not given	Loss (1)	not given	Loss (20)
1963	not given	38	—	—	not given	44	not given	34	not given	Loss (40)
1964	not given	57	—	—	not given	38	not given	69	not given	Loss (50)
1965	3066	201	—	6.5	1151	111	935	78	980	12
1966	3452	256	12.6	7.4	1174	114	1079	63	1199	79
1967	3747	283	8.5	7.6	1312	132	1258	101	1177	50
1968	3871	308	3.3	8.0	1374	170	1502	106	995	32
1969	4007	471	3.5	11.8	1381	223	1661	133	965	115
1970	4619	615	15.3	13.3	1410	262	2120	204	1089	149
1971	5287	781	14.5	14.8	1498	304	1643	259	2146	218
1972	5901	879	11.6	14.9	1583	385	1815	329	2503	165

NOTE: Accounting adjustments (e.g. to eliminate profits on inter-group sales) are taken into this column although some part of such adjustments relate to the William Heinemann Ltd and Heinemann Educational Books Ltd figures. This means that the 'Rest of Group' column gives only an approximate indication of the aggregate result of the other companies; it also includes the results of the WH and HEB overseas companies.

APPENDIX D

WILLIAM HEINEMANN LTD
Sales and Profits before Tax 1962–72

	1 Sales of Books	2 Subsidiary Rights Revenue	3 Total Sales (1 + 2)	4 William Heinemann Profit before Tax	5 Pan Profits on Dividends	6 Total Profit before Tax	Ratios Sales Increase over Previous Year (Column 3)	Ratios Profit Margins (4 over)
	£000	£000	£000	£000	£000	£000	%	%
1962	682	69	751	(66)	—	Loss (66)	1.9	N/A
1963	710	72	782	44	—	44	4.1	N/A
1964	764	74	838	38	—	38	7.1	N/A
1965	1041	110	1151	111	—	111	N/A	9.6
1966	1064	110	1174	114	—	114	2.0	9.7
1967	1178	134	1312	132	—	132	11.8	10.1
1968	1252	122	1374	170	—	170	4.7	12.4
1969	1216	165	1381	163	60	223	0.1	11.8
1970	1241	169	1410	170	92	262	2.1	12.1
1971	1350	148	1498	192	112	304	6.2	12.8
1972	1410	173	1583	233	152	385	5.7	14.5

1962 } See Note
1963 }
1964 }

NOTE: The Audited Accounts for 1962–64 shows Profits before Tax but they omit Sales. The sales figures for these 3 years, as shown above, have been taken from internal accounts and are not on a comparable basis to the sales figures for 1965 onwards.

APPENDIX E

THE HEINEMANN GROUP OF PUBLISHERS
Summary of Sales and Profits 1972–82

YEAR	HEINEMANN GROUP CONSOLIDATED ACCOUNTS				WILLIAM HEINEMANN LTD (UK only)		HEINEMANN EDUCATIONAL BOOKS LTD (UK only)		THE REST OF THE GROUP (See Note 2)	
	Sales	Profit before Tax	Sales Increase on Previous Year	Profit % on Sales	Sales	Profit before Tax	Sales	Profit before Tax	Sales	Profit before Tax
	£000	£000	%	%	£000	£000	£000	£000	£000	£000
1973	7533	1164	27.7	15.5	1928	449	2117	360	3488	355
1974	8637	1242	14.7	14.4	2241	382	2407	356	3989	504
1975	10927	1802	26.5	16.5	2749	718	2997	411	5181	673
1976	14595	2887	33.6	19.8	3098	857	3562	618	7935	1412
1977	16914	3079	15.9	18.2	4141	1051	4220	818	8553	1210
1978	21388	3629	26.5[1]	17.0	4436	1200	6755	914	10197[1]	1515[1]
1979	21934	2807	2.5	12.8	4323	553	7937	641	9674	1613
1980	23613	1208	7.7	5.1	4263	342	8800	740	10550	126
1981	28148	3172	19.2	11.3	5332	667	10358	1251	12458	1254
1982	30468	3787	8.2	12.4	5913	744	9692	135	14863	2908

NOTES:
(1) Ginn Sales and Profits (£2138000 and £722.000) were consolidated in their first full year within the group, but HEB Nigeria Sales were no longer consolidated as Heinemann's shareholding in the Nigerian company was reduced to less than 50%.

(2) Accounting adjustments (e.g. to eliminate profits on inter-group sales) are taken into this column although some part of such adjustments relate to the Wm Heinemann and Heinemann Educational Books figures; so the 'Rest of the Group' column gives only an approximate indication of the aggregate results of the other companies; it also includes the results of the WH and HEB overseas companies and (after 1978) Ginn.

WILLIAM HEINEMANN LTD
Sales and Profits before Tax 1973–82

	(1) Sales of Books	(2) Subsidiary Rights Revenue	(3) Total Sales	(4) Wm Heinemann Profit before Tax	(5) Pan Profits or Dividend	(6) Total Profit Credited in Wm Heinemann Accounts	(7) Ratios Sales Increase Over Previous Year (Col. 3)	(8) Profit % of Sales (Col. 4/3)
	£000	£000	£000	£000	£000	£000	%	%
1973	1717	211	1928	268	181	449	21.8	13.9
1974	2044	197	2241	285	97	382	16.2	12.7
1975	2471	278	2749	392	326	718	22.7	14.3
1976	2748	350	3098	480	377	857	12.7	15.5
1977	3395	746	4141	692	359	1051	33.7	16.7
1978	3740	696	4436	805	395	1200	10.7	18.1
1979	3548	775	4323	367	186	553	(2.5)	8.5
1980	3473	790	4263	250	92	342	(1.4)	5.9
1981	4596	736	5332	534	133	667	25.1	10.0
1982	5028	885	5913	568	176	744	10.9	9.6

APPENDIX G

	(1) Tilling Funds Invested in the Heinemann Group (Share Capital, Reserves and Loans)	(2) External Borrowings (mainly Bank Overdrafts)	(3) Total Funds Employed at End of Each Year [(1) + (2)]	(4) Profit before Tax and before Charging Interest to Tillings	(5) Profit before all Interest	(6) Return on Tilling Investment [4 over 1]	(7) Return on Total Funds [5 over 3]
	£000	£000	£000	£000	£000	%	%
1973	3739	912	4651	1218	1315	32.5	28.2
1974	5962	1283	7245	1246	1434	20.9	19.8
1975	7069	885	7954	1922	2091	27.2	26.2
1976	8388	1305	9693	2973	3169	35.4	32.6
1977	9676	1319	10995	3207	3297	33.1	30.0
1978	11409	906	12315	3726	3807	32.7	30.9
1979	15478	1731	17209	3172	3357	20.5	19.5
1980	19362	1750	21112	1825	2127	9.4	10.1
1981	21598	1345	22943	3872	4034	17.9	17.5
1982	22986	2128	25114	4263	4426	18.5	17.6

NOTE: The return on funds calculations in columns 6 and 7 are based on capital etc. in use at the end of each year. An alternative method would be to calculate percentage profit returns on the average of capital etc. employed at the beginning and end of each year. This method would result in higher returns being shown, e.g. in 1976 the figures of 35.4% and 32.6% would become 38.5 and 35.9 respectively.

THE HEINEMANN GROUP OF PUBLISHERS LTD
Sales and Profits of Overseas Subsidiaries and Associated Companies in 1982

	Sales	Profits before Tax
	£000	£000
Subsidiaries		
Australia	2234	215
New Zealand	566	46
Asia	1756	169
East Africa	554	51
USA	325	(27)
South Africa	–*	17
Heinemann & Zsolnay	1032	50
	6467	521
Associated Companies Overseas		
Nigeria		61†
Caribbean		27
		609

* No stocks held in South Africa; books supplied to booksellers directly from the UK.
† This represents the group's 40 per cent share of the annual profit.

BIBLIOGRAPHIC REFERENCES

[Names in square brackets indicate location of the documents, but not necessarily the ownership of the copyright.]

Chapter 1

1. P. Chalmers Mitchell, quoted in *William Heinemann, a Memoir* by Frederic Whyte (Cape, London, 1928) pp. 33–4, 37–9.
2. William Heinemann, *The Bibliographer*, vol. 5, pp. 173–4.
3. Max Beerbohm, 'Whistler's Writing', in *Yet Again* (Chapman & Hall, London, 1909) pp. 112–16.
4. Robert Hichens, in reprint of *The Green Carnation* (Heinemann, London, 1894) pp. 33, 47, 49, 80, 122, 135–6.
5. Robert Hichens, *Yesterday* (Cassell, London, 1947) pp. 70–2.
6. Rudyard Kipling to William Heinemann, 10 December 1892. [Princeton]
7. ibid. 3 December 1892. [Princeton]
8. Ann Thwaite, *Edmund Gosse: a Literary Landscape, 1849–1928* (Secker & Warburg, London, 1984) pp. 1–3.
9. Edmund Gosse to William Heinemann, 12 December 1891. [Harvard]
10. ibid. 15 January 1895 [Harvard]
11. Arthur Waugh, *One Man's Road* (Chapman & Hall, London, 1931) p. 236.
12. Alfred A. Stevens, *The Recollections of a Bookman* (Witherby, London, 1933) p. 63.
13. Henry James, 'Wolcott Balestier – a Portrait', *Cosmopolitan Magazine*, May 1882 – quoted in Angus Wilson's *The Strange Ride of Rudyard Kipling* (Secker & Warburg, London, 1977) p. 161.
14. Leon Edel, 'A Young Man from the Provinces', in *Rudyard Kipling: the Man, his Work, and his World*, edited by John Gross (Weidenfeld & Nicolson, London, 1972) p. 67.
15. Arthur Waugh, op. cit. pp. 192–3.
16. ibid. pp. 196–7.
17. ibid. pp. 204–5.
18. Henry James, 'Wolcott Balestier', a biographical sketch in *The Average Woman* (Heinemann, London, 1892), pp. x–xi.

19. Edmund Gosse, *Century Magazine*, April 1892.
20. *The Times*, 22 November 1892.
21. ibid. 23 November 1892.
22. Rudyard Kipling to William Heinemann, 6 December 1892. [Princeton]

Chapter 2

 1. *Publishers' Circular*, 28 July 1894.
 2. ibid. 7 July 1894.
 3. ibid.
 4. ibid. 12 January 1895.
 5. Hall Caine to William Heinemann, 18 May 1896. [Harvard]
 6. Ernest Whyberd, 'Mr William Heinemann – Publisher', *Press and Pavilion* (Heinemann House Journal), No. 5, p. 28.
 7. Hall Caine to a Mr Goldstein, 20 December 1913. [Fales, New York]
 8. Hall Caine to William Heinemann, 11 August 1897. [Harvard]
 9. ibid. 27 August 1897. [Harvard]
10. Hall Caine to Bram Stoker, 11 October 1897. [Fales, New York]
11. Hall Caine to a Mr Goldstein, 20 December 1913. [Fales, New York]
12. George Sampson (revised by R. C. Churchill), *The Concise History of English Literature* (Cambridge University Press, Cambridge, 1970) p. 647.
13. H. G. Wells to William Heinemann, 22 May 1899. [Illinois at Urbana-Champaign]
14. ibid. 7 August 1897. [Illinois at Urbana-Champaign]
15. William Heinemann to H. G. Wells, 20 September 1909. [Illinois at Urbana-Champaign]
16. H. G. Wells to William Heinemann, 7 October 1910. [Heinemann archive]
17. Joseph Conrad, 'To my Readers in America', preface to US edition (Dodd Mead, New York, 1914) p. ix.
18. Joseph Conrad to William Blackwood, 12 April 1900, in *Joseph Conrad: Letters to William Blackwood and David S. Meldrum* edited by William Blackburn (Duke University Press, Durham, North Carolina, 1958) p. 91.
19. F. M. Hueffer (Ford Madox Ford), *Joseph Conrad: a Personal Remembrance* (Duckworth, London, 1924), p. 53.
20. Joseph Conrad to Edward Garnett, 26 March 1920, in *Letters from Conrad: 1895–1924* (Nonesuch Press, London, 1928), p. 169.
21. F. M. Hueffer, op. cit., p. 149.
22. Joseph Conrad to F. N. Doubleday, 21 December 1918, *Joseph Conrad: Life and Letters* by G. Jean-Aubry (Heinemann, London, 1927) vol. 2, p. 215.
23. William Heinemann to Henry Holt, 15 May 1897. [Heinemann archive]

24. Violet Powell, *Flora Annie Steel: Novelist of India* (Heinemann, London, 1981) p. 98.
25. ibid. pp. 115–16.
26. Flora Annie Steel, *The Garden of Fidelity* (Macmillan, London, 1929) pp. 265–6.
27. William Heinemann, 'Fashion in Fiction?', *Literature*, 23 June 1900.
28. F. M. Hueffer to D. H. Lawrence, 15 December 1909; handwritten copy made apparently by Lawrence. [Heinemann archive]
29. Violet Hunt in *D. H. Lawrence: a Composite Biography, vol. 1, 1885–1919*, edited by Edward Nehls (University of Wisconsin Press, Madison, Wisconsin, 1977) pp. 127–8.
30. D. H. Lawrence to Sydney Pawling, 11 April 1910. [Heinemann archive]
31. D. H. Lawrence to Frederick Atkinson, 14 June 1910. [Texas]
32. ibid. 24 June 1910. [Texas]
33. ibid. 15 July 1910. [Texas]
34. *Phoenix: The Posthumous Papers of D. H. Lawrence*, edited by Edward D. McDonald (Heinemann, London, 1961) p. 233.
35. ibid. p. 232.
36. D. H. Lawrence to Louie Burrows, 30 January 1911. [Nottingham, Boulton 80–2]
37. ibid.
38. D. H. Lawrence to Edward Garnett, 18 December 1911. [New York Public Library]
39. ibid.
40. D. H. Lawrence to Louie Burrows, op. cit. [Nottingham, Boulton 80–2]
41. D. H. Lawrence to Edward Garnett, 22 August 1912. [New York Public Library]
42. Walter de la Mare to Edward Garnett, 1 July 1912. [Texas]
43. William Heinemann to D. H. Lawrence, 1 July 1912. [Texas]
44. D. H. Lawrence to Edward Garnett, 3 July 1912. [New York Public Library]
45. *Phoenix*, op. cit. p. 233.
46. Compton Mackenzie, *My Life and Times: Octave Four, 1907–15* (Chatto & Windus, London, 1965) p. 191.
47. Desmond Shawe-Taylor in *The Life of George Moore* by Joseph Hone (Macmillan, London, 1936) pp. 488–9.
48. A. St John Adcock, 'William de Morgan', *The Bookman*, August 1910.
49. William de Morgan, *It Never Can Happen Again* (Heinemann, London, 1909) vol. 1, p. 289.
50. Clotilde Graves, quoted by Frederic Whyte in *William Heinemann: a Memoir* (Cape, London, 1928) p. 237.

51. Joseph Conrad to John Galsworthy, 2 October 1903, in *The Life and Letters of John Galsworthy* by H. V. Marrot (Heinemann, London, 1935) p. 159.
52. John Galsworthy to Sydney Pawling, 28 August 1911, in H. V. Marrot, ibid. p. 317.
53. John Galsworthy to William Heinemann, 17 June 1910. [Heinemann archive]
54. ibid. 16 December 1914. [Heinemann archive]
55. W. Somerset Maugham, preface to *Mrs Craddock*, written for 1928 edition.
56. Ted Morgan, *Somerset Maugham* (Cape, London, 1980) p. 89.
57. ibid. pp. 117, 124.
58. W. Somerset Maugham to William Heinemann, 4 November 1911. [Heinemann archive]
59. ibid. 6 August 1914. [Heinemann archive]
60. Desmond MacCarthy, *Pall Mall Magazine*, May 1933.

Chapter 3

1. Ernest Whyberd, 'Mr William Heinemann – Publishers', *Press and Pavilion* (Heinemann House Journal), No. 5, pp. 26–a.
2. George Jefferson, *Edward Garnett* (Cape, London, 1982) p. 75.
3. William Heinemann to Edward Garnett, 5 July 1901. [Hilton Hall – Garnett archive]
4. William Heinemann to *Publishers' Circular*, 14 November 1900.
5. William Heinemann interviewed by William Archer, *Real Conversations* (Heinemann, London, 1904), pp. 183–5.
6. Edward Craig, introduction to *An Almanac of Twelve Sports and London Types*, reprinted from the original woodblocks (Whittington Press, Andoversford, 1980).
7. Joseph Conrad, 'Stephen Crane', *London Mercury*, December 1919.
8. Henry James to William Heinemann, 26 February 1909. [Heinemann archive]
9. ibid. 2 March 1909. [Heinemann archive]
10. H. Montgomery Hyde, *Henry James at Home* (Methuen, London, 1969) p. 141.
11. Henry James to William Heinemann, 24 July 1903. [Heinemann archive]
12. ibid. 16 October 1914. [Heinemann archive]
13. Upton Sinclair, *The Autobiography of Upton Sinclair* (W. H. Allen, London, 1963) pp. 117–18, 120.
14. ibid. pp. 130–1.
15. ibid. pp. 82–3.
16. Upton Sinclair to William Heinemann, 29 July 1911. [Stanford]
17. ibid. [Stanford]

18. Jack London to William Heinemann, 22 January 1911. [Huntington]
19. ibid. 22 January 1911. [Huntington]
20. William Heinemann to Jack London, 11 February 1911. [Huntington]
21. Jack London to William Heinemann, 1 March 1911. [Huntington]
22. William Heinemann to Elizabeth Robins, date illegible. [Fales, New York]
23. ibid. 24 March 1897. [Fales, New York]
24. ibid. quoted in a letter from Elizabeth Robins to Florence Bell, 14 January 1898. [Fales, New York]
25. William Heinemann to Constance Garnett, 19 July 1911. [Hilton Hall – Garnett archive]
26. Virginia Woolf, 'Mr Bennett and Mrs Brown', *Nation*, 1 December , p. 342, 1923.
27. Constance Garnett to William Heinemann, 5 April 1915. [Heinemann archive]
28. William Heinemann to Edward Garnett, 23 December 1915. [Hilton Hall – Garnett archive]
29. Joseph Conrad to Edward Garnett, 26 October 1899, *Letters from Conrad: 1895–1924* (Nonesuch Press, London, 1928).
30. Constance Garnett, 'The Art of Translation', *Listener*, 30 January 1947.
31. Edmund Gosse to William Heinemann, 12 May 1900. Evan Charteris, *The Life and Letters of Sir Edmund Gosse* (Heinemann, London, 1931), pp. 270–1.
32. *Publishers' Circular*, 23 July 1898.
33. William Heinemann to Elizabeth Robins, 15 February 1899. [Fales, New York]
34. P. Chalmers Mitchell, quoted in *William Heinemann, a Memoir* by Frederic Whyte (Cape, London, 1928) p. 192.
35. Magda Heinemann to Elizabeth Robins, undated. [Fales, New York]
36. Gwen Gabriel, typewritten memoir of William Heinemann. [Heinemann archive]
37. William Heinemann to Elizabeth Robins, 3 October 1904. [Fales, New York]
38. *The Times*, 17 January 1905.
39. Hall Caine to Sydney Pawling, 22 February 1913. [Harvard]
40. *The Times*, 25 January 1907.
41. William Heinemann to Elizabeth Robins, 9 May 1903. [Fales, New York]

Chapter 4
1. Nigel de Grey, quoted in *William Heinemann, a Memoir* by Frederic Whyte (Cape, London, 1928) pp. 278–9.

Bibliographic References

2. Michael Holroyd, *Lytton Strachey. The Years of Achievement 1910–1932* (Heinemann, London, 1968) p. 340.
3. George H. Doran, *Chronicles of Barabbas* (Methuen, London, 1935) p. 314.
4. *Publishers' Circular*, 18 November 1893.
5. *The Times*, 10 May 1895.
6. *The Athenaeum*, 3 December 1892.
7. ibid. 11 November 1893.
8. *The Author*, 1 October 1901.
9. *Publishers' Circular*, 23 July 1910.
10. James Hepburn, *The Author's Empty Purse* (Oxford University Press, London, 1968) p. 97.
11. Elizabeth Pennell, quoted by Frederic Whyte, op. cit. pp. 207–9.
12. William Heinemann to Joseph Pennell, 9 September 1913. [Library of Congress]
13. ibid. 2 December 1913. [Library of Congress]
14. ibid. 2 October 1914. [Library of Congress]
15. ibid. 7 October 1914. [Library of Congress]
16. Joseph Pennell to William Heinemann, 4 September 1913. [Heinemann archive]
17. ibid. 16 December 1919, extract from letter in catalogue of sale of William Heinemann's correspondence at the American Art Association, New York on 13 January 1922 (Lot 356).
18. William Heinemann to Rudyard Kipling, 11 October 1897. [Heinemann archive]
19. Marguerite Steen, *William Nicholson* (Collins, London, 1943) pp. 62–3.
20. William Nicholson to William Heinemann, July (but no further date). [Heinemann archive]
21. Rudyard Kipling to William Heinemann, 3 August 1899. [Princeton]
22. Ann Thwaite, *Waiting for the Party* (Secker & Warburg, London, 1974) pp. 221–2.
23. Derek Hudson, *Arthur Rackham* (Heinemann, London, 1960) pp. 87–8.
24. *A Catalogue of the Caricatures of Max Beerbohm* (Macmillan, London, 1972).
25. Max Beerbohm, 'The Spirit of Caricature' in *A Variety of Things* (Heinemann, London, 1928) pp. 144–9.
26. Hugh Trevor-Roper, *A Hidden Life: the Enigma of Sir Edmund Backhouse* (Macmillan, London, 1976) p. 210.
27. ibid. p. 212.
28. Sir Douglas Mawson, quoted by Frederic Whyte, op. cit. p. 284.
29. Edmund Gosse to Sir Alfred Bateman, 25 September 1895. Evan Charteris, *The Life and Letters of Sir Edmund Gosse* (Heinemann, London, 1931) p. 251.

30. George Bernard Shaw to William Heinemann, 26 September 1895, extract from letter in catalogue of sale of William Heinemann's correspondence, op. cit. (Lot 366).

Chapter 5
1. Michael Meyer, *Henrik Ibsen*, vol. 3, 1883–1906 (Hart-Davis, London, 1971), p. 156.
2. ibid. pp. 165–6.
3. ibid. pp. 178–9.
4. ibid. p. 179.
5. George Bernard Shaw, *Collected Letters* (edited by Dan H. Laurence (Reinhardt, London, 1965) p. 292.
6. *Theatre and Friendship: Some Henry James Letters* with a commentary by Elizabeth Robins (Cape, London, 1922).
7. Leon Edel, *Henry James: the Treacherous Years* (Hart-Davis, London, 1969) p. 25.
8. George Bernard Shaw, op. cit. p. 397.
9. Elizabeth Robins to William Heinemann, undated. [Fales New York]
10. Holbrook Jackson, *The Eighteen Nineties* (Grant Richards, London, 1922) pp. 213–14.
11. *The Times Literary Supplement*, 25 October 1917.
12. George Bernard Shaw, quoted in *William Heinemann, a Memoir* by Frederic Whyte (Cape, London, 1928) p. 166.
13. ibid. pp. 167–8.
14. J. W. Lambert and Michael Ratcliffe, *The Bodley Head, 1887–1987* (Bodley Head, London, 1987) p. 104.
15. William Heinemann, *The First Step* (John Lane, London, 1895), prefatory note.
16. *Saturday Review*, 2 April 1898.
17. ibid. 9 April 1898.
18. Padmini Sengupta, *Sarojini Naidu* (Asia Publishing House, London, 1966) p. 28.
19. ibid. p. 29.
20. 'Nightfall in the City of Hyderabad' in *The Golden Threshold* (Heinemann, London, 1905) pp. 90–1.
21. Sarojini Naidu to William Heinemann, 27 July 1911. [Heinemann archive]
22. ibid. 17 August 1911. [Heinemann archive]
23. ibid. 14 September 1911. [Heinemann archive]
24. ibid. 5 October 1911. [Heinemann archive]
25. 'Invincible' in *The Broken Wing* (Heinemann, London, 1917) p. 36.
26. *The Garden of Kama* (Heinemann, London, 1901) p. 124.

27. Elizabeth A. Sharp, *William Sharp, a Memoir* (Heinemann, London, 1910) p. 222.
28. ibid. pp. 422–3.˙
29. John Freeman, 'Edmund Gosse', *London Mercury*, July 1923.
30. Edmund Gosse to William Heinemann, 10 August 1907. [Heinemann archive]
31. ibid. 2 September 1907. [Heinemann archive]
32. ibid. 29 August 1907. [Heinemann archive]
33. ibid. 31 October 1907. [Heinemann archive]
34. ibid. 10 November 1907. [Heinemann archive]
35. Ann Thwaite, *Edmund Gosse: a Literary Landscape, 1849–1928* (Secker & Warburg, London, 1984) pp. 436–8.
36. Holbrook Jackson, (Grant Richards, London, 1922) p. 42.
37. Richard Le Gallienne, *The Romantic '90s* (Putnam, London, 1951) p. 139.
38. Max Beerbohm to Reggie Turner, 27 July 1912, in *Letters to Reggie Turner*, edited by Rupert Hart-Davis (Hart-Davis, London, 1964) p. 216.
39. *Zuleika Dobson* (Heinemann, London, 1911) p. 17.
40. David Cecil, *Max: a Biography* (Constable, London, 1964) pp. 312–13.
41. Max Beerbohm to William Heinemann, 3 July 1911. [Heinemann archive]
42. Max Beerbohm to Sydney Pawling, 16 November 1911. [Heinemann archive]
43. Bohun Lynch 'Max Beerbohm', *London Mercury*, June 1920.

Chapter 6
1. William Heinemann interviewed by William Archer, *Real Conversations* (Heinemann, London, 1904) p. 188.
2. ibid. pp. 186–7, 189.
3. ibid. p. 178.
4. ibid. p. 179.
5. *The Athenaeum*, 3 December 1892.
6. *Publishers' Circular*, 26 June 1909.
7. John Connell, *W. E. Henley* (Constable, London, 1949) p. 316.
8. ibid. p. 300.

Chapter 7
1. *Publishers' Circular*, 5 September 1914.
2. F. Tennyson Jesse, quoted in *William Heinemann, a Memoir* by Frederic Whyte (Cape, London, 1928) p. 292.
3. Philip Gibbs, *Crowded Company* (Allan & Wingate, London, 1949) pp. 110–11.
4. *Enid Bagnold's Autobiography* (Heinemann, London, 1969) pp. 128–9.

5. Reginald Kingsford, *The Publishers' Association, 1896–1946* (Cambridge University Press, Cambridge, 1970) p. 53.
6. Edmund Gosse, *A Plea for Books* (Heinemann leaflet, 1918).
7. *Publishers' Circular*, 25 March 1916.
8. William Heinemann to Paul Warburg, 16 June 1920. [Heinemann archive]
9. Frederic Whyte, op. cit. p. 314.
10. ibid. pp. 293–4.

Chapter 8

1. F. N. Doubleday, *The Memoirs of a Publisher* (Doubleday, New York, 1972) p. 214.
2. ibid. p. 213.
3. *The Bookseller*, December 1920.
4. F. N. Doubleday, op. cit. p. 227.
5. ibid. p. 219.
6. *The Bookseller*, April 1921.
7. Edmund Gosse to C. S. Evans, 20 June 1922. [A. Dwye Evans]
8. F. N. Doubleday, op. cit. pp. 217–18.
9. Edmund Gosse to C. S. Evans, 3 April 1922. [A. Dwye Evans]
10. F. N. Doubleday, op. cit. pp. 231–2.
11. *Publishers' Circular and Booksellers' Record*, 6 January 1923.
12. F. N. Doubleday, op. cit. p. 228.
13. F. N. Doubleday to Theodore Byard, 5 July 1923. [Heinemann archive]
14. F. N. Doubleday, op. cit. p. 223.
15. ibid. p. 224.
16. ibid. pp. 224–5.
17. Arnold Gyde's private journal, 29 September 1939. [Dr Humphrey Gyde]
18. Theodore Byard to Sam Everitt, 20 April 1923. [Heinemann archive]
19. F. N. Doubleday to Theodore Byard, 25 June 1923. [Heinemann archive]
20. C. S. Evans to Eric Pinker, 17 April 1928. [Heinemann archive]
21. Theodore Byard to F. N. Doubleday, 20 April 1923. [Heinemann archive]
22. *The Times*, 2 July 1921.
23. *The Bookseller and the Stationery Trades' Journal*, May 1922.
24. C. S. Evans to F. N. Doubleday, 31 August 1923. [Heinemann archive]
25. Theodore Byard to Arthur W. Page, 27 July 1923. [Heinemann archive]
26. ibid. 9 August 1923. [Heinemann archive]
27. Extract from autobiographical notes by A. S. Frere given to Edward Thompson. [Heinemann archive]
28. Theodore Byard to F. N. Doubleday, 11 May 1923. [Heinemann archive]
29. F. N. Doubleday to Theodore Byard, 4 September 1925. [Heinemann archive]

30. Theodore Byard to F. N. Doubleday, 30 October 1923. [Heinemann archive]

31. J. Johnston Abråham, *Surgeon's Journey* (Heinemann, London, 1957) pp. 258–9.

Chapter 9

1. Grace Cranston, 'A Personal Impression of the Move from Bedford Street to Kingswood' – typewritten paper. [Heinemann archive]
2. J. Galsworthy, printed speech. [Heinemann archive]
3. Grace Cranston, op. cit.
4. Theodore Byard to F. N. Doubleday, 27 January 1928. [Princeton]
5. F. Yeats-Brown, 'The Factory of the Future', *Spectator*, 10 March 1928.
6. F. N. Doubleday to Theodore Byard, 14 April 1927 [Heinemann archive]

Chapter 10

1. Arnold L. Haskell, *In His True Centre* (A. & C. Black, London, 1951) p. 87.
2. ibid. p. 83.
3. ibid. p. 77.
4. ibid. p. 91.
5. ibid. p. 80.
6. Grace Cranston, 'Captain Arnold Gyde', *Press and Pavilion* (Heinemann House Journal), No. 6, p. 5.
7. Arnold L. Haskell, op. cit., p. 93.
8. James Whitall, *English Years* (Cape, London, 1936) pp. 313–14.
9. ibid. pp. 314–17.
10. ibid. pp. 332–3.
11. Frank Swinnerton, *Authors and the Book Trade* (Gerald Howe, London, 1931) pp. 35–6.
12. John Masefield, *C. S. Evans, 1883–1944* (Heinemann, London, 1945 – commemorative booklet printed privately) p. 2.
13. David Higham, *Literary Gent* (Cape, London, 1978) p. 170.
14. Arnold Gyde's private journal, 27 March 1939. [Dr Humphrey Gyde]
15. ibid. 17 April 1939. [Dr Humphrey Gyde]
16. ibid. p. 36, undated. [Dr Humphrey Gyde]
17. Theodore Byard to F. N. Doubleday, 31 January 1928. [Princeton]
18. Beatrice Webb, *The Diary of Beatrice Webb*, edited by Norman and Jeanne MacKenzie, vol. 4, 1924–43 (Virago, London, 1985) p. 297.
19. C. S. Evans to J. B. Priestley, 25 July 1928. [Heinemann archive]
20. J. B. Priestley to C. S. Evans, 26 July 1928. [Heinemann archive]
21. J. B. Priestley, interviewed in *Strand Magazine*, April 1930.
22. *The Times*, obituary, 16 August 1984.

Bibliographic References

23. J. B. Priestley to A. S. Frere, 7 June 1946. [Heinemann archive]
24. *Margin Released* (Heinemann, London, 1962) pp. 230–1.
25. *Midnight on the Desert* (Heinemann, London, 1937) pp. 9–10.
26. Francis Brett Young to C. S. Evans, 29 September 1937. [Heinemann archive]
27. Jessica Brett Young to C. S. Evans, 4 December 1937. [Heinemann archive]
28. *Daily Mail*, 24 February 1933.
29. *The Times*, obituary, 29 March 1954.
30. Jessica Brett Young, *Francis Brett Young* (Heinemann, London, 1962) p. 12.
31. Ted Morgan, *Somerset Maugham* (Cape, London, 1980) p. 289.
32. Compton Mackenzie, *The Author*, Spring 1954.
33. Desmond MacCarthy, 'The English Maupassant', *Nash's Pall Mall Magazine*, May 1933.
34. Ted Morgan, op. cit. pp. 384–5.
35. Rupert Hart-Davis, *Hugh Walpole* (Macmillan, London, 1952), p. 316.
36. ibid. pp. 316–17.
37. W. Somerset Maugham, *Cakes and Ale* (Heinemann, London, 1950 – new edition), introduction.
38. A. S. Frere to Hugh Walpole, 17 April 1931. [Heinemann archive]

Chapter 11
1. W. Somerset Maugham, *The Summing Up* (Heinemann, London, 1938) pp. 190–2.
2. John Galsworthy, quoted by Storm Jameson in *Journey from the North* (Collins & Harvill, London, 1969) vol. 1, p. 158.
3. Storm Jameson, ibid. p. 183.
4. Storm Jameson, 'Writers, Publishers, and Booksellers', *The Bookseller*, 6 October 1933.
5. Q. D. Leavis, *Fiction and the Reading Public* (Chatto & Windus, London, 1932) p. 34.
6. Gerald Bullett, 'Bestsellers – Why and How?', *The Bookseller*, 3 October 1934.
7. C. S. Evans to Clemence Dane, 29 June 1943. [Heinemann archive]
8. Sheridan Morley, *A Talent to Amuse* (Heinemann, London, 1969) p. 195.
9. *The Times*, obituary, 29 March 1957.
10. Edna Ferber to A. S. Frere, 14 April 1952. [Heinemann archive]
11. *Henry Handel Richardson: Some Personal Impressions* edited by Edna Purdie and Olga M. Roncoroni (Angus & Robertson, Sydney, 1957) pp. 34–5.
12. Frank Swinnerton, *The Georgian Literary Scene* (Heinemann, London, 1935) p. 305.

13. *The Times*, 19 April 1954.
14. Q. D. Leavis, op. cit. p. 7.
15. Denis Mackail, *Greenery Street* (Heinemann, London, 1925) pp. 120–2.
16. Thomas Kelly, *History of Public Libraries, 1845–1965* (Library Association, London, 1973) p. 491.
17. *The Publisher and Bookseller*, 14 October 1932.
18. John Galsworthy, *The White Monkey* (Heinemann, London, 1924) p. 202.
19. *The Publisher and Bookseller*, 21 July 1933.
20. ibid. 6 November 1935.
21. C. S. Evans to G. J. Heath, 22 November 1929. [Heinemann archive]
22. A. S. Frere-Reeves to F. N. Doubleday, 14 February 1928. [Princeton]
23. Reginald Pound, *Arnold Bennett* (Heinemann, London, 1952) pp. 340–1.
24. Q. D. Leavis, op. cit. p. 7.
25. Malcolm Bradbury, *The Social Context of Modern English Literature* (Blackwell, Oxford, 1971) p. 212.
26. C. S. Evans, letter to *The Bookseller*, 19 September 1934.
27. Arnold Gyde's private journal, undated 1937. [Dr Humphrey Gyde]
28. John Galsworthy, concluding sentence to the preface of *The Forsyte Saga* (Heinemann, London, 1922) p. ix.
29. David Higham, *Literary Gent* (Cape, London, 1978) pp. 170–1.
30. *The Times*, 1 February 1933.
31. R. H. Mottram, *For Some We Loved* (Hutchinson, London, 1956) p. 173.
32. Virginia Woolf, 'Modern Fiction' in *The Common Reader* (Hogarth Press, London, 1925) First Series, p. 187.
33. Quentin Bell, *Virginia Woolf* (Hogarth Press, London, 1972) vol. II 1912–41, p. 185.
34. John Galsworthy, 'Authors and their Public', *The Author*, April 1925.

Chapter 12

1. *The Publisher and Bookseller*, 31 October 1933.
2. Richard Aldington, *Life for Life's Sake* (Cassell, London, 1968) pp. 323–6.
3. *Selected Letters of Thomas Wolfe* edited by Elizabeth Nowell (Heinemann, London, 1958) pp. 146–7.
4. ibid. p. 148.
5. ibid. pp. 139–40.
6. *Notebooks of Thomas Wolfe* edited by Kennedy and Paschal Reeves (University of Carolina Press, Chapel Hill, 1970) vol. 2, pp. 689–90.
7. C. S. Evans, 'Cheap Books and Authors' Royalties', *The Author*, Winter 1931.
8. David Higham, *Literary Gent* (Cape, London, 1978) p. 170.
9. Nicola Beauman, *A Very Great Profession* (Virago, London, 1984) p. 5.
10. ibid. p. 3.

11. Beatrice Kean Seymour, 'Apologia as a Novelist', *The Bookseller*, 2 March 1934.
12. Kathleen O'Brien, 'The Task of the Patient Author', *The Author*, Autumn 1930.
13. Niall Rudd, *T. E. Page: Schoolmaster Extraordinary* (University of Bristol Classical Press, Bristol, 1981) p. 30.
14. ibid. p. 31.

Chapter 13
1. *The Times*, 11 April 1935.
2. ibid. 23 November 1937.
3. Allen & Overy, solicitors, to William Heinemann Ltd, 27 January 1938. [Heinemann archive]

Chapter 14
1. C. S. Evans to Enid Bagnold, 10 September 1937. [Heinemann archive]
2. ibid. 1 March 1939. [Heinemann archive]
3. Enid Bagnold to C. S. Evans, 1 January 1939. [Heinemann archive]
4. Marjorie Bowen, 'The Future of the Novel', *The Author*, April 1925.
5. Jane Aiken Hodge, *The Private World of Georgette Heyer* (Bodley Head, London, 1984) p. 29.
6. Maurice Baring, *Have you Anything to Declare?* (Heinemann, London, 1936), p. 1.
7. Hilary Spurling, *Secrets of a Woman's Heart: the Later Life of Ivy Compton-Burnett* (Hodder & Stoughton, London, 1984) p. 130.
8. Graham Greene, *A Sort of Life* (Bodley Head, London, 1971) pp. 191–2.

Chapter 15
1. Simon Raven, preface to *The Best of Gerald Kersh* (Heinemann, London, 1960) p. vii.
2. Gerald Kersh, 'In the Lyons Den', column in unknown US newspaper, 29 September 1949.
3. Arnold Gyde to Jessica Brett Young, 4 December 1944. [Heinemann archive]

Chapter 16
1. A. S. Frere to John Masefield, 2 November 1949. [Heinemann archive]
2. Thomas Kelly, *History of Public Libraries in Great Britain, 1845–1965* (Library Association, London, 1973) p. 491.
3. H. L. Hall to Louisa Callender, 13 February 1946. [Heinemann archive]
4. H. L. Hall, 'Pioneer in Australia', *Press and Pavilion* (Heinemann House Journal), No. 4., April 1957, unpaginated.

5. Memorandum by A. Dwye Evans to other board members, 30 August 1955.
6. Arnold Gyde's private journal, 23–4 June 1952. [Dr Humphrey Gyde]
7. Minutes of Heinemann Group Management Committee, 9 April 1959.

Chapter 17

1. A. S. Frere interviewed by Walter Allen, *New Statesman and Nation*, 13 April 1957.
2. J. B. Priestley to A. S. Frere, 19 April 1949. [Heinemann archive]
3. Garson Kanin, *Remembering Mr Maugham* (Hamish Hamilton, London, 1966) p. 11.
4. Georgette Heyer to Lady Avebury, 1 November 1958. [Heinemann archive]
5. Georgette Heyer to A. S. Frere, 12 October 1954. [Heinemann archive]
6. ibid. 15 March 1958. [Heinemann archive]
7. Nevil Shute, letter to *The Author*, Autumn 1951.
8. Anthony Powell, *A Question of Upbringing* (Heinemann, London, 1951) p. 2.
9. Pamela Frankau to A. S. Frere, 2 February 1948. [Heinemann archive]
10. ibid. 28 March 1949. [Heinemann archive]
11. A. S. Frere to Pamela Frankau, 22 January 1954. [Heinemann archive]
12. Fred Hoyle to Janice Robertson, 30 April 1963. [Heinemann archive]
13. Pamela Frankau to A. S. Frere, May 1958. [Heinemann archive]
14. Pamela Hansford Johnson to Olivia Manning, 24 May 1951. [Heinemann archive]
15. Olivia Manning to Louisa Callender, 26 February 1952. [Heinemann archive]
16. F. J. W. to Olivia Manning, 28 May 1952. [Heinemann archive]
17. Olivia Manning to Francis King, 2 January 1965. [Texas]
18. Rebecca West to A. S. Frere, 13 June 1952. [Heinemann archive]
19. John Lodwick to A. S. Frere, 28 January 1953. [Heinemann archive]
20. ibid. 4 April 1953 [Heinemann archive]
21. John Lodwick to Jonathan Price, 16 September 1956. [Heinemann archive]
22. John Lodwick, *The Butterfly Net* (Heinemann, London, 1954) pp. 42–3.
23. Dymphna Cusack, letter to *The Author*, Autumn 1952.
24. Erskine Caldwell, *In the Shadow of the Steeple* (Heinemann, London, 1967) p. 149.
25. Erskine Caldwell interviewed by Haskel Frankel in *Books*, 6 February 1965.
26. Frank Yerby to A. Dwye Evans, 1 June 1965. [Heinemann archive]
27. Max Catto to A. Dwye Evans, 4 June 1964. [Heinemann archive]
28. Elleston Trevor to Mark Barty-King, 29 September 1970. [Heinemann archive]

29. Eric Ambler, *Here Lies: an Autobiography* (Weidenfeld & Nicolson, London, 1985) pp. 231–2.
30. Hubert Nicholson to Roland Gant and David Machin, 27 March 1965. [Heinemann archive]
31. Roland Gant to Hubert Nicholson, 15 April 1965. [Heinemann archive]
32. A. S. Frere to Audrey Lindop, 12 April 1957. [Heinemann archive]

Chapter 18
1. Ray Bradbury, *The Social Context of Modern English Literature* (Blackwell, Oxford, 1971) pp. 222–3.
2. *The Bookseller*, 22 August 1940.
3. Memorandum from A. Dwye Evans to A. S. Frere, 28 February 1946.
4. Fredric Warburg, *All Authors are Equal* (Hutchinson, London, 1973) pp. 139–41.
5. ibid. pp. 142–3.
6. A. S. Frere interviewed by Walter Allen, *New Statesman and Nation*, 13 April 1957.
7. Minutes of Heinemann Group Management Committee, 9 April 1959.

Chapter 19
1. Henry Miller to Jonathan Price, 2 February 1958. [Heinemann archive]
2. Richard Aldington to A. S. Frere, 20 November 1945. [Heinemann archive]
3. Richard Aldington to Arnold Gyde, 21 November 1945. [Heinemann archive]
4. Richard Aldington to A. S. Frere, [Heinemann archive]
5. ibid. 12 September 1948. [Heinemann archive]
6. ibid. 21 February 1949. [Heinemann archive]
7. ibid. 16 April 1950. [Heinemann archive]
8. A. S. Frere to Richard Aldington, 21 April 1950. [Heinemann archive]
9. A. S. Frere to George Millar, 11 January 1945. [Heinemann archive]
10. W. Somerset Maugham to A. S. Frere, 22 April 1954. [Heinemann archive]
11. Sylvia Plath to her mother and Warren, 11 February 1960, *Letters Home* (Faber, London, 1975) p. 366.
12. Sylvia Plath to her mother, 25 February 1960, ibid. p. 368.
13. H. G. Wells, *Mind at the End of its Tether* (Heinemann, London, 1945) p. 17.

Chapter 20
1. *Sunday Express*, 7 March 1954.
2. Report of trial in *The Bookseller*, 23 October 1954.

Bibliographic References

---

3. ibid. 16 October 1954.
4. ibid.
5. Shorthand notes of summing-up by Mr Justice Devlin, 18 October 1954, p. 4.
6. Report of second trial in *The Bookseller*, 4 December 1954.
7. ibid.
8. *The Times*, 27 October 1954.
9. *Sunday Times*, 5 December 1954.
10. *New Statesman and Nation*, 4 December 1954.
11. *The Times*, 3 December 1954.
12. Graham Greene, 'The John Gordon Society', *Spectator*, 9 March 1956.
13. A. S. Frere to John Gordon, 8 March 1956. [Heinemann archive]

Chapter 21
1. R. O. A. Keel to Lionel Fraser, 11 December 1962. [R. O. A. Keel]
2. Lionel Fraser to Peter Ryder, 25 March 1960. [Heinemann archive]
3. Peter Ryder to Lionel Fraser, 28 March 1960. [Heinemann archive]
4. Fredric Warburg, *All Authors are Equal* (Hutchinson, London, 1973) pp. 287–8.
5. *Observer*, 26 November 1961.
6. ibid. 25 February 1962.
7. A. S. Frere interviewed by Walter Allen, *New Statesman and Nation*, 13 April 1957.
8. Graham Greene to Lionel Fraser, 1 June 1961. [Heinemann archive]
9. Graham Greene, letter to *Observer*, 26 July 1961.
10. Lionel Fraser to A. S. Frere, 19 December 1961. [Keel]
11. Graham Greene to A. S. Frere, 16 October 1962. [Keel]
12. Graham Greene, *The Comedians* (Bodley Head, London, 1966) p. 5.
13. Georgette Heyer to Derek Priestley, 9 January 1963. [Heinemann archive]
14. Jane Aiken Hodge, *The Private World of Georgette Heyer* (Bodley Head, London, 1984) p. 168.

Chapter 22
1. *Guardian*, 20 October 1961.
2. Ted Morgan, *Somerset Maugham* (Cape, London, 1980) p. 604.
3. Robin Maugham, *Somerset and all the Maughams* (Longman and Heinemann, London, 1966) p. 211.
4. Roland Gant to Olivia Manning, 12 June 1968. [Heinemann archive]
5. Frank Yerby to Roger Smith, 2 October 1979. [Heinemann archive]
6. J. W. Lambert, 'Priestley: Rebel and Squire', obituary in *Sunday Times*, 19 August 1984.
7. A. S. Byatt, 'Monica Dickens: a New Assessment', *Nova*, March 1970.

8. Monica Dickens to Charles Pick, 2 September 1966. [Heinemann archive]
9. ibid. April 1967. [Heinemann archive]
10. Monica Dickens to Roland Gant, 5 February 1968. [Heinemann archive]
11. Marcelle Bernstein, 'He has Lived Happily Ever Since', *Sunday Times* colour supplement.
12. Paul Gallico to Charles Pick, 8 October 1962. [Heinemann archive]
13. ibid. 22 January 1969. [Heinemann archive]
14. ibid. 24 June 1974. [Heinemann archive]
15. A. Dwye Evans, letter to *The Times Literary Supplement*, 13 September 1963.

Chapter 23
1. Michael Johnston, *Book Publishing* (Jordan, London, 1983) p. 2.
2. Peter H. Mann, *Book Publishing, Book Selling, and Book Reading* (Book Marketing Council, London, 1979), p. 7.
3. *Public Library Book Spending in the United Kingdom* (Book Trust, London, 1986), pp. 2–4.
4. Peter H. Mann, op. cit., p. 17.
5. Lionel Foot, 'A Day in the Life of a Country Traveller', *Hot off the Press* (Heinemann House Journal), No. 2, June 1982.
6. Ian Norrie, *Mumby's Publishing and Bookselling* (Bell & Hyman, London, 1982) pp. 101–2.

Chapter 24
1. Morris West to A. Dwye Evans, 12 December 1961. [Heinemann archive]
2. Morris West, quoted by Brian Johns in 'Second Calling: the Formative Years of Morris West', *Nation*, Sydney, 10 August 1963.
3. C. P. Snow, introducing *A Small Town in Germany* to members of the American Book of the Month Club, 9 July 1968.
4. Anthony Burgess, *Little Wilson and Big God* (Heinemann, London, 1987), pp. 367–8.
5. ibid. p. 369.
6. ibid. p. 402.
7. ibid. p. 420.
8. Fay Weldon, speech at the Booker Prize Award Ceremony, *The Times*, 27 October 1983.
9. Edward Upward to James Michie, 1 September 1961. [Heinemann archive]
10. Stephen Spender, advance publicity quote for *In the Thirties*.
11. John Lehmann, advance publicity quote for *In the Thirties*.
12. J. D. Salinger to Pat Cork, his agent, 26 May 1962. [Heinemann archive]

13. Richard Condon, 'Adventures of a Middle-aged Novelist', *Books and Bookmen*, October 1964.
14. Nicolas Freeling to David Burnett, 9 April 1975. [Heinemann archive]
15. Nicolas Freeling to Roland Gant, 8 August 1980. [Heinemann archive]
16. David Machin to Chinua Achebe, 22 April 1965. [Heinemann archive]
17. Chinua Achebe to David Machin, 13 May 1965. [Heinemann archive]
18. Alan Scholefield, probably publicity handout, undated. [Heinemann archive]
19. Graham Greene, introduction to *The Bachelor of Arts* (Nelson, London, 1937), pp. vi–vii,
20. R. K. Narayan responding to the presentation of a citation awarded by the American Academy and Institute of Arts, 18 January 1982.
21. Richard Church to Derek Priestley, 19 October 1964. [Heinemann archive]
22. Paul Scott to John C. Willey, 14 November 1972. [Heinemann archive]

Chapter 25
1. Graham Watson, *Book Society* (Deutsch, London, 1980), pp. 157–8.
2. ibid. p. 156.
3. ibid. pp. 156–7.
4. J. B. Priestley, 'Damn the Authors!', *New Statesman*, 6 January 1961.
5. Richard Findlater, *The Author*, Winter 1972.
6. ibid.
7. *The Author*, Summer 1981.
8. Giles Gordon, *The Author*, Spring 1987.
9. Jonathan Raban, *The Author*, Spring 1987.
10. Harold Macmillan to Geoffrey Eley, 26 April 1973. [Heinemann archive]
11. Ian Chapman to A. Dwye Evans, 18 April 1973. [Heinemann archive]

Chapter 27
1. *The Times*, 10 October 1968.
2. Fredric Warburg to A. Dwye Evans, 15 October 1968. [Heinemann archive]
3. *The Times*, 24 February 1969.
4. 'Profile of Frederic Warburg', *The Times*, 16 November 1968.

Chapter 28
1. Colin Thubron interviewed by Nicholas Shakespeare, *The Times*, 25 July 1985.
2. Lionel Fraser to Charles Pick, 24 August 1962. [Heinemann archive]
3. Michael Wolff, 'Work Behind "last of classic biographies"', *East African Standard*, 28 October 1966.

Bibliographic References

4. Martin Gilbert, progress report, 29 April 1970. [Heinemann archive]
5. Michael Holroyd, preface to revised edition of *Lytton Strachey* (Heinemann, London, 1973) p. 10.
6. ibid. pp. 16–17.
7. ibid. p. 20.
8. Michael Holroyd to Joyce Pearson, 5 September 1964. [Heinemann archive]
9. Arthur C. Fields to Roger Manvell, 18 February 1970. [Heinemann archive]
10. A. Dwye Evans to Enid Bagnold, 9 March 1964. [Heinemann archive]
11. Enid Bagnold to A. Dwye Evans, 11 March 1964. [Heinemann archive]

Chapter 29
1. *Private Eye*, 2 July 1982.

INDEX

(Compiled by Meg Davies, Society of Indexers)

Note: Entries and sub-entries are arranged alphabetically, word by word.

Index

[667]

Index

Index

Index

Dahl, Roald, 381
Daily Chronicle, 28, 124
Daily Telegraph, 113, 119
Dane, Clemence, 150, 201, 242, 301
  Broome Stages, 224–5
  Call Home the Heart, 401
Daudet, Alphonse, *The Nabob*, 78
David & Charles (publishers), 546, 616
David-Neel, Alexandra, *My Journey to Lhasa*, 239
Davies, Hunter, *The Beatles: the Authorised Biography*, 610–11
Davies, Nicholas ('Nico'), 274, 299, 429, 579
Davies, Peter, 273–4, 299, 579
Davies, Peter, Ltd, 253, 273–4, 312, 319, 373, 386, 415, 418, 489, 501, 579–80, 581, 613
Davies, Rhys, *Things Men Do*, 361
Davis, B., *Food Commodities*, 553
Davis, Maxine, *Sex and the Adolescent*, 403
Dawson, Coningsby, *The Garden Without Walls*, 89–90
Dawson Scott, C. Amy, 39
  Wastralls, 53
De Goncourt, Jules and Edmond, *Renée Mauperin*, 78
De Grey, Nigel, as manager, 88–9, 161
De la Mare, Walter, 14, 44–5, 202
De Morgan, William,
  An Affair of Dishonour, 50
  It Never Can Happen Again, 49–50, 147
  Joseph Vance, 49
De Quincey, Thomas, *The Posthumous Works*, 9
Dehan, Richard,
  The Dop Doctor, 50–2
  That which has Wings, 52
Delafield, E. M., *The War-Workers*, 159
Delavenay, Emile,
  D. H. Lawrence: the Formative Years, 1885–1919, 413
  D. H. Lawrence and Edward Carpenter, 413
Dennis, Geoffrey, *Coronation Commentary*, 276–9, 405
Dennis, Nigel, 603
Dent J. M. (publishers), 7, 33, 34
Desai, Anita, 468, 541, 619
  Clear Light of Day, 521–2
Dettmer, John, 52, 59, 60, 161, 184, 299, 312, 492, 579
Deutsch, André, 490–1
Devlin, Mr Justice Patrick, 407, 409
Dick, Bernard F., *The Apostate Angel*, 512
Dick-Read, Grantly, 270, 386, 586
Dickens, Monica, 450–1, 468

Follyfoot Farm series, 562
  Kate and Emma, 451
  The Listeners, 451
  One Pair of Hands, 450
Dickson, Carter (Carr, John Dickson), 263–4
direct mail selling, 63, 64, 236–7, 469, 542–6, 561
discount, to booksellers, 233, 312, 320, 461, 463
Dobson, Austin, 14, 106, 142
Dodd, Mead, and Co. (publishers), 277
Dodge, J. D. and Viner, G. (eds), *The Practice of Journalism*, 559
Donaldson, Frances, *Freddy Lonsdale*, 390
Doran, George H., 89–90, 198, 251
Dostoevsky, Fyodor,
  The Brothers Karamazov, 80
  novels, 79–81
Doubleday (publishers), 36–7, 149, 543–4
Doubleday, Doran, and Co (publishers), 242, 251–2, 492
Doubleday, F. N. ('Effendi'), 171–6, 178–80, 205, 226, 235–7, 242, 252, 492
  failing health, 189, 192, 251, 254
  and Frere-Reeves, 183–7
  and Kingswood, 189–93
  and William Heinemann, 37, 167–9
Doubleday, Florence, 184–5, 293
Doubleday, Nelson, 167, 168, 174, 251
Doubleday, Page and Co,
  control of Heinemann, 167–70, 173–5, 177–81, 195, 226–7
  sale of Heinemann shares, 249, 250–1, 293–4, 423, 437, 442
  and *The World's Work*, 183–6
Douglas, Lloyd C., 274
Douglas, Lord Alfred, 12–13, 359
Douglas, Norman, *Venus in the Kitchen*, 403
Dowthwaite, Maurice, 474
Doyle, John, 403
drama, 56, 82, 117–25, 180, 224, 382–3, 401, 550
Drama Library, 382, 585
Dreiser, Theodore, 376
Drucker, Peter, *The Practice of Management*, 552, 559
Du Maurier, Daphne, 291
Duckworth, Gerald (publishers), 7, 44, 46, 53, 260, 340–1
Dudeney, Mrs Henry, *The Maternity of Harriet Wicken*, 53
Duffield (publishers), 43
Duncan, Andrew, *The Reality of Monarchy*, 588
Duncan, David, *Dark Dominion*, 338

Index

Index

Gardner, Erle Stanley, 357
Garnett, Constance, 79–81, 448–9
Garnett, Edward, 14, 34, 36, 44–5, 53, 60–1,
    68, 79–80, 248
Garnett, Richard, 78, 133
    Essays of an Ex-Librarian, 133
Garside, R. M., 486
Garstin, Crosbie, 246
Gaskell, T. F. and Cooper, Brian, *North Sea
    Oil – the Great Gamble*, 595
Gatfield (accountant), 59
Gauguin, Paul, *Intimate Journals*, 238
Gauld, Alan, *Mediumship and Survival*, 589
Gazette du Bon Ton, 150–1
Gibb, Marian, *Guide to Marie Chassevant's
    Method of Musical Education*, 116
Gibbs, Philip (later Sir Philip), 305
    Ordeal in England, 279–80
    The Pageant of the Years, 392
    Realities of War, 158
    The Soul of War, 157–8
Gibran, Kahlil, 399, 441, 566
    The Prophet, 290, 483
Gide, André, 370
Gielgud, John, 382–3, 585
Gilbert, Martin, 600–2, 619
Gill, Eric, 240
Gilmour, Ian (later Sir Ian), 413
Ginn & Co (publishers), 550, 566, 612, 615
Gittings, Robert,
    John Keats, the Living Year, 383, 400
    Young Thomas Hardy/The Older Hardy,
    550
Gladstone, W. E., 3, 148
Glazebrook, Ben, 423
Glover, T. R., 269
Gobineau, Count Arthur, *The Inequality of
    Human Races*, 109
Godden, Rumer, 274, 376
Godwin, David, 616
Goethe, Johann Wolfgang von, *Wilhelm
    Meister's Theatrical Mission*, 78
Goff, Martyn, 466
Goldberg, Audrey, *Body Massage for the Beauty
    Therapist*, 558
Golden Pine editions, 132
Golding, Louis, *Give up your Lovers*, 291
Goldschmied, Elinor and Trimmer, Eric, *The
    First Seven Years*, 586
Gollancz, Victor, 291, 436, 497, 583
Golon, Sergeanne, *Angélique*, 355
Goncharov, *A Common Story*, 16, 79
Goold, G. P., 587
Goolden, Barbara, 359–60
    The China Pig, 360

Gordon, George, 242
Gordon, Giles, 535
Gordon, John, 405, 413–14
Gordon, Rex, *Utopia 239*, 338
Gordon, Richard,
    'Doctor' books, 453, 468
    The Sleep of Life, 453
Gordon, William, 318
Gorki, Maxim,
    The Orloff Couple and Malva, 81
    Reminiscences of Leonid Andreyev, 81
    Reminiscences of my Youth, 81
Gosse, Edmund, 22, 39, 59, 91–2, 106, 120,
    289
    as advisor, 14, 15–16, 18, 19, 77–9, 82,
    170–2, 201
    and authors, 23, 113–14, 118–19, 126, 132,
    138
    The Autumn Garden, 133
    belles-lettres, 132–5
    Books on the Table, 132
    Collected Poems, 133
    Father and Son, 134–6, 598
    Gossip in a Library, 132
    Hypolympia, 133
    The Life and Letters of John Donne, 133
    personality, 14–15
    Plea for Books, 161–2
    The Secret of Narcisse, 133
    Silhouettes, 132
Gosse, Edmund and Garnett, Richard, *English
    Literature: an Illustrated Record*, 133
Gosse, Nellie, 14
Gould, Gerald, 229–30
Gould-Davies, Tony, 545–6
Gower Mews, London, 489, 579
Graham, Billy, *Peace with God*, 377
Graham, Harry, 202
Graham, Helga, *Arabian Time Machine:
    self-portrait of an oil state*, 595
Grand, Sarah (Frances McFall),
    The Beth Book, 10
    The Heavenly Twins, 10, 17, 90
Grant, Duncan, 605
Grass, Gunther, 569
Graves, Clotilde, *see* Dehan, Richard
Graves, Robert, 169, 289
    Fairies and Fusiliers, 159
Great Educators Series, 9, 116
Great Peoples Series, 109
99 Great Russell Street, 195–6, 210–11, 235,
    270, 298, 305, 349–50, 418, 489.
    friction with Kingswood, 320–7, 328
Green, Julien, 337
Green, Sir Owen, 616

Index

Index

Index

Hill, David, 479
Hill, Enid, 385
Hill, Eric, *Where's Spot?*, 564
Hill, James, *Teeline*, 552
histories, 107–11
Hlasko, Marek, 337
Hobson, Laura Z., 512
Hodder & Stoughton (publishers), 49, 55,
    179, 286, 369, 496–8, 501
Hodge, Jane Aiken, 286–7
Hogben, Lancelot, 454
    Beginnings and Blunders, 587
Holden, William (Bill), 456, 466–7, 500
Holderness and Lambert, *School Certificate
    Chemistry*, 272–3
Holland, Julian, *Spurs, the Double*, 402
Hollis, Christopher, *The Seven Ages*, 607
Hollis, Nigel, 467–9, 509, 615–16
Holmes, Valentine, 277
Holroyd, Michael,
    Augustus John, 605–6
    Lytton Strachey, 603–5
    Lytton Strachey by Himself, 605
Holt, Henry, 38
Holt-Jackson (library suppliers), 461
Home, William Douglas, *Collected Plays*, 401
Homes, W. & R., 461
Hope, A. D., 399
Hope, Christopher, 619
Hope, Laurence (Nicholson, Adela),
    The Garden of Kama and Other Love Lyrics,
    128–9
    Indian Love, 129
    Stars of the Desert, 129
Hopkins, Antony, *Talking About – Symphonies*,
    402
Hopkinson, Sir Tom, *Treasures of the Royal
    Photographic Society*, 586
Horder, Sir Thomas, 172
Horgan, Paul, 289
Hough, Richard, *Advice to a Grand-daughter*,
    607
Hoult, Norah,
    Poor Women, 266
    Time, Gentlemen, Time!, 266
Houlton, Mark, *An Introduction to Cost and
    Management Accounting*, 559
house rules, 343–4
Howells, W. D., 97
Hoyle, (Sir) Fred, 343–4, 383, 550
    Frontiers of Astronomy, 368
Hudson, Derek, *Arthur Rackham – his life and
    work*, 402
Hudson, Edward, 89
Hudson, Nick, 472–4, 549

Hueffer, Ford Madox, 35–6, 41–2
    It was the Nightingale, 36
Hugo, Victor, *Notre-Dame of Paris*, 78
Hume, Martin S., *The Spanish*, 109
Humphreys, Christmas, *Zen Buddhism*, 403
Hunt, Ralph Vernon, 539, 541
Hunt, Violet, 42
    White Rose of Weary Leaf, 53
Huntington, Gladys, *Madame Solario*, 362
Hutchinson (publishers), 7, 407
Huxley, Aldous, 260
Hyde, Douglas, *I Believed*, 398–9
Hyde, H. Montgomery, *The Life of Sir Edward
    Carson*, 390
Hyperion Press Art Books, 402

I Can Read series, 574
Ibsen, Henrik, 76, 78, 117–22, 125, 137, 171
    Collected Works, 121
    A Dolls's House, 117– 119
    Ghosts, 117
    Hedda Gabler, 118–19
    The Master Builder, 119, 120
illustrators, 101, 103, 137, 379, 402, *see also*
    Beerbohm, Max; Nicholson, William;
    Oxenbury, Helen; Rackham, Arthur
India, sales to, 316–17
Inglis, Brian, 589–90
Inskip, Thomas KC, 276
'instant' books, 454–7, 466
Integrated Clinical Study series, 578
International Library, 9, 16, 79
Ireland, Peter, 484, 564, 615, 618
Irvine, Ian, 620, 621
Irving, Clifford,
    Fake, 608
    Howard Hughes, 608–9
Irving, Clive, Hall, Ron and Wallington,
    Jeremy, *Scandal '63*, 454–5
Irving, (Sir) Henry, 117, 123
Irving, Lawrence, 303
Irving, Washington, *Rip van Winkle*, 103
Irwin, John, 471
Isham, Col. Ralph H., 387–8
Isherwood, Christopher, 503
Ishikawa, Satomi, 565
Ismay, Lord, *Memoirs*, 395

jackets, 52, 101, 499, 536
Jackson, Cora, 67
Jackson, Holbrook, 32, 121–2, 136
Jackson, Stanley, 475–6
    The Sassoons, 607
Jacobs, Mendl, 319, 475
Jacobson, Dan, 574

Index

Index

Index

Index

Index

Morrison, Arthur, *A Child of the Jago*, 148
Morrison, G. E., 110
Morrow, William (publishers), 523
Mortimer, John, *The Wrong Side of the Park*, 401
Mortimer, Raymond, 15
Moser, (Sir) Claus, *Survey Methods in Social Investigation*, 384
Moult, Thomas, 288
Mowat, Farley, 454
Mudie, Charles, 16
Mudie's subscription library, 7, 16, 18, 26–7, 231, 311
Muggeridge, Malcolm, 328, 340
Muir (accountant), 59
Muir, Frank, 541
  A Book at Bathtime, 590
  The Frank Muir Book, 468, 590
Muller, Renee, 324
Munro, Leslie, 185, 234, 312, 328, 366
Murray, Gilbert, 78
Murray, John (publishers), 95, 145, 314, 491
Murry, J. Middleton, 80, 183
music publishing, 401–2, 585

Nabokov, Vladimir,
  The Image and the Search, 364
  Lolita, 364, 413
Naidu, Sarojini, 126–8
  The Golden Threshold, 126
  The Bird of Time, 127
  The Broken Wing, 127–8
Naipaul, V. S., 479
Naldrett Press, 373, 378, 402
Nansen, Fridtjof,
  In Northern Mists, 112–13
  Through Siberia: the Land of the Future, 113
Narayan, R. K., 468, 520–1, 619
  Malgudi Days, 521
  The Man-Eater of Malgudi, 520
Nash, Ogden, 185
Nationwide Book Service, 544–6, 616
Nelkon, Michael, 381–2
Nelson (publishers), 54
Nelson and Warne (publishers), 143
Net Book Agreement, 90, 145–6, 543
Nettle, Keith, 548
Nevinson, H. R., 32
New American Library, 369
New Review, 32, 34, 100, 147–9
New Windmill Series, 381, 475
New Zealand, sales to, 318, 320, 473, 474
Newman, Ernest, 230
Ngugi, James (later Ngugi Wa Thiong'o), 475, 478

Weep Not Child, 519
Niall, Ian, *The Poacher's Handbook*, 403
Nichols, Beverley, *Father Figure*, 608
Nicholson, Adela, *see* Hope, Laurence
Nicholson, Hubert, *Patterns of Three and Four*, 361–2
Nicholson, (Sir) William, 59, 96, 98–101
  An Almanac of Twelve Sports, 65, 99
  An Alphabet, 98–9, 271
  Characters of Romance, 101
  Clever Bill, 101
  designs colophon, 64–6, 101
  London Types, 101
  The Square Book of Animals, 100
  Twelve Portraits, 99–100
  The Velveteen Rabbit, 101
Nicklaus, Jack, *Golf my Way*, 588
Nicoll, Helen, *Meg and Mog* series, 563
Nicoll, Robertson, 55
Nordau, Max, *Degeneration*, 113–14
Norman, Henry, 149
Norrie, Ian, 489
North American Review, 147
Northcliffe, Lord, 146
Notes for Authors, 560
novels, 180
  historical, 284–7, 335, 353–5, 502
  romantic, 509–10
  see also 'three-deckers'
Noyce, Wilfrid, *South Col: One Man's Adventure of the Ascent of Everest*, 403

O'Brien, Kate,
  The Land of Spices, 267
  Mary Lavelle, 267
  Pray for the Wanderer, 267
  Without my Cloak, 266
O'Brien, Pat, *Outwitting the Hun*, 158
Obscene Publications Act 1959, 412
obscenity, 71, 275–6, 405, 407–12
Observer, 44
Octopus Books, 449, 460, 566
Octopus Group, 619–22
Odinga, Oginga, 478
Oliver, B. F., 175, 192–4, 251–3, 299, 301, 321–2, 328, 371
omnibus editions, 68, 449–50
O'Neill, Hugh, *Stone for Building*, 595
Orford, Ann, 318
Orwell, George, 337, 368, 381, 449–50, 539
  Nineteen Eighty-Four, 370
Osborne, Bob, 621
Ouida (de la Ramée, Marie Louise), 171
  The Tower of Taddeo, 23–4
  Under Two Flags, 23

Index

Index

Polak, Hans, 579
pop-up books, 373, 563–4
Pope, Dudley, 574
Positioning in Radiography, 270
Post, L. A., 268, 385
Postema, Robert, 561
Potok, Chaim, *The Chosen*, 514
Potter, John, 621–2
Potter, Stephen, *Anti-Woo*, 590
Pottinger, David T., 268
Pottle, Frederick A., 387, 388–9
Pound, Reginald, 241–2
    Arnold Bennett, 390
Powell, Anthony, 619
    Afternoon Men, 340
    A Dance to the Music of Time, 341, 444, 468
Powell, E. Alexander, *Fighting in Flanders*, 158
Powell, Graham, 314
Powell, Margaret, *Below Stairs*, 579
Powell, Violet, 38–9, 224, 341, 444–5
Price, James, 570–1
Price, Jonathan, 349, 391
Price, Willard, *The Amazing Amazon*, 403
prices
    1890–1920, 26–9, 48, 54, 142–3, 144–7, 160
    1921–45, 179–80, 207, 212, 261–2
    1945–61, 309–10, 324–5, 336, 365, 415, 420
    1961–83, 459, 483–5, 534, 560–1, 566
Priestley, Derek, 312, 313, 431, 462, 579, 581
Priestley, J. B., 206–9, 215–16, 294–5, 299, 309, 376, 381, 410–11
    Angel Pavement, 206, 208
    Blackout in Gretley, 301
    and Bodley Head, 427, 430
    Festival at Farbridge, 312–13, 334
    The Good Companions, 206–9, 236, 261–2, 334, 448
    Margin Released, 208
    Midnight on the Desert, 209
    plays, 209, 224, 334
    The Prince of Pleasure, 447, 572
    value to Heinemann, 242, 313, 447–8, 468–9, 487, 531, 534, 613
Priestley, J. B. and Hawkes, Jacquetta, *Journey down a Rainbow*, 334
printing, *see* typesetting; typography; Windmill Press
Private Eye, 614–15
prizes, literary, 466
production, 61–3, 98, 179, 192–3, 321–5, 454–5, 480–5, 586
profit margins
    1890–1920, 17, 58, 87, 159–60

1921–45, 180, 187, 250, 296–7, 304
1945–61, 309, 415–16, 640
1961–83, 438, 440, 473, 483, 525–6, 566–8, 578, 580, 616, 642–7
promotion, 112, 134–5, 185–6, 213, 361, 439, 454–6, 560–1
    see also advertising; publicity
pseudonymous works, 10, 13, 23–4, 50–2, 76, 107, 115, 128–9
Public Lending Act (PLR), 535
public relations, 466–7
Public School Verse, 289
publicity
    1961–83, 446, 459–69, 531, 561
    1890–1920, 53, 56, 63–4, 112
    1921–45, 196, 199, 211, 234–5
    1945–61, 312–13, 323, 335, 368
Publishers Association, 66, 145–6, 160, 164, 179, 233, 242–3, 459, 538, 584
Publishers' Circular, 27–9
Pugh, Alice (first secretary), 7, 88
pulp publications, 183, 184–5, 271
Putnam, 151, 177, 373, 611
Puzo, Mario,
    The Dark Arena, 514–15
    The Godfather, 514
Pyramid series, 562–3

15 Queen Street, London, 418, 466, 480, 492
Quiller-Couch, A., 133

Raban, Jonathan, 535–6
Rabbets, Eric, 326
Rackham, Arthur, 63, 96, 103–5, 169, 271
Radzinowicz, Sir Leon, 550
Raimond, C. E., *see* Robins, Elizabeth
Rainbird, George, Ltd, 447, 592
Ramsay, Margaret (Peggy), 382
Randle, Ian, 479–80
Randle, Leslie, 611
Range, D. L. (Peter), 474, 486, 488–9, 493, 540, 614
Ransome, J. Stafford, *see* Lewis, Caroline
Raven, Simon, 302
Read, (Sir) Herbert, *Art and Society*, 240
Read, Piers Paul, 574
Reade, Charles, 6
Reader, W. J., *Fifty Years of Unilever*, 594
readers, 14, 38, 42–5, 60–1, 157, 197–8, 200–3, 203–4, 299–300, 328, 330, 360
Rebman Ltd, 152, 187
Redgrave, (Sir) Michael,
    The Actor's Ways and Means, 383, 401
    Mask or Face – Reflections in an Actor's Mirror, 401

Index

Index

Index

Spears, Sir Edmund, *Prelude to Dunkirk*, 228, 395

Spender, (Sir) Stephen, 504

Spillane, Mickey, 622

sponsorship, 592–4

Spoor, Alex, *White Collar Union*, 595

sports books, 116, 373, 378, 402, 588

Spurling, Hilary, *Handbook to Anthony Powell's Dance to the Music of Time*, 444

Spycatcher (Wright), 13

Squire, J. C., 169, 192, 200, 287–8

staff association, 584

Stainsby, Charles, 586

Standish, Robert, 579

Star Editions, 369–70

Steel, Flora Annie,
  A Book of Mortals, 38
  The Garden of Fidelity, 39–40
  On the Face of the Waters, 38, 39–40

Steel, Flora Annie & Gardiner, Grace, *The Complete Indian Housekeeper and Cook*, 38

Steen, Marguerite, 99–100

Stein, Gertrude, 46

Steinbeck, John, 291–2, 313, 449–50, 539, 622
  The Grapes of Wrath, 292
  Once There Was a War, 395

Stendhal, *The Chartreuse of Parma*, 78

Stephen Crane Omnibus, 68

Stephen, Herbert, 148

Stephenson, Kenneth, 486–7, 488

Stepniak, Sergei, 79

Stevens, Alfred, 18

Stevenson, R. L., 21, 149, 282

Stewart, Andrew, 476

Stocks, Mary, *My Commonplace Book*, 579

Stocks, Ralph, *The Cruise of the Dreamship*, 239

stocks, unsold, 309, 416, 438–9, 470–1, 525

Stoker, Bram, 20, 30, 123
  Personal Reminiscences of Henry Irving, 123

Storm, Lesley, *Roar Like a Dove*, 401

Stott, Mary, *Organization Woman*, 595

Strachey, James, 604

Strachey, Lytton, 89, 603–5

Straub, Peter, 582–3

Straus, Roger, 423

Streatfeild, Noel, 271

Strindberg, August, 46

subsidiary companies, 370–7, *see also The World's Work*

Sunday Express, 405–6, 413–14, 443

'Sunlocks, London', 3–4

Suskind, Richard, 609

Sutherland, Graham, 402

Sutro, John, 413

Sutton, Ethel, 196, 330

Swanton, E. W., *West Indies Revisited*, 402

Swift, Graham, 619

Swinburne, Algernon Charles, 106, 128, 131–2
  Complete Poetical Works, 289
  Letters, 132
  Posthumous Poems, 132
  Springtide of Life, 105
  Works (Bonchurch edition), 132, 289

Swinnerton, Frank, 202–3, 230, 256–7, 291, 294

Symington, T. and Carter, R. L., *Scientific Foundations of Oncology*, 578

Symons, Arthur, 14, 81–2, 126, 136–7, 148
  The Fool of the World and Other Poems, 137
  Poems, 137
  Studies in Elizabethan Drama, 137
  The Symbolist Movement in Literature, 136–7
  Tragedies: The Harvesters, The Death of Agrippina, Cleopatra in Judea, 137

Tack, Alfred, 377–8

Talbot de Malahide, Lord, 387–8

Talbot, F. A., 116

Taller, Herman, *Calories don't Count*, 586–7

Tarkington, Booth,
  Growth, 227–8
  The Heritage of Hatcher Ide, 228
  The Plutocrat, 228

Tauchnitz, Baron Christian Bernard von, 20, 22, 23, 281, 370

Taylor, Frank, 609

Taylor, Frank Sherwood, 272–3

Taylor, Selwyn, 577

Tazewell, Charles, *The Littlest Angel*, 378

Tempest, Margaret, 379

Temple, M. H., *see* Lewis, Caroline

Temple Smith, Maurice, 569–71

Tennant, Emma, 565

Terry, Ellen, 59–60

Tey, Josephine, 274, 622

Thalbourne, Michael, *A Glossary of Terms used in Parapsychology*, 588

Thames & Hudson (publishers), 572

Thiong'o, Ngugi Wa, *see* Ngugi, James

Thomas, A. Noyes, 386

Thompson, Edward, 380, 382, 491–2, 548, 550, 585

Thompson, Nicholas, 619

Thompson, Sylvia, *The Hounds of Spring*, 266

Thorne, Anthony, *Cabbage Holiday*, 355

Index

Index

Index